ALANBROOKE

ALANBROOKE

David Fraser

With a Prologue and Epilogue by
ARTHUR BRYANT

COLLINS
St James's Place, London
1982

William Collins Sons & Co Ltd
London · Glasgow · Sydney · Auckland
Toronto · Johannesburg

First published 1982
©David Fraser 1982
ISBN 0 00 216360 8
Photoset in Imprint
Made and Printed in Great Britain by
William Collins Sons & Co Ltd, Glasgow

This story
of one of the greatest of Gunners
is dedicated to
The Royal Regiment of Artillery

CONTENTS

LIST OF ILLUSTRATIONS

LIST OF MAPS

ACKNOWLEDGEMENTS

This book could not have been written without the collaboration, in its preparatory stages, of Sir Arthur Bryant, to whose invaluable advice, encouragement and wisdom I am deeply indebted. As I am, too, to his *Turn of the Tide* and *Triumph in the West*, many passages from which he has allowed me to include in my biography.

I must equally acknowledge with gratitude all the assistance and confidence extended to me by the family and Trustees of the late Viscount Alanbrooke, and especially Viscount Alanbrooke, the Hon. Mrs Macdonald and Mrs Hill. They have generously made available to me an assembly of documents, recollections and advice which has been invaluable, as well – in the case of the Trustees of the Alanbrooke Settlement and the Executors of Lord Alanbrooke's Will – as granting unlimited access to the Alanbrooke papers themselves, lodged in the Liddell-Hart Centre, King's College, London. I particularly appreciate the gesture of Lord Alanbrooke in making available to me over 1300 letters between his father and mother, which have greatly illumined the Field-Marshal's character.

At the Liddell-Hart Centre my warm thanks are due to successive archivists, most recently Elizabeth Bennett and Patricia Methuen, but previously and very especially Julia Shepherd, who carried out the great work of cataloguing and classification which has enabled the Trustees to agree terms of access to the Alanbrooke papers.

An invaluable part of the Alanbrooke papers is a collection of biographical material, including records of interviews with a number of men and women, some of great distinction, who knew the Field-Marshal well. The collection of this material was entrusted first to Mrs Astley, who had been Lord Ismay's secretary during the Second World War, and then to the late Mrs Long; and the devoted and imaginative work done places any biographer enormously in debt.

I am also in debt to those many friends, colleagues, subordinates and associates of Lord Alanbrooke who have honoured me with their impressions, their memories and their views. I hope that, where appropriate, due acknowledgement is sometimes made in the body of the book: but I know well that there are many more who have contributed, with a sentence or a trenchant word, to some of the insights I have tried to attain. To all I extend my gratitude.

From the start the Royal Regiment of Artillery and successive Master Gunners have given me their confidence, encouragement and support. If this book does anything to improve public knowledge of one of the greatest of all Gunners its author will have been amply rewarded. The Regiment's assistance has been particularly demonstrated by Major-General Hughes, who has read a number of chapters, supplied information and advice, and done all that man can to prevent the solecisms of one who is not an Artilleryman.

The manuscript has been read in whole or part by Lieutenant-General Sir Ian Jacob and Benita Stoney. Sir Ian has given me authoritative and welcome counsel on the course of the war and Alanbrooke's part in it: as an outstandingly distinguished member of the War Cabinet Secretariat, as well as a personal diarist of note he has been uniquely enabled to do so, and has also permitted me to quote from his own diary. Benita Stoney, Lord Alanbrooke's granddaughter, has helped me in three irreplaceable ways: she has worked tirelessly on her grandfather's personal correspondence, she has checked typescripts against original documents in the case of the diaries and notes in the Alanbrooke papers, and – last but not least – she has criticized and commented on drafts with taste, vigour and an exactitude and objectivity of which the subject of the biography would have highly approved. Her contribution has deserved my very sincere gratitude.

The Public Record Office has been able to yield most of its secrets under the thirty-year rule, although, of course, the authors of the *Grand Strategy* volumes of the *History of the Second World War* had access to documents regardless to this rule. I am particularly grateful to Group-Captain Arthur Peers for the devoted work he put in on the files at the PRO. Having mentioned the *Grand Strategy* volumes I cannot neglect to pay my personal tribute to the authors of this splendid work to which I have made incessant reference, and from which I have received, with gratitude, permission to quote.

I am grateful to Viscount Montgomery for permission to quote from his father's letters and memoranda; to Mr Charles Hammick for permission to quote from the First World War diary of Major P. H. Pilditch and to Lady Nye for permission to quote from the unpublished memoir of her husband by Mr A. Harrison.

I owe a particular debt to the late Dr David Bannerman, and, after his death, to his daughter Lady Gibbon, for making available to me letters from Lord Alanbrooke, as well as vivid recollections and assessments of the Field-Marshal in the field of ornithology.

Many hands have been concerned with the typing of draft after draft of this work. I wish particularly, however, to record my appreciation of the splendid and tireless work put in by Paul Blaber and Penny Lewis at different periods of the book's evolution. I pay a particular tribute to Ted Birkett for his enthusiastic work on the maps.

Finally I owe an unpayable debt to my wife who has had to live with the frustrations, setbacks, excitements and alternating fits of depression and enthusiasm which the production of a biography over a period of several years can induce, and has throughout been tolerant, constructive and wise.

PROLOGUE

by Sir Arthur Bryant

IT IS NEARLY a quarter of a century since the public learnt that it was a professional soldier, presiding over the Joint Committee of the British Chiefs of Staff – the operational heads of the Royal Navy, Air Force and Army – who, at Churchill's side, and in conjunction with the American Chiefs of Staff, played the leading part in co-ordinating and directing the strategy and world-wide operations of our Forces during the decisive years of the war. The launching in February 1957 of *The Turn of the Tide*, in the presence of the three wartime Chiefs of Staff and more than four hundred generals, admirals and air-marshals, was the publishing sensation of the year. It was hailed by Attlee – Churchill's Deputy Prime Minister and successor – as 'the most important publication of the Second World War', and by Field-Marshal Montgomery as 'the inside story and faithful picture of the two greatest figures on the British side'. The then Regius Professor of History at Oxford called it 'this marvellous and memorable work . . . the most important that has appeared about the late war', and another Professor 'a momentous, magnificent book'. In America it and its sequel, *Triumph in the West*, published two years later, were both 'Books of the Month Club' choices with a huge circulation.

Their popularity was based on a diary throwing a dazzling light on the inner councils of those who had directed the war at its highest level. In it General Sir Alan Brooke, Chief of the Imperial General Staff from 1941 to 1946, had recorded, night after night, the anxieties, problems and decisions which for more than three and a half years had faced him and his colleagues. For the diary – a classic source-book of military history – had the quality common to all great diaries of instant communication, conveying to its readers the shocks, frustrations and hazards which had confronted the little group of men who, after Japan's and America's entry into the war, at the supreme and lonely pinnacle of responsibility and power, had little by little wrested the initiative from the enemy and overcome his immense initial preponderance of force.

For, in the words of Hugh Trevor-Roper, Alanbrooke's diaries possessed 'a tenseness, a clarity and vitality which make every detail sparkle; we see the sparks, we feel the atmosphere, whether it is an atmosphere tense with frustration or warm with excitement'. And they revealed, for the first time, the full nature of the partnership between the brilliant professional soldier and the great national leader without whom, as I wrote at the time, 'there would have been neither turn of the tide nor triumph in the west'. As Churchill's wartime Secretary of State for War, Sir James Grigg, put it, reviewing what he termed 'this faithful and accurate picture of the two greatest figures on the British side, . . . to Churchill first and Alanbrooke second our countrymen can never be sufficiently grateful'.

In the Introduction to *The Turn of the Tide* – the strategic narrative in which and its sequel, *Triumph in the West*, I set the jewel of Lord Alanbrooke's diaries – I tried to assess what the world owed to that partnership. 'In the summer of 1940 the Prime Minister's courage made this country the hope of the world.' 'You ask,' he said when the German armies were driving through the broken lines of France, 'what is our aim? I can answer in one word: Victory – victory at all costs, victory in spite of all terrors, victory, however long and hard the road may be.' His resolve to attack the colossus dominating Europe at any point within reach was then the only policy. So long as the Navy held the narrow seas and the RAF the air above, the enemy, for all his immense strength, could bring Britain no lower than she already was. Every attack on her mighty adversary, however daring, could serve only to revive and rouse her people's courage and offensive spirit.

Churchill was an orator, a poet and a sage with a taste for splendour and good living, an aristocrat who possessed the common touch that the English like to see in their rulers. For all his eighteenth-century eloquence and Victorian imperialism, he was the ideal champion for a people whose favourite song was 'The Lambeth Walk', and whose pet hobby a flutter on a horse. They liked his cigar, his glass of brandy, his bulldog face and figure, the twinkle in his eye. They loved his humour, his way of pronouncing foreign names, his indomitable courage. Above all, he had the power to touch chords in men's hearts that transcended politics. His sense of history never failed. He believed in a Providence which worked through human instruments and, like Elizabeth and Cromwell, he made the people he led believe in it too. He bade them be 'unyielding, persevering, indomitable, in the overthrow of another continental tyranny as in the olden times'.

Prologue

The Prime Minister's virtues as a war leader were immense. The higher the tide of trouble rose, the higher rose his courage. His nerves never failed, and the worst of disasters left his sleep and appetite unimpaired. He had the imagination to foresee dangers and opportunities that others would have missed and the drive to ensure that neither took the country unawares. He would never take No for an answer. For five years he was a spur in the flanks of every military and civil commander in the land.

His failings as a leader were impatience and impetuosity. The qualities which made him so great in adversity – the insistence on fighting back at all points, the obsession with attack, the tireless energy, the soaring imagination – sometimes made him essay enterprises which, had he not been dissuaded, could have ended in disaster. Nor, since he always threw the whole of his heart and head at the nearest fence, was he good at choosing between conflicting objectives – a choice which became increasingly important as Britain's resources and those of her allies began to offer a chance of wresting the initiative from the enemy. After 1941 any needless dispersal of force, any commitment which could drain away resources that might be needed at the decisive point at the decisive moment, might have deferred victory for a long time and, perhaps, for ever. Churchill's eloquence and persistence then became something of a problem to his military advisers. It was hard for them to concentrate and build up reserves and a striking-force for the future when he was always seeking, and with such intensity, to use them at once against the nearest foe.

It was in checking these tendencies that Alan Brooke proved the necessary counterpart to his leader. In contrast to the latter's sweeping Edwardian impatience for inconvenient details and his 'method of suddenly arriving at some decision as it were by intuition, without any kind of logical examination of the problem', Brooke's whole career had been a training in adapting means to ends. He had the imagination to see what was possible and the practical knowledge to know how, when and where it could be made so. He saw the war steadily and never, whatever the pressure of the moment, lost sight of the global picture. He had the ability – the hallmark of the born strategist – to grasp all the essentials of a problem at once. 'He was more qualified,' wrote James Grigg, 'than any other soldier, or possibly than any other sailor or airman, to look at the war as a whole.'

Before Alan Brooke appeared on the strategic scene in December 1941, the enemy, with his infinitely greater strength, had enjoyed the initiative, and Britain had been saved, not only by her people's courage, but because she had as leader a man whose instinct was to fight back whatever the odds. Henceforward, by that leader's side was one who not only hit back, but knew exactly where to hit to hurt most. Within eight months of Brooke's assumption of the chairmanship of the Chiefs of Staff Committee, Germany had ceased to call the tune to which Britain danced and began to be forced to dance to hers. To Churchill's lightning flashes of inspiration and the courage that refused to admit defeat yet sometimes endangered victory by spurring him to attack prematurely, Brooke brought what Wellington, who also possessed it, saw in Marlborough – a cool, clear and steady understanding.

In all their arguments and differences, though they sometimes failed to realize it, the Prime Minister and his CIGS were the complement to one another. Churchill had the iron nerves, the splendid good humour and robust resilience of perfect health; the inspired instinct for the right word and the power to simplify great issues so that others could see them in the same clear terms. In his first speech as Prime Minister he had declared that the policy of his Administration would be 'to wage war, by sea, land and air, with all our might and with all the strength God can give us'. It was a promise faithfully fulfilled. The root of the matter was in him. 'War,' he wrote, 'is a constant struggle and must be waged from day to day.' He never for one moment gave up doing so. And he did it with a flame of hope which communicated itself to the whole nation. He saw what was necessary, and, with his prescient imagination, often long before it was required, but his expectations outran what was achievable and sometimes caused him to seek what in the circumstances of the time was impossible.

To correlate the Prime Minister's prophetic vision with the realities of what was immediately practicable thus became Alan Brooke's task. For this he was far better suited than his predecessor, Sir John Dill, who, for all his brilliant gifts and noble character, allowed himself to be drawn into endless arguments and was worn down by these clashes. Like most soldiers, Alan Brooke knew little of politics and instinctively distrusted those who practised them. But he had the gift which is at the root of all politics, as of all professions which concern the management of men: of distinguishing between what is practicable and im- practicable, and because of it was able to establish a successful *modus operandi* with his great, though mercurial, chief. It was he who gave to the Chiefs of Staff Committee and the Joint Planning Staff serving it, over which from March 1942 to the end of the war he presided, the full cohesion and power of which it was capable. For, as General Fraser in his brilliant biography makes plain, 'in presenting that united military advice which was so signal an achievement of the British system in the Second World War, the Chiefs of Staff were managers of a highly efficient process.' Controlling and using it at high pressure, Alan Brooke, as Chairman of the Chiefs of Staff Committee, made it what its creators had intended – an expert precision-instrument for directing a vast, complex war machine. In his hands it became that rarest but most potent of all military weapons – a Council of War operating with the consistency and speed of a single will.

In planning strategy Churchill and Brooke were the complement of one another. Churchill's task was to mobilize a whole people, inspire it with his resolve for victory and ensure that its effort was used with maximum force and effect. That of Brooke and his fellow Chiefs of Staff was to bring to the council table first-hand experience of the techniques of modern war and prepared plans which, before they could be translated into action, they had to pit – often for many weeks of argument – against their chief's brilliant, though at times insufficiently thought out, proposals. That there was controversy between the Prime Minister and his CIGS – who, as Chairman of the COS Committee bore the brunt of his onslaught – was inevitable; no military adviser would have been of any use to Churchill without. Brooke's supreme service to him, to the nation and to the Allied cause was that he never gave way on essentials or allowed himself to be deflected by eloquence or pressure from what he knew to be militarily right. Once, when his opposition to some cherished project had particularly infuriated him, the Prime Minister told General Ismay that the CIGS hated him and would have to go. When Ismay, acting as peacemaker, reported this to Brooke, the latter replied: 'I don't hate him, I love him, but when the day comes that I tell him he is right when I believe him to be wrong, it will be time for him to get rid of me.'

Churchill never did. For nearly four years he tolerated Brooke's constant restraint and, where necessary, opposition, because he knew at heart, for all his attempts to beat him down, that if his adviser refused to yield on a professional matter he was probably right. Though a perpetual, and frequently invaluable, critic of every measure which he and his colleagues put forward, Churchill was, *au fond*, their indispensable partner, patron and backer. No War Minister can ever have appeared so formidable to his military advisers; none, in reality, ever interfered with them less. Though he disputed with them every move of the game, in contrast to the autocrat who misdirected Germany's strategy there was no instance, after Alan Brooke became Chairman of the Chiefs of Staff Committee, of Churchill's using his unchallenged political power to overrule them.

For on essentials Brooke never gave way. So long as he remained CIGS he was resolved that purely military decisions should only be taken by those who were officially and professionally responsible for them. The Prime Minister found in him a companion whose wit and flexible mind he enjoyed as much as Brooke did his. But he also found him immovable and uncompromising on any matter in which his soldier's knowledge convinced him that he was arguing from insufficient premises. After each tremendous argument in War Cabinet or private session came the unvarying and outwardly imperturbable reply: 'Sir, we will examine the point you have raised at the Chiefs of Staff Committee in the morning and report on it immediately.' No entreaties or abuse could move him, nor, to whatever lengths the Prime Minister went, could he circumvent this quick-minded, unyielding soldier. With his instinctive liking for a fighter, Churchill respected this quality in him, even when it thwarted him. Though the two men had many a hammer-and-tongs argument, they resumed their friendship as soon as the storm had passed. Both were too magnanimous for it to be otherwise. On every essential point, in Sir James Grigg's words, they 'argued themselves into agreement before final action was taken'.

It was Churchill who chose Brooke, Churchill who used him and who, even when he disagreed with him and passionately believed himself right and Brooke and his fellow Chiefs of Staff wrong, had the wisdom and magnanimity to be guided by them. Yet the constant, inescapable presence of that unresting genius imposed a heavy strain on his advisers. Like a transformer, they had to break down, so that it could serve practical military ends, the high tension of his dynamic power. It had proved too much for Brooke's predecessor, and most people who had worked under the Prime Minister expected that it would prove too much for Brooke. And under the surface his diary reveals just how great the strain was.

For this reason Brooke's vivid picture in his diary of Churchill was much resented, and fiercely criticized, in some quarters as marring the portrait that, in his old age and fame, had been drawn of the great War Minister by a popular Press and grateful public – of a man invariably right and without human imperfections. What, in the mingled exasperation and admiration of his day-by-day entries, Brooke shows us is the real Churchill – the man who rallied a defeated nation in storm and disaster; passionate, impetuous, daring, indomitable, terrible in anger and pursuing every expedient – sometimes brilliant, sometimes, for he was prepared to try almost everything, fantastic – that could bring about victory. Inevitably, seeing him so constantly, he portrays his weaknesses as well as his strength. In the last years of their partnership both Churchill and Brooke – the one over seventy, the other in his sixties – were desperately over-strained and tired. Each was usually too exhausted to realize that the other was in the same state. If Churchill, as Brooke shows, was unaware of the strain he was imposing on his subordinates, Brooke, too, tended to forget that military responsibilities were only one of the Prime Minister's many cares and that he came to the strategic debates he describes in the diary exhausted by Parliamentary and political duties. This sometimes makes him appear unjust to him.

Yet Britain's finely tempered mechanism of Defence Minister, War Cabinet and Chiefs of Staff, in permanent debate to achieve agreement in decision and action, proved a far more effective instrument for victory than Germany's political dictatorship and subservient military machine. Brooke's chronicle of verbal battle enables us to hear the dynamo at work and watch its processes. Those who complained that the sound was harsh and grating – whether they complained of Brooke or of Churchill – missed the point. Out of that clash of counsel came, with astonishing smoothness, the ordered movements of the great national effort which won the war.

Its triumph was partly due to the Chairman of the Chiefs of Staff Committee's tact, skill and firmness in welding them, despite differences of opinion, into a single-minded, decisive Council of War, whose will prevailed because it was unanimous. But it was ultimately due even more to Churchill's respect for constitutional forms and, despite all appearances to the contrary, to a deep-seated humility – born of the vicissitudes and setbacks of his stormy career – which caused him to recognize, even though he might never admit it, that his approach to military problems needed the corrective of cooler judgements. Where he differed from Hitler and his own predecessor of the First World War, Lloyd George, was that, though well aware that soldiers could make blunders and for ever on the watch for them, he knew that in a dispute on a purely military question between a civilian, however able, and a soldier, the latter, if master of his profession, was more likely to have the correct answer. Having chosen the best and stoutest Service advisers he could find, though constantly probing and prodding them, he knew he could rely on their resistance if he went too far, and always deferred in the end to their considered and united opinion. The historian, G. M. Trevelyan, touched the heart of the matter when he wrote of *The Turn of the Tide*:

> So far from lowering my estimation of Winston the book, to me, has raised it. Napoleon fell because he would never take counsel; his marshals were only his servants, whereas Winston treated his generals as his advisers. This habit of taking counsel, combined with his own personal qualities, is what won the war.

Yet if the picture drawn in Alanbrooke's diaries in *The Turn of the Tide* and *Triumph in the West* is, in the broad perspective of history, fair to Churchill, it is, in the same perspective, unfair to Alan Brooke himself. For the self-portrait that emerges from those two books was contained in a diary compiled in the heat of pressing events. It reveals how the diarist saw himself and those around him, but not how they saw him. The side of Alanbrooke's character which emerges from his journal is one that was never seen by those who worked with him and which was therefore far from being that of the whole man. In contrast to the portrait he paints of himself – impatient, irritable and, at moments of exhaustion, anxious and even querulous – he was, by the testimony of all who served with him, habitually self-controlled, calm and imperturbable. 'I am feeling very weary and old,' he wrote in his diary a few weeks before D-Day, 'and wish to God this would finish!' No one working with him at the time could have guessed it. To the members of the War Cabinet, to his colleagues of the Chiefs of Staff Committee and to the commanders in the field he seemed a man of iron without nerves or feelings.

The contrast between Alanbrooke's outward bearing and the uninhibited self-revelation of his journal is thus bewildering. As autobiography, the diary is a distorting mirror. It not only presents a personality quite different to the selfless, though stern and reticent, soldier who, unmoved by disaster and pressure, directed Britain's armies from the winter of Singapore to the summer of Lüneburg Heath. It reflects the unguarded moods of a deeply

24

emotional and self-repressed man carrying an almost intolerable burden and releasing feelings that he could not reveal to anyone except the deeply loved wife for whom his diary was kept. It was a safety-valve for irritation and anxiety in a life of constant frustration and strain. Alanbrooke was not, as may seem at times from its pages, a disagreeable man expressing disapproval of his colleagues and contempt for every view but his own, but an intensely sensitive and tired human being, tried and exasperated almost beyond endurance by the burden he was carrying and which, because he bore it so efficiently, he was never allowed to lay down.

In one respect at least Alanbrooke's wartime diary reflects his character justly. Though hypercritical of others and intolerant of what he regarded as inefficiency or stupidity, it reveals him as almost totally without personal ambition. Apart from his resolve to win the war as quickly as possible and with as few mistakes and casualties, his only wish was to live in a world at peace, to be reunited with his wife and family and to pursue his hobbies of bird-watching and fishing. He had no axe to grind, either professional or political. It was this, as much as his unique ability and strength of mind, that gave his counsels such weight, particularly with his political chief. However unpalatable his advice – and it was frequently very unpalatable – the Prime Minister always knew that it was disinterested.

A diary has limitations, too, as history. It is not a comprehensive assessment of events calmly and dispassionately seen in retrospect but an account of them written on the spot amid the passions and anxieties they evoked. Alanbrooke's nightly entries, brilliant and graphic first-hand reporting though they often were, were not balanced situation reports on the strategic situation; he had neither time nor occasion for such at the end of crowded days which often continued from daybreak until his release from Churchill's side in the small hours of next morning. As the journal of any man of action must be, his diary is a record of conflict. It portrays him in continual verbal battle with adversaries – albeit colleagues and allies – upon whom, in the pursuit of duty, he was seeking to impress his views of what was the right strategy to pursue in order to defeat the Axis with the smallest possible loss of time and life.

In letting his diary tell his story, Alanbrooke allowed a picture of himself to emerge very different from the polished portrait of memoir writers. And in the post-war autobiographical notes which, without altering the original record, he later added to his diary, he drew attention to his contemporary misjudgements. Thus he tells us how mistaken he was in supposing that the Prime Minister's powers were failing in the strained months before D-Day or in imagining that he had not grasped the fallacy in Eisenhower's strategic arguments before the German Ardennes offensive. By doing so with his habitual disinterestedness he tilted the record against himself.

This is where Sir David Fraser, in his biography of his famous fellow soldier, has provided such an invaluable corrective to Alanbrooke's wartime diary. He presents him, not as he drew himself in his exhausted and harassed midnight diary entries in *The Turn of the Tide* and *Triumph in the West*, but as he was, and was seen to be, by those who served and worked with him in those years of strain and testing. As Sir David justly observes, 'A reader of Alanbrooke's diary and nothing else would find an emotional, hasty and intolerant man, immoderate in expression. On the contrary, in his professional dealings Alanbrooke was an excellent listener, calm, rational, and persuasive.'

No one could have been better equipped than General Fraser to complete the unfinished task, begun by me more than a quarter of a century ago, of making Alanbrooke's life better known to his countrymen. Himself a Grenadier, with a distinguished military career which carried him to the highest reaches of his profession, a past Vice-Chief of the General Staff, he was, both by experience and sympathies, the ideal biographer of a soldier, described as 'regimental as a button-stick', who in his early thirties had proved himself a Gunner of genius in the great barrage-duels of the First World War, and in the years of preparation between the wars had become recognized as one of the country's foremost staff-trained commanders. In his magnificent concluding chapter, summing up his career and achievement, General Fraser ranks him as 'the outstanding soldier of his generation, a superb professional and the prime military architect of Britain's success in the Second World War . . . He fought with tenacity, courage and skill for a realistic strategy and for a path that would lead most surely and economically to victory. He fought colleagues, he fought Allies, he fought Ministers, he fought Churchill. He fought successfully.'

Yet his biographer is not blind to his faults or mistakes. 'Alanbrooke was certainly not infallible in his judgements of men,' he writes. 'He was by temperament remote, and he did not find it easy to get on terms with those he did not already know well . . . His character, like Wellington's, was of the kind which saves lives by thought and study; and by disdain of gesture. His prudence and self-discipline were the consequence of devoted study of his profession. They did not stem from a cold temperament . . . He could be impulsive and exaggerated, but he kept this for his diary and for his private moments.'

For while judging him primarily as a soldier – and by the highest standards of his profession – General Fraser is equally sympathetic to the other side of his character – his 'love of nature, of birds, of colour and beauty and the high, wild places . . . Alanbrooke was a great man, and a whole man. He could love and be moved, as well as fight and decide. He had passion and compassion as well as strength and will . . . To many of those who only knew him in the Army, he was, or could be, forbidding, although he was totally without pomposity or affectation. To those whose acquaintance or friendship was other he was a different human being, warm, amusing and affectionate.' It was this which caused Churchill's physician, Lord Moran, companion of many of Alanbrooke's wartime journeys, to describe him as 'a simple, gentle, selfless soul – a warning to us all not to give up hope about mankind'.

Perhaps, as I feel David and I would agree, it was a poet – a contemporary of that other great Anglo-Irish soldier, Wellington – who, in his character of the 'Happy Warrior', came nearest to defining the enigma of this firm, unflinching, meticulous, yet gentle and lovable, soldier.

> Who, doomed to go in company with Pain,
> And Fear and Bloodshed, miserable train,
> Turns his necessity to glorious gain.
> In face of those doth exercise a power
> Which is our human nature's highest dower . . .
> He who, though thus endued as with a sense
> And faculty for storm and turbulence,
> Is yet a soul whose master-bias leans
> To homefelt pleasures and to gentle scenes.
> Sweet images! which wheresoe'er he be
> Are at his heart; and such fidelity
> It is his darling passion to approve;
> More brave for this that he hath much to love.

CHAPTER I

'The Unforgiving Minute – 1944'

THIRTEENTH APRIL 1944 – He arrived at the front door of the War Office in Whitehall about 9 a.m. Only the Secretary of State for War, the members of the Army Council and their immediate subordinates were allowed to use this imposing entrance, which opened upon marbled hall and staircase, their grandeur reduced but not extinguished by visible precautions against air raids. His 'Good morning' to the attendant porter as he galloped towards the stair was loud and sharp, like the crack of a high velocity piece of artillery. He wore the khaki Service dress and badges of rank of a Field-Marshal, a man immaculate but somewhat round-shouldered, dark and a little sallow. His eyes were restless and observant. He moved fast.

His office, the office of the Chief of the Imperial General Staff, was on the second floor, in one of the four six-sided rooms set in the corners of the building at each level. A huge window gave on to Whitehall. The adjoining room held desks for his Military Assistants and his Aide-de-Camp. None could see him except by way of these competent watchdogs, who prepared with unfailing dispatch his folders for meetings, the associated papers to illumine any incoming document or telegram, his programme for the day. The work was done punctiliously. Their master tolerated nothing less than perfection and, above all, speed of thought and deed. His greatest virtue was not patience.

The CIGS reached his desk one minute after entering the building. In the 'In' tray was always a situation report on the progress of operations from every front, land, sea and air. There were also a large number of telegrams. Some of them covered the fighting in the active theatres of war. Others were from the British Military Mission in Washington. Yet more were copies of signals to the Foreign Office. Every telegram would be marked by his personal staff so that his eyes could go straight to the point of greatest importance. He read and absorbed at great speed. At 10 a.m. his briefing team appeared, led by the Director of Military

Operations, and the Director of Military Intelligence. Placed
before him at his desk were the folders for the day's Chiefs of Staff
Meeting at 10.30 a.m. The Chiefs of Staff met every day and often
several times a day. For each item on the Agenda there was a folder,
with the supporting papers placed behind the particular document
to be considered – a Planners' paper, a telegram from a
Commander-in-Chief, a Memorandum from the Prime Minister.
In the front of the folder was a brief prepared by the General Staff.
He glanced rapidly at each folder, reading his brief with
extraordinary speed, already familiar with every argument but
checking that the salient points, shorn of irrelevance or repetition,
were arranged in a way that he could use. If he was dissatisfied a
sharp comment or question would come in his strong, rather nasal,
voice.

Briefing could not take long. Accompanied by his Personal
Staff Officer he then raced to the front door and was driven to
Great George Street, where the War Cabinet had their sessions,
where their Secretariat, including the Military Secretariat, worked,
where the Chiefs of Staff met. A secret and elaborate subterranean
warren had, with foresight, been developed before the war; and in
these cramped and not inappropriate surroundings, reminiscent of
the nether regions of a warship, Ministers and Chiefs of Staff
discussed for long hours filled with anxiety, cigar smoke and
fatigue.

Arriving at Great George Street he took the Chair, for he was
not only professional head of the British Army but Chairman of
the Chiefs of Staff Committee and their principal representative
and spokesman. Seated at the table were the First Sea Lord, who
had joined the Chiefs of Staff the previous October, and the Chief
of the Air Staff, who had been longest a member of the Committee.
They were sharply contrasting types, these men in dark and light
blue uniforms respectively – the one bluff, extrovert, quick-
tempered and formidable, with force and combative charm, very
much the fighting sailor, the Commander: the other younger than
any in the Committee, quiet, courteous, master of his subject,
intelligent, unruffled and decisive. Also at the table was the head of
the Military Secretariat of the War Cabinet. As Principal Staff
Officer to the Minister of Defence he had no formal responsibility
for decisions taken, but his relationship with the Prime Minister –
Minister of Defence as the latter also was – meant that his counsel
was invaluable. This Committee constituted the British Military
High Command in all but name.

In the background sat the junior secretaries, the minute takers. They recorded the discussions and the decisions, in prose which could smoothly mask anger and contention. As each item on the Agenda was completed, a minute taker would slip away to set that particular record in hand. After the meeting's conclusion the Secretary would wrestle with the drafts, struggling to produce, as has been written – 'what he thinks that they think that they ought to have thought'. Whatever the time and whatever the pressures the minutes, irreproachably typed, would be on desks next morning.

On this day, the Chiefs of Staff discussed the threat of German pilotless air weapons against England: the shooting of German prisoners of war by Yugoslav partisans: how the city of Rome was to be fed when captured: the policy for communicating information to the Russians about the impending invasion: the shipping situation in the Mediterranean: the control of secret operations in the Balkans: the potential of Australia as a base in the war against Japan: and many other matters.

A Committee had recently toured the world to study the requirements of war in the Far East. They had produced a report, and this morning attended the Chiefs of Staff Committee to present it and answer questions raised upon it. The report was comprehensive: the Committee had visited North America, Hawaii, Australasia, Burma and India.

He returned to the War Office after a brief lunch. The afternoon was generally the time of day for visitors and interviews. Today was no exception. First came a General who had been Second-in-Command to the 'Chindits', whose mercurial leader had been killed in the previous month. They had a long talk about the Burma campaign. Next came the Financial Adviser to the Viceroy of India. They discussed the internal situation in India, and in particular the grave dangers which the grain and food shortage could produce. India was the main base for operations in Burma. Any internal crisis there could have immediate repercussions upon the war. The Viceroy was a close friend and frequent correspondent.

Then two Americans called. There were serious differences of view between the British and American Chiefs of Staff, and between President and Prime Minister. The CIGS's own views had been strong and consistent. He was regarded by the Americans as the most intransigent of the British. His visitors today were the Deputy to the United States Chief of Army Staff and the Under

Secretary of State for the Department of the Army. They talked for an hour until he had to excuse himself for a forthcoming meeting of the War Cabinet. The papers and folders had been mounting on his desk. They would be handled with extraordinary dispatch, because only minutes elapsed between his visitors' leave-taking and his own departure once again for Great George Street and Cabinet at 6.30 p.m.

The length of proceedings at Cabinet tended to be governed as much by the mood of the Prime Minister as by the complexity of the issues before the meeting. This was an average day. The Cabinet discussed manpower at the conclusion of the War against Germany. Industry, reconstruction at home, and the requirements of the Armed Forces in occupying the territories of their defeated enemies would all compete. He had folders and briefs for each item of Cabinet, as for Chiefs of Staff Meetings. He spoke when invited, crisply, authoritatively and in a way which inspired invariable respect. He never wasted a word. Cabinet ended at 8.15 p.m.

Now came moments of relaxation. He dined at Boodles Club with an old friend and Hampshire neighbour. After dinner the CIGS returned to Great George Street.

At 10.30 p.m. the Defence Committee of the Cabinet met. This was the Committee of Cabinet Ministers most nearly associated with the running of the war, sitting under the Prime Minister's Chairmanship, with the Chiefs of Staff in attendance. The meeting was largely concerned with the correct bombing policy to adopt in preparation for the forthcoming invasion of France. Discussion focused on the so-called 'transportation' plan, particularly supported by the British Deputy to the Supreme Allied Commander, who argued strongly for attack to be concentrated against German centres of communication so that the German reserves would have maximum difficulty in moving against the Allied forces once landed. The opposing point of view advocated continuous attrition of the German aircraft industry, so that the Luftwaffe would be incapable of action against the beachheads and invasion forces; air attack against the Allied concentrations was still the threat most feared by some. At that time the CIGS inclined to the latter viewpoint. The Prime Minister, too, veered to it: he feared the effect on French opinion of the French civilian casualties which the 'transportation' policy would necessarily produce. But the balance of opinion favoured the other. The meeting closed at midnight, having agreed that the 'transportation' plan should continue, the matter to be reviewed a week later.

He had been feeling very tired for some weeks – for the first time he felt 'stale'. After the meeting the Prime Minister detained him, and they talked for a further half-hour during which he successfully slipped in a request for a week's leave. At 12.30 a.m. he returned to his flat in Whitehall Gardens.

He had lived this life since early December 1941. When he had assumed office Japan was on the point of striking, and within weeks Britain had suffered the loss of most of her Empire in the Far East. In Europe no military power had existed west of the Russian steppe except that of Britain's enemies. In the Mediterranean a small British Army had confronted a German-Italian force in North Africa, in a campaign which had swung to and fro, sometimes seeming remote from the places and issues which would bring victory or defeat in the end. He had lived through this 'dark night' and witnessed the gradual transformation of the war situation which 1942 and 1943 had brought forth. He had struggled without ceasing – above all against unrealism, against strategic vision unhooked from logistic and operational fact. Now, in spring 1944, the struggle was about to bear fruit. The Germans were about to be brought to battle once again in France. The Allies were about to invade. He had been waiting and working for this since 1940.

For the Allies had now to do what no one had done since William the Conqueror, and that which Philip of Spain, Louis XIV, Napoleon and Hitler had all attempted in vain. In two days they had to transport across the stormy tidal waters of the Channel, without hurt from U-boat, mine, E-boat or Luftwaffe, nearly 200,000 armed men and land them with 20,000 mechanical vehicles on open beaches along a fifty-mile stretch of fortified coast, negotiating a complex network of undersea obstacles and immobilizing shore defences of immense strength. Ever since November, when Germany's most original-minded commander had been sent to reorganize the Channel defences, half a million troops and conscript workers had been toiling to strengthen the 'Atlantic Wall'. The tidal stretches before the beaches had been strewn with steel and concrete wrecking devices, the sands and roads into the interior had been mined and barred by fortifications and tank traps, while every accessible landing-place was enfiladed by the fire of hidden batteries, and the level spaces behind the coastline studded with wooden posts to prevent airborne landings.

33

The hard core of the Allies' problem was logistic. It lay in the fact that a single division in the battleline was assessed as needing some 600 tons of supplies a day and that, until Cherbourg could be reached and captured, everything for the invading forces would have to be landed on open beaches. So would their reinforcements. Even with the two artificial harbours, secretly pre-fabricated in Britain during the winter, it was going to be a race against time to build up strength fast enough to hold off and ultimately break the defenders.

With so much to achieve and at stake it was inevitable that those responsible should have fears for the issue. Even the Americans, who two years earlier had wished to embark on invasion before their forces had been trained and equipped, and before almost any of the logistical wherewithal to make it possible was available, were now assailed by doubts.

The weeks and days before D-Day were never free from such doubts. To the CIGS, a realist whose pragmatism was often streaked with melancholy, the doubts were gnawing indeed.

The day was not yet over, nor could he sleep without a further act. He opened a small, brown leather-bound volume and began to write:

'April 13th, a tiring day . . .'

and then painstakingly recounted the actions and visitors of the last twenty-four hours. The diary, when complete, would be handed to his beloved wife, a record of a nightly conversation with her and an outlet for the exhaustions, the emotions and often the frustrations of his heart.

But the diary was not enough. A letter must be posted early next morning to Hampshire where his family were based, and whither he would go for a day at the end of the week. The day was now recounted in letter form, carrying to his wife the narrative of his time and the expressions of his love. Only when diary and letter were both written could he at last rest. It was like a thousand other days. He who lived them was a man of great although often disguised sensitivity: the exact opposite of the bluff extrovert beloved by caricaturists of British Generals. In four of the most dramatic years of its long history he was the head of the British Army, responsible for its performance, its survival and its honour on battlefields from the Channel to the Irawaddy.

Professional advice was tendered in the name of a Committee. Official minutes convey little of the individual's part in persuading or guiding a meeting. The story of a Chief of Staff has not the same sort of individual drama as attends the sole decisions of a Commander in battle. The CIGS's part was to determine, to discuss, to harmonize, to represent. His responsibilities ranged across the entire war effort: his sphere of interest was the world. The stage on which he performed was that of the highest direction of the war. His story is the story of the war. Fortunately for Britain it is also the story of an Ulsterman of outstanding stamina, intelligence and strength of will, a professional soldier of well-tempered steel, a supreme realist. A man of clear head and great heart; Irish breeding and an Irish heart. Alan Brooke.

CHAPTER II

Deux Patries

THE COUNTY OF FERMANAGH lies in the far west of the ancient province of Ulster: Feor-magh-Enagh, 'the country of the lakes'. Its landscape is dominated by windswept Lough Erne which gives the county, formed as such on the shiring of Ulster in 1585, its familiar name. For centuries, however, it was known as Maguire's country, the territory of a large and formidable tribe, descended from the 'Guarii' of antiquity: the Maguires.

During the autumn of 1641 the great Irish rising began.

The party in England which had destroyed Strafford – the party of John Pym – was riding high. Dominating Parliament, it was soon to challenge the King beyond hope of conciliation, and had meanwhile brought down his greatest servant. Strafford in Ireland had governed with that combination of harshness, efficiency and justice which characterized the man. He had checked, amid huge indignation, the ruthless exploitation of the native Irish by the English adventurers who had arrived with Elizabeth's Essex, and by the land-hungry Scots of the Ulster Plantation. Now Strafford's enemies were in the places of power. He had tried, when recalled from Ireland, to get appointed as his successor a man who understood Ireland, with some comprehension of the Irish view. He had proposed a Dillon, an Ormonde. Instead, two representatives of those English adventurers whose greed Strafford had bridled were established as joint Lords Justice in Dublin, and the supremacy of the English over the Irish Parliament was asserted in London. A principal element in the policy of Pym's party was the demand for rigorous enforcement of penal laws against Roman Catholics, and the scene appeared set for an attempt to extinguish in Ireland the people's dearest remaining possession, the old religion. On the night of 23rd October the native Irish rose.

They failed to achieve complete surprise. During the night of the 22nd Sir William Parsons, one of the Lords Justice, had received warning from an informer that Lords Maguire and

Macmahon were to seize Dublin itself. He acted. Several hours before the rising was due to start a young man was found disguised and hiding in a cock loft and arrested for urgent questioning: the second Baron of Enniskillen, Connor Roe Maguire.

The rising started in Ulster, although it spread to Munster and became for a while general. The O'Neills swept through the Plantation, seized Carrickmacross and Newry, besieged Monaghan, advanced on Drogheda. But fortresses and castles held out with their garrisons, bases for later reconquest and retribution. Frightful atrocities, born of despair and fear and magnified in the telling, produced, as the tide turned, a counterwave of cruelty and repression. The rising did not take long to fail.

For those who had led or inspired it there could be little hope. Young Maguire, sent to England in 1642, was brought to trial in London on 11th February 1645. He had struggled hard. He had escaped once and been recaptured. He had prayed to be judged before his peers in Ireland; but Judge Bacon had ruled that, 'A baron of Ireland was triable by a jury of this Kingdom'. He had challenged all twenty-three jurymen and secured a day's adjournment. The outcome was not in doubt. Found guilty of high treason he was hanged at Tyburn on 20th February, and his lands were declared forfeit. In consequence, Henry Brooke, first of Colebrooke, was granted 30,000 acres of Fermanagh.

Henry Brooke had held Donegal Castle and the surrounding district against the rebels, and had reaped his reward. He had inherited Donegal from his father, Basil Brooke, an Elizabethan captain of ancient Cheshire lineage who had come to Ireland on campaign and had received grants of land. He was knighted in 1664.

He married first a Wynter of Dyrham in Gloucestershire, a daughter of Captain John Wynter who had sailed with Drake, and by that marriage bred a son, Basil, ancestor of the Brookes of Donegal. Henry Brooke married, second, a daughter of Lord Docwra, another fierce old Elizabethan soldier in Ireland. Thirdly, he married a St George of Carrickdrumruisk in Roscommon, by whom he had a son, Thomas, who inherited Colebrooke.

Thomas, second Brooke of Colebrooke, was Member of Parliament for Antrim Borough. He served in the Army of Charles II and James II, but was dismissed from the Service, with other Protestants, by Tyrconnel during the latter's period of power, and was attainted, together with his half-brother Basil, in James II's time. When James II's reign ended in revolution and civil war, Thomas became major in the Regiment of Lord Drogheda, his brother-in-law, and fought for William III throughout the Irish War. His descendants, father to son, have held Colebrooke to this day.[1]

Without the Irish Regiments the story of the British Army would be impoverished. It would be poorer still without those officers of the Anglo-Irish ascendancy and of the Ulster Plantation who have provided the Army with many of its most illustrious names. Wellington, Gough, Montgomery, Alexander, Cavan, Dill, Gort, O'Connor, Templer – the roll-call echoes down the last two centuries like the music of some noble ceremonial march.

Field-Marshals and Generals reach the pages of published history. Often related to and certainly far outnumbering them are the others, the Regimental officers provided for Britain's wars, generation after generation, by these hardy, uncompromising and patriotic warrior families. Second to none were the Brookes of Colebrooke. They had come to Ireland with swords in their hands, unashamedly. They tenaciously defended the authority of the British Crown and the Protestant succession with which their own fortunes as a family had been intertwined. Not only loyalty but leadership in their community and zest for military service came as naturally to them as breathing. They had the stimulus which comes from challenge, and from more than a touch of insecurity.

Life in Ireland could never be placid or predictable. These families came to identify themselves closely with the country of their adoption, whose prosperity and stability they promoted, whose quirks they enjoyed, whose humour and sentiment they increasingly shared; but ancient native bitterness survived, feeding on every misfortune, every inequity. 'They' had risen in '41. 'They' rose again in '98. Danger and instability were never far below the surface of elegance, amusement and affection. The Anglo-Irish were determined simultaneously to enjoy being Irish and being different. They lived with a challenge.

Such an atmosphere breeds fighting men. In the Napoleonic wars Sir Henry Brooke, later created first Baronet of Colebrooke, had three brothers holding high rank in the Army, of whom one, Sir Arthur Brooke, succeeded General Robert Ross in command of the expedition which burned the Capitol of Washington in 1812. A second brother, Francis Brooke, led his Regiment, the 4th Foot, in many of the battles of the Peninsular War, was one of the first into Badajoz and took temporary command of Sir John Lambert's brigade at Waterloo, a battle in which his nephew, Sir Henry Brooke's eldest son, was killed.

This Sir Henry Brooke's second son, Arthur, served in the Royal Navy and succeeded as second Baronet of Colebrooke. Typical of the family were the five sons of his youngest brother, George Brooke, of whom three joined the Army and two the Royal Navy. Typical, again, were the family of Sir Arthur Brooke's second son, Sir Harry Brooke of the 92nd Highlanders – the Gordons – whose eldest son, James, and whose third son, Henry, were killed in that Regiment in the Great War of 1914–18, the first-named winning the Victoria Cross; and whose second son, in the Indian Army, was very severely wounded, while the youngest son, in the Navy, was killed in 1917. Twenty-six Brookes of Colebrooke served in that war: twenty-seven served in the war of 1939–45: and in those wars, or from wounds received in them, twelve died.

Sir Victor Brooke, third Baronet of Colebrooke, eldest son of Sir Arthur Brooke, succeeded his father at the age of eleven in 1854. He married Alice Bellingham, daughter of Sir Alan Bellingham, third Baronet of Castle Bellingham in County Louth, head of a family with deep roots in Northumberland, which had removed to Ireland early in the seventeenth century. His forebear, Henry Bellingham, had served in a regiment of cavalry raised for the suppression of the rebellion in 1641, and the next Bellingham, Thomas, was Colonel of another cavalry regiment which he himself raised for William III in the Irish War. The Bellinghams matched the Brookes. Their ancestral memories were the same.

Victor Brooke and Alice Bellingham married young – he twenty-one, she appreciably younger. In the fifteen years of their marriage between 1864 and 1879 eight children were born. Four years later, to the unconcealed dismay of his mother, arrived a ninth and last child, a sixth son: Alan Francis Brooke.

The youngest Brooke was born in a small chalet at Bagnères-de-Bigorre in the French Pyrenees, not far from Pau. In 1868 Victor and Alice Brooke had started the habit of spending the winters in the South of France, returning to Colebrooke only for the summer months. Pau was a fashionable resort, particularly popular with the British, with a famous Hunt enjoying country at the foot of the Pyrenees known already as 'the Leicestershire of France'. The climate was agreeable, there was excellent ibex shooting, good fishing in the mountain streams. The British colony was exclusive, but growing. There was sun, sport and pleasant society; and Alice Brooke was a woman of outstanding beauty, charm and artistic sensibility who could enjoy it fully. She claimed delicate health: and this, with her frequent confinements, gave her ample reason to spend as much time as possible in this congenial atmosphere and away from the damp rigours of Ireland. Victor Brooke, too, had lung trouble and for that reason had needed to spend long periods in a dry climate.

In 1879 the Brookes bought the Villa Jouvence in Pau, and henceforth Victor Brooke visited Colebrooke more and more rarely. He became an absentee landlord; and his estates were to some extent neglected and impoverished through that neglect, although on his annual return he was always received with affection as well as respect. Meanwhile the Villa Jouvence became his home. At the hottest time of the year the Brookes would leave the Villa Jouvence, not for Ireland, but for a rented chalet in the cool of the hills. At Bagnères, some forty miles from Pau, in 1883, they had taken the Chalet Geruset. It was a hot summer, and Alice Brooke was advised not to return to Pau for her confinement. Thus Alan Brooke was born on 23rd July in a small village of the Bigorre, a harsh and hardy district of the high Pyrenees.

Alan was a delicate child. He tended to have long attacks of fever in the spring of his early years, confined to bed for weeks at a time. He had, too, a dreamy and elusive quality, with enormous eyes in a fragile, white face. Victor Brooke was a stern and somewhat remote father in the mould of the times; but his heart went out immediately to his youngest son.[2] Alice adored him; and Alan, for his part, responded to his mother with a love which was a fundamental part of his character and which never diminished. Throughout her life he wrote to her of all his doings. He never acquired the reserved concealment of affection which was normal at the time even in devoted families – or never where she was concerned. She was his 'own darling'; every twinge of ill-health·or pain, described to him, was enough to produce a passion of commiseration from the depths of the heart. No sufferings were like her sufferings, no sympathy like hers. 'She had the faculty,' he wrote near the end of his life, 'so rare amongst humans, to be able to enter entirely into all one's activities, aspirations, disappointments, successes and failures and to throw herself wholeheartedly into one's life. She was consequently not only the most perfect mother but one of the very best of companions.' 'I place her,' he said, 'on a plane above all other members of my family.'[3] To her his letters as a stalwart cadet or Artillery subaltern would end as 'Your ever loving little son,[4] your Benjamin'. Such extreme devotion, frankly expressed and carried into manhood, has often attracted critical comment from pundits of psychological fashion. It has been equated with a fixation, a twist of the personality. It is hard to imagine such in Alan Brooke. He may have seen his mother, both at the time and in retrospect, with simple eyes of adoration. She undoubtedly bequeathed to him a capacity for tenderness, a concern for others, and, ultimately, a gift for companionship which were the attributes he most prized in her.

Alan, as a child, lived in a world of his own. His character was withdrawn and remote. Outward things did not seem particularly to affect him, so that he accepted rules or inhibitions without concern. To his brothers and sisters he was outstanding in his apparent self-sufficiency. He could keep himself occupied for hours, totally absorbed in what he was doing, in his own private life.

This concentration did not seem to extend to lessons. Here was his principal trouble, and here his teachers found difficulty in securing his attention. Indeed it seemed for long to be almost impossible to teach him to read – although a visit to an oculist at the age of seven, which proved his eyes to be out of focus, showed that there was a physical contribution to his slowness. On the other hand he was, from the start, good at mathematics; and he was always quick and clever with his fingers, making or mending things. Observers thought him much more like the Bellinghams than the Brookes. He loved drawing – an inheritance from Victor Brooke; and all his life he drew with fluency and wit. He drew what he saw, with quick, accurate observation, but as he grew older and his natural sense of fun became more extrovert and robust he also drew scenes of absurdity, caricatures and cartoons of humour and skill.[5]

Alan started his life as a Frenchman. Having been born at Bagnères he had ultimately to be naturalized. But beneath this formality was a reality. He spoke French before he spoke English. His early education was undertaken by German and French governesses and he was fluent in both languages. In English, on the other hand, spelling and some of the finer points of grammatical usage eluded him to the end of his days. He was shy – and, of course, not a little ashamed – of these 'shortcomings', but they were part of the boy and they remained part of the man. There was

41

something unmistakably French – indeed Gascon – in Alan Brooke, which must have come from the atmosphere and which mixed with Anglo-Irish blood to produce ultimate distinction. His rapid speech – likened later in his life to a machine-gun – his speed of perception, thought and action, his impatience and his peremptory quality may have owed something to Irish blood, but they owed much, too, to the environment of France. He was much with 'old' Laurent, the butler at the Villa Jouvence, who would take him fishing, and came to run Alice Brooke's establishment completely, from housekeeping to the engagement of servants, from cookery to the keeping of bees. Long afterwards when he and Alan met, a cousin recalled that they 'would always embrace like true Frenchmen'. 'I always felt,' Alan said to the people of Bigorre when he visited them at the end of his life, 'that I had *deux patries.*'

When the boy was eight years old his father died, and he was taken to see the body. Although his father's early death removed his direct influence, Victor Brooke's character was to be significantly reflected in that of his youngest son. Victor Brooke was a renowned sportsman and naturalist, devoted to all aspects of nature, who published learned zoological articles, and showed himself a profuse correspondent from every quarter of the globe. He was a tireless traveller while health permitted. In India George and Charles Trevelyan were among his friends. He took as deep an interest in the peoples and history of the sub-continent as he did in its flora and fauna. His sporting prowess and his love of the wild were matched by great zest for life and profound religious feeling.[6] Contemporaries spoke of 'that bright eager nature'. All this would be echoed in Alan. Victor Brooke never took a leading part in politics but he was an effective and lucid speaker. He strongly opposed Irish Home Rule, drawing on his conviction that it would be against the interests of all and, as he publicly expressed it, 'would leave a legacy of hate that no time would heal'. It was said that none of the bitter feelings of the Irish land question touched his property; and two thousand people followed his body to its grave at Colebrooke.

Alan experienced further bereavement, and saw two more corpses – a coachman's son and his own mother's brother – within the year. Then a young man, a carpenter's son, died of a haemorrhage in front of him; and a woman, one day, was flung out of a dogcart and suffered severe injuries before his eyes. His reactions to sorrow or to shock were inward. His brothers and sisters felt that they never knew what was going on in his mind.

Yet, looking back on their childhood afterwards, they reckoned that the sad things made a very deep mark. The urgent, pleading note in his voice was remembered as he reached that point in his prayers where he sought God's power to ward off calamities. Rabies was prevalent at one time in Pau, and Alan returning from a picnic on his bicycle was bitten by a Pyrenean dog. He said no word of concern until three weeks later something like quiet relief appeared, and he said:

'Now is there no longer a danger of my going mad?'

There was another side to the withdrawn and self-possessed little boy, which found its inspiration at Colebrooke. When Victor Brooke died his eldest son, Douglas Brooke, succeeded to the baronetcy and the estate. Eighteen years older than Alan he became as a young father to him; and Douglas's son, Basil Brooke,* born in 1888, became as a small brother. The position of baby of the family was succeeded by the responsibilities of a senior. Basil Brooke and Alan were sent to the same school in Pau, run by a German for the sons of English families, and the young Basil, a boarder, spent the Christmas and Easter holidays at the Villa Jouvence. But in the summer holidays they went together to Colebrooke, a beautifully placed Georgian house built of the local grey stone, the Cole Brooke itself running down from the hills.

Here he began to acquire that profound love and knowledge of nature and of all country pursuits which was to remain throughout his life the characteristic which often struck his acquaintances most. Douglas Brooke was his mentor; and although a stern disciplinarian towards his own sons, in the manner of Sir Victor, to Alan he was the kindest of instructors. Here at Colebrooke Alan learned to shoot and to fish, and to become more companionable. Colebrooke became his home in a way which his father's infrequent visits had never enabled it to be. It stood, always, for something separate in his life, surrounded by a unique enchantment.

He became, in effect, a member of his eldest brother's family. Yet, apart from his mother, the outstanding figure in his affections was his next brother – Victor Brooke, fifth son of his father, but ten years older than Alan. Of Victor he wrote that 'he became my hero', and it was Victor whose enthusiasms and achievements inspired him most.[7] Victor added a romantic quality to life. He was good at all things, invariably aiming at difficult physical and intellectual goals and, by skill, courage and self-discipline

* First Viscount Brookeborough.

achieving them. Not only to Alan but to the whole family he was a paragon.

Gradually Alan's character became more rounded. He learned to ride well, and, mounted by the kindness of two American ladies, started his hunting career with the Pau Hunt. He exercised his periodic responsibilities as chaperon to Basil, on their journeys alone from France to Ireland, with scrupulousness and exact discipline, threatening dire punishment should Basil fail to observe his instructions. 'It is to be "Uncle" Alan' he had, at the age of eight, told Basil, and he maintained order firmly. They shared even the most bizarre occupations. 'I've a great treat for you, Basil, a vulture to skin,' Alan excitedly told him at the start of one holiday at Pau when Basil arrived to stay. In an outhouse was the dead vulture, and an array of surgical instruments neatly set out by Alan. Basil's part was humdrum although carefully planned. Lady Brooke's scent spray, filled with disinfectant, was also on the bench. 'Now your job,' said Alan to Basil, 'is to keep spraying my hands and forearms and if one louse (the vulture was crawling with them) gets on to my clothes you'll never forget it.' Basil was deeply flattered at the high nature of the task.[8]

Lady Brooke had kept Alan at Pau – ostensibly for his health, and he had, indeed, remained delicate – and never sent him to a public school in England. The education at his school in Pau was, as he recalled it, excellent. But there were comparatively few boys – mostly English and American with a small number of French – and, although games of hockey, football and cricket were played with conscientious regularity, Alan felt, as an adolescent, that through unfamiliarity with team games or through a sense of innate difference he had missed something of value. It is questionable whether the feeling was well-based. He was not, and never felt, one of the herd. He learned admirable French and German: and he had Colebrooke.

Shy, reserved and without any outward sign of possessing much drive or ambition, not manifestly keen on emulating the daring exploits of his older brothers and sisters, Alan's future did not strike his mother as particularly promising. 'I want one day to see a tablet on this house stating that you were born here,' she used to say as they drove past the Chalet Geruset in her carriage and pair, but without great conviction. He first felt drawn towards the profession of doctor or surgeon, but by the age of sixteen it had been decided that he should seek entry to the Army. After six months' very hard work at a 'cramming' establishment at

Roehampton he went up for the entrance examination to the Royal Military Academy at Woolwich; and, although depressed about his chances and gloomily aware of his inadequacies, particularly in Latin, he 'crawled in with the tail-end – 65th out of 72', as he later described it – 'At any rate I was over that fence'.

The Royal Military Academy – 'the Shop' – trained 'Gentlemen Cadets' for commissions in the Royal Artillery and Royal Engineers. It was an intensely competitive establishment, comprising a two-year course, strenuous both physically and intellectually, and grading cadets in an ultimate 'passing out order' likely to have a significant effect upon their future lives. The top 'slice' of successful cadets were normally given commissions in the Royal Engineers, the number varying according to vacancy, and the remaining candidates in the Royal Regiment of Artillery. Within the Royal Regiment, however, there was again intensive competition. A 'good place' probably meant a commission in the Field Artillery, a lower place in the Garrison Artillery or some other less coveted branch.

In the summer the cadets went into camp under canvas at one of the training grounds familiar to generations of British soldiers. Brooke, whether at Woolwich or in camp, always found time to write at length and in the most exact detail to his mother. She had a natural gift of interest and comprehension of all her son's doings, so that when he recounted every minute of the military day he did so as to one whose attention, he was confident, would never wander. 'My dear little Pet,' he wrote from camp at Perham Down on Salisbury Plain in July 1902, 'I shall keep a kind of diary here for you in my letters': and a diary it was, enriched by drawings of increasing skill, and showing, too, an emergent taste for achievement and success.[9]

Life at a camp like Perham Down was a mixture of field exercises involving hard infantry work, rifle shooting, riding, tactical instruction and sport. Brooke, deprived, as he felt at the time, of the benefits of a public school background, took little part in team games; but he had developed into a fine horseman, and he was a skilled shot. He was a cadet highly commended for his accuracy, zeal and powers of application, and a very good draughtsman. He was an expert linguist and won a silver medal offered by the French Ambassador for a competition in the French language. More than any of these accomplishments he felt – and expressed – a new sense of being able to assess his fellow men. He had grown up with few friends beyond his immediate family and no exact contemporaries within it. When he passed out of Woolwich, as a particularly well-regarded cadet, he had not only absorbed its training but had developed an ability to mix with others, to give and receive friendship and to sum up character. At this, one of the greatest gifts of corporate education, he was a late starter, and learned fast. Another facet had developed and would always remain: 'He is restless,' a contemporary recalled, 'and lives on his nerves.'

Brooke improved his competitive placing at Woolwich as the course went on. He worked his way up to 15th in Academy order and hoped for a commission in the Royal Engineers. He worked hard – perhaps too hard – in the summer of 1902, had frequent headaches and complained of 'the beastly bad luck dogging me at present'. Whatever the reason he dropped two places in his last term: only fifteen Engineer commissions were granted; and he therefore took the second place in the list of cadets commissioned in the Royal Artillery, a high place enabling him to select the branch of his choice, the Field Artillery. 'A thoroughly good, all-round cadet who should make a smart Field Artillery officer,' his final report stated. 'He is a very good horseman,' a certificate added. The ultimate parade was taken by the veteran Field-Marshal and Gunner Lord Roberts who, in an address of typical understanding and frankness, chiefly aimed consoling words at those whose placing had not justified their attaining the Arm or Branch of their choice.[10] On 24th December 1902 the Secretary for War, St John Brodrick, signed a commission of King Edward VII appointing Alan Francis Brooke to the Royal Regiment of Artillery. With his commission Brooke retained the typically forbidding written notification which had accompanied it, calling his attention to an Article in the Royal Warrant for Pay and Promotion –

> 100. An officer shall not be permitted to remain in our Army unless during the first three years of his service his retention is shown to be in every way desirable.

against which a wag scrawled on Brooke's copy –

> Take care, or they will make a Grenadier of you,[11]

no doubt in ribald allusion to a current scandal in that Regiment of Guards, in which a Brooke cousin was serving, and which had required the attention of Lord Roberts himself.

CHAPTER III

The Subaltern

THE FIRST THREE YEARS of Brooke's military life were spent in Ireland, the next eight in India. In both countries his life was much occupied by sport. In Ireland, he joined a battery stationed at Fethard in Tipperary 'with kennels of the Tipperary Hounds, hunted by Burke, only a mile from the barracks; a trout stream running through the village, and many snipe bogs in all directions'; and later removed to Waterford to relieve another battery 'which, as a result of a public-house brawl had shot a man outside the barrack gates'.[1] The months were crowded with hunting, steeple-chase and point-to-point riding (with considerable success), shooting and fishing. Every detail and triumph was relayed to his mother 'with *worlds* of love', 'with the vastest of hugs' to his 'dear little pet',[2] although he sometimes deferred telling her about his rides over steeplechase fences until after the event, to avoid her worrying. His letters to her, whether from Ireland, India or elsewhere were long, descriptive, regular and brimful of affection.

This was the pattern of military life at that and indeed subsequent times. Officers were paid little, and were generally hard up unless – which was unusual – endowed with generous private means. Men like Brooke, youngest of a large family and backed by a somewhat inpoverished Ulster estate, were generally short of cash. Yet the basic elements of life and of field sports were still inexpensive. Gunner officers were encouraged to hunt the battery horses. Hospitable landowners were 'at home' to the officers of Ireland's garrisons. Brooke acquired a motorcycle and got home to Colebrooke whenever he could.

Sport was considered an excellent formative of character. To ride well was a prerequisite of efficiency in an officer, and sport promoted competent and courageous riding. Sport developed, too, speed of reaction, judgement and physical fitness. It would have astonished Brooke and his contemporaries had it been suggested that their lives were over-full of play for servants of the Crown. They would have indignantly enquired in what duty they were failing.

Such indignation would have been reasonable. Together with the sport, the expeditions, the fun there went a scrupulous discharge of Regimental duties. To fail in care for the men of the battery or – the supreme sin – the cleanliness and effectiveness of the guns was unheard of, care for the battery horses was a sacred trust. Artillery practice was a matter of keen competition between batteries, and the professional skill of the Royal Artillery, far from being regarded as a tiresome irrelevance to the pursuit of leisure, was a matter of pride to every Gunner. The Army had only recently emerged from the sobering experiences of the Boer War. There was a certain relaxation in the air, but it would be succeeded, as the decade advanced, by the sense of another shadow. Whether in Ireland, England or India, British soldiers rode, roistered and enjoyed themselves; but, at least at the Regimental level, they also paid scrupulous and increasing attention to their professional competence. The Boer War had woken the Army up.

This was congenial to Brooke. He threw himself with great intensity into all he did, developing his powers of observation and his physical skills while at the same time using, whether encouraged or not, a quick and enquiring mind. He was a soldier, and as with everything he took up in life he determined to master the business. He had been noted, at Woolwich, as 'one who thought things out for himself and did not take them for granted', and from the start of his military career he developed an objectivity which is not the universal characteristic of his profession or those who rise therein. 'This is an excellent battery,' he wrote of that in which he served in 1905, 'thoroughly and carefully instructed in every way'; while in 1907, at Practice Camp in India, 'I was not impressed by the standard of artillery shooting as compared to what I had been used to at home.'[3]

Soon after receiving his commission, he designed and submitted to the War Office, with skilfully executed drawings, a timed percussion fuse (it was returned with the thanks of the Secretary of State but adjudged 'not sufficiently promising to justify the carrying out of any trials').[4] His mind was restless and critical. He made copious written notes on military lectures or articles which interested him. He studied military history, as was not only obligatory but fashionable among intelligent officers at the time, and began – at first painfully – to write well when he produced the periodic obligatory piece. Among other writings an essay on the Valley Campaign in the American Civil War (a war whose relevance to the age had been preached to a generation of

British officers at Camberley by Colonel Henderson, the biographer of 'Stonewall' Jackson) survives, clearly written, lucid, objective and – as ever with Brooke – accompanied by superbly drawn maps. He became a qualified interpreter in both French and German in 1904.

In 1906 Brooke thought it was time he saw more of the world. He volunteered for service in India, and in November of that year was ordered to take over a draft of the East Lancashire Regiment, and superintend their movement from the Curragh, outside Dublin, to Bombay. The draft, as was not uncommon with drafts, was drunk. 'In fact,' Brooke recalled later, 'two men were so bad that they had to be stretched across the top of a side car and brought up the rear of the drunken mob I had to march through Newbliss to the station, singing obscene songs at the top of their voices.' He embarked at Southampton, and on 26th December arrived at Bombay, and travelled to join the 30th Royal Field Artillery Battery at Meerut, in the Punjab.[5]

There now began what Brooke, like many an officer of his generation, could later describe as the happiest and certainly most carefree years of life: eight years in the India of the British Raj, before 1914. It was, for an Artillery subaltern, a country in which every variety of experience, travel and sport was to be obtained, and cheaply – the India of 'Kim', garrisoned by a large, British-officered Indian Army alongside another, large, British Army. India's defence, in the aftermath of the Boer War and before a new threat produced a sharply different British strategic policy, was regarded as the primary task of the British Army. The chief threat was considered to be the thrusting south-facing ambition of Imperial Russia, restless player of the 'Great Game'.

The Royal Artillery, wherever stationed, was at that time divided into brigades, each artillery brigade normally consisting of three Field (or two Horse) Artillery batteries and an Ammunition Column. All batteries were horse-drawn; but Horse Artillery, whose function was the support of the cavalry, were armed with a lighter gun, equipped with a superior breed of troop-horse, and, by a long tradition in the Royal Regiment, constituted a *corps d'élite* to which officers of particular promise from the Field Artillery would be posted, thus receiving the coveted 'jacket'. Each brigade of artillery – although the organization and deployment were seldom as tidy as the theory demands – directly supported a Cavalry or Infantry Division; and these divisions, British and

49

Indian, were distributed throughout the Military Districts of the Raj. Four batteries, two of RHA and two of RFA, were stationed at Meerut.

From the first Brooke loved India. Every view from the train from Bombay to Meerut, with peacocks and parrots and every sort of wildlife, delighted him and was the subject of immediate note and drawing. He had already begun that interest in photography which lasted all his life. He loved India's wild places, its mountains, jungles and great rivers and was utterly content, alone or with one companion, on the shooting trips he organized whenever time and his means permitted. 'I found,' he said, after a journey through Travancore, 'an inspiration and an insight into the problems of life. In those many happy days spent wandering in Kashmir, Ladek, Sewalk, Central Province, Bhopal and Travancore I did more towards laying down the foundation of the religious concepts that have guided me through life. In those surroundings I have felt nearest to my Maker and best able to appreciate His greatness.'[6] It is not uncommon for a superb natural environment to induce a sense of awe, and of the smallness of men before the mysteries. In Brooke's case this sense remained a constant part of his being. His observations of nature, of animal and plant life, later, above all, of birds, had from the beginning been acute. What flowered in India was an associated reverence and self-questioning.

His years were crowded with sport. Pigsticking from the start, and later the hunting of jackal with a pack of 'long dogs' he organized in 1912, occupied much of his spare time. He speared a wolf in January 1909 – a rare feat: riding out after jackals with one friend, armed with hog-spears, they put up a wolf and after a mile's run Brooke caught and killed him. And there were the shooting trips; the meticulously prepared journeys over the wildest parts of India in pursuit of the 'Ovis Amon', bear, ibex, the Kashmir stag, the Tibetan wolf. Every trip was carefully planned and costed, conducted as far as possible on foot to save horseflesh and money, and administered on the most austere basis. The 'shooting trip' if it could be organized, was for Brooke the high point of the year. That of 1907 involved covering about 1000 miles, over half of it on foot, in eighty-six days. Undertaken with one companion it cost Brooke the equivalent of £55. He had always to be careful over money, and it was in his nature to worry about it.

Then there was the quest at every opportunity for tiger and panther in the jungles of India; and adventures of following up wounded animals in tall grass, the imprudences, the scares, the escapes. And there were the Regimental Races, the Polo, the Cup meetings. Brooke enjoyed it all hugely. 'I was determined,' he said, 'to enjoy every minute of life to the full,' and his energy and achievements were considerable. All of it was recounted to his beloved mother. Yet the self-questioning, accompaniment of maturity, increased. 'From the very start,' he wrote, 'I had experienced pangs of regret and repentance when a hunt was brought to a successful end by the destruction of some wild creature . . . strange feelings of deep dissatisfaction with oneself at the very moment of elation at having accomplished the task one had set one's heart on, and which had in many cases entailed much physical effort, discomfort and suffering.'[7] More and more his letters home reflected an increased sensitivity about killing. Increasingly he found that by replacing the rifle by the camera he obtained 'all the skills of the chase without any of the personal reproaches at its outcome'. He exemplified the sentiment in one letter home:

> My shikari suddenly saw the black back of a bull bison close to us. I crept up to about 40 yards from him and examined him carefully. All the better feelings were for leaving him, but a desperate struggle was going on inside me. It was practically my last chance, a very tempting shot. I decided to shoot him, got ready and had the rifle on him ready to shoot when he turned a little more broadside on. But he turned the other way and started grazing towards me, he looked absolutely glorious and somehow I could not bring myself to shoot him when in the back of my mind I felt I did not really want him. So I changed my mind and decided to let him off and to take a photograph instead . . .[8]

Nevertheless his 'kills' continued to thrill him.

Sport was only one aspect of life. Brooke was working, with a determination and thoroughness which was to be his personal hallmark, at the study of his profession. Even when on leave he would read military subjects several hours a day. 'Power of command, horse management, keenness and knowledge of gunnery. He was exceptional at all,' said his Battery Commander at that time.[9] He qualified in Urdu in 1908, and in Persian in 1910. He also turned his thoughts to the Indian Staff College at Quetta and decided, in January 1909, to try for the next November Entrance Examination.

The decision, reached when staying at Government House in Calcutta with his adored brother Victor who was Military

Secretary to the Viceroy, Lord Minto, was taken under a cloud. Brooke had recently been on leave in England and had visited several aurists to seek advice on increasing deafness in the left ear. They were unanimous that he should not subject his ears to heavy noises, if he was to avoid complete deafness: and that he should leave the Royal Artillery. A possible solution, or at least stay of execution, might be to 'try for the Staff', and this Brooke decided to do.

It involved very high pressure. He had just passed in Urdu. Now he needed, under the current rules, to pass his promotion examination to Captain before applying to take the Staff College Examination itself. From that moment 1909 'became a year of continuous work'. In June he passed the Promotion Exam, which comprehended papers in Topography, Fortification, Tactics, Organization, Law, Military History and Sanitation. The first hurdle was cleared. It was next necessary to be attached to the Staff for a short period, and then August and September were spent 'cramming' under a well-known and exceptionally able but mildly alcoholic preceptor at Murree.

> I am now hard at it all day from 7 a.m. till 10.30 p.m. with only stops for meals and one hour's exercise at 7 p.m.[10]

In the midst of this Brooke heard that he had got his 'jacket'. He was to join 'N' Battery, Royal Horse Artillery, known as 'The Eagle Troop', at Ambala, and to move with it to Practice Camp at the beginning of October. This was to be immediately followed by manoeuvres. On the one hand the posting to the Royal Horse Artillery was something to which Brooke had aspired for the last five years, for which he had been strongly recommended, and which he certainly did not wish to sour by implying to his new commander and comrades, the elite of the Royal Regiment, that his principal concern was quickly to leave them for the Staff College. On the other hand the examination was to start on 15th November and every minute mattered. In the event Brooke went to Practice Camp and on manoeuvres with the Eagle Troop; was given a week's leave off manoeuvres for a final cramming at Murree before he sat the papers; and, like many another before and after, failed the examination by failing the paper in Military Law. Thereafter he happily laid aside all thoughts of taking the Staff College Examination or of leaving his splendid new 'family' of 'N' Battery; and ultimately went, with a nomination rather than after examination, to the Staff College at Camberley in 1919.

And the deafness? Brooke wrote in 1950:

As for the ears, I gambled on them and hoped that the ear specialists might have been wrong. They were wrong, and I have now reached my 67th year with reasonable hearing left, in spite of having continued to shoot and remained close to Artillery in action on very many occasions.[11]

So much for the inauspicious medical and academic beginnings of the future Chief of the Imperial General Staff and Master Gunner of St James's Park.

Comradeship is the outstanding quality of a good army. Brooke had, from first joining the Royal Regiment, not only attracted the consistent praise of his superiors but made a mark on all who knew him as outstandingly likeable, witty in rejoinder, an excellent companion. His friends meant much to him.

He served in Eagle Troop until 1914 – 'five of the happiest years of my life' he called them. He seemed now to give little evidence of that withdrawn and inscrutable quality which had marked his childhood, nor of the shyness which he later claimed had haunted his youth. Nevertheless he was seldom a man of much outward display. He gave, at that time and later, a certain impression of being uninterested in people except at an agreeably superficial level, absorbed only in practical or professional pursuits. Yet his letters and later recollections showed a sensitive and thoughtful nature, deeply grateful for the friendships he enjoyed, and very perceptive. His sensitivities however, like those of most British subalterns, did not extend to all. In possession of a catapult on a train journey 'I used to amuse myself shooting natives on the backside as they stooped over'.[12] In spite of his warm affection for Indian companions in sport or personal servants, in his general attitudes he was a young man of his time.

Brooke paid several visits to the States of the Native Princes where a different and fascinating India could be found:

Early in the year (1910) I proceeded to Bhopal for a ten-day shoot . . . We were the guests of Colonel Abaidullah Khan the second son of the Begum of Bhopal. He was kindness itself. Our visit included paying our respects to the Begum. She received us from behind a 'purdah' screen but was a most charming personality.

And in December that year:

I received an invitation to go to Gwalior for the Christmas week. I knew that this week would be at least 50% social, but I wanted to establish contacts with the Maharajah Scindia, and Oureat, a Frenchman who was head of the 'Animal Department', a sort of glorified gamekeeper who ran all shoots and looked after all the jungles. I had hoped that when my photographic flashlight equipment had been perfected I should be able to try it out on some of the very plentiful Gwalior tigers.

The Maharajah Scindia was a great character, full of energy and enthusiasm, not beyond having a drop too much at his wonderful banquets and balls. The balls were usually fancy dress ones, and as I had no kit I was taken by him to a room in the palace and told to choose a kit for myself. His favourite dance was 'Sir Roger de Coverley' so every second dance was one. We all lived in the guest house, which was filled with a variety of people from all over India – [13]

'I knew that this week would be at least 50% social, but . . .' Brooke was candid and unkind about the society which India afforded, as far as Englishwomen were concerned:

The Meerut week has been in full swing. Dances and a regular rush of society with the whole place crowded out. It is the side of India that I dislike more than words can express. I love the wild uncivilized part, the living in the jungle and the crawling about after buck . . . But the social side consists of a bevy of women, any one of which is uglier than the next, painted up to the nines and rejuvenated, and all wearing a most abominable self-conscious expression which does not shine at its best on a sunburned complexion! After this harangue you will probably hear by the next mail that one of these beautiful fairies has absolutely captivated me . . .[14]

But it does not appear to have happened, although his reactions were not always so caustic – 'One's feelings,' he wrote, with ostensible facetiousness, referring to the relationship with women as opposed to friendship with men, 'continually jumping and changing in a manner most injurious to health . . .' and, ruefully, after an outburst of youthful cynicism, 'I know that I shall soon again be a silly moth flitting around some beautiful creature knowing jolly well the whole time that I shall singe my wings.' Social life in India was full of 'longueurs', and he was never patient: but there is little to show that he was not as susceptible as most men.

But his ideals, although he was reticent, were high, and his imagination probably romantic to a degree unsuspected by his fellows. His letters seldom refer to his reading, but in one he described *The Choir Invisible* as the only book he had ever read three times. It is a story, by James Lane Allen, of romantic love and renunciation, with vivid descriptions of adventure, but also with a theme of fusion between spiritual and physical passion which belongs more to the age of chivalry than to the eighteenth-century Kentucky of the tale's setting. The (illicit) object of the hero's – unspoken – passion gives him Malory's *Morte d'Arthur* as the book 'he would always need'. She is spiritual mentor as well as object of adoration. 'As he read the nobler portions of the book the nobler parts of his nature gave out their immediate response.' The hero is torn between the knightly and spiritual virtues – 'the white wheat of the spirit' and the 'red tares of the flesh' which he hugs as a 'whole inflaming bundle against his blood'. He treads, with much pain, the path of virtue to the end. The book, admirably and perceptively written, clearly struck a powerful chord of sympathy in Brooke. It expounds the power of true love, the danger of idealizing the beloved rather than seeing her clear as human and individual, and the pain of virtuous choices. It may be a 'young man's book'; anyway this particular young man read it again and again.

However he was already pledged. Six-month leaves in Europe were granted at regular intervals to officers serving in India. On the first such taken by Brooke, in 1908, he became engaged to a beautiful Irish girl, Jane Richardson, a neighbour, daughter of Colonel John Richardson of Rossfad in Fermanagh. Marriage on a subaltern's pay and Brooke's slender means was impossible. Promotion was slow, dependent on seniority and vacancy, with little movement in the higher ranks. It was the system, and accepted as such: Brooke's eleven years as a subaltern, leading to promotion only because of war, were perfectly normal. It meant, however, that the engagement had to remain 'secret' – or at least unofficial. They were engaged for six years.

'The side of India that I dislike.' There was no doubt of the side he loved. His sporting expeditions crowd his letters, but increasingly not the game to be stalked, but the majesty of their environment provided the fundamental excitement.

> On reaching Lamayorou [in 1907] we met a Monsieur Toussaint, a judge in Madagascar, taking six months' leave studying Buddhist religion in Tibet and Burma. I found him most interesting and visited the local monastery with him. I had been asking him about the pictures of wild-looking gods on the

side walls of the temples, and he had informed me that the lamas, whilst according the place of honour to Buddha at this end of the temple, did not like to cast out the old gods and had placed them on the side walls: at this point we arrived at the door of the temple, looking out on to range upon range of snow-topped Himalayas. He stopped; and waving his arms shouted *'Voila, les Dieux changent et les montagnes restent!'*[15]

He probably spoke for Brooke.

So life in India continued, hard work, hard play, companionship and professional pride. Brooke attended the Durbar of 1911, an unforgettable spectacle, apotheosis of British India. He took part in the great Review, with 50,000 troops on parade, the RHA batteries on the traditional right, and leading the march and gallop past the King-Emperor.

Cavalry Manoeuvres, Artillery Practice Camps, 'Staff Rides' – what was the object of this activity? Where was now the main threat, perceived or unperceived, which alone could give ultimate point to such a life? At home, and far outside the concern of a Gunner subaltern, exactly this had been fiercely debated ever since the dust settled after the Boer War. Although he probably was unaware of it Brooke's 'happiest, carefree years' since receiving his commission had been marked by a fundamental shift in British policy.

The conflict over the correct strategy for the Empire between 1902 and 1914 was generally conducted as one between the supporters of a Maritime or a Continental strategy. By the former it was contended that the maintenance or gaining of supremacy at sea would absolutely protect the United Kingdom from invasion, and would deter or prevent any attempt upon her overseas possessions, with the exception of India. The task of the Army would be to defend India: even garrisons abroad could safely be reduced, since if command of the sea were exercised they would be unnecessary, while if it were lost they could not possibly be adequate. If any land force were to be retained for offensive action it should be small, amphibious, capable of being used as a projectile exploiting flexibility and surprise, fired by the dominant strategic arm of the Navy.

This view was popular. It represented the conventional wisdom. The dominant role of sea power in history, largely exemplified by the course of the Napoleonic Wars, had not only been recently expounded by Admiral Mahan – it had been accepted and taken as a challenge by Imperial Germany. A great German naval expansion was set in hand. For the first time since

Trafalgar Britain's supremacy at sea was at risk. How could there be argument as to the best course to follow, or the priority to adopt? The early years of the Committee of Imperial Defence were predominantly devoted not to debate but to consolidation of this point of view. Men like Lord Esher, who envisaged that Committee as ultimately possessing executive authority over the Services comparable to the Ministry of Defence of our own day, were convinced of the correctness of a maritime philosophy. Its supporters had fashion in their favour, and in terms of British national or imperial defence against a nineteenth-century background this was comprehensible.

At the heart of the situation was a paradox. It was German maritime ambition which brought the likely enemy to the forefront of planning; and this planning was initially obsessed with the maritime aspect of the threat. Yet the course of events which focused the minds of British strategists on the possibility of European war, against a European enemy, also produced, as a rational reaction to this possibility, a policy of Alliances. There was a realistic sense that Imperial Germany would best and perhaps could only be deterred from adventure by the prospects of a combination of European Powers in arms against her. The Entente was born, and from it as night follows day came the expectation of France that she would not stand alone if attacked. By that could only be understood 'attacked on land'.

Those convinced of the strategic wisdom of an almost solely maritime philosophy contended that Britain's naval power alone represented, as Esher put it, the 'value of the Entente to France in war'. But to a Continental Power – then as ever – threatened by invasion, the protracted and attritional effects of sea power might be ultimately decisive to the destiny of her British ally, but were immediately irrelevant to the defence of her own frontiers. A long drawn-out throttling of Imperial Germany could have no attractions for a possibly occupied France. It was defence of the land that mattered.

Thus Britain, in a series of jerky and often half-disowned initiatives described in terms of 'contingency planning', was drawn by the Entente into implicit political and moral commitments on which it would one day be impossible to renege. A predominantly maritime strategy was rational in terms of national and imperial defence. In terms of Allied solidarity, in deterrence of Imperial Germany, it would never meet the case. Nor can it be argued that this situation could have been avoided without ultimate disaster, given the premise that Germany was to be confronted one day. Without the British Army, born as it was from the seeds planted between 1906 and 1914, France would, without question, have been beaten by Germany. Maritime power could have saved Britain. It would not have saved the Entente. The inexorable logic of events was drawing Brooke and every young soldier of his generation to France.

It was not popular, even if it could be afforded, that subalterns should marry, but by 1914 Brooke and his Janey decided that, obstacles or not, marry they would. Permission had to be sought. Ronald Adam, a brother subaltern in Eagle Troop, was in the same case and they decided to apply together. 'Who'll break the ice?' said Adam. 'I will,' said Brooke, and did.[16]

Home leave was agreed, and the date of the wedding fixed for July at the bride's home at Ballinamallard in Fermanagh. Brooke prepared everything – bungalow, garden, 'buggy', furniture, for his return as a married man. He had just, somewhat to his regret, taken over command of the Ammunition Column which supported each Brigade of Artillery, and which each subaltern took turns to command for a year. He had been home in 1913 also, visiting Lady Brooke in St Jean de Luz, and spending several weeks in Ireland: however, the leave which he began in May 1914 was planned to be for four months, and to cover his marriage, honeymoon and return. He expected to be back in September, and as usual travelled via Marseilles to call on his mother, and then via England to Ireland. He saw his brother Victor, by now Second-in-Command of the 9th Lancers, while in England. He was not to see him again.

The wedding took place on 28th July. At the church door one of the ushers, Commander Archdale of the Royal Navy, approached the bridegroom. 'I won't be able to come to the reception after the Service,' he said . 'I've been recalled by the Admiralty.'

The honeymoon started in County Down. A knock on a hotel bedroom door on the evening of 5th August produced a telegram.

Be prepared embark for India about 11th August at Southampton no family will be conveyed. Acknowledge and state whether you are in possession of a return ticket to India and if so by what ship on what date. Pack saddle.[17]

Six years of engagement: six days of marriage: then August, 1914.

CHAPTER IV

France and Flanders – I

FOR A SOLDIER nothing is worse than to be separated from his kit and to lose his boots, and this was Brooke's recurrent fate. On first joining his battery in India in 1907 he had lost 'a leather kit bag containing all my boots and shoes, one pair of jackboots, three pairs of brand new Peel boots, a pair of Wellingtons and many others' during the rail journey from Meerut to Agra to take part in an important Review.[1] In 1940, before embarking from Dunkirk, 'came the difficult moment to decide what to abandon. I had a brand new pair of Huntsman breeches and an equally new pair of Maxwell's Norwegian boots. However I thought this would be an awkward attire to swim in . . . I therefore very reluctantly stripped these off.'[2]

So it was in 1914. All Brooke's uniform, equipment, horses and saddlery were in India. He secured one ready-made suit of uniform, and – without belt or revolver – embarked on the transport *Somali* on 11th August. In packed conditions, an assortment of officers, warrant officers and civil servants, suddenly recalled to India, sailed to Port Said without any intermediate stop. Brooke had, unsuccessfully, asked leave from the War Office to be retained at home, sharing with all his generation the fear that in so short a war the Army in India would be 'out of it': many officers on leave from India were retained to help the raising of Kitchener's 'New Army'. Wireless orders reached *Somali*, however, that officers of certain Divisions and Brigades in India were to disembark in Egypt to await the arrival of their units. It looked as if Brooke might meet his command and his comrades half-way from India rather than catching them at the start of their long voyage towards the war; for to France they were bound.

Accordingly on 24th August Brooke disembarked at Port Said and moved to Cairo where he attached himself to a battery of Royal Horse Artillery at Abassia. No situation could have been more wretched to a young man, although, as always with Brooke, enjoyment of the present kept breaking through. He was just married and had immediately been parted from his bride: he was separated from his possessions, his friends, and his command. The future was obscure; and great events were taking place in Europe. Characteristically, Brooke engaged an instructor in Arabic and started to learn the language – 'as I felt that if we were to fight in the Middle East the knowledge of this language might be of use'. Equally in character he spent a lot of time at the zoo, bought a Baedeker guide, explored Egypt and 'succeeded in having a most interesting time in spite of the continual uncertainty of plans from day to day'. Grief compounded loneliness and uncertainty. The name of his beloved brother, Victor, appeared among the dead in the first casualty list Brooke saw. Victor was 'my ideal of a man' he afterwards wrote – 'I owe him more than any other man'. Bereavement and isolation were exacerbated by an initial absence of letters from home, the postal services being in the disarray normal at the start of a war; and by anxiety for the suffering of his mother.[3]

On 17th September light broke. Brooke heard that a Horse Artillery Battery and Ammunition Column would probably pass by Port Said next day. He went there and on the 18th found his beloved Eagle Troop in one transport and in another the Ammunition Column. Here, again, was his personal command, in which he was known, as his Quartermaster-Sergeant recalled fifty-two years later, as 'a Commanding Officer to whom one could take all problems and be sure of support and solution'. He caught the convoy by two minutes, found that a brother officer, Adam, had brought all his uniform and equipment, and learned that their destination was Marseilles. The Ammunition Column, with its 17 wagons and 29 mule carts, its 120 men, 98 horses and 58 mules, had disembarked by the end of September and, after a tremendous Marseilles welcome – streets packed, and cheering crowds – made its slow way by train northward through France. A three-week hardening-up period for men and horses, after the cramped inactivity on board, was spent in camp near Orleans. During these weeks, of course, no sporting opportunity was missed, and he wrote how, 'We have borrowed a couple of ferrets from the Chateau close to here and are going to ferret a few rabbits tomorrow afternoon'.[4]

'We went to see some German officer prisoners,' he wrote in his letter of 8th October 1914.[5] 'I had a talk with them and they seemed to be quite well satisfied with the way they were being looked after.' Brooke's references to the enemy in his letters were never tainted by that very understandable hatred which loss and misery exacerbated by propaganda were so freely to generate. To him the German soldier was, from first to last, 'the old Bosch' (sic). As the war progressed Brooke often referred to its horrors, grateful as so many have been then and since for a certain numbness of feeling which comes to the soldier. 'The sights up there,' he wrote from the Ypres Salient in November 1917, 'are beyond all description; it is a blessing to a certain extent that one becomes callous to it all and that one's mind is not able to take it all in.' But he never made the horrors a cause of personal resentment against a brave enemy. He knew, without relish, that both sides were suffering alike. German activity was described objectively, with soldierly appreciation, or – where it was outwitted – with the satisfaction of a victor combined with the elation of the successful hunter, and in sporting terms. There will always be many who find such habits of mind completely alien. To fight they need to hate. Such was not Brooke's way.

On the night of 30th October the Ammunition Column finally began its journey towards the front.

When Brooke arrived in France the tide of the great German advance had already ebbed at the Battle of the Marne. The Germans had then withdrawn to the Aisne, where the French and British forces following up found them already well-entrenched. The advance had been too leisurely, and the withdrawal too deliberate to permit the sort of counter-offensive for which the Allied Commanders hoped: one which would have enabled the French and British troops to drive a retreating enemy from hastily prepared positions, and to resume mobile operations in pursuit of a beaten invader. In fact, at the Battle of the Aisne, the Germans were well prepared, and showed clearly what modern weapons in well-sited and co-ordinated defensive positions could do. The Allies abandoned the idea of frontal attack and advance, as had the Germans earlier. Instead, each contestant hastily moved his weight northward to seek his opponent's flank. The 'race to the sea' was on. The critical point of the campaign was shifted to Flanders as each moved as rapidly as possible to forestall the danger of envelopment, and to seek, in turn, to envelop. This led to the encounter battle we know as First Ypres; and, because it was indecisive, to an extension of the deadlock at appalling cost.

Thus the British Army had been withdrawn from the Aisne front in mid-October and moved northward. The subsequent forward movement, together with a French Group of Armies under Marshal Foch on the British left, was conceived as an out-flanking eastward advance. It soon met a corresponding German westward thrust in much greater strength than had been anticipated, itself envisaged by the Germans as an envelopment, with the right flank marching down the coast. The Germans were determined to prevent any move to cut them off from the Channel ports and, in the words of General von Falkenhayn, the new German Chief of Staff, 'to force a favourable change in the whole situation on the Western Front'. It was the last occasion on that front when two opposing armies met, each initially thinking of itself as carrying out an offensive.

The battle had been joined on 20th October. The outer flank was largely stabilized by the flooding of the country in the battles on the Yser. On 30th October, however, the same day that Brooke and his Ammunition Column far to the south had started their journey from Orleans towards the war, a major German offensive took place with fresh forces against the British line in front of Ypres. The climax was reached the following day. Battalion after battalion of the British Regular Army was annihilated, or so reduced by terrible casualties that never again in the war did it possess the same character. It has been said that the old British Army died at First Ypres. It was certainly not in vain. The last German attacks, still with an overwhelming superiority of numbers, were held on 11th November. Thereafter there were developed defensive systems of ever increasing strength and complexity, on both sides, 'from Switzerland to the sea'.

When Brooke finally reached the front and reunited his Ammunition Column with its parent Artillery Brigade, the First Battle of Ypres was nearly over. He found his Brigade supporting the Indian Corps, near the southern end of the British front against which there were no further serious German attacks, the main enemy effort being directed further north and towards Ypres itself. Life in that first winter of the war was a matter of cold, wet and monotony for an Artillery subaltern, most of whose activity consisted of covering many miles in the saddle daily between the batteries of the brigade and Artillery Headquarters, ascertaining the needs of the guns and organizing their supply. In November Brooke was promoted Captain, after more than eleven years' service. Leave to England started as the front solidified, and Brooke returned for the first week in 1915 to his beloved Janey, and again at the end of February; relieving patches of light in a life he described as a 'mixture of boredom, fear, discomfort, cold, wet and endless drabness', for Brooke was certainly not one who in retrospect idealized the personal sides of war. Janey would come over to London from Ireland, and there were snatched times of happiness in the ensuing four years, filled with visits to relations, concerts, theatres, the sense of escape, the unreality of 'leave'.

In January 1915 Brooke was delighted to be made Staff-Captain, Royal Artillery, in the 2nd (Indian) Cavalry Division. The Staff-Captain was, in effect, Adjutant to the Commander, Royal Artillery, at that time normally a Colonel in command of a Horse Artillery Brigade. Brooke revelled in the responsibility. 'My new Commander' (Colonel Askwith) he wrote,

> . . . was a very charming person to meet and live with but certainly not one of the world's workers. He had looked upon his profession as a means of providing him with an easy-going life connected with horses, hunting and good friends; his dislike of work was so deeply ingrained that it almost hurt him to see anybody else work. I very soon found that if things were to run smoothly I should have to do most of his work for him as well as my own.[6]

So it was: and when their Artillery Brigade was moved to support another division in the attack on Neuve Chapelle which began on 10th March 1915, and was combined with two other Field Artillery Brigades to give Brooke the supervision of some fifty-four guns, 'I had my hands full,' he wrote, 'as my Colonel played patience most of the time he did not take much of the load off me.' But he relished the challenge, found all things interesting and began to gain an indispensable education in the handling of Artillery; and Artillery dominated the war of 1914–18 on the Western Front. 'I am fit as can be,' he wrote then, and was to write in similar vein throughout the war, 'and am enjoying life immensely.' He kept a diary throughout 1915.[7]

Brooke's diary and letters showed him, as he always was, reflective. He had a quick eye for the striking and the absurd. He also thought deeply about the lessons of war. For an Artilleryman – and Brooke held only Artillery appointments throughout the war – one of the first impressions of the early stages of war was of shortage of ammunition. Brooke ascribed this to a lack of pre-war understanding of the primacy of fire-power. Nobody, he thought and wrote, had appreciated how guns would dominate the battlefield, nor how impossible manoeuvre would become without absolute superiority of firepower (cf. Chapter V). He also, like all his contemporaries, criticized the premises on which preparations for war had been based, and this no doubt helped give him that sceptical attitude towards strategic planning assumptions which was to stand him in good stead in later life.

For those responsible for our preparations had always been instructed to assume that war, if it happened, could not possibly last long. The terrible power of modern weapons, the immensity of the forces certain to be deployed, the consequent strain on the economies of the combatant nations and the disruption of all civilized processes were thought to be incompatible with a protracted struggle. War would be ferocious, dramatic, decisive – and, inevitably, short. Above all, operations would be marked by a high degree of mobility and a negligible consumption of materiel.

This sort of failure of prophecy is not unusual or surprising. It would have been startling and highly inconvenient for the authorities to have accepted, in the pre-1914 planning period, the possibility of a long war with almost limitless British participation, and to have based plans thereon. The implications of conscription, the mobilization of industry and the menace of blockade would all have required not only examination but contingency action of a politically divisive and unpalatable kind. Nor was the official line without sound argument. The French Plan XVII, under which the war opened with a French offensive, did not achieve the instant – or any other – degree of success anticipated by the French High Command. The German Schlieffen Plan, the 'giant wheel', foundered on the ill-judged opportunism of the commander of the German right wing. But none of this might have happened. Decision might indeed have been as swift as in 1870. British involvement might have been limited to a short, sharp, single fight conducted, by definition, on the principles of open warfare by a small, largely Regular force. Instead, the exhausted Armies of the early battles settled down to a long and murderous siege – a siege where the defender could, furthermore, prolong battle by withdrawal to yet another fortified line.

In any siege manoeuvre ceases. There may, at the moment of the breach, be tactical skill of a high order in actual combat; and this was true in many of the great efforts to breach – the attempted breakthrough battles – of the war. But major manoeuvre is excluded. Each contestant knows where his foe eats, sleeps and is supplied, and where he will be tomorrow. The situation is static. In these circumstances virtually the only tactic was and is to pound with indirect fire, for the enemy's positions will be contrived to protect him from direct. In the First World War that indirect fire was principally artillery fire, and the war saw an immense development of Artillery in all armies. For four years the Artillery art was Brooke's unremitting concern.

The Artillery art is that of applying the principle of concentration of force in space and in time, by exploiting the fact that a shell moves faster than the fleetest of men, vehicles or horses; and that a huge quantity of shells can thus be concentrated on simultaneous or on a succession of targets without the movement of a single one of a large number of dispersed guns. Fire can be produced, thickened up, switched, lifted or called off without the physical movement of anything but a projectile.

The art has prerequisites. First there needs to be a sufficient number of the guns themselves of varying ranges and calibres, supported by a sufficiency of ammunition, so that the physical effect required for a particular tactical situation can be achieved without waste. Artillery resources, like all resources in war, are always in limited supply and to apply them uneconomically is to be short when the crunch comes. The British Army of 1915 had good support artillery, but was short of heavy and medium artillery. Above all, however, there was a serious shortage of ammunition of all types, a consequence of false assumptions about duration and intensity of conflict. This experience burnt itself on to Brooke's heart. He was prepared to write personal memoranda about Artillery ammunition to the end of his active military life.

The second prerequisite of successful gunnery is a projectile which will have the desired effect on arrival. These developed throughout the war. It was not until 1917 that high explosive shells were provided with instantaneous percussion fuses which caused the projectile to detonate on impact but above the ground. Before then, an unavoidable delay in the operation of the fuse led to penetration before detonation, as a result of which the shell expended more of its energy on disturbing the ground than on destruction above it. Shrapnel, the standard issue for the close support artillery in the anticipated mobile operations which did not materialize, although it burst high and scattered destruction, was of limited use against entrenched troops in concealed positions. The result was that artillery fire churned up ground, creating ever larger shell holes as the calibre of gun became heavier. As great masses of artillery came to be deployed this destruction of the battlefield itself, substituting mud, water and holes for terrain, became a factor of supreme tactical significance. In the subsequent stages of an attack the impediment to movement created by the very fire which had sometimes enabled the opening stage to succeed, was itself decisive. A great weight of artillery fire might pulverize the enemy's front line and support trenches, and the first assault waves might fight their way to their objectives, sometimes even with comparatively little loss. Such actions were intended only as a prelude. The aim was to break through, to end the deadlock, to develop open warfare and mobile operations. Yet the follow-up echelons of the attacking force and the replenishment columns of the first waves (by then hanging on to their gains in face of the inevitable German counter-attack) would be struggling through frightful conditions created by our own artillery fire, while the enemy would be re-supplying and reinforcing the critical points over comparatively clean ground, and sealing the breach. So it was at Neuve Chapelle, in March 1915, Brooke's first major battle as Staff-Captain, when the objectives were taken quickly in most cases but the initial attack was held while subsequent attempts at exploitation gained little ground at the cost of heavy losses.

The third prerequisite for the effective use of Artillery is a system of control and communications. So flexible an arm is capable of maximum effect only if information and orders can be instantly transmitted and if control be centralized at the optimum level of command. In the First World War this presented peculiar difficulty. Communications beyond word of mouth were mainly by telephone, and not only were telephone systems rudimentary but lines could be expected to last little time under the weight of the enemy's artillery fire. 'We were completely deficient of any kind of telephone exchanges,' Brooke wrote about Neuve Chapelle, 'as we had lines from our three batteries, from the two Field Artillery Brigades, the Ammunition Column and Divisional Headquarters, complete confusion existed until I improvised a form of exchange made up out of the small bayonet socket joints which cables were provided with at that time.'[8] The problem of communication – and not only for the Artillery – dominated the war. Many of the more facile criticisms of command decisions, made of that war in modern times, might have been modified by a greater perception of the difficulties and delays which were inherent in the passage of news.

The fourth prerequisite of the Artillery art is intelligent planning, planning which is systematic and yet robust, which accepts that in battle things go awry and the unexpected always occurs, and which yet provides a certain fixed and predictable pattern of support on which all can rely. Brooke became not only a master-planner but an innovator.

The fifth prerequisite is observation. Air observation from aircraft and balloons was increasingly developed. Ground observation posts on the Western Front were difficult to obtain, vulnerable, often crowded because of their scarcity. A typical atmosphere is conveyed in a diary of an Artillery subaltern in the New Armies, writing of April 1915:

> The subalterns of the 9th, 16th and 70th batteries all used the top storey room inside the cowl-shaped roof to observe from, and they fired their 18-pounder batteries against the triangle trenches now and then but not very much as ammunition was now very short.
>
> There were only three holes in the roof for observation purposes, so I only got a look now and again. Really the place is hopelessly overcrowded and one unlucky shell might put several batteries temporarily out of action by killing or wounding their observers. The firing is done by passing the firing orders to telephonists.
>
> . . . the mending and maintenance of these telephone wires which run haphazard over the ground and are frequently shot to pieces by shells seem to be the most risky part of a gunner's life out here.[9]

And such OPs were also, of course, the focus for visiting commanders whose only other vision of the front would be on an exposed firestep in a forward trench. A great part of Brooke's life as an Artillery Staff Officer supporting troops in the line was taken in the selection, visiting and organization of observation posts.

From these Artillery observation posts, and from them alone, the ground between the two front lines could be seen.

> 'I shall never forget,' wrote Brooke, 'the ghastly sights . . . the space intervening between the trenches was covered with dead and dying. The wounded lay in a scorching May sun throughout the day without water and writhing with agony from their wounds. At night a few of them were brought back, but during daylight nothing could be done.'

He was describing the Battle of Festubert in May 1915:

> A series of abortive attacks which seldom penetrated the enemy front line and resulted in one of the worst shambles in No-man's-land that I have ever seen.[10]

After the battles of Neuve Chapelle and Festubert Brooke spent much of the summer of 1915 in reserve. But after returning from a week's visit to his mother, still living at St Jean de Luz, he found orders posting him as Brigade Major, Royal Artillery, to the 18th Infantry Division.

It is a supreme benefit for any officer to find himself, at an impressionable age, working closely with a master of the art of training troops for battle and a skilled and realistic tactician. This now befell Brooke. The 18th Division was commanded by one of the most thorough and effective commanders on the Western Front, Major-General Maxse. Maxse was later to command XVIII Corps in the Fifth Army, at that critical moment in our country's history when the Germans broke through the British line in March 1918. When Brooke joined his staff he had been for only four months at the Western Front with his 'New Army' Division which he had formed in England in October 1914, after handing over command of the 1st Guards Brigade in France. Maxse, a Coldstreamer, was a trainer of the most thorough kind. He believed in the exhaustive explanation of every tactic, every theory. He believed in unremitting practice; every set-piece attack planned by the 18th Division was incessantly rehearsed on ground specially selected for its similarity to the future battlefield. He believed in physical fitness and stamina, and made demands of calculated severity in training the units of his division, expecting and obtaining the highest standards. He believed in discipline rooted in confidence and self-respect, but did not ignore its outward manifestations on which he insisted with well-known rigour. Above all, he believed in thoroughness.[11] He had been attached to and deeply impressed by the Prussian Guard before the war. With his abrupt and sometimes unconventional manner he had set the indelible mark of his character upon his entire division.

Brooke reported to Maxse on 20th November. The meeting was typical of both men. Maxse barely said 'good morning', and looked Brooke up and down critically.

'I don't like your hat.'

Brooke was not, however, prepared to be put down from the start.

'Neither do I,' he said, 'and if you give me a week's leave I shall go home and buy a new one.'[12]

No week's leave, and no new hat, but no further testing attack until a few days later when the Brigade Major, RA accompanied his Divisional Commander to the trenches, and 'perched on a stick that was protruding out of the hurdle revetment' alongside the

68

General, who monopolized the firestep built for a single sniper. Maxse exposed most of his upper body above the parapet and pointed out various German trenches while Brooke turned his head in the required direction. 'Keep your head still!' said Maxse. 'You're no good as a deer stalker,' an observation which somewhat stung the experienced Brooke. And, a little later as the stick which supported Brooke broke off and he dropped to the bottom of the trench – 'There you are: bobbing about like a bloody sparrow!'[13]

Brooke came deeply to admire Maxse, as did all who served him. With his gift of mimicry he also caught the great man's manner perfectly, and at the Staff College, long after the war, Brooke imitating Maxse with humour and affection was one of his most demanded acts.[14] He was now as active and as interested as even he could wish. Not only did he serve an outstanding Divisional Commander but his immediate superior, the Commander Royal Artillery, was a brilliant Artilleryman, Brigadier-General Casimir Van Straubenzee, 'one mass of energy' as Brooke described him. There was now in progress a great expansion of strength in men, equipment and munitions. New Army Divisions had, throughout 1915, been sent in large numbers to the front. The British Army which had deployed six divisions to France in 1914 now had at its disposal over sixty divisions formed in four Armies – and this despite the severe casualties of First Ypres, Neuve Chapelle, Loos. 'The gradual building-up,' Brooke noted, 'had reached a stage when large scale offensive became possible.'

The 18th Division was already deployed in Picardy, east of Albert, alternating periods in the line with periods in reserve. Now in 1916 from all over the Western Front formations converged on the same point: men, guns, vehicles, horses, trains, drawn, as has been said, 'like iron filings by a magnetic force', to one unforgettable arena; the Somme.

The Battle of the Somme in 1916 and the battles in Flanders of 1917 known as Third Ypres have profoundly marked the British collective memory. The names cause revulsion. Yet the decisions to be made were complex and their treatment with hindsight has sometimes done little justice to the appalling nature of the strategic and tactical problems involved, to the political struggle endemic in holding the Western Alliance together at all, or to the despairing note struck again and again, both at the time and in retrospect, in German accounts of the same battles. The fearful cost in life and suffering; the apparently indecisive strategic results, imply tragedy with terrible clarity. Tragedy gains, however, little from caricature.

Brooke, as Brigade Major Royal Artillery, played a vital part in the Artillery preparation and conduct of the Battle of the Somme in the 18th Division sector of attack, and both his own impressions and the course of operations in that sector emphasize a number of points which can too easily be forgotten. First, the quality of British formations differed greatly, if only because of the huge expansion of the Army since the outbreak of war, and the tiny number of highly trained commanders and Staff officers. Brooke was fortunate in serving in a division formed and trained by Maxse, and with a staff instilled universally with their commander's own devotion to the troops. Maxse had led the way in the physical hardness, shooting skill, discipline and caring administration which marked the division. He had also prepared the division for the battle with his usual thoroughness, creating exact replicas of the objectives in rest areas behind the lines and taking the assault troops through extensive familiarization exercises so that every man felt as versed as was possible in the part he was to play.[15] This was not true of all divisions.

Second, the ground over which the attack was to be made differed considerably, sector by sector. The 18th Division formed part of General Congreve's XIII Corps on the extreme right of the British battlefield, with a French Army on its own right. The attack, on the right flank, was northward, over slightly rising fields towards the villages of Montauban and Mametz. The terrain was comparatively straightforward, the objectives clear. In the centre of the British line near Fricourt and, above all, on the extreme left at Beaumont-Hamel, it was a very different story.

A picture is evoked by the phrase 'the first day of the Somme', a picture of line after line of British Infantry climbing out of the front-line trenches to be cut down by the unsilenced German machine-guns even before reaching the enemy protective barbed wire, itself uncut in spite of the unceasing preliminary bombardment and the certainty of our Intelligence Staffs that no serious wire obstacles remained intact. There is terrible truth in much of this picture. Numerous observers have referred to 'the infernal pounding from the enemy's howitzers' which 'concentrated on our communication trenches and forming up places'.[16] As for the wire – if and when reached – it was often found to be gapped in such a way as to concentrate the assault troops at bottlenecks on the most

I JULY 1916. 18 DIV. ATTACK

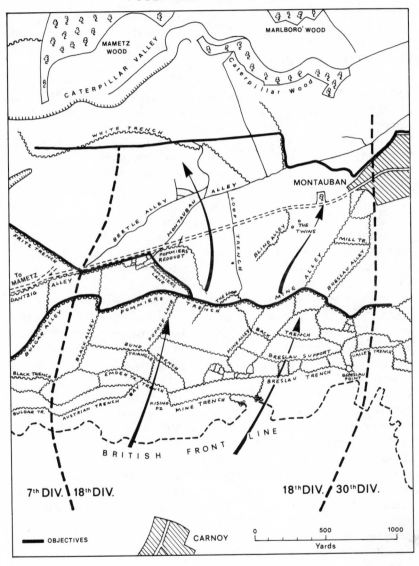

MARLBORO' WOOD

MAMETZ WOOD

CATERPILLAR VALLEY

CATERPILLAR Wood

WHITE TRENCH

MONTAUBAN

BEETLE ALLEY

MONTAUBAN ALLEY

LOOP TRENCH

BLIND ALLEY

THE TWINS

MILL TR.

FRITZ TRENCH

POMMIERS REDOUBT

To MAMETZ

ALLEY

DANTZIG

POMMIERS LANE

THE LOOP

MINE ALLEY

BRESLAU ALLEY

POMMIERS TRENCH

BULGAR ALLEY

BLACK ALLEY

POPOFF LANE

BUND TRIANGLE TRENCH

MINE VALLEY BACK TRENCH

BRESLAU SUPPORT

VALLEY TRENCH

BLACK TRENCH

EMDEN TR TRENCH

BAT TRENCH

KISING PZ.

MINE TRENCH

BRESLAU TRENCH

BRESLAU POINT

BULGAR TR.

AUSTRIAN TRENCH

BRITISH   FRONT   LINE

7th DIV. 18th DIV.

18th DIV. 30th DIV.

▬ OBJECTIVES

CARNOY

0   500   1000

Yards

exposed ground. Over much of the front the enemy's tactical obstacles were still a formidable help to the defence: his concealed artillery batteries (a large number of which had been forbidden to shoot until the main Allied assault was known to have started in order to avoid earlier retribution) had been by no means silenced by our own counter-bombardment preparations, immense though they had been and thorough though their planning. Perhaps most significant, the rate of our own close support barrage for the advancing Infantry was such as to enable the shaken German defenders to man the remnants of their smashed front and support trenches, the rims of shell holes and mine craters and to bring murderous machine-gun fire to bear on men advancing in the open, after the British barrage had passed them by. As ever, the German fire positions and preparations for enfilade and concentration of fire were expertly planned, just as their soldiers did their duty with unfailing discipline and skill.

Yet the picture is extraordinarily uneven. In Brooke's part of the front – XIII Corps and 18th Division sector – there was swift British success. The wire cutting was done with trench mortars employed exclusively thereon, as well as with shrapnel or high explosive penetrating shell; and was extremely effective. The first objective was taken in twenty minutes and men were holding triumphant impromptu sing-songs in the captured enemy trenches. Above all, Brooke himself had proposed and gained at least partial acceptance of a new system of supporting fire. Brooke knew that many of the enemy machine-guns were and would be sited in shell holes between the main trenches. His system was based on the principle of lifting by fixed increments of a specific number of yards, regulated by the predicted rate of our Infantry advance. His Artillery operation order provided for the first five lifts to be bombardments of specific trench lines, and thereafter for the barrage to 'creep' by lifts, at ninety-second intervals, of fifty yards. It was the first 'creeping barrage' and a great success. Brooke wrote of the battle with profound satisfaction – 'The Division practically went straight through to its objective without a hitch.'[17]

The idea of such a type of barrage was French. In the preceding March Brooke had taken a French Colonel Herring round the 18th Division sector. The 'creeping' or 'rolling' barrage in exactly the form adopted was described to Brooke by Herring. It became, as he said, 'famous and universal'. His very individual contribution, however, was to develop the system by converting it into clear maps, so that the barrage could be set out, with its timings and implications 'on the artillery board and fire orders worked out from it'. This device had much occupied Brooke in the weeks before 1st July and the result became standard, with tracings given to each Artillery Brigade showing battery lanes, lifts and timings.[18]

The Battle of the Somme, after its first bloody days, was continued at intervals for several months, with 18th Division Artillery periodically supporting other formations. As far as the close support barrages were concerned, 'by now' wrote Brooke 'the map procedure was working like magic and being copied on all sides'.

The continuation of the fighting appeared to Brooke entirely necessary and to be expected. Some of his descriptions were vivid.

The battle goes on practically unceasingly, with continuous attacks on various smaller German strong points, and in most places we have been gaining ground gradually. Yesterday and the day before the General and I went up to study our new front. Our line runs more or less on the top of a ridge from which one gets a very good view of the country all round. On our left we could see Mametz wood, and continual scrapping going on for it. One could see the Germans scuttling backwards and forwards at the far end of the wood in a continual hail of shrapnel.

Yesterday we arrived just in time to see in the distance one of our attacks on Contalmaison; it was a wonderful sight. To begin with the heavy Artillery were pounding the village. Great columns of smoke and brick dust were flying up into the air, some of them about three times as high as the ruins of the chateau. The whole village was wrapped in a cloud of smoke, lit up by flashes of bursting shell. This went on for some time, and then the shrapnel barrage became intense, rows of white puffs of smoke and the ground whipped up into dust by the shrapnel bullets, and away in the distance we could see our infantry advancing in lines towards the village. One felt as if one was in a dream, or that one was watching some extraordinary cinematograph film, and that it could not all be true.

You could see the German shells bursting in amongst our lines and men fall down, but the remainder seemed to move on as if nothing were happening. We then began to see small columns of Germans legging it out of the far side of the village, running like hares followed up by our shrapnel fire, with dust flying all round them. It seems extraordinary that any of them were left alive.

Then close down under us we saw a party of 30 or 40 of our men leave their trenches and start a flanking movement in the village. They ran along until they topped a rise, and then came under heavy fire from a trench held by Germans standing up on the fire step of their parapet, shooting. The ground all round our small party went up in spurts of dust, and the whole party went down like ninepins. I thought they had all been wiped out, but watched through my glasses and saw them gradually crawl into some shell holes and from there down a fold in the ground, and shortly afterwards we could see them carrying on a bombing match with the German garrison of that trench.

The noise was unimaginable. We were carrying on a pretty heavy bombardment on our front, and the Germans were retaliating fairly freely. One continuous series of 'cracks' from our 18 pr. batteries close up, busy wire-cutting on the German second line. More distant were the heavier guns, and the continuous screech and whistle of our shells going over our heads and German high explosive shells, both on the ground with columns of dense black smoke, and in the air with creamy-coloured smoke-burst, and in the midst of it all, the infantry moving about in and out of the captured German trenches as if nothing were happening, some of them comfortably huddled up in a corner of the trench, sleeping; others peacefully boiling a little tea in their cooking pots and smearing plum and apple jam with the clasp knife on ration biscuits; others again quietly reading some penny novel.[19]

The confidence, the drama and yet the sense of normality conveyed by Brooke's hurried letters, describing a hectic life, a fluctuating battle, local successes and a personal job obviously well done may not convey the usual picture of the Battle of the Somme, with terrible casualties rewarded by so little ground gained – and by no immediately perceptible strategic advantage. Brooke had no doubt about the nature and scale of such sacrifices. The waste and folly of war always sickened him: but he showed, at the time, no doubt about the need. The rewards were not, at once, apparent: they may fairly, however, be deduced from the words of Ludendorff about 1916 – 'The German Army had been fought to a standstill and was utterly worn out.'[20]

Such a method of making war – attrition – clearly fell short of the 'breakthrough' for which the Allied leaders hoped. Yet it did not appear to an intelligent participant like Brooke as mindless, callous or irrelevant. The expensive renewal of successive assaults, the call for further sacrifices in pursuit of a great object was not a novelty in the history of warfare. Few would deny that there were appalling tactical errors – as in most battles – made on the Somme in 1916. The losses were huge and tragic. Every loss is tragic and a single casualty is huge to the family which bears it. But this was not a new phenomenon. The casualties of Waterloo had been huge. The real difference lay in the protracted nature of events. In previous ages suffering and loss had been as proportionately great, but a concentrated day of battle had been rewarded by clearcut victory. In the wars now undertaken by great industrial nations, with manpower fully mobilized, the struggle would almost certainly assume, at some points at least and for some time at least, the nature of attrition. In the First World War this, for reasons of tactics and terrain, took place on the Western Front. In the Second World War it took place in the East.

Thus in 1916, the breakthrough – the great opportunity for which a mass of cavalry had been kept in reserve behind successive points of attack – never came. The state of the ground was, apart from all else, unconducive to it. On 8th September (when supporting the Canadian Corps in the centre of the Somme front) Brooke wrote 'the ground up near the front line is like nothing on earth! Along the Pozières ridge the surface of the ground is just like the pictures of the moon, all the craters of the shells touching each other, the surface is literally ploughed up by shell, not a square foot anywhere that has not been churned up . . . a scene of absolute desolation and destruction. Broken debris everywhere, everything seems broken except the morale of the men in the deep narrow ditch of a trench running through this desolation, and they are as cheery as sandpipers.'[21] Brooke was awarded the Distinguished Service Order for his part in the Somme fighting. Commenting on 1916 afterwards, he wrote:

> We had made great progress in the co-ordinated control of artillery. We were, however, still obsessed with the idea that the total destruction of all enemy defences must be achieved before the attack. We were, therefore, still wedded to lengthy preliminary bombardments of several days which sacrificed all the advantages of surprise. We had still to learn that predicted artillery fire was possible, without previous registration, and that the main advantage to be derived from artillery fire was in its power to neutralize the hostile rifle, machine-gun and artillery fire as opposed to the destruction of trenches and obstacles.[22]

In February 1917 Brooke left the 18th Division and was posted as 'Staff Officer RA' to the Canadian Corps; in effect Chief of Staff to the Commander of the Corps Artillery. His responsibilities were now correspondingly enlarged; and he had a particularly free hand. In 18th Division his immediate superiors had been first Major-General Van Straubenzee and then Brigadier-General Metcalfe, both expert Gunners and very experienced soldiers (although the latter once remarked 'Brooke is magnificent, he does everything – but I wish he'd sometimes tell me what he is doing for I *am* the CRA').[23] Now his commander, a newspaper editor in private life, 'was full of bravery and instilled the finest of fighting spirit in the whole of the artillery under his command' wrote Brooke, 'but as regards the tactical handling of artillery he knew practically nothing'.[24] Brooke would write all orders, having found even discussion of planning impossible, and ensure that his superior had a copy. They were never questioned; and in Brooke's view were seldom understood.

His personal standing was thus enhanced and the professional task itself was greater. The preparations were well under way for the great Canadian attack at Vimy, by four divisions, due in April. All Divisional Artilleries would be centrally controlled at Corps level, the Corps Commander being General Byng, whose ADC was Brooke's nephew Basil. The allocation of positions, establishment of communications and supply lines by road and rail, ammunition dumping systems and, finally, the actual Artillery Plan now fell to Brooke. He was helped by the fact that the Corps Chief of Staff, Major-General de Blaquiere Radcliffe, was himself a Gunner. The Artillery Commander's professional limitations were admirably offset by his faith in Brooke, but confusions could occur. Brooke belonged to the Corps Headquarters 'B' Mess, while his commander dined in 'A' Mess with Byng who would sometimes casually mention something he wanted done, in the matter of artillery, to his Artillery Commander. The latter would always agree, with little comprehension, and when told later by Brooke that the matter was confused, would simply say 'the Corps Commander wants it done'. 'I had to wait till he had gone to bed,' wrote Brooke, 'and then went up to see Byng myself and had the matter put right.'[25] Byng once asked a very senior Artillery General about Brooke. 'He is a marvel' was the answer, 'and the best we have got.' Byng called him 'Uncle'.[26]

The attack on Vimy Ridge on 9th April was an outstanding success, Brooke putting again into effect to general acclaim his barrage system. He made, according to a Canadian Artillery Staff Officer working at the subordinate headquarters, 'his initial and greatest reputation as a gunner staff officer in the 1st Canadian Corps in the artillery plans he drew up for and executed in the capture of the Vimy Ridge by the Corps in April 1917'. It was one of the epic actions of the war; and the concentration of artillery was, on the frontage of attack, over twice as great as on the Somme. That summer in Artois saw further heavy fighting by the Canadian Corps and extracts from the Official History indicate graphically the sort and scale of artillery usage which Brooke was now directing. In the attack on Hill 70 in August:

> It was hoped by the full use of artillery power in all stages of the battle to reduce Infantry casualties to the minimum. Concentrations of fire both by heavy and divisional artillery were to be laid on the probable lines of advance of the enemy's counter attack formations and on their assembly areas . . . and forward artillery observers with the leading infantry, and air observers in 2 seater Sopwiths had the special task of watching the back areas for enemy concentrations . . .
>
> Heavy thunder showers which fell during the afternoon of the 14th cleared in the evening and the night was fine but dark. At zero hour, 4.24 a.m. dawn was just breaking when the barrage crashed on the German defences.
>
> The creeping barrage was formed by 8 field artillery brigades. Four hundred yards ahead of the creeping barrage was a jumping barrage of 4·5 inch and 6 inch howitzers, and beyond that a moving barrage of heavy howitzers which dealt in succession with the enemy strong points.
>
> The machine-guns creeping barrage, inaugurated so successfully by the Canadian Corps on the Vimy Ridge assault was to be repeated: on the front of assault 160 Vickers guns, in four groups, were to lay barrages along the objectives and to be ready to answer subsequent SOS calls.
>
> The ammunition expenditure shows the scale of the Artillery support. From zero hour to midnight on 15th August, 67,000 rounds of 18 pdr and 12,000 rounds of 4·5 inch howitzers were fired by the artillery of the 1st Canadian Division alone; the 18 pdr total averaged 713 rounds per gun.
>
> At a time when the Western Front was being combed by the Germans to meet the great demands for Flanders five of their divisions had been engaged and broken up by three Canadian Divisions in a few days.[27]

'It was a great success and ran like clockwork,' wrote Brooke.

Brooke was taking more and more to flying, finding the observation from aircraft as fascinating as it was useful. When in the line he walked incessantly, inspecting the front line, the conditions of battle which the artillery would need to support, and the battery positions themselves. A badly camouflaged battery detected from the air was soon acquainted of the fact. When in reserve he always found it possible to relax, to grow fruit in the garden of a billet and revisit it triumphantly to gather some later in the year. Old friends played their usual vital part in war, suddenly relieving monotony or sadness with an unexpected contact. There was a mass of work beside the incessant tramping – which Brooke loved – flying, driving and visiting. There were also lighter moments, horse shows, even games of golf in calmer periods behind the lines.

In October 1917 the Corps was moved north to take part in the closing stages of the battle known as Third Ypres. Its course had become a protracted tragedy. After initial success, including Second Army's victory at Messines, the weather had broken prematurely and the low-lying Flanders battlefield of the Ypres Salient became more and more difficult terrain over which to attack. The decision to continue the battle has been the subject of bitter contention ever since, but continued it was until, after savage fighting between 26th October and 13th November, the Canadian Corps, at least fresh to that particular holocaust, captured their final objectives, the ridge and village of Passchendaele. Brooke, on first arrival in the Ypres Salient, had been appalled at the conditions.

> Mile upon mile of mud and swamp with practically no roads. Just before our attack I attended a conference which Douglas Haig ran at Canadian Corps HQ. I could hardly believe that my ears were not deceiving me! He spoke in the rosiest of terms of our chances of breaking through. I had been all over the ground and to my mind such an eventuality was quite impossible. I am certain he was misinformed and had never seen the ground for himself.[28]

Nevertheless, he was able to write on 8th November, 'You will have seen details in the papers of our attack on Passchendaele. It was a complete success and the crowning of the hard fighting which this Corps has had during the past few weeks.'[29] Then 'Third Ypres' came to its bitter end.

After Christmas 1917 Brooke returned for a short Staff Course at Cambridge, and was able to take rooms and live together with his wife. It was an intensive* and happy three-month course but it was interrupted. On 21st March 1918 the last great German

---

* Thorough as ever, his notes on the course cover nearly 300 methodically organized pages.[30]

offensive of the war 'Operation MICHAEL' was launched on the Western Front, the main blow being directed in the area of the Somme and the sector held by the British Fifth Army. It was soon clear that the German offensive had achieved a major success.

Open warfare, the aim of the attacker for four years, was once again a reality. All officers on the Staff Course were recalled. Brooke, however, did not find himself directly involved in those dramatic days of late March and early April; and in June he was appointed temporary General Staff Officer I (Lieutenant-Colonel) Royal Artillery at the Headquarters of First Army. Here he acquired the new experience of handling Long Range Artillery, railway mounted guns and so forth; and could take advantage of the attachment to First Army of a flight of Bristol Fighters to increase still further his understanding of the potential of aerial observation, liaison and control of artillery.

In the autumn of 1918 the tide finally turned. The peace with the Russian Bolsheviks in 1917 had enabled Germany to make one final effort on the Western Front in March. It had failed to achieve strategic success. Now the United States was in the war, its power increasing on the Western Front all the time, its potential vast, its people unwearied. In a series of offensives, British troops at last had the unprecedented sense – at least in some sectors – of weakened resistance before them. The Armies advanced. When he wrote a letter on 10th October the end was nearer than Brooke imagined.

> One trip up to Lens where I wandered among the ruins . . . such ruin and such desolation. I climbed on to a heap of stones which represents the place where the Church once stood, and I looked down on the wreckage. One could spend days there just looking down picturing to oneself the tragedies that have occurred in every corner of this place. If the stones could talk and could repeat what they have witnessed, and the thoughts they had read on dying men's faces I wonder if there would ever be any wars.*[31]

Brooke felt little triumph and less hatred. He was curious about the German occupation as French territory was liberated.

> So far I haven't come across any case of brutality to the civilians,

---

* Twenty-one years later Brooke revisited the same spot. 'Stones had remained silent,' he said, on re-reading his previous letter. 'We were starting the Second World War.'

but they all complain of the thieving habits of the Bosch and certainly the houses and chateaux round about show signs of it; even the plush upholstering of chairs has been cut off and sent to Germany, also tapestry off the walls and pictures out of their frames.

On the other hand one finds certain signs of the Bosch which sometimes point to his not being quite as black as he is painted. Today [30th October 1918] I had a long walk round Douai cemetery, looking at all the graves, French, English, Russian, Italian and German all equally well cared for . . . in the middle of the cemetery the Germans had put up a big stone monument, like this [he sketched it]. On the three corner stones are three medallions with the French, English and German crests, each face turned towards the respective country. On each frontal face at the top is written *Pro Patria* and at the bottom on each side:

A LA MEMOIRE DES BRAVES CAMERADES
DEN GEFALLNEN KAMERADEN ZUR EHRE
IN MEMORY OF BRAVE COMRADES[32]

The battles of August to October 1918 are seldom dramatized. The Somme and Third Ypres – and the many other expensive and strategically inconclusive encounters of the preceding four years – are those which tend to set the pattern of British popular imagination about the First World War. Yet these culminating battles were also very costly, and the efforts they demanded from the British Army were very great. Over 350,000 British and Imperial casualties were suffered in three months. They purchased total victory. That victory must, in justice, be attributed not only to the concluding battles themselves, which once again restored 'open warfare', but also, and fundamentally, to the process of attrition, terrible though it was, which had preceded them. It was not for nothing that the Germans, on the other side of the hill, had ceaselessly reported that their army was bleeding to death on the ridges east of Ypres and in the rolling fields above the Somme. The mistakes and the tragedies are part of our history. Also part of that history, however, is the fact that in autumn 1918 the German Army was beaten, on level terms, decisively, and every British soldier knew it. 'Haig,' said a German appreciation, 'contributed the most to prevent a German victory. Thus he really remained "Master of the field".'[33]

On 3rd November Brooke returned to England for leave. His

eldest child, a daughter, Rosemary, had just been born. He was in London when the Armistice was announced and watched the crowds. 'That wild evening jarred on my feelings,' he wrote. 'I felt untold relief at the end being there at last, but was swamped with floods of memories of those years of struggle. I was filled with gloom that evening, and retired to sleep early.'[34]

CHAPTER V

Lessons of War

WHEN THE WAR HAD BEGUN Brooke had been thirty-one years old. His adult life to that point had been carefree. He had enjoyed to the full the interests – largely outdoor and physical – of a young man. He had been an enthusiast for the Army, marked as an excellent and aspiring professional, but it was the enthusiasm of youth, of a learner. In personality, despite his own averred shyness and some remaining signs of the 'inwardness' and self-contained character so apparent in his childhood, he had been known and loved as the best of companions, sharp in tongue, witty and bold; and, in heart, tastes and appearance, young.

There comes to every ambitious man, particularly in so hierarchcial a life as the Army, a point when having hitherto seen the profession from below, whether critically or admiringly, with the freedom and irreverence of youth, he begins to feel himself a part of its management, involved not as a learner or aspirant, but as a senior, keen and able to think constructively, to exert influence and personally to take a hand in directing the way the profession should go. A major war, to those who survive it, acts as such a watershed. The young officer who disembarked his Ammunition Column in the South of France in 1914 was not only four years older when the war was over, but, like all his contemporaries, was a different person. He had seen great suffering, mistakes and successes. He had felt with poignancy the loss of a generation of friends and beloved members of his own family. He had hated the waste and destruction endemic in war and would continue to hate them: but on how to wage it he had formed strong opinions, and would now increasingly be in a position to give them effect. His future professional development, as well as many of his emotions, were inevitably charted by those terrible yet stimulating years. In 1919 he had already made a personal list of extracts from military history and the reflections of some of the great Captains and had placed against them a number of remarks drawn from his own experience of the recent war.

The character of Brooke, tempered by war, was generally

82

regarded as one of strength and severity. He was, when he gave his friendship, the most charming of companions, and the most thoughtful and entertaining of comrades. The young officer of Indian days bent on 'enjoying every moment of life to the full' was by no means dead. But outwardly he could be forbidding. He could unnerve with his rapidity of thought, speech and action. His contempt for inadequacy was very apparent. He could be hot-tempered. He suffered fools not at all and, quick in everything, was quick to make judgements of men, which were not always fair but which he, with characteristic generosity (for he could be as generous as he was modest), never hesitated to change and confess as error if later circumstances so persuaded him.

The sensitivity of the youngest, adored child of the family, 'your little Benjamin' was never eradicated. Gentleness was there; but, like every soldier, he had to evolve a shell around it and the shell was hard.

He had little sympathy with weakness in himself or in others whether of body or character. 'Headache? There's no such thing,' he would say sharply to his family[1] (he who had suffered with every twinge of his mother's as if it were his rather than 'his own little pet's'). He had a strong puritan streak and disliked what he regarded as moral as well as physical flabbiness. In appearance he was immaculate. Not surprisingly he seemed formidable. Yet friends soon found behind that impression a man with a deep awareness and love of nature, a ready wit, an artistic facility with pencil and camera – he could seldom get through a meeting without a quick pencil sketch of some of the participants – and a thoughtfulness for others the more appreciated because so absolutely without ostentation. He was a patient listener: perhaps because he himself always needed a listener – an intimate and totally understanding ear, as his mother's had been, to which he could allow escape the inner ferment behind the stern, calm exterior.

In 1919 Brooke was delighted to be selected as a student on the first post-war Staff College Course at Camberley. He had spent a desultory although not disagreeable few months in France in the immediate aftermath of war at the beginning of 1919. 'Oswald Birley, on returning from leave home,' he wrote, 'found a French officer's shoot near Valenciennes which he proceeded to run for the owner during his absence. We had several good days of about thirty brace before the owner returned. His return never upset

Birley in the least and he calmly invited the owner to join us in our day's shooting. He accepted this invitation graciously, but turned out to be a desperately dangerous shot . . .' And – 'Gosling, commanding AA guns, who had been Master of the Essex Hounds, had gathered together several Belgian dogs that usually pull carts . . . with this pack we had several amusing days, hare hunting among the shell holes of country surrounding Valenciennes.'[2]

The Staff College, to Brooke as to most officers, was a thoroughly formative influence; particularly so, soon after a major war when considerable experience both of Instructors and students could be pooled. The Staff College, too, is traditionally the place where Regular officers of a generation, likely to rise in their profession, meet each other and form those friendships which come from being under simultaneous and demanding intellectual pressure, from sharing an experience. Brooke's course was full of names already renowned for their careers at the front – Gort, Freyberg, Foss (to name but three with the Victoria Cross) and many more. But he was most drawn by temperament to an Instructor, the Head of his Division, a man whom twenty-three years later he was to succeed as Chief of the Imperial General Staff, John Dill.

> I know [he wrote long after] no other soldier in the whole of my career who inspired me with greater respect and admiration. An exceptionally clear and well-balanced brain, an infinite capacity for work, unbounded charm of personality, but above all an unflinchable [sic] straightness of character: these were the chief characteristics that made up one of the most remarkable soldiers of our century . . .[3]

Brooke was a distinguished Staff College student, remembered by his contemporaries with awe for his knowledge, mental dexterity and – to his own surprise – eloquence. The students had to give lectures to the whole course, and Brooke's first effort 'almost made me ill with fright, I wrote out every word of it, and withdrew to the locked drawing-room where I spouted away, repeating it till I was word perfect'. 'He gave [a contemporary recalled] an absolutely first-class lecture, without referring to a note. There was no criticism possible.'[4] Yet there was no humbug in Brooke's anxieties. He was very self-critical, and although confident in his capacity as a soldier, he had no vanity. Indeed it was the mixture of ability, modesty and wit – his ready gift of repartee, his love of affectionate and accurate mimicry – which made him an irresistible companion. This period was also his first experience since marriage of normal family life and he adored his children (a son, Thomas, was born in 1921), his letters full of 'great romps' with them, children described, as by most fathers, as uniquely enchanting, their weights and dimensions meticulously tabulated. There came one moment of especial grief. In July 1920 his mother died in her house at St Jean de Luz, where he had last visited her in the previous August. He had maintained until that moment the habit of writing everything to her, and she had kept volume after volume of the often beautifully illustrated letters which spanned the first twenty years of the century.

To Brooke his mother was irreplaceable. By others of the family her enormous charm and power to attract – to 'get people running to her' whenever she wished – was viewed with mixed feelings: but to him she was unique, the perfect listener, the perfect correspondent, an inspiration, utterly adored.

After leaving the Staff College Brooke spent three years on the General Staff of the 50th Northumbrian Division, a Territorial Division whose Headquarters were at Newcastle. Some months were spent in the search for a house, after which, installed at Warkworth some thirty miles north of Newcastle, Brooke settled down to a happy life full of sport and offering many opportunities for the bird-watching and photography which were becoming an increasing passion. The professional side of life was darkened by industrial strife and the fear of revolution. In the aftermath of the Bolshevik Revolution in Russia few nations felt immune from the virus, which had, until mastered, infected much of Central Europe. The Territorial Army had been converted on a voluntary basis into a Defence Force to enforce law and order in extreme circumstances. In 1921 those circumstances were thought to be imminent. While Brooke was discussing with Commanding Officers at the Depot the question of what men in which units would be likely to volunteer for the Defence Force:

> The whole sky was suddenly lit up red by flames of the big RAF hangar on the Town Moor which had been set alight by some hotheads . . . There was a fairly strong Communist branch in Newcastle.
> Practically the whole of the 50th Division joined the new 50th Defence Force Division . . .

And a little later:

On May Day the Communist branch had planned a demonstration of which we had all details. Twelve platforms (11 Communist and 1 Sinn Fein) were to preach sedition on the Town Moor finishing with chorus singing of 'The Red Flag' and 'The Internationale' with a view to inciting the crowd to riot and to a pillaging of the Newcastle shops.

The Depot looked out on to the Town Moor and I had our one and only tank warmed up ready to sally forth if necessary, and a strong inlying platoon held in readiness to accompany it. I then sent out Intelligence officers to mingle with the crowds and report progress. The whole of Newcastle turned out, fathers, mothers, prams, babies . . . they walked round to see the various Communist platforms as if they were going round the cages at the zoo! From the Communist point of view the day was a dead failure, the crowd returned peacefully to Newcastle, the tank engine was stopped, the inlying platoon dismissed and perfect peace continued. By 8th June the crisis was over, the Defence Force was disbanded and the original Territorial Division reformed.[5]

Apart from this brush with duties in aid of the Civil Power, Brooke had an enjoyable but undemanding time in his first appointment away from guns – perhaps the last undemanding time of his professional life, largely spent in a house let to the family and belonging to his wife's sister near Catterick (whither the 50th Division Headquarters had moved) with his wife and two young children.

In January 1923 Brooke returned to the Staff College as an Instructor, and the family returned to Camberley.

His fellow Instructors, or many of them, had careers ahead of them as well as fine fighting records behind them. Some had been fellow students. If the Staff College is a place of student friendships, perhaps the strongest ties and mutual assessments are formed between those who compose the Directing Staff. There was Gort, a fellow student, a future CIGS, a man of immense courage, directness and enthusiasm whose fate would be crossed with Brooke's in the future. There was Adam, a brother officer from RHA days, a future fellow Corps Commander in 1940, a future Adjutant-General and colleague on the Army Council. There was Thorne, an incomparable Regimental soldier, another future formation commander in the dark days of 1940. There was Paget, a future Commander-in-Chief, perhaps the best trainer of soldiers the Army would possess for a generation. There was Anderson, an Army Commander in North Africa in the war that was to come: Riddell-Webster and Neame, men who would reach the top. There was Montgomery, of sharp and intolerant judgement, who formed a profound respect for Brooke, indeed a love and an awe which were to serve both men and their country well. There was the remarkable Fuller. To all of them he was and remained 'Brookie' all his life.

These men formed a generation of great distinction. They were completely dedicated and professional in their approach. Without exception they studied deeply. They had all had wide and direct experience of war, and were united if by nothing else in the conviction that, if it ever came again, it must be fought by skilled and well-trained troops and commanders. Their influence in the next fifteen years was uneven, their conclusions not always unanimous; but in their several ways, their hour would come. Nor did Brooke appear at that time as a solitary star in the constellation. Most of them shone very brightly indeed.

Brooke's war had been entirely spent with the Royal Artillery. He had become a recognized expert in the handling of artillery and had thought deeply about it. His theories on its evolution found expression in a series of lectures he gave when an Instructor at the Staff College and which in turn formed the basis for a sequence of published articles in the *Journal of the Royal Artillery* between 1925 and 1927. In spontaneous effusions, Brooke – who always endearingly confessed himself (as one who had known French and German before his mother tongue) 'not quite at home' with some aspects of English usage – could be repetitive, ungrammatical and inelegant. Tautology abounded. He could never spell. When writing formally, on the other hand, he expressed himself admirably and with style. In these articles he traced with thoroughness the background to artillery organization and equipment before the war. He next described the evolution of the various types and weights of artillery as the war progressed, exposing what he regarded as fallacies and false steps, and setting out his own views. Finally he produced in very clear and cogent terms his summary of lessons.

These 'lessons' represent the distillations of Brooke's experience as a Gunner, for they reflect, to some extent, his views on the future of warfare and since he was already a 'coming man', as a Staff College Instructor and an acknowledged expert, his influence was a reality albeit still at a comparatively junior level. They also display a characteristic of Brooke's. Whatever was the job in hand he thought about it thoroughly and single-mindedly.

In the First World War he had been a Gunner and his expertise was concentrated thereon. His mind was like a searchlight's beam pointed in the particular direction of his duty. When his duty came to cover the strategy of the entire British Empire the beam lost nothing in penetration by needing to embrace all points of the compass.

The first deduction Brooke made from his experiences he described as 'standing out in a class entirely by itself' in terms of importance. 'In our pre-war conceptions,' he wrote, 'we had failed to appreciate the true influence of fire-power in modern battle.' He deduced from this that the proportion of what he called 'fire-power producing arms' must be increased, and – very importantly – that 'the manoeuvre of fire-power in battle must receive closer study'. And he continued – perhaps ominously:

> If we remember the tendency prevalent in times of peace to seek mobility at the expense of fire-power we shall find sufficient reason for a closer study of this important question.

Brooke, like most of his generation, still saw in his mind's eye the absolute immobility imposed upon the front by the use of a great weight of artillery as well as by the emplaced machine-gun. When he wrote of 'fire-power producing arms' he primarily meant artillery. He had seen the futility of infantry daylight attacks across broken ground in the face of an unbroken enemy, and he had seen the possibility of infantry advance when – and only when – supported by an artillery programme which permitted them to reach objectives silenced by artillery fire. He dreaded the natural tendency in peacetime manoeuvres, when the devastating effect of artillery and other fire cannot be realistically simulated, to behave as if that effect did not exist. Brooke saw an adequacy of well-co-ordinated artillery as the only antidote to the fearful casualty lists which his generation had suffered or survived.

Brooke disputed the thesis that the war had become 'an artilleryman's war' purely because of the static conditions, the stalemate of the trenches. With what some would certainly regard as special pleading he stood the argument on its head.

> If we reconsider the events of 1914 we shall, I think, see that it would be more accurate to argue that the conditions of static warfare were originally produced through a deficiency of fire-power. The loss of mobility in the operations subsequent to the race for the sea can be attributed mainly to lack of artillery

ammunition and consequent impossibility to support any further attacks.

Not all would agree with this analysis of First Ypres and its aftermath, although clearly lack of artillery power (on both sides) contributed to the exhausted inertia into which the front then settled; but so did many other factors (not least the flooding of the outer flank in the Yser battles) and Brooke's deduction was simplistic. It was really to say no more than 'had one side *or other* had a much greater superiority of fire-power a decisive victory might have been won, which was not won'. But that tends to be true of all drawn battles. Brooke was surely seeing matters too narrowly from an Artilleryman's angle.

Brooke tackled the question of the tank head-on. He paid tribute to the new weapon in discussing later phases of the war. 'The successes gained were mainly attributable to the new arm. Unquestionably the use of tanks in our offensive of 1918 had both a direct effect on the operations through their own action and an indirect one by rendering the new tactical handling of artillery possible.'

He then entered forceful caveats.

'If we examine the German offensive operations of 1918, employing somewhat similar artillery tactics without the assistance of tanks, we find that they met with equal tactical successes.' He stated boldly that the importance attached to the tank's success in the closing offensives had led some to the heresy of 'comparing the success obtained by a limited number of tank personnel at Cambrai with the failures of large numbers of artillerymen at Ypres'. Brooke denounced this as a false analogy: 'The density of artillery employed to support these tank attacks did not vary appreciably from that employed in supporting the infantry attacks.' The artillery, in other words, had been the dominant arm: the tank had simply replaced the infantry by an armoured means of moving assault troops across fire-swept ground. He ended his section on the tank:

> There can be no doubt of the fact that the introduction of the tank has reduced many of the tasks formerly asked of the Artillery, but it has at the same time created new ones in the necessity of providing protection for the tanks themselves. We are still confronted by the same problems of fire and movement but under a different shape.

Different shape or not, Brooke showed no doubt about the

answer. Tanks did not affect the necessity 'for a proportional increase in Artillery'. In a section on 'the manoeuvre of fire-power in battle' he saw the higher commander's control of manoeuvre almost exclusively in terms of his application and control of the artillery fire-power available to him.

As Brooke continued his 'lessons' he made it plain that in his mind, at that time, future battles would, to a large extent, resemble those he had experienced, tanks or no. His analysis of the handling of artillery, of its control, of the importance of counter-battery work was thorough and convincing. As to the attack itself:

> In a deliberate attack some sort of moving curtain of fire must be provided in advance of the assaulting troops. This curtain may either be provided from a stationary point of origin, such as the artillery deployed to support an attack, or from an armoured point of origin moving with the attacking troops, such as tanks in support of an attack.

The tank, therefore, is envisaged as producing close fire support – the artillery role – for the attacking infantry, who will need to occupy the objective; or as the assault force itself, requiring artillery support. Brooke recognized that the close support fire which could be given by tanks working closely with infantry would be superior in accuracy and immediacy to anything which the traditional artillery arm could provide. But he concluded his 'lessons' with a reiterated warning against 'sacrificing fire-power to mobility'. Mobility itself depends 'on our own fire producing arms'. He thought of the tank as one of these.

Tactically this was well thought through, admirably argued and sound as far as it went. Was there further to go? In the same bound volume of the *Journal of the Royal Artillery* which contains Brooke's concluding thesis a very different note is struck by a very different author. In an article called 'The Tactics of Penetration', Colonel Fuller launched a devastating attack on the barrenness of operational thinking in the recent war. The article immediately takes the reader from the minor – albeit vital – problems of tactics to the fundamental principles of war: surprise, concentration, deep penetration and envelopment. In criticizing the equal distribution of tanks along the front in the battle of Cambrai – as opposed to the alleged Tank Corps suggestion of concentrating at one point with a break-in echelon and a reserve, exploitation echelon – Fuller acknowledged the tactical success achieved by the tanks, but criticized the limited operational consequences, due to failure to concentrate force and exploit the penetration. He uses words which show him to be the author of the 'heresy' attacked by Brooke in his 'lessons' (published in a later article).

> At Ypres 120,000 gunners entirely failed to accomplish what in this battle [Cambrai] was done by 4000 tank soldiers.

Brooke's response to that, as we have seen, was that the tanks had enjoyed at Cambrai comparable artillery support to that afforded at Ypres – simply a new arm had been added and the scales of success tipped thereby. But the real difference between the two attitudes of mind of these men was more fundamental than implied in the scoring of debating points on Cambrai and Ypres. It was better indicated in the flavour, if not the specific detail, of some of Fuller's closing paragraphs:

> ... tanks could form offensive flanks and strike at the rear of the enemy, the enemy between the two points attacked. Have we learnt this lesson yet? I much doubt it. Have we learnt that the decisive point of attack is the rear of the enemy's army . . .?

Fuller was, in this article, harping on the theme of 'the dual attack'. But the real message was the necessity and renewed possibility of deep penetration, the necessity of concentration, the primacy of manoeuvre and the feasibility of obtaining operational victory through the power to exploit tactical success. The two writings – Brooke's and Fuller's – in juxtaposition make a dramatic contrast. The one, Brooke, is thorough, tactically convincing, conservative, judicious in expression and conveys to the reader's eye a battlefield modified but similar to those of immediately previous experience. He does not go further. The other, Fuller, is immoderate, brilliant and imaginative. Yet he conveys not so much a different concept of the tank considered as a tactical weapon, but, rather, a new and significant vision of the strategic and operational possibilities of the internal combustion engine with armoured protection combined. It is a vision of manoeuvre, and a vision of the future.

Indeed, one of Brooke's own illustrations, quoted above, was also used by Fuller to make his point. The Germans in March 1918, Brooke wrote, without tanks, 'met with equal tactical success', fairly attributing this to their use of surprise and of the short, hurricane bombardment of vital points rather than the protracted destruction of the objectives themselves whereby both surprise and subsequent mobility had so often been lost. But Fuller used the same example, with a different and significant deduction. The Germans were unable to gain victory through the exploitation of that breakthrough, because they lacked the means to produce mobility effectively. That, to Fuller, was the real lesson of March and April 1918. The concepts of the two men were not inconsistent with each other at a limited level of argument but they thought in different dimensions, and with different landscapes in their minds' eye.

It was Fuller whom the Germans read and re-read in those years. 'The engine of the tank,' wrote Guderian later, under the heading *Feuer und Bewegung*, 'is as much a weapon as its gun.' Fuller was a prophet (although he disclaimed the description, calling himself a 'missionary'), an original, one of the truly interesting minds and characters of his military generation. The debate in which he took so seminal a part and the stance of his contemporaries therein is critical to the understanding of British military leadership in the coming war.

Brooke had not been eighteen months at Camberley when tragedy struck him hard. He liked driving fast cars, as highly strung men often do, and he possessed a large Bentley in which he indulged the taste. He did not drive well. His wife tended to be nervous; but in fact he was not driving particularly fast with her one day in April 1925 on a slippery road when a bicyclist, turning unexpectedly across the road in front of the car, caused Brooke to brake, skid, turn round, and overturn. It was an open car, with only a hood as roof. Brooke, with the steering wheel stoving in his chest, broke several ribs and a leg but survived. Janey, with paralysis following a broken vertebra, contracted pneumonia after the consequent operation and died a few days later.

It was a shattering blow. They had been completely unlike – he precise, scrupulous for detail; she beautiful, affectionate, vague, 'Irish' with a happy-go-lucky temperament. It had been clear to all how much he adored her, taking immense pains with the preparation of small presents for her, attentive and devoted. It was thus that soldiers who knew them at that time recalled them. The family was close-knit, the children very young.[6]

For many months after his wife's death and his own recovery Brooke withdrew into a complete shell. His children were too young to be companions, and his own taut and inherently shy disposition made it difficult for him to replace for them a mother's affection. He was not the sort of man who could be both father and mother in such a situation, and they, as they grew older, found him strict and withdrawn. They stood in considerable awe, which he lacked the skill and perhaps the inclination to dispel. A niece, his sister's daughter, Pamela des Voeux, came to give devoted help in running his household. He almost certainly felt not only grief but guilt over his wife's death. The children reminded him of the tragedy, and although he undoubtedly loved them, told them stories, drew for them, the reminder seemed sometimes intolerable. Not unnaturally his son, at least, responded with the development of a nervous tension which derived from Brooke and which the boy got inadequate comfort to dispel. The family had been well served by faithful attendants and it was an added blow that an adored nursery governess had to leave them also at exactly the moment of their mother's death. To the children the domestic staff became something of a refuge and a link with their mother.[7]

To others he retreated behind a mask, seldom lowered. 'I very much wish I could have been finished off myself at the same time,' he wrote two full years later. He rarely spoke to anyone except at and about work. He developed a pronounced stoop and rarely smiled. His gifts of wit and capacity for laughter seemed, at least for a while, to have gone as if for ever. He himself found that the only course was, as he put it, 'to immerse myself as soon as possible in work, and to let absorption in my profession smother pangs of memory'. With determination he continued to drive the Bentley extremely fast. Within himself he entered a dark night of loneliness and emptiness which would last four years. The inward, uncommunicating reaction to sorrow which others had observed in him as a child was again manifest. It would take a strong light to dispel it.

After four years at Camberley Brooke went, at the beginning of 1927, to the newly constituted Imperial Defence College, then situated at 9 Buckingham Palace Road, as one of the first batch of students. The Imperial Defence College was formed to develop understanding of the conduct of war and the preparation of Defence Policy among selected officers of the three fighting Services, the Civil Services, and the Dominions. Brooke, who was to return to it as Army Instructor in 1932, believed in it profoundly. It was the first time that he found it necessary to widen his reading and thinking from the operational sphere to the whole business of war, and its higher direction. He found this intensely interesting and his tough and often irreverent mind was admirably suited to the sort of questioning of accepted rubrics which the

Imperial Defence College needed to engender. The Course passed quickly.[8]

At its end Brooke returned 'to Regimental Duty' and although he found it agreeable after so long spent on the Staff, or at places of instruction, to be close to soldiers and guns again, he felt restless. He was a Brevet Lieutenant-Colonel, but still a Major in the Regimental list of the Royal Regiment. Promotion seemed sluggish, life somewhat drear. He was often intolerably lonely. He thought of a complete change of scene and profession, and had looked at the possibilities of leaving the Army and emigrating to New Zealand before his selection for the Imperial Defence College. He was slightly encouraged by the offer of command of a medium Artillery Brigade in India early in 1929, and by notification of his impending promotion to Lieutenant-Colonel. But those days were slow-paced for his entire generation with their wealth of experience and their ideas: and the faster their minds the slower seemed the pace.

The clouds soon dispersed. Instead of the medium brigade in India he was offered, from February 1929, the post of Commandant of the School of Artillery at Larkhill. It meant a step from Regimental Major direct to Brigadier, a post where his profound knowledge of and thoughts on artillery tactics and development could find expression, and in professional terms a most congenial environment.

Although he was subsequently, for nine months, to be 'Inspector of Artillery', a now defunct post for which he had little use in view of its almost complete absence of influence, Brooke's appointment as Commandant at Larkhill marked the climax of his career as an Artilleryman. He was long remembered for his work there, all of which reflected his strength and personality.[9]

He pulled down a large part of the camp. It was at that time a messy and muddy place of condemned huts and unmaintained roads. Using, no doubt, every device in and round the regulations to get his way and to finance it, he created, in a remarkably short period, a well-ordered and personally designed camp with tree-lined avenues and proper shops. He was, they said, the first Commandant who immediately inspected the quarters of the civilian staff, and saw for himself how deplorable they were. He moved them into soldiers' married quarters, removing the soldiers into newer quarters whose completion he accelerated. He rode ceaselessly round the camp with his Adjutant, who was described as 'a fiery sword darting here, there and everywhere supervising

Alanbrooke's mother,
Alice Bellingham, Lady Brooke

Colebrooke

Jane Richardson,
Mrs Alan Brooke

With Gunners of the 30th Battery Royal Field Artillery, 1909

On the Artillery Staff of the Canadian Corps, 1917

The C.I.G.S.

the work Brooke had ordered'. His eyes missed nothing. The quality of life of every soldier or civilian at Larkhill was improved.

Brooke's changes to the curricula at the School were all in line with his philosophy of soldiering – thoroughness in training, especially the training of leaders. 'Young officers' courses, for officers joining the Royal Regiment, were started in his time and under his stimulus. The tactical as well as the technical aspects of gunnery provided another of his main themes; and, as always, the importance of the collaboration of all Arms. He imported lecturers from the other main Arms and Services to lecture – a normal practice now, an innovation then.

As to teaching methods, Brooke himself would give a lecture on 'how to lecture' which deeply impressed all who heard it. He had been struck, on a visit to the French *Cycle d'Instruction* at Versailles, by the imaginative system of visual aids, and he developed these. He encouraged the use of several speakers on a theme, to vary that which can become monotonous. Every detail of training and presentation was exhaustively thought through.

All respected his ability, his fairness and his depth of professional knowledge. All, without exception, stood in awe of him. Whether in personal or professional matters he was strict. He never sought popularity, nor made particular efforts at human contact. 'He was not a mixer,' civilian members of the old Larkhill Staff recalled long afterwards, 'nor was he a martinet. A pure and simple soldier . . . as regimental as a button-stick.' That, indeed, in every appointment or under any strain was Brooke. Quick in perception, indifferent to display, empty of the slightest ostentation, thoroughly professional, determined to get his way when he saw his way clearly, a man of steel, but sensitive behind it all. Furthermore his merit was recognized. 'Great ability, devotion to duty and charm of manner. He is an outstanding officer and highly educated professional soldier far above the average of his rank': thus his confidential report at the beginning of 1930 and the whole series of annual encomia echoed the same.

He had, by a rare stroke of unconventional sense at the War Office, been promoted some ninety places to get the appointment, and his first day as Chairman of the Annual Artillery Conference saw him addressing the assembled Artillery Commanders of the Army, many of them seven to ten years his senior. When he stood up the conversational buzz continued. He waited, very still, for it to stop: and waited a further thirty seconds in perfect silence before he started to give his plans and policy. Senior or junior, all were instinctively impressed and little criticism was heard. He was, by sheer force of personality and self-evident knowledge and ability, master of all he confronted.

But he also understood, and would always understand (although sometimes forget) that a little tact and subtlety can be necessary to get results. Believing as he did in the necessity to keep tactical and technical policy in step throughout the Artillery he started courses for the Commanders, Royal Artillery of the various divisions. The majority were, of course, his seniors. He announced that his object was to hear the latest views of CRAs on tactics to ensure that the School was on the right lines.

> 'I don't think many of them had given much thought to tactics or their development; they certainly had few ideas on the subject,' said Brooke. 'As a result I had little difficulty in getting them to accept mine.'[10]

Brooke's service at Larkhill was probably one of his happiest times from a professional point of view. It could hardly be otherwise for there now came to him another joy so complete, entrancing and profound that it coloured the whole of life. It lasted until death.

Brooke was forty-six in 1929. Benita Lees, eldest daughter of Sir Harold Pelly, Baronet, of Gillingham in Dorset was nine years younger, widow of Sir Thomas Lees, Baronet, of South Lytchett Manor also in Dorset. Her husband had died of wounds received in the Dardanelles campaign in 1915. There had been no children of the marriage, the baronetcy had passed to her brother-in-law, and she had been living at home with her parents.

Benita was a woman of striking looks; calm, energetic where energy was required, capable and kind. Their acquaintance started in 1928. The following summer, 1929, they visited Colebrooke together. By the autumn their letters had warmed from practical discussion of arrangements to meet for races, parties, the theatre; and warmed also from 'Dear Brigadier Brooke . . . Yours sincerely, Benita Lees'. On 10th September Benita's letter thanking him for a day watching the Schneider Cup began 'My dear, dear Alan'. It was clear to her by then that he was deeply in love. 'Darling Benita' he wrote on 26th September, 'Every day you mean more and more to me . . . and I also wonder how I could face life without you.' Her letters gave him hope:

> . . . it would have been better to have waited longer and not to have discussed anything in the frame of mind we were in. However I daresay it's all right and we'll get on in the cool and

collected way necessary! . . . . Thank you so much for everything you are and all you've given me,

Benita[11]

Two days later:

> I do hope all is going well and that you don't feel your hair wants smoothing! I can't think of where to lay my hands on a snapshot but promise if some horror comes to hand you shall have it for what it is and you may do what you like with it – which will probably be to tear it up; the ultimate end, too, I hope of my letters though I'm very glad to think they are so safe with you – but then everything is I know – one feels that, dear Alan . . . God bless you . . . thank you for all your dearness,

Benita

By 30th September she had accepted him.

The 'hair smoothing' was surely a significant phrase between them – it indicated the calm she brought to that high-strung impatient nature. He used it in a letter of 21st September.

> After all, no amount of 'hair smoothing' gets work done . . .

but on 14th October he was more explicit while still defensive on this aspect of what had clearly become their love:

> I can't ever explain what balm and comfort you bring – partly because there is apparently nothing in my life that can have needed either or does need either – but I do know that a greyness has been there over everything all these years and that though it's been painted over by interests and various activities you are taking it away and each time with you brings a fresh glimpse and feeling of heavenly light and glow of new life and joy.

To him she was dissolving the shadows in which he had lived since the appalling moment when he had found himself alone. To her there was in him that sense of safety and security – 'Safe with you but then everything is, I know', and the theme recurs again and again, not only in their courtship and awakening to each other but through all their years. 'I never tell you what I think of you,' Benita wrote on 20th October, 'but I hope you can feel what I *do* think brings a strong feeling of absolute trust and safety.' Furthermore she sensed something not only perceived by a lover's eyes. 'When driving that man,' recalled his driver in the Second World War, who shared many of the air raids with him and had known him a long time, 'I always felt safe.' And in spite of his more nervy and irritable disposition she obtained peace from the underlying

97

strength of the man. Her sister, she reported in a letter of 16th October, said, 'You were so soothing – and you *are* my darling: just like a wonderful piece of deep, calm still water with lights right down in it.' The best of Alan Brooke and the heart of their relationship is in those words.

Their period of engagement to be married was short. First the wedding was projected for the following spring, but Brooke grew more and more impatient and the day was finally fixed as 7th December 1929. Few days passed that autumn without letters, just as few days saw them separated throughout life without a letter from him, or (in the Second World War) a diary entry intended for her eyes alone. He idolized and idealized her. In November:

> . . . I am so awfully proud of you and so filled with admiration for the way in which you have made use of your life. And my own darling you are so wonderfully modest about it all . . . today with you was just heavenly, and I felt as we were going along that I was just gliding through life with you beside me, and what a wonderful, wonderful thing your help was to me, how you had tuned up all my ideals to a much finer pitch for me.

Benita's common sense deprecated too much praise.

> 'Modest' was a word you used . . . I would like you to realize before you have a disappointing eye-opener that I may be quite a successful cats-paw but have practically no initiative.

She had written earlier:

> My part will be to try and make other things smooth so that the whole of your energy can go into your job whatever it is . . .

Her modesty, however, was real and not false:

> 'I'm not at all, all you think,' she wrote on 12th November. 'It's only that – as always – a big nature draws out a little one – like my puny one – and clothes it with some of its own influence and sees it through eyes that don't look for smallness . . .'

Each was fulfilled and magnified by the other, and so it remained.

Indeed Benita evoked in her Alan a spirit in the tradition of courtly love, both dedicated and humble, laying his achievements at her feet and vowing to do so in the future, doing all things, explicitly, for God and her – *Pour Dieu et Elle* as was Christian of Brunswick's battlecry when charging with the Winter Queen's glove in his helmet. He wrote: 'I feel that in any work or anything that I may do your part will be by far the greater and finer for having inspired me towards it.' Probably few who knew the professional man, thorough, hard and relentless in the pursuit of duty, perceived the romantic inner self. It was, however, a constant part, consistent with the small boy whose thoughts were concealed but had shown such devastating feeling when they had emerged.

They immensely enjoyed the exploration of each other's thoughts and personalities. Both had suffered. Both were mature. In his case there was a very particular and pervasive sense of coming into light from darkness:

> 'I am continually marvelling,' he wrote in early October, 'at my completely transformed outlook on life generally due to your existence, the increased interest in everything and the complete *joie de vivre* which I had entirely lost.' And a little later he wrote of 'That perfectly ghastly feeling of being absolutely alone in life which this house used to give me when it was empty . . . the deadly loneliness of it you have absolutely dispelled'.

Dispelled indeed it was. 'I simply loved wandering about in your thoughts,' he wrote at the time they became engaged. Her thoughts were as sensitive as his own. But she was also practical and commonsensical, and he loved her as well for that. Planning for the house and garden which would be their home – a very charming home, Syrencot House at Figheldean – she showed knowledge of at least one of his weaknesses. Benita to Alan, 8th October:

> When you wrote about tulips and antirrhinums I never noticed the fact that they wouldn't be out together – partly because I thought, subconsciously, you wanted the latter to follow on and to cover up the dead leaves of the tulips – and partly because I was thinking how like you to be worrying out the right spelling because you wanted that word – instead of hiding behind 'snapdragons'!

It was impossible to be a correspondent of Brooke's without discovering his incapacity to spell.

They referred to 'our garden' not only in that actual sense but as the private world they shared where all others were intruders. At first it was, of course, so new and precious that they delayed as long as they could telling the world of their engagement. 'In spite of them all and what they may say and do our "garden" just remains "our garden" where you and I are and no one else is allowed in. The rest can run about outside and we can talk to them over the garden wall.' Thus Brooke. Nevertheless 'the rest' appeared universally delighted. Very important was the matter of talking to Brooke's children. Benita praised him for his achievements with them single-handed. He deprecated her praise, and to some extent he may have been just to do so. 'I feel very ashamed of myself,' he wrote, 'for not having done more for them at a time when they quite unknowingly made life much more difficult.' They had made him feel guilty and inadequate and there can be little doubt that they had instinctively sensed his consequent withdrawal, more cold than warmth. Now all was to change for them too. Benita was from the very beginning an admirable stepmother. 'The result is quite delightful,' she wrote of what she generously ascribed to his upbringing of them. 'We'll try to give them a good time these holidays, darling, to start happily – I do want to get to know them really well straight away – ' and she had fairly written, 'How I get on with them depends entirely on me and I'm much the same always.' She got on splendidly with them, they calling her 'Mum' from the start.

Brooke's second marriage brought to him and to his wife complete happiness. His letters thenceforward never failed to express the joy and peace he found in her. Hers echo equal joy, and also convey throughout his life her sense of trust and the strong safety she found in him. Both believed that Providence had enabled them to find each other. Brooke sometimes appeared impatient with, or at least did not attach immense significance to the formalities of his religion, but his belief in God as a support and benevolent unchanging guide was a fundamental part of his existence. So it was clearly with Benita too. Whether in religious feeling, in sense of duty, in humour or in love he and she were at one. Their last exchange of letters before their marriage conveys the spirit of young lovers:

> I . . . still find it hard to fully grasp the fact that *you* are to be actually here with me: it seems far too wonderful to be true. Oh! My darling, I do *bless* you for your love and for the happiness you have given me and I do pray God from the *very* bottom of my heart that I may be worthy of you. Good night my *very* own darling, *your* 'belonging' Alan.

and Benita:

> My own dear darling Alan, I really wonder why all this wonderful love has come . . . I just love you with my whole being and admire you more and more every day, and I do thank God that you are here and that you have given me this heaven on

earth. My darling God bless you *always*. This brings all my love my own darling belonging,

your Benita

Perhaps the fairest note on which to end this account of their courtship and betrothal is struck by Benita's father in his letter of warm welcome to Brooke on being told in early October that she had made up her mind. With paternal feeling but with justice Sir Harold Pelly wrote:

> ... She is sensible, wise, capable, good and beautiful. All this and a good deal more you know, and will grasp more and more the longer you know her, and I think (if I may say so) you must be a remarkable man to have gained her love.

Remarkable or not, he was at least distinguished in two aspects of his married life. First his ardour and his articulate expression of it never showed abatement. Second he always, with an out-pouring which could only be sincere and spontaneous, showed his sensitivity for Benita's feelings, cares, pains or pleasures and unaffectedly put her first. This did not dim with time and custom. 'My own blessing,' he wrote in 1931, 'when you are away from me I realize more than ever how you are just *all* and *everything* to me': and 'I was glad to hear that you have been having your rests regularly, but you did not report whether the blinds were down and whether you slept . . . ?' Twenty-five years after their wedding, he was still showering lines of love upon her, and expressing his loathing of leaving her even for a short time, and his loneliness without her, in terms as ardent as when engaged or just married.

The small change of love, perhaps, but an integral part of Brooke. He had always needed love and intimate, total communication with a woman. He was incomplete without it and in Benita he found it. His natural reticence and inwardness as well as his outward austerity had to be counterbalanced by love and it is hard to believe that such a character could have accomplished what he did, whatever his discipline and dedication, without the light and warmth he found away from his professional duty. This highly articulate passion was no leaping flame – it glowed hot and steady all his life. Every letter after their marriage echoes the same theme: 'I do thank God,' he wrote in 1935, 'that He allowed you to be on this earth. I cannot begin to tell you, my beloved one, how grateful I am for all the happiness you have brought into my life.' 'I feel that I am wasting life when I miss opportunities of being with you,' he wrote again and again, until the last.

Now Brooke's life was balanced, natural and full again. His spirits were restored, his back straightened, he could again be heard singing the little Irish songs he loved as he pursued whatever he was doing in his home, for he was never inactive for a minute, generally working to music on the radio. His elder children were delighted and reassured by the presence of Benita, and overjoyed by two babies, a daughter Kathleen and a son Victor, born in 1931 and 1932.

CHAPTER VI

The General

IN 1932 BROOKE RETURNED to the Imperial Defence College as an Instructor. It was gruelling work, most weekends being absorbed in the preparation of schemes and a 'Directing Staff Solution' to the strategic problems under study. At that time the syllabus of the Imperial Defence College was essentially practical in emphasis, concerned less with the background of world affairs than with the actual issues which confronted Defence Planners in the British Empire, and would confront them and their superiors in war itself. Brooke's ideas, in the light of his future, remain of interest.

The study of the higher direction of war was, like all other military and politico/military questions of the period, much dominated by the experience of the war so recently won. Problems were considered in some depth. Lectures were given by experts of international renown, debates were conducted, and syndicates were formed to study explicit questions and produce answers, ultimately measured against the solution evolved by the collective wisdom of the instructor Establishment.

The first problem discussed was how to produce a co-ordinated strategy. Fresh in many minds was the situation of 1914 when the Navy and the Army appeared to have different and contradictory views of how the war should be fought by Britain, a dissension which had been simmering, unresolved, in the pre-war years and which had led to hasty, uncoordinated and in some cases ill-judged propositions in war itself.

Second, was the question of Imperial co-ordination at both the political and military level. It was taken for granted that the Empire – officers from all parts of which attended the College – could and would act as a strategic entity. The problem was how to ensure that the entity should be both secure and effective. The associated question of the organization of action with non-Imperial Allies received, perhaps naturally, less attention.

Third, was the question of national machinery to give effect to the solutions. Machinery was considered from every point of view, particularly with regard to the highest political direction and the necessity, or not, of a small 'War Cabinet'. Consideration was also given to the relationship between such a Cabinet and its strategic advisers and commanders in the field; and to the matter of transition to war. Brooke had listened to many lectures on these subjects in 1927. It is probable that those which impressed him most were given by Sir Maurice Hankey and Lord Haldane, who between them had covered almost the whole gamut of 'higher direction'. In particular, each had dealt comprehensively with the question of whether to create a Minister – and Ministry – of Defence. When, in 1934, Brooke himself came to produce 'Directing Staff Solutions' for various illustrative war contingencies the language he used was in many cases Hankey's. The experiences of the Second World War were largely to confirm his views.[1]

On the question of a united and indivisible approach to strategy, it was generally agreed that this would be achieved by the agency of the Chiefs of Staff Committee, 'COS', or, as sometimes described 'COI (Imperial) S'. The Chiefs of Staff Committee had been created after the war as a subcommittee of the Committee of Imperial Defence, itself an essentially advisory body, charged with a general oversight of the strategic problems facing, or likely to face, the Empire; and conceived as politically bi-partisan to the greatest degree which could be attained in peacetime. Brooke, together with his immediate colleagues, saw the Chiefs of Staff Committee as becoming the 'supreme Military Council', producing strategic advice for the political leadership on a joint basis, representing the collective wisdom of those who would have the actual responsibility for execution – the professional heads of the Services. They envisaged the Committee of Imperial Defence fading away in actual crisis, or, at the most, providing some of the nucleus of a 'War Committee', itself probably becoming a small War Cabinet. They believed that the Chiefs of Staff should issue directives to the commanders in theatres of war; and they also took the view that there should, where more than one Service was concerned, be a Supreme Commander in each theatre of war. They saw this pyramid – War Cabinet, Chiefs of Staff Committee, Supreme Commanders in the field – as executing the agreed Imperial strategy. The Service Departments would be responsible for the enormous tasks of administration and would have no direct Departmental hand in the conduct of operations.

The Chiefs of Staff Committee would be served by a Joint

Planning Staff – permanently established, and additionally conducting a dialogue with the operational staffs of the three Services. The War Cabinet would be served by a Permanent Secretariat, deriving from the Secretariat of the Committee of Imperial Defence. All this would produce a united approach to strategy and a continuity of strategic thought and direction. It would also produce authority and simple, clearcut lines of responsibility. In fact it was, in almost all particulars, what the Second World War produced and later generations retained.

On the second question, that of Imperial co-ordination, there was general agreement that the Committee of Imperial Defence should have Imperial representation, and that the Chiefs of Staff Committee 'must be an Imperial body'. This was not spelled out, and would become increasingly inappropriate to the full independent status of the Dominions. Some, however, went much further. Fuller (who was to be successfully flattered, as the father of armoured philosophy, by Hitler, and who was to make political judgements in favour of Fascism prejudicial to his future employment) lectured most forcefully, arguing for an 'Imperial Solution', an 'Imperial Council' ('the CID having failed us') and the need for a 'true Imperial General Staff', which would be Inter-Service as well as Inter-Dominion. Fuller envisaged a 'Great General Staff', separate from the Service Departments, the latter responsible for administration and for carrying out the orders of the former.[2]

On the question of co-operation with Allies, teaching and opinion at the College appeared unanimous. It was opposed to placing our forces under a 'foreign commander'.

The third great question was that of machinery. Three matters were regarded as paramount.

First, there was the issue of authority – who would resolve different claims on resources? Here there emerged unanimity, and it was perhaps the most explicit and determined view which the generation produced. The position of the Prime Minister was paramount. He alone could run a War Cabinet – which, it was envisaged, the Chiefs of Staff would invariably attend. No subordinate Minister could conceivably possess the authority since war affected not simply the Services but all Departments of State and all aspects of the life of the nation. In this they echoed the sage words of a previous wartime CIGS.*

* *Soldiers & Statesmen 1914–1918*. FM Sir William Robertson. He had written in 1915: 'The responsibility for co-ordinating the many and varied

Then, should there be a Ministry of Defence? The opinion of the pundits who lectured – notably Hankey and Haldane – and at the College was absolutely opposed to the creation of uch a Ministry. Churchill had at an earlier stage appeared somewhat in favour, being – quite rightly – concerned with the creation of what he called 'a common Staff brain' and the avoidance of divided counsels in strategic advice. Fuller advocated a Ministry of Defence, pouring typically astringent scorn on a system which 'when inter-Service problems arise . . . refers them back to those who separately have failed to solve them'. But the weight of opinion was hostile to a Ministry of Defence. The whole question had been exhaustively examined by Parliamentary Committees, notably that chaired by Lord Salisbury, and the idea was widely regarded as based on fallacy, although some thought it possibly the right eventual solution. But each Service, argued Hankey, was so complex in its requirements in war – and probably in peace – that it needed a Minister. One Minister alone could not possibly be loaded with all the administrative work, and if junior Ministers were created major issues would nevertheless be brought to the top, and the Minister of Defence still be overloaded. If a Minister were superimposed on the three existing Service Ministers and Departments there would be no economy.

In fact this concept – spelled out in a 'Directing Staff Solution' to the problem of 'Higher Direction of War' when Brooke was Instructor at the College – was very much what happened. It is true that there was, in the Second World War, a 'Minister of Defence' in the sense that the Prime Minister gave himself that additional appointment. There was, however, no 'Ministry' – there was a powerful Secretariat and a strong joint staff apparatus. The impossibility of any but the Prime Minister playing the lead role was recognized, at least after Churchill had come to the head of the Government. More recent developments have nothing to do with the life of Brooke.

The third main issue under the heading of 'machinery' was the question of a separate Air Ministry, and, indeed, of a separate Air Force. This had been argued when Brooke was a student, and he also attended a College debate in 1930 and took copious notes on the subject. The question centred on the control of air forces. The view of some – the 'Naval syndicate' led – was that air forces

aspects of military policy rests with the Prime Minister, who is ex-officio Minister of Defence.'

formed part of naval or military operations and constituted, simply, another arm for their prosecution. Separate command would thus be unsound. As to those operations which could be regarded as solely aerial – 'Does the Defence of London or an attack on Paris,' they rhetorically enquired, 'demand a separate Service?' This was the battle which Trenchard had consistently fought for the life of the young Service, and feelings ran high.

Brooke noted all the arguments very fairly and thoroughly. His own views were typically practical. The Royal Air Force and the Air Ministry existed. It was better to make the existing system work than try to argue from principles which themselves might one day be made obsolete by technology. Furthermore, he believed that unless the development of air forces were under single and dedicated control that development would be slowed down – 'divergent lines of technical development lead to slow progress'. As to the allocation of resources and the argument that a separate Service could lead to disharmony with the overall military or maritime strategy, Brooke appears to have been somewhat impatient. It was in his nature – and in his experience – to believe that arguments between men of goodwill aiming at the same national objective could be resolved by reason. He disliked the assumption that distinction must imply confrontation.

> 'Are CAS and CIGS *bound* to disagree?' he noted. 'They *may* disagree on *principle* in which case the PM will have to adjudicate. *But is that not his job?* The ultimate military control of the next war must be political as it has been since the days of Pitt.'[3]

To Brooke the allocation of all resources in war, including air resources, must conform to an overall strategy laid down by the War Cabinet, advised by the Chiefs of Staff. Details of command and subordination in the field might differ, theatre by theatre: but at the centre there could be no ambiguity. The Chiefs of Staff would advise, both collectively and individually. They were the responsible heads of the Services. The War Cabinet, under the authority of the Prime Minister, would decide. The Chiefs of Staff would execute. All this came about.

Finally – with a less satisfactory sequel – the political authority would lay down the *object* of the war, what the fighting and the sacrifice was to achieve, an object which should never be lost from view. In an admirable lecture on 'The Preparation of a Combined Appreciation' (to be presented to Ministers on the recommended conduct of an imaginary war) Brooke drove that lesson, Clausewitz's lesson, hard home: 'War is a political act.'

When Brooke left the Imperial Defence College in April 1934 he assumed, and held for eighteen months the command of the 8th Infantry Brigade. It was unusual for an Artillery officer to get such a command – in fact there had been a recent War Office order restricting Infantry Brigade commands to Infantry officers. Brooke's star was sufficiently in the ascendant for an exception to be made in his case.

The 8th Brigade – a brigade at that time consisted of four battalions, all supporting arms being commanded on a divisional basis – was based in Plymouth. Brooke found the work absorbing. He had served, whether at Regimental duty or on the Staff, almost entirely as a Gunner. Now he had to study Infantry work, from first principles, if he was to be able to guide, criticize and inspire. He read voraciously and was soon to find that, given the study and depth he put into the task, the handling of the Brigade on manoeuvres presented him with few difficulties. He loved command – and his life, with its long periods of Instructorships as well as on the Staff, had been short on Command experience. He organized a Battlefield Tour studying among other actions the Battle of the Aisne and drawing not only exhaustive lessons from what occurred but making his officers think about the differences, or lack of them, advances in technology in the intervening twenty years might have produced in similar situations. He was an untiring trainer.[4]

If there was much to learn there was much to impart as well. Brooke had a very poor opinion of the approach to the training of the British Infantry subaltern. He wrote:

> They were sent to their Battalions from Sandhurst quite unfit to command a platoon, and as far as I could see the most usual method to teach them was to put them direct into a platoon to learn for themselves under the very doubtful tutelage of a Platoon Sergeant.[5]

To Brooke this was anathema. He had studied war and lived through it, and believed that the tactical handling of troops is an art to be learned and not an automatic inspiration. He also believed that the tactical handling of small bodies of Infantry, because the component parts of such bodies are human rather than mechanical, requires more study, training and instruction than in any other arm of the Service. Unable to make official headway, he formed his own Brigade school for young officers, drawing the instructors from the 'best officers and NCOs available within the Brigade'.

Later, he took his ideas further. When the Director of Military Training (a post Brooke himself was to fill in 1936) held a conference in 1935 Brooke – who had just been promoted to Major-General but was left in command of his brigade for a few more months – spoke forcefully. In his view it was essential that on leaving the Royal Military College a young officer should have some sort of 'post-graduate' specialized training to fit him to command a platoon. Other speakers objected that it was 'experience with their men, in their units' that the young officers needed most and needed early. To Brooke, however, it was inherently wrong to place the lives of men, even for a short while, in untrained hands. The matter did not reach any final or universally accepted solution (it never has) but at least Brooke, later in his life, had the supreme satisfaction of seeing the establishment of a School of Infantry. He had to wait to become CIGS before attaining it. When Director of Military Training in 1936 he managed to obtain the support of all Infantry Brigadiers for such a school, but found the then CIGS, General Deverell, adamant against the idea. It had not been necessary in the past so why was it necessary now? Brooke withdrew, but never dropped the project and generations of Infantrymen owe much to his tenacity.[6]

Two more of Brooke's opinions survive from his period with his Infantry Brigade. First he spoke with passion of the need for more and better training at night, believing that on the modern battlefield the Infantryman came into his own at night, and perhaps only at night. Brooke believed that the infantry training of the Army should be largely orientated towards fighting in darkness – not as a difficult exception to the norm but as something to be prepared for, welcomed and initiated. He wished the training manuals to be entirely revised with this emphasis. His colleagues were divided on the subject. Some were strongly of his mind, others – remembering the disorganization and chaos of certain night operations in the war – believed that they could never be more than limited and exceptional. On the whole Brooke carried his point.[7]

His other recorded view at about the same time raises echoes of his earlier writings on armour. At a conference he discussed 'the attack'.

Armoured fighting vehicles also appear to present a doubtful solution to the problem of the attack. Their fate in the conflict between armour and fire-power is in the balance, they are unlikely to be present in sufficient numbers in the early stages of a campaign, *and it is open to argument whether tanks do not on the whole favour the defence when employed in close co-operation with Infantry* [author's italics].[8]

This was, to say the least, lukewarm. But his brigade thought the world of him. 'He was a thinking soldier,' said an officer in it, 'he was head and shoulders above the ordinary officer of his rank at that time. We all thought he should be higher. You felt his presence. He filled a room.'[9]

Brooke was soon to leave his brigade on promotion. His first appointment as Major-General was to be Inspector of Artillery in November 1935. 'This appointment,' he wrote, 'held no authority of any kind.'[10] The Inspectors of the various Arms were subordinate to the Director of Military Training, although of the same rank, and the Inspector of Artillery did not even possess the right of direct access to Artillery Commanders whose units' technical performance he was expected to assess. Brooke felt his ability to influence the handling of Artillery or anything else to be minimal in such a post, which contrasted most unfavourably with the recent happiness of command.

Fortunately it did not last long. In August 1936 Brooke was appointed Director of Military Training, a War Office Directorate offering great scope, and central to the task of training the Army for war. The Press noted his appointment formally in the usual way; the *Evening Standard* described him perceptively as resembling 'a benevolent eagle'.

He had acquired a family house called Ferney Close at Hartley Wintney in Hampshire, and it was to be his home and his base for many of the coming years: his refuge and his private paradise.

The Army in which Brooke had now obtained a position of influence, and whose development he was increasingly to affect and ultimately to dominate was far from sure of itself.

The first and simplest contributory factor to malaise was the so-called 'Ten Year Rule'. This, largely and paradoxically attributable to Winston Churchill when in office in 1929 as Chancellor of the Exchequer, had provided a working assumption, on which the Armed Forces were to plan their shape, size, equipment programmes and forward budgets; there would be no major war for ten years. The Chiefs of Staff did not dissent. The assumption was reviewed annually. Although the development of sophisticated equipment was already a protracted business it was simpler than it has since become. The Ten Year Rule meant, in effect, that the Army would get ten years' notice of war, and it was a convenient implication that in ten years huge changes and expansions of both organization and materiel could, if necessary, be undertaken. The Ten Year Rule was an admirable device under which to impose economy; and a very successful way of ensuring stagnation, preparing unpreparedness and discouraging all parts of the military machine. It was, furthermore, irrational. It could only be based upon a certainty of the course of events in potentially hostile countries, and an equal certainty about how political intentions might develop in those countries. Any Government which believes it can foresee with certainty the designs of others – or is confident that such designs will take ten years to change – is unwise. Of the Services suffering from this the Army came off worst.

The second major point of contention was the role of the Army in war. There was a natural revulsion from the great offensives of the Western Front only a few years past, with their huge losses, accompanied by conditions of protracted stalemate. To the British there seemed – as there had seemed before 1914 – at least a strategic choice. If we were not directly threatened, it was asked, why should we not concentrate upon the defence of our own shores and our own Empire? There was, however, a discernible countervailing sentiment (probably stronger in the country than in the Cabinet) that we would, in honour, need to become physically involved in Continental war, if such ever came. Few people, before 1934, thought that it would. Meanwhile doubt on the Army's function stultified its progress.

The next development which dominated military thinking was the threat from the considerable increases made in air power. The United Kingdom would clearly be directly threatened in a future war in a far more savage, even decisive, way than ever before. Air Defence, although starved of much that was needed, was recognized as one of the main pillars of British strategy. Offensive air power based in the United Kingdom could be built up as a deterrent force. The role of the Army, therefore, was to provide – mainly by Territorial Units – the ground based, gun and searchlight element of Air Defence: to secure overseas possessions, principally India where a large British Army in addition to the

Indian Army was maintained: to defend the United Kingdom itself, against raids, variously estimated but defined for most of the time as possibly in the order of 10,000 men, sea or air landed (major invasion was considered only a remote possibility): and – possibly – to provide an Expeditionary Force to the Continent, the advantages and disadvantages of which were increasingly debated. By the time Brooke became Director of Military Training, however, a catalyst had appeared in the form of Adolf Hitler. Germany had left the Disarmament Conference in 1933, and a Defence Requirements Committee reported to the British Cabinet early in 1934. Quoted in the report was an assessment by the Chiefs of Staff that Germany might be ready for war by 1938 or 1939. Few people in public life thought this far-fetched. Few had previously thought the Ten Year Rule unreasonable, and it was now abandoned. The ill effects of such a policy cannot be righted overnight. A five-year rearmament programme was recommended to the Cabinet. Only a part of the necessary financial allocation was agreed, and rearmament proceeded sluggishly and unevenly, nowhere more so than in the Army.

Another contributory factor to malaise was internal, and concerned the whole question of mechanization and the role of armoured forces. First there was a straightforward issue between those who regarded the tank as an overrated instrument which would be inherently vulnerable to well-sited defences, so that business would go on much as before; and those who believed that the combination of the internal combustion engine and armoured protection had introduced a new era in land warfare, of which the tank battles of the previous war had given only minor indication. The practical point at issue between these two schools of thought was the extent to which horsed cavalry should be unhorsed and mounted in armoured vehicles.

The second strand in this debate concerned the employment of the armoured forces themselves. Were they to be regarded as supporting the infantry and used, in effect, as very close support artillery to reduce strong points so that infantry mobility could be maintained without the grievous losses of the past? Or should they be 'let off the leash', entrusted with bold operational movements, careless of flanks and of the progress or lack of it on other parts of the front, if a front existed? Would the battle move at infantry pace and in unbroken lines, or could it more resemble the operations of fleets at sea – or, indeed, at an immensely faster pace, the manoeuvres of the great Captains of previous ages?

Within a small but important circle this debate dominated the period. As to the efficacy of the tank as a weapon system and the place, if any, of the horse there could only be one outcome. The defenders of horsed cavalry as the mobile arm in Western European war, or most other contingencies, were so self-evidently out of date, that 'mechanization' was a foregone conclusion, and the horsed cavalry regiments of the Army were scheduled to be converted to armoured fighting vehicles and to lose their horses. This programme was limited only by finance, and lasted well into the Second World War. Indeed, Army policy, once determined, was possibly immoderate in disposal of the horse, in that infantry transport, for example, became entirely motorized; at least in some campaigns this was of questionable value if the infantry themselves had to move at marching speed. It is noteworthy that the German Army, pioneers of armoured warfare in practice, retained most of their horsed transport throughout the war in order to save fuel and workshop capacity for that which they regarded as fundamental – the armoured formations.

As to the second strand in the debate – the proper employment of armoured forces – extreme views could be found on both sides of the argument, and views became identified with individuals. Personalities tended to obscure judgement. The British had led the field in the development of the tank, and they continued for a while to lead in theoretical discussion of its use. In 1927 an experimental mechanized force had been established on Salisbury Plain, with a battalion of tanks, a battalion of machine-gunners in cross-country vehicles, a tractor-drawn field artillery regiment and a mechanized company of Engineers. The essence of this force, embryonic though its organization and equipment may have been, was that it was a mobile formation of several arms. The degree of protection differed unit by unit; but all could move and fight together. Then the 'mechanized force' gave way to the 'Tank Brigade' which was entirely composed of tanks and which was based on the premise that a tank force did not require the co-operation of other arms. From 1937 the battalions of the Royal Tank Corps were brigaded annually for training on Salisbury Plain for this purpose, and in 1934 the brigade was organized on a more permanent basis. There was, therefore, a separate and tactical issue – whether tanks should form part of a mobile body of all arms or should form an independent and self-sufficient force.

But the essential issue was whether such a force – entirely tank or composed of all arms – should be envisaged in deep operational manoeuvres: or whether the tank would not be best and perhaps solely employed in support of the infantry. The prime exponents of the tank as symbol of a new era in warfare were the now retired Fuller and Captain Basil Liddell-Hart. Fuller was a visionary. He had, through his lectures and writings, considerable influence – on none more than on a certain German officer struggling for the future of armoured forces within the attenuated Reichswehr and now the growing Wehrmacht, by name Guderian. Fuller's fundamental thesis was that the ability to move armour–protected weapons, at the pace provided by the internal combustion engine and across country, restored manoeuvre to the tactical battlefield and made obsolete much of the enforced experience of the war of 1914–18. Fuller had been offered command of the original experimental force of 1927, but had ultimately declined it through somewhat petulant dissatisfaction with some of the circumstances which would surround the appointment.[11]

Liddell-Hart, who had published a history of the war in 1930, had also produced a number of books on operational themes, discussing tactics, in particular Infantry tactics, with originality and acumen. He had been greatly encouraged by Maxse, Brooke's old commander and mentor. On mechanization and its implications his mind was close to Fuller's. Both envisaged major operational movements aimed at the nerve centres of the opposing forces. Liddell-Hart, unlike Fuller, was constant in belief that mobile operations should be conducted not by tanks alone but by balanced formations of all arms. He was a prolific military theorist, historian and biographer.

In 1936 when Brooke went to the War Office as Director of Military Training, Liddell-Hart, who had been invalided from the Army from war injuries in 1924, was Military Correspondent of *The Times*. In this capacity he had considerable influence. But it was not only through *The Times* that Liddell-Hart had a high reputation in military circles throughout the world. His writings and his voluminous correspondence with all, of whatever nationality, interested in the development of strategy and tactics had given him a wide variety of contacts – and led to the amassing of a huge and original library of relevant papers – so that he was regarded in a good many quarters as a somewhat contentious 'guru' of the military art, albeit a 'guru' who, in spite of dedication, showed sometimes more emotion in his approach to his subject than the scientific detachment he preached.

The argument was not simply that of a handful of imaginative revolutionaries struggling without success against the conservatism of their superiors. As early in 1927 the CIGS himself had addressed the officers of the original mechanized force and had used uncompromising language:

> A force of this description you can use as a swinging blow coming round the flank. It is an armoured force intended for long distance work. It may be necessary to employ it as an armoured force for close work, but essentially what I am aiming at is a mobile armoured force that can go long distances and carry out big operations and big turning movements. In a force of this kind you must have quick decision . . . the Commanding Officer must be far forward . . .[12]

And much more to the same effect. Thus the professional head of the British Army. It might have been Guderian – or Liddell-Hart – himself. Nevertheless the CIGS in question – General Milne – had not carried through his own ideas to any significant degree. He tended to start a matter boldly and grow more cautious about any idea as it developed. Although he had brought Fuller (whose influence is clear in the words quoted above) to the War Office with him, as his Military Assistant, mechanization moved at a snail's pace. Much of this was, of course, due to the innate conservatism of those who disliked parting with their horses and exploited every means of delay in so doing. It could almost be said that a significant part of the officers of the Army took the view – 'we can't argue in logic against mechanization, but do it as slowly as possible'. Military conservatism, generally dominant in conditions of financial constraint and a long peace, was powerful. Because it was doomed to failure there was bitterness. A good deal of this was directed at Liddell-Hart, who was not only the most articulate and enthusiastic proponent of mechanization but was known to be consulted, very widely, by politicians and editors interested in military affairs.

Brooke was of a generation of gifted and able officers who had survived and pondered the war, read widely, discussed deeply. Could there be among such men instinctive allies of the military conservatives to whom Liddell-Hart, Fuller and their school were anathema? Unfortunately there could. Among a number of the chief proponents of reform was to be found an intellectual arrogance which did not make their propositions more acceptable, which led to easy counter-attacks upon the more extreme of their claims, and which tended to divide opinion between those who associated all that was traditional with what was obsolete on the one hand, and all that was innovatory with what was unsound and disloyal upon the other.

The crunch came in 1937 when Mr Leslie Hore-Belisha was appointed Secretary of State for War. Hore-Belisha was an ambitious politician with a strongly developed sense of public relations. He became genuinely interested in the case for Army reform, including the pace of mechanization. He was confident that he could help the Army, not least by stimulating the sort of publicity at which he was adept. He was entirely out of sympathy with the senior officers of the Army and they in turn found his manner and methods offensive. He thought the Generals crass, and they found him vulgar and incompetent.

Determined to make changes in personalities, because rightly sensing that changes were needed, he naturally looked for advice. He then took a disastrous step. He effectively made Liddell-Hart a personal consultant on Army matters. Furthermore it soon became known that the consultations he principally carried out were about the appointments of senior officers, whose careers to advance, how to get rid of X, whether Y was as stupid as he looked. The issue of whether an officer happened to take the 'Liddell-Hart view' of strategy and tactics suddenly appeared to colour the prospective careers of all.

This was lamentable on a number of counts. Liddell-Hart had a somewhat doctrinaire approach to his chosen subject. His personal relations with intelligent soldiers started by being good, but he tended to write the history of battles, campaigns and commanders with the sort of omniscience an Examiner brings to the marking of some pretty sub-standard papers. His theories were by no means always consistent, and while some encountered mere prejudice others failed to convince, and failed with at least some able although less articulate men. His influence now made the future command appointments of the Army appear matters of whim. Few thoughtful soldiers did not welcome change – and radical change was required. But the private conversations and correspondence of Hore-Belisha and Liddell-Hart (and these things became not only known but exaggerated) were such as to undermine all respect for the selection process. The general effect was that dislike of Hore-Belisha came to know no bounds and extended to the good things he did – and there were many, for he was dynamic and courageous. The dislike of Liddell-Hart's influence and position as an *éminence grise* sometimes extended to virtually all of Liddell-Hart's fundamental ideas themselves. The man's indiscretion frustrated his brilliance. Brooke and his friends were bitter on the subject.

As can often happen in so volatile a situation many of the appointments made under the aegis of Hore-Belisha were unsuccessful (as he quickly found) even in their object of bringing into association with him kindred spirits with enthusiasm for reform. He got rid of the CIGS (Deverell), which was probably right, but replaced him by Gort which was probably wrong, judged by his or any other criteria. Gort had invariably maintained close and cordial relations with Liddell-Hart who admired him. He was universally respected as a highly professional soldier, a serious student of war, and a superb leader, one of Brooke's original 'band of brothers' at the post-war Staff College. But he lacked the width and speed of mind of a number of officers of whom Wavell, Dill, and Brooke himself were but a few who were all his seniors in age. He was not generally considered a man with a strategic cast of mind, appropriate to the higher direction of war. Finally – although this would have been true of any of them – he was so much the opposite of Hore-Belisha in character and personality that intense dislike was generated between the two, and the Army suffered thereby. 'Many first-class officers were written off as useless,' wrote Brooke of this time, 'and a feeling of mistrust soon permeated throughout the Army'.[13]

Out of this general ferment following a long period of stagnation came for Brooke an admirable opportunity. At the end of 1937 a 'Mobile Division' – the first forerunner of the Armoured Divisions of the future – was formed in Southern Command in England. Brooke was given the command. He was delighted. In some ways the appointment, given the atmosphere of the day, was surprising.

In spite of the fact that by now Liddell-Hart was an avowed opponent of British land participation in Continental warfare he had taken a particularly keen interest in the Mobile Division. He had preached the gospel of mobility on a grand as opposed to purely tactical scale, and had done so on the basis of mechanization, and the mechanized mobility of whole formations. The creation of the Mobile Division seemed a major step down the road which the British had first pioneered but which had been followed only hesitantly – through discord, conservatism and parsimony – since the inauguration of the first mechanized force ten years before. It was natural that Liddell-Hart and his closest associates would have strong views on the commend. It was also natural that Brooke's would not be a name to command itself, in spite of his acknowledged professionalism, thoroughness and quickness of intelligence. Brooke was considered very much the distinguished Artilleryman who had distilled the lessons of war from a Gunner's angle; he was not to be counted among the prophets.[14] His writings, lectures and general reputation placed him, in the eyes of at least the extremists of the 'tank school', among the conservatives. He was marked by the visionaries as pedestrian. They remembered his teachings at the Staff College, his profound belief in the well-organized barrage he had done so much to develop, his concept (at that time) of tanks distributed along the front of attack to help the infantry forward. All this was the antithesis of that operational mobility and manoeuvre in depth in which they rightly believed.

It was inevitable that Liddell-Hart should recommend that the command of the Mobile Division should go to one of those prime believers in the tank who had been fighting for its existence and development over the years; of these General Hobart was the best known, and the most doctrinaire. Hore-Belisha was of the same view. Brooke's name came up. 'Essentially deliberate in his methods as a tactician,' wrote Liddell-Hart to Hore-Belisha,[15] 'that tendency would be a handicap in his handling of mobile troops. Moreover from what I have gathered in recent conversation of his ideas on the role of the Mobile Division I have found no idea beyond a repetition of the use of the Cavalry Division in 1914. The vital need is for someone who will produce fresh ideas . . .'

All this was part of a general post in the senior ranks of the Army. Hore-Belisha, who was simultaneously trying to find ways of getting rid of the CIGS (Deverell) and to avoid accepting his recommendations, discussed posts with Gort – at that time Military Secretary – and, invariably, with Liddell-Hart. In the event Gort's recommendation of Brooke's name for the Mobile Division – accepted as a *pis aller* by the CIGS who had stubbornly supported the claims of General Houston, Inspector-General of Cavalry – was in turn accepted by Hore-Belisha who extracted as a 'concession' the appointment of General Hobart as Director of Military Training in succession to Brooke. It was an extraordinary way of doing business, but Hore-Belisha's regime at the War Office was marked by an atmosphere of intrigue never seen before or since.

Of more significance than the circumstances of his appointment to command the Mobile Division is the question whether, in fact, Brooke was a sound choice and whether the criticism that his mind was too conservative for the task has substance. He had, as recently as when commanding an Infantry Brigade, spoken dubiously of the tank, as possibly favouring the defence. The cause of mechanized forces of all arms in offensive operations had already been set back by some false lessons drawn from manoeuvres a few years before, in which there was at least a suspicion that results had been rigged, and that the 'cavalry lobby' had been successful in nobbling at least one influential senior officer. Since then tank experts and armoured enthusiasts had been too much missing from the central direction of affairs. Was Brooke's appointment another example of half-heartedness towards the whole concept of mechanized operations? It is true that at no point had Brooke yet given evidence that he had a real insight into the strategic and operational opportunities, as opposed to the tactical advantages, which the tank and the general progress of mechanization were to produce. To that extent the critics of his appointment were justified. On the other hand he brought to the appointment a sense of tactical realities which was much needed. Brooke was severely practical. Although he may not have 'seen a vision' as had some of the military prophets he was certain that when required to fight a battle – as opposed to exploitation or pursuit – the tank would need the support of other arms: and it thus followed that a formation with overall operational mobility must, within itself, contain a tactical balance of arms.

In this Brooke was undoubtedly right, and was proved right by subsequent experience. The true argument – and it required a comprehension not so much of mechanization as of history – was or should have been between those who envisaged armoured formations concentrating and exploiting so that force could be applied by striking, in the German phrase 'with the clenched fist rather than the open palm', and those who pictured them as formations providing supporting elements for use at as many points as possible, to strengthen fundamentally less mobile troops in a slow-moving battle. It was this latter heresy which the proponents of the tank had so vigorously opposed through the years of frustration, and which some of Brooke's earlier thinking and writing led them to connect with him. There is no evidence, however, that Brooke in 1937 in the least subscribed to it, whatever his earlier views had been. Indeed, in the Mobile Division he specifically directed that tanks were not to be used piecemeal.

Brooke, writing of the task he faced, saw it as both tactical and human.

> There was on the one hand the necessity to evolve correct doctrines for the employment of armoured forces in the field of battle, and on the other hand some bridge must be found to span the gap that existed in the relations between the extremists of the tank corps and the cavalry. There was no love lost between the two . . .[16]

The first part of the problem he saw in practical terms, the co-operation and logistic support of all Arms in operations in which all shared tactical mobility. Brooke had devoted considerable thought to the concept of how best to use the mobile division when Director of Military Training, and a distinguished and original senior officer of the Royal Tank Corps, Vyvyan Pope (later Brooke's Chief of Staff in II Corps), had been his chief assistant. His ideas had probably evolved at that time. Now he was able to develop from these ideas the more detailed tactical concepts which needed to be applied within the Mobile Division itself. The Second World War was to produce many deplorable examples of the mishandling of armour: in most cases, however, they derived less from incomprehension or inexperience of new technology than from neglect of the eternal principles of war. Those who failed were not so much rooted in anachronism as ill-educated in war itself. Brooke, on the other hand, was both well-read and wise. He also had the advantage of serving in the Southern Command under Wavell, a shrewd counsellor and friend.

The second part of Brooke's problem – the human relations between Tank Corps and cavalry – he was admirably fitted to handle. He was universally respected as a thoroughly professional soldier. As a Gunner he was, as he expressed it, 'a neutral'. He understood, from a human point of view, the sadness of the cavalry at losing their horses, their own concept of panache, 'and becoming dungaree mechanics' – Horse Gunner and fine horseman that he was, how could he not? But he also saw clearly that it was armour that 'was destined to play a major part in future war', and that the rapid melding of Tank Corps and previous cavalrymen into a united armoured force, was the task. He gained the absolute support of the best of both camps. He helped to overcome the natural prejudice of those in the Tank Corps who, as he put it, 'were apt to look upon the cavalry as amateur soldiers who only thought of polo, hunting and racing and never took their profession seriously'. As one who had been adept and enthusiastic at all mounted sports but whose professionalism was universally recognized, he was well equipped so to do. He paid unstinting tribute to the breadth of mind of those who supported him, particularly to Willoughby Norrie, commanding the 1st Cavalry Brigade, Tilly, commanding the Tank Brigade, and his GSO I, Crocker: and in general he referred afterwards to 'the wonderful spirit with which the cavalry faced this very great change'. Of some he wrote, restrainedly:

> There always exist . . . some men who fail to rise to the occasion, and being unable to absorb the bitterness that faces them endeavour to embitter the lives of those that surround them.[17]

His time in command of the Mobile Division did not last long. He was fifty-five. In July 1938 he was selected for promotion to Lieutenant-General and for command of a new 'Anti-Aircraft Corps', to be established with a Headquarters at Stanmore together with the Air Defence of Great Britain Headquarters of the Royal Air Force. Brooke was to take command of five Anti-Aircraft Divisions – two existed, and three more were to be raised.

> 'Here again,' he wrote, '. . . new ground to break . . . a new and complicated Corps to raise and an expansion of over 100% in one year. My brain was getting used to mental gymnastics, first Artillery techniques at the Artillery School, then Higher Direction of War at the IDC, followed by a change to Infantry work with the 8th Infantry Brigade, leading to a return to Artillery Training and organization as Inspector of Artillery, general training matters as DMT, Armoured Forces as Commander of the 1st Mobile Division, and now Anti-Aircraft work at a time when the air threat to this country was becoming daily more menacing.[18]

The Air Defence of the country, like most other aspects of our preparedness for war, had suffered from starvation of resources, confusion of counsel, divided responsibilities and, until fear lent impetus, indifference. The far-sightedness and dedication of those officers of the Royal Air Force who had made it their business to concentrate their energies upon the air threat and the appropriate response were ultimately to save the country.

The name of Dowding, then Air-Marshal, Air Officer Commanding in Chief Fighter Command and Air Defence of Great Britain, was soon to take its place in history. It was with

Dowding, and for operational matters under Dowding, that Brooke was now to work. He found the Air-Marshal, despite the nickname 'Stuffy', an entirely charming collaborator, and conceived for him an unchanging admiration. It was also thus as regards the general co-operation he enjoyed. 'It was the first time that I worked directly under the Royal Air Force,' he wrote, 'and I could not have asked for better treatment or greater cordiality on all sides.'[19]

This was typical of Brooke. Throughout his life and in every rank and sphere he tended to speak warmly of the collaboration he received – except in those cases where narrow-mindedness or feebleness of purpose diminished it, when he could be astringent as any. But there was in this quiet, quick-witted, somewhat imperious soldier, who 'thought fast, talked fast, moved fast' as wartime subordinates were to recall, a warmth and a total dedication to the task and to his country which drew co-operation from men of whatever type or Service who shared his aims. It was hard to be with Brooke and not to share his breadth of vision, and his determination to concentrate on the real aim whatever the incidental difficulties or irritations. This perception of essentials and concentration on them was a hallmark of the man; another was a combination of determination to achieve those essentials with a shrewd tactical sense of how to do it. He could be flexible in method – or prepared to be, for he never played his cards before he had to – yet steel-like in ultimate purpose: *suaviter in modo, fortiter in re*, although a good many of his colleagues and subordinates of the war years might have questioned the *suaviter in modo*. Yet Brooke, like all great men, knew where to draw the line, where to concede and where to stand. So dedicated, adroit and intelligent a soldier, combining high qualities of mind and character with obvious integrity attracted the co-operation of others, for which he typically gave the sole credit to them. 'I was very lucky,' wrote the restrained Dowding, 'to have such a courteous and considerate comrade in arms.'[20]

The Army's role in the Air Defence of Great Britain was complementary to that of the Royal Air Force. It was to provide heavy Anti-Aircraft guns, and searchlights to illumine the night sky. Early warning would be supplied by the radar chain, in an early stage of that great invention, and would be supplemented by an observer corps and a system of communications intended to convey the movement of enemy aircraft once over British territory.

But the prime task of the Army was the searchlight and the gun, and men to operate both.

As in all other spheres the requirement had been examined, re-examined and progressively increased as fear rose over the international situation and the intentions of Germany. Immediately after the First World War the pattern had been set, but implementation had been negligible.

In June 1936 the Committee responsible, known as the 'Reorientation Committee', had put the requirement at 76 anti-aircraft Batteries, each of eight heavy anti-aircraft guns; and searchlight companies to provide about 2500 lights. There were at that time 60 effective guns and 120 searchlights in the whole country. The same Committee, in June 1937, alarmed at the increase of the Luftwaffe which had given further impetus to their deliberations, increased the requirement by almost exactly double. Over 1200 guns were required and nearly 5000 searchlights. The first and desperate problem which faced Brooke when he took up his new command in July 1938 was one of equipment. On paper the Anti-Aircraft Corps was to be expanded from two to five divisions, covering the whole country: these divisions needed guns.* Anti-Aircraft guns in widely separated batteries and detachments, the maintenance of them, and the great number of searchlights required, necessitated huge numbers of men. The manning of Anti-Aircraft Defences had, from their inception, been considered a suitable task for the Territorial Army – an entirely volunteer force, then as now, who in return for modest remuneration gave up their free time to the nation's needs. Now a major expansion was to take place. Brooke's problem was to man his command, and to ensure that the men were properly treated and cared for. The decision of the Government in 1938 to introduce conscription created anomalies in this regard. Politically, the conscript had to be seen to be 'well-treated' in all respects. This was admirable, but the goodwill of the Territorial Volunteers (who had responded in heartening numbers to the recent call for expansion) tended to be taken somewhat for granted, and the more so as the situation developed. A trenchant letter from Brooke (who had by then been accorded the status of a Commander-in-Chief, and his Anti-Aircraft 'Corps' redesignated 'AA Command') to the Director-General of the Territorial Army shows the sort of problems which arose:

* For further discussion of Brooke's view on the type of gun see Appendix I.

Recent international events have enabled us to fill up our AA units very rapidly with the best elements of all classes of the population. These men, appreciating the urgency of pushing ahead with AA training and organization, have accepted the sacrifice of most of the leisure-time hobbies and amenities which go to lighten the daily round, and have put in an immense amount of voluntary unpaid work.

In addition, they have accepted a normal peace liability and abnormal war liability, both having a financial effect on their domestic budgets. The normal peace liability includes an annual camp of 15 days or 8 days. In accepting this, they took stock of the emoluments of all kinds available from Government sources, and of their employers' concessions, with their eyes open. In accepting the financially more serious war liability, their general view was that in war everyone will have to 'do his bit', and that as all will be in the same boat, a general financial upset will be inevitable.

Now what has actually happened?

Under the pressure of a deteriorating international situation, the Government rushed through legislation which enabled it to embody all the AA troops for the extended period of one month, in batches. This extended period serves two ends, firstly increased peace-time security against sudden air attack, and secondly (but only incidentally) facilities for intensive training. In fact, however necessary these special measures may be, it cannot honestly be contended that there yet exists a state of war. In other words, the AA troops are being required to honour a liability for which they did not contract.

Many men are seriously hit, both financially and in their domestic arrangements, by being called on to do a month. Those in skilled and semi-skilled occupations, normally earning from £3 to £5 a week, are badly out of pocket, since employers can hardly be expected to extend their existing concessions in order to make good what the Government ought to provide. Household budgets, providing for hire-purchase of houses, furniture, cars, etc., leave no margin for unexpected set-backs of this nature . . .[21]

There was then the problem of command and control. Brooke took prompt action over the tactical aspects of this, sometimes ahead of official authorization, acquiring, for instance, Brompton Road underground station as a Headquarters for the guns defending London, building command posts into the lift shaft and running communications, secure from bombing, along the underground railway. But transcending the tactical issues was the question of responsibility and higher command. Inevitably the ubiquitous Liddell-Hart had interested himself in this problem and had offered his advice to the Secretary of War, together with the customary flow of admonition as to who would or would not be the best men for the jobs.

Liddell-Hart had first discussed the matter with Hore-Belisha in May 1938 – two months before Brooke took up his appointment. He had rightly diagnosed that little could be achieved fast while there was excessively divided responsibility at the top. He produced a paper recommending a single Command covering the whole country which, as we have seen, came into being. He further proposed, however, that a 'Director-General Anti-Aircraft' should be created, with a seat on the Army Council and direct access to the Secretary of State. This would create a new Department 'taking over' Liddell-Hart recorded in his own memoirs 'the various branches in other departments which were at present dealing with the different matters'. He also argued (an argument generally very acceptable to Hore-Belisha) that such a reorganization would convince the public that Hore-Belisha was taking the danger seriously. 'The idea,' wrote Liddell-Hart, 'excited his imagination.'[22]

Such devices are generally highly inefficient and Brooke was scathing about this one. In dealing with an activity such as Air Defence there is attraction in the idea of creating a separate machine, finding a gifted individual and granting him distinctive powers. Yet what are his problems? He needs equipment – those branches of the General Staff dealing with the operational requirements on which production is to be based do not work in closed cells, but in close collusion with others. Few equipments can be absolutely isolated and to inject a requirements branch separate from all others is merely to confuse business. Such an overlord needs men. The Organization branches of the General Staff and the Manning branches of the Adjutant-General's Department – to say nothing of the Director-General of the Territorial Army – would have their work duplicated, or confused, or nullified.

A 'Deputy Chief of the Imperial General Staff – AA' was, however, created, with a new Department. Brooke wrote:

> The inevitable happened, a 'war office' within the War Office grew rapidly, with a duplication of General Staff, AG and QMG departments. *I began to find it more and more difficult to get anything done.*[23]

In this instance the 'new Department' had not, in fact, gone the whole way that Liddell-Hart had advocated, as he indignantly told Hore-Belisha when they discussed the matter in June 1938; so perhaps it suffered from the additional drawback of a half-measure. Needless to say Liddell-Hart soon disapproved of Brooke's appointment to the command at Stanmore, and criticism of his – and other – promotions in the sphere of anti-aircraft duly appeared in *The Times*. Anyway the end of this particular and rather tragic chapter was in sight. At the end of May Liddell-Hart had written in a 'note of reflection':

> I am coming to feel that, from a long-term point of view the most damaging step I've ever taken was to go in with him [Hore-Belisha]. Previous to that I was in an unassailable position, standing apart yet on good terms with most of the rising generation of soldiers . . .

Few would dissent. By mid-July, after some disagreements, Liddell-Hart took a silence between the two men as 'tantamount to the dissolution of the partnership'.

It was strange how this original, gifted and patriotic man, who loved the Army, who studied history and its lessons with passion and who was fearless and eloquent in advocating progress and operational innovation could err wildly when dealing with practical, organizational or human aspects. Yet perhaps it is not strange. The military historian or commentator provides an indispensable goad to established thinking, and holds up an often properly unflattering mirror to the establishment itself. But if he lacks all experience of actual administration he tends to propose elegant and unworkable solutions to such matters as command and organization, where pragmatism and a knowledge of the machine from the inside are preferable to even the most luminous imagination.

In March 1939 the President of France paid a State Visit to England. An incident at the time is best told in Brooke's words and exemplifies a not untypical confusion of thought in Whitehall.

> The climax was reached with President Lebrun's visit. I was summoned to a Council of the CID, Chatfield was in the chair, as Minister of Co-ordination of Defence, Chamberlain had sent Wilson to address us. He said that as a result of the 'slaps in the face' which we had been giving Hitler, he might suddenly launch a 'mad-dog attack' on London; on the other hand, as the

President of the French Republic was with us, the Government was anxious to impress him with our strength against aerial attack. He then asked me what I could do as Commander of the AA Defence to meet these requirements. I informed him that he had stated two requests which could not be met by the same action. If he wished to defend London, we must deploy guns for this purpose, but in that case the President would see nothing unless he toured the whole of London to visit these guns. On the other hand, if he wished to impress the President, it would be possible to deploy searchlights throughout London and to carry out some illuminating practices, but in this case the security of London would not be provided for. Which did he want?

He then stated that the security of London was the matter of real importance. I told him that in that case, if a state of emergency was declared, the Territorial personnel could be called up and guns deployed according to plan. He replied that it was not desirable to declare a state of emergency, could we not call for volunteers amongst the Territorials to man these guns. I had to explain to him that it was not easy to call for volunteers amongst what was already a voluntary movement. Should we do so we should probably obtain a loader at one gun, a layer at another, an ammunition number at a further one, etc., namely a distribution of personnel that would render the manning of the guns quite impossible. I recommended that the regular AA guns from Aldershot be deployed as a temporary measure. This was not considered adequate, and we were left in committee all day to find some better solution, which we failed to do. Finally, at about 7 p.m., my original plan was accepted by the Prime Minister, mainly owing to the fact that he was in a hurry, having to dine in the Mansion House with the President.[24]

Brooke, however absorbed in duty, was never far in heart from the countryman, fisherman, lover of birds. He had more and more substituted photographing game birds for shooting them, ultimately fitting a cine-camera with the stock of a gun and taking his place in the line with this unlethal instrument. On fishing, at which he was particularly expert, one of his Staff at Stanmore who shared his enthusiasm recalled a lunchtime conversation at a time of particular intensity.

He informed me that, contrary to most experts who use a very wide range of different flies, he had been using one type only, merely varying the size to suit conditions, and had had as much success as with the other method. In response to my interest he said he would give me one of his flies. A week passed, and I naturally thought the matter had been driven from his memory by pressure of work, but the next day he presented me with a box containing the fly.

It would be difficult to overstate my admiration of a mind which, under so terrible a burden of responsibility, can have the thoughtful consideration to remember a promise given quite casually on a matter of no inherent importance at all.[25]

Perhaps the gesture was not all that exceptional and the appreciation overstated. But it was entirely characteristic. 'More than anything,' a subordinate at that time wrote to him later, 'I remember your unfailing courtesy and pleasantness to junior officers and your regardless courage in fighting, when necessary, the powers that be.'[26] Throughout his life – and throughout the coming war – Brooke invariably found time for letters, gestures and actions of friendship, or affection or sympathy whatever his preoccupations and however exhausting his day. He was generous-hearted. He wrote to an officer previously senior to him, but who next found himself under Brooke's command in Anti-Aircraft Command and then retired with little recognition. The reply came back: 'I have never received such a nice letter as yours or one by which I set such store. I always knew it would be easy to work under you and it was for that reason and knowing your ability that I never from the word "go" felt badly over your going over my head.'[27]

Brooke's tenure of command at Stanmore only lasted thirteen months, during which, in May 1939, he was appointed Colonel Commandant, Royal Artillery. He was a tireless visitor of every part of his command and undoubtedly laid foundations on which others could build. He handed over to General Pile, who held AA Command throughout the war. Brooke was, to his delight, designated to succeed Wavell as Commander-in-Chief Southern Command, with Headquarters at Salisbury. It was August 1939.

British War Plans, which included the dispatch of an expeditionary force to France, and which had been agreed in detail with the French General Staff, envisaged a leading echelon of one Army Corps of two divisions, based on the Aldershot Command under Dill. This echelon was complete. A second echelon was to consist of a second Army Corps, also consisting of two divisions – the 3rd and 4th Infantry Divisions – based on the Southern Command. Neither these divisions nor the Corps Headquarters had received the same priority as those in the Aldershot Command, and II Corps was not only deficient of much material, had not yet received all its new 25-pounder Field Guns and lacked virtually all anti-tank equipment, but its Corps communications units and general command structure were totally unpractised, unready for war. Nevertheless it was, at the last moment, decided to include II Corps in the British Expeditionary Force – the BEF. On 31st August Brooke was told that he had been selected for Mobilization Appointment No. 1000, Commander II Corps, required to assume duty as soon after mobilization as he considered necessary. Southern Command was handed over to General Fisher, and Corps Headquarters Staff began to be cobbled together at the White Hart Hotel in Salisbury. War was declared on 3rd September. The 4th Division of II Corps was commanded by Johnson, a winner of the Victoria Cross in the First World War, sixty years old and beyond the age at which Divisional Commanders should generally operate in modern times, but a magnificent man in spite of his years who had the trust of his division as an 'unflappable' fighter, sound as a bell in all matters pertaining to Infantry training. The 3rd Division was commanded by Montgomery. He had been waiting to take over the appointment and Brooke hurried the date forward. He knew Montgomery well, and needed the energy and drive which would be brought by him to the training of a relatively raw division. But time was needed. 'The more I saw of II Corps the more convinced I became that it was quite unfit for war in its present state,' wrote Brooke. 'It would require a long period of running in.'[28]

However it was decreed that II Corps must proceed to France 'to give the French confidence in our intentions' although Brooke was assured that it would be for a while retained in Western France for a period of completion and training. Thus on 28th September Brooke embarked from Southampton. That night, on the voyage to Cherbourg, he began to keep, for the wife to whom he had just bidden farewell, a private diary of his thoughts and experiences. Written in a succession of small leather lock-up pocket books, bought at a Salisbury bookshop out of remaindered stock from the *Queen Mary* and consigned, as each was completed, to his wife for safe keeping, 'my evening talk with you on paper' as he called it, it became an inseparable companion, a safety valve for repressed irritation, anxiety and frustration, and a reflection of a self that few suspected in this most reticent of professional soldiers. He needed, as ever, to talk to his 'listener', and the diary was necessary to fulfil this need. It replaced the detailed and diary-form letters to his mother of the First World War. Once again he knew that his irritations would be soothed when voiced, his sensitivities understood, his apparent petulance dissolved in the love, understanding and good sense of the reader for whose eyes the pen worked.[29]

The sensitive, withdrawn child had become the popular, hard-riding and sporting yet thoughtful young officer. That young officer had gone through the fire of the First World War and developed into the shrewd, thorough and entirely professional senior who set a mark of efficiency and high standards on everything he touched. He had come to inspire awe in most, not excluding members of his family. But he had never, even when suffering most from personal tragedy or professional frustration, lost the power to attract and amuse, to mimic, recount or, above all, sympathetically to listen. He was, as he had always been, the officer 'Regimental as a button-stick', the comrade in a joint venture of markedly 'courteous and considerate character', the commander whose presence invariably brought reassurance whatever his private feelings. He was also the man whose outstanding and most memorable characteristic would be recalled by an old friend as 'his complete knowledge and deep love of everything to do with nature',[30] and, very simply, by another as 'the most lovable human being I have ever known'.[31] Inwardly vulnerable and high-strung, outwardly calm and stern, in appearance aquiline, round-shouldered but impeccable, contemptuous of ostentation or affectation, quick witted, and as able a soldier as even his own Ulster had produced he returned, that September, to war and to France.

CHAPTER VII

France and Flanders – II

THE WAR HAD three great acts of drama.

The first act started in September 1939 and ended in June 1940. This appeared, Hitler and the Nazis notwithstanding, something of a continuation of the war of 1914–18: the same enemy, the same major Ally, the same successful initial enemy campaign in the East – although this time Russia instead of being an Ally was the enemy's accomplice in crime. In the West the act started differently. There was no early German offensive, no immediate inoculation by fire, no Mons, no Le Cateau, no Marne and no First Ypres. But there was, at least to Brooke, a certain sense of *déja vu* – both saddening and, as things turned out, misleading. Yet only twenty-one years had separated the end of one war from the start of the next, and in a full professional life that is but an interlude.

The second act began in June 1940 and lasted exactly one year. During that year Britain stood alone. The aim seemed unequivocal – to survive and to continue the fight. The United States was generous and friendly, but formally neutral. The Soviet Union, where Stalin regarded the United Kingdom as Bolshevism's ultimate enemy – a position he did not seem inwardly to abandon – had a nervous weather-eye cocked on Germany, but had not failed to send fulsome congratulations on German victories against Britain and France in the West. Meanwhile the Russians carried out their own quiet acts of brutal and unscrupulous aggression in Bessarabia and the Baltic States. The remainder of Europe was either occupied by the German Army, was actively hostile or was generally cowed by German power; and there was at that time a widespread disposition in the world at large to recall the misconduct rather than the benevolence of the British Empire. The Empire itself was united; but the vast extent of British possessions posed problems as much as it produced strength. Perhaps not since 1776 when Britain had simultaneously faced a transatlantic Colonial war and a direct threat of invasion of the homeland and the Colonies – and faced it without Allies of any kind – had the situation been so grave. This was the time of defiance and of unity. It was a new experience. It was dissimilar to anything in the previous war. It was as stimulating as it was dangerous.

The third, and by far the longest act, began with the invasion of Russia by the Germans in June 1941 and only ended with the final defeat of Japan over four years later. It was in this period that Brooke came to the pinnacle of his profession and made his supreme contribution. The act began with the end of British isolation. The Germans engaged for us another Ally; and soon the Japanese were to do the same and make the war global.

War is a political activity. Unless there is a valid policy for which it is being waged, and unless that policy governs the means applied to waging it there is a vacuum of purpose and, as Fuller once wrote, 'Means monopolize ends'. As the third act unfolded the policy of the Western nations became less rooted in rational aims than in victory, without regard to its aftermath. Western military power grew mightily, the strategic outcome was inevitable albeit delayed, but the aim of war – Clausewitz's 'extension of politics by other means' – became cloudy while that of the Soviet Union remained clear and hard as crystal for those prepared to see.

The aim of the first act, on which Brooke and his II Corps were now to embark as part of a once again 'contemptibly little' British Expeditionary Force, was comparatively clear: to inflict a military defeat upon Germany sufficient not only to protect the nations of Western Europe from further territorial encroachment, but to force a withdrawal from conquered Poland, a disgorging of the other fruits of conquest. War had been declared to honour a 'guarantee' to Poland and nothing less than a complete change in the nature and direction of German policy would suffice as a war aim. Germany must repent and withdraw. She must come to Canossa. Unless there were to be a collapse of the home front she would only be brought thither by defeat in the field, and since she had swiftly settled matters in the East this meant defeat in the field by Britain and France. If the Western Powers were not to accept the peace overtures made to them after the defeat and partition of Poland no other aim appeared rational.

A dispassionate observer would not have rated the Allies' military chances high. Although in theory the Germans could have been attacked while their hands were full in Poland, the state of the French Army and the nature of its tactical doctrine made such a policy improbable, to say the least. The French, even more than the British, were determined not to repeat the massive attacks nor to incur the huge casualties of the earlier war. Their thinking was entirely defensive. An immense system of fortification – the Maginot Line – had been constructed along the Franco-German frontier, to make that frontier impenetrable. Such fortifications could have had their uses if serving to minimize troops required to hold ground, to maximize their protection and their fire-power, while freeing mobile troops for offensive or counter-offensive manoeuvre. So sound a concept played little part in French thinking. Although the French Army – unlike the British – disposed of a considerable number of tanks, they had no concomitant doctrine of concentration, of all-arms co-operation or of the operational offensive. Such ideas had been mooted in the French Army but had found little favour.

The British were making too small a contribution to have more than a marginal effect upon the general strategy. The commander of a force of four divisions – or even of ten as the BEF became before the blow fell – has little overall influence on general strategy when co-operating with a huge Continental army, with some ninety divisions, such as that of France. Nor have the General Staff who direct him from home, nor have the Government whom they serve more than proportionate influence, and the proportion in this case – as in 1914 – was minuscule. But even if British influence on the strategy to adopt had been powerful, there is not the slightest reason to suppose that the outcome would have been greatly different in terms of achieving the initial aim – to inflict a defeat on Germany. There was nothing in accepted British doctrine, and nothing in what they knew of their own capabilities and what they could all too clearly perceive of their Allies to suggest that an early offensive – or perhaps any offensive – would or could succeed. If the war went on the Boches would come – probably, as before, through Belgium. One would meet them in defensive positions on some appropriate line, facilitated by the impregnable Maginot Line covering the right-hand sector of the front. The defensive was stronger than the offensive so the enemy would bring about their own defeat by beating their heads against the Allied Wall. Meanwhile one waited, conserved manpower, built up strength and prepared for a long war.

There was a great deal of building up to be done. The equipment, tactical doctrines and habits of mind of the British Army – particularly in the lack of armoured and anti-armoured capability and philosophy – made them largely unfit for modern war in spite of the small-scale experimentation already discussed. For the most part there was a generation gap in thinking and a distressing disparity of professionalism between Germany and her principal enemies, Britain included. The efforts of the gifted men of Brooke's generation had not borne sufficient fruit in 1939. They had been smothered by the dead hand of economy; by the lack of perception of threat; by aversion from the disagreeable necessity to disturb popular sentiment; and – it must be said – by that cult of the amateur which had affected the Army, as in previous (though not all) periods of its history – a dangerous cult, fashion being one of the most powerful of pressures on human affairs. It is probably also the case that some of Brooke's contemporaries, although they had emerged from the First World War with high professionalism, had suffered a hardening of the mental arteries produced by the routine, the concentration on minutiae and the tendency to conservatism which peacetime too frequently induces.

The general strategy had been inevitable. In the Staff talks which had preceded the war the French had made it clear that, if hostilities came, the military objective would be the defence of French territory. As to Poland, her ultimate fate would depend on the outcome of the war. The 'guarantee' was considered by its supporters as a warning, criticized by its detractors as a provocation to Hitler. It could hold no salvation for Poland.*

For Brooke the first eight months of the Second World War constituted his sole experience of high command on active service. He greatly enjoyed the challenge of bringing a freshly formed and completely unfit Corps to an attainable pitch of efficiency in the time which was unexpectedly vouchsafed. The assurances Brooke had received that his Corps would be kept for a while in reserve in Western France had been ignored, as such assurances tend to be, to no surprise of its commander. But the delay in the German offensive provided a respite, and the autumn, winter and spring were spent in training, in the preparation of a defensive position on the Franco-Belgian frontier to face the anticipated enemy attack through the Low Countries and in discussion of the best plan of operations to adopt when that attack came. Training – and especially the training of Montgomery's 3rd Division, 'the Iron Division' – went ahead well, and Brooke oversaw the gradual

* The British Chiefs of Staff were entirely opposed to the guarantee to Poland when given in March 1939.

evolution of a Corps at least capable of taking the field within the limitations imposed by hopelessly inadequate anti-tank (and most other) equipment and by a certain boredom in standing on the defensive in a theatre of war for months on end without being attacked or seeing action. 'The King realizes that the Troops must have been having rather a monotonous time,' wrote Sir Alexander Hardinge, Private Secretary, in reply to a letter Brooke had written to King George about II Corps, 'though they have no doubt been able to put in some valuable work on improving the defences.'*

The preparation of defences was a matter inextricably mixed with what plan to adopt.

The major planning issue was whether, in the case of German invasion of Holland, Belgium or both (or of Dutch accession to German demands, which would be regarded as the equivalent of invasion) there should be a forward movement by French and British forces, covered by presumed Belgian action on the frontier. Such a movement, which was ultimately decided upon and which took place in the event, would aim to give depth to the defence of France and to encourage Belgian co-belligerence (for Belgium was maintaining a policy of strict neutrality, and overt preliminary arrangements were impossible). Belgian policy had swung in 1936 from close links with France to a very exact non-alignment, and information on plans in case of attack could only be conveyed by unorthodox means. These means were to some extent employed. Understandings of a sort were reached. But there was an immediate and dangerous lacuna in any Allied plan to adopt a forward defensive position in Belgium – the absence of machinery for continuous political and strategic co-ordination with the host nation, the owners of the battlefield.

Brooke's initial reaction had been instinctively opposed to a move forward into Belgium in case of attack. By November, however, he recognized an advance to the line Antwerp–Namur would be a sensible way of shortening the front to be defended, provided that the advance was made in time. 'On balance,' he wrote in January, when, for a moment, a Belgian request for assistance seemed imminent, 'I think we should score by going in if invited' (to Belgium).[1] But he was deeply uneasy. He did not

* King George encouraged such correspondence from his Corps Commanders. He felt the need to be kept intimately informed. Gort also encouraged this direct link. Brooke found the drafting a slight problem. 'I am not used to writing to Kings,' he told Benita, 'and did not know how to begin or end.'

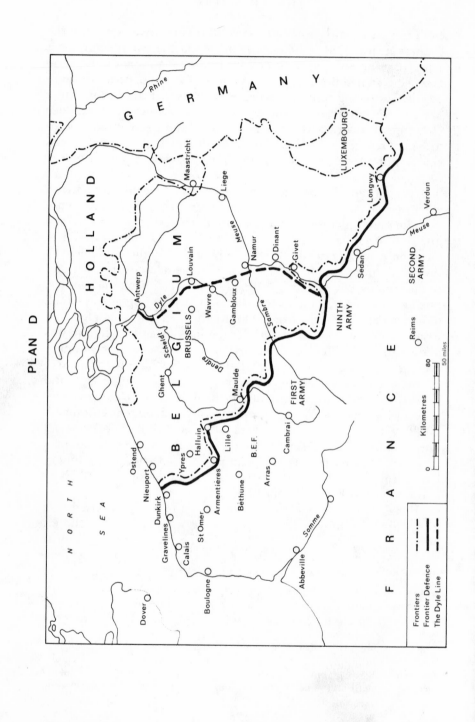

PLAN D

believe that Belgian power to delay the German advance in the Belgo-German frontier area would amount to much, or that the Dutch could put up an effective resistance. No Belgian invitation was received and he did not like the idea of moving from a prepared to an unprepared position in a country with which there could have been no military contact at field commanders' level. He did not believe – and this was crucial – that the mobility, equipment, anti-armour and anti-aircraft capability of the Allied left wing could match a German offensive of the kind seen in Poland, if met in open field. Above all, he was sceptical of the capabilities of the French Army on whom the flanks of such a movement would depend. Indeed, he had visited the Maginot Line, and had also had occasion to renew his contacts with French soldiers.

On 5th November I had an experience which began to crystallize out [sic] the worst fears I had gradually been forming as regards the inefficiency of the French Army. I had been requested by Gort to represent him at a ceremony to be given by General Corap, Commanding 9th French Army, on that point of his front where German emissaries of peace had come over with the White Flag in 1918. This was the Corap who became famous in 1940 for crumbling under the first blows of the German advance, and who was relieved by Giraud in the first few days of the attack.

This ceremony took place round a monument on which was inscribed *Ici triompha par sa tenacité le Poilu*. There were speeches by Corap and the Préfet, followed by prayers by priests of three denominations, catholic, protestant and jewish. Wreaths were presented by ladies to Corap and myself to lay on the monument, and finally Corap requested me to stand alongside him whilst the guard of honour, consisting of cavalry, artillery and infantry marched past.

I can still see those troops now. Seldom have I seen anything more slovenly and badly turned out. Men unshaven, horses ungroomed, clothes and saddlery that did not fit, vehicles dirty, and complete lack of pride in themselves or their units. What shook me most, however, was the look on the men's faces, disgruntled and insubordinate looks, and although ordered to give 'eyes left' hardly a man bothered to do so.

After the ceremony was over Corap invited me to visit some of his defences in the Fôret de St Michel. There we found a half-constructed and very poor anti-tank ditch with no defences to cover it. By way of conversation I said that I supposed he would cover the ditch with the fire from anti-tank pill boxes. This question received the reply '*Ah bah! On va les faire plus tard –*

allons on va déjeuner!' and away we went to *déjeuner* which was
evidently intended to be the most important operation of the day.
I drove home in the depth of gloom – [2]

This was no narrow Francophobe writing, but a man who
loved France and the French as one who had spoken their tongue
before his own, who would one day tell them that 'he had always
felt . . . he had *deux patries*'. He had visited Verdun at the period of
its greatest agony in 1916 and been impressed to the depths of his
being by the indomitable character of the French Army and people
– at that time. The contrast shattered him.

Thus all things, unpreparedness, the quality of Allies and the
unsoundness of plans combined to give Brooke a pessimistic view
of the likely future. Furthermore – unlike various visiting pundits
from London – he was certain that it was on the Western Front that
the major blow would fall. The winter's inactivity had induced in
some the comfortable assumption that the European theatre could
be regarded as militarily stable. Not so Brooke.

> 'Thus ended 1939,' he wrote, 'a year which had seen . . . the
> beginning of what has been known as the "phoney war" period.
> It may have seemed phoney to those comfortably established at
> home: from my point of view it was anything but phoney. To find
> oneself in command of a formation unready for war both from
> the point of view of training, equipment and deficiency of
> modern weapons such as tanks, aircraft, anti-tank weapons and
> anti-aircraft weapons. To be confronted with plans which were
> definitely unsound in the event of attack. To become less and less
> confident of the fighting value of one's Allies. On top of it all to
> have the firm conviction that the Germans must attack sooner or
> later. Such a combination of circumstances certainly did not
> provide the peace of mind and lack of anxiety which might well
> be connected with the conception of a "phoney war".'[3]

Compounding much of Brooke's pessimism was his lack of
confidence in Gort, his own Commander-in-Chief. The relationship was on the whole an unhappy one between two noble men.

Gort was suddenly given command of the BEF on the outbreak
of war. He had been CIGS – a post which, of all posts, demanded
continuity in the transition to war – and had been replaced by
General Ironside, who had been recently brought back from
Gibraltar. Ironside, however, had been given to understand that
he would command the BEF, in spite of the clearly superior claims
of Dill, commanding Aldershot Command and normally regarded
as Commander-in-Chief designate of an Expeditionary Force.

There was thus a general post in key appointments the day war began; a crazy proceeding.

Gort was a fighting man above all things. To him, as his Chief of Staff, General Pownall, recorded,[4] Brooke was a pessimist, failing to exude or spread confidence. Brooke's – and Dill's, his fellow Corps Commander's – manifest scepticism about the agreed plan, a plan largely dictated by the French supreme command to which Gort owed constitutional obedience, was an irritant to the Commander of the BEF. He knew that both Brooke and Dill, widely regarded as broader minded and more intelligent, thought him inadequate to his task. His position was difficult and he understandably hesitated to exercise a Commander-in-Chief's authority towards them. For his part, he could see the weakness of the British Expeditionary Force's position as well as they. He had always been a very thorough reader of military history, an absolutely dedicated and widely read student of war, and he recognized the dangers of open warfare against such an Army as the German as clearly as any. But he had his orders, he was utterly loyal by instinct and conviction to the concept of Allied unity of command, and his duties were to obey his instructions and to encourage all with whom he came in contact. He had little patience with those who seemed to him to radiate gloom. He contemplated replacing Brooke.

Brooke regarded Gort as inadequate to his responsibilities, incapable of taking a broader view or of recognizing the strategic peril of the situation. He was filled with foreboding and yet his Commander-in-Chief seemed determined neither to share it nor to annul it. There was an optimism in some quarters at GHQ which, to Brooke, flew in the face of the realities.

Nobody, least of all Brooke, could fail to love Gort's spirit or deny him personal loyalty, admiration and affection. On a joint visit to the French front near Metz, 'I think he [Gort] had a terrible longing . . . to take a patrol out himself. His eyes were still twinkling with the excitement of it. He is the most inspiring person I have ever met when discussing questions related to the handling of a battalion in war.'[5] But Brooke never revised his view of Gort's deficiencies as a Commander-in-Chief. He repeatedly referred to his absorption in detail and his refusal to look at strategic issues. To which Gort might have replied that there was little to be gained by looking at them – they were plain and depressing. His duty was to lead, fight and inspire.

Both men, in their estimate of each other and of the situation, were at the same time correct and unjust. To Gort Brooke was a pessimist, a faint-heart, where he wanted warriors who would disregard odds.* Yet Brooke's assessment of the situation was accurate. Furthermore, Brooke's ability to infuse confidence in those below him, whatever his misgivings, was in fact enormous. When the storm broke and when the British Army was as near annihilation as it has ever been, a young cavalry subaltern, in what seemed a desperate situation, recalled two minutes' conversation on a visit from his immaculate Corps Commander, gleaming boots and belt, a rapid staccato voice, a demeanour of utter calm, with the words, 'He was one of those whose brief presence was sufficient to make one perfectly sure that all would come right in the end.'[6] Brooke's strategic judgement was sound, and his power of command impeccable.

To Brooke Gort was 'a queer mixture, perfectly charming, a very definite personality, full of vitality, energy and *joie de vivre* and gifted with powers of leadership, but he fails to be able to see the big picture . . .'[7] This may also be true. Certainly Brooke was far from alone in his estimate, and – which he did not say but many others did – there is no doubt that his mind, like that of Dill's, worked faster and ranged more widely than Gort's, thorough though the soldierly instincts of the latter were. Yet when the crunch came it was Gort's decision, and Gort's alone, which in May 1940 was to save the BEF. Unsupported, to some extent in defiance of his formal instructions, backing his hunch about the futility of further reliance on Allied plans, he saw one thing might be done: the Army might be saved to fight again. He acted on that insight and showed unflinching willpower in so doing. Gort's skill in the handling of a large army, or the planning for it, may be questioned. There are, however, many occasions in war when will is more important than skill. At a vital moment Gort showed will, and many were thus saved for ultimate victory.

The months of inactivity dragged on in France. Brooke had been joined on his personal staff by Captain Ronald Stanyforth and Captain Barney Charlesworth as Aides – he became devoted to both.

As always, he enjoyed his casual encounters with the French

---

* In fact Dill was a good deal more depressed and pessimistic even than Brooke. Dill was the only senior member of the BEF who had been on the Staff of GHQ in the First World War and was naturally consulted by those at Gort's Headquarters as to how things should be run.

population. He took a photograph of the three French children of
the owner of his billet, showing them one of his own family and
evolving a brief pen-friendship between their children:

Le 9 Janvier 1940

Dear little English friend,
    I don't know you but I have seen your pretty photo and your
name is Catherine like my cousin's . . . Your Daddy is a great
General, you must be proud. Mine is only Lieutenant. After the
war your Daddy told me that I shall go to England near you
during the holidays. I am very happy . . . I kiss you.
                               Mary-Rose de Wavrin

To which Kathleen Brooke made suitable reply:

J'espere venir en France quand je sais parler la langue. Je
t'embrasse.

He found interest, though no particular comfort, in visiting the
scenes of earlier personal encounters and vanished tragedies in his
vicinity, Aubers Ridge, Festubert, Neuve Chapelle. Especially
interesting were occasional tours, during his travels, of historic
battlefields – Bouvines, (1214) Mars-la-Tour and Gravelotte
(1870).
    There were two short leaves at home; reminding him as always,
when returning from Benita, of 'the incompleteness of everything
in life when you are not there to share it with me'. All his letters
displayed the loneliness of a man of fifty-seven still profoundly in
love. Separation was hell. His evening diary was a necessity – 'I do
love my little talk with you.' It has been found by some surprising
that Brooke, throughout the war, kept his daily diary for Benita, as
well as writing to her with the greatest regularity whenever parted.
It filled a profound need. His entire heart was in his home and
family and he was and felt dependent on the warmth and security
he found only there. His letters dwelt hungrily on family and every
word expressed loneliness and love.

    . . . Such a treat this evening receiving your parcel and in it the
    frame with my beloved Pooks and Ti! I just *loved* getting it,
    though it gave me a most desperate longing to have them here
    just for one large hug. I have installed them on the small table
    beside my bed alongside of your photograph. But just at the
    present moment we are having a little family gathering as I have
    put both your photograph and that of the Pooks and Ti on the
    table I am writing at, so that we are all together while I have a talk
    with you.

Our evening talks [he wrote ten days later] as you say take a long time to travel across from one chair to another, but for all that they are something quite sacred to me, the one moment when we seem to draw very close together, when I can make you say things to me and almost imagine you then saying them, and then answer back on paper.

Years had in no way diminished what he drew from her faith.

. . . and with it all I cannot tell you what an inspiration and help you are to me, darling, even at this distance. Your letter breathes that divine confidence in God which radiates from you and is an inspiration to anybody that comes in contact with you.

I have been reading the Bible regularly since I got back, from where we left off, but what I should rather like would be to feel that I was reading the same bit as you are. We could do it if you select a bit to start on well ahead so that I have time to receive your letter and start on the date you name with the chapter you mention, and we can read a chapter or half chapter every evening.

At last I slipped off and imagined you at my side and we had a very nice little short walk and a lot of conversation together about the carpet of anemones that have come out and on the delays of the trees in coming out. I felt very close to you.

To him she stood for family life and everything peaceful, beautiful, orderly and sane. Every detail about the children was sought and treasured:

That beloved Pook's little love affair and telling you the great secret of her first proposal of marriage! The beloved little angel I do wish I could see her and her lovely eyes all lit up by the exciting idea of her forthcoming wedding! And that dear old Ti not wanting to be left out of the wedding business . . .

Which way does she sleep now? [he enquired of Pooks] with her head near the basin or near the chimney? I should like to know so as to imagine her in bed.

At times I rather wonder whether it is myself that is out here. It seems such a different person, and only half a person.

This was the inner man, seen and sensed by so few: the outer man was he who recorded in his letter of 23rd November that he had 'a trying day. Started by having to tell off Monty good and proper for a most offensively worded instruction . . .' That interview has been amply described, not least by Montgomery himself.[8] It was recalled by Brooke's Staff as having been heard through closed doors, the Corps Commander's voice as vibrant and a good deal louder and even sharper than usual, at the end of a corridor.

Every month brought its 'invasion imminent' scares. Nevertheless, plans for Scandinavian 'side-shows' – ultimately taking the form of military response to the German invasion of Norway, which itself was a pre-emptive move to possible Allied occupation of the Norwegian ports – threatened to drain troops from the 'static' Western Front, where Brooke was sure the main blow would soon fall. In April, Brooke's eldest son, Tom, already in the Army, was taken seriously ill with appendicitis, followed by the development of peritonitis. Brooke interspersed visits to the casualty clearing station at Rouvroy with sittings to a War Office portraitist in Arras. On 8th May Tom had taken a turn for the worse and was in great danger. The surgeon reckoned 'he has a good fighting chance of pulling through', and on the 9th Brooke wrote, 'Tom much the same, visited him twice . . . but very, very weak.'

On 10th May the British Prime Minister, Neville Chamberlain, resigned, after damaging attacks on him in the House of Commons. The King entrusted Winston Churchill with the task of forming a National Government. On the same day Operation SICHELSCHNITT, the German offensive in the West, at last began.

Such an offensive, which Brooke had insistently predicted, was the outcome of the radical thinking now dominant in the German High Command, largely because of the conversion to it of Hitler himself in the aftermath of the Polish campaign. Learning, as they avowed, from those same British 'visionaries' whose ideas we have already discussed, and encouraged by General Von Seeckt, reorganizer of the limited post-Versailles Reichswehr, some of their younger officers had experimented during the twenties with ways of using tank groups and motorized support groups in conjunction, first for mobile defence and later for attack. The same ideas had germinated in Britain, but through lack of conviction and financial feed the growth had been sickly as well as contentious. The difference was that in Germany, when major rearmament began under Hitler, their experiments resulted in the creation of three armoured or 'Panzer' divisions in which fast tanks with mobile supporting arms were grouped together, not for co-operation with infantry against fixed fronts, but for swift independent action in a war of movement. These divisions had played the leading part in the unopposed occupations of Austria

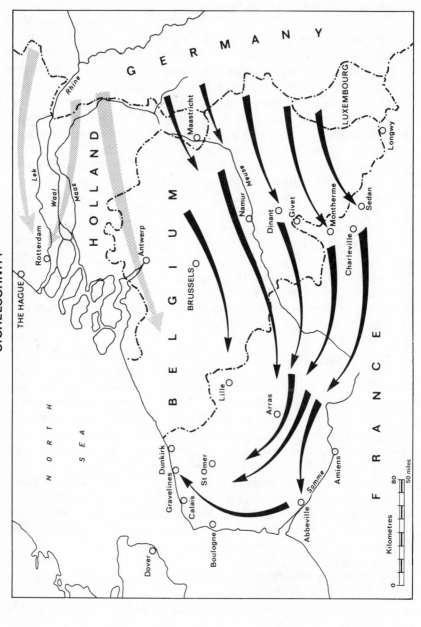

"SICHELSCHNITT"

and Czechoslovakia; and more recently, in war itself – greatly increased in number – they had shown their devastating effect when boldly handled in the campaign against Poland. The early successes of German arms in the Second World War, especially against France and Russia, derived less from a superiority of materiel or of numbers (indeed in some cases there was inferiority) than from an attitude of mind, an understanding of manoeuvre more genuinely historical than that of the military conservatives who had regarded the new theories with scepticism. Above all there was a willingness to take risks, an opportunism in execution which itself demanded the initiative of Commanders and Staff Officers, still admirably brought up to the traditional independence of mind of the German General Staff.

Yet all German opinion was not on one side. With the fresh creation of a fully equipped Reichswehr many of the more senior German Generals had reverted to the view of war which had dominated their formative years. Now that they once again enjoyed possession of heavy guns and masses of conscript infantry they tended to frown on the theories of younger enthusiasts and, like the French, to favour the employment of tanks in small tactical groups for the support of infantry. In Poland the 'blitzkrieg' had triumphed over an unmechanized enemy without strongly prepared defences, but the German High Command no more contemplated using it against the Maginot Line than did the French contemplate an all arms concentrated attack on the Siegfried Line. Nor, impressed by the strength of French defensive armaments, were the Germans anxious to expose their army on the Belgian plain; they wished – or at least they began instinctively by wishing – to be attacked rather than to attack. The stalemate mentality was almost as strong in Von Brauchitsch and Halder, the Commander-in-Chief and Chief of Staff of the German Army, as in the prudent Gamelin.* They had been trained in the same school. And they were to be almost as astonished as their enemy at the speed and scope of their own success, as often as not seeking to rein in their leading armoured thrusters, uneasy in their balance overall.

Hitler's mind had also been conditioned by his experiences in the First World War, but in a different way: he feared above all the repetition of a war of attrition. For the Western democracies, with the hope of ultimate American help, a static war spelt steadily

* General Gamelin, Chief of the French General Staff.

growing strength. Hitler, therefore, was truer to an older German – or, indeed, Napoleonic – tradition, that of the knock-out blow against one enemy before an overwhelming combination could be raised by several. He had grasped the immensely increased importance of the air weapon and its interaction with the operations of land forces, and during the Polish campaign he had first seen the power of the tank. Four days after the start of that offensive he had stood amazed by the side of Guderian, the pioneer of Germany's independent Panzer divisions of all arms. They had surveyed the smashed Polish battalions that had contested the crossing of the Vistula. 'Our dive bombers did that?' he asked. 'No,' replied Guderian, 'our Panzers'. When Hitler learned also that the casualties in Guderian's four divisions had only amounted to 150 killed he could hardly believe him.

Now Hitler was certain not only that German morale had recovered from the humiliation of earlier defeat but that his own intuition was as infallible in war as in peace, in operations as in politics. This personal assurance would cost Germany dear. In the meantime it was rooted in fact. He had brushed aside his Generals' fears of attacking in the East with 'the great French Army' in their rear. He had been right. He had shown contemptuous disbelief in the power of an isolated state like Poland to withstand the assault of a rearmed and resurrected Reich. He had been right. Now he was convinced that his estimate of the inertia and cowardice of the French was equally right. They could be dealt with in the same manner as the Poles. Since Britain and France would not acquiesce in his Eastern conquests and make peace, an offensive in the West would settle the matter for good. Only the weather delayed the offensive, first designed by Hitler for early November 1939, until the memorable 10th May.

Gamelin, effectively the French Supreme Commander, had anticipated this. But the delay not only gave a breathing space. It had also led to a reappraisal of German plans of attack.

For the German plans for the offensive were not those the French High Command had anticipated. In February, following a forced landing of a German aircraft and a Staff officer, captured papers had disclosed to the Belgian and Allied Governments details of the proposed German attacks. These – variations of the 1914 'Schlieffen Plan', the 'giant wheel' through Belgium and Holland – had then been replaced by a more original project first propounded by Lieutenant-General Von Manstein, at that time Chief of Staff to the Commander-in-Chief Army Group A (Von

Runstedt) in the centre of the front.* The new plan would involve not an enveloping movement round the Allied left wing, as in 1914, but a thrust by concentrated armoured forces through the Ardennes to cross the Meuse between Dinant and Sedan in the centre of the Allied line. Parachute troops would assist in the overrunning and neutralization of Holland. Belgium would be invaded – but with weaker forces on the classic routes north of Namur towards Brussels than on the Luxembourg–Sedan axis.

French and British forces would probably advance to meet the German right wing. This advance could play into German hands. As they moved towards the Scheldt and the Dyle the German *Schwerpunkt* would break in behind them with the mass of the German Panzer divisions. The hinge on which the Allied advance pivoted would be smashed, and the Allied forces cut in two. Schlieffen had preached that the more vigorous the French offensive in 1914 against the Franco-German frontier the more it would facilitate the 'swinging door' closing on their left. Now the door could be hinged on the other doorpost. And the tactical instrument for the movement – the combination of air and armour – lay to hand in a way which it had not for the exhausted German marching divisions of 1914.

The point of main attack would be the ground held by Corap's Ninth Army.

There was no reason why the contingency of a main German thrust in the centre rather than on their northern wing should not have been taken into full consideration by the Allied High Command – which in effect meant Gamelin. Although it was correctly estimated that the Germans would have no hesitation in attacking Belgium and Holland if not granted immediate transit facilities, the assumption that the enemy's weight must be in the north, as in 1914, rested on shaky foundations. The Maginot Line, it is true, was an improbable area of frontal assault. But there was also an apparent belief that the terrain east of the Meuse in the centre of the front would be virtually impassable to the mass of armoured formations, with which it was presumed – again correctly – that the German attack would be led. Although there are certain defiles which need to be forced, and certain approaches, particularly to the banks of the Meuse, which canalize and delay an

---

* The genesis of the German plan has been the subject of much literature. Hitler himself, if not its originator, was early attracted to it and depressed by the conventionality of the first General Staff concept. But then the Army Command disliked the adventure anyway.

enemy, there is nothing in the general character of that part of the Ardennes which makes it impracticable for the passage of mechanized, or any other, armies; and it is curious that at least some circles in the High Command seemed to regard the sector as if it formed part of the Himalayas. At one moment early in the war Gamelin appeared to recognize this, and to see the future with uncanny clarity. But the moment passed.

Nor was this all. Much Intelligence from many sources – including some very accurate Belgian assessments conveyed to the French – indicated during the first months of 1940 a main thrust astride Sedan, between Givet and Longwy in the area of the Southern Meuse and the extreme south of Belgium. The location by Intelligence of the bulk of the German armoured formations in the area of the Eifel, although not conclusive, was consistent with the same assessment. Much has been written of this – from the Allied viewpoint – disastrous campaign. It is easy to have hindsight. It must, however, be said that if a major element of the art of war is to consider all contingencies, particularly the least convenient, and at least mentally to prepare for them, then that element was missing in Gamelin. Indeed General Georges himself (ostensibly the Commander of the 'Armies of the North East' but by-passed by Gamelin vis-à-vis the BEF as often as not, and thoroughly out of accord with his chief) observed à propos of the planned forward movement into Belgium and Holland:

> Our defensive manoeuvre . . . will have to be conducted with the thought that we must not be drawn into engaging in this theatre, in face of a German move which might be merely a diversion, a major part of our forces. If, for example, the main enemy attack came in our centre, on our front between the Meuse and the Moselle we could be deprived of the necessary means to repel it.

Sage and moderate words. Nevertheless the bait would be taken and the trap sprung.

When the blow fell on 10th May the Armies duly advanced into Belgium in accordance with 'Plan D', the finally agreed Allied plan whereby French and British troops would move forward from France: on the left into Holland to the assistance of the Dutch with the French Seventh Army (Giraud); in the centre to adopt a defensive position on the general line Antwerp–Namur, east of Brussels; and on the right to extend the new defensive position south to the French frontier near Givet. The British sector of responsibility would be on the general line of the River Dyle, south of an agreed line with the Belgian Army running east-west to the north of Brussels, and north of the French First Army (Blanchard) whose southern boundary would be the River Sambre. South of the French First Army was Corap's Ninth Army holding, or at least occupying, the line of the Meuse. It was here that the *Schwerpunkt* of SICHELSCHNITT was to fall.

GHQ of the BEF remained at Arras and Gort, with a small staff which included his Chief of Staff and his senior Staff Officers, established himself in a prepared command post at Wahagnies, just south of Lille. It is difficult to defend this step which had only been conceived shortly before. A commander is needed at the centre of his communications – this provides his 'centre of gravity' – with the ability to visit any part of the battlefield as freely and conveniently as possible and even, if facilities permit, to exercise temporary command from a mobile command post, to command 'from the saddle'. To set up, however, a command post only some twenty miles forward of his main Headquarters while still about equidistant from the front was to have the worst of all worlds. Nor did successive moves of this command post nearer to the battle, as awful days succeeded each other, while understandable in a commander of Gort's fighting temperament, do much to facilitate his task. It must, however, be said that that task, combining as it did the role of Commander-in-Chief with that of Army Commander co-ordinating the movements of his Corps, was thoroughly overloaded. Nevertheless Gort should surely have left his main GHQ, with his Chief of Staff, to function as such, if nothing else.

Whatever the inadequacy of Gort's command arrangements, however, nothing could have counter-weighted the chaos and breakdown of the chain of authority nominally superior to him, both as planned and in the event.

The BEF deployment was in the north-centre of the French General Billotte's Army Group. This Army Group was accepted as a co-ordinating authority by the Belgian Army only on 12th May, two days after the invasion began. It also had, in the north, French Seventh Army (Giraud) advancing to meet the Germans in Holland. Georges had wished to retain Giraud in reserve but had been overruled. Seventh Army moved into Holland and sharply rebounded. From the first the collapse of Holland, and the early involvement of what could have been a reserve, was to extend and threaten the northern flank.

It is, in fact, something of a euphemism to describe Billotte's authority as that of an Army Group Commander. Higher Command – whereby hitherto Gamelin had only partially and grudgingly conceded any authority over the BEF to Georges – was an important element in the coming defeat. It became plain, as it always should have been plain, that 'Plan D' – advance into Belgium and Holland by three armies and liaison, largely *ad hoc*, with the Belgian Army – would need a commander on the spot without other preoccupations. The task fell to the inadequate and unsupported Billotte.

Within the BEF two Corps – Brooke's II Corps and General Barker's I Corps (Dill had returned home to become VCIGS) – were deployed on the 'Plan D' line east of Brussels, with Brooke's Corps in the northern area including Louvain. III Corps (Adam) was retained in depth in the area of the River Scheldt. Two divisions were kept in GHQ reserve. At least on the map, the BEF had some initial depth and balance. Its main line of communication ran westward into France, to a base in the area of Le Mans. Its flanks rested on Allies. The pattern of the forthcoming campaign would be dominated by the cutting of those communications and the collapse, first at a distance and then nearby, of those flanks.[9]

The initial move forward of the BEF went well, deliberately unhindered by German air attack. Difficulties were chiefly produced by lack of effective liaison with the Belgians, with consequent confusion over routes to be used and frontages to be adopted. There was much irritation at the lack of co-ordination. It could hardly have been otherwise. A smooth-running Alliance system can hardly be forged on the day of war. There was also the inevitable friction with GHQ, whose attempts to provide co-ordination 'from the back seat' were uninformed and unsuccessful. Nevertheless II Corps reached its deployment line and started to prepare defences as ordered. News from the front was bad. 'The air was full of rumours of the rapidity of the German advance, and of German victories,' wrote Brooke on 12th May. By the 13th II Corps was deployed on its appointed line, with 3rd Division (Montgomery) holding the Corps front and 4th Division (Johnson) in support. News was received on the same evening that the Belgian Army had been ordered to withdraw to the Antwerp–Louvain–Wavre line; that held by the Allied forces in fact. First contact with the Germans took place on 15th May. 'Several minor attacks on 3rd Division front,' wrote Brooke, 'with minor penetrations in each case.' But there had already been reconnaissance of some rearward lines of defence should erosion of the flanks force the BEF to withdraw – and by 15th May news from the flanks was already very disturbing. On that day the Dutch forces capitulated.

'It was,' observed Montgomery with a reminiscent chuckle towards the end of his life, 'a real shocker of a campaign.'[10] It was, conversely, one of the most swift, brilliant and decisive ever fought by German arms. To those at the other and defeated end it was shocking indeed.

First came the rapid – and, to Brooke, unsurprisingly rapid – advance of the German right wing through Holland and Northern Belgium, quickly overtaking any very thorough preparation of defensive positions on the line of the River Dyle and south of it to Namur. Yet the Germans in front provided the least of concerns. Far to the south, in the area of Sedan, in the French Ninth Army sector, the German armoured spearheads of Army Group 'A' (Von Runstedt) had achieved a complete breakthrough by 15th May. Thereafter, in the south, the German advance was a triumphant procession, delayed solely by the demands of fuel or exhaustion, or the nervousness of the High Command; and only occasionally impeded by isolated pockets of resistance from a disintegrating French enemy. Initially there had been some hard fighting. Now, after a mere five days, it was a question of pursuit, which should, according to classic German doctrine, be 'to the last breath of man and beast'. Nevertheless even Hitler, convert to military radicalism that he was, suffered periodic fits of alarm at the awe-inspiring speed of his own armies' advance and the theoretic vulnerability of their flanks.

For the troops in Belgium the threat which this collapse posed to the southern flank of the French First Army was clearly the most immediate. German armoured forces were advancing westward behind its deep flank, and withdrawal was inevitable. On the evening of the 15th orders were given for all the forces in Belgium to be withdrawn west of Brussels by stages, to the line of the Scheldt. To the men of the BEF this was inexplicable and disappointing. There had been some hard fighting, chiefly by the 3rd Division in front of Brussels, and no ground lost. They were not yet to know that far to the south – for north of Namur little success attended the limited German attacks – the whole Allied front had been ripped open.

The next fourteen days were, for Brooke, a protracted nightmare. He had first of all the straightforward task –

straightforward in terms of definition rather than accomplishment – of extracting his Corps from contact and establishing it on a series of defensible lines, using communications which were often rudimentary or non-existent, and frequently achieving deployment only by personal visit and verbal order. Then he had the problem of co-ordination. The nervous system of his southern neighbour, the Commander of I Corps, was unequal to the strains of the situation, and Brooke found the powers of GHQ to co-ordinate movement and deployment were severely limited.

All the time there was an appalling cloud of uncertainty hanging over the situation on the flanks. News from the French Ninth Army had begun to circulate as rumour on 14th May, and, although the full scale of the calamity was obscure for some time, it became gradually plainer to the Command of the BEF that not only were communications with their own base about to be cut by a fast moving enemy but the chances of maintaining any sort of coherent front with the bulk of the French Army appeared daily more remote. SICHELSCHNITT was cutting its swathe through the Allied defensive system exactly as intended.

Then there was the situation in the north. Here Brooke's flank depended on the fortitude and movements of the Belgian Army. He had formed a poor opinion of their capabilities. His interview with King Leopold, in an attempt to straighten out an initial misunderstanding in occupying the Dyle position on 12th May, has been often described. In Brooke's own words:

As I came in Roger Keyes withdrew and left me alone with the King.

I explained to him my difficulties concerning the 10th Belgian Division in English, I found him charming to talk to, and felt that I was making progress in getting matters put right, when I suddenly heard a voice speaking in French from behind my right. On turning round I found an officer there who did not introduce himself to me, but went on speaking in French to the King. His contention was that the Belgian Division could not be moved, that the whole of the BEF should be stepped further South and be entirely clear of Brussels. I then turned on him in French and told him that he was not putting the full case in front of the King, since he had not mentioned that the 10th Belgian Division was on the wrong side of the Gamelin Line. He then turned to me and said – 'Oh! Do you speak French?' I assured him that I did, and that I happened to have been born in France.

By that time he had interposed himself between me and the King. I therefore walked round him and resumed my conversation with the King in English.

This individual then came round again and placed himself between me and the King, and the King then withdrew to the window. I could not very well force my presence a third time on the King, and I therefore discussed the matter with this individual whom I assumed must be Chief of Staff. I found that arguing with him was sheer waste of time, he was not familiar with the dispositions of the BEF and seemed to care little about them. Most of his suggestions were fantastic! I finally withdrew, and on going out I met the French General Champon, who was the appointed Liaison Officer between French and Belgian forces. I told him about my interview and asked him who the individual was whom I had met with the King. He told me that his name was Van Overstraeten and that he was the ADC to the King with the rank of Major-General! I asked him where the Chief of Staff was so that I might see him in connection with this matter. He then told me that it was quite useless my bothering to see him, as Van Overstraeten had taken all control in his hands and that he could get the King to do just what he wanted!

The impression this interview left in my mind was that the King, whilst being a charming person to meet, had little backbone and no inclination to assume the responsibilities which he could not escape in his position. Of Van Overstraeten I formed the very lowest opinion, and cannot imagine how the King could have been satisfied to allow him to obtain such an ascendancy over him, and such misplaced power.

I left the Belgian GHQ with many misgivings in my heart.[11]

Misgivings justified or no, certainly misunderstandings – by no means all of them the fault of the Belgians – marred co-ordination of withdrawal on the northern flank. But as the withdrawal continued the first preoccupation of the BEF was to cover, by some means, the southern flank of the westward withdrawal against a northward swing of the German forces penetrating towards the Channel. For Brooke it was a case of juggling with the divisions and brigades allotted to him, improvising some sort of co-ordination with his fellow Corps Commanders and keeping a weather eye cocked on the north where a Belgian collapse would threaten the BEF with total encirclement.

The rearward movement started, for Brooke, on 16th May. His Corps had consisted of 3rd, 4th and 50th (Martel) Divisions, but the latter had been withdrawn for another task by GHQ on the

15th, so that the first withdrawal consisted of bringing the 3rd Division westward through a temporary position held by 4th Division on the Charleroi Canal, and redeploying west of Brussels on the line of the River Dendre.

On 18th May, the Corps safely redeployed, Brooke attended a GHQ conference at Renaix where he was able to see that events were proving too much for his neighbour to the south, the Commander of I Corps (Barker) from whom a series of alarmist reports had flowed during 17th May. 'Barker,' wrote Brooke, that evening, 'is in a very difficult state to deal with . . . he sees dangers where they don't exist . . . whenever everything is fixed he changes his mind shortly afterwards.' Re-reading his diary long afterwards, Brooke hated the apparent criticism of an old friend, realizing that he was in fact suffering partial nervous breakdown. But it emphasized to him, if such emphasis were needed, the necessity for iron nerves in war, and the transcendence of the qualities of robustness and will. He was proving again that he possessed them. Wherever he went he spread confidence; and in spite of the chaotic communications and disruption of any sort of routine he generally managed to get four or five hours' sleep in the twenty-four. He was, recorded his personal staff, 'rather silly' in his inattention to bombs: 'a most imperturbable man' who rarely showed his feelings.

The next step was to be a withdrawal to the line of the River Scheldt where III Corps (Adam), hitherto held in depth, would be on Brooke's left and I Corps on his right. 4th Division would pass to III Corps command; 50th Division would revert to II Corps command; and 1st Division (Alexander) would pass from I Corps to II Corps. The BEF would be united, with three Corps in the line. In spite of mistiming between the withdrawal of I Corps and its neighbours, the line of the Scheldt was occupied by the evening of 19th May.

Already, however, GHQ was contemplating the by now inevitable worst. As II Corps withdrew towards the Scheldt on 19th May Brooke attended a conference at Armentières.

'It was a momentous one!' he wrote that night. 'The news of the French front was worse than ever, they were attempting one further counter-attack to try and restore the situation. Should this fail, it looks as if the allied forces will be cut in the centre. The BEF communication to the sea will be completely exposed, and so would our right flank.

'GHQ had a scheme for a move in such an eventuality towards

Dunkirk, establishing a defended area round this place and embarking all we could of the personnel of the BEF, abandoning stores and equipment.

'I preferred pivoting on our left, which is secure and in contact with the Belgians. To swing our right back on to the River Lys and up the new but empty canal to Ypres, and thence by the Ypres canal to the sea. By this means, I feel that at any rate we can keep the BEF as an entity and not have it destroyed by bits. If we let go our hold on the Belgians now I feel certain they will stop fighting and both our flanks will be exposed, in which case there will be little hope.'[12]

On 21st May Gort visited II Corps HQ at Wambrechies behind the Scheldt. The BEF must again withdraw, this time to the old 'frontier defences' prepared by them the previous winter. 'It could only be a temporary measure,' wrote Brooke, 'entailing further withdrawals.' For the 'frontier defences' were also threatened by the fact that the German westward advance to their south had turned the British right wing already. On the 23rd Brooke visited all Divisions and found them well established on the frontier line. Nevertheless on that day he found the situation depressingly plain. He wrote that evening 'nothing but a miracle can save the BEF now and the end cannot be very far off. We carried out our withdrawal successfully last night back to the old frontier defences . . . but, when the danger lies in our right rear, the German Armoured Divisions have penetrated to the coast: Abbeville, Boulogne and Calais have been rendered useless. We are cut off from our sea communications, beginning to be short of ammunition, supplies still all right for three days but after that scarcity. This evening the Germans are reported to be pushing on to Bethune and on from St Omer, namely right in our rear.'

On 22nd May he wrote to Benita – from whom occasional life-saving letters arrived – 'the chances of this letter getting off just at present are very poor as our lines of communication to the rear have been interfered with by German tanks'. And on the 24th:

The anxiety and responsibility is the wearing part of it. The strain of keeping a cheerful exterior when one is feeling just the reverse is perhaps the hardest of all. And yet I feel that it is of vital importance. Gloom at the Corps HQ during a crisis such as the present would be fatal, and the unpleasant situations must be met with a smile. Come what may, my darling, I still have the most implicit (sic) faith in God . . .

To all around him he radiated confidence and control.

The mass of refugees, threatened by remorseless air attacks, compounded every problem of movement. 'This continual sight of agonizing [sic] humanity,' wrote Brooke, 'drifting aimlessly like frightened cattle becomes one of the worst of daylight nightmares. One's mind, short of sleep, is continually wracked by the devastating problems of an almost hopeless situation, and on top of it one's eyes rest incessantly on terrified and miserable humanity, cluttering the lines of communication on which all hopes of possible security rest.'

Meanwhile Adam's III Corps was withdrawn from the line, allotted 5th and 50th Divisions and directed to make a limited southward attack against the great German corridor stretching from the Ardennes to the sea in conjunction with a (presumed) attack by the French from the south. The concept might have been elegant and correct. It bore, however, all the marks of what German Staffs expressively describe as a plan developed *auf dem grünen tisch* – i.e. a manoeuvre sounder in theory than practice. The relative strength of forces, the insecurity of the Allied base of attack, the lack of any other threat against the mass of the German Armies, and the latter's consequent ability to deal with any temporary setback if it occurred, could never have made this manoeuvre more than a forlorn hope, even had it taken place as strongly as planned. The immediate effect for Brooke was that II Corps again became the left wing of the BEF; and 4th Division reverted to his command.

And now of immediate concern was not only the south – the deep flank – but a widening gap between the British and Belgian Armies in the north, and what Brooke reckoned was an imminent attack on his left, on the axis Menin–Ypres.

At this time – between 24th and 26th May – the Belgians, using their accredited and very senior British Liaison Officer, Sir Roger Keyes, as intermediary, made several impassioned pleas for a British counter-attack against the German forces opposing them, German formations in some cases moving north and north-westward across the British front, which itself was not under serious attack. These appeals met no success. Although there was a theoretic case for such a movement, it would have been unsound and could have been disastrous. By then it could only have served to expose and unbalance the formations of II Corps, which were in a coherent but overstretched defensive position, and which, it was abundantly clear by then, could only hope for extrication.

Nor was there any stake to be won. The joint Franco-British

counter-attack against both flanks of the German penetration south of the BEF had been called off, for obvious lack of effective resources. It had been proposed by the French High Command, in manifest ignorance of the real situation and the capacity for manoeuvre of even such formations as existed. The decision not to destroy troops in futile gestures, which could have had no conceivable effect on the strategic outcome, was as correct as it was courageous. It was made by Gort. No less correct was the determination not to be drawn into manoeuvres with inadequate forces against the Germans attacking the Belgians in the north. They could not possibly have affected the strategic result in that sector. They might temporarily have delayed it. They would certainly have made the subsequent extrication of II Corps more hazardous. None can say what situation would then have faced the Army, but one thing was already clear. To save the British Expeditionary Force, together with as many as possible of its Allies, must now be the dominant aim. It was this that Gort saw clearly. It was for this that he – faithful to a fault in loyalty to Allies – had called off the southern 'counter-attack'. It was for this that neither he nor Brooke would be drawn into demonstrations on the Belgian front.

> 'I had few illusions by then,' Brooke wrote on 25th May, 'as to the fighting value of the Belgians.'[13]

The Belgian Army was having a hard time, subject to bombing attacks without respite. Unable to withdraw by day because of the enemy mastery of the air, and unable to obtain from his British Allies any relieving action, on 27th May King Leopold requested a ceasefire.

This action has been and will no doubt remain a matter for often acrimonious debate. The legend that the King's action was taken without attempt to notify his Allies has for some time been discredited. There are those who remain convinced that the King was certain of German victory, and believed that his duty lay in saving Belgian lives by a surrender which had become inevitable. If by 'victory' is meant victory in the campaign of 1940, the King's certainty was justified. Nobody in their senses could, by 27th May, imagine that the Germans had not won the campaign: all that remained was to determine the scope of the prize. If, as his critics aver, King Leopold believed in ultimate German victory he must be condemned for lacking the gift of prophecy, the unforgivable sin at the bar of history; but, even on that assumption, hardly for lack of logic at the time. It must, moreover, be borne in mind that in response to Gort's unflinching determination to save the Army, and to maintain that as his sole aim, the British Government had also accepted the inevitable and confirmed, on 26th May, the instructions to withdraw and evacuate the BEF. They had not informed the King of the Belgians. Only on the 27th – the day of the Belgian capitulation – was that judged vital. 'It is now necessary to tell the Belgians,' wrote Churchill. 'We are asking them to sacrifice themselves for us.'[14] With the British rightly determined to leave, it is as churlish as it is irrational to make much of the Belgian capitulation.* No comparisons with 1914 will do. In that year the line held, the French Army was capable of the counter-offensive, and the fortitude of King Albert had been rooted not only in courage but in justified confidence.

Meanwhile, for II Corps, the sudden disappearance of the Belgian Army, although not wholly unexpected, left the northern flank in the air. Brooke's first concern was to extend his left to cover the ground north of Ypres, and to do this he switched the incomparable 3rd Division from the south to the north, moving by trucks in darkness across minor roads parallel and very close to the front, and through what was likely to be a mass of disorganized refugees and stragglers. The latter included stragglers' vehicles, for discipline in much of the French Army had broken down. To add to the confusion lunatic asylums were no longer containing their inmates.

'The main Armentières-Lille road,' wrote Brooke later, describing 27th May, 'was practically blocked with 4 lines of traffic moving against me towards Armentières, two rows of horse-drawn vehicles and two rows of motorized ones. The drivers were unshaven, and with the growth of several days on their faces, their clothes were covered with mud, I saw no officers in charge or any attempt on the part of NCOs to control the mob. With great difficulty, by travelling mostly on the footpath, I managed to work my way back to Lomme with the sickly smiles of dribbling lunatics in corduroy occasionally looming up in the failing light at the car window.

'The sight of that uncontrolled mass of French Army vehicles sent a cold chill through my heart, as I thought of Monty and his

* It is particularly churlish when we consider that as early as 20th May King Leopold, judging the strategic situation accurately and foreseeing the British dilemma of how to maintain contact with Allies on both flanks, explicitly stated that he did not feel he could ask for any actions by the BEF to maintain contact with him which would prejudice their safety, or their front with the French.

3rd Division carrying out their precarious night move. This mob of vehicles might well bring the 3rd Division to a standstill should they overflow on to the roads I had allotted to it.'[15]

But the 3rd Division was not brought to a standstill. It reached the left of the Corps front on time, extending into the vital gap, and joining hands on the left with a French Division, a remnant of the original French Seventh Army which had advanced into Holland under Plan D. Meanwhile attacks of increasing ferocity were developed on the Corps front south of Ypres, chiefly falling on Brooke's 5th Division* on the Ypres-Comines Canal.

Astride what was now a shallow bridgehead were the German armoured forces of Army Group A which had reached the sea at Abbeville and branched north to besiege Boulogne and Calais, with capacity to attack the shrinking Allied force from the south; and the forces of Army Group B (Von Bock) from east and north-east, who had been pressing throughout against the front of the BEF, had brought about the capitulation of the Belgian Army and had occupied Holland. Brooke's line of withdrawal from the 'frontier defences' was now northward, virtually across the German front and at right angles to the previous axis of retreat. The line in front of Ypres was vital.

Brooke could not know that with regard to the southern threat an order had been given on 24th May that the German armour should be halted on the line of the canal which runs from Gravelines through St Omer to Bethune, giving a breathing space until the 27th, when the Armoured Groups again resumed a north-eastward advance. In the north his most immediate concern was a report on 28th May that a German column had entered Nieuport, some twenty-five kilometres along the coast north of Dunkirk, by now the designated focus of embarkation. A brigade was hastily diverted to a blocking position. Brooke's later account conveys the atmosphere then too widely prevailing:

> This was a disconcerting bit of news, I thought that I had checked the German advance Westward in the battle that had been raging in the Ypres-Comines area, but here was a new force which had evidently been advancing along the coast. I sent off instructions at once to divert Hawkesworth and his 12th Infantry Brigade from Dixmude to Nieuport, and remainder of 4th Division to follow, so as to cover perimeter defence from Furnes to Nieuport.

* Under General Franklyn. 5th Division had passed to the command of II Corps after cancellation of the south-directed 'counter-attack'.

On returning to my new Command Post at Vichem, I received a dispatch rider sent from Monty with the same news about the Germans being in Nieuport. Monty had picked up this information from Herbert Lumsden's Armoured Cars; he knew enough about my plans to realize at once the importance of this new and unexpected development. He had consequently sent off a dispatch rider at once, and in order to make doubly certain that the news should reach me he also dispatched his GSO 1 'Marino' Brown in a car. A very wise precaution which unfortunately ended in a tragedy. The roads were very badly congested with disorganized elements of the French Army which had lost all discipline and were completely out of control. We have only the account of Brown's chauffeur as to what happened. Apparently the road was so badly jammed with French transport vehicles that it was impossible to pass. Knowing the urgency of the message he was carrying, apparently Brown got out of his car leaving it on the side of the road with his chauffeur, and proceeded on foot in order to regulate the traffic and to induce some discipline into the French transport. Shortly after he had been left, the chauffeur heard a revolver shot somewhere up the road, and a little later he was informed by one of our men that there was a dead Colonel lying on the side of the road. He went to see and found that Brown had been shot dead! Further details remain shrouded in mystery and will never be cleared. Probably Brown had difficulty in clearing the road, he was known to have a hottish temper and he may well have used the rough of his tongue on some of this rabble. This may well have resulted in one of these demoralized Frenchmen drawing a revolver and shooting him. It was a real tragedy as he had a brilliant future in front of him.[16]

In such an atmosphere, nevertheless, II Corps replaced the Belgian Army and moved its exhausted divisions to their appointed places on the east or south-east of the shrinking perimeter around Dunkirk.

On 29th May Brooke was ordered to hand over command of II Corps and to return home, to be available for the task of reforming new armies. He obtained agreement to remain in command until he had brought his Corps into the perimeter covering the embarkation. Even so it was as hard an order as he had ever had to obey, and he 'felt like a deserter not remaining with it till the last'.[17] He handed over command to Montgomery on the beaches of La Panne, for the first time showing emotion, with tears streaming down his cheeks.[18] Adam, who had been able to observe the situation and reflect on it deeply, later described Brooke's handling of his Corps throughout the momentous days between 10th and 29th May 1940 as 'perfect'.[19] He was always where required, outwardly unperturbed, patching up gaps as they appeared, reassuring high and low alike by his quiet, assured demeanour, his apparent confidence that all would come right in the end, his quick reactions and decisiveness however exhausted, and his invariably impeccable appearance. None mistook his determination.

> I received a message from General Bougrain, commanding 2nd DLM informing me that he had received orders from General Blanchard that he was to proceed to La Panne to embark his Division! He proceeded to state that he was conforming with this order and moving his Division at once!
>
> I got Neil Ritchie to draft out an order to him telling him that I gave him a direct order that he was NOT to commence moving before midnight. Explaining that if he moved sooner he would completely throw out all arrangements for the retirement of the II Corps.
>
> I then got hold of his liaison officer, who was to carry back this message and told him: 'that if his General disobeyed my order, and I caught him, I should have him shot'. He did disobey this order, but took good care that I did not catch him, so that I did not have the satisfaction of shooting him![20]

Inwardly he could release himself to the diary which he nightly maintained. He had, throughout, no news of his son, left in a dangerous condition when the advance into Belgium began. He did not know whether Tom was alive, dead, improved in health or overrun by the German advance. Brooke was also suffering from toothache, for which he had been under treatment interrupted by the German attack on 10th May. No hint of this or any other concern was allowed to disturb the calm, and the power to induce calm in others of this resolute man. In 1940 Brooke showed, as he was never again to have the same opportunity to show, that ability to think clearly, accurately and fast in circumstances of danger and confusion, and that ability to impose his will on others and on circumstances which are the hallmarks of the great captain.

He gained another priceless asset for his own and his country's future – an insight into the abilities in war of some subordinate commanders, notably Alexander and Montgomery.

He knew both well, from Staff College times. In those earlier days he had not formed a high opinion of Alexander's intelligence. Having now seen him under stress he was impressed by the quality which such crisis had most demanded – imperturbability. This quality, and a charm which compelled loyalty and co-operation in others, more than compensated in Brooke's eyes for what he regarded as a certain emptiness of imagination, a certain lack of profundity. Montgomery he had always thought of highly – much more highly – from the point of view of professional ability. He knew him as prone to egotism, to misjudgement in personal matters, as tending to say foolish and impetuous things; but as a soldier of swift understanding, total calm in crisis and iron will he regarded Montgomery, of those he had seen at close quarters, as having no peer.

On 30th May, having with a heavy heart said goodbye to all his divisions, Brooke went down to the beach at La Panne by Dunkirk and was carried out to an open boat. With his Military Assistant and ADC, they paddled to a destroyer and climbed aboard. Adam was on the same boat and remembered that Brooke fell on his bunk and there remained fully dressed in a state of collapse. Physically he had been unresting since the retreat began. Mentally he had adjusted with his customary skill and speed to ever changing threats and circumstances. He had just had to leave his command to an unknown future. He still knew nothing of his son.

The agony went deep. For four years, between 1914 and 1918, Brooke and his generation had lost the flower of their con-temporaries in holding a line in Europe for ultimate victory against the German Empire, and in keeping the forces of that Empire from the Channel ports. Now, in three weeks, the entire sacrifice seemed nullified. Against the same enemies, and unassisted (except by the compliance of Soviet Russia), that same Germany – yet in reality a new and more menacing Germany – had reversed the previous verdict and wiped the slate clean. Brooke had been shattered by much of what he had seen of the soldiers of the France he loved – so different from what he remembered. He had no illusions about the weaknesses in equipment, training and concepts of the British, though his admiration for the character and calm of the British soldier was reinforced by his experiences. In this he was generous – in fact the performance of units and formations of the British Army had been uneven and while some had maintained its highest traditions others had not. As for the German enemy, his comment in his diary of 23rd May was professional and characteristic: 'The success they have achieved is nothing short of phenomenal. There is no doubt that they are most wonderful soldiers.'

Given the psychological and doctrinal unpreparedness of the Allies – for that, rather than material inferiority was the key to the disaster – nothing, after the great breakthrough at Sedan and the crossing of the Meuse, could have altered the outcome of the campaign. Arrows drawn on maps for hypothetical manoeuvres against the German flanks were meaningless. Heroic actions by individual units and formations – and there were many – were too disconnected to be effective. The will of the men to execute co-ordinated manoeuvres and the robustness of the High Command to enforce them were alike shattered. The wildest dreams of the exponents of a new mobility in warfare had been realized. The nervous system of much of the defence was paralysed by the speed and effectiveness of the armoured and air attacks. There was nothing to do but save what could be saved and start again.

Brooke made a brief visit to Admiral Sir Bertram Ramsay, an old friend, who was handling the enormous enterprise of improvised evacuation, from a Headquarters in Dover Castle. He told Ramsay how things were across the Channel, and gave him the unpalatable news that several more days were needed. After sending a telegram to Ferney Close he drove to London, lightened a little in heart by having seen Ramsay. 'I know no other sailor,' he wrote, 'whom I would sooner have seen responsible for extracting my old Corps and the BEF. Providence was indeed kind that we should have known each other so well before this critical interview on which so much depended.' The drive through Kent was, of course, pure joy. The contrast of the tranquil beauty of England with the desolation of war in another land is something unforgettable to any who have experienced it. To Brooke it would remain an exquisite memory.[21]

After a visit to Dill, who had become CIGS, and giving an account of Gort's situation and of the conversation with Ramsay, Brooke went home. He took a train to Hartley Wintney. He was utterly exhausted and had to walk up and down the compartment to stay awake and prevent overshooting the station. His wife, Benita, was on the platform, with the two younger children, Kathleen and Victor. At last there came rest and a few days of peace. Like most officers he had been badly shaken by the scale of the reverse and was extremely depressed.

On 2nd June Brooke went to London to see what his next duty was to be. When he heard it from Dill he later described the moment as one of his blackest in the war.

Return to France to form a new BEF.[22]

The task appeared to most Englishmen the next logical step in a war in which a battle in the Low Countries had indubitably been lost, but in which the mass of the French Army was, it was presumed, still in the field, capable of organizing another line and of accepting the revived Army of its Ally through another port and for another campaign. There was still the sense that 'the front', as twenty-two years before, must be 'over there', and somewhere holding. It was not only natural to think in terms of organizing a new British Army to provide reinforcement: it would also clearly be a precondition of the continued struggle of France herself. Behind this dogged refusal to accept defeat stood the galvanic will of the new Prime Minister, Churchill, whose attempts to breathe courage into a paralysed Government of France had occupied much of his time since assuming office, and to whose character it was totally alien to give in. 'In defeat, defiance' was the opening phrase of one of his recipes for life. To Churchill high stakes were worth placing on the table if there were a chance thereby of keeping France in the war.

This was unquestionably right. To Brooke, however, there was no such chance. He had seen the disintegration of the French at too close hand to be able to resurrect belief in their powers of continued resistance. He was certain that France was totally beaten, at least insofar as the campaign being fought was concerned. There is a point at which realism demands that which can seem defeatism to the optimist. Brooke had reached it. Nevertheless the attempt had to be made. 'You are the only man for the job and we all know it,' wrote Montgomery to him, imploring him to send for the 3rd Division if he wanted it: 'We thank God we were under no one else in the last encounter.'[23]

A considerable number of British troops were still in France, south of the great German 'corridor' to the sea, north of which the Dunkirk evacuation had taken place. Some 100,000 had been engaged on duties on the lines of communication: from there a mixed force under Brigadier Beauman had been formed, and placed under the French Tenth Army – the western of a string of shattered French Armies which, at least on the map, were by now deployed along the general line of the Seine and the Aisne eastward from the Channel to the northern part of the now outflanked Maginot Line. There was also the 52nd Division (Drew) which had been landed to reinforce this new attempt, and of which one brigade had already been placed under the orders of the French Tenth Army: some elements of a Canadian Division, also intended for a 'reincarnated BEF', had already been landed; and the remnants of the 1st (and only) Armoured Division, which had lost much of its equipment and supporting infantry in the defence of Calais and had then withdrawn west of the Seine. Additionally, the 51st (Highland) Division (Fortune) had been detached from the original BEF for duty in the Maginot Line before the German offensive started, and had then been transferred to the westward flank of the French Armies, south of the 'corridor'. Forbidden by the French High Command to withdraw across the Seine, it had been first penned in the Havre Peninsula and then surrounded at St Valery en Caux. The Division was forced to surrender on the day Brooke returned to France.

In Whitehall Brooke had been told what might be 'scratched up' and sent out after him. He had seen the Secretary for War, Anthony Eden, who asked whether he was satisfied with what was being done for him.

Brooke told him that he was far from satisfied. The mission had no military value and no possibility of success. On the political merits of the gesture Brooke made plain he could pass no comment. On the military factors, however, he wished to leave Eden entirely clear. Another disaster would be the most probable outcome of any plan to build up anew in France. He then left the room, gloomily aware that the political motive was judged paramount, but certain as an individual that it, too, had not the slightest chance of satisfaction.[24] His written instructions from Eden, with their formal reference to the right of the French Supreme Command to delegate immediate command of the British Force to a 'subordinate French Commander not below the Commander of a Group of Armies' exuded a spirit remote from the total collapse of which Brooke had been so recent a witness. 'Brooke left me in no doubt as to what he thought of the situation,' recalled Eden later, 'but had a happy knack of strong criticism without raising rancour.'[25]

Brooke was made Knight Commander of the Order of the Bath, and received the accolade from the King on 11th June. On 12th June he said another goodbye to his family, all the more bitter for the sense of participation in a futile gesture. The next evening, with a small staff, he arrived at Cherbourg. Three days earlier Italy, too, had declared war on France.

Brooke first gave orders to press on with the evacuation of all

Line of Communication troops not essential to the maintenance of a force of four divisions, which was to be the theoretical strength of the reformed BEF. He discovered that the unfortunate 51st Division had already been surrounded and forced to surrender: he extricated its remnants and ordered their evacuation. He then made contact with the French, and on 14th June reported early in the morning at Orleans to General Weygand who had assumed the supreme command from Gamelin, summoned, as it was widely believed Marshal Foch himself on his death bed had recommended, to save France in her hour of trial.

Weygand was frank. The French Army had ceased to be able to offer organized resistance. Paris had been evacuated. There were no reserves left. The sole military strategy left to the Allies, and agreed at an Inter-Allied War Council, was to cover Brittany by holding a position in front of Rennes, its flanks resting on the Gulf of St Malo and the mouth of the River Loire. Instructions would be issued to the French Army Commander under whom some British troops were still deployed to concentrate them near Le Mans, where Brooke could take them under command. Weygand was later to dispute that he had given Brooke so grim a picture of French disorganization. It is impossible to believe that Brooke misunderstood him. Brooke's French was perfect, and he described the conversation fully in his diary that night. Colonel Archdale, a member of Brooke's staff at the time, was outside the door but recorded how Brigadier Swayne (in command of the British Mission with General Georges) –

> Came out and told us that Weygand had stated categorically that an armistice was imperative.

Furthermore – surely the essential point – the grim picture was correct.[26]

Together with Weygand Brooke drove to see Georges, still the Commander of the 'North East Front'. On the way Weygand remarked 'This is a terrible predicament I am in'. He made it clear that he was referring to a failure which was in the process of marring an otherwise uniformly successful career.[27]

Georges demonstrated on the map that the French forces as a coherent whole had ceased to exist. Then where, asked Brooke, was the Army necessary to defend Brittany – a front he measured before their eyes as 150 kilometres, requiring at least fifteen divisions? Britain might somehow produce four. Where were the others?

There were none. The plan was characterized as 'fantastic' by Weygand, 'romantic' by Georges. It had, however, been agreed by the Inter-Allied Council and must be regarded as an order. Brooke undertook to comply but to report to the British Government. Weygand did not say that he had already advised the French Government to seek an armistice.

Brooke then sent General Howard-Vyse, the British Liaison Officer with Weygand, home with a simple message, reinforcing a telegram he sent from Georges' Headquarters asking that the 'Brittany plan' should be reconsidered, since Weygand, Georges and he were at one on its absurdity. Howard-Vyse was to see the CIGS, to tell him to stop any plans to send more British troops to France and to prepare to evacuate the rest. Brooke had been clear from the outset of the adventure that this would be its end. The Brittany plan was a gesture of defeated men. The French Commanders were already discussing capitulation and recognized its inevitability. Three days later it occurred.

Brooke's advice was accepted in London later that day. He made it clear that Weygand must be told that the British Army would no longer be under his orders. Once again plans were hurriedly made for embarkation, this time by Cherbourg, covered by a force holding the neck of the Cotentin Peninsula, with other elements of the British Line of Communication troops moving to the nearest ports convenient.

At Le Mans on the evening of 14th June, when Brooke had completed his plans for evacuation, an important contact was made. In the words of Churchill 'on the night of 14th June, as I was thought to be obdurate [about the proposal for evacuation] he [Brooke] rang me up on the telephone line which by luck and effort was open and pressed this view upon me. I could hear quite well and after ten minutes I was convinced that he was right and we must go.'[28]

In fact the call originated from London, the CIGS having telephoned Brooke from 10 Downing Street. Brooke later described his own impression of the conversation. Dill had asked about dispositions, and in particular what was being done with the 52nd Division which was due to cover the embarkation from Cherbourg and then withdraw itself. Brooke told him.

'The Prime Minister does not want you to do that.'

'What the hell does he want?'

Churchill then came on the line and these two, whose relationship

167

forms so large a part of this story, first spoke to each other.

> He told me that that was not what he wanted. I had been sent to France to make the French feel that we were supporting them. I replied that it was impossible to make a corpse feel, and that the French Army was to all intents and purposes dead . . . He insisted that we should make them feel we were supporting them . . . he asked whether I had not got a gap in front of me . . . and whether the division could not be put into the gap? I told him that . . . it would again inevitably result in the throwing away of good troops with no hope of achieving any results.
>
> Our talk lasted for close on half-an-hour, and on many occasions his arguments were so formed as to give me the impression that he considered that I was suffering from 'cold feet' . . . This was so infuriating that I was repeatedly on the verge of losing my temper. ['You've lost one Scottish Division,' Brooke was heard saying. 'Do you want to lose another?'] Fortunately while I was talking to him I was looking through the window at Drew and Kennedy (CRA 52nd Division) sitting on a garden seat under a tree. Their presence there acted as a continual reminder of the human element of the 52nd Division and of the unwarranted decision to sacrifice them with no attainable object in view.
>
> At last, when I was in an exhausted condition, he said 'all right, I agree with you!'
>
> I think it is the only time in all the work we subsequently did together that he made use of those words.[29]

This conversation made a strong impression on Brooke. With all the admiration he came to conceive for Churchill he deplored the great man's tendency to interfere with tactical decisions of commanders in the field, and to use the force of his powerful will to influence them in directions contrary to their better judgement. 'The strength of his power of persuasion,' wrote Brooke, 'had to be experienced to realize the strength that was required to counter it.'

To Brooke 'interference' with the judgement of a commander in the field in the exercise of his responsibilities was deplorable. In this case he, Brooke, was the commander. His judgement was admirable, and he knew it. His courage had never been impugned, and his temper would be quick to react to any critical implication on that score. There was plenty more such interference before final evacuation. Yet, from Churchill's point of view, the political need to support the French might yet help save something of France or of French arms. He did not know Brooke. What if here, indeed, was a faint-hearted General, by now accustomed only to defeat, incapable of resolution in the face of odds? He would need fire breathing into him, and the only idiom to use would be reference to actual examples, the details of the battlefield. Furthermore Churchill's method of getting at the truth, of finding conviction, was by opposition and argument, the more vigorous the better, a system with which his professional advisers never truly came to terms.

Brooke on this occasion was right – and accepted by Churchill as right. He was often to be right. But he had had his first encounter with a will which, if misdirected, could run away, but which, if diminished in its dynamism, would have accomplished nothing of that which in the next epic years had to be done. Such men need advisers of integrity, skill, but above all strength of character to stand up to the flood of eloquence and vigour which can wash away sound argument and balanced plans unless the latter are expounded with unremitting clarity and courage.

Brooke described himself at the end of this conversation as 'in an exhausted condition'. Nothing is more exhausting than these struggles of the will. Hitler, who had the same dynamism, eloquence, and readiness to interfere in operational detail, seldom lost such an encounter – fortunately for Germany's opponents. But Hitler could not accept persuasion without sense of personal diminution. Churchill, on the other hand, with no less willpower and strength, was supported by his own profound sense of the traditions of Parliament and Cabinet, of corporate decision and of personal accountability. He growled at his military advisers, tried them to the limits of their endurance, could be idiosyncratic, perverse, unfair and wrong. But in the last resort he never overruled them on a professional issue. For this to work he needed men of the highest quality, and with robustness which matched his own. On 14th June he found one.

There were, however, more anxious days ahead. On 16th June, while embarkation from various ports was under way and when Brooke had moved his Headquarters back to Redon, north of St Nazaire and towards the south of what would have been the unrealized 'Brittany line', he heard from Dill that Weygand was not satisfied with Brooke's departure from his agreement to hold Brittany. This was deplorable, since Brooke had specifically asked on 14th June that Weygand be informed from London of the withdrawal of British troops from his command, and thus of the end of involvement on their part in the 'Brittany plan' – which Weygand had personally described as fantastic. Dill had himself told Brooke on that day that 'the Brittany scheme was off', and evacuation had been agreed. 'Satisfied' or not with Brooke's co-operation Weygand's forces were, on the next day, to hear Marshal Pétain's broadcast which could only lead to the end of all resistance against the Germans. It might have been at least as appropriate to convey this intention to the British, who still had large numbers of men and quantities of equipment in France, as to express dissatisfaction with British non-participation in an empty plan. It has been said that Pétain's broadcast was consistent with a French Governmental decision to fight on unless honourable terms could be obtained. Nobody who, like Brooke, had seen the dark cloud of defeat engulfing the French Army could possibly believe that such a broadcast, in which the Marshal spoke of the need to stop the fighting, could be followed by continuing operations of war. It was the end. 'Looking back on those days,' wrote Brooke, 'I thank Heaven that from my first contacts with Weygand I appreciated the imminence of the disaster and in spite of opposition from home took the dispositions I did. Had I not, I feel certain that we should have saved very little of the British forces at that time in Northern France.'[30] It was not the least of Brooke's services. In his diary of 16th June he wrote, 'I do not mind what accusation may be made against me. If I were faced with the same situation again I should act exactly in the same way.' 'On the whole my plans are working out as I meant them to,' he wrote that evening to Benita, 'I am feeling wonderfully fit.'

By 18th June Brooke was aboard an armoured trawler – *Cambridgeshire* – having taken ship at St Nazaire. Plymouth was reached on the 19th, and having taken the midnight train to London, he reported to the CIGS the next morning.

He was greeted with an enquiry as to why he had not saved more vehicles and equipment. These were, indeed, great losses, but to Brooke the essential, as at Dunkirk, was to save the soldiers who could form the basis for reconstituted armies and further campaigns. It was under a week since he had set out on his journey from Cherbourg to Weygand's Headquarters. In five nightmare days he had rescued three fighting divisions, which, had he carried out the Government's original instructions, would all have suffered the fate of the 51st (Highland) Division and been forced to surrender. His prescience, decision and moral courage had made possible the evacuation of nearly 160,000 British and Allied troops and more than three hundred guns. For the efficiency of this second evacuation, which brought the total of men carried out of

France to more than half a million, great credit was due to the Lines of Communication chief, General de Fonblanque, who died, worn out by his exertions, a few days after reaching England. 'To my mind,' Brooke wrote, 'the country owes him and his staff a great debt of gratitude.'[31] But the will and vision that had saved the rest of the British Expeditionary Force had been Brooke's. The vision – criticized by some as premature and defeatist – was of a beaten France and of only Britain resurgent. The will was that of acting upon the vision and, without delay, saving the human material necessary for national revival. 'I had always heard that he was stubborn,' wrote Archdale, 'and this was a moment when we thanked God for it.'[32]

CHAPTER VIII

The Lord High Constable

AT THE CORONATION OF QUEEN ELIZABETH II thirteen years later, Brooke, by then a Field-Marshal and a Viscount, held the office of Lord High Constable of England, an office now vested in the Crown except at Coronations, and one which in origin, with that of Earl-Marshal, involved the command of the armies of the Sovereign in the defence of the Realm. In 1940 Brooke was to exercise that function in deadly earnest. For now Britain appeared alone except for the unflinching support of her Empire. Invasion seemed inevitable. There were a large number of men under arms at home, but the arms themselves were primitive and inadequate, and the level of training and organization left much to be desired. The only commodity not in short supply was enthusiasm.

Brooke spent the six days after his return from France at his Hampshire home, during one of which he was summoned to Downing Street to lunch with the Prime Minister. 'It was the first of many meals we had together,' he recalled, 'and left a vivid impression on my mind. We lunched together at a small table for two, and he cross-questioned me about my last trip to France, my impressions of the French and details of my final evacuation.'[1] Then on 26th June Brooke returned to harness, taking up the appointment of General Officer Commander-in-Chief, Southern Command, which he had relinquished to go overseas in the autumn of 1939. At that time, for a man with his love of sport and nature, it had seemed the most attractive command in the British Army. But at midsummer 1940 its prospects were of a very different kind.

The forces in Southern Command consisted of a single Corps Headquarters, one Regular division – the 4th – and two Territorial divisions. The coastline Brooke had to defend stretched from West Sussex to Wales. He wrote after his fourth day at his Headquarters, Wilton, 'The more I see of conditions at home, the more bewildered I am as to what has been going on in this country since the war started. It is now ten months, and yet the shortage of trained men and equipment is appalling . . . There are masses of men in uniform, but they are mostly untrained: why I cannot think, after ten months of war. The ghastly part of it is that I feel certain that we can only have a few more weeks left before the Boche attacks.'[2]

For the next three weeks, Brooke worked unceasingly to strengthen the coastal defences and – what he regarded as more important – to form a reserve for mobile operations. 'My days,' he wrote, 'were spent touring the coastline, visiting defences and formations, changing unsuitable officers, and trying to instil a greater war atmosphere.' He established a central striking force on Salisbury Plain, organized Exercises, attended conferences for Divisional and Area commanders, and inspected the beach defences of the entire south coast from Plymouth to West Wittering. As usual he was restless, tireless and impatient of the slightest complacency or lack of energy. 'Called up late last night,' he wrote on 30th June, 'and invited to lunch at Chequers with PM to see Paget' – Ironside's* Chief of Staff. 'Suggested Paget should come here instead, which he did. Had long talk with him, telling him what I wanted for the defence of Southern Command, namely, another Corps HQ, another division, some armoured units and a call on bomber squadrons. Some of these things I may get. At any rate, I rubbed into him the nakedness of this Command taken in relation to the new situation in Western France.'[3]

For it was from across the Channel against Southern England, not across the North Sea against East Anglia – the area where at the moment the defending forces were most strongly concentrated – that Brooke expected the attack to come. Like all his fellow countrymen he was sure that come it would. It was for this anticipated moment that the Prime Minister was pouring his huge energy and boundless love of country into organization, leadership, and – most memorably – exhortation. For a while German arms had seemed irresistible: Churchill was determined that the effects of shock must be at once dispelled. He recognized that while there was enthusiasm it needed to be warmed and articulated, and where there was defeatism and apathy it must be extirpated. He broadcast to the nation on 14th July:

> And now it has come to us to stand alone in the breach and face the worst that the tyrant's might and enmity can do.

Three days later he visited Brooke at Southern Command, 'in

* Field-Marshal Lord Ironside, on handing over as CIGS to Sir John Dill, had become Commander-in-Chief Home Forces.

wonderful spirits' wrote Brooke, 'and full of offensive plans for next summer. We had a long talk together, mostly about old days and his contacts with my two brothers Ronnie and Victor of whom he was very fond.' Brooke was in great private anxiety about his son Tom who had been evacuated from his field hospital in France soon after the German attack, but was still desperately ill and requiring blood transfusions on 13th July.*

The two men spent some four hours together driving round the command. The meeting had significant consequences. Two days later Brooke was sent for by Eden, Secretary of State for War, and directed to assume command of all Home Forces. If invasion came it was now to be Brooke who would direct the land battle to defeat it.

The day before Brooke's meeting with Churchill, Hitler had issued Führer Directive No. 16. Even the preamble was cautiously phrased:

> Since England in spite of her hopeless military situation shows no signs of being ready to come to an understanding, I have decided to prepare a landing operation against England and if necessary to carry it out. The aim of this operation will be to eliminate the English homeland as a base for the prosecution of the war against Germany and, if necessary, to occupy it completely.[4]

Hitler's conditional approach was consistent with his state of mind. He had never wanted war with the British Empire, and he had miscalculated the reactions which his Eastern policy would ultimately provoke. After the brilliant success of the battle of France he hoped for, and attempted to obtain, some sort of British acceptance of the status quo in Europe. He could see no rational British interest in refusing peace. Peace would have freed his hand for his real preoccupation – a war of conquest and expansion in the East where he had both ambitions for Germany and disquiet over Russian intentions in the long term. Failure to persuade the British meant that Germany had an unsubdued enemy to the west. That enemy possessed an air force whose offensive capacity could disturbingly increase; and that enemy would impose on Germany the necessity to allocate major resources to war at sea. Furthermore, behind that enemy lay always the shadow of support from the United States with its huge industrial potential. Peace with the British Empire was the greatest prize Germany could

---

* Tom recovered and returned to service with the Royal Artillery.

obtain in the summer of 1940. If not peace there must be neutralization.

Peace had been spurned. The Directive addressed the question of timing.

Preparations for the entire operation must be completed by the middle of August

and the preconditions, of which one was regarded as paramount:

The English Air Force must be so reduced morally and physically that it is unable to deliver any significant attack against the German crossing.[5]

Planning was set in hand, and Operation SEELÖWE took shape – the great War Game which was never played except upon the map.

On Brooke's appointment to the Command-in-Chief congratulatory letters poured in. Such messages are customary, and it is friends and supporters who write them so that their tone is naturally partial. Nevertheless these letters – from family and old family friends, previous subordinates (and superiors: Gort wrote in terms which in view of his own inevitable disappointment and sense of anti-climax after Dunkirk were typically magnanimous), Field-Marshals, comrades like Van Straubenzee from the old 18th Division days in 1916, old Gunners from Eagle Troop – all convey a sense of inevitability. 'It was bound to come' is a recurring phrase; and, in one form or another, the sentiment 'we feel the country is in good hands'. 'You brought with you to GHQ,' wrote General Paget, Chief of Staff, when himself leaving a few months later, 'a sense of purpose, a decision, and a grasp of essentials which have been an inspiration to us all.' Benita, too, received a massive correspondence, quoting remarks about Brooke which made her glow with pride. An enjoyable accolade came to him from the Dean of Enniskillen, sometime Rector of Colebrooke:

I do hope I may live to see you when you have finished with Hitler. It will beat the night that Colonel Ronnie [Brooke] came back after the South African War. Brookeboro' was full of lighted tar barrels and Orangemen and Nationalists were all shaking hands with one another. Half the crowd did not get home until next day . . .

Reminiscence mingled with confidence and relief:

'There came to me so vividly,' a lady wrote, 'the picture of you when you stayed with us at our shooting place in the north, after

"SEELÖWE" SEPTEMBER 1940

the Great War. We had an impromptu Fancy Dress Dinner and
you appeared as a Rajah and sat on the floor and sang songs.'

When Brooke took over, Headquarters Home Forces were at St
Paul's School in London, although there was nowhere there to live
and for a while he slept at his Club – first the Naval and Military
(bombed shortly afterwards) and then the Army and Navy Club in
Pall Mall. His first days were spent in touring the country, visiting
the various Army Commanders and discussing their dispositions
and the state of the forces in their respective commands.

It was characteristic of Brooke that he combined at this time of
supreme responsibility, just as he did later as CIGS, an exterior of
confidence and complete calm, with inner anxieties, self-
questioning and uncertainty. The latter he confided only to his
diary – his safety valve. To all others he was the same energetic,
imperturbable and immaculate soldier that he had always been –
quick in temper (although he never lost it) and quick in speech, a
man who reassured by his personality but who had little patience
with the slow or the half-hearted. To some extent this stilling of
inner doubt and display of outer confidence is the function of every
commander. The tougher the situation and the more intelligent
the commander, the harder the task. Brooke certainly found it
hard. 'The idea of failure,' he wrote, 'was indeed appalling enough
to render the load of responsibility almost unbearable.' And again
– 'To be periodically wracked with doubts as to the soundness of
one's dispositions, and with it all to maintain a calm and confident
exterior is a test of one's character the bitterness of which must be
experienced to be believed.'[6] 'Bitterness' was a curious and surely
an inaccurate word to use. But the theme, although obvious, can
too easily be forgotten. The loneliness of the leader is great. In
Brooke's case, too, a certain melancholy of disposition lay deep
beneath the powerful exterior and behind the joy of family life. He
hid it, but it was always fermenting within. Yet to colleagues and
subordinates he was the embodiment of calm and charm, able to
forget the anxieties of office, and never talking 'shop' in his
moments of relaxation in Mess or Club. Members of his staff spoke
later of the 'cheerful, light-hearted atmosphere' which Brooke
brought to GHQ Home Forces.

If loneliness was profound for a field commander, so was it in
greater measure for his superior, the head of the Government. Of
course there was also challenge, stimulus and exhilaration – and
men incapable of enjoying as well as suffering in such conditions

are probably unsuited to their roles. But however tempered by exultation when a success, perhaps illusory, is achieved or a danger, perhaps exaggerated, is averted, strain and loneliness are always there. Brooke relieved them in his diary. Churchill relieved them by giving free rein to impetuous proposals, to periodic and unjust ill-temper, and to unconstrained interference in every sphere which caught his eye, ear or imagination. That this produced irritation will appear in these pages. It must be seen against the background of the huge burden upon the Prime Minister, and as a minor counter-weight to the magnificence with which that burden was borne.

Ironside, the previous Commander-in-Chief, had had a concept. Brooke liked it not at all. The main feature was a static defensive line, with anti-tank ditches and pill-boxes roughly parallel to the coast and well inland. There were also massive concrete road blocks at the approaches to most towns and many villages – a system Brooke had encountered in France, and which he regarded as unsound.

Brooke believed that the defence of the country must rest on different principles. A light line of defence would need to be held on the coast, to impose as much delay as possible on enemy landings. The main effort, however, would need to be made by mobile reserves, energetically handled and launched in counter-attack before the enemy could become established. A static line of defence would demand too many troops to man it. Instead the enemy's points of effort would need to be identified and hampered as far as possible, and then driven into the sea by quickly concentrated forces. Apart from troops manning coastal defences Brooke assessed his requirement at twenty-two divisions, eight of them armoured, as well as twelve 'County' divisions, ten Army Tank brigades (for the support of infantry), eight further independent Infantry brigades or brigade groups and an airborne brigade. These forces were never assembled in full, since the demands of overseas theatres soon overtook the requirements of home defences. But Brooke's concept was accepted in principle and he stood at the head of a rapidly increasing Army.

For this to work there had to be accurate assessment of the areas of main threat, so that the resources at the Army's disposal could be wisely deployed. Brooke carried out a lightning tour of the coast, visiting and assessing all areas and all senior commanders. Travelling by air he was able quickly to get round, and equally quickly to make up his mind. It was clear to him that the vulnerability of naval surface ships to land-based air attack meant that an invasion fleet could not be intercepted and defeated by the Navy unless it was routed far from any sort of air cover. Indeed he 'soon discovered' as he wrote, 'that the Home Fleet had little intention of coming further south than the Wash'. Whether this would in fact have been observed as a limitation Churchill, for one, indulgently doubted, saying that 'he never took much notice of what the Royal Navy said that they would or would not do in advance of an event since they invariably undertook the apparently impossible without a moment's hesitation whenever the situation so demanded'. Furthermore Brooke's 'discovery' hardly did justice to the Home Fleet, which had already detached cruisers on station round the south and east coasts under the Nore Command. Churchill's assessment was probably sound, but these were days before the interaction of air and sea power and the vulnerability of the Fleet had been terribly demonstrated.

If the invasion were launched in the south-east its success or failure would primarily depend on the air battle and on the operations of the Army if attacking formations got ashore. From every point of view it was in the south-east, Brooke was sure, that the battle would develop. One of his principal worries was the prospect of German airborne forces dropped on the South Downs and intercepting the movement of mobile British counter-attack forces directed at the invasion beaches.[7] Another nagging concern was the mental unpreparedness he thought he found among the people. In spite of the dangers which threatened them he reckoned they had failed to adjust mentally. Efforts were made, enthusiasm and self-sacrifice were apparent but to too many, thought Brooke, invasion was, from some instinctive rather than rational cause, still unthinkable. And they behaved accordingly. Perhaps Brooke, the Irishman by blood and the Frenchman by childhood upbringing, was in this less ultimately perceptive than his unprofessional and ill-informed compatriots. There was a certain confidence that the worst could not possibly happen. It was not sustained by reason but it may have owed a good deal to a subconscious sense of history. Germans didn't cross water: Britannia ruled the waves. It was irrational but pervasive. Race meetings continued.

Meanwhile, across the Channel, Operation SEELÖWE took shape. Thirteen divisions were to be landed in the first echelon, supported by the two airborne divisions whose intervention was so particularly feared by Brooke. Nine Panzer and motorized divisions were to follow up, to break out of the initial beachheads. In all, forty-one divisions were to be committed. The frontage of assault was to be the south-east coast between Folkestone and Bognor. The break-out would establish the German Army on the Surrey hills south of London, a line running from the Thames Estuary to Portsmouth – a line to be reached in ten days.

British Intelligence and German capabilities and intentions were not far apart. The GHQ appreciation of the German invasion effort was kept under incessant review. On 27th November it was thought that between twenty-five and twenty-nine divisions would be initially committed of which between four and seven would be airborne – the latter an exaggeration within an overall total of considerable accuracy. The points of attack would, it was thought, be primarily in the Eastern Command, which was true: although this was at first believed to include possible landings in East Anglia and thus to straddle London. This was not the German intention, and on 13th September Brooke noted that the invasion area looked as if it would be from the Thames to Plymouth – correct in the east, excessively extended in the west as we have seen. On the same day he wrote 'everything looks like an invasion starting tomorrow [14th]'.

SEELÖWE had indeed been ordered, in a German directive of 1st August, to be ready on 15th September. Indicators had seemed to the British to give an earlier possible invasion day. On 7th September Brooke dined, as he regularly did, with his cousin Bertie, 'Boy' Brooke – Lt.-Gen. Sir Bertram Sergison Brooke – commanding the London District, to whom he was very close in spirit and able to discuss matters with a freedom and intimacy greater, probably, than with any other serving officer except Dill. The Commander-in-Chief's instinct was that the invasion was about to begin, and before dinner he had issued the order placing Eastern and Southern Commands in a state of readiness. Dinner with a cousin and old friend was a particular comfort that night. It was always a real relief from the strain of responsibility to have an evening with him and to talk of other subjects than war. In fact SEELÖWE had, on 3rd September, been put off to the 21st. Brooke's note on the 13th of 'an invasion starting tomorrow' was at that moment only a few days wide of the mark. Three days later, on 17th September, Hitler directed that the operation be indefinitely postponed.

The key to this direction lay in the first precondition for

invasion established in the Führer Directive of 16th July and already quoted: 'The English Air Force must be so reduced morally and physically that it is unable to deliver any significant attack against the German crossing.' This had not been achieved. The story of the Battle of Britain is imperishable. It need not be retold in these pages. Suffice it to say that Hitler's first requirement was never attained and the German High Command, lukewarm from the start, never had to set SEELÖWE to the test.

The plan was kept in being, and Hitler, through the winter, periodically referred to the possibility of it needing again to be implemented. In the United Kingdom the sense of release, not unnaturally, lagged behind the Führer's somewhat volatile intentions. Nevertheless Brooke noted on 3rd October 'I am beginning to think that the Germans may after all not attempt it'.[8] The nightmare would often recur, however. On 17th October he referred to evidence from shipping movements and radio interception of 'an impending invasion of some kind or other'.[9] The shadow of invasion remained, but there was ever diminishing substance in the threat. At the end of 1941, when the Germans had already invaded Russia and a new phase of the world struggle had begun, Churchill, as a 'proving' exercise, directed a special high-level committee to assume a German defensive on all other fronts and to plan, from the enemy's viewpoint and with forces as they then existed, a new invasion of England. Drawing, perhaps, on the wisdom of hindsight the 'Invasion' team dispensed with preliminary operations to destroy British air-power. They dispensed with Hitler's first precondition – not, of course, that they had been assisted by distribution of the Führer's Directive No. 16 in the first place. They set out to achieve maximum surprise by the extensive use of airborne forces and major attacks on the Early Warning Systems, combined with a hurricane twenty-four-hour assault on the defensive fighter bases. Their final deduction was that no plan would offer the German High Command a sufficient chance of success. The possibility of invasion thereafter provided a minimal factor in British planning, and had indeed been considered of diminishing seriousness throughout 1941, especially after the launching in June of the great German adventure in the East, Operation BARBAROSSA. The preparation of this plan had been instituted by Führer Directive No. 21 of 18th December 1940, and on 9th January 1941 preparations for SEELÖWE had been, by order, discontinued.

*

Brooke's greatest battle as the Commander of the land defences of the Kingdom, in what would have been the most critical campaign in the Army's history, was thus never fought. Exercises have been conducted, war games played and books written on what the outcome might have been. Brooke did not attempt an exact appraisal after the event. 'I did not consider our position a hopeless one,' he wrote in retrospect, 'far from it.'[10] At the time, in the summer of 1940, with his sense that only about half his divisions could be regarded as fit for more than rudimentary operations, that his 'mobile reserves' moved in requisitioned buses and that everywhere there was a shortage of all types of equipment, his views probably went no further than a diary entry of 8th September. 'I wish I had more completely trained formations under my orders. But for the present there is nothing to be done but to trust God and pray for His help and guidance.' In every week his working day started early and often finished late at night. A few hours were sometimes snatched at Ferney Close with Benita. 'Spent afternoon in paradise with you and the children, those two delicious wee souls,' he would write.[11] His sense of unity with Benita was all the sharper for strain and peril, as was his association of it with religious faith. 'It is impossible to live with you,' he wrote in September 1940, 'without seeing God's divine beauty radiating from you at all times. I do thank Him for having allowed me to meet you, and through you to be able to get so much nearer Him.'[12]

Increasingly, through 1941, Brooke's preoccupation was less with the preparation of defensive battle against a German invader than with the fitting of the Army in the United Kingdom for war, wherever war might next be waged. The security of the Realm had, of course, still to take first place, but it was felt less and less directly threatened. It was Brooke's duty, nevertheless, to keep the question of that security before the eyes of authority. There were inadequacies which continued to nag at him, but which were too deepseated to have tackled in the immediacy of danger in September 1940. One of these was the overall Command System.

Brooke's chief disquiet with the Home Command arrangements lay in the division of authority. He later wrote:

> There was, however, one point above all others that constituted a grave danger in the defensive organization of this country, there was no form of combined Command over the three Services. And yet their roles were intimately locked together. Who was deciding the claims between the employment of destroyers

against hostile landing craft, as opposed to anti-submarine protection on the Western Approaches? Who would decide between conflicting calls of the Army for bombers to attack beaches, as opposed to Navy wanting them for attack on hostile fleets? Who would decide whether Fighter Command should protect our bombers attacking hostile aerodromes, or attend to the calls of the Army on the beaches against hostile bombing attacks? These are only a few of the various contingencies that were certain to arise, and did, in fact, repeatedly in every exercise that we ran. There were far too many Commanders; the Navy had the C.-in-C. Home Fleet, C.-in-C. Nore, C.-in-C. Portsmouth, C.-in-C. Plymouth, C.-in-C. Western Approaches. The Army had the C.-in-C. Home Forces; and the Air Force had the AOC.-in-C. Fighter Command; the AOC.-in-C. Bomber Command, and the AOC.-in-C. Coastal Command, There was no co-ordinating head of this mass of Commanders beyond the Chiefs of Staff Committee and the Admiralty, the Air Ministry and War Office.

It was a highly dangerous organization; had an invasion developed I fear that Churchill would have attempted as Defence Minister to co-ordinate the action of these various Commands. This would have been wrong and highly dangerous, with his impulsive nature and tendency to arrive at decisions through a process of intuition, as opposed to 'logical approach', heaven knows where he might have led us!

He held periodic Conferences of Commanders-in-Chief, which were attended by all the coastal Naval Cs.-in-C., such as Nore, Plymouth and Portsmouth, thus giving the Naval side too great a preponderance in these discussions.[13]

Brooke believed that a supreme command for all forces concerned in the security of the Kingdom was necessary. Whether, in fact, a Supreme Commander – one man – could in such circumstances have exercised power in all dimensions may be debatable. Some would regard it as impossible. Probably the Chiefs of Staff Committee itself, responsible for operations world-wide, would not have been able to focus solely on the invasion question. But although the functions of the Services had an immediate reaction upon each other, and in particular air power was critical to the success of both maritime and land operations, it is still questionable whether a single Commander could have held sufficient expert and acceptable authority. Perhaps a Committee of Commanders-in-Chief, each exercising command over all the functions of his own Service might have provided an acceptable middle point between that diversity of command which Brooke deplored and that concentration of authority in single hands which he advocated – and which he was instrumental in effecting overseas in the future.

He was, however, uncompromising on the point. 'There should only have been three Service Representatives,' he wrote after one of what he described as the 'somewhat futile conferences of commanders-in-chief' run by the Prime Minister. 'These three Service Representatives should have been under a Supreme Commander responsible to the Chiefs of Staff Committee.' On the evening of 17th June 1941, he entered in his diary, 'At 12 noon one of the PM's meetings of Cs.-in-C. which in the long run turns out to be mainly a meeting of rather moth-eaten old admirals!' No doubt this was most unfair.

His own Headquarters was at St Paul's School, but a Battle HQ in Whitehall had been constructed for GHQ Home Forces, with the Chiefs of Staff meeting in the same building and the Prime Minister possessing a flat in it. 'Its only fault is . . . its proximity to Winston,' Brooke commented wryly. Already, from periodic visits to Chequers, he was finding Churchill's energies and the idiosyncratic plans of that fertile mind one of the most exhausting aspects of his work. But he, like all, found stimulus too, and thoughtfulness. Churchill, knowing the great amount of travelling Command of Home Forces entailed, had obtained for Brooke's use a special Headquarters train, an enormous asset particularly when he could not fly.

Then there was the matter of command of air forces.

On the question of air power in support of the Army Brooke held very strong opinions, which at their most extreme included advocacy of a virtually separate Army Air Force or an Air Force with units under Army formation command. There was, among many military commanders who had experienced the effectiveness of German dive-bomber and Panzer co-ordination, a widespread belief that this co-ordination derived from exactly such subordination of Air to Army Commanders at field level, and that the Germans managed such things a great deal better. Some thought Brooke had almost an obsession on the subject; it was certainly true that the system of obtaining air support in the BEF, except from the designated 'Air Component' under Gort's command, had been laborious.

In fact, however, the German system[14] corresponded closely to that which ultimately became the accepted basis of Army Air co-operation in the British Services. Luftflotte zones of responsibility corresponded to those of Army Groups. A decision would be taken, at the appropriate level, on the general thrust of Army support operations between the air and military commands concerned. Thereafter the Luftwaffe missions were agreed in very general terms. The method of executing these missions was entirely for the Luftwaffe commander concerned, the ground force commander having stated the purpose to be achieved at a joint conference.

This was broadly the system to be adopted by the British. Furthermore, the German system of close air support stressed flexibility and the principle of concentration, so that the maximum forces could be assigned to the point of main effort. Dispersal of command inevitably involves loss of concentration although it can, obviously, lead to greater speed of response in local situations. The only exceptions to the above during the Second World War appear to have been the formation of certain specific Luftwaffe reconnaissance units under Army Command during 1942: but no exception was made in the case of ground attack or 'interdiction' – that is isolation of the battlefield by a bombing and strafing policy aimed at preventing the movement of enemy reinforcement and support. German Army and Air Command Headquarters were located together where possible and each placed liaison officers with the other. Certainly some specialized ground attack air groups were formed. They themselves were concentrated under General Freiherr von Richtofen in Poland and in France, and used to support the main point of attack – a concept entirely contrary to the dissipation of resources by allocating them to individual Army formations to command.[15]

Brooke only occasionally, and with explicit reluctance, went to the extreme of referring to the desirability of a separate Army Air Force, but two connected matters bothered him. First he felt that the Royal Air Force placed insufficient emphasis on support of the Army, and changed the pilots assigned to Army co-operation squadrons with such frequency that the task would not be well done if battle was joined – and the experiences of France and Belgium had convinced him of its vital importance. Second, he believed that both a cause and a consequence of this was that Bomber Command, and the whole policy of strategic bombing, had an excessively high priority for the results likely to be achieved. He first put his views in a somewhat abrasive interview with Portal, Chief of the Air Staff, to whom he in February 1941 proposed a meeting, and who, through a misunderstanding, thought the Commander-in-Chief Home Forces was summoning him, the CAS, to come to see him – an impropriety of which Brooke would never have been guilty. Portal, with typical modesty, nevertheless appeared at St Paul's. The two men reached if not agreement at least a *modus vivendi*. Portal never denied the importance of Army Air co-operation, of Joint Training and of continuity of pilot assignment within the limits of the possible: but those limits were tight. He (rightly in the event) concluded earlier than his colleagues that invasion was unlikely, and his thesis was that it was in the air that the only offensive could at that time effectively be carried out against Germany and that it must, therefore, be pressed in order that the enemy's defensive resources could be pinned, would need to be augmented and could be increasingly attacked. Furthermore there was a minimum strength below which Fighter Command must not fall.

There were other concerns. On 13th September 1940 Italy invaded Egypt. To the Italians this war in the Mediterranean and on its littoral was to be a taste of glory. To the Germans, soon to be directed primarily to the East with the mass of their forces, it was at first a sideshow: then a theatre of some limited significance where unexpected tactical success seemed for a short period to open possibilities of conceivable (albeit far-fetched) strategic advantage; and, ultimately, one which turned into a drain on resources and a menace to their southern flank after the United States became involved in the war. To the British it was the only field of engagement, the only place where for a while we had a chance to fight. In these circumstances it was natural that the pugnacious instinct of Churchill should lead to pressures to reinforce the Army of Egypt at high cost to the security of the United Kingdom base. This, in the event, was both courageous and justified, but diversion of resources could not fail to meet reservations from Brooke. His criticism of dispersal of effort turned out mistaken in strategic terms. Not only was the threat of invasion actually behind us – or very nearly so – but the brilliant victories over hugely superior Italian forces achieved by General O'Connor and the Desert Army in the winter of 1940/1 shone like a solitary star in a dark sky. They marked the first step in a progression which was to end in the invasion of Italy and deep German involvement in the Mediterranean; and they had a profound effect on Italian morale and on neutral and particularly Spanish and Turkish opinion. In all this, as in the events of the terrible summer of 1940, Churchill's influence was decisive.

Brooke's reservations were a good deal more powerful when, to help counter an Italo-German invasion of Greece, an expeditionary force was diverted thither early in 1941 from the British Middle East Command. It failed, achieving only the weakening of British forces in the Western Desert. 'Are we again going to have "Salonika supporters" as in the last war?' Brooke asked in his diary about the Greek adventure. 'Why will politicians never learn the simple principle of concentration of force at the vital point and the avoidance of dispersal of effort?' It is the cry of field commanders down the ages, not invalidated by the fact that very often 'the vital point' appears that for which the speaker is responsible. Applied to Greece the criticism is only half a true bill. The motive of intervention in Greece was the rational one of reassuring Turkey, sustaining Greece, drawing in a stronger German effort and, with luck, embroiling the Germans in a difficult campaign. Brooke's rhetorical question – 'When will politicians ever learn . . .?' was unfair. Although Churchill was naturally anxious to help Greece if it could be done, he made clear that if local strategic advice were against it the British Government would not press. He sent Dill, the CIGS, together with Eden, to take stock. They recommended in favour. Only after their visits to Athens and with the full endorsement of the Commanders-in-Chief in the Middle East was the Greek adventure determined. It failed, and it weakened our forces in the Western Desert at a crucial time.

Brooke's other preoccupations lay chiefly with training, equipment and the quality of commanders at all levels. He was dissatisfied with what he regarded as the softness of the British Army, compared to its texture of only twenty years before against the same enemy. He set out to harden it, to train it in all weathers and conditions, and only to advance men who would do the same and whose minds he judged to be adapted to the new pace of warfare. He organized intensive exercises, and ran frequent conferences on all aspects of modern war. He replaced large numbers of commanders, including friends of long standing. He constantly lamented the shortage of gifted Army and Corps Commanders as the Army expanded, and he wielded the pruning knife sharply to make room for younger men. He was probably sometimes unfair: no commander can be infallible in such matters. It is, however, essential to have at a critical time one who is sufficiently ruthless to back his judgement against the instincts of tranquillity or affection. Brooke had the strength to be un-compromising and yet gentle in such matters. One commander who had been replaced left Brooke's office in tears, but could only say as he left the room 'what a wonderful man!'. Brooke, in the fullest sense, was a man of sympathy.

Not only British troops and personalities were involved. The United Kingdom was the chief base for whatever main effort against Germany lay ahead. French forces under General de Gaulle, Polish forces under General Sikorski, and an increasing number of forces from other countries of the British Empire were concentrating under the strategic direction of the British High Command. In the case of the Empire, Canada was chiefly engaged in contributing to the Army of the United Kingdom, while Australia, New Zealand, South Africa and India were to be powerfully engaged in the Mediterranean theatre and, when Japan entered the war, in the Far East. Meanwhile Brooke found some aspects of the Canadian contribution unsatisfactory. On 19th April 1941 he watched a Canadian Corps Exercise. He wrote that evening in his diary:

> Rather depressed at the standard of training and efficiency of Canadian Divisional and Brigade Commanders. A great pity to see such excellent material as the Canadian men controlled by such indifferent commanders.

and he commented later:

> Unfortunately, as long as MacNaughton* commanded the Corps there was not much chance for improvement. He could not see the deficiency in training and was no judge of the qualities required by a Commander. Matters improved radically at a later date, when Harry Crerar took command.[16]

MacNaughton appeared to Brooke to be over-exact in his interpretation of his charter as to how Canadian forces were to be

---

* General Andrew MacNaughton. There is evidence that MacNaughton thought Brooke prejudiced against him because of professional differences during service with the Canadian Corps in the First World War in 1917, as well as at the Imperial Defence College where they were fellow students on the first Course in 1927. There is no record of this in Brooke's own letters or diaries and on the personal level he always wrote of MacNaughton with admiration, regretting only that the latter's ultimate removal from Command (which Brooke regarded as inescapable) seemed to create bitterness and to rob him of one he regarded as an old friend.

employed and under what conditions of independence. Brooke complained that they were the most difficult to deal with in that respect. He ascribed this largely to MacNaughton, recording with asperity how the latter, on an exercise in January 1941, had complained that one division of the Canadian Corps had been temporarily employed with another Corps – which was 'not in accordance with the Charter governing the employment of the Canadian corps'. This, to Brooke, showed MacNaughton's 'warped outlook', and he later recorded his view of him as 'a man of exceptional ability where scientific matters were concerned, but lacking the required qualities of command. He did not know his subordinate commanders properly and was lacking in tactical outlook. It stood out clearly that he would have to be relieved of his command.' In fairness, however, the position of a commander acting as part of a force primarily composed of other national troops yet responsible also to his own Government is seldom easy – as Brooke, of all men, knew well.

He saw much of the Poles. Brooke profoundly respected the fighting spirit of these excellent men, and they had been entrusted with the defence of part of the Scottish coast. They were naturally eager for new and superior equipment, and were not easy to persuade that they had a respectable place in the queue for scarce military commodities. Brooke did his best, visiting them often and always with enjoyment. This was particularly so because of the admiration and affection he conceived for Sikorski, their commander. Sikorski's information from Eastern Europe was extensive and accurate, and Brooke gained both from him and later from General Anders, who had been a prisoner in Russia, a clear picture of the savage hardships inflicted on the Poles by the Russians as well (from Sikorski) as a perceptive view of the likelihood of the German attack on Russia, a view which coincided with Brooke's own hunch on the subject. 'I would not be surprised to see a thrust into Russia,' he noted in his diary on 15th March 1941. Brooke greatly mourned Sikorski's later death in an aircrash. 'His death,'* he wrote, 'was one of the primary contributory causes towards the final Polish tragedy.'

* In view of the speculation and research devoted to the death of General Sikorski, and the understandable suspicions that it had been arranged by those who wished to see Poland less than free, it is of interest that Brooke asked personally to study all the papers in the case, and, right or wrong, was convinced that the accident had derived from mechanical failure and not from man's design.[17]

Brooke, like many others, was therefore early informed on the horrors being inflicted on Poland by Russia, although the full measure of those atrocities only gradually came to light. The deportations, mass murders, torture and degradations exceeded the harshness of the German occupation – and this against a nation with which the Soviet Union had not even a nominal quarrel.

As opposed to Sikorski, admiration for General de Gaulle was restrained. Brooke saw him often from August 1940 onwards and his views were uncompromising. 'Whatever good qualities he may have had were marred by his overbearing manner, his megalomania and lack of co-operative spirit. He is supposed to have said at that time *"Je suis la France!"* Whether he did or not he certainly adopted that attitude. In all discussions he assumed that the problem of the liberation of France was mine whilst he was concentrating on how he would govern France as its Dictator as soon as it was liberated. Added to these disadvantages his Headquarters were so completely lacking all sense of secrecy that it became quite impossible to discuss any future plans with them.'[18]

The Commander-in-Chief was inevitably drawn not only into operational policy in the highest sense, with frequent and personal contact with Churchill and his Ministers, but into questions of resource allocation and production; questions which often suffered from becoming an auction, a matter of whim rather than logic, and which were exposed to the influence of strong and interested personalities. For none of these did Brooke develop such a powerful loathing as for Lord Beaverbrook, who had been placed in charge of Aircraft Production by Churchill, over whom he seemed to exert some influence. Churchill thought the country needed what he described as 'his [Beaverbrook's] vital and vibrant energy'. This energy was grafted on to a combat aircraft programme which has also been described as 'a triumph of far sighted planning and industrial organization'.[19] Beaverbrook's achievement, in the view of at least some of the Air Staff, was to disrupt a carefully phased programme based on a proper balance between aircraft types, front line and reserves, trainers and spares, and to commit by *diktat* every resource to the production of the maximum number of fighters, regardless of back-up. Brooke, who had his own differences with the Air Staff, knew and cared deeply about a sensible aircraft programme. He distrusted Beaverbrook's activities. His distrust was not mitigated by the latter's next achievement – diversion of much needed armoured plating from tank production in order to build small armoured cars (inevitably called 'Beaverettes') for use by Home Guard protectors of individual factories – a curious tactical concept, uncoordinated with Home Forces Command. The two men were fellow guests at Chequers on 17th August 1940, Brooke's first visit. 'After dinner,' recorded Brooke, 'he sat at the writing table, pouring himself out one strong whisky after another, and I was revolted by his having monkey-like hands as they stretched out to grab ice cubes out of the bowl. I felt those hands were typical of the man. The more I saw of him throughout the war the more I disliked him and mistrusted him. An evil genius who exercised the very worst influence on Winston.' Brooke may have been fastidious in his antipathy. He was certainly not alone. After the war was over he was interested to learn from Eden that he, too, had always regarded Beaverbrook as Churchill's evil genius.

Yet it has been alleged that Beaverbrook's dynamic energy was exactly what was required. It is probably true that aircraft production, design and the planning of force structure has seldom been under such intelligent and dedicated control as in the years before and at the start of the Second World War, and to inject a 'rogue' factor into a complex system generally produces sensation rather than lasting improvement. Nevertheless Beaverbrook achieved remarkable things, not only in fighter production, but in the dispersal of factories. He, and his mentor, Churchill, were single-minded in their view that without enough fighter aircraft we would lose the war quickly, but they were not very obviously wrong. Furthermore Beaverbrook was a man who did not believe that scarce resources should be allocated by priority. He believed that approach to be a recipe for continuing scarcity. It was necessary, in his view, to set up strong men to fight their respective corners – and then the general outcome would be greater overall, in spite of some anomalies along the way. This sort of philosophy, cynical and robust, was anathema to Brooke.

Beaverbrook was not the only object of Brooke's aversion. Of a man who, as CIGS, came to be regarded as a model mix of firmness and co-operation in his dealings with the Cabinet, it must be said that this did not come naturally. When a particular anti-invasion exercise to test the reactions to the landing of airborne forces in the London Parks was debated – and prevented – by a number of Ministers, on the grounds that it could affect public confidence, Brooke exploded. He referred to Sir Henry Wilson's unflattering descriptions of 'The Frocks' in the First World War as absolutely true to life, 'The more I see of politicians the less I think of them'.[20]

The building up of the Army brought many professional issues before the Commander-in-Chief where strong feelings as well as convictions were aroused. A few may be mentioned. One was the plan to form special Commando units, by drawing selected men from battalions and training them hard in the techniques of raiding. Brooke opposed it, and never changed his view. He admired the work done in 'Combined Operations', initially by Sir Roger Keyes: he was, however, convinced that raiding forces should not have been divorced from the Army, but rather that each division should have maintained a comparable Commando patrol.

Another issue was airborne forces. Brooke believed in them profoundly. He believed in the threat they posed in the context of invasion, and in their offensive capacity, used to create chaos behind the front and to fight, in conjunction with ground mobile forces, battles of encirclement by the use of a third dimension. He laid the basis for the creation and expansion of the British Airborne Forces whose story, part triumphant part tragic, belongs to a later part of this tale.

Of all his personal encounters, those with the Prime Minister were the most demanding – combining the heights of exasperation and exhilaration. Visits to Chequers were dreaded by Brooke, for the fatigue they involved – Churchill's late hours were notorious. Then there were the projects. Of these the 'Trondheim Plan' is worth describing at some length in Brooke's own words, at this point, since it provided a pattern for so many similar excursions in the future.

The German attack on Russia had started on 22nd June 1941, thus ending what has been described as the second act of the war. By October the Russian position seemed desperate. Since every serious soldier in Britain was convinced of the impossibility of a British landing on the French coast, where the Germans had at least four times as many divisions as the British could hope to land and could certainly build up at a faster rate, the Prime Minister turned his mind to Norway. Here, he argued, if a lodgement could be made – a thing which only he believed possible so far outside the range of British fighters and in the face of German air-power – it would have the double effect of distracting German attention from Russia and easing the difficulties of escorting the convoys which

Britain and America were sending to Murmansk round the North Cape of Norway.

Brooke's diary then ran:

> 3rd October 1941. At midnight received special messenger from the War Office with orders to carry out examination for attack on Trondheim and preparation of plan of attack. The whole to be in by next Friday! Also that I was to dine tonight at Chequers and spend night there to discuss plans. I motored back to London in the morning and spent most of the afternoon studying details of the plan.

> At 6 p.m. picked up Dill at the War Office and drove to Chequers discussing details with him on the way. Dudley Pound, Portal and Attlee formed the party. We sat up till 2.15 a.m. discussing the problem, and I did my best to put the PM off attempting the plan. Air support cannot be adequately supplied and we shall fall into the same pitfalls as we did before.

> 4th October. Resumed discussion at 11 a.m. and went on till 1 p.m. I think PM was beginning to weaken on the plan. Returned to London and made arrangements for conference on Monday to start discussing plan. Finally motored home in time for dinner. Very weary after hard week short of sleep.

He later wrote:

> The plan for the capture of Norway had already been examined by the Chiefs of Staff Committee, and had been turned down as impracticable owing to insufficient air support for the operation. Now, at Chequers, I, in my capacity as Commander-in-Chief Home Forces, had received orders from him [Churchill] to prepare a detailed plan for the capture of Trondheim, ready to the last button. A Commander for the expedition was to be appointed by me and the plan was to be sufficiently ready only to require the order to start. I was given one week to prepare it. I said that, if I was to do so, I must have the Commander-in-Chief Home Fleet, Air-Officer-Commanding Fighter Command, Air-Officer-Commanding Bomber Command, Minister of Transport and several others at my disposal for repeated conferences during the week. I was told that they were all to be made available.

> It was an unpleasant assignment. I had been told by Dill of the results of the Chiefs of Staff inspection of the problem, and I felt convinced that I should arrive at similar conclusions. It was going to entail a great deal of wasted work on the part of many busy people.[21]

The diary continues:

6th October. Left home 8 a.m., foggy. Conference at 11 a.m. in Cabinet War Room at which I presided. Following were present: Commanders-in-Chief Home Fleet, Fighter Command, Bomber Command, Coastal Command, Army Co-operation Command, Quartermaster-General, Minister of Transport, my own staff etc. The more we examined the problem of Trondheim, the more certain I am that it would be folly to attempt it . . .

Then:

9th October . . . The whole morning had been taken up with another of my meetings preparing Trondheim operation . . . Our final survey of the operation convinced us more than ever of its impracticability. I now have been warned to attend Chequers next Sunday again at 6 p.m. I have to start for Newcastle the same night.

And later:

Sunday 12th October. After having made all arrangements to go to Chequers and for special train to collect me at Wendover station at 1.45 a.m., I suddenly received message during afternoon that PM wanted us at 10 Downing Street instead. Went there at 6.30 p.m. All Chiefs of Staff, Tovey, Sholto, [Douglas], Paget and I attended. PM very dissatisfied with our Appreciation. He then proceeded to cross-question me for nearly two hours on various items of the Appreciation, trying to make out that I had unnecessarily increased the difficulties. However, I was quite satisfied that there was only one conclusion to arrive at. Finally left at 8.30 p.m., dined at club and embarked on train at 11 p.m.

Of this meeting – in the course of which, according to General Paget, the Prime Minister, looking angrily at him and Brooke, remarked, 'I sometimes think some of my generals don't want to fight the Germans!' – Brooke wrote subsequently:

At 6.30 p.m. we assembled at 10 Downing Street. The PM was already in the Cabinet Room, and I saw at once from his face that we were in for the hell of a storm! He had with him what he used to classify as some of his 'colleagues', usually Anthony Eden, Attlee, Leathers on this occasion, and possibly a few others. On my side of the table I had the various Naval and Air Commanders-in-Chief who had collaborated with me, Paget, who was nominated as commander of this Expedition, and some of my Staff.

When we were all assembled he shoved his chin out in his

aggressive way and, staring hard at me, said: 'I had instructed you to prepare a detailed plan for the capture of Trondheim, with a commander appointed and ready in every detail. What have you done? You have instead submitted a masterly treatise on all the difficulties and on all the reasons why this operation should not be carried out.' He then proceeded to cross-question me for nearly two hours on most of the minor points of the appreciation. I repeatedly tried to bring him back to the main reason – the lack of air-support. He avoided this issue and selected arguments such as: 'You state that you will be confronted by frosts and thaws which will render mobility difficult. How can you account for such a statement?' I replied that this was a trivial matter and that the statement came from the 'Climate Book'. He at once sent for this book, from which it at once became obvious that this extract had been copied straight out of the book. His next attack was 'You state that it will take you some twenty-four hours to cover the ground between A and B. How can you account for so long being taken? Explain to me exactly how every hour of those twenty-four will be occupied?' As this time had been allowed for overcoming the enemy resistance on the road, removal of road-blocks and probable reparation to demolition of bridges and culverts, it was not an easy matter to paint this detailed picture of every hour of those twenty-four. This led to a series of more questions, interspersed with sarcasm and criticism. A very unpleasant gruelling to stand up to in a full room, but excellent training for what I had to stand up to on many occasions in later years.

The meeting finished shortly after 8.30 p.m. and for the second time Winston had been ridden of Trondheim* . . .[22]

Yet such trials, confided to his diary often in savage terms, were offset by other perceptions about Churchill, again and again breaking like shafts of sunlight through the clouds. 'He is most interesting to listen to, and full of the most marvellous courage, considering the burden he is bearing (July 1940). 'He has a marvellous vitality and bears his heavy burdens remarkably well. It would be impossible to find a man to fill his place at present' (October 1940). 'PM suffering from bronchitis, came down to dinner in his "siren-suit", a one-piece garment like a child's romper suit of light blue. He was in great form and after dinner sent for his service rifle to give me a demonstration of the "long port" which he wanted to substitute for the "slope". He then

---

* 'It was not long,' added Brooke later, 'before he made a third attempt.' It is fair to add that a possible British invasion of Norway gave the Germans some concern during that winter.

followed this up with some bayonet exercises' (March 1941). And perhaps most happily, since it was at the conclusion of one of Churchill's 'Tank Parliaments' sessions (May 1941) when he collected ideas from assembled experts and where discussion was liable to go off the rails, and Brooke apt to fume:

> It is surprising how he maintains a lighthearted exterior in spite of the vast burdens he is bearing. He is quite the most wonderful man I have ever met, and is a source of never-ending interest to me, studying, and getting to realize that occasionally such human beings make their appearance on this earth. Human beings who stand out head and shoulders above all others.

Brooke, later in life, was adamant that entries in his diary were his sole relief and in no sense represented a just or considered view. They were written for the eyes of his wife alone – 'my nightly talk with you on paper'. They were explicitly dedicated to her. A diary entry is evidence of the state of mind of the writer on a particular evening. It is imperfect evidence of the facts it records and can imperfectly reflect the writer's true self. A man's irritations when exhausted are atypical of him, and of none more than Brooke. When there is passion felt on vital subjects, dispute can turn men savage. Diaries do not argue – they assert, with brevity and exaggeration, the emotion and prejudice of the minute. Perhaps the last word on the subject should lie with General Ismay, the Prime Minister's Representative on the Chiefs of Staff Committee:

> The dogmatic, sometimes wounding, and often unjustifiable comments which he [Brooke] makes from time to time on his war comrades, cannot be regarded as considered judgements. There is however a danger that posterity, not knowing the circumstances, will take the assertions and criticisms in the diaries at their face value, and will get the idea that Brooke was self-satisfied, self-pitying, ungenerous and disloyal. He was none of these things. On the contrary, his selflessness, integrity and mastery of his profession earned him the complete confidence, not only of his political chiefs and his colleagues in Whitehall, but also of all our commanders in the field. On that account alone, he was worth his weight in gold. In the course of my eighteen years' service in Whitehall, I saw the work of eight different Chiefs of the Imperial General Staff at close quarters, and I would unhesitatingly say that Brooke was the best of them all.[23]

Brooke had largely reconstructed the Army, making the untrained and in some cases demoralized forces into an Army fit for operations at home or abroad. He had rigorously combed out senior commanders, while still dissatisfied in that regard.

During his first year as Commander-in-Chief Home Forces he covered 35,000 miles in his own car, many more thousands in the cars of other commanders, great distances by train and 14,000 miles by air. He had lived with the ever-present albeit diminishing threat of invasion, of the knock-out blow to end British history. In retrospect, Brooke's continuing anxiety about invasion after the Germans turned on Russia seems excessive. In July 1941 he still insisted that invasion might come suddenly. This was regarded with some scepticism in other quarters, and with hindsight bears little relationship to German intentions or capabilities. But many people expected Russia quickly to collapse, and the main strength of the German Army to be again deployed in the West.

He greatly enjoyed his tours. Getting out of an office provided contact with humanity – with the often mercifully humorous Britain of 1940 and 1941. He moved into the bar of a darkened hotel in Savernake Forest with his driver, their billet during an exercise nearby. 'Mind my bloody bottles,' called out the barmaid in the gloom as Brooke's unidentified shape entered. 'Mind her bloody bottles, Sergeant,' said Brooke, turning to his driver. Sergeant Parker, the driver, was very close in spirit to Brooke. 'I've never known a greater gentleman,' he later said, adding: 'It was obvious the great majority of people were frightened of him.' It was always Parker's hand he would shake first, and after whose family he would enquire after returning from some trip abroad.[24]

There had been few but precious days of relaxation. He often managed to take Sundays with the family at Ferney Close, 'such a paradise'. From his nephew Basil's wife he would receive letters with news of Colebrooke which gave him '*such* joy'. Sometimes fleeting contacts with friends and family would be worked into his tours. 'I felt hardly flattered by Augusta Bute's comparison of me with her father when he was young,' he wrote to Benita after one such. 'He was a Papist for whom we had little use!'[25] Lady Bute was his first cousin, a Bellingham niece of his mother, and in spite of this rather intemperate reaction about his uncle it had always been observed that Alan had more Bellingham than Brooke in his appearance. Wherever he went he tried to find occasions to mix a little of the things he loved with the things he had to do. A diary entry on 14th May 1941:

Discussed defence arrangements [for Scapa Flow] with Binney, then left with Kemp for main island and proceeded to visit two new aerodromes near Twatt and their defences. From there on to the cliff near Kitchener's Memorial, where we watched a peregrine falcon on her nest, also fulmars and guillemots. Back to Stromness for lunch and then to Kirkwall aerodrome to emplane for Shetland. Very good fly over except for occasional snow squalls. After one hour's flight, landed south end of island and had tea with Black Watch. Then inspected defence of south end of island, and from there to Cunningham's Headquarters in Lerwick. After dinner, at 9 p.m. started off for the Bird Sanctuary on the Isle of Noss. Blowing fairly hard, sea rather rough, and odd snow storms, but most interesting. Wonderful 600 ft cliff covered with gannets, guillemots, kitti-wakes and a few cormorants. Also fulmars in the air and an odd great skua diving down on to the gannets. We took with us the Town Clerk who is a great bird authority and had worked with the Kearton brothers in the old days. Got back to Lerwick after 11 p.m., bitterly cold but a very interesting evening.

On one occasion a trip was organized to the Farne Islands. Brooke was hung with cinematograph impedimenta, and eagerly stepping from the small naval vessel on which he had been ferried he lost his footing and disappeared (equipment and all) beneath the waves to the consternation of everybody, very particularly including the young naval officer in charge.[26]

In June 1941:

A weekend of bird photography with fly-catchers, young swallows, house martins and young sparrow hawks, again did marvels in temporarily wiping out the war and all its anxieties.

And a month later:

The weekend of 5/6th July was a red letter day from the point of view of bird photography. I discovered a wryneck nesting in a large nesting box I had put up for woodpeckers. This was a great find and I proceeded to put up a hide and took coloured film. It may well be imagined that such an important event as a wryneck nesting in the garden put the war and all its troubles right out of my mind during those happy hours. I returned to my work a new man.

And in August, after watching an exercise by Polish forces in Scotland:

After the exercise drove on to Milden to shoot with Ivan Cobbold for 3 days. Arrived back about tea-time, all guns still out shooting. They arrived back for a late tea, consisting of

Cobbold, his wife, daughter and two boys, John Astor, Bertie Brooke, Humphrey de Trafford, and Astor's boy.

He wrote later:

> Then followed three lovely days shooting with 281, 132 and 160 brace of grouse. Days during which the war receded into the dim distance! On 25th August I picked up my plane in Montrose and flew back to shoulder the burdens again.[27]

It is a remarkable fact that Brooke, on the vast majority of days during the war, whether as Commander-in-Chief or later, not only completed a diary entry for Benita's eyes but wrote to her as well. Often diary and letters covered the same ground – but he seemed to get satisfaction from writing of his love as often as possible, and he found it not a chore but a relief to pour himself out at such length. His letters contain much about family affairs and domestic arrangements, but they also describe his days and the way they had been filled. Both diary and correspondence can be criticized for indiscretion and at times for less than a perfect sense of security. However, this was his way and the fault, if it was fault, was indispensable to the man's performance and thus to his service to his country.

His letters would be written however late the hour or exhausting the day. Again and again, as the war proceeded, can be found letters which quickly recount a hectic string of meetings, interviews, reports and meetings again and –

> It is now 11.30 p.m. and just home.

But still he had to write, 'It is very late and I am very sleepy so this is just a short word of love.'

Benita made rare and precious visits to London from Ferney Close, where she was fully occupied with two small children and the maintenance of a home for his occasional weekends or Sundays. Sometimes a child would come too, and these were Brooke's oases in the desert of war.

> 'I cannot tell you how much I enjoyed my lunch with you and Mr Ti [Victor] today! It was just a bit of heaven interspersed in a very drab day. First the joy that very impetuous greeting by the wee Ti hunting me out, then finding you like a bit of heaven that I longed to wrap my arms around – ' He wrote of
> 'those two beloved wee things, they are a source of endless joy and amusement to me, probing into their minds and watching

their reactions to this wonderful world (in spite of all wars) which they have been born in'.

'I love the feel of him [Victor]' he wrote after another visit, 'in the toy department, his little hand almost quivering with excitement on mine, pulling gently (like a fish on a line!) in the direction in which he wants to go!'[28]

In October 1941 Brooke submitted to the CIGS, Dill, a proposed list of new appointments to Army and Corps Commands. But more considerable changes in the High Command of the Army were afoot. Dill had had an unhappy time. He could not get on terms with Churchill or his methods of work. He had had a very painful period in his personal life. He lived on his nerves and was exhausted. On 13th November he told Brooke that his departure from the office of CIGS was, he was sure, imminent. He made clear that he hoped Brooke would succeed him, although there were other contenders, such as General Pile. Brooke had already heard from Pownall (VCIGS) that Pile was a possibility and that Beaverbrook was pushing the idea – an idea that Brooke regarded as thoroughly unsuitable.

The diary entry for Sunday 16th November is probably one where instantly recorded impressions convey the truest record!

> Spent morning putting goat cart together again after its painting. [This was a goat cart he had made for the children on odd Sundays at home] At 5.30 p.m. left for Chequers. Found party consisting of Mountbatten, the 'Prof', Pug Ismay and self. Mrs Churchill was there for dinner.
>
> After dinner PM took me off to his study and told me that as Dill had had a very hard time and was a tired man, he wanted to relieve him. That he would be made a Field-Marshal and Governor of Bombay.
>
> He then went on to say that he wanted me to take over from Dill and asked me whether I was prepared to do so. It took me some time to reply, as I was torn by many feelings. I hated the thought of old Dill going, and our very close association coming to an end. I hated the thought of what this would mean to him. The thought of the magnitude of the job and the work entailed took the wind out of my sails. The fact that the extra work and ties would necessarily mean seeing far less of you tore at my heart strings. And finally a feeling of sadness at having to give up Home Forces after having worked them up to their present pitch.
>
> The PM misunderstood my silence and said: 'Do you not think you will be able to work with me? We have so far got on well

together.' I had to assure him that these were not my thoughts, though I am fully aware that my path will not be strewn with rose petals! But I have the greatest respect for him and real affection for him so that I hope I may be able to stand the storms of abuse which I may well have to bear frequently!

He then went on to explain the importance he attached to the appointment, and the fact that the Chiefs of Staff Committee must be the body to direct events over the whole world. He also stated his relations with me must from now on approximate to those of a Prime Minister to one of his Ministers.

Nobody could be nicer than he was, and finally, when we went to bed at 2 a.m., he came with me to my bedroom to get away from the others, took my hand and looking into my eyes with an exceptionally kind look, said: 'I wish you the very best of luck.'

I got into bed with my brain in a whirl trying to fathom the magnitude of the task I am about to take on. I have no false conception as to the magnitude of this task and of the doubts whether I shall be able to compete with it. If it was peace time I should love to try it, but in war the responsibility is almost overwhelming. The consequences of failures or mistakes are a nightmare to think of.

I pray God from the very bottom of my heart that He may give me guidance, and be at my side in the times I may have to go through.

And then I have you. Oh! my darling, as my lighthouse in all stormy seas. Bless you for the help which you are to me.

Many many thoughts kept galloping through my head and by 4 a.m. I was still tossing about without sleep.

CHAPTER IX

Chief of the Imperial General Staff

BROOKE BECAME CIGS on Christmas Day, 1941. Since Dill was undertaking a farewell term, Brooke had several weeks' indoctrination, and first took his place in the War Office on 1st December.

The congratulatory letters, telegrams and messages flowed in. Field-Marshals wrote, old Artillerymen wrote, de Gaulle wrote. Brooke felt that he might have appeared somewhat ungracious in his acceptance of office, and wrote to the Prime Minister to say so. The reply struck the perfect note:

> My dear Brooke,
>
> Thank you for your letter. I did not expect that you would be grateful or overjoyed at the hard, anxious task to which I summoned you. But I feel that my old friendship for Ronnie and Victor, the companions of gay subaltern days and early wars is a personal bond between us to which will soon be added the comradeship of action in fateful events.
>
> Yours sincerely,
>
> Winston S. Churchill

In fact, Brooke had not been Churchill's first choice as CIGS. The Prime Minister had thought of General Nye, and Beaverbrook had pressed on him the presentational advantage of a man promoted from the ranks, as Nye had been. Nye, although to prove a VCIGS of outstanding merit, was far younger and less experienced and would have been in an impossible position. Nye himself was in no doubt of the right choice – Churchill discussed the matter with him in November and he told the Prime Minister that Brooke was the 'only one conceivable choice'. Churchill's response was prescient:

> When I thump the table and push my face towards him what does he do? Thumps the table harder and glares back at me – I know these Brookes – stiff-necked Ulstermen and there's no one worse to deal with than that![1]

Nye apart, there were other eyebrows lifted at the appointment of Brooke. Portal, for one, reckoned he might prove too abrupt. He changed his mind, although right to the end Portal sometimes thought him tactless, with his frequent contribution of 'I flatly disagree'. But by then Portal, like all others, recognized him as the one man large enough and strong enough for the job, and utterly fair minded in it. Churchill had had misgivings. 'I don't think we'll get on' he had said. But in a sunlit moment months later he said to the Secretary of State for War: 'Brooke was the right man – the only man.'[2]

The family poured messages on him – Basil Brooke, the companion in vulture skinning, and now a prominent Ulster Minister writing to 'Dearest Uncle', the family filled with pride and love, his sister Hylda, now Lady Wrench, beginning as she often did, '*Mon précieux petit Cognac*'. Brooke was still at times the 'little Benjamin' of the family. Lady Wrench would finish a letter: '*Oh mon chéri que Dieu te benisse et te garde, si tu savais comme je t'aime.*' It is probable that the most agreeable letters whether from loved ones such as she, or remote acquaintances, were those which invoked images of a carefree past to add to their rejoicing:

> 'My mind has been going back,' wrote his sister, 'to your long ago birthdays and to the wonderful cake castles Laurent used to make with their fairy turrets and the little ponds with duck floating on them . . .'

and from another correspondent on a different note:

> Do you remember marching down from Meerut to Moultan en route for Karachi? The writer has a very special reason for remembering one incident during that march – it concerns yourself Sir. Your papers for entry to the Staff College were due in and there had been some little delay with them. Due to some stupidity on my part (I was Colonel's Clerk in those days) the papers nearly missed the boat altogether! I well remember that when you were recounting certain high spots in my pedigree to me those Irish eyes were NOT smiling. Captain Boucher was the Adjutant at the time. His telling off was just like a gentle breeze compared to the hurricane I had from you.[3]

Montgomery's congratulation was terse: 'The whole Army wants you on that job.' And General Loyd, who had taken over from Paget as Brooke's Chief of Staff at Home Forces, wrote simply, 'You have the Army 100% behind you.' As usual Gort, now commanding in Gibraltar, wrote generously: 'Everybody in

Gibraltar, myself included, is delighted to serve under your leadership.' Brooke always answered personal letters from high or low promptly, and generally in his own hand. Indeed, in the following year, having received a letter with some helpful suggestion for the prosecution of the war from an assistant cook in the Merchant Navy, the writer was astonished to receive a reply in the strong handwriting and customary green ink of the CIGS:

> I regret not having answered your letter of 13th [August] earlier but this was due to absence in Egypt and Russia. I read your letter with great interest and was much impressed with the spirit in which you put forward your suggestions. I can assure you that your proposal will be carefully examined. With many thanks for your kind assistance . . .[4]

Brooke, like Wellington, believed in the swift and punctilious dispatch of business, and no correspondent could ever have detected in the CIGS, whatever his preoccupations and responsibilities, any touch of pomposity, impatience or patronage.

The post of Chief of the Imperial General Staff, which Brooke now assumed, had had a comparatively short history. The name imperfectly described the function, but he became in effect the senior military member of the Army Council and the professional head of the Army.*

The CIGS's second function was to act as the Army member of the Chiefs of Staff Committee. This Committee, established in 1923 as a subcommittee of the Committee of Imperial Defence, had, by formal warrant, 'a collective responsibility for advising on defence policy as a whole'. When the Second World War began the Committee of Imperial Defence (whose function had been advisory rather than executive) passed into history. A War Cabinet was reborn, and the Chiefs of Staff Committee came into its own as the joint body charged with the supreme direction of military operations, responsible collectively to the Government. It consisted of the three Chiefs of Staff of the three Fighting Services.

Two facets of the Chiefs of Staff Committee stand out. First, in and before the war of 1914–18 it had not existed. Co-ordination of military plans between the two Services had not, therefore, been systematic, and there was no tradition of reconciling opposed philosophies. Second, the global nature of the Second World War, as well as the new dimension added to warfare by air power, made

---

* For background to the creation of the post see Appendix II.

such reconciliation – or resolution – essential. In the First World War, as far as the Army was concerned, the overwhelming effort was on the Western Front. In the struggle of 'Easterners' against 'Westerners' the latter had carried the day at all points. Although subsidiary campaigns – in the Dardanelles, in Mesopotamia, in Palestine – were undertaken, it was on the Western Front that principal resources had been committed. Operational recommendations and decisions on that front lay with the Commander-in-Chief. The CIGS had had, as a prime function, to support the man on the spot, which in the cases of Robertson and Haig he did with efficiency and conviction. In the Second World War, on the other hand, there were a considerable number of permutations of strategy, each making different demands on the allocation of resources. There were decisions to be made on the relative priorities of different theatres of war, from the Far East to Europe, and within Europe between the Mediterranean and the Western Front. There was the question of our sea communications, and of the consequences, not only for the nation's survival but for its ability to support any overseas operations at all, if those communications were not secured. There was the question of the best use of air power. In such matters, more complex than hitherto, the 'collective responsibility for advising on defence policy' lay – and in the view of all its members rightly lay – with that Committee each of whose members was the professional head of his own Service, supported as to his advice by the collective expertise of that Service, and himself responsible for the Service's effectiveness and well-being.

Brooke had studied the higher direction of war at length when at the Imperial Defence College. He was convinced, as were all his colleagues during his time on the Committee, that no 'Great General Staff' (as conceived by Fuller, cf. Chapter V), divorced from the Service Departments, would be satisfactory or acceptable. In his view the votes that counted in the Chiefs of Staff Committee were those of the heads of the Services, each connected to the body of his own Service. In effect each was Commander-in-Chief of his Service, and therein lay his strength.

Brooke – and all of them – extended this view to the Chairmanship of the Committee. The idea was periodically canvassed of an 'independent' chairman, standing apart from the presumed parochialism of his colleagues when some matter of inter-Service contention was in debate. Brooke and his fellow Chiefs would have none of it, and Churchill supported them. In their view they had a duty to resolve a problem if it could be resolved by reason – tempered by such compromise as conscience could permit. If it could not be so resolved then a major point of strategic priority or of principle must be at stake. In that case it could, and should, only be resolved at the political level. If a matter were professional they hammered it out until it was presentable. If it involved wider issues of principle they were always ready to lay it before the Prime Minister with each propounding his own case. Their Chairman existed as one of themselves, to preside over their deliberations but most certainly not as their superior. He was their representative spokesman – and thus *de facto* the senior strategic adviser to the Government – on certain occasions; but he spoke on such occasions with their authority. At Cabinet all attended.

This collective identity was achieved only after hard and sometimes bitter dispute, but it played a vital part in the history of the Second World War. It was assisted by the personalities concerned. Brooke served on the Chiefs of Staff Committee with two First Sea Lords – Admiral Pound and Admiral Cunningham – and with one Chief of the Air Staff, Air-Marshal Portal. All were men personally congenial to each other, and however tough their conduct of debate their mutual respect and affection became profound. Brooke, Portal and Cunningham were the same sort of people, fighting men by instinct, countrymen at heart, keen fishermen, quick-witted, unostentatious. The Chairmanship was for the Prime Minister to select from among the three Chiefs of Staff. On 5th March 1942, within three months of becoming CIGS, Brooke was nominated Chairman in place of Admiral Pound, who continued loyally to serve as First Sea Lord under his chairmanship. Brooke remained Chairman of the Chiefs of Staff Committee until the end. He had been sharply critical of Pound's chairmanship, sleepiness and inexpeditious conduct of business on the occasions when, from Home Forces, he had attended the Committee. He regretted his strictures when he realized that the devoted old Admiral was dying. On his first day as Chairman his heart was touched by seeing how Pound – normally late for meetings – had scrupulously arrived early in order to sit in the First Sea Lord's place and thus quietly to emphasize his ready vacation of the Chair.[5]

The Second World War thus marked the debut of the Chiefs of Staff Committee as an instrument for the control of war. It was, above all, in and through the Chiefs of Staff Committee that Brooke made his contribution to history.

The Committee's composition has already been described. Attendance at meetings of the Committee, however, was variable, with a number of other officers or officials invited to attend, some on an almost permanent basis. The Committee was served by subcommittees and joint staffs, mirroring its own composition, of which the most important were the Joint Planning Committee and the Joint Intelligence Committee. Each of these consisted of a Director of Plans or a Director of Intelligence of each of the three Services. In the case of the Joint Planners the three Directors of Plans headed a Joint Planning Staff, in the sense that it was not drawn from the Single Service Staffs in the Service Ministries but had an independent existence from them and negotiated with them. Directors of Plans would consider a policy or planning document which had already been discussed between the Services and with all other interested Ministries or bodies in Whitehall. They would attempt to produce an agreed paper or to define the points of fundamental as opposed to peripheral disagreement, and in so doing they would be representing their Chiefs of Staff. The Directors of Intelligence had a similar function of exchange, co-ordination and reconciliation: because of the nature of Intelligence and the variety of the sources of information which compose it, the Joint Intelligence Committee was chaired by an official of the Foreign Office, and was not supported by an integrated set of Joint Intelligence Teams like the Planning Staff but by a system of subcommittees drawing on a wide spectrum of agencies.

Other Committees, too numerous to catalogue, answered to the Chiefs of Staff Committee, of which mention should be made of the Principal Administrative Officers Committee consisting of the Senior Logistics Officer of each Fighting Service, supported by a Joint Administrative Planning Staff. Three additional points and personalities require particular note.

First the entire system was flexible. In theory an idea would be launched (from on high, or from the Staff or from overseas; very frequently from on high). It would be subjected to analysis and consultation with all Ministries, staffs or agencies whose interests could be affected or who could be required to contribute. Drafts would be produced and debated, and ultimately a paper would be presented to the Chiefs of Staff. The process could, and frequently had to, be considerably abbreviated, and the lines with other parallel work had to be kept unravelled. This demanded above all a very skilful and clear-headed Secretariat. The Secretariat (deriving from the Secretariat of the Committee of Imperial

Defence, and from the original genius of Hankey) not only recorded proceedings and ensured that consequential action was taken. They not only saw to it that business was attended to without delay so that decisions could be timely – itself a major art where the programmes of busy men are concerned. They were also responsible that all parts of the machine serving the War Cabinet were meshed; that, where the attendance of a particular notable from a concerned Ministry was necessary at short notice, he was present and briefed; that where the calendar did not permit of more than one stage of business although reason and difficulties might demand at least four, one stage was made to suffice; that what had been agreed or disagreed was known to all who needed, and was not known by those who did not; and that the Secretariat of the War Cabinet (of which the Chiefs of Staff Secretariat in effect formed the Military Secretariat) was sufficiently apprised, for the information of the Ministers, of the proceedings of their professional advisers. The importance of this Secretariat and the brilliance of its principal members may not have constituted the most flamboyant stuff of history, but its contribution was unrivalled.

Second, it should be noted that to the Chiefs of Staff Committee there came to be added another member, who attended 'when appropriate', the 'Chief of Combined Operations' (CCO). Admiral Lord Louis Mountbatten occupied this post from March 1942 until his appointment as Supreme Commander in South East Asia Command eighteen months later. It was not an inclusion which Brooke thought appropriate although he enjoyed Mountbatten's enthusiasm, while giving vent to periodic explosions of irritation.

Third, no description of the Chiefs of Staff Committee and its working would be accurate without reference and tribute to the personality of General Ismay.

Ismay was formally head of the Military Secretariat: he had been an early member of the Secretariat of the Committee of Imperial Defence, which had 'fathered' or been transmuted into the War Cabinet Secretariat and he knew Whitehall forwards, backwards and sideways. When Churchill became Prime Minister he promptly (and rightly) assumed the additional office of Minister of Defence, and henceforth Ismay was also entitled 'Principal Staff Officer to the Minister of Defence'. As such he attended, as of right, all meetings of the Chiefs of Staff Committee. Such a post could have been a source of constant friction.

Instead it provided an unfailing emollient. Had Ismay sought to intrude his personal views as opposed to those of the Chiefs of Staff, or to act as their spokesman in place of their Chairman; had he used his friendship with and access to the Prime Minister, to whom he was entirely congenial (as he was to all), in order to extend his own influence as many would have been tempted to do, bitter mistrust would have been sown. Instead this man of complete integrity, using his gifts of charm, patience, tact, humour, and a pliancy which was never weakness on a point of principle, made business between Churchill and the Chiefs of Staff Committee effective. Ismay knew – none better – when and how Churchill could be handled on particular issues. He knew his Chiefs of Staff – corporately and individually – and they knew him and trusted him and loved him. To Brooke, who admired him deeply, he was an indispensable part of the machine. He interpreted strong men to each other without usurping the authority of any. Although having a seat at the Chiefs of Staff table he never signed the documents which represented their professional advice and theirs alone.

When the Committee's deliberations required executive instructions to field or fleet commanders it was customary for the Single Service Staffs to act on remit from the Chiefs of Staff Secretariat, who would record that a particular Chief of Staff had been so invited. In the case of Supreme Commanders abroad, instructions were generally initiated by the Secretariat itself. When a paper was required to be provided to the Prime Minister or the War Cabinet – and this was very frequent – it would be placed before the Defence Committee of the Cabinet (select Ministers chaired by the Prime Minister) or before the War Cabinet itself. Again, the attendance was flexible, and again stages could be eliminated and corners cut. Sometimes Churchill as Minister of Defence would himself hold a meeting with the Chiefs of Staff alone. War is probably the most complex of human activities and no method of directing it can be perfect. It has been a frequent temptation in democracies to look with envy at alien methods, where the whole military and administrative machinery of the state has been concentrated in one pair of hands. Such dictatorial systems have clear and seductive attractions, when the needs of the moment appear to demand speed of decision, and authority rather than consultation. Yet beneath autocracy private empires and mutually suspicious cabals flourish even more vigorously than within more free societies, to the general disadvantage. Nor is there any evidence that failures – and all wars record failures – in British conduct of the Second World War stemmed from lack of authority in its central direction. Taken all in all it may surely be said that the system which evolved was admirable for its purpose, and that the errors which occurred derived from human rather than organizational fallibility.

It remains to mention the extension of the system which followed the United States' entry into war.

The British Chiefs of Staff, by using the military missions attached to Dominion High Commissions in London as well as by direct contacts with their opposite numbers in the Dominions and with the Commander-in-Chief in India, were able to represent to the Americans the whole Empire – although there was much initial disquiet on the part of Australia and New Zealand about the representation of their views, both political and military, after Japan attacked. A British Military Mission in Washington largely reflected in microcosm the British Chiefs of Staff organization. As the need to co-ordinate strategy became clearly a matter not of periodic meetings at the summit (although these were necessary and occurred) but of continuous work, there was born the Combined Chiefs of Staff Committee, based in Washington, on which Dill was the permanent British Member, sitting opposite the Chairman of the American Joint Chiefs of Staff. The Combined Chiefs of Staff came to be served by a Combined Staff, analogous to the Joint Staffs at home. A plenary meeting at a 'summit' of the Combined Chiefs would be attended by the Chiefs of Staff Committees of both nations; thereafter the professional advisers of the two great Western Powers would meet together with President and Prime Minister to argue out and receive the ultimate endorsement, and to take the next step along the hard road.

The machinery of Government, even Government at war, makes dry stuff, dissected. There was nothing dry in practice in the way the machine worked. The personality of Churchill, his restless energy, his determination to be involved in every aspect of the national war effort, his passionate interest in military history and military affairs, and his fertile imagination made life for the Government's professional advisers often tempestuous but never dull. Churchill, on assuming office, had wished to surround himself with a personal 'Cabinet' of unofficial advisers, mostly men who had supported him in the political wilderness, and who would have had no Ministerial or professional responsibility.

Such a system would have been disastrous, not least because Churchill's judgement of dependable counsellors was by no means infallible. In the end, however, and largely due to the tact and adroitness of Ismay, he settled down with and came deeply to trust 'the machine', however much he growled at it. After some particular passage of arms Brooke would return to the War Office fuming. 'Impossible, quite impossible,' he would snap at a General Staff Director summoned to hear the worst. 'That man! That man!' Then a tired but infectious smile would touch his austere features and he would quietly say, 'But *what* would we do without him?'[6]

Thus Brooke, on taking over as CIGS, had the twofold task of devoting his mind and energies to the grand strategic questions of the hour, and the readiness of the Army to play its part in their resolution; and of establishing and enforcing a relationship with all Army Commanders or Commanders-in-Chief which would ensure his authority and therefore his discharge of responsibility.

The Chiefs of Staff Committee was concerned with the overall direction of war. The demanding nature of such business meant that Brooke, as CIGS, delegated most of the running of the General Staff Directorates in the War Office to his Vice or Deputy Chief. Although he held overall responsibility, his own days were not spent on the affairs of the Army except the most fundamental questions of principle or of personalities. They were spent in discussion with his colleagues, the heads of the other two Services; increasingly with Allied Chiefs as the war progressed; and, above all, with the Prime minister. Yet his personality could be felt throughout the War Office. He now more than ever 'Talked fast, moved fast, thought fast'. He expected others to do the same. He at once agreed to the reorganization of his private office in a way which made it as briskly efficient as himself. He was peremptory. 'Hurry, man, hurry!' he would call to a General, spotted in the War Office corridor and summoned by name as a thought came to the CIGS's mind.[7] Above all, he exercised from the first day an absolute and unquestioned authority over Army Commanders in the field. In the Second World War, not only because of its nature, the number and variety of theatres of operations, and the comparative complexity of the strategic problems, but also because of the personalities involved, the CIGS had to be and was in fact if not in name the Commander-in-Chief of the Army. Thus Brooke exercised general superintendence over what was already and would increasingly be a huge expansion and modernization of the British Army. It was not an Army of concentrated and uniform divisions in one theatre as in the First World War. Instead it was deployed world-wide, with all that implied in separate and complex logistic support, costly both in infrastructure and men. Brooke was responsible overall for this vast enterprise. His method of discharging the responsibility was to select colleagues and subordinates wisely, and to trust them, while remaining accessible and with sensitive antennae for the principal problems – or those likely to attract the Prime Minister's enthusiastic or disparaging attention. In all this Brooke had the unfailing support of the Secretary of State for War, P. J. Grigg who took over from Captain David (later Lord) Margesson early in Brooke's tenure of office. Brooke, in his turn, did his utmost to help Grigg whose path was not always easy, as when his Parliamentary Secretary (Mr Duncan Sandys), in Brooke's view, sought to undermine Grigg's authority by misusing his position as Churchill's son-in-law. Brooke's personal record of these manoeuvres (as he saw them) was severe: he invoked Eden's help to straighten matters out.[8] At all times his relationship with Grigg was close and cordial and their mutual trust was entire.

Brooke selected Commanders, or argued the selection of his nominees with a sometimes querulous Churchill. Once selected he supported them to the hilt. Even when he had some inner doubts he took the part of Commanders in the field, unless or until he became convinced they were mistaken or inadequate. Where he trusted their operational and tactical judgement he never attempted to override it. If they, in turn, sought to step outside their proper sphere or to use improper channels of communication he showed them who was master in no uncertain terms. The achievements of the successful theatre and Army Commanders in the Second World War have been amply recorded and justly praised. Behind and above each, guiding, supporting or admonishing stood Brooke.

Towards Commanders in the field Brooke started as he meant to continue. Churchill liked to send personal messages to these Commanders and to receive equally personal replies on matters of substance and sometimes of detail. Brooke wrote to Auchinleck in the Middle East a few days after taking Dill's chair:

> I sent you a wire as regards your private telegrams to the Prime Minister. It is, of course, very desirable that you should send private telegrams direct to PM in reply to his and to keep him

informed as to the general course of events, yet I do not think that this should in any way affect the normal channel which should exist between you and the War Office. The extensive use of private telegrams has caused confusion here at times owing to important messages never reaching either DMO, DMI or myself. In addition the flow of military information and instructions connected with the use of reserves, etc., direct between you and the PM is apt to make my position difficult at times.

I therefore hope that whilst maintaining the necessary flow of information by direct messages to the PM you will ensure that such a procedure does not affect the normal channel of communications to me which should exist between us.

The message was clear.[9] Furthermore, in the nine days before so writing, Brooke had had but little chance to find his position 'difficult at times'. Nor was he the man to accept an inherited difficulty on the report of others. One occasion sufficed. He never failed to make plain to all Commanders in the Army who stood at the Army's head. It was periodically necessary to impress upon a somewhat reluctant Churchill the same point. Nor, hard though he and his colleagues tried, was it always possible to interpose between the Minister of Defence and Commanders in the field on matters of high policy. In fact Brooke spent a great deal of time advising them, in long personal letters in longhand, on how to present their views to Churchill, how to deal with the vigorous probes of the Prime Minister in a way which would gain support rather than provoke exasperation. In such correspondence Brooke was a helpful, understanding and wise counsellor. Yet from first to last he never tolerated questioning of his authority. When Montgomery, the war safely over, proposed the establishment of some post on his staff in Germany, using the language of demand rather than request, the victorious Field-Marshal received from the CIGS a reply which started with the uncompromising words 'I dislike the whole tone of your message and have not been accustomed to receiving such . . .' Nor was it only Army Commanders who felt the lash. Mountbatten, as Supreme Commander South East Asia, once sent Brooke a telegram using the words 'If the Army cannot from their resources assist me with a suitable Chief of Staff . . .' The response was icy. 'I take exception,' signalled Brooke, 'to the tone of your telegram, which fails entirely to take into account the fact that there are other active fronts beyond South East Asia.' He would accompany such exchanges with a friendly letter, and apply a salve: but he cut first.

Brooke was not an easy master to serve. He was demanding, intolerant where he 'took against' a subordinate and thought him below his very exacting standards. Yet behind the dedicated, apparently rigorous professional man was that other entirely human side, as there always had been. Soon after his arrival at the War Office in the mornings he tended to pay a regular call to one of its wash-places, on leaving which he would often be ambushed by a particular member of the ancient and admirable tribe of messengers who serve the establishment:

'Well Guv'nor, how are things going?'

the latter would often ask, and as often the CIGS would stop and say:

'Well, I'll tell you.'

Then Brooke would stand and talk – for a good many minutes – freely and informatively and give out a little of himself in such informal surroundings, talking of his chief concerns, talking of the country's dangers and chances, talking simply as one man to another, talking about the war.[10]

As CIGS Brooke showed, magnified and extended by the scale of the task, exactly the characteristics, with all their remarkable qualities and a few human imperfections, which he had brought to all duties throughout his life.

He was impatient and hasty with some subordinates and could be ruthless to those whom he thought inadequate.[11] He was hardest on seniors, most approachable to comparative juniors. The latter remembered him as a stern taskmaster but invariably courteous and never overbearing. To Generals and the like, however, his manner could be forbidding in the extreme. He had a habit of continuing what he was doing, completely absorbed, without apparently noticing another's presence until he would suddenly raise his penetrating gaze and utter a staccato question or phrase. But if they showed that they were good enough they not only survived but gave their Chief their absolute devotion, for the perceptive among them – and few who were not stayed the course on the General Staff – knew that whatever the stresses under which Brooke laboured he would fight the battle for what he thought right with absolute integrity and unwavering strength. Nevertheless Brooke, although as ever the best of companions to the few included in his intimacy, was never what is known as a 'clubbable' man. He did not induce relaxation. It was remarked that when the Chiefs of Staff travelled together, perhaps to some major conference, Brooke seldom put in more than a brisk formal appearance at any social gathering. On other occasions there would be a whisper as he approached: 'The CIGS'. Then his appearance was remembered afterwards as having an electric effect on even exalted Staff Officers, who clicked to attention, their carriage stiffer, their manner rather more formal, their answers quicker than when talking to one of the other Chiefs. The respect felt for him by those in the General Staff and in Whitehall generally was thought by observers to be second only to that extended to Churchill himself. If he had to bite he bit hard. General Browning, who commanded an Airborne Division and later an Airborne Corps was summoned to see the CIGS. He had been 'writing to politicians' said Brooke. Browning was himself a formidable superior, but he emerged from a few minutes interview, scarlet in the face, gathered his Staff Officer waiting in the outer office and hastened away. 'Come on,' he said, 'I've had the biggest dressing down of my life – but My God he's a great man!'

The art of strategy is to determine the aim, which is or should be inherently political: to derive from that aim a series of military objectives to be achieved: to assess these objectives as to the military requirements they create, and the preconditions which the achievement of each is likely to necessitate: to measure available and potential resources against the requirements: and to chart from this process a coherent pattern of priorities and a rational course of action. Brooke summed up the elements of the task as prevision, preplanning and provision. He did not on the whole originate ideas. Unlike Dill he was not particularly imaginative, which may have made him more robust. He received ideas and put them through the realistic computer of his mind, came to a judgement, and expressed it with a clarity which nobody exposed to it ever forgot, and with a strength and balance hard to withstand. He absorbed with great speed and complete attention, so that the work he got through was prodigious. Although the demands of strategy and major war-making policy, the concerns of Chiefs of Staff Committee and War Cabinet, took much of Brooke's time, the General Staff obtained his broad views on major issues of Army policy and then Nye, the VCIGS, would relieve him to the maximum degree possible of concern with detail. He rarely attended throughout full meetings of the Army Council, the formal body which, under the chairmanship of the Secretary of State for War, ran the Army. He left it to his colleagues, Nye and General Weeks, a brilliant businessman turned General, who had been imported to the War Office as Deputy CIGS. These would represent his views – although on formal business affecting some point 'neutral' to the General Staff (as, for instance, when it was proposed by Adam, the Adjutant-General, that saluting should be discontinued out of barracks or off duty!) Nye and Weeks would give their own independent views when Brooke was there. On such occasions Brooke tended to support Adam on the Adjutant-General's own ground (on the saluting issue he did so, and was outvoted by other members including Nye), probably to some extent by an instinct to let the responsible Council Member have his own way, possibly by a rather less defensible loyalty to an old brother officer of 'N' Battery. It can be a point of criticism against Brooke that mistakes made in the organization and manning of the Army, and in its interior economy and discipline in the Second World War – and there were a significant number – were not particularly attended to by the Army's professional head. As an example General Slim, in a trenchant paper from Fourteenth Army about the Infantry, its neglect in peace and maltreatment in war in spite of its paramount importance, strongly attacked the massive abandonment of the Regimental system in reinforcement, so that men were 'rebadged' without sense or sympathy, a policy which however theoretically flexible was more than counterweighted by loss of Regimental identity and of morale. Many agreed with him. Brooke stood back from such questions, but they mattered. The fact is that his military preoccupations were global and strategic, and there were not enough minutes in the day for them also to be organizational and domestic. His main arena was the Chiefs of Staff Committee.[12]

At the Chiefs of Staff Committee he attained mastery without delay. He started with genuine modesty. 'I'm new to this,' he said to an attendant and junior Joint Planning Staff Officer before the first meeting he attended. 'If you see me making a fool of myself, say so!'; and to the same, six months later, without affectation, 'How am I doing?'[13] He was always at his best with younger people.

He was exceptionally bad at finding the right document in the 'pack' of flagged documents before him. 'Where is it? I know I've got the thing somewhere!' he would mutter. He was, however, a master of timing. He would often sit with half-closed eyes, giving to others a feeling of inner tension and profound concentration. At other times he would fasten his gaze on the speaker, staring at him intently, absolutely still. When he intervened it would never be too early or too late, so that his point was made decisively in time, and with lucidity and brevity. He never wasted a word.[14]

Where Brooke was, as sometimes happened, criticized for tactlessness it would more generally be by Service officers with their instinctive sense of hierarchy than by Ministers, to whom political hard knocks are common currency. Brooke's often brutal and decisive rejections sometimes shocked the courteous Ismay, or even Mountbatten. To Eden, on the other hand, he always appeared to strike exactly the right note – rocklike and uncompromising on what was professionally right, utterly rational in exposition, never losing sight of essentials and always keeping matters exactly in balance.[15] To some Brooke appeared obstinate to the point of error: to others tenacious to perfection. These are reverse sides of one coin. All agreed that he was incapable of dissimulation, weakness or ambiguity. It was such a man that Churchill needed. Churchill had enormous vision. He could and often did impressively surpass his supporters in his imaginative span. He was capable of seeing the war as a whole and envisaging how it might be won. But in relating resources to options, so that what was strategically desirable could be actually effected and sustained, Churchill, above all men, needed strong, objective and completely professional advice, robustly conveyed. He had the imagination and the energy and the faith: he needed not stimulus but discipline. It was inevitable that this discipline of inescapable facts had to be provided by his professional advisers, the Chiefs of Staff Committee. In providing it they needed frequently to adopt what appeared obstructive and unimaginative attitudes. But to hammer out a rational strategy involves absolute realism, just as its implementation needs not only resources but inspiring leadership. Churchill's leadership was inspiring indeed. It was the responsibility of others unflinchingly to inject the realism. At the forefront in the discharge of this responsibility was Brooke. All knew that to win the Chiefs of Staff Committee it was necessary to win Brooke. 'It's no good putting that up. The CIGS will never accept it,' Mountbatten would say. Or 'It's all right. I've got the backing of the CIGS.'[16] The CIGS seldom made a note. When listening, he would sometimes 'doodle' on a piece of paper – sometimes excellent sketches of his companions, but more often designs of swords – Crusader swords.[17]

CHAPTER X

Dark Winter

THE STRATEGIC SITUATION which Brooke inherited was very different from when he had taken over his previous appointment. A fundamental change in the world drama had taken place the previous summer. Operation BARBAROSSA, the attack on the Soviet Union, had begun in June 1941. It had started with impressive tactical successes. In spite of the numerical superiority of the enemy, both in men and armour, the German forces had fought a series of brilliant penetrating and encircling battles against the Red Army in the western districts of Russia, capturing huge numbers of prisoners, claiming over 12,000 tanks destroyed or taken.

These initial victories were spectacular. Indeed German campaigns on land had been so continuously successful that there appeared a sort of inevitability about them. To this was added a generally low opinion of the likely quality of Russian opposition. The Red Army had acquired a poor reputation for efficiency in the Winter War of 1940 against Finland: and it was known that the Officer Corps had been savagely diminished and demoralized by the great purges of the 1930s. Brooke had not been sanguine about Russian chances of holding out. The crucial question was whether she could. If not, it looked like being a very long war. Fear that Soviet resistance might lapse dominated much of Churchill's thinking, and of Roosevelt's perhaps even more. The Foreign Secretary, Eden, was about to visit Moscow, and Brooke's first days of office were largely occupied in preventing him taking in his pocket a promise to send two British divisions to fight on the South Russian front, a concept as laborious in administrative terms and ineffectual as to potential results as it was unsound in strategic priority.[1]

Yet it is easier to appreciate with hindsight than it was in the second half of 1941 that the German Eastern offensive was on too grand a scale for the limited resources available. It was true that BARBAROSSA was carried out by a very large number of divisions. Of these, however, only some twenty were armoured – and the tank numbers of each had been halved since the campaign in France and the Low Countries. 2700 German tanks had led the Blitzkrieg of May 1940. 3500, only 800 more, set out into the incomparably vaster spaces of Russia. The transport echelons of the armoured divisions were motorized. The great majority of German divisions were marching infantry with mainly horsed transport. The ordinary German soldier marched into Russia on his feet, and marched out again. The lack of roads, and their poor condition except when the weather was fair, was a critical factor. All this had, of course, been appreciated, and the German plan was based on cutting off and destroying the Red Army before it could conduct a deep withdrawal. But the Germans underestimated Russian resilience, Russian materiel both in quality and quantity, and the huge reserve of semi-trained manpower, employable in mass, drummed up from the Eastern districts of the Soviet Union.

The space to be covered, if decisive results were to be achieved against an enemy with plenty of room behind him, placed a premium on speed. Speed demanded energy, which was plentiful, luck which was variable, and a higher degree of cross-country all-weather mechanical performance than the German Army possessed. By December 1941 the German spearheads were still short of vital objectives, their lines of communication were greatly extended and their supply laborious. The Russian winter was serving its traditional purpose. The Red Army, in spite of great losses, was still in the field and starting a series of counter-offensives with massed manpower which were having a shattering effect, in bitter weather, on the Germans, largely unready for winter war. External supplies from Western Allies would play an increasing part in Russian success. Space and time were on their side. On the Eastern Front the Wehrmacht was ordered to stand, fight and freeze where it was. On 19th December Adolf Hitler dismissed Field-Marshal Von Brauchitsch and assumed personal command of the German Army. By the end of February that Army would already have suffered over one million casualties in BARBAROSSA. A severe oil shortage was making itself felt, and that factor alone was likely to make a campaign directed on the Caucasus with its oilfields attractive and even necessary. Beyond the Caucasus lay the Middle East.

The Battle of Britain had saved the country from invasion. The British Army, hastily expanded as a counter-invasion force, had now for some time been regarded as, once more, an expeditionary

Army for operations overseas. There was only one theatre where the enemy's land forces and those of the British Empire were engaged – the Middle East. Considerable reinforcements had been sent to North Africa from Brooke's Home Army during the preceding year.

The British Middle East Command was alert, and would become more so as the Germans reached the Caucasus, to the potential threat to their northern flank either through Persia or through a cowed or acquiescent Turkey. But the enemy at the gate was in the Western Desert. There the tide had ebbed and flowed. The German Afrika Korps had joined the Italian Army, composing a force under General Rommel which had, from the start, shown dazzling qualities of enterprise and audacity. Meanwhile on the British side General Auchinleck had replaced General Wavell as Commander-in-chief Middle East, responsible for a theatre which extended from Persia to Eritrea as well as including the entire North African shore. In the Western Desert, the Desert Army had been named 'Eighth Army' under the command of General Cunningham.

A British numerical superiority in tanks and aircraft had been built up for an offensive – Operation CRUSADER – launched in mid-November. The equipment of nine divisions, including some 700 tanks, had been assembled. By the time Brooke took over as Chief of the Imperial General Staff, the high point of the battle was approaching. Cunningham, an exhausted man, had been replaced by General Ritchie. Considerable casualties had been incurred by both sides, but the German siege of Tobruk had been lifted and the Germans were shortly to withdraw with greater proportionate losses. A significant slice of the North African desert had been cleared of the enemy. It was a victory. Yet a decisive result – the enemy's destruction – had not been achieved, although it would be some weeks before hope was abandoned. For a while Auchinleck's letters and signals still gave news of forward movement, prisoners taken, and the hope of catching the German/Italian forces under Rommel by a major manoeuvre. The mood did not last.

The only major offensive open to Britain was the strategic bombardment of Germany. There had been powerful differences of opinion about the best philosophy of attack. At the beginning of the war there had been a deliberate policy of avoidance of civilian casualties, and selection of only military targets. The escalation of conflict which began in the summer of 1940 had removed such moral constraints, and now not even lip service was paid to them

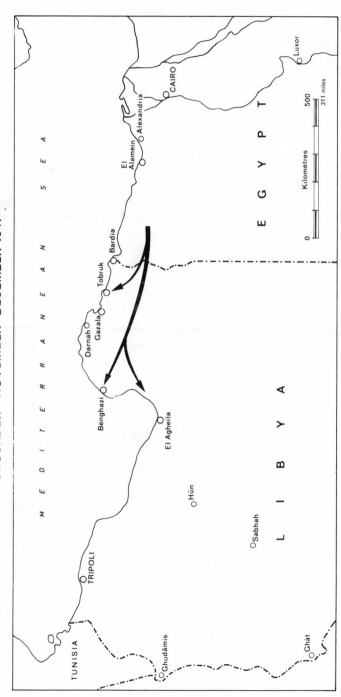

"CRUSADER" NOVEMBER-DECEMBER 1941

by the combatants. On the British side, from the winter of 1940, a policy of area bombing was consciously adopted, and in June 1941 the Chiefs of Staff had agreed that the morale of the German civilian population was the most vulnerable point of attack and that this morale had to be broken, with its presumed effect on German military morale, before a major land offensive on the mainland of Europe could be envisaged. Even then the size of the bomber force, whose increase was not proceeding at the pace planned, as well as the difficulties of targeting accuracy, made the bomber offensive an indecisive affair. There were divided counsels between those who put the attack on population centres – particularly those housing industrial workers – first, and those who believed that the most profitable target was the German transportation system. A July 1941 directive to Bomber Command had ordered concentration on both. Underlying both was the belief that by destroying industrial plant, by making it impossible to move materials except slowly and laboriously, and by inducing despair and terror in the workers themselves the German economy could be shattered.

This never happened to the extent hoped for. It was certainly not significantly under way at the end of 1941. Churchill, although devoted to this offensive, was, and remained, a sceptic as to the decisive effect likely to be attained by bombing alone. Nevertheless, Britain was attacking.

At sea the Battle of the Atlantic, on which depended British supplies from a friendly United States, had taken a temporary turn for the better before Brooke took office. The importance of transatlantic traffic could not be exaggerated. Stretching neutrality to the limits and beyond, the American people had started to turn their immense productive capacity to the manufacture of war materiel for embattled Britain. In the previous twelve months they had sent to her 2800 aircraft, 1000 tanks and nearly 13,000 trucks. 'We shall give every possible assistance to Britain' President Roosevelt had publicly proclaimed to the American nation in June 1941. American entry into the war must surely come: meanwhile the Germans took every precaution, and meekly accepted every distortion of generally accepted rules of neutrality, to delay or avert the day.

If supplies were to come to Britain the German U-boat fleet had to be mastered. It had increased fivefold since the summer of 1940 when Britain declined peace overtures and showed to Germany that she was in for a long war. Its toll on shipping had risen from about 100,000 tons a month to more than 300,000. The British Merchant Marine had lost nearly eight million tons or more than one-third of pre-war tonnage. But the U-boat menace in the Atlantic was by now briefly diminished. Defensive measures, air power and evasive routing had forced the Germans to confine submarine operations to the mid-Atlantic, and greatly to reduce them. Now they turned in force to the Mediterranean and the far north.

The submarine, which would reappear with devastating results when American shipping also became a target, was not, however, the only threat in the Atlantic. The German surface fleet which, apart from two old battleships fit only for use in the Baltic, had entered war with two battle cruisers and three commerce-raiding 'pocket battleships' had been reinforced by the most powerful warship afloat, the 42,000-ton *Tirpitz*. Her effect was to tie down, based in the Orkneys, two of the Royal Navy's fastest battleships, to pursue her should she break northwards into the Atlantic. *Bismarck*, *Tirpitz*'s sister ship, had done so during the summer, had sunk the Royal Navy's huge battle cruiser *Hood* and had finally herself been sunk. Thus the Atlantic convoys were threatened from the northern end of Europe's conquered coastline, while to the south the battle cruisers *Scharnhorst* and *Gneisenau*, after sinking twenty-two British merchant ships in the spring, lay in Brest awaiting an opportunity to break out, whether for offensive action or to seek escape from the incessant watch by submarines and reconnaissance aircraft which the British maintained. The European seaboard from the North Cape to the Spanish frontier was in German hands. Yet the situation in the Atlantic was by now temporarily better for Britain than it had been. It would remain the key to all.

Very different, however, was the Mediterranean. There the Italian fleet operated under-shore based air cover from a central position. Although it had difficulty in sufficiently protecting Italian convoys, it posed a formidable threat. The Mediterranean sea routes to the East became virtually impossible. Except for an occasional convoy escorted by a major fleet, Britain had to supply her forces in the Middle East and maintain her communications with India and the Far East round the Cape of Good Hope. This multiplied fourfold the length of the voyage to Egypt and doubled that to India, imposing an immense strain on shipping. The Mediterranean fleet itself, based at Alexandria, had to be supplied through the Suez Canal across 13,000 miles of ocean, while the

Western Mediterranean was covered by a small battle squadron based on Gibraltar. The Mediterranean fleet covered the northern flank of the Desert Army. It was a dwindling force. Only three battleships and three cruisers remained of its original strength, and of these, a fortnight before Brooke took office, one of the battleships, *Barham*, was sunk by U-boats. U-boats at the same time sent to the bottom the sole Mediterranean aircraft carrier *Ark Royal*.

With the entry of the Soviet Union into the war the Royal Navy had additionally to undertake escort of convoys carrying arms and supplies to Russia along a nightmare sea route to Murmansk, threatened by submarine, shore-based aircraft and warships waiting in the northern fjords. The overall position at sea was, therefore, comparatively, albeit temporarily, stable in the mid-Atlantic; highly dangerous in the Mediterranean; and provided incessant strain on the route to Russia. To meet the situation the Royal Navy had, in November 1941, nine serviceable battleships and battle cruisers, and four fleet carriers. Two other battleships were refitting in home ports and three more, immune from air raids, in America. Two new battleships were expected to be ready within the year and another, *Duke of York*, was on the point of commission. Of the nine capital ships two were at Alexandria, two at Gibraltar, two on the convoy duty in the Atlantic which the threat of German surface raiders made necessary, and one, watching *Tirpitz*, lay at Scapa Flow. The new, powerful *Prince of Wales* and the battle cruiser *Repulse* had just been dispatched to Singapore, in an eleventh-hour attempt to deter Japan. The Admiralty was coping, but it was at full stretch, and any increased burden on our maritime resources would pose problems as severe as at any time in British history.

Unless overseas visits or catastrophe made it impossible, Brooke took one day off a week, either Saturday or Sunday, and went to his home at Ferney Close. There he was able to withdraw from the anxiety and ferment of affairs. He had an admirable capacity for relaxation, and for switching from one form of intense activity to another, finding relief in the contrast. Some bird-watching or photography, the ever present love and calm provided by Benita and the adoration and fun of his two young children restored his spirits completely. He never forgot a parent's duties, all the more important in the comparative scarcities of wartime. 'I've got an itchy back,' he would say to his small son Victor ('Ti' to him) 'scratch it please.' The subsequent scratching, reaching up under his Service Dress tunic, would lead to the discovery and extraction of a 'Comic'. And always, for them, he would draw the 'nonsense' drawings he had always enjoyed.[2]

He was able to take over the flat at No. 7 Westminster Gardens which had been occupied by Dill: and his Aide-de-Camp Captain 'Barney' Charlesworth, the perfect confidant and friend, furnished the flat from his own resources and ran the personal side of Brooke's life with quiet efficiency. In the flat Brooke generated cheerfulness and good humour. He was able completely to dismiss the stress of office – or seem to. He radiated charm and relaxation. He liked good food and a glass of wine, though he seldom drank spirits, and would give small dinner parties, talking of anything except war. Most weeks he lunched one day with Adam, who had become Adjutant-General in June 1941. The two were able to help each other's morale by shared reminiscent contact with an earlier, easier world.[3] After such lunches Brooke would often steal an hour and hunt for ornithological books and bird prints in Hatchard's, or in the second-hand shops of Charing Cross, before returning to the War Office or the Cabinet Room for the rest of the day, the evening, and sometimes half the night.

> Do write to me occasionally and tell me about some things such
> as birds and fish and not human beings which can think of
> nothing better than continually waging war,

he wrote to an old friend in Scotland soon after taking over as CIGS.

> We must go off and catch a salmon together or I shall go mad![4]

Brooke attended his first Chiefs of Staff Committee meeting on 1st December. Concern principally focused not on Russia, nor on the air offensive against Germany, nor on the Atlantic, nor on North Africa, the Mediterranean, the Western Desert. A new threat occupied the Chiefs of Staff. This was the possible enlargement of the war by the entry into it of a new enemy, Japan: and by the simultaneous acquisition of a new and ultimately dominant Ally, the United States.

The United States, concerned with the Japanese occupation (with French connivance) of French Indo-China, had instituted a crippling trade embargo against Japan in the autumn of 1941, facing that martial people with the inescapable alternative of abandoning their protracted campaign in China or seizing by force necessary raw materials. The embargo was so savage in its effects on Japan's imports that it virtually constituted an ultimatum. Britain, and Holland's Government in exile in London, had joined the United States. Their possessions in Malaya and the Dutch East Indies were therefore a natural target for Japan if her decision were for war rather than withdrawal. Many circles in Japan were profoundly anxious but, given the nature of the internal power balance in Tokyo and Japanese military capabilities, given the preoccupation of Britain and Russia in other theatres, given the German occupation of Holland and the virtual immobilization of France, the decision might well be for war. Negotiations were attempted but failed. The chief deterrent would, it was thought, be that exercised by the presence of the American Pacific fleet. Intelligence and Planning Staffs were hopeful that Japan would not risk war with this fleet in being. If she were to do so, it was forecast as a step-by-step affair. A certain complacency reigned. For the United Kingdom the worst contingency, of course, would be Japanese invasion of British and Dutch possessions without the certainty of American involvement.

In an act which must rank as ultimately the most providential in the entire war Japan struck simultaneously at Malaya, Hong Kong and the Philippines and delivered a pre-emptive strike at the · American fleet at its base at Pearl Harbor, all on 7th December. By a fortunate circumstance Germany and Italy soon thereafter declared war on the United States, settling any doubt that might have arisen in that matter. Thus did the war become global, and thus was formed the great coalition of powers, created by their enemies, which would by a combination of space, tenacity and greatly superior resources assuredly triumph in the long term.

Meanwhile the first operational crisis to meet the new CIGS at the end of his first week was sharp indeed. The winter turned suddenly very dark. Blows from the new assailant in Asia came thick and fast. Seven out of America's nine battleships in Pearl Harbor – or nearly half her capital ships – were sunk or put out of action. On the same day part of the small RAF and RAAF contingent in Malaya was destroyed on its airfields, and Japanese troops landed in Southern Thailand near the Malayan frontier. Next day an enemy detachment, crossing the narrow Kra Isthmus, reached the shores of the Indian Ocean, seized the British landing-ground at Point Victoria and cut the air route by which the reinforcements from India and Europe were flown to Singapore.

'This has entirely upset the balance in the Pacific and leaves the
Japs master of the ocean until we can assemble some forces there,'
Brooke wrote after a late sitting of the Chiefs of Staff two days after
Pearl Harbor. 'We, therefore, examined possibilities of sending
British battleships to restore the situation.'[5] But next morning,
10th December, brought tragic news. *Prince of Wales*, which the
Prime Minister had told Stalin could 'catch and kill any Japanese
ship', had been sunk, together with *Repulse*, by torpedo-carrying
aircraft while trying, without air cover, to intercept a fleet of
transports off the Malayan coast. Churchill had hoped that these
great ships would pose a menace to Japanese maritime movement
in the South Pacific, affecting events by their unseen presence as
Tirpitz and *Bismarck* had done in the North Atlantic. Now they
had been committed and were no more. 'It means,' Brooke wrote
that night, 'that from Africa eastwards to America through the
Indian Ocean and Pacific we have lost command of the sea.'

It had long been accepted that sooner or later America would find
herself at war, probably with both Germany and Japan. Staff
conversations had been held as early as August 1940 and had
defined as a 'general aim to pass to the general offensive in all
spheres with the utmost possible strength in the spring of 1942' –
which explicitly included the idea, as soon as blockade and air
bombardment made it feasible, of re-establishing a 'striking force'
on the Continent.

Further Staff conversations in January 1941 had clarified
positions and had led to a written report. It had been agreed that in
case of war by both Britain and America against the European Axis
Powers and Japan, the former should be regarded as the prime
enemy, and the European theatre treated as vital, followed in
importance by the security of the Far East, including Australia,
New Zealand and Singapore. Little more was done to co-ordinate
plans in the Far East. It was provisionally agreed that it would be
regarded as divided into a Pacific area proper, an American
responsibility: a 'Far Eastern area'; and Australia/New Zealand.
The responsibility for the last two, and the evolution of a command
structure, was left obscure. There was a general British
disposition, endorsed by the War Cabinet's Defence Committee,
to defer to American views on all matters connected with the
Pacific, and an American instinct to defer to the British on
European matters, although this would not survive the point,
comparatively late in the war, where American effort east of the

Atlantic became first equal to and then greater than that of the British Empire.

The report emanating from the January 1941 discussions had also dealt with machinery, envisaging a 'Supreme War Council' – of President, Prime Minister and their colleagues – advised by a Combined Chiefs of Staff formed by the United States and United Kingdom Chiefs in joint deliberation. It was reaffirmed that there should be united action in the air offensive against Germany, and that the ultimate aim should be the build-up of sufficient force for a land offensive on the European mainland. Meanwhile – and somewhat at odds with this – the British aim was described, with whatever realism, as 'to create such intolerable conditions in Germany by an ever-increasing force of bombers that the German armies would be forced to return and the regime be overthrown'. The Americans, with some justice, formed the view and never wholly lost it until the event that at least some of the British believed the war might be won without direct and costly trial by land battle in the West.

Joint Missions from each country were discreetly established in the other's capital. This was strong meat for an officially neutral nation, and President Roosevelt could only move within the limits of his own political situation as he perceived it. Nevertheless material aid was unstinted, within the ever-developing potential of American industry. After the launch of BARBAROSSA Anglo-American collaboration received impetus from the attempted co-ordination of assistance to Russia, exemplified by the visits of Mr Harry Hopkins to London and Moscow in July 1941.

In the following month, August 1941, there had been a meeting between President and Prime Minister, and the 'Atlantic Declaration' was produced in terms which left little doubt that a great coalition would ultimately be formed. Parallel military discussions took place, at which it was already clear that the United States Chiefs of Staff viewed with profound mistrust, as a diversion, the British concentration on the Middle East: a possible North African expedition had already been mooted by the British. It still seemed to many in America that they could best assist from a position of one-sided neutrality. To Germany it remained essential to delay American entry into the war. In the Far East, policy throughout 1941 was based on the premise that Japan would not risk war simultaneously with an undefeated Britain and with the United States. A working assumption was also made that if such did occur the British would send a fleet to the Far East, and would have been freed to do so by American reinforcement of the Atlantic; American reinforcement of the Atlantic did in fact begin in June 1941. The chief American effort was envisaged as likely to be in the Atlantic and Mediterranean, with the Far East regarded as 'a diversion'.

Now, after the drama of 7th December, all was changed. Would the agreement to 'deal with Germany first' survive the shattering blow to American security and prestige dealt by the naval disaster which had precipitated her, unprepared, into war? How and where could the next steps be taken and the situation stabilized at essential points – and what were they? Disaster always brought out the best in Churchill. He was never better than when all was going awry. He determined to take counsel with Roosevelt. On the day after Japan struck he obtained, with the King's permission, the Cabinet's agreement that he should cross the Atlantic; and was somewhat chagrined by a telegram from Washington suggesting that for security reasons it might be better to postpone his visit till the New Year. But he was not to be deterred, and by 12th December he had got his way and was off, with hatches battened down against the winter gales, in the newly-commissioned *Duke of York*. He took with him the Minister of Supply, Beaverbrook, the First Sea Lord, Pound, and the Chief of Air Staff, Portal, leaving the new and still only acting CIGS as Chairman of a caretaker Chiefs of Staff Committee in England with the Vice-Chiefs of Naval and Air Staff as his colleagues. Brooke was naturally disappointed but being hardly in the saddle, it was only, he wrote, to be expected.

Before Churchill sailed, however, Brooke persuaded him – at a meeting in Downing Street on the afternoon of 11th December – to take as permanent head of the British Military Mission in Washington the man whom above all others the CIGS trusted and admired, his predecessor, Dill.

'This agreement,' he wrote, 'was not arrived at without a good deal of discussion . . . I had to press for this appointment and point out to him that, with Dill's intimate knowledge of the working of the Chiefs of Staff Committee and of our strategy, there could be no better man to serve our purpose in Washington at the head of our Mission. Thank Heaven I succeeded in convincing Winston, as few men did more in furthering our cause to final victory than Dill. From the very start he built up a deep friendship with Marshall and proved to be an invaluable link between the British and American Chiefs of Staff . . . I look upon that half-hour's discussion with Winston at 10 Downing Street on 11th December as one of my most important accomplishments during the war or at any rate among those that bore most fruit.'[6]

Churchill had not been impressed by Dill, and took a lot of persuading. The choice was particularly providential because the American Chiefs of Staff began by regarding Brooke himself as somewhat abrasive, with his terse, uncompromising manner; and although they came undoubtedly to admire him it was in some cases a reluctant admiration, not unmixed with suspicion to the very end. Dill, on the other hand, made an instant impression of intelligence, courtesy and tactful integrity.

Not that he found it easy going, at least to start with. Different methods of working made their own difficulties, and to the British Washington was an organizational nightmare.

'There are no regular meetings of their Chiefs of Staff,' Dill wrote to Brooke on 3rd January,

> and if they do meet there is no secretariat to record their proceedings. They have no joint planners and executive planning staff . . . Then there is the great difficulty of getting the stuff over to the President. He just sees the Chiefs of Staff at odd times, and again no record. There is no such thing as a Cabinet meeting, and yet the Secretaries for War, Navy, etc., are supposed to function. People like Harry Hopkins have no clear functions, and I feel, though I don't know, that the Chiefs of Staff rather resent his privileged position in which he can give advice on any conceivable subject. It seems to me that the whole organization belongs to the days of George Washington who was made Commander-in-Chief of all the Forces and just did it. Today the President is Commander-in-Chief of all the Forces, but it is not so easy just to do it.[7]

The voyage in *Duke of York* was marked by the production of a remarkable series of papers by Churchill which he passed to the Chiefs of Staff for their comments, and which evolved a British position for the forthcoming meetings. It is easy to criticize, with justice, many of Churchill's interventions in the running of the war, particularly his ignorance of logistic factors, his natural buoyancy which led him to goad commanders towards premature offensive moves against their will, and his general dislike for those aspects of reality which impeded his grand design for victory. These defects made him a most imperfect strategist in the practical sense, and often a sharp thorn in the sides of men no less anxious than he to beat the enemy. But it is equally easy to forget his vision, and that Ismay – admittedly a devoted admirer but an admirer, too, of the Chiefs of Staff – said of Churchill: 'In his grasp of the broad sweep of strategy [he] stood head and shoulders above his professional advisers.'[8] In his papers aboard *Duke of York* he showed it.

He concentrated attention in Europe upon the Mediterranean 'The North-West African theatre is one most favourable for Anglo-American operations.' He argued that 'a campaign must be fought in 1942 to gain possession of or conquer the whole of the North African shore . . . thus giving free passage through the Mediterranean'. He summed this up as the main offensive effort in the West in 1942: 'occupation of the whole of the North and West African possessions of France . . . further control by Britain of the whole North African shore from Tunis to Egypt, thus giving, if the naval situation allows, free passage through the Mediterranean to the Levant and the Suez Canal.' 'These great objectives,' he wrote, 'can only be achieved if British and American naval and air superiority in the Atlantic is maintained, if supply lines continue uninterrupted and if the British Isles are effectively safeguarded against invasion.' He saw the German crisis clearly. 'Hitler's failures and losses in Russia are the prime facts in the War at this time.'[9]

As to the Pacific, Churchill recognized that Japan had temporarily the upper hand. Sea power would be the key and it would be necessary to build it up, with carrier-borne air power. He accepted that to give priority to seaborne aircraft could retard the bomber building programme. He envisaged progressively regaining island bases to bring offensive air power ever nearer to Japan itself, culminating in assaults on Japanese cities. He did not prophesy the desperate defensive campaign for India and the reconquest of Burma which came about.

All this was consistent with the Chiefs of Staff's own views. As usual they stressed the details and the constraints as well as those threats they always feared Churchill might brush aside too lightly. They pointed out cautiously that at least a minimum of protection was still necessary for the United Kingdom. They underlined the inevitable increase in our naval commitments, already under heavy additional pressure because of the Russian convoys. There would now be an additional and major burden in the Far East. The Atlantic traffic was still vulnerable to surface raiding. They referred to possibilities open to the Axis Powers, which would need countering: a move against Gibraltar, the establishment of U-boat bases in West Africa, Japanese submarines in the Indian Ocean. They underlined the potential threat to the Middle East were the Germans to become masters of the Caucasus. Above all they reminded the Prime Minister that it would only be possible to reinforce the Far East at the expense of the Middle East. They envisaged, however, a long-term policy of 'tightening the ring round Germany', taking every opportunity of knocking Italy out of the war, clearing the Mediterranean, and mounting ultimate concentric operations on land against Germany from the west by the United Kingdom, from the south by the United States and from the east by the Soviet Union, who must in the meantime at all costs be sustained. Churchill had already looked forward to 1943 and beyond with prescience and vigour. He proposed the invasion of Sicily and the securing of a foothold on the mainland 'with reactions inside Italy which might be highly favourable'. At all times, however, he was clear that the war could only be won 'through the defeat in Europe of the German Armies or through internal convulsions in Germany'. He suggested that plans be made for landings, in the summer of 1943, in one or more of the following: Scandinavia, the Low Countries, France, Italy and the Balkans – 'the actual choice of which four or five to pick can be deferred as long as possible'. He envisaged an invasion Army of forty armoured divisions ('the local populations will rise') covered by command of the sea and superior air power, their path prepared by a bombing offensive. 'We might hope to win the War,' he wrote, 'at the end of 1943 or 1944.' With the German Armies supreme in Europe and European Russia and the Japanese fast overrunning British and American possessions in Asia, with China an uncertain ally, the Royal Navy at more than full stretch and half the American capital ships at the bottom of the sea this was the way to talk. Nevertheless the Chiefs of Staff's caution was sufficient slightly to cool the British position now agreed. In 1943 'the way *may* be clear for a return to the continent'.[10]

The subsequent conference with the American President and Chiefs of Staff, first in a historic series, was called ARCADIA. The principal difference between the two sides which emerged concerned the Mediterranean. To the Americans it was, and long remained, a diversion. The British, they thought, were obsessed with it because of their Imperial concern with the route to India, and their own position and possessions in East Africa and the

Eastern Mediterranean. But to the Americans it was a long route to take to the heart of Germany, and they placed all their emphasis on the great and decisive effort which would have to be made in Western Europe, and the need for economy in other theatres. Their armed forces for operations on land were embryonic. They needed time to build up.

Nevertheless some sort of overall concept was agreed, although it left much to later debate and interpretation. In all the circumstances this was inevitable. ARCADIA was not a well-prepared conference, but it was probably better to press on with it than delay it. One or two specific gains, from the British point of view, were established. The concept of 'Germany first' was reaffirmed, as was the general principle of 'encircling Germany' – which, given Russian participation, could mean as much or as little as desired. Continuation of a bombing offensive and a blockade, and attempts to 'subvert' were also agreed. The support of Russia to keep her in the war was accepted as essential. 1943 was regarded as the year when it was hoped major landings could take place somewhere in Europe. None of this added up to a plan. It was also agreed, however, that planning should proceed for a combined expedition in North Africa which, if it took place, would ultimately join hands with a victorious British Army advancing from the desert. This operation was named GYMNAST. It was recognized that it could not take place before May 1942 at the earliest.

In the Far East one positive proposal was agreed. It was a bad one – 'wild and half-baked' as Brooke described it. There would be set up a Supreme Command known as ABDA (American, British, Dutch, Australian) to cover all forces operating in a vast area of the Far East including Burma to the west, the Dutch East Indies, the Philippines, Malaya and Hong Kong and virtually the whole of the China Sea. Wavell, currently Commander-in-Chief in India, was appointed to the Command. By separating Burma from the Command in India which must sustain it, the area's boundaries on its western flank made no sense. As to the rest there was not yet any coherent chain of command agreed, on an international basis, to which Wavell could report. The position of the Dutch, the Australians and the New Zealanders was anomalous. They were not members of the Combined Chiefs of Staff yet their possessions or homelands were threatened. Overshadowing this, of course, was the fact – not yet so horrifyingly apparent as it would be in a few weeks – that there was absolutely nothing Wavell could do to affect the issue in an area where the Japanese had achieved complete surprise, were as dynamic as their opponents were too frequently supine, and where Allied reinforcements were inadequate or non-existent. Such as could be made available inevitably came from the troops earmarked for the Middle East, and a pull-devil, pull-baker contest developed between the two theatres of war, both dependent on a long and vulnerable supply line. ARCADIA decisions on where Wavell should hold were either self-evident – for example to hold Burma and Australia as essential – or impossible to carry out. There were other considerations.

'My view,' wrote Dill to Brooke on 28th December, 'is that it would be a grave mistake to appoint Wavell.' Dill felt strongly that no British General should be given responsibility 'for the disasters that are coming to the Americans as well as ourselves'. 'After all,' he wrote, 'the Americans let us in for this war in the Far East.' This was true – but in so doing they let themselves in for war against Germany, and Brooke as well as Churchill thanked Providence for the fact.[11]

One very positive achievement stemmed from ARCADIA – the formal establishment of the Combined Chiefs of Staff already described. Co-ordination of Allied strategy is invariably difficult. In 1942 it was assisted by the fact that the two principal Western combatant nations were English speaking, and of roughly equivalent military strength at that time. It was not always perfectly efficient, and some mistrust persisted until the end and after, but few can doubt that such mistrust would have multiplied in at least equal proportion to the number and diversity of the participant nations.

Meanwhile at home Brooke, within a fortnight of entering on his duties, found himself left, under the Deputy Prime Minister, Mr Attlee, in charge of the British war machine in London 'to grip' as Churchill put it, 'the tremendous problems that awaited him', while his political chief and colleagues crossed the Atlantic to settle in conference with the Americans how those problems could be solved. 'Had a real good afternoon at the office,' he wrote on the day they sailed from the Clyde, 'and at last began to get level with some of my work.' It was all the heavier because the Vice-Chief of the Imperial General Staff was with the Foreign Secretary in Moscow, the Deputy Chief with the Prime Minister and Dill on the high seas, and the Director of Staff Duties on a mission to the Middle East. Almost every night that month Brooke was forced to return to the office after dinner to wrestle till midnight or after with seas of paper. The amount he had to read was so great that it affected his eyes.

While the Chiefs of Staff in mid-Atlantic debated long-term policy, as far as the immediate present went the next few weeks were a strategist's nightmare. Three days after the Prime Minister sailed, Brooke wrote in his diary 'Far East situation far from rosy! I doubt whether Hong Kong will hold out a fortnight and Malaya a month.' The garrison of the former – six British and Canadian battalions without air cover, facing the assault of a strong division – had been driven from the mainland on to the congested and heavily bombed island. The Philippines were invaded on the day after the sinking of *Prince of Wales*, and Borneo, with its Dutch and British oilfields, a week later. On 18th December Penang, on the west coast of Malaya, after being struck by dive-bombers, was occupied by the Japanese, now advancing swiftly down both sides of the peninsula towards Singapore. Singapore, apart from its unique significance as a symbol of British Imperial authority in Asia, had always been accepted by both British and Americans as a crucial piece upon the board, the base for an Allied fleet. There was none other for a very long way. 'We have laid down,' wrote Brooke on Christmas Day, 'that first of all in importance comes security of this country and its communications, and after that Singapore and communications through the Indian Ocean.' Upon these communications rested not only the security of India but to a large extent, because substantially nourished by India, the Middle East. Meanwhile, on 18th December, a dreadful naval disaster occurred in the Eastern Mediterranean. Following the loss of *Ark Royal*, *Barham*, *Prince of Wales*, and *Repulse*, Admiral Cunningham's two remaining battleships, *Queen Elizabeth* and *Valiant*, were holed in Alexandria harbour by time-bombs affixed by Italian frogmen. This brought the loss or disablement of British and American capital ships in a month to fifteen, or nearly half their combined battle strength in all oceans. Next day, while trying to intercept a convoy of German and Italian supplies bound for Tripoli, three British cruisers and four destroyers from Malta – the 'K' force which the Prime Minister had induced the Admiralty to base on the island and which had done splendid work – were caught in a minefield. A further cruiser was sunk in the same week by U-boats. Simultaneously a German Air Corps withdrawn from Russia – where flying had temporarily become impossible – opened an all-out assault on Malta. Except for the island's defiant guns and empty harbour nothing remained in the two thousand miles between Gibraltar and Alexandria of Britain's mastery of the Mediterranean but three cruisers and a handful of destroyers and submarines. In supply of the African theatre the Axis Powers had the upper hand. Yet those near Brooke remembered him at this time, as ever, resilient and cheerful, able to seem to put aside worry and make light of disaster in a way which all found comforting. A visiting Staff Officer, who had served Brooke previously, offered tentative commiseration on his difficulties. 'Oh, we're not doing too badly!' said Brooke with a chuckle, 'we've only lost about a quarter of the Empire.'[12] He kept expressions of despair for his diary. To all around him he was the epitome of confidence and strength.

In North Africa Operation CRUSADER had spent its force. Churchill was still thinking in terms of a great victory in Libya. Cyrenaica had indeed been cleared. The next move, however, was to be made by Rommel. Brooke had been hearing from Auchinleck about the recent fighting, and about the latter's dissatisfaction with some facets of the British Army. In Auchinleck's view tactical sense was defective in too many of the British Armoured Corps Officers, and he said so. 'Gott – an Infantryman – and Campbell – a Gunner – have been the outstanding leaders. I admit to being seriously disturbed at the apparent lack of tactical ability in our RAC [Royal Armoured Corps] Commanders,' he wrote to Brooke. He frequently returned to the theme. 'Many Cavalry Officers are not fitted mentally or by training to take command in modern war,' he wrote in March.[13]

Auchinleck expanded on other weaknesses. Our cruiser tanks, he wrote, appeared mechanically inferior to those of the enemy. Our tanks were out-gunned – particularly by the enemy's anti-tank guns which could out-range and destroy them, and behind screens of which the Germans were adept at manoeuvring their Panzer units. And in tactics, as well as a general lack of sound practice, there was too often a failure to understand the necessary co-ordination of all arms. He discussed some organizational changes he had in mind to improve this situation of which the most radical, which flowered somewhat later, was the proposal to make the brigade group of all arms, rather than the division, the basic unit of manoeuvre. Anti-tank guns would be integral to Infantry battalions. Brooke assented to most of this.[14] It was the Commander-in-Chief's responsibility, but specific points like the lack of all-arms co-ordination had preoccupied Brooke for a long time, and as he had already shown in command of Home Forces he held a far from complacent view of the quality of British tactical leadership in higher command.

In general, Auchinleck's letters during January were optimistic in tone. He seemed cheerful and he paid generous tribute to the co-operation he had received from the other two Services: nevertheless he raised a certain disquiet in Brooke's mind. It seemed that matters in the desert, where he had never been, looked different on the spot than when viewed in London. CRUSADER had been a significant victory. It had not been decisive, but it had been sufficient for the British and American authorities to discuss a North African enterprise with which the Desert Army, without setbacks, could ultimately link hands. Now Auchinleck was producing operation instructions (of which he sent a copy to Brooke on 21st January) saying in his covering letter 'should circumstances make it necessary to withdraw from Cyrenaica'. 'Needless to say I hope the necessity will never arise,' he had added. Brooke, in the green ink reserved by the War Office custom to the CIGS, side-lined the sentence with a prescient and perhaps mistrustful exclamation mark.[15]

Whatever Brooke's uneasiness at what he sensed in some parts of Auchinleck's thinking, he did not at all dissent from the strictures on the state of training and particularly the training of commanders. Since much of Auchinleck's Army had passed through his own hands as Commander-in-Chief Home Forces he had no illusions. Compared to the enemy the British Army and its leaders were ill-trained, with certain admirable exceptions. Much of the reason lay in defective systems. The British organization had necessitated hasty expansion on an inadequate professional base, and that base was itself too often archaic and amateur. There was no tradition of a unified doctrine, an accepted 'corpus' of tactical principles from top to bottom such as had always been absorbed from the first day of his field training into the bloodstream of the German soldier. The defect persisted. If an Army is to perform well for any length of time in war – and in the first battles – it must have not only a well-established tactical and operational doctrine but a strong cadre, including reserves, of officers and non-commissioned officers brought up in that doctrine. Britain had little of these things. Nor was Churchill always wrong in regarding lack of boldness as endemic in British military thinking.

Brooke's early weeks in London, while his colleague Chiefs of Staff and the Prime Minister were in America, gave him a sound baptism of fire not only because of the speed and drama of unfolding events but because he acted as Chairman of the Chiefs of Staff Committee during the time and gained experience in handling it, and in looking at strategic issues from the Chair. Two issues, one brutally immediate and one curiously unrealistic, stand out.

The first was shipping. In early January Attlee asked the Chiefs of Staff to confirm that they were fully apprised of the shipping situation. Brooke replied that they were, and that it meant formations and reinforcements urgently needed in the Middle and Far Eastern theatres could not be transported, apart from its effect upon munitions and supply. The shortage of shipping and the vital nature of the war for the protection of our sea communications impressed itself more vividly than ever on his mind. It lay behind his strong endorsement of a 'Mediterranean' strategy which would ultimately reduce passage time and tonnage requirements for North African and Far Eastern operations.

The second issue was that which would dominate, often with bitterness, the strategic debate of the next two years – the opening of a 'Second Front' in Western Europe. Already the Joint Planning Staff had been instructed to devise an operational plan in outline and the Chiefs of Staff Committee gave it preliminary consideration on 2nd January. Its assumptions and tone reflected a certain – perhaps knowingly artificial – optimism about the circumstances in which such a front could and would be opened. Thus, German morale was assumed to be near broken before the attempt would be made, and the German war machine already near collapse, through the effect of attrition in Russia and from the devastating results of the bomber offensive. A prime operational aim once the Army – only reckoned as about fifteen divisions, a fraction of that ultimately to be employed – had landed was to advance rapidly to the Ruhr and thus ensure that the German Army in the West could be decisively beaten before managing an orderly withdrawal to the Reich. The tone of the paper was somewhat bland to one who, like Brooke, had a high opinion of German resilience and was sceptical of the results of the strategic air operations. He contented himself with saying that the aim and nature of tactical operations envisaged after the landings needed further study, and that he did not approve of them as given. The plan was remitted to Commanders-in-Chief to examine and refine. It was described as an outline plan 'for operations on the continent in the final phase'. Brooke believed it improbable that operations could be deferred until the assumption of the paper – Germany so weakened as to need but a *coup de grâce* – was satisfied.

On 17th January 1942, the Prime Minister returned after his month's absence. The contact he had made and the indomitable assurance spread abroad by his personality had been of the utmost value. He had every reason for satisfaction with his journey. The concept of 'Germany first' had been reiterated in spite of the emotional blow struck by Japanese aggression at American sentiment: it had been agreed that the Americans would build up a great force in the United Kingdom for operations in Europe. The evolution of an agreed operational plan and sequence had eluded him and his advisers: but these were early days.

CHAPTER XI

Grand Strategist – 1942

BROOKE'S INTELLECT was a precise instrument. He saw issues and their interrelationships very clearly, and he divided essential from peripheral factors as tidily as the untidy business of war permits. In speech he was warm and emphatic: in thought he was cold.

He had to think and act in three different dimensions. First he had to decide what he believed should be the long-term strategy of the Western Allies. Second he had so to manage the machinery of war – the higher direction – that first his professional colleagues, next his Ministerial superiors (which meant above all Churchill), and lastly Britain's Allies would come to accept his point of view or persuade him of theirs. Third he had to deal with current operations, and particularly those for which Britain had sole or primary responsibility; this activity turned not only on resources and operations but on the competence and personality of commanders in the field. The first dimension was conceptual – the art of the grand strategist. The second involved skills of persuasion, and needed great lucidity and forcefulness of presentation. The third dimension required speed of perception and decision and a sufficient degree not only of professional brilliance but of ruthlessness. In all three dimensions Brooke showed himself a master.

The major strategic problem confronting the Allies, after Japan's attack had brought into being the grand Alliance, was where, when and how to engage the German Army in battle on a large scale. At the ARCADIA Conference it had been agreed that the defeat of Germany should continue to take priority – in political terms a difficult and courageous decision for the United States. The American Army would take time to expand from a minuscule peacetime base. But when it had expanded – and while it was expanding – it must be ready to fight and win.

There was little disposition in America – and here Brooke did not dissent – to believe that Germany could be subdued by bombing and nothing else. She could be weakened but not brought to surrender. Nor was there belief that blockade alone could reduce a Germany so comparatively secure in the raw materials needed for war as the Reich appeared in 1942. She had well-known weaknesses, but her skill in the production of substitutes was recognized; and oil, the largest single inhibiting constraint on the German war machine, could become plentiful if a successful campaign were mounted in the Caucasus. Furthermore, the balance of power at sea had been tilted so alarmingly against the Allies by Japanese aggression on the one hand and the speed of the German U-boat building programme on the other that sea blockade as an offensive weapon was far away. Indeed, for a Britain dependent on sea movement for survival, the battle of sea communications was again defensive and desperate. To win it was a precondition of the people's life as well as necessary for the prosecution of all other operations.

A nation can be defeated by invasion, bombardment or blockade. The latter two would, in Brooke's view, bring no ultimate decision against Germany. Only invasion could be contemplated as the final act in the drama. It seemed improbable, early in 1942, that Germany could ever be successfully invaded from one direction only. For the Russians, already preparing against renewed German offensives in the summer of 1942, ultimate victory unaided by Western efforts was unthinkable; while defeat, if those efforts were not major and timely, was very thinkable indeed. For the Western Powers invasion and successful subsequent operations against a Germany without preoccupations on other fronts was equally unthinkable. The first requirement for a successful invasion, therefore, was that the Russian war effort should be sustained. The Russian campaign must continue to bleed the German Army. Thus far little divided Britain from America, nor Brooke from the American Chief of Army Staff, General George Marshall. The two men did not meet until April. But both were agreed that the continent of Europe must be invaded and the German Army brought to battle and defeated, and both were agreed that in achieving this the efforts of Russia were crucial. Yet when planning moved beyond joint resolve to sustain Russia sharp differences arose. These differences appeared to Brooke under two main heads – about the degree of weakening and dispersal which must be forced upon the German armed forces before any successful invasion by the Western Powers could be contemplated: and about the resources which would be required in terms of the size and skill of the invading land forces themselves, of air cover, of speed of build-up and smoothness of maintenance and, in consequence, of shipping. On these matters he and Marshall thought differently.

The strategic debate swirled round code names. BOLERO was the build-up of American forces in the United Kingdom for operations in Europe (although in some American documents it was incorrectly used as shorthand for cross-Channel operations). There was no substantive disagreement between Allies on BOLERO. All agreed that the United Kingdom must be the main base for Continental invasion, although Marshall emphasized the necessary connection between BOLERO and some specific operation.

SLEDGEHAMMER was the code name for operations in Continental Western Europe in 1942.

ROUNDUP meant major cross-Channel operations in 1943.

The North African operation – a landing in French possessions by British and American forces with the aim of eventually joining hands with the Eighth Army operating from a conquered Tripolitania, and thus clearing the whole North African littoral – was first known as GYMNAST. Originally conceived as an early entry 'by invitation' it was soon recognized as carrying its own problems. When Churchill, at the winter ARCADIA Conference, had first mooted it he believed that Auchinleck's CRUSADER offensive would shortly bring British troops to the borders of Tunisia. A landing in February was envisaged. This was not to be. Reverses in the Western Desert removed for a while one of the plan's basic assumptions – a successful Allied pressure along the North African coast from the east. Resources, too, lagged behind hopes. Shipping devoted to an early GYMNAST involved severe penalties elsewhere. American troops would not be ready in sufficient quantity and with sufficient support. As 1942 wore on GYMNAST ceased to be an immediate expedient, a vigorous Allied blow to offset something of the indignities inflicted on Allied prestige, and instead came into competition with SLEDGEHAMMER and then, by implication, with ROUNDUP itself as a major operation.

In the debate Brooke took as the point of origin of his arguments the fact of shipping. BOLERO and invasion would make enormous demands on shipping. Therefore the demands of other theatres must be reduced, through a step-by-step strategy. For unless the Mediterranean and the Suez Canal could be used by Allied shipping, the Cape route to India and the Far East, in the

face of a hostile Japan, would add an intolerable percentage to the
tonnage required for the minimum needs of war in Asia: and the
Middle East theatre, itself, would also continue to produce a
disproportionate requirement for shipping. In the British view, it
was impossible to assume that a Middle East theatre could be
discounted, under any strategy. Egypt apart, there was the threat
from the north to consider, a threat to Persia and Iraq from a
German Army which might soon stand poised and triumphant in
the Caucasus: and that meant loss of vital oil. Thus, to Brooke, if
shipping was one of the keys to successful invasion, the
Mediterranean was the key to the availability of that shipping.
This meant clearing the North African coast, thus ensuring the
safety of Malta and the secure passage of convoys from Gibraltar to
Alexandria.

To Marshall this meant a number of things, all of them
unpalatable. First he doubted the strength of the relationship
drawn by Brooke between the effect of a free Mediterranean
passage on shipping resources on the one hand, and the
requirement of those resources for cross-Channel invasion on the
other. The Channel is a short passage. To Marshall it must often
have seemed that the British created difficulties, first postulating
the necessity of a Mediterranean campaign and then showing how
voracious of shipping such a campaign inevitably must be. Was not
Brooke's preoccupation with the Mediterranean passage simply a
British dogma – 'The route to India' – understandable in terms of
Imperial defence but at variance with that concentration on the
defeat of Germany first which both nations had agreed? Indeed
Marshall would use the 'shipping factor' against Brooke in
pressing for cross-Channel operations at the expense of
'diversions'.

Next, Marshall was concerned that a Mediterranean campaign
would sadly disperse Allied resources. He had put his great heart
and great skills behind the creation of new American Armies. They
would take time to form. The British Army in the United
Kingdom had now reached a respectable size, and with American
help its equipment was becoming formidable. Were these assets to
be spread round the periphery of occupied Europe? Surely, as
Marshall saw it, they should be massed in Britain, whither every
available American soldier, tank and aeroplane would be sent for a
united thrust by the shortest sea passage and the shortest land
route to the enemy's vitals – the heart of the Reich itself. To
Marshall this was consistent with concentration, a basic principle

of war. Furthermore air cover would most easily be provided near rather than remote from a main base.

Third, Marshall was acutely aware of the factor of time, in domestic political terms as well as in its effect on the performance of Russia. In this the President was powerfully behind him. It seemed to them that only an early invasion of Western Europe could produce the sort of diversion of German resources which the Russian Armies needed; and they needed it soon. It further seemed to both President and his Chiefs of Staff that the American public would inevitably be impatient for action and for results. They would wish the action to be directed clearly and offensively against Germany, by no circuitous route and not long delayed. Marshall believed a significant effort in the Mediterranean would delay cross-Channel invasion, probably beyond 1943.

Marshall was also very conscious of a further point where domestic pressures could sway policy. He had loyally held his colleagues to the Allied theme: 'Germany first'. If decisive action had to be deferred, the 'Pacific lobby', whose principal and vigorous exponent was Admiral King, Chief of Naval Staff, would come into their own, supported by a public opinion soured by an apparently sluggish strategy, too Fabian for American taste.

Thus the way to Allied consensus was hard. When Churchill and the Chiefs of Staff returned from the ARCADIA Conference they left behind them in their American colleagues a certain sense of having been 'outsmarted'. With their natural desire to get to grips with the enemy as early and as directly as possible, the American Chiefs of Staff reflected uneasily that their President and Commander-in-Chief had perhaps been a victim of Churchill's powers of persuasion, and that they had themselves been outmanoeuvred by British professionals with well-prepared positions and superior staff work to back them. The result was British emphasis on North Africa which, as they considered it from various angles, both the loyal 'Westerner' and soldier, Marshall and the equally determined enthusiast for the Pacific, King, joined in disliking. This happened to coincide in February with a cooling towards GYMNAST on the part of the British Chiefs of Staff, for very different reasons. Rommel had launched his counter-attack, and in North Africa Britain was once again on the defensive. It was, in Brooke's view, of little value to occupy French possessions in North West Africa – assuming that this could be done without serious initial opposition – if we lost Egypt at the other end of the Mediterranean. Temporarily, at least, GYMNAST was out of favour with both British and American Chiefs of Staff in February and March 1942, and it was agreed by all that no shipping should be reserved for it.

But the reasons were different and the differences fundamental. To the British GYMNAST was for a while impracticable. To the Americans it was in its very concept a diversion. There was, there had to be, a shorter cut to victory. In spite of the pessimism on the point at ARCADIA, BOLERO must be made to lead to a major offensive in Western Europe in 1942. American Planners, under the direction of General Dwight Eisenhower, Chief of the War Plans Division in the War Department, examined the matter. They concluded that an invasion could be launched in the autumn of 1942, with a subsequent thrust line Calais-Arras-Paris.

It was not in dispute that the main forces employed would need to be British, since the massive build-up of American Armies would not have reached a very high point. The decisive voice would thus be British. To Brooke the whole matter was unreal. Apart from the practicability of landing – and he considered the American planners naïve about the difficulties of opposed landings – he held to the view he had put forward when the British Chiefs of Staff had first considered a British Planners' paper in January, that the operations after landing were unrealistic in view of the Allied forces which could be disembarked and sustained, and the rate of build-up against them. The British Planners had concluded that no such operation could take place unless the German armed forces were by then profoundly weakened in strength and morale. Since few regarded this as likely, there was here the first basic disagreement in assessment. The two conflicting planners' 'appreciations' were exchanged in March 1942, and the Combined Chiefs of Staff, the forum for professional Inter-Allied co-ordination which had emerged from ARCADIA, called for a reconciliation.

The results of this initial piece of international Staff work were disagreeable to the American Chiefs. It looked to them as if the British, having over-persuaded the President towards unwise courses, were now capable of twisting the minds of their own subordinates in the Combined Staffs. For the Combined Planners reported that there was so serious a shortage of shipping for offensive operations that operations against the Continent were not possible in 1942. Such operations might be possible in 1943 – but even then only if Russia were containing the bulk of the German armed forces. There was a further factor from the British viewpoint. British forces were already deployed and engaged in large numbers in various overseas theatres. To concentrate all disposable force at this juncture for cross-Channel operations (and no lesser concentration could have made sense) was to risk defeat elsewhere; and to no purpose.

Various new positions in the dance were adopted, as realism broke through on one side and enthusiasm on the other. At one moment in March the American Chiefs of Staff appeared again to agree that no large-scale land operations were possible in 1942 except in Russia. Simultaneously the British Joint Planning Staff produced a paper on offensive operations based on different assumptions. If a 'sacrificial effort' were required in 1942 to help Russia, it could take the form of a bridgehead established on the Continent – SLEDGEHAMMER – in the early summer of 1942. Only cross-Channel operations, as being the most economical in shipping, were envisaged, employing some ten divisions. The Planners argued in favour of this operation, fearing an early Russian collapse: nobody doubted that the spring would see the resumption of the offensive by Germany on the Eastern Front.

In their very different ways both Brooke and Marshall thoroughly disliked what the Staffs, whether national or combined, now put before them. Brooke – who became Chairman of the British Chiefs of Staff Committee on 8th March – condemned the whole idea of a 'bridgehead', or premature sortie in 1942. The German Army was still intact. Its rate of build-up against a bridgehead would surpass anything the Allies could produce. We should have another and worse Dunkirk. Nor was he impressed by a surprisingly optimistic estimate of their chances produced at the same time by the British Commanders-in-Chief who would mount such an undertaking. His fellow Chiefs of Staff were less emphatic. Brooke was adamant.[1]

For his part Marshall was unimpressed with Combined Planning so far. Eisenhower argued to him the many advantages of a major cross-Channel attack as early as possible. It was clear that these advantages would not emerge satisfactorily from the Combined Planning machine, and Marshall agreed that a plan for such an attack should be produced independently by the American Chiefs of Staff and then, bypassing the Combined Planners and the British Mission in Washington, be taken up with the 'highest British authorities'. Marshall addressed to the President a memorandum to this effect on 1st April; and thus he and Mr Harry Hopkins, the President's influential aide and adviser, travelled to

London on 8th April with the 'Marshall Plan' in their pockets. The substance of this plan was that maximum Allied forces should be concentrated in the United Kingdom for an 'Emergency' offensive in 1942 – one which would take advantage of opportunity, or be mounted to help Russia in dire necessity – and for a 'full-scale' invasion not later than 1st April 1943.

Discussions took place in London between 8th and 14th April. It was Brooke's first meeting with Marshall. Although they came to have high esteem for each other both men were at first wary.

> 'The more I see of him the more I like him,' wrote Brooke.[2] But later 'there was a great charm and dignity about Marshall which could not fail to appeal to one. A big man and a very great gentleman who inspired trust but did not impress me with the ability of his brain.'[3] As to the 'Plan' – Brooke wrote 'His plans for September of 1942 were just fantastic!'[4] and later 'It was not possible to take Marshall's "Castles in the Air" too seriously! It must be remembered that we were at that time literally hanging on by our eye-lids! Australia and India were threatened by the Japanese, we had temporarily lost control of the Indian Ocean, the Germans were threatening Persia and our oil, Auchinleck was in precarious straits in the desert, and the submarine sinkings were heavy. Under such circumstances we were temporarily on the defensive and when we returned to the offensive certain definite steps were necessary. We were desperately short of shipping and could stage no large scale operations without additional shipping. This shipping could only be obtained by opening the Mediterranean and saving a million tons of shipping through the elimination of the Cape Route. To clear the Mediterranean, North Africa first must be cleared.
>
> 'We might certainly start preparing plans for the European offensive, but such plans must not be allowed to interfere with the successive stages of operations essential to the ultimate execution of this plan.'[5] This note, written long after the event, nevertheless probably reflects with accuracy Brooke's state of mind. His opinion of Marshall remained constant. 'A great man, a great gentleman, and great organizer, but definitely not a strategist.'

However Brooke's afternote gives more than his opinion of Marshall, and his by then firmly formed views on the 'progressive' strategic path which must be followed before an invasion could be launched in Western Europe. There is also a strong note of indulgence: 'It was not possible to take Marshall's "Castles in the Air" too seriously.' Brooke was confident these operations *could* not take place, as events and detailed study would establish. Thus it was not vitally important what was done with such ideas in the meantime. Let planning continue, if by that means accord could be maintained. When the British, having considered the American proposals at the level of Prime Minister and Chiefs of Staff, returned their final answer they gave an impression of more harmony than really existed. It is a British characteristic to find a formula of agreement in order to preserve some sort of unity in an organization, while postponing a crunch of opinion until real decisions on action have to be taken. It is an American characteristic to take at literal value the written word. Each attitude has its virtues. Each can give to the other side an appearance of insincerity on the one hand, of pedantry and unrealism on the other.

So it was after the London visit of Marshall and Hopkins. At a meeting on 14th April the British Chiefs of Staff agreed that 'plans should be prepared' for major operations in Europe in 1943 'on the lines of his [Marshall's] paper'. Any operations in 1942 would be recognized as 'sacrificial' and only contemplated if Russia were on the point of collapse. In their meetings with Marshall the Americans and British each adopted a point previously regarded as the preserve of the other: Marshall stressed the importance of shipping resources, from which, however, he deduced the primacy of cross-Channel operations and the necessity of avoiding 'dispersions'; while the British firmly reminded their Ally that Japan must be held all the time, and that the effort to do so produced certain minimum requirements in conflict with the resources required for a policy of 'Germany first'. These were important points, but not yet necessarily contentious. They depended upon interpretation. At a Defence Committee meeting on the evening of 14th April, Marshall expressed before Churchill his relief that 'agreement had been reached on basic principles for a frontal assault on the enemy in Northern France in 1943'. Brooke had assured him that 'we all agreed on 1943'. Whatever the fate of SLEDGEHAMMER, ROUNDUP at least seemed assured. Some forty-eight divisions were envisaged, not later than 1st April 1943.

Yet on 16th April the British Chiefs of Staff met again, the day before Marshall's departure, and that evening Brooke wrote in his diary:

> Important COS meeting at which we discussed plans for this year's invasion of the continent in collaboration with the Americans, and also plans for 1943. These plans are fraught with the gravest dangers. Public opinion is shouting for the formation of a new Western front to assist the Russians. But they have no conception of the difficulties and dangers entailed! The prospects of success are small and dependent on a mass of unknowns, whilst the chances of disaster are great and dependent on a mass of well established military facts.

It is clear, and he emphasized it both then and later, that Brooke had no intention of supporting such an invasion unless he were to believe that the balance of forces could lead to its success. It is equally clear that Marshall believed the formal endorsement of ROUNDUP in 1943 had laid the ghost of 'dispersions' which could annul it. Of these he regarded the Mediterranean as the foremost. As to SLEDGEHAMMER – operations in 1942 – the issue both in London and between the Allies was left somewhat in the air, and no doubt this was for the moment the best place for it. SLEDGEHAMMER would be considered if Russia was in desperate straits. Brooke, pragmatic as ever, regarded this as the worst situation in which to mount it. 'Should Germany be getting the best of an attack on Russia,' he wrote in April, 'the [public] pressure for invasion of France will be at its strongest, and yet this is just the most dangerous set of circumstances for us.'[6] In such an event German reserves would be unpinned, and in hand for the West. The other circumstance which could touch off SLEDGEHAMMER would be a German collapse. Few people believed in this.

Nevertheless SLEDGEHAMMER planning for a 'bridgehead in '42' was, by War Cabinet direction, continued; and Brooke said, noncommittally, that he would 'give it a fair run'. Only British troops would be involved. The British position, therefore, was one of authority. Marshall, on the other hand, reasonably believed that he had obtained Allied endorsement of major operations in Western Europe at least by spring 1943, and agreement that no obstacles should be allowed to prevent them. The bitter misunderstandings which clouded the summer arose from the fact that what to Brooke could be a precursor of a successful cross-Channel invasion – a triumphant Mediterranean campaign – was to Marshall a dispersion of our forces which would inevitably delay it. In the event both turned out to be right. The Mediterranean operations of 1943, which eliminated Italy from the war, assisted to weaken and disperse the Germans. At the same time these operations led to the postponement of cross-Channel operations, as Marshall feared – but, in Brooke's judgement, ensured their success.

On 15th February Singapore fell. Its loss was regarded and described as one of the most devastating reverses to British arms in our history. It was clear that a blow, perhaps mortal, had been dealt to British prestige in Asia. Now the Japanese threatened India, to every Briton symbol of the very existence of Empire.

The initial strategy to be adopted against Japan might need to be defensive. It still had to be concerted. 'Defensive' admits of interpretation. Initially ARCADIA produced the short-lived ABDA command to which Wavell was appointed. It was envisaged that in this command the southward advance of Japan would be halted on the 'Malayan barrier', and that Burma to the west and the Dutch East Indies to the south would act as the spine and shoulders of the defence. By 25th February, ABDA was at an end. The Japanese had shown superior fighting qualities on land to their opponents. They controlled the sea and the air. No naval bases were available to the Allies except at the points of a great triangle, Hawaii, Australia and Ceylon. The Japanese dominated South East Asia, posing a distant but perceptible threat to Australia and an immediate menace to Burma, the gateway of India. They could operate a fleet from Singapore and from the Philippines.

The British response to this situation was inevitable. There were no options. The Defence Committee, meeting on 16th February, recognized that we must concentrate on the defence of Australia, India, Burma and Ceylon. The Dutch East Indies could not be effectively helped. It was not unnatural that the Australian Government immediately requested that two Australian divisions deployed in the Middle East should return to Australia, and, in spite of British pleas that one should reinforce Burma, to Australia they returned. During March the Dutch East Indies, island by island, were occupied by the Japanese. Australian fears were entirely understandable. The 7th Australian Division (that whose diversion to Burma had been refused) 'might have saved Burma' noted Brooke. He described the Australians as 'parochial' over their security.[7] This was hardly just. It is unlikely that one division would have stemmed the tide in Burma; and it is in nature to be 'parochial' about home security. Brooke, as Commander-in-Chief Home Forces, had seldom given an inch, except under great pressure, on the strength of the garrison of the United Kingdom under threat. In fact the Japanese had decided that invasion of Australia was beyond them, and a policy of maritime interdiction of Australia from the United States (they rightly appreciated that Australia would be an Allied Main Base) would serve them better. Matters did not, however, appear in that light in Canberra. The Australians not only felt with justification that they were in the front line; they believed the Pacific had been neglected in British calculations before the blow fell.

Once again it was vital to agree the principles of strategy with the Americans. One of the most crucial issues was command responsibility. Roosevelt took the initiative. In February he referred in a telegram to Churchill to 'our two flanks, the right based on Australia and New Zealand, and the left on Burma, India and China'. The United States would take prime responsibility for the right flank, the British for the left. In March he followed this up with a further development whereby the 'right flank'– broadly the Pacific area – would be an American responsibility: the 'middle area' would extend from Singapore westwards to include not only the Indian Ocean but the Mediterranean and would be a British responsibility; and a 'third area' – the joint responsibility of both nations – would include the Atlantic and a future front on the European Continent. There was general British assent. On 17th March General Douglas MacArthur was appointed to the Supreme Command of the 'South West Pacific'.

The situation in the British zone of responsibility would, it was rightly reckoned, ultimately turn on sea power in the Indian Ocean. The Japanese were pressing the British to a long withdrawal in Burma, but much more devastating would be an amphibious descent on the coast of India or upon Ceylon, for Ceylon was a vital base for the fleet. The danger of too rigid a division of areas of responsibility at sea was that it could preclude concentrated action against a concentrated Japanese fleet. And a concentrated Japanese fleet in the Indian Ocean was what Brooke most feared.

For this reason, and in spite of the policy of 'Germany first', the British Chiefs of Staff considered carefully in early April the relative priorities of the Middle East and Indian theatres. They decided that both depended on sea communications in the Indian Ocean (since India still to a large extent nourished the Middle East Command) and both depended on oil from Abadan, and therefore on the security of Persia against a southward German move from the Caucasus. On these premises, the Japanese potential to strike disabling blows in the Indian Ocean was for the moment greater than the threats posed to Persia or to Egypt by the German Army in Russia, or by the Afrika Korps in the Western Desert. It was thus agreed that the first priority would be to build up strength in the Indian Ocean and to protect Ceylon. Five of the older battleships and three aircraft carriers had already been sent thither from the Mediterranean. The second priority would be to concentrate on renewal of the offensive in Libya after Auchinleck's recent recoil. Libya would have priority over any Japanese land or amphibious threat except to Ceylon. As for Persia the best immediate policy was to hope that the Russian front would hold. As if to emphasize the point Colombo and Trincomalee were heavily raided by air and bombarded from the sea by Japanese forces on 5th and 9th April.

Brooke was now Chairman of the Chiefs of Staff Committee, *primus inter pares*, and the maritime situation in the Indian Ocean disturbed him the more because he did not believe the First Sea Lord was sufficiently active in seeking co-ordinated action with the United States: 'Without such a plan,' he wrote, 'we run grave risks of being defeated in detail.' Yet Pound, despite effort, could get little from Admiral King. In the event the Japanese raid marked the limit of Japanese westward expansion. Thereafter the High Command in Tokyo concentrated their maritime efforts upon the Pacific.

Threats may actually pass some time before the danger seems over. The British fleet had withdrawn from Colombo, and avoided air attack in harbour. No maritime disaster was suffered in the Indian Ocean, and the threat to India was maintained only by Japanese land forces through Burma. The Japanese had decided against invasion of Australia. Yet because of the vulnerability of Ceylon the British Eastern fleet was based at Kalindini on the Kenyan coast. Wavell, Commander-in-Chief in India, was deeply concerned at the threat of air and amphibious attack against the Indian coast, and indignant at the proposed withdrawal of troops or non-arrival of reinforcements – the more so because the equivalent of seven Indian divisions were serving outside India and there was domestic pressure for their return. The Australians also pressed, throughout April, for the diversion to Australia of some British divisions, en route to the Middle East theatre. Such were the preoccupations of the Chiefs of Staff. The Prime Minister helped them play these conflicting and highly political, as well as strategic, issues. He said that we would see how the threat to Australia appeared when reinforcements rounded the Cape. This temporizing was successful.

These dark days in the Far East coincided with Marshall's first visit to London, where discussion had concentrated on the European and Mediterranean theatres: yet the span of Brooke's concerns could never be narrowed. On 10th April he entered in his diary:

> A very busy day which started with usual COS meeting mainly concerned in trying to save India from the Japs; a gloomy prospect with loss of command by sea and air. Lunched with Adam and in evening had another COS meeting to discuss Joint Planning Staff report on Marshall's scheme for invasion of Europe. Then out to Chequers for dinner and the night. Harry Hopkins and Marshall there, also three Chiefs of Staff. We were kept up till 2 a.m. doing a world survey but little useful work.[8]

The problem of reinforcement for India was compounded by an expedition to occupy Diego Suarez in Madagascar – Operation IRONCLAD – an operation which Brooke regarded as unnecessary. IRONCLAD took place successfully on 7th May, on the same day that the American fleet frustrated a Japanese attempt on Port Moresby in the battle of the Coral Sea. But the Australians did not regard this as decisive. In May Dr H. V. Evatt, the Australian Minister for External Affairs, was in London. He questioned the entire policy of 'Germany first'. Australia, he said, had not been represented at the Anglo-American meetings where this policy had been formulated and reaffirmed. Was it not superseded by the advances of Japan?

In Brooke's view the answer was a categoric 'no'. He had already sensed that the Japanese would not attempt an all-out offensive against Australia or India, and would concentrate on securing their position in the Pacific. The matter was concluded by the battle of Midway in early June. Four Japanese carriers were sunk for the loss of only one American carrier in this engagement in the Central Pacific, one of the decisive battles of the war. Thenceforth, the Japanese stood on the strategic defensive. Midway ended the rise of Japanese power. On the Indian frontier the British had completed the withdrawal from Burma into Assam on 20th May. In the Far East, from now on, the high point of danger was past, and the tide would run the other way.

In the Far East, as in Europe, however, the tide looked as if it

253

would run too slowly for some American taste. The Americans envisaged the reconquest and protection of island after island, to act as springboards for further advance, and projecting air power, and consequent protection of the fleet as well as bombing capacity, ever nearer Japan itself. But to Eisenhower, in the General Staff in Washington in February 1942, this was a 'slow, laborious, indecisive type of warfare . . . something that will keep us from going to Russia's aid in time'. To Brooke, on the other hand, it was the sort of practical, calculated strategy to which he himself invariably turned. He came to regard its chief practitioner, the Supreme Commander, General Douglas MacArthur, as the finest Allied strategist of the Second World War. This admiration was cumulative. It certainly did not exist when MacArthur, at the outset, pressed for a major Pacific 'second front' to a point that would have fatally diverted resources – especially shipping – from the Atlantic, the Mediterranean and the build-up for European invasion. MacArthur even suggested that such an offensive would do more than anything to help Russia since 'it would secure her Eastern frontier'. Her Eastern frontier was not Russia's greatest concern in 1942 and it is hard to believe that MacArthur was serious. No such arguments could, in the event, divert the Combined Chiefs of Staff from the overriding principle of 'Germany first'.

In May Mr Molotov, the Soviet Foreign Minister, visited Britain and the United States. He was under directions, among other things, to press the Western Allies on the matter of a 'Second Front' on the Continent of Europe. The timing of the visit was well-judged. The German offensive in the East had opened, and Russia was likely to be again hard pressed during the summer. It is probable that the Soviet Government appreciated a certain underlying disharmony in the attitudes of London and Washington so that there would be room for influence and for manoeuvre; and there was a popular groundswell of sympathy for Russia and her struggling Armies which left-wing circles in the democracies, including those in ideological sympathy with Moscow, were not slow to exploit.

Molotov passed through London on his way to and from Washington. In Washington he found the President unduly expansive. Roosevelt authorized the Soviet Foreign Minister to report 'that we expect the formation of a second front this year'. An official statement referred to the 'urgent tasks of creating a second front in Europe in 1942'. Marshall tried to have mention of 1942 deleted, without success. It was indeed a rod made by Roosevelt for his own – and his Allies' – back. It was a very stretched and disingenuous interpretation of the position by now reached between the Allies on SLEDGEHAMMER, and Britain was not privy to it. Dill wrote to Brooke on 18th May that Marshall had said to him wryly that day 'I have so many battles to fight I am never quite sure whether I am fighting you or the President or the Navy!'[9]

In London on his return journey Molotov received colder comfort about a second front, although an Anglo-Russian Treaty was signed. Churchill told him that as regards operations in 1942 'we are making preparations' – and this, both in planning and in our raiding policy, was strictly true. However, the Prime Minister, to the satisfaction of his Chiefs of Staff, also made it clear that such operations might not be feasible. It would depend upon circumstances. No promise could be given in the matter. Molotov had to be content with that and Roosevelt's more forthcoming attitude; and on the following day the War Cabinet agreed that SLEDGEHAMMER should not be attempted unless, first, it would succeed, and second the forces landed could maintain themselves in Europe against all likely counter-attack. An impeccable conclusion, but perhaps somewhat more definite than that with which the Soviet Foreign Minister was permitted to depart.

Before the end of May, however, the first shadows fell despite what might have seemed a clear sky at the end of Marshall's visit to London.

On 27th May, Brooke spent the morning with the Chiefs of Staff and the home Commanders-in-Chief discussing the command organization which should be recommended for ROUNDUP. Argument moved in two dimensions – how Allied positions and relationships were to be established in the Command structure, and whether there should be a Supreme Commander of land, sea and air forces involved. After a brief interval, in which he bought his small son Victor a bicycle and held three interviews, he attended a meeting at Downing Street with the Prime Minister and his own colleague Chiefs. It was at this meeting that SLEDGEHAMMER was, as far as the British were concerned, effectively put down. The facts of the situation as regards landing craft, and the limited numbers of men and tanks which could be put ashore in the assault echelons, were set before the Prime Minister. Churchill had no difficulty with the matter. He had no appetite for fruitless ventures on a large scale. He did, however, again revert to one of his favourite obsessions – a landing in North Norway. Brooke had never had patience with this idea, whose strategic potential he regarded as non-existent. The Chiefs of Staff agreed to examine the matter – code name JUPITER.

More importantly, however, after the meeting Churchill sent a message to Roosevelt. In this he mentioned the conclusions reached about landing craft and undertook to send Mountbatten to Washington to explain the problem further. The sense that the British had little further interest in SLEDGEHAMMER came through clearly. He referred to the battles starting in Libya (Rommel had attacked on 26th May). One sentence in the message struck a jarring note in Marshall's heart. 'We must never let GYMNAST pass from our minds. All other preparations would help, if need be, towards that.'

The Americans were right in assuming, as they did, that the British had by now decided that SLEDGEHAMMER was not worth further serious consideration. The British had, as an alternative, set in hand studies of two major raids on the European coastline. One – the larger – would involve some four divisions and was christened IMPERATOR. The second would be on a smaller scale, consist of a short sharp foray to Dieppe, and be carried out during the summer. The Prime Minister saw little purpose in IMPERATOR (its only ostensible justification, as a scaled down SLEDGEHAMMER, would have been if the Russians were in despair, and it would have been inadequate in those or any other circumstances) but authorized preparation of the Dieppe raid – code name RUTTER. But this was far from the concept of SLEDGEHAMMER.

On the other hand the British had not, as the Americans now suspected, concluded that ROUNDUP itself was impracticable.

June 1942 was a crucial month for Allied strategy. It appeared to the Americans that, within weeks, the British were in their hearts reneging on the position reached at the end of Marshall's visit. Mountbatten had been charged with explaining to the President and the American Chiefs the problems of cross-Channel operations, and had gone to Washington. He succeeded in impressing his point upon Roosevelt. The latter, however, drew a gloomy deduction from these difficulties. If cross-Channel operations were so complex, by 1943 they might be altogether infeasible because by then Russia would have collapsed. The President's mind, like the Prime Minister's, worried at the question of how and where the Allies could engage the German

Army soon rather than ultimately. To the alarm of his advisers, but consistent with his message from Churchill, he started thinking again about GYMNAST. There was a further point which Mountbatten had pressed both in London and in Washington. Any attempt at SLEDGEHAMMER would not only rule out raiding and amphibious training for the future because of the limited numbers of landing craft: it would also slow down preparations for 1943 itself.

By now a crunch had come, and in the open. The British War Cabinet had found the arguments against SLEDGEHAMMER conclusive. They hoped that the United States would perceive the virtues of GYMNAST – in 1942. As far as SLEDGEHAMMER went this was not inconsistent with the position reached by Marshall in London; 1942 had always been questionable. But it brought GYMNAST again into the forefront of the debate, and those who, like Marshall, believed that GYMNAST would inevitably lead to the delay of ROUNDUP until after 1943 could argue that, in its implications, any plea for GYMNAST was inconsistent with decisions already agreed.

Only personal contact could restore a measure of understanding. Churchill decided to go to Washington, taking Brooke with him. A journey by flying boat brought the British party to Washington after twenty-seven hours' flying on 18th June. It was Brooke's first visit to America.

When the Combined Chiefs of Staff met on 19th June, Brooke first addressed the concerns the President had expressed as he had listened to Mountbatten – that, if resources were so constraining, any offensive effort mounted by the Allies might be too late to save Russia from collapse. Everything turned on how likely that collapse was, and how much reliance could be placed on the Russian front holding.

Brooke discussed the various ways in which the Western Allies could help that front by bringing other pressure to bear. He dismissed SLEDGEHAMMER, after describing its limitations. It would be inadequate in scale, and probably unsuccessful. The best course for the time being was to concentrate in the United Kingdom the largest British and American forces possible. If the Russian front held they could be employed offensively in the best way circumstances at the time indicated. If Russia collapsed the United Kingdom base would, from their presence, be secure. This was BOLERO – build-up. As to future campaigns the Combined Chiefs of Staff agreed that the principle offensive effort should be on the Continent, as early as conditions allowed; and that GYMNAST should not at present be undertaken.

This represented the one – or the most evident – moment of wavering by Brooke on the urgency and logical place in grand strategy of a Mediterranean campaign. He was seldom inconsistent, but this was an inconsistency. He wrote after the war:

> I could not get either Marshall or Stimson to realize that operations across the Channel in 1942 *and 1943* [author's italics] were doomed to failure. We should go in with half-trained divisions against a superior number of war-hardened German divisions and the Germans would have the facility of reinforcing that point at a rate of 2 to 3 divisions for every one we might put in.[10]

The mention of 'Stimson' places this criticism in the context of summer 1942. Yet although Marshall was undoubtedly more optimistic there is no indication that Brooke, at that time, tried to persuade the Americans of the inherent impracticability of ROUNDUP. Indeed he referred at the time to general agreement on that matter. Again, after the war he wrote:

> I could *never* [author's italics] get Marshall to appreciate the fact that North Africa and Italian operations were all part of a strategy preparing for the ultimate blow.[11]

This was probably fair as regards Marshall's reservations about GYMNAST. But in June 1942 Brooke made no attempt to press GYMNAST on Marshall. The reason was that he was too uncertain of how the campaign in the Middle East might go, and thus uncertain of whether GYMNAST was timely or even would be practicable. These were realistic doubts. They should, however, be remembered in assessing claims that Brooke consistently saw the clearance of North Africa as an *indispensable* preliminary to cross-Channel operations.

If that were so he could hardly have agreed with Marshall on 20th June that all forces should be concentrated in the United Kingdom; that cross-Channel operations – without mention of preconditions – should be the paramount task of the 'United Nations'; and that GYMNAST should for the while be dropped.

GYMNAST was not dropped. The reason lay not in the combined or individual professional advice of Marshall and Brooke but in the private meetings Roosevelt and Churchill were conducting at the same time at Roosevelt's residence, Hyde Park.

Brooke wrote in his diary on the evening of 20th June:

> . . . we fully appreciated that we might be up against many difficulties when confronted with the plans that the PM and President had been brewing up together at Hyde Park. We fear the worst and are certain that North Africa and North Norway plans for 1942 will loom large in their proposals, whilst we are convinced that they are not possible . . .

GYMNAST had no support in the American military hierarchy. Brooke opposed it because of the immediate situation in the Western Desert. Marshall opposed it because he regarded such plans as leading to the inevitable postponement of ROUNDUP. It must in justice be said that only Marshall was right.

Nevertheless Roosevelt and Churchill had indeed been at work together, agreeably isolated from their professional advisers. Roosevelt had, on 19th June, received a paper from his Secretary for War, Mr H. L. Stimson. It was a cogent and well-expressed document. It argued again the 'Marshall case' for concentration at one decisive point – Western Europe. It argued strongly against 'diversions', Mediterranean or otherwise. And it argued that the British had inadequate faith in the struggle in the West. Only America could lead – the British, with fearful memories of a Continental war of attrition, and with an Empire to defend, would always try to hold her back.

Against this, Roosevelt had been persuaded, and was to be persuaded again, by Churchill, of the impracticability of early cross-Channel operations. He saw clearly that no arguments for the principle of concentration of force could balance likely failure. Yet he was convinced that American soldiers must, before the end of the year, see action. They must be blooded. Their Commanders must start learning 'on the job'. He was in this frame of mind when Churchill saw him and unfolded again the strategic attractions of GYMNAST. Roosevelt was converted. But Churchill also reiterated British support for ROUNDUP. He acted as a counter to Stimson. British hearts were in cross-Channel operations. But these could not be precipitate, and we too were impatient for earlier action. It was probably as well that the Prime Minister had no CIGS with him, since he started enthusiastically to outline the large numbers of dispersed landings which might take place on the day of invasion, an idea which would have horrified the Chiefs of Staff. This was an unimportant personal excursion. What mattered was that with Roosevelt he struck the right and the successful note.

When President and Prime Minister met their military advisers on 21st June a paper was drafted which endorsed BOLERO, and paid lip service to the clear strategic advantages which a successful SLEDGEHAMMER would produce. Nevertheless a paragraph ended:

> If on the other hand detailed examination shows that, despite all efforts, success is improbable we must be ready with an alternative.

And plans for GYMNAST were to be completed in all detail, while decisions to put them into effect would remain in suspense.

There was enough in this for everybody, and Brooke had no reason for disquiet. SLEDGEHAMMER could clearly have now no more than a shadowy and conditional existence in anybody's mind. GYMNAST was alive – but without firm date or commitment. ROUNDUP, failing SLEDGEHAMMER, was blessed in principle as the necessary consummation of all. The crunch had come – and, like most crunches gone again for a while. On 25th June the British party left America. On the same day the Combined Chiefs of Staff agreed that a Commander for both GYMNAST and ROUNDUP be nominated.

For the British delegation the Washington Conference had been grimly overshadowed by the course of the war in the Western Desert. Rommel had launched a successful attack on 26th May and Eighth Army was in full retreat. One incident stood out. Brooke recalled it afterwards. It took place during a conference with President, Prime Minister, Brooke, Dill, Ismay, Marshall and Hopkins on the afternoon of 21st June:

> Churchill and I were standing beside the President's desk talking to him when Marshall walked in with a pink piece of paper containing a message of the fall of Tobruk. Neither Winston nor I had contemplated such an eventuality and it was a staggering blow. I cannot remember what the actual words were that the President used to convey his sympathy, but I remember vividly being impressed by the tact and real heartfelt sympathy which lay behind the words. There was not one word too much nor one word too little.
>
> Marshall at once got to work to see what he could do to furnish some tangible signs of their sympathy in the shape of active assistance . . .
>
> 'I always feel,' added Brooke, 'that the Tobruk episode in the President's study did a great deal towards laying the foundation

of friendship and understanding built up during the War between the President and Marshall on the one hand and Churchill and myself on the other.'[12]

Certainly American regard for Brooke increased as, at meeting after meeting, they got to know him better and appreciate his skill and his professional expertise. Most of them, however, right to the end, stood in a certain and somewhat resentful awe of his uncompromising attitude, and rapid, authoritative speech supported by facts and arguments hard to contest. He did not show the diplomatic skill or charm of Dill. Brooke's charm – enormous charm – was reserved for his personal relationships, his unprofessional moments. He did not show it when expounding strategy or putting the British case on the prosecution of war. At such moments he was bleak, lucid and without a touch of dissimulation. In this directness and force of argument lay his greatness. A lesser man, however intelligent, under pressure of political superior or Ally, could bend a little in search of compromise. If an operational point were at stake, and the fate of servicemen possibly to be placed at hazard on an unsound venture Brooke would never bend – even a little. 'I flatly disagree,' would be his rejoinder. That would be that.

The Washington meeting edged the two Western Powers towards an agreement, but did not yet achieve it. July saw both British and Americans again urgently considering their positions. In London the War Cabinet again formally agreed that, except in most improbable conditions, SLEDGEHAMMER could not take place. ROUNDUP should be the focus of planning, and the Americans should be led towards GYMNAST.

In Washington suspicion of GYMNAST was unabated. There might be no SLEDGEHAMMER: this was virtually certain after the Washington Conference. But to the American Chiefs GYMNAST's principle significance was that it would represent a diversion, and probably delay ROUNDUP, deny it though the British might. Marshall and King flew to London on 18th July to clear matters up as far as they could. Both men were unconvinced of the merits of GYMNAST. Both had, without success, sought to persuade Roosevelt that the British should be given an ultimatum – to be more convincing in enthusiasm for early cross-Channel operations or to see the United States adopt a policy of 'Japan first'.

Nevertheless the discussions in London, which included a formal meeting of the Combined Chiefs of Staff, led to an agreed memorandum. It was in some ways a curious document. It contained a somewhat circular argument, exemplified by the following three paragraphs:

> That no avoidable reduction in preparations for ROUNDUP should be favourably considered so long as there remains any reasonable possibility of its successful execution before July 1943

but

> that if the situation on the Russian front indicates such a collapse or weakening of Russian resistance as to make ROUNDUP appear impracticable of successful execution, the decision should be taken to launch a combined operation against the North and North West coast of Africa at the earliest possible date before December 1942

and finally

> that it be understood that a commitment to this operation (GYMNAST) renders ROUNDUP in all probability impracticable of successful execution in 1943 and therefore that we have definitely accepted a defensive encircling line of action for the Continental European theatre, except as to air operations and blockade; but that the organization, planning and training for eventual entry in the Continent should continue . . .[13]

In other words, if ROUNDUP looked unpromising we should accept its postponement and go for GYMNAST, appreciating that the choice depended on the state of the enemy in the next few months, and that this, in turn, primarily depended on events on the Eastern Front.

This gave Brooke virtually all he wanted – except agreement on reasoning. He was certain that the next two months (a decision was required by September) would not produce such a weakening of the German Army in the East as could permit recommendation of ROUNDUP. This was now agreed as automatically implying GYMNAST – rechristened TORCH. In the Western Desert Rommel's menacing advance on Egypt appeared to have reached its limits, so that Brooke was reasonably free of his previous anxiety, that which had caused his temporary coolness towards the Mediterranean design – fear of losing Egypt at one end of that sea while spending resources on occupying Algeria and Tunisia at the other. Marshall was less happy. In spite of the wording of the agreed document that ROUNDUP had priority until external factors killed it, he was convinced that the British had long decided it was unsound. Marshall reckoned ROUNDUP would die not from its own weakness but from British obsession with TORCH and the Mediterranean. As late as August Marshall considered that TORCH represented an abandonment of the strategy agreed in April. But by then time pressed, and in September the firm decision for TORCH was made, and ROUNDUP's deferment until after 1943 accepted. 'There will be another tremendous row with Stalin,' wrote Churchill to Roosevelt on 22nd September. Only in July had Stalin been told that SLEDGEHAMMER, regardless of the Roosevelt-Molotov conversation, was not to take place.

In the question of 'Germany first' the British Chiefs of Staff were by no means always united on method during 1942, but the need to establish a common position with the Prime Minister and ride him off unsound preoccupations such as a North Norwegian campaign concentrated their minds wonderfully, as did the necessity to prepare and present an agreed British position to their American colleagues. There were other issues on which they had to resolve their differences. They had to make sure that the equipment programmes of their own Services were adequately protected against claims of others, diplomatically and even strategically desirable though these sometimes were. The greatest claimant was, of course, the Soviet Union to which Beaverbrook, in Brooke's view, had over-committed British resources without thought of consequence.[14] There were others. The Foreign Office was always anxious to support Turkey, and to encourage her to resist possible Axis demands. It was proposed to divert to her military equipment needed by the hard-pressed British Army. Brooke successfully resisted.[15]

The principal issue which caused contention between the Chiefs of Staff was not where we should or could make our chief operational effort. It was rather how we should use air power, and in what priority. The rival claimants were the Navy – for the Battle of the Atlantic, on which our survival and the possibility of future overseas operations undoubtedly depended: the Army, which continued to believe that in future land campaigns, wherever conducted, offensive air support might be inadequate because of lack of priority given by the Air Force to the task; and the Royal Air Force itself with its twin preoccupations of defending the United Kingdom and bombing Germany.

This battle ebbed and flowed through summer and autumn. It was temporarily settled by the Prime Minister in September, at the same time as orders for TORCH were issued. Consistent with the minimum requirements for the Air Defence of the United Kingdom (about which there was no contention) the expansion of Bomber Command and the intensification of bomber effort were to proceed. The Battle in the Atlantic would be (and to a large extent was) assisted by greater United States intervention. The Army's demands were less easily satisfied, largely because the General Staff had drawn incorrect lessons from the German successes of 1939 and 1940. They believed too simply that the answer was the dive-bomber, probably under direct Army command.[16] In fact the dive-bomber (of which a number were bought off the shelf from America) was out-moded by the fighter bomber of the later war years. Portal had never placed a low priority on Army co-operation but he was quietly adamant that it should be carried out with the most effective machines, and under sound principles, when it occurred. He was as strong on his own ground as Brooke invariably was on his; and this was Portal's ground. Brooke girded at this a good deal. He wrote to Benita on 23rd March: 'I had an unpleasant COS meeting which entailed a hammer and tongs battle with Portal trying to get Army air requirements out of him' – a theme which would not go away for a long time.

There was, however, a more fundamental debate. 'I had a hammer and tongs with Portal in the COS this morning and did not get much further with our arguments,'[17] he was to write in his evening letter of 22nd October. His diary for the day recorded:

> He [Portal] wants to devote all efforts to an intensive air bombardment of Germany on the basis that a decisive result can be obtained in this way. I am only prepared to look on the bombing of Germany as one of the many ways by which we shall bring Germany to her knees.

This latter argument was in response to a powerfully written memorandum submitted by Portal. It argued that two courses of action could not be simultaneously pursued, for lack of resources: the creation of sufficient land and air forces to invade Western Europe before breaking German industrial power on the one hand, and the destruction by a bomber offensive of that power followed by an Army of occupation landing in an already shattered Europe on the other. Portal argued that attempts to do both would lead to an indecisive compromise. He argued that emphasis on the bomber offensive, greatly increased for the purpose, would be more economic and more certain. His colleagues disagreed. Brooke argued that, while certainly intensifying the bomber offensive, we should 'exert pressure on the German military and economic machine from every quarter', and 'should take full advantage of the sea and air bases in North Africa to exert a heavy pressure on Italy with a view to turning her into a serious liability for Germany'. Brooke never believed that the strategic air offensive could so shatter Germany that the Army would have a clear and unopposed run on returning to Europe. Nor was it conceivable that the Americans would wait for such a moment, could it in the event ever come. Portal's paper was rebutted.

There was little doubt that the more immoderate supporters of the bomber offensive claimed for it advantages which events were convincingly to disprove. On the other side is the point made perhaps most vividly by Albert Speer, German Minister of War Production – that whatever the economic consequences for Germany the Allied offensive created a new front in a third dimension, and drew off huge resources to meet it.[18] That this was a profound factor, although not a decisive one, in the weakening of Germany cannot be doubted. It is also true that the Allied bomber offensive threw the Luftwaffe on to the defensive and kept it there. The desperate need for air defence fighters diverted German production from the sort of aircraft which might have had a powerful effect on Allied operations later in the war, and in the vulnerable days of invasion. Whatever the strategic effect, the avowed object was the destruction of the amenities and the wherewithal to live in the industrial areas, thus making them uninhabitable. It was not, Portal said emphatically, to kill civilians in the largest numbers *per se* – had this been so there were more economic methods than the bombing of heavily defended industrial cities; but the targeting policy was carried to lengths of inhumanity which it would not have been possible to defend under any earlier conventions, even in conflict. That such kindly, sensitive men as Portal and Brooke believed in the policy bears simple witness to the brutal influence imposed upon the principal actors of all nations by the Second World War. Nor were the military men unsupported. Air-Marshal Harris, the Commander-in-Chief Bomber Command, and the Air Staff, were never discouraged by their superiors on moral grounds. The Foreign Secretary, Eden, in April 1942 explicitly recommended 'for its psychological effect' the bombing of the 'smaller towns not too heavily defended' – and the object was, in the context, specifically the civilian population.[19]

By late summer 1942, therefore, progress had been made along the lines which Brooke advocated. Early invasion was, from whatever cause, no longer under consideration and there was general, albeit in some places grudging and temporary, acceptance of 1944 as the probable year of return to France. Maximum co-operation in the Battle of the Atlantic was agreed as an aim. A campaign to clear the North African coast had been endorsed, and American forces were committed to it – an absolute necessity in view of the relations with France which would arise. The air bombardment of Germany would continue, increasingly on an Allied basis. Russia would be sustained by material supplies where possible. The Mediterranean strategy would draw German land forces to the south, and if Italy could be shaken from the Axis would draw many more, all to the benefit of the Eastern Front and the ultimate invasion from the west. In the United Kingdom American and British land and air forces would assemble, creating a vast main base for offensive operations, both in the Mediterranean and in Western Europe, a base from which an active policy of raiding would be carried out. In the Western Desert the British Eighth Army, re-equipped and refreshed, would take the offensive. Many difficulties, operational and diplomatic, would impede smooth and rapid progress towards this goal. It was, however, Brooke's goal, at least in its main elements, from the start, and he only occasionally wavered. It was also Churchill's original goal, and although he brought imagination rather than calculation to the debate the imagination was fiery and persuasive.

Most persuasive of all to the President, the man on whom these decisions turned, was the question of timing. In July 1942 he dismissed any idea of reverting to a primarily Pacific policy. He only asked where American soldiers might go into action that very year, and demanded that they should. This, above all, was decisive for TORCH.

Thus, after nine months, the initial course of strategic action which Brooke had believed sound from his first week in office, was agreed. Negotiation with the Americans had been hard. In it both Churchill and Brooke had played complementary and indispensable parts. Churchill had worked on Roosevelt's imagination, and on his impatience to commit American forces to battle. He had also, both in December 1941 and again in a minute he sent to the

Chiefs of Staff just before the arrival of the American deputation in July, expounded what he regarded with justice as the real strategic implications of the North African operation – its offensive possibilities against the Southern flank of Europe.

This would have been insufficient without Brooke's firm attitude to any premature cross-Channel operations. On this he was like a rock. He would not at first, like Marshall, accept that ROUNDUP was inevitably postponed by TORCH; but he accepted without demur that this was 'in all probability' so. Anyway he believed ROUNDUP would be impracticable not because of any diversion of Allied strength to TORCH but because of the unbroken strength of Germany.

Roosevelt now had no intention of being diverted from TORCH in favour of a Pacific strategy in the short term, but there were shadows over long-term plans. They derived from the terms of American consent to TORCH. It had been described as a 'defensive encircling line of action' for the European theatre. Yet, by American reasoning, if the Western Allies had accepted an explicitly defensive posture against Germany throughout 1943, after undertaking TORCH it might be better, might indeed be a logical corollary to concentrate offensive power in the Pacific. The principle of 'Germany first', to which TORCH had seemed to the British an important contribution now again appeared placed, and placed by TORCH itself, at risk.

From August onward therefore, transatlantic debate continued. It now largely turned not on the fact but on the significance of TORCH. If it was merely to 'close the ring' round occupied Europe, while air bombardment continued, and to liberate shipping for other operations still open to debate, then clearly the Americans could argue (and continued to argue) that it was not essentially a land offensive against Germany in the strategic sense. If, on the other hand, TORCH, and the clearance of North Africa which was assumed to follow, could be seen as leading to an offensive against Southern Europe, a complementary and preliminary step to an invasion of the West, then matters would be different.

The argument had at least the effect of concentrating British minds. Although an early underlying motive of clearing North Africa had been to create a 'launch pad', and to exploit the possible effects of success in Italy – and neutral Turkey – there had been prime emphasis on the consequent release of shipping: and shipping could be used anywhere. The need to demonstrate to the Americans that TORCH could, in the British view, imply no departure from the principle of 'Germany first' led to emphasis upon the offensive opportunities which its success would produce. Nevertheless it was only by degrees that Brooke and his colleagues came to see that onward movement from North Africa must be continuous if Allied strategy was to remain in concert, and this onward movement had most certainly not yet been agreed. Furthermore Brooke was at every stage cautious. In discussing the question of a possible invasion of Italy he again adverted to the point that German powers of resistance must be reduced before 'large-scale' land operations could be contemplated. For Brooke feared above all things a premature and unsuccessful return to the mainland of Europe.

Throughout this debate Brooke had shown his outstanding characteristics. The American points had been cogent. They had argued for a short sea passage, for concentration of resources, and for urgency. Brooke's response rested on fact and logic. Brooke was adept at deploying facts and drawing conclusions from them which he challenged any to deny. The shipping question could be resolved when planners got down to details. As for dispersal of resources, what counted was the balance of resources assembled by each contestant at particular points. It was no use concentrating all available resources for a cross-Channel invasion if the rate of build-up and reinforcement of the Armies once landed could not match that of their enemies. Brooke was convinced, as were all his colleagues on the Chiefs of Staff Committee, that no invasion could at present succeed in the face of the anticipated rate of German reinforcement. European east-west routes were comparatively good, in spite of the bombing offensive (whose prime targeting, as has been said, was on population centres and civilian morale). German troops could concentrate against beachheads faster than their opponents could land. They could do so even while Russia still occupied much of German strength – much more so if Russia neared or reached collapse. Brooke, like all commanders in the 1940 campaign, had a vivid picture before the eye of German resilience, speed of response and fighting efficiency. He reckoned that the Americans had no knowledge of the modern German soldier and seriously underestimated him. Brooke also formed the view that the American concept of operations after landing was hazy. But his chief objection to Marshall's ideas was that they were impracticable until two preconditions were met. The first was a major weakening of Germany; this would take time, bombs and Russians to achieve. The second was the assembly of sufficient resources, notably shipping.

Thus the accent of Brooke's response to Marshall throughout 1942 was on practicability, and to that extent – since he regarded the American concepts as impracticable – he at times undoubtedly appeared negative, one whose heart was not in the great venture. By apparent contrast Churchill's promotion of exactly the same Mediterranean and North African strategy, which he had put to the Chiefs of Staff on *Duke of York* in December 1941, had been very positive. Churchill had dwelt on the exciting prospects a conquest of North Africa would expose. He had referred to the possible implications for Italy. If Italy were knocked out of the war, every Italian division throughout Europe would need replacing by Germans. He had seen the chance of dispersing the German armed forces, to counter a wide range of Allied options for invasion of the Southern flank. This was a strategy which would exploit command of the sea. He had appreciated that the effect of this on German land and air forces would be more far-reaching, and could probably be more immediate, than an invasion of France at which Churchill's underlying instinct, like Brooke's reason, revolted until the time was ripe. Churchill sometimes argued for early invasion when under great Allied or Parliamentary pressure, but he greatly feared a costly disaster in the West and he was always half-ready to be persuaded. Churchill's and Brooke's minds were complementary, with the former producing the visionary, the latter the prosaic elements. Brooke, helped by the sensitive antennae of Dill, came also to see that too 'defensive' a construction placed upon TORCH would be self-defeating. The clearance of North Africa must be presented as an opportunity for offensive operations; but – here he showed his dominant characteristic, caution – such operations must be limited in extent unless the German Army were morally and materially weakened.

Brooke, as a strategist, was the exact reverse of the opportunist or the gambler. He was a calculator, and he only played to win. He was not a great originator. His two great strengths were his realism – his practical grasp of what would and would not work, a grasp which demanded a completely clear understanding of the relationship between essential tasks and available resources: and his firmness of purpose, so that although he was prepared to modify a line he never vacillated. He developed from factors on which he felt he could depend a clear argument and he then stuck to it. The invasion of Western Europe must not take place before those preconditions had been met which would ensure its success. All pleas that deferment might further imperil Russia met the bleak response that Russia would not be helped by an inadequate diversion leading to Allied defeat in the West, and that such would be the consequence of premature action.

In the Far East there had been similar pressure. Churchill expressed personally to Wavell the hope that a dramatic offensive could be undertaken in the autumn of 1942. The American Chiefs of Staff argued the urgency of sustaining China (and keeping Chiang Kai-shek in the war) just as they argued for the relief of Russia. Again Brooke and his colleagues were adamant. The reconquest of Burma would be an operation of great complexity. It would demand shipping resources if, as seemed probable, it included a major amphibious element. It would demand mastery of the Indian Ocean, sufficient troops, and the laborious development or capture of forward bases. It could not be undertaken in 1942 nor before the completion of Operation TORCH. ANAKIM, as the Burmese offensive by seaborne assault was christened, would be undertaken, but not before the 1943 monsoon. In all this, like Wellington, Brooke showed the greatest military quality of a strategist – objectivity. He looked at facts as they were and not as they would more agreeably be, and he drew correct and exact conclusions.

CHAPTER XII

'The Conscience of the Army'

FOR BROOKE 1942 was his hardest year. The struggles to achieve an agreed Allied strategy have been described. From day to day the CIGS also watched the conduct of British soldiers on the various battlefronts. His was the ultimate responsibility. It was he that Churchill would on occasion excoriate before the Cabinet for reverses to the British Army, or for the shortcomings or apparent timidity of some distant general. If Brooke had faltered in the waging of the soldiers' battle in the war of Whitehall he would have betrayed the fighting men. He was the conscience of the Army.

This responsibility meant, above all, assurance that commanders in the field were the right men doing the right thing. There were three of outstanding importance. At General Headquarters, Home Forces, Paget had taken over from Brooke. He was always a kindred spirit. Brooke was devoted to this vigorous, austere yet lively Light Infantryman and trusted him completely in what might yet prove to be the most crucial theatre of all if the Russian front were to collapse and Germany turn again her undivided attention to Britain. And it was in Britain that the forces for future invasion were being prepared.

In the Far East, after the short-lived and ill-conceived ABDA project, Wavell had returned to Delhi. He was again Commander-in-Chief, India. In Burma Alexander had taken command of the Army and the retreat. Brooke had few anxieties there. His view of Alexander was always somewhat ambivalent. He admired his charm, his calm, his detachment and his nerve: yet he sometimes confessed in the privacy of his diary to finding a certain emptiness in Alexander, as if the exterior belied the inner man. At the Staff College Brooke had at first dismissed Alexander: 'No brains.' He had revised the terse over-simplification of that estimate – yet at times he seemed to have doubts and to return to it. Soon after taking office, during Wavell's temporary removal, the question of the Command-in-Chief in India had arisen, and Brooke had noted:

I feel Adam is the only possible selection but am afraid I may

have Gort pushed on me! And I am convinced he is unsuitable.
The other alternative is Alexander who has not got the brains and
Paget who should be left with Home Forces.[1]

It was not Brooke's most perceptive note, on, perhaps, more
than one count. Anyway he never stinted his admiration for
Alexander's ability to get men working together, particularly in
Italy.

With Wavell there was a complete sympathy, which echoed the
days of the Mobile Division on Salisbury Plain, with Wavell as
Brooke's wise superior and counsellor at Southern Command.
Brooke found it hard to communicate easily with his fellows in the
higher ranks of the Army. With the young he could relax and talk
of other things: with generals he tended to be forbidding unless he
knew them really well and they had earned his full trust. He
received their respect, their admiration, on occasions their
affection; but he had a warm personal relationship with few. One of
the few – always – was Dill, perhaps the only serving soldier for
whom Brooke showed unreserved admiration. A second was his
cousin 'Boy' Brooke – Bertie – whom ties of family as well as
lifelong friendship set apart. A third was Adam, now Adjutant-
General, the companion of 'N' Battery and of youth. A fourth was
Wavell. He found Wavell's taciturnity as a companion a trial, but
as a correspondent he valued him greatly. To Wavell in India
Brooke would write freely about every anxiety whether it
concerned that area or another. Perhaps because of this affinity
Brooke was more generous than he might have been to Wavell's
performance. In the withdrawal from Burma, as well as on other
occasions in the future, Wavell was reckoned by some to show an
excessive detachment, a certain lack of grip. Certainly his
directions to Alexander in Burma were ambiguous. Nevertheless
Wavell and Dill were Brooke's wartime confidants.

In the Middle East, the theatre of operations on which so many
British hopes and fears were concentrated, was Auchinleck.

From his first days in office Brooke's mind had inevitably been
bent very largely on the Middle East, in spite of the successive
hammer blows suffered from Japan. The clearance of North
Africa, delayed though decisive operations might be by the rival
claims of the defence of India and Ceylon, was nevertheless
Brooke's – and Churchill's – constant aim. For this there had to be
a successful campaign in the Western Desert. Instead, the
triumphs of CRUSADER quickly evaporated, as the Eighth Army

was forced, by German counter-attack, to withdraw: by 7th February it was back at Gazala. 'Nothing less than bad generalship on the part of Auchinleck,' Brooke confided to his diary on 30th January – no measured verdict, but an indication of a seed of disquiet and irritation which, just or not, would grow. Furthermore he wrote not of Ritchie, the Army Commander, but of Auchinleck, the Commander-in-Chief, whose Headquarters were in Cairo and whose concerns were not only with the Western Desert but with a huge area including Persia and Iraq, and with the possible threat of a German southward advance from the Caucasus towards oilfields vital to Britain.

Auchinleck had certainly shown the breadth of outlook necessary in the Commander-in-Chief of such a theatre. Soon after assuming command in 1941 he had sent to the Prime Minister an admirable appreciation of the whole situation.[2] He was always concerned – as was natural to one of the Indian Army's greatest sons – with the threat to India from the east as well as with the possible drive of the Germans into the Middle East to his rear. India was an essential support to his own forces based in Egypt. 'We can't hold the Middle East without India,' he wrote to Brooke in May 1942.[3] Auchinleck rightly considered matters on a large map. He spoke of 'what *I* call the Middle East – Turkey, Iraq, Iran, Afghanistan and Arabia'. He had shown a certain initial pessimism about Libya, writing to Dill in his earliest days: 'I am expecting to see us back around Mersa Matruh before long.' But his vision was never narrow. He believed that the way to ultimate victory lay via the Adriatic into Hungary, Bohemia and Bavaria.

Nevertheless Auchinleck had been encouraged – indeed spurred – by Churchill, with sound instinct, to concentrate his energies upon the enemy at his door. 'Defeat the Germans in the Western Desert . . . all your armies would therefore be free in conjunction with Wavell's to give their right hand to the Russians and to animate and even draw in the Turks. Nothing can compare with this,'[4] the Prime Minister had written to him in August 1941, striking a note in sympathy with Auchinleck's long-term views but with exuberant disregard of logistics, shipping and virtually every other strategic reality at that time. Churchill, whatever the hyperbole, had already reckoned that not only the Turks but possibly GHQ Middle East needed animating. These exchanges bothered Auchinleck. Dill had warned him of the difficult times he would have in satisfying Churchill's impatience and voracious zest for detail, and in reconciling this with his duty to his command and to his conscience. He never failed in the latter, but he took the pinpricks hard. They were irritants to a Commander on the spot. 'It would have seemed more consistent with accepted principles of strategy and commonsense to have engaged the Tobruk garrison in heavy and continuous action before or during the climax of the attack upon Sollum,' Churchill had signalled to him in July 1941.[5] Such operational advice from the fortress of Whitehall is easier to give than receive. And there was a constant stream of requests for information on detailed matters such as tank numbers. 'His [Churchill's] sharp thrusts . . . *do* worry me,' Auchinleck wrote to Dill in November 1941, 'and I can't help it.'[6]

Auchinleck's own appointments and judgements of men had not improved the regard in which he was held at home. Cunningham, of whom he had written to Churchill in September 1941, 'he gives me great confidence', had cracked and been replaced at the head of Eighth Army by the untested Ritchie. In the circumstances Auchinleck had no wide choice, and it was entirely to his credit that thereafter he supported Ritchie to the hilt and beyond. Unfortunately Auchinleck's very qualities of loyalty to and trust in subordinates got in the way of a ruthlessness which might have served his country – and himself – more enduringly. When he started to have inner doubts – as with Ritchie – he ended by shielding the Army Commander from what appeared command errors by himself assuming more and more direct control. This he was urged by Churchill to do, and in the terrible summer of 1942 ultimately did in full, assuming formal command of Eighth Army, and replacing Ritchie. The two functions were impossible to combine: but even before officially replacing him Auchinleck was apt to stand too close behind his chosen subordinate, which inevitably tended to blur responsibility and undermine confidence.

In other appointments Auchinleck's views did not allay the doubts in Brooke's heart. He had asked for General Corbett as his Chief of Staff, in place of General Smith who was, Brooke agreed, excellent but in need of rest. Corbett 'will blow away a lot of cobwebs' Auchinleck wrote enthusiastically to Brooke on 1st March.[7] Brooke was not so sure. Corbett proved a conspicuous failure, although Auchinleck considered him at one point for command of Eighth Army – an extraordinary choice. Even in his comments on officers of that Indian Army he knew best (and Corbett had come from the Indian Army) Auchinleck did not show judgement which hindsight can endorse. He had urged on Brooke the necessity for Wavell, in Delhi, to have an Indian Army Chief of Staff, and Wavell had suggested the name of Slim as one of two possible choices. 'Personality is needed. Neither have the reputation, personality and experience which would give the Indian Army full confidence in their ability,' Auchinleck wrote to Brooke authoritatively – and on the figures of the Indian Army he was indeed regarded as the supreme authority. He may have been right but it is legitimate to doubt it, although naturally there was no demur at the time.[8]

As to contacts with Whitehall, Brooke's assumption of office helped Auchinleck by interposing a more determined CIGS into the space between Premier and Commander-in-Chief. But well before the operational drama of the summer of 1942 a personal crisis occurred. Churchill asked that Auchinleck should return to London for consultation. With the British back on the Gazala line, the situation in the Mediterranean critical to future Allied plans, and with the new problems created by the enlargement of the war this request was entirely reasonable. Auchinleck said that his responsibilities prevented his return. The war situation – it was early March – was too dangerous.

This position, from which Auchinleck would not be shifted, infuriated Churchill. He was already disappointed in what he regarded as Auchinleck's defensive outlook, and was naturally chagrined at the turn of events after the initial triumphs of CRUSADER had evaporated. He made his first moves towards replacing this stubborn Commander-in-Chief. On 19th March he wrote to Brooke:

> In case we reach a complete deadlock with General Auchinleck it would be right to consider the claims of Lord Gort.[9]

Brooke was still defending Auchinleck and would for some time continue to do so. His views on Gort were, as we have seen, not such as to make him receptive to that suggestion. 'I sincerely hope,' he replied, 'that we do not reach a complete deadlock with General Auchinleck. I should certainly not recommend Lord Gort to replace him. Having served under him in France . . . he will make a first class commander for a small force, of a division to a Corps, where a determined commander is required for a dangerous operation. He has, however, definitely not got the knowledge or ability to perform the duties of Commander-in-Chief in a large and difficult Command such as the Middle East.'[10]

Brooke expressed the opinion that if change were really necessary – and he was by no means convinced yet that it was – it would be best to bring back Wavell and send Auchinleck to India, where he would be excellent. In view of Churchill's previous impatience and inability to get on terms with Wavell this, of course, was never a practicable possibility and Brooke must have known so. Meanwhile he found the duty of defending Auchinleck increasingly irksome. 'It is very exhausting this continual protection of Auchinleck,' he wrote in his diary at the end of March, 'especially as I have not got the highest opinion of him.' The two men had been on the first Imperial Defence College course together in 1927 and were old acquaintances but they were not particularly close in spirit. However 'Marshall in great confidence told me of your stout defence of the Auk', Dill wrote to him on 23rd April. While Auchinleck held the Command the CIGS would be behind him.[11]

Defence of the Commander-in-Chief continued to be needed throughout April and May as Churchill demanded an offensive which Auchinleck refused to undertake until he was ready. It was intensely irritating to Auchinleck that, as he put it in a letter to Brooke on 7th May, his 'forecasts' on the possible timing of operations were taken by the Prime Minister as programmes to which he should adhere. Sometimes he fumed at Brooke himself, on one occasion taking leave to doubt whether a particular signal could possibly have had the CIGS's approval, so ignorant did it seem (he said) of local difficulties and so inconsistent with an earlier personal and understanding message. Brooke soothed him. The signal was a diluted version of a much more aggressive one drafted by Churchill, and new factors had arisen in the interval between the sympathetic message and the harsh one.[12] So the cut and thrust went on. Desperate for the possession of the Cyrenaican airfields in order to help the relief of Malta, London was pressing for the earliest possible resumption of the attack. Auchinleck declared he could not attack before 1st June, and he would not be moved. The visit of Sir Stafford Cripps as a Cabinet emissary from the Prime Minister, with General Nye, Vice-Chief of the Imperial General Staff, far from shaking Auchinleck convinced his two visitors that he was right.

Right or wrong – and in fact almost certainly right – Auchinleck's tactics in communicating his thinking and his intentions had the effect of provoking Churchill, and making Brooke's task of defending the Commander-in-Chief even harder.

On 6th May Auchinleck not only proposed delaying his offensive to 15th June but gave certain conditions under which it would have to be postponed until August. A few days earlier a Middle East signal had taken a broad view of the strategic situation, and envisaged the possibility of standing on the defensive in the Western Desert and diverting all available forces for the defence of India against the Japanese. To a Prime Minister desperate for success against Rommel and looking to that success as a pressure point in the difficult propulsion of the Americans towards the Mediterranean; and to a Chiefs of Staff Committee profoundly concerned for Malta, such signals – above all from the Commander-in-Chief to whom all looked for victory in the desert – appeared grossly out of tune with political and grand strategic realities. Auchinleck seemed to Brooke and his colleague Chiefs to minimize or fail to understand the importance of Malta, and to overstate the difficulties of the operational situation confronting him.

He was urged, if necessary, to take risks with the security of Egypt if he could thereby provide a chance of earlier relief to Malta. Whether or not this was practicable guidance to follow, patience with Auchinleck was running out in London during May 1942 and confidence in his Command and Staff was at a low level. 'I am not happy at all from all I hear of the situation at Middle East Headquarters,' Brooke wrote in his diary on 19th May, 'Auchinleck's Chief of Staff is nothing like good enough for the job, and yet he insisted on selecting him. On the other hand I do not feel Neil Ritchie is a big enough man to command the Eighth Army and I fear that the Auk is also losing confidence in him.'

On 26th May Rommel attacked.

The victorious German operations at Gazala and throughout June 1942 have often been described, and in an earlier chapter we saw how the fall of Tobruk found Prime Minister and CIGS in Washington, stunned by the disaster. Auchinleck relieved Ritchie on 25th June and decided to try to stabilize the front at the most defensible point covering the Delta–El Alamein. To the Alamein poisition a largely disorganized British and Imperial Army streamed back, with all those doubts inevitable in shaken troops about the leadership which had brought them to such a pass. Auchinleck proposed his own resignation which was declined. Brooke wrote on 8th July that Churchill in a Cabinet Meeting 'ran down Middle East Army in a shocking way, and criticized

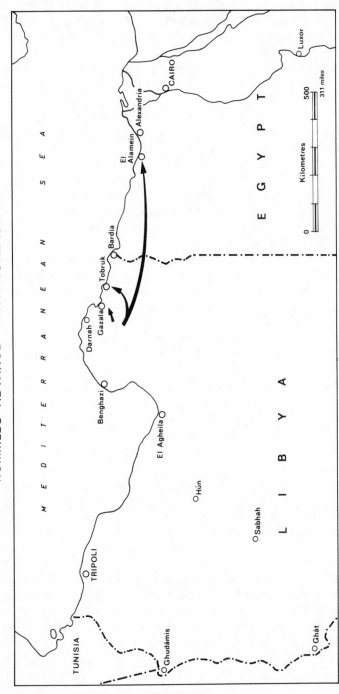

ROMMEL'S ADVANCE   MAY - JUNE 1942

Auchinleck for not showing a more offensive spirit. I had an uphill
task defending him and pointing out the difficulties of his present
position . . . After being thoroughly unpleasant during the Cabinet
Meeting, with that astounding charm of his, he came up and said to
me: "I am sorry Brookie if I had to be unpleasant about Auchinleck
and the Middle East".'[13]

To Auchinleck himself Brooke did his best, in spite of
profound misgivings, to provide support. He wrote on 17th July:

> I should like you to realize how much I feel for you in the difficult
> times you have been through, and to know that you can rely on
> me to do all I can to help you from this end[14]

and Auchinleck replied with gratitude on 25th July in a letter
which showed plenty of spirit:

> 'We undoubtedly gave the enemy a rude shock but we failed in
> our object which was to break through' (this followed one of the
> exhausted counter-attacks on the 'Alamein line'). Commenting
> that 'the Eighth Army will need a Commander of its own again
> some day I suppose', Auchinleck observed that Gott might do
> the job well. 'It is not easy filling a dual role,' he wrote, 'however
> Corbett is doing excellently in Cairo.' He mentioned in the same
> letter the possibility of having to withdraw from forward
> positions, 'but I hope this will not be necessary'.[15]

After a few breakthrough attempts with insufficient force behind
them, the overstretched Axis forces, having suffered some well-
administered knocks, settled for a temporary stalemate. Their
communications and lines of supply were tenuous, those of their
adversaries, within sixty miles of Alexandria, were simple.
Auchinleck, with tactical skill, and boundless courage and
stamina, held his hastily adopted front and inflicted heavy
casualties on his enemies. The moment of extreme danger was over
for the British Army, and with the prospect of major reinforcement and build-up the initiative was again theirs. In the desert, as
in a fencing bout with foils, the right of attack passed from one side
to the other as if by rule.

The loss of Egypt, the 'Worst Case', had been examined in both
Chiefs of Staff Committee and Cabinet on the 2nd and 3rd July. It
was not unreasonable for the British to prepare contingency plans
for action if the enemy broke through the Alamein position, but
there is no reason to doubt Auchinleck's confidence that he could
stop them doing so in the future as he had just succeeded in doing.
Contingency plans for withdrawal tend to become known,

however, and in an Army whose morale is fragile they can be dangerous. As at Tobruk, so at El Alamein, there was a certain ambiguity in Auchinleck's words about withdrawal, if not in his mind.

It was in the immediate aftermath of this situation that Brooke decided to visit Egypt. He found it unfortunate that Churchill was determined to take the same road, en route to Russia to break to Stalin the news – inevitably disagreeable – of Allied intentions for the rest of 1942 and for the future. Brooke had first headed off a visit of Churchill to Cairo on 1st June, saying how unfair it would be to Auchinleck. When he obtained leave to go in August he first hoped strongly to be alone, and to size things up for himself. 'Had to go round to the PM at 7 p.m. for about an hour to receive last minute marching instructions,' Brooke wrote to Benita on 29th July.[16] 'The old ruffian is quite jealous that he is not coming along with me!' In such matters the old ruffian had a tendency to get his way. Brooke was also to go to Russia. This offered at least a possibility of learning about operations on the Eastern Front from the Russians themselves. 'The only way in which I knew Russian dispositions was through German messages which we intercepted,'[17] Brooke wrote afterwards. Fortunately this was knowledge of remarkable extent. Brooke had visited the miracle workers of ULTRA in April '. . . went to see the organization for breaking down ciphers. A wonderful set of professors and genii. I marvel at the work they succeed in doing.'*[18]

But at the beginning of August the urgent task which confronted the professional head of the Army was to see what needed setting to rights in the Middle East, and, although he would have preferred to do so alone, it was not to be. Prime Minister and CIGS travelled separately, however, and by different routes. Brooke made a brief stop in Malta. Later he wrote:

> I was specially anxious to visit Gort in Malta as I knew he was in a depressed state, feeling that he had been shoved away in a corner out of the real war, and in danger of his whole garrison being scuppered without much chance of giving an account of themselves. His depression had been increased by the fact that he

---

* Brooke wrote later: 'Unfortunately secrecy will never make it possible to describe this organization or to pay full tribute to it. The results it achieved played a large part in rendering ultimate victory possible.' This particular omission has now been rectified. It is remarkable that he also mentioned his visit and its object in his evening letter to Benita.

insisted on living on the reduced standard of rations prevailing in the island in spite of the fact that he was doing twice as much physical and mental work as any other member of the garrison.* Owing to the shortage of petrol he was using a bicycle in that sweltering heat and frequently had to carry his bicycle over demolished houses. I wanted to tell him about the plans for new command in the Middle East with an advance westward, combined with American-British landings in North West Africa moving eastward, destined to meet eventually. I wanted to make him feel that if all this came off he would find himself in an outpost of an advance instead of the backwater he considered himself in. I felt certain that to be able to look forward to something definite would do much to dispel his gloom.[19]

In fact Gort had been governing and commanding Malta in desperate days for the island when its importance was paramount. The successes of convergent Allied Armies in North Africa would relieve Malta, but hardly enhance its importance or give to its warrior leader a sense of participation in greater events than those he was then surviving. A more stimulating message might have been given had Brooke known every secret of the German High Command. In the spring of 1942 it had been agreed by Hitler and Mussolini that Malta was to be invaded from Sicily by four airborne divisions, with a seaborne expedition guarded by the Italian fleet as soon as a bridgehead had been secured. The operation – HERCULES – planned for July, had been postponed until September, after the capture of Tobruk, on the ground that it would involve needless loss if, as then seemed possible, Rommel could take Egypt and the Canal without it. Hitler's heart had never been in it.

On 3rd August Brooke reached Cairo. The day, the first of a momentous visit, was recorded by him that evening:

Finally we descended at about 6.30 a.m. and found a large gathering on the aerodrome awaiting PM who was due shortly.

We did not wait for PM but drove on the 25 miles to Cairo and the Embassy where I had a shave, bath and breakfast. PM then turned up delighted with his trip and looking remarkably fresh.

At lunch Smuts turned up having flown up from Pretoria. He was astounding good value and full of wit in answering PM's remarks.

After lunch snatched ¾hour's sleep before going to meet

* But it would have been inconceivable to Gort, the quintessance of a Regimental officer who put himself last, to do anything else.

Auchinleck who was coming back from the front, and had a short talk with him before attending one of his C.-in-C. meetings. At 5.30 p.m. he came to the Embassy and we had a long interview with the PM after which he [the PM] called me in for further talks. He is fretting that there is to be no offensive action till 15th September and I see already troublesome times ahead!

After dinner, when I was dropping with sleepiness, PM again called me in and kept me up till 1.30 a.m. Back to the same arguments that Auk must come back to the Command of ME and leave the Eighth Army. Exactly what I have always told him from the start!

Then he argued strongly for Gott to take over [Command of 8th Army] whilst I know that Gott is very tired. Finally suggested that I should take it over! I shall have a job to convince him that I am unsuitable for the job having never been trained in the desert.

This was the first of Churchill's suggestions for a command for Brooke. It gave him, he wrote later, 'desperate longings'. It is hard to believe, however, that the CIGS could have been selected thus for a subordinate command, or that any new Commander-in-Chief (let alone Auchinleck, who was not assumed to be superseded when this particular conversation took place) would have found their relative situations tolerable. But Brooke's emotions were very understandable. Whether, personal position vis-à-vis others apart, he would have been the right man to command Eighth Army must be a matter of speculation. His 'having never been trained in the desert' can be discounted. Neither had Rommel nor Montgomery. Brooke would certainly have imposed his will; and that needed doing. But he was a self-questioning, sensitive man and he was not by instinct a 'Regimental soldier', a soldiers' general. Even some of his greatest admirers would have been dubious. Brooke, said Paget, 'had little understanding of the average soldier or day-to-day life of Regiment or Unit'.[20] The Secretary of State P. J. Grigg, whose regard for Brooke was immensely high, was also retrospectively sceptical. 'He commanded the admiration and respect of officers,' wrote Grigg, 'who recognized in him a master of his profession, but rarely did he arouse affection, for he was too insular and rarely offered friendship – regarding subordinates as cogs in the machine.'[21] How different was this image from the intensely human, modest, loving and lovable man disclosed to his real intimates, his family, his children! 'Too insular' – 'No man is an island' yet some set more insulation around themselves than others. Most men are at least two men, but in Brooke the contrast between the austere and remote professional and the sensitive, witty and sympathetic private person was so sharp that few who knew only one of the two selves could easily credit the existence of the other.

For the command of Eighth Army Brooke pressed the name of Montgomery. He had absolute faith in Montgomery's tactical ability. He knew that he was self-confident to a fault, thoroughly resilient and ruthless in getting his own way. Eighth Army needed such a man. Brooke was dubious as to whether Auchinleck and Montgomery could work together – and with the Germans at the gates of the Delta the eyes of both Commander-in-Chief and Army Commander would, for the while, be on the Western Desert. Auchinleck, he felt, would try excessively to steer a subordinate – as he clearly, though perhaps necessarily, had done with Ritchie. Montgomery would not take to such treatment. Rather to Brooke's surprise, however, Auchinleck accepted the idea of Montgomery as Army Commander.

Churchill demurred strongly. Brooke's diary for 4th August recorded:

> After dinner I was dragged off into the garden by PM to report results of my day's work. As I expected my work was not approved of! Montgomery could not possibly arrive in time to hurry on the date of the attack! I told him no one else could. He then pressed for Gott. I told him that I had discussed him with Auchinleck who did not consider him up to it, and also that he was too tired . . . However he kept me arguing till 1 a.m.

Next day Brooke toured Eighth Army. His visit to General Gott, commanding a Corps, confirmed his impression that he needed a rest and would not, or at least not yet, be suitable as an Army Commander. Eighth Army Headquarters did not make a favourable impression. Brooke had not yet decided whether it was imperative that Auchinleck should go. The balance of his opinion was shifted that way by his day in the desert, when he reckoned that Auchinleck was too much under the influence of General Dorman Smith, an imaginative officer, widely mistrusted, whose flood of ideas, in Brooke's view, needed a very perceptive sifting of which he felt Auchinleck incapable. Both at Army HQ and at GHQ new blood was needed. Churchill, however, supported by his own enquiries, was still persuaded that Gott would be the best choice. Sixth August was an important day for Brooke and best told in his own words:

> One of the most difficult days of my life, with momentous decisions to take as far as my own future and that of the war was concerned. Whilst I was dressing and practically naked, the PM suddenly burst into my room. Very elated, and informed me that his thoughts were taking shape and that he would soon commit himself to paper! I rather shuddered and wondered what he was up to!
>
> Ten minutes later he burst into my room again and invited me to breakfast with him. However as I was in the middle of my breakfast by then he asked me to come as soon as I had finished my breakfast. When I went round he made me sit on the sofa whilst he walked up and down. First of all he said he had decided to split the ME command in two. A Near East taking up to the Canal, and a Middle East taking Syria, Palestine, Persia and Iraq. I argued with him that the Canal was an impossible boundary as both Palestine and Syria are based administratively on Egypt. He partially agreed, and then went on to say that he intended to remove the Auk to the Persian-Iraq Command as he had lost confidence in him, and he wanted me to take over the Near East Command with Montgomery as my Army Commander! This made my heart race very fast. He said he did not require an answer at once, and that I could think it over if I wanted. However I told him without waiting that I was quite certain it would be a wrong move. I knew nothing about desert warfare, and could never have time to grip hold of the show to my satisfaction before the necessity to attack became imperative.
>
> Another point which I did not mention was that after working with the PM for close on 9 months I do feel at last that I can exercise a limited amount of control on some of his activities, and that at last he is beginning to take my advice. I feel, therefore, that tempting as the offer is by accepting it I should definitely be taking a course which would on the whole help the war the least.
>
> Finally I could not bear the thought that Auchinleck might think that I had come out here on purpose to work myself into his shoes.
>
> PM was not pleased with this reply but accepted it well.

Continuing on the same theme:

> After lunch Smuts asked if he could see me for a bit, and we retired to a quiet room. He then started on the same story as the PM in the morning, telling me what importance he attached to my taking it (the Command of the Near Middle East) and what a

wonderful future it would have for me if I succeeded in defeating Rommel. I repeated exactly what I had said to PM. Thanked him for his kindness and told him that he really did not know me well enough to be so assured that I could make a success of it. However he answered that he knew I had taken a leading part in saving the BEF in France. At last I got him to agree that Alexander was a better selection than me.

I have been giving it a great deal of thought all day and am *quite* convinced that my decision was a right one and that I can do more by remaining CIGS.[22]

This was indeed a momentous decision. The Middle East Command was Brooke's if he chose. At that moment it gave promise of being the most active and historic for the British Army at a critical moment in its history. Brooke declined it.

There can be little doubt that he was right, but neither can there be doubt that the decision was painful. The satisfaction of Command differs in kind from that of a Staff appointment however influential or exalted. Whitehall was an exhausting and often frustrating place, and the conflicts and compromises necessary there were needles in Brooke's flesh, able though he was at managing them. He was a superb CIGS, and by August 1942 he probably knew it. But he often longed for more freedom, and challenge of a different kind.

In fact Brooke was not only virtually indispensable as CIGS, but was already so outstanding as Chairman of the Chiefs of Staff Committee, and as their chief spokesman in Cabinet and to Churchill, that the entire war effort must greatly have suffered had he left his post. Furthermore, as matters turned out, he would have been wasted in the Middle East. The critical area in that Command remained the Western Desert, and the dominant influence therein should be the new Army Commander, not the Commander-in-Chief.

In the diary entry quoted above Alexander was mentioned, for the first time, as a natural successor to Auchinleck. It is clear that Brooke's mind had by now become reconciled to the fact that Auchinleck must go. Furthermore not only the diary but notes written afterwards reveal a dominant motive. Brooke was determined to get Montgomery, sooner or later, to command Eighth Army although he accepted, with some misgiving, the choice of Gott to serve under Alexander as the final selection 'package' put to the War Cabinet on 6th August.[23] In fact Gott's tragic death, shot down the following day in an aircraft flying to

Cairo, meant that Montgomery's appointment took place immediately. Brooke was always pretty certain that Auchinleck and Montgomery would not work well together, and the logic of that belief, as well as the poor impressions he had received since arrival, led him to agree with any solution which took Auchinleck from Cairo.

This was a culmination of a long summer of disquiet at aspects of Auchinleck's command. Brooke realized that Churchill could no longer be expected to support a man in whom he had lost confidence. As to Alexander, Brooke, as we have seen, had his own views and they differed somewhat from those of Churchill to whom Alexander was the ideal general, a man with panache, a figure to whom a certain natural aura of romance attached itself, harmonious with the Prime Minister's own character. To the more dissective mind of Brooke Alexander was, above all, imperturbable and a man who would trust subordinates and keep a fair balance between interests – and, later, Allies: and who would, in turn, be trusted by all. As early as May Churchill had wanted to bring him back to play some part in the Middle East.

Of particular importance to Brooke was the fact that Alexander could be discouraged from seeking to direct too closely his new Army Commander, and would be receptive to that discouragement. For Brooke had neither doubts nor illusions about Montgomery. 'I knew that Monty was far better qualified to command the Eighth Army than Alex, and I did not want Alex to be encouraged to interfere with Monty,' wrote Brooke in his diary on the evening of 8th August. He regarded Montgomery as, without question, the best tactical commander in the Army. 'I never interfere with Monty in tactical matters,' Brooke observed to a colleague in the War Office, 'he's generally right'; but then, with a twinkle, 'and he doesn't let you forget it!'[24] For the CIGS was also sharply aware, as he had been from the days when he had firmly commanded in his Corps this gifted, energetic and idiosyncratic soldier, that Montgomery possessed a powerful strain of egocentricity and an assurance which was indispensable when well-directed but which could appear provocative and ill-mannered when not. So it continued. 'Monty still requires the occasional kick on the backside,' Brooke wrote to Wavell about their fellow Field-Marshal as late as 1944, 'and I am trying to make certain he gets it!'[25]

But that Montgomery was now the man for the Eighth Army Brooke had no question, and his confidence was reinforced by the vigorous and impressive briefing on his future plans which Montgomery gave to the Prime Minister and CIGS shortly after taking over, and during their second visit to Cairo on return from Moscow. It has been argued that Montgomery's plans were not original: that he claimed too much personal credit for them; and, indeed, that Auchinleck himself had foreseen the future run of events and the best way to meet them with equal prescience. This may be partly so. The essential fact, which Brooke saw clearly and which greatly relieved him, was that Montgomery, by his force of personality and his strength of will, had put fresh heart and fresh confidence into the Army. He restored morale, and he allowed no voice to drown or even challenge his own. At crucial moments in war this power of the commander's will is all-important, transcending the brilliance or fallibility of operational concepts. With Alexander and Montgomery in the British Army's most significant theatre of war Brooke at last felt that he had done all he could. Montgomery had zest for battle and such a man was needed. 'Do you *enjoy* fighting battles, Franklyn?' Brooke had broodingly asked the General commanding in Northern Ireland on a visit in July 1942: 'I don't. I think Monty does.'[26]

Outwardly Auchinleck, as was his way, took the decision that he was to go with uncomplaining dignity. He had refused on several occasions to attack before he was ready (as would Montgomery refuse) and he was at ease with his conscience on that score. He knew that he had done his best, and dealt the Axis forces some effective blows when the position was stabilized at El Alamein. He had no qualms about planning for further withdrawal if, as he did not believe likely, it were forced upon him. At all costs he would keep the Army in being and prevent any tactical reverse in Egypt from becoming a major strategic defeat opening the road to Persia, Iraq, the Indian Ocean. He rated the latter, at last resort, more important than Egypt. So did the Chiefs of Staff. The 'centre of gravity' of Auchinleck's strategic thinking was well to the east.

Auchinleck declined the proposed new Persia/Iraq command offered him. He did not believe its boundaries made sense, and he felt his removal implied lack of confidence in him – which it did. He regarded this as unjust – the outcome of incomprehension by those in London of the problems of the Desert War. They did not appear to him to understand the difference made to numbers by equipment quality – nor how superior were the German anti-tank guns in particular. They did not appear to understand the need for training and acclimatization of new units – and for modification of new equipments – to make them ready for battle. They appeared to ignore, perhaps as unpalatable, the tactical superiority the German commanders so frequently displayed: yet he had described it faithfully and at all times striven to correct it.

To Brooke alone Auchinleck showed his bitterness. Brooke regretted his refusal to take the Persia/Iraq command. It was a command, Brooke wrote on 8th August, 'where he might restore his reputation, as active operations are more than probable'. Whether, on this assumption, it was consistent to offer the command to one in whom Churchill had lost confidence was more debatable. 'I am not certain we are not better off without him,' Brooke's diary continued. He regarded it as 'unsoldierly' in Auchinleck to turn down a command in war – 'like an offended film star'. Brooke had a stormy interview on 9th August with Auchinleck. 'I tried to soften the blow as much as I possibly could. In the end I had no alternative but to turn on him and put him in his place,' Brooke recorded afterwards, 'he left me no alternative.'[27] It was a disagreeable task, but no man since Wellington had stood at the head of the Army more capable than Brooke of describing to even the most exalted their failings in plain words. 'I had to bite him back as he was apt to snarl, that kept him quiet,' he wrote.

Auchinleck bore no trace of animosity against Brooke. In spite of 'this unpleasant day' Brooke wrote that 'our relations remained of the best and he could not have been more charming than he was in after years'.[28] Auchinleck recognized the CIGS's quality throughout the war. 'I hope it doesn't mean that you are not going to stay where you are,' he wrote to Brooke on congratulating him on a Field-Marshal's baton two years later. 'You must!'[29] Brooke's ultimate judgement was succinct: 'Auk was a fine commander but a poor judge of men.'[30] Brooke did not like overruling commanders in their choice of subordinates, but he never found cause to change this criticism of Auchinleck. Initially, however, he went further. In February 1943, the question came up of Auchinleck's suitability as Commander-in-Chief, India (Wavell was to be Viceroy) and Brooke signalled to Wavell:

> I have lost all confidence in him as a commander. He is bad in the selection of men to serve him and has a faulty conception of modern war.[31]

Some of the reason for this particularly damning verdict, which contradicted his usual qualified encomium of a 'fine commander', no doubt stemmed from their sharp exchanges of 9th August. But another part cause must have been a note which Montgomery wrote after taking command of Eighth Army, and which both Brooke and Churchill saw. The substance of much of this note corresponds to the account published in Montgomery's *Memoirs* but there were some savage additional paragraphs.

> The condition of Eighth Army as described above is not over-painted; it was almost unbelievable. From what I know now it is quite clear that the reverses we had suffered at GAZALA and East of it, which finally forced us back to within 60 miles of Alexandria, should never have happened.
>
> Gross mismanagement, faulty command, and bad Staff work, had been the cause of the whole thing.
>
> But the final blame must rest on General AUCHINLECK for allowing an inexperienced General like RITCHIE to mishandle grossly a fine fighting Army and for allowing a policy of dispersion to rule.
>
> Divisions were split up into bits and pieces all over the desert; the armour was not concentrated; the gunners had forgotten the art of employing artillery in a concentrated form.
>
> If changes in the higher command had not been made early in August we would have lost EGYPT.
>
> Actually they were made only just in time.[32]

Montgomery wrote in a personal letter at the same time – 'Auchinleck should never be employed again in any capacity.'[32a] Many an old desert hand would have regarded some of this as exaggerated. There had certainly been bad times. Auchinleck's expression of intentions with regard to Tobruk, for instance, had contained a certain ambiguity which was remembered against him when that port fell to Rommel. The dividing of formations in 'bits and pieces' was the result of his conviction that armour and infantry needed to be handled in intimate combination at a lower level than that of division, a conviction he had discussed in frequent letters to Brooke. There was little doubt that Eighth Army had suffered from lack of 'grip', and Montgomery was exactly the man to provide it. Yet in denying all credit to his predecessor's fighting achievements Montgomery spoiled a case by overstatement and showed the ungenerous side of his character. Trusting Montgomery's tactical and professional perceptions as he did, it is clear that Brooke accepted his findings in their entirety where a pinch of salt would not have been out of place.

There is one small, sad postscript. When the 'Africa Star' was struck, an 'Eighth Army clasp' was approved to be worn on the medal ribbon by certain qualifying soldiers. Auchinleck wrote to Brooke in January 1944 from India (in the same letter in which he told Brooke how indispensable he was) asking him to intervene, since he had heard that the clasp was only to be awarded to those who had served at or after the October 1942 battle of Alamein, Montgomery's great victory. Auchinleck felt and wrote strongly:

> I think this is doing a great injustice to those brave men who under Cunningham and Ritchie fought and broke Rommel in November and December 1941 . . .
> They did this, as you know yourself, with inferior armament and equipment and with practically equal numbers . . .
> Again, after Tobruk fell, the men who held the Germans at Alamein surely laid the foundations for the final victory of the 8th Army?[33]

Wavell also pressed the claims for some additional distinguishing mark for those who had fought in the original Desert Army. Brooke replied to Auchinleck in March that he had supported this request to the Prime Minister, but that the appropriate Committee declined to accede to it, giving as their reason that to extend the period as proposed would 'inevitably involve a clasp for earlier operations'. Auchinleck had asked that the Eighth Army clasp should cover all who fought with that Army since its creation. Brooke supported what on the face of it looked like better justice; he anyway thought such 'clasps' a mistake.[34] But in the event the men who fought under Cunningham, Ritchie and Auchinleck only wore the Eighth Army clasp if they survived to serve under Montgomery on or after 23rd October 1942. It is ironic that had such a warrior as Gott been wounded instead of killed in his air disaster he would not have qualified.

Meanwhile other great encounters awaited Churchill and Brooke. Command had been changed in the Middle East. Alexander and Montgomery were sent for. Prime Minister and CIGS immediately set out for Moscow, planning to revisit Egypt on their return journey. Brooke undertook many long-distance flights during the war. They were uncomfortable – usually in a converted Liberator bomber where the CIGS found a bed in the bombrack. They were, however, high adventures and in spite of the frustration of much of the business of conference, he always had zest for new sights, new wildlife and new country. On this occasion he flew from Cairo to Tehran, where he changed to a Russian plane and pilot, who was, Brooke noted, 'light hearted' and apt to execute a manoeuvre in the air over the airfield at take-off as a farewell to his friends. The flight to Moscow passed near the Caucasus, where the German advance had already penetrated, and Brooke was surprised to see from the air how minimal were Russian defensive works in the Southern Caucasus. He was more impressed by glimpses from the aircraft of egrets, herons and duck in the Volga delta.

This was Brooke's first visit to the strange and Oriental world of which the Kremlin was the centre. He was fascinated by his first meetings with the Russians and by watching the effect of Churchill and Stalin upon each other. Afterwards he described it vividly:

> It had been a long and tiring flight lasting some fifteen hours. I was longing for a bath, light dinner and bed. It was not to be – as I stepped out of the plane I was handed a message from Winston to come at once to dine with him, to go on to the Kremlin at 11 p.m.
>
> Tired as I was I would not have missed that meeting between Stalin and Winston for anything in the world. Everything of that meeting is still vivid in my memory. We were shown into a sparsely furnished room of the Kremlin which reminded me of a station waiting room. I think the only picture on the wall was that of Lenin. Stalin, Molotov and the interpreter entered and we sat at a long table.
>
> We were soon involved in heated discussions concerning Western Second Front and Winston had made it clear that such an offensive was not possible for the present but would be replaced by operations in North Africa. Stalin then began to turn on the heat and through the interpreter he passed a lot of abusive questions such as: 'When are you going to start fighting? Are you going to let us do all the work whilst you look on? Are you never going to start fighting? You will find it is not too bad if you once start!' etc. Stalin spoke gently and quietly, not looking Churchill in the face.
>
> The Prime Minister crashed his fist down on the table and poured forth one of his wonderful spontaneous orations . . .
>
> Stalin stood up sucking at his large bent pipe, and with a broad grin on his face stopped Winston's interpreter and sent back through his own 'I do not understand what you are saying but by God I like your sentiment!'[35]

Brooke reckoned afterwards that Stalin's insults had been

deliberate, to discover Churchill's character; and that however fundamentally incompatible were the Soviet and Western leaders' policies and methods the meeting at least established in Stalin's mind that he was dealing with a man of determination and fighting spirit; and that this was good. It may be so. It is likely that Churchill overestimated the accord which he had achieved, or which ever could be achieved with the Russians although his illusions lasted less long than those of others. Brooke, too, wrote of 'a certain mutual understanding which grew up between these men and which greatly facilitated the co-ordination of our plans'. Even this assessment probably exaggerates the degree to which personal sentiment as opposed to ruthless calculation played any part in the Russian dictator's policy. Stalin was described by another onlooker at the time as 'like a gently smiling Tiger in a Tea shop'.[36] Brooke's diary entry after the meeting was probably accurate:

> He [Churchill] appealed to sentiments in Stalin which do not, I think, exist . . . altogether I felt we were not gaining much ground . . .
>
> Personally I feel our policy with the Russians has been wrong from the very start . . . we have bowed and scraped to them, done all we could for them, and never asked them for a single fact or figure concerning their production, strength, dispositions, etc. As a result they despise us and have no use for us except for what they can get out of us.[37]

In Moscow Brooke again met the Polish General Anders, who called on him in his hotel.

> When he came into my hotel sitting room he beckoned to me to come and sit at a small table with him. He then pulled out his cigarette case and started tapping the table and speaking in a low voice. He said 'as long as I keep tapping this table we cannot be overheard by all the microphones in this room!' I must confess that till then I had not realized that my sitting room was full of microphones.* I learned to realize that all rooms in Moscow had ears. Anders then proceeded to tell me that, hunt as he might, he could not discover a large consignment of Polish prisoners which comprised most of the men of distinction in most walks of life. He had followed one clue half way across Siberia and then it fizzled out. He said he was certain that they were either being liquidated in one of the Siberian convict camps or that they had

---

* This lack of realization does not bear very impressive witness to the quality of the CIGS's preliminary briefing, unless British Intelligence was more naïve than is usually supposed.

been murdered. It turned out that he was correct. This was the batch of prisoners that the Russians murdered* and that the Germans found later on, Goebbels exploiting this find to the utmost.[38]

But Brooke himself had shown the Russians plainly the sort of man he was. He was pressed at length by Marshal Voroshilov as to why all possible divisions could not be concentrated in England and shortly landed on the coast of France. After long factual explanations of the problems of opposed landings, which met little comprehension, he eventually and bluntly said that the Americans and British had come to definite conclusions on the subject and were not prepared to alter them. Voroshilov said he could not, of course, press further.

The party returned to Cairo for their second visit – that visit during which Montgomery made so favourable an impression and lifted the spirits of his superiors, as he had already restored the morale of his command. Brooke felt fresh confidence, now, in the commanders of the British Army throughout the world.

In India Brooke could count on what he at least regarded as the rocklike presence of Wavell: below Wavell, in command of Eastern Army facing the Japanese, was General Irwin, an officer who would be replaced in the following year, and whose character did not inspire universal liking, but whom Brooke, who knew him well, tended to support. In the Persia/Iraq Command, to whose importance a dimension was added by the decision greatly to increase the capacity of the Iranian port, railway and road systems in order to carry a much larger tonnage of supplies for Russia, General Maitland-Wilson, a tried and trusted old friend, was in charge. Some alleged that he had aged and lost his edge: this was not Brooke's impression. In Egypt Alexander and Montgomery formed a team in which Brooke had high confidence, as he did in Paget, commanding in the United Kingdom. The high point of German success was over when Rommel was halted by Auchinleck at El Alamein, and the tide turned in the Caucasus: and the high point of Japanese success had been reached at the battle of Midway and after completion of the British withdrawal from Burma. In future there would be victories at gathering pace. New men betokened a new mood.

While Brooke was in Cairo another blow had fallen – but one which would have educative effect however tragically purchased.

* At Katyn.

The Canadian raid on Dieppe – the only substitute for SLEDGEHAMMER the British were prepared to consider in 1942 – had ended with heavy casualties. Brooke had regarded the experience such a raid would produce as essential for the greater amphibious operations to follow. Churchill's personal doctor, later to be Lord Moran, recalled the news breaking in Cairo:

> The Dieppe raid was, it appears, a fiasco; three-fifths of the Canadians – about 3000 men – were either killed or taken prisoner . . . 'It is a lesson,' the CIGS grunted, 'to the people who are clamouring for the invasion of France!'[39]

But for a while the spectre of premature invasion of the Continent was laid. Operation TORCH, the Anglo-American landings in North Africa, had been approved and ordered by President and Prime Minister. Montgomery prepared his plans to deal with the expected – and final – attempt by Rommel to advance into Egypt, and the subsequent offensive battle which Montgomery himself intended to fight, in classic form, when he was ready and strongly superior to the enemy. With a lighter heart Brooke returned to London.

Now back at home it was, for the CIGS, a question of waiting, desperately hoping for a decisive victory for the British Army whose head he was. As Chairman of the Chiefs of Staff Committee he had plenty to occupy his mind. Apart from the campaigns of the Army the crucial battle was still in the Atlantic. There, the first half of 1942 had been appalling. The 'free hand' against American shipping given to the German U-boats by the enlarging of the war, amply exploited by the rate of U-boat build, had led to the loss of $3\frac{1}{2}$ million tons of Allied shipping in exchange for what proved to be a mere 4% of U-boat strength destroyed. Of the 8 million tons of shipping lost in 1942 $6\frac{1}{4}$ million were lost to submarines. The Germans had concentrated in northern waters, leading to the difficult decision to cancel, in June, convoys sailing to Russia. In the second half of 1942 the tide began slowly to turn and in May American shipbuilding rates overtook losses. But in June the First Sea Lord still pointed out that 'our whole war effort was hampered by lack of shipping'. This was Brooke's own conviction and constant theme.

As the year turned to autumn Brooke looked back on months of ceaseless strain. Although he now felt able to deal with the mercurial genius of Churchill as well as any professional soldier could hope to, he had had serious misgivings at first. After a few weeks as Chairman he had considered whether or not it was his duty to resign in the hope that another might work better with the Prime Minister. Ismay told Churchill, who was rather moved. 'General Brooke – resign? Why no – I'm very fond of him, and I need him!'[40] Nevertheless the two men, with their powerful characters and dissimilar temperaments, were already a trial to each other. Ismay recalled one meeting at which he considered the CIGS not only at his most uncompromising but also intolerably rude to the Prime Minister. When the Chiefs of Staff withdrew Ismay was alone with Churchill. 'Brooke must go!' Churchill said. 'I cannot work with him. He hates me. I can see hatred looking from his eyes!' Ismay sought Brooke.

> 'The Prime Minister says he can't work with you and that you hate him.'
> 'Hate him?' said Brooke. 'I don't hate him. I *love* him. But the first time I tell him I agree with him when I don't will be the time to get rid of me, for then I will be no more use to him.'

Ismay received permission discreetly to quote this reaction and did so.

> 'The CIGS says he doesn't hate you. He loves you! But if he ever tells you he agrees when he doesn't you must get rid of him as no more use.'

Churchill's eyes filled with tears, and he gently murmured:

> '*Dear* Brooke!'[41]

Moran later wrote of the relationship between the two men and the strain it imposed on both – Brooke exhausted by Churchill's hours, profusion of impracticable ideas, and unjust criticism of the Army in front of Ministers; Churchill frustrated by Brooke's bleak refusals to make imaginative leaps of reasoning, or take risks with the lives of soldiers unless absolutely supported by the logic of facts. Yet Moran also quotes a question he put after the war to Churchill:

> 'Did you ever think of getting rid of Alanbrooke?'
> He became serious. 'Never!' There was a long pause. 'Never' he repeated with complete conviction.[42]

The recollection of Moran surely reflects the relationship more enduringly than expressions of mutual irritation by two great and very different patriots under stress. Neither fully appreciated the other's inner difficulties, while recognizing his qualities. Brooke could not sympathetically enter into the imaginative, sometimes erratic and fallacious but essentially artistic and romantic attitudes which characterized Churchill. For his part Churchill showed little understanding of the sensitivity and tension concealed behind Brooke's austere exterior. This tension continued to be relieved in the daily outpourings to Benita in diary and letter, and to her alone. Brooke's letters throughout 1942 showed ever heightened love and longing for her presence, admiration for her fortitude if ill or in difficulties, passionate solicitude that echoes his early letters to his mother in her apparent suffering long ago. 'Half a week nearer seeing you again,' he would write on a Wednesday, and after some minor mishap:

> 'I keep on wondering, my darling, how that darling finger of yours is. I do *hope* it is not aching too much? Whenever I look at the flowers I think of you and your pluck not saying anything about it and just nursing your finger. And my eyes fill with tears and I long to give you a vast hug.' His emotional dependence on her was complete.

> As usual my darling you are being my mainstay and anchor in life. Without you I should be able to do nothing. Your example and life is the most wonderful inspiration to me, and my whole life just hinges round you.[43]

He made very clear how deep was the pain when he had to forgo a visit to Ferney Close.

> 'The worst of it was,' he wrote soon after becoming CIGS, 'that I myself had to decide that it was essential to have a Chiefs of Staff Meeting tomorrow, it was an awful wrench! A flow of excuses came flooding into my mind and had to be sent out.'

And later:

> I just *longed* to leave the Empire to lose itself and dash down.[44]

He had black moments, but only in his diary did he permit depression to appear. On 31st March he wrote:

> During the last fortnight I have had for the first time since the war started a growing conviction that we are going to lose this war unless we control it very differently and fight it with more determination. But to begin with a democracy is at a great handicap against a dictatorship when it comes to war. Secondly, a government with only one big man in it, and that one man a grave danger in many respects, is in a powerless way. Party politics, party interests still override larger war issues. Petty

jealousies colour decisions and influence destinies. Politicians still suffer from that little knowledge of military matters which gives them unwarranted confidence that they are born strategists! As a result they confuse issues, affect decisions, and convert simple problems and plans into confused tangles and hopeless muddles. It is all desperately depressing. Furthermore it is made worse by the lack of good military commanders. Half our Corps and Divisional Commanders are totally unfit for their appointments, and yet if I were to sack them, I could find no better! They lack character, imagination, drive and power of leadership. The reason for this state of affairs is to be found in the losses we sustained in the last war of all our best officers who should now be our senior commanders. I wonder if we shall muddle through this time like we have in the past? There are times when I wish to God I had not been placed at the helm of a ship that seems to be heading inevitably for the rocks! It is a great honour to find oneself entrusted with such a task, and the hope of saving the ship a most inspiring thought and one that does override all others. But may God help me and guide me in my task.

For most of the war he was profoundly lonely. He was also, like all with heavy responsibility, increasingly tired and his weekly day at home was jealously to be guarded for its recuperative effect. It often had to be forgone. 'Terrified of rumours of weekend at Chequers,' he wrote on 23rd July, and the note often recurred. Another relief was if a visit to Northern Ireland, to Colebrooke, could be woven into the pattern of his military life. He had written to Lady Brooke – Cynthia, his nephew Basil's wife – in April, 'The last few months since I took over this job have been about the grimmest in my life. We seem to lose a new bit of the Empire almost every day.' But in July, after visiting a large-scale exercise in Ulster British and American troops, he was able to write: 'How I loved every minute of my visit. It is heavenly joy looking through that narrow door on to that lovely sunlit garden.'

Colebrooke refreshed him as always and as nowhere else, except where his own Benita herself was.[45]

Brooke's letters to Benita naturally meant even more to him when abroad. He wrote from Cairo:

I am imagining that this is the house you stopped in with the Allenbys and keep wondering whether by any chance you lived in this room! I like to imagine to myself that you did.

Again all my love, my darling, from your devoted old Alan.[46]

His weekend diary entries would be brief and characteristic:

Walked with children to Andrew's cottage to ask him about Kingfisher's nest. Spent afternoon photographing missel-thrush.

Not only summonses to Chequers, and meetings extended long into the night, marked the Prime Minister's commerce with his chief strategic adviser. Brooke was lucky if he could take a few days' leave undisturbed. After a visit to the Infantry Battle School at Barnard Castle in September 1942 he had greatly looked forward to three days' grouse shooting on the Yorkshire moors with his Aide-de-Camp, Barney Charlesworth. The exasperation of the evening letter to Benita was pardonable:

> When we arrived here about 5.30 we found a telephone message from the PM saying that he wanted to speak with me on the scrambler* at 7 p.m. As the nearest scrambler is 15 miles away it meant ½ hour drive each way. To make it worse he changed the time to 7.30 p.m. so that I did not get back till 8.30 p.m. All he wanted were my reactions to a wire he had received! As I had not seen the wire it was not easy to answer. He then expressed surprise I had not seen it, and seemed to expect that I should be followed by a series of DRs chasing me on the moor.
>
> I had to have the message sent up by the night mail; and have now got it. At 12.30 I am going back to that scrambler to tell him what my reactions to it are. I should also like to tell him what my reactions are to the way he cannot even let me have 3 clear days without being badgered![47]

'Badgered' Brooke had been. The message was from Alexander, and there was nothing in it that could not have awaited his return to London. At his first telephone conversation Churchill asked how he could, when he had read the signal, communicate his views. 'How? Will you send a telegram? Have you got a cypher officer with you?'

'My temper was beginning to get worn,' wrote Brooke later. 'I replied "No, I do not take a cypher officer to load for me . . . I shall come back here tomorrow morning and continue this conversation with you on the scrambler . . ."'[48] Yet he blamed himself afterwards, for in response to Alexander's telegram (which concerned the timing of the forthcoming offensive) Churchill, although Brooke believed he had successfully dissuaded him, nevertheless sent a 'hurrying' signal which was ignored by the

* Secure telephone.

imperturbable Alexander. He would not have been troubled had Brooke been in London.

At last a day came when the Prime Minister's importunity could happily be endured. He wrote to Benita on 4th November:

> PM sent for me at 10.20 – wanted to discuss good news! At 3.30 p.m. he sent for me again! It is now 12.30 and I have only just arrived. He is busy sending telegrams to Stalin, Roosevelt, Dominions, Commanders, etc!! Very anxious to ring Church bells! I had to ask him to wait a bit to make certain we did not ring them too soon!

It was not too soon. On the night of 23rd October a mighty artillery barrage had opened the battle of Alamein. Eighth Army's hour had come. For some days the course of battle seemed uncertain to those anxiously waiting at home. Churchill's impatience needed curbing and Brooke, as ever, had to play the decisive part in curbing it. On 29th October, he wrote to Benita (whose state of health was giving him anxiety to which half the letter was devoted):

> I have had another unpleasant day. I was woken up with a telegram the PM wanted to send to Alexander which I did not agree with! Then during the COS I was sent for by the PM and had rather a row. Then at 12.30 we had a COS meeting with him and Smuts, Eden, Attlee, Oliver Lyttleton attending. There Smuts agreed entirely with me and all went well. In evening Cabinet at 5.30 and this evening whilst dining with Bertie [Sergison-Brooke] another call from PM to come at 11.30 p.m. when he was very nice and showed me some cheerful wires he had received.[49]

The 'cheerful wires' were highly encouraging interceptions of German signals. The 'row' had turned on Churchill's desire to send to the Middle East a message of exhortation. The Prime Minister thought he already detected signs of irresolution, and he was concerned that victory should be apparent before Operation TORCH – the landings in North Africa – took place on 8th November. Churchill's original draft queried tactical details. Brooke's advocacy turned this into an unexceptionable – if unnecessary – message of support to Alexander 'whatever the cost, in all the measures which you are taking to shake the life out of Rommel's Army and make this a fight to a finish'. Brooke had his own inward doubts, his lonely anxiety, but he was determined that the Commanders in the field should not be harassed. It had not been easy, and his diary expands upon it:

> ... Anthony Eden had come round late last night to have a drink with him [Churchill] and had shaken his confidence in Montgomery and Alexander, and had given him the impression that the Middle East offensive was petering out!
>
> During the COS meeting, just while we were having a final interview with Eisenhower,* I was sent for by the PM and had to tell him fairly plainly what I thought of Anthony Eden's ability to judge a tactical situation at this distance!

In fact Montgomery had in hand his decisive blow, Operation SUPERCHARGE, which was delivered on the night of 1st November. This led to the breakout of the victorious Eighth Army and to Alexander's telegram of 4th November: 'Eighth Army has inflicted a severe defeat on the enemy's German and Italian forces under Rommel's command in Egypt. The enemy's front has broken . . .'

Details of Montgomery's intentions for SUPERCHARGE came by signal to the War Office during night-time, and were passed by telephone to Brooke in his flat by the Duty Officer. There was a pause. 'Are we scrambled?' asked the CIGS. He knew the answer. 'Well, shouldn't we be?' he continued. Next morning, Brooke's reputation for tolerance of error not being high, the man in question, when sent for to report to the CIGS, assumed that his days of that particular duty were over. But – 'You were a young fool. Don't do it again,' closed the matter.[50] It was a time for triumph and happiness. 'All news continues to be good. I can't tell you what a relief it is!!' wrote Brooke to Benita in his letter of 4th November. 'If this had failed and all my planning in Cairo come to nothing I should have been at my wits end and have had nothing left but to go and let someone else try and do better!' Now even Brooke's cautious nature felt rejoicing, for on 3rd November he had seen the ULTRA text of intercepted signals from Rommel which stated that his Army was in total disarray and that he could only hope to 'extricate remnants'.

Brooke had also had anxious moments about security. The details of the impending offensive had only been known to a tiny circle. Brooke, who received the plan on 14th October, had told Churchill and obtained a promise to communicate to nobody, but

---

* General Dwight Eisenhower was the designated Allied Commander for Operation TORCH.

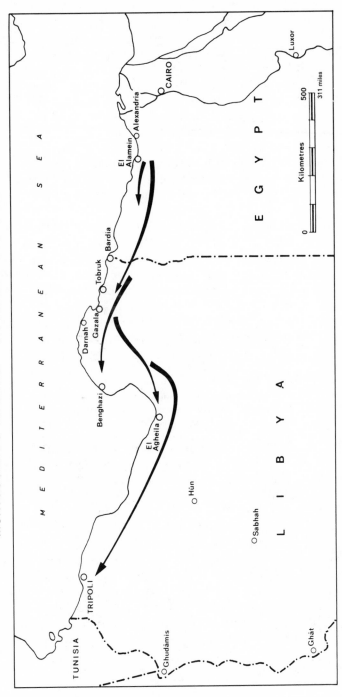

MONTGOMERY'S ADVANCE   NOVEMBER – DECEMBER 1942

MEDITERRANEAN SEA

Luxor

CAIRO
Alexandria
El Alamein

Bardia
Tobruk
Darnah
Gazala
Benghazi
El Agheila

TRIPOLI

TUNISIA
Ghudāmis

Hūn
Sabhah
Ghāt

EGYPT

LIBYA

Kilometres
0   500

311 miles

he then discovered that Churchill had told Eisenhower who was in London for the final preparations for TORCH. Brooke fumed:[51] 'It is absolutely fatal to tell any politician a secret. They are incapable of keeping it to themselves,' he wrote in his diary. He was also appalled to find that P. J. Grigg, the Secretary of State for War – the only man in the War Office apart from Brooke who knew what was about to occur and when – had told two other officers. 'I was genuinely astounded,' Brooke wrote afterwards. 'I thought he would have been quite safe.'[52] Grigg 'could not have been nicer' when the indignant CIGS rebuked him. Churchill, too, was recorded in the diary entry for 22nd October as being 'very nice and repentant'. In fairness, however, it must be said that diaries are not necessarily secure, and that the same entry ran: 'I had been expecting that Monty's attack might start last night. Probably will be tonight instead.'

As to the exchanges at that time with the Prime Minister, the best word perhaps came on 29th October, a day of many meetings of which the last took place at 11.30 p.m. Churchill asked whether Brooke would not have preferred to have accepted his offer made in August, and now to be commanding in the Middle East. 'Yes,' said Brooke, and meant it. Churchill said: 'Smuts told me your reasons and that you thought you could serve your country best by remaining with me, and I am very grateful for this decision.'

And Brooke recorded in his diary:

> This forged one more link between him and me. He is the most difficult man I have ever served but thank God for having given me the opportunity of trying to serve such a man in a crisis such as the one this country is going through at present.

For Brooke, although exasperation would struggle with affection to the end, recognized the need to accommodate the ways of his incomparable chief. When Churchill, against all protocol and sense, would address a minute or a query direct to one of Brooke's subordinates in the War Office, the Director of Military Operations or the Director of Military Intelligence – 'Prepare the answer,' Brooke would say, 'and if I agree I'll sign it!' He never remonstrated.[53] Not on such points, but on great strategic issues would he do battle with the Prime Minister, and always in pursuit of the same cause, the successful prosecution of the war and the support and honour of the British Army in the field. Now, due very largely to his strength of will and purpose, that cause had been advanced by a mighty step. 'Brooke,' wrote Ismay, 'was the most difficult and in a way unsympathetic CIGS [I] had ever had to deal with. But the best.'[54]

Now at the other end of the Mediterranean the second act of the drama was taking place, whose opening had been at El Alamein. The consummation of Brooke's cherished ambition – the clearance of the North African coast – was under way.

TORCH had not had an easy birth. It was the first truly Allied operation, in the sense of being, from the planning stage, under the overall direction of an Allied Commander-in-Chief and an Allied Headquarters responsible to the Combined Chiefs of Staff. It had suffered from the problem of American disquiet with the concept itself, and with its place in the strategic scheme of things, a problem which would not easily disappear. Indeed to many Americans, in the words of their official History, TORCH had the effect of 'limiting and unsettling American plans for helping all Allied Powers and conducting all-American operations, and thus gradually blurred the outlines of American strategic planning'. Such scepticism apart, however, there were a number of uncertainties.

The first of these concerned the attitude which the British and Americans would find among the French forces and population of the French North African possessions. TORCH was conceived, initially, as an occupation 'by invitation' of friendly territory. It had been assessed that resentment against the British, after their destruction of a French fleet, made it essential that the expedition should appear as American as possible. An American Commander, General Eisenhower, was appointed, a man who, whatever his quality as a field commander, was adept at inspiring co-operation, trust and affection. It was correctly decided that no French forces of de Gaulle should be included in the expedition, and that de Gaulle's Headquarters should not be informed of what was afoot – a measure made necessary by security, if nothing else. This caused Brooke no trouble. He disliked de Gaulle and distrusted those elements in the British Foreign Office, including the Foreign Secretary, who believed that de Gaulle would command significant support from Frenchmen in the event.[55] He had rejoiced to see Churchill (whose views were similar) 'put down' Eden when the latter had tried to press for a Gaullist part in an expedition to 'liberate' Madagascar earlier in the year.[56] As early as 12th May he had been approached by de Gaulle, with a view to co-ordinating the Gaullist subversive organization in France with plans to re-enter the Continent, and in reporting these approaches to his colleagues had strongly recommended that de Gaulle should be told nothing of plans to deal with the French Army. 'Even the disclosure to General de Gaulle that we were negotiating with the French General Staff would be disastrous' minuted Brooke on the general subject of 'support to the French Army in occupied territory', and the Chiefs of Staff agreed. But the Allies hoped that French anti-German opinion might rally French forces (which were not inconsiderable) and French sentiment round an acceptable and distinguished pro-Allied figure, and General Giraud was cast for the role and covertly left France to play it. In the event the French in North Africa were, to the Allies' discomfiture, loyal to 'the Marshal': Giraud received no recognition; and only the fortuitous presence in Algiers of Admiral Darlan, who had played a leading part in the Vichy Government, solved the problem. Darlan accepted Giraud as a Deputy, and in return for certain assurances directed the French forces to cease resistance two days after the initial landings. This providential act received less than its meed of gratitude from the Foreign Office to whom Darlan was the 'antithesis' of that 'international decency' for which the nation was being exhorted to fight.[57] The Allies of Stalin appear in retrospect slightly comical in the striking of such righteous attitudes, and Brooke had little difficulty in the matter of Darlan. Mercifully neither did Eisenhower, and TORCH did not lead to a war between the Atlantic Allies and France. The political situation was further eased by the assassination of Darlan on Christmas Eve, and his 'succession' by Giraud.

TORCH, therefore, was beset by political uncertainty. Operationally there had also been dissension. The plan envisaged landings on both the Atlantic and Mediterranean coasts, the former being technically more difficult and subject to climate, but the latter necessitating massive movement through the Straits of Gibraltar, which the American Chiefs of Staff feared might be closed behind the expedition by a German operation through Spain, or by Spanish hostility. Brooke thought this danger chimerical, but all this took time to resolve, so that the scope and nature of the forthcoming campaign – if it were, indeed, to become a campaign rather than an unopposed occupation of friendly territory – were at issue between the Allies in a way which caused inevitable delay. Reversing their frequent roles the British pressed always for an earlier and the Americans for a later date. On 21st September a landing on 8th November was agreed.

The strategic object was, in Brooke's mind, completely clear: a giant step forward towards the clearance of the North African coast. The operational object should be the rapid occupation of Tunis and the forestalling of major German reinforcement, so that the business should be quickly over, and Rommel's Army facing Montgomery in the Libyan desert find a large force established to their westward. The operational object was not achieved. The advance towards Tunis was checked by German forces rushed to the theatre. The first Luftwaffe units disembarked at Tunis the day after the Allied landings, and on 11th November German troops marched into unoccupied France. German attention was now to be turned fully to their Southern flank. The fact that the Tunisian campaign took months to complete was recognized by Brooke with hindsight as no bad thing. 'Had we cleared Tunis of Germans and Italians in the early stages,' he wrote after the war, 'we should not have derived the immense benefits of the battle of Tunis . . .'[58] Benefits they were indeed. When Tunis ultimately fell more than 230,000 of the enemy became prisoners.

At first, however, Brooke fretted at what seemed Eisenhower's slowness, and absorption in the complexities of politics in Algiers rather than concentration upon 'gripping' a campaign which needed urgent leadership at and from the front. In this he probably underestimated those complexities, and the fact that Eisenhower alone had been given power to wrestle with them: but Brooke's instinct was sound, that the battle needed firm control and decisive initiatives if opportunities were not to be lost. It was echoed frequently on later occasions.

There had also been problems about the command arrangements. In some form these were to continue, particularly in respect of those French forces who were now directed to fight with the Allies. The British forces, under the command of General Anderson, had initially been assigned to Eisenhower under a directive which followed previous patterns, giving Anderson direct access to Whitehall if he disagreed with his instructions. Eisenhower, standing out for a principle to which he was nobly dedicated, objected to this. Anderson's instructions were amended to make it clear that right of reference to the British War Office would be wholly exceptional. It was referred to as an 'unlikely event', surrounded by conditions which Eisenhower found tolerable and which Brooke accepted; and the right was never invoked.

The landings took place as planned; but progress was slower

than was hoped, and a front was stabilized. In the Western Desert Eighth Army's advance was inexorable but deliberate. Tripoli, at the beginning of December, was still in Axis hands. North Africa seemed to be sucking resources into an indecisive theatre. Furthermore, the significance of the North African campaign was indissolubly linked with the question of what should follow it.

The matter was given impetus by renewed impatience on the part of the Prime Minister. In a general report on the future conduct of the war, which Churchill studied in November, the Chiefs of Staff anticipated, *inter alia*, amphibious operations to occupy (possibly) Sardinia or Sicily after the successful completion of a North African campaign. Churchill was far from satisfied. When in Moscow in August he had given Stalin a private understanding which went well beyond the agreement of the Chiefs of Staff. He had indicated that there would be a Second Front in Europe in 1943 (although in September he had retracted this). Nevertheless he was conscious of a powerful pressure to help the Russians more obviously and instantly. 'You must not think that you can get off with your "Sardines" in 1943' (referring to Sicily and Sardinia) he growled at Brooke on 3rd December. 'No – we must establish a Western Front, and what is more we promised Stalin we should do so when in Moscow.' 'No,' replied Brooke, '*we* did not promise!'[59] Nevertheless, Churchill drew personal conclusions from the improved situation on the Russian front. He suggested that matters in the East were so bad for Germany that the Western Powers could reasonably assume no reinforcements could be drawn thence to face an invasion. He suggested that the operations in the Mediterranean could be over by June 1943, and an invasion of Western Europe launched in August or September.

To this the Chiefs of Staff, united, opposed hard facts. The available shipping and the relatively slow build-up of forces meant that in 1943 an invading Anglo-American Army would be outnumbered by some two to one by the German Army in the West – and to achieve even this ratio implied calling off any amphibious operations in the Mediterranean in exploitation of TORCH. Brooke put this to the Prime Minister just before Christmas, expanding the Chiefs of Staff point of view with his ruthless lucidity. 'As the paper we put in,' recorded Brooke, 'went straight against Winston, who was pressing for a Western Front whilst we pressed for amphibious operations in the Mediterranean, I feared the worst. However, the meeting went well from the start, and I succeeded in swinging him round.'[60] 'We had avoided the grave danger of Winston siding with the Americans,' he wrote later, 'there was of course always the chance that he might swing round again but I felt fairly safe.'[61] Brooke was by no means safe and Churchill returned to the charge more than once in the following weeks, but to no avail. The British position was established – exploitation of TORCH by such operations as could be mounted in the Mediterranean: intensification of the strategic bomber offensive: no invasion of Western Europe before 1944. Brooke was confident that no other path would have been right to tread. He was certain that the ultimate invasion must follow a weakening and stretching of the enemy's land forces, for which he now regarded operations in the Mediterranean theatre as offering an opportunity. The altercations with Churchill helped show him how vital it was to stress the offensive possibilities TORCH could produce, if the Americans were to be kept wholeheartedly committed to the European war. As so often, persuading the Prime Minister was gruelling work, but it helped clarify the mind.

Furthermore the Americans themselves were by now sceptical of the possibilities of ROUNDUP 1943. Their planners asserted in December that 'even if movements to North Africa were stopped in January 1943 convoy restrictions would permit no more than half a million Americans to be assembled in the United Kingdom and made ready to cross the channel by July [1943] – about eight divisions with supporting troops'.[62] There might, it was thought, be twelve by September – to which could be added some thirteen British divisions. Yet mid-September was regarded as the last possible time of the year for cross-Channel invasion – and the Allies had accepted a requirement for the operation of some forty-eight divisions.

On 22nd December Brooke recorded in his diary:

> Roosevelt has sent message to Winston suggesting a meeting in North Africa somewhere near Casablanca about 15th January. We shall consequently soon be travelling again.

CHAPTER XIII

Casablanca and After

ISMAY LATER RECALLED 1943 as 'the year of conferences'![1] Of these the first, named SYMBOL, was held at Casablanca in January, between President and Prime Minister and between the American and British Chiefs of Staff. It had been the original hope of the Western leaders that Stalin could be induced also to attend, but he made it known that the operational situation on the Eastern Front precluded his leaving the Soviet Union. Furthermore Stalin's interest – his only interest – in Anglo-American deliberations lay in how early and how strongly they would result in an offensive against Germany which would take pressure off Russia. It was clear that he did not believe his presence necessary to affect that matter.

Casablanca was the first full meeting of the Combined Chiefs of Staff, with both sides represented by principals rather than the British by Dill and members of the Joint Staff Mission in Washington. These conferences between the British and Americans were the milestones along Brooke's road of grand strategy. He did not relish them. 'They do a lot of good in securing greater understanding between us,' he wrote in his diary of one such later in the year, 'and yet – they fall far short in so far as our basic convictions remain unaltered . . . compromises emerge and the war is prolonged, whilst we age and get more and more weary.'[2] Brigadier Jacob, who had handled all the arrangements on behalf of the British War Cabinet and Chiefs of Staff Secretariat, reckoned that Brooke was exhausted by the end of the Casablanca Conference.[3] And in his letter to Benita of 23rd January Brooke wrote, 'We have finished the first job and thank Heavens for it! It has been 10 of the hardest and most difficult days I have had since taking up the job.' The Conferences, for Brooke, were not only milestones. They were also battlefields.

The strategic situation in January 1943, however, was very different from that which had faced British and Americans a year before in the immediate aftermath of Pearl Harbor. In Brooke's first diary entry for the New Year he reminded himself of how it had looked to him in the beginning:

> Glancing back at 1st January last year . . . I could see nothing but calamities ahead; Hong Kong gone, Singapore going, Java, etc., very doubtful, even Burma unsafe. Would we be able to save India and Australia?
>
> Horrible doubts, horrible nightmares, which grew larger and larger as the days went on till it felt as if the whole Empire was collapsing round my head.
>
> Wherever I looked I could see nothing but trouble. Middle East began to crumble, Egypt was threatened. I felt Russia would never hold, Caucasus was bound to be penetrated and Abadan (our Achilles heel) would be captured, with the consequent collapse of Middle East, India, etc.
>
> After Russia's defeat how were we to handle the German land and air forces liberated? England would be again bombarded and threat of invasion revived. Throughout it all Cabinet Ministers' nerves would be more and more on edge and clear thinking would become more and more difficult.

This diary 'recollection' was a fair summary of Brooke's earlier views recorded at the time. It shows very frankly the pessimistic strain in his character. He was vigorous, robust and objective, a man who would never give in. But he was so temperamentally averse from living with false hopes, and so suspicious of any hint of unrealism in measuring aspirations against facts that he was inwardly not only cautious but sometimes gloomy. In this note he showed clearly that he had underestimated Russian powers of recuperation (although in January 1942 they were already evident) and had been more downcast about the Middle East than the situation at that stage warranted. Of course Brooke, writing on 1st January 1943, emphasized the dark side of the year before in order to point up, with prudent exhilaration, the contrast. Nevertheless he did not much exaggerate his own earlier forebodings.

His diary entry for 1st January continued:

> And now! We start 1943 under conditions I would never have dared to hope for. Russia has held, Egypt for the present is safe. There is a hope of clearing North Africa of Germans in the near future. The Mediterranean may be partially opened up, Malta is safe for the present. We can now work freely against Italy, and Russia is scoring wonderful successes in Southern Russia.
>
> We are certain to have many setbacks to face, many troubles and

many shattered hopes, but for all that the horizon is infinitely brighter.

From a personal point of view life is also a bit easier with 13 months of this job behind me. I feel just a little more confident than I did in those awful early days when I felt completely lost and out of place.

I pray to God that He may go on giving me the help he has given me during the last year.

Certainly this did not overstate the transformation of the strategic situation. In Russia, which was to Germany the critical theatre of operations, Stalingrad with the entire German Sixth Army had been cut off from the main German Southern front by Russian counter-offensive moves in November 1942. On 2nd February the remnants of Sixth Army surrendered – an appalling blow to German arms and a turning point in the war. In the Far East heavy naval losses had been inflicted on the Japanese in a series of engagements, and MacArthur's strategy of moving from island to island had led the enemy to evacuate Guadalcanal in the Solomon Islands at the same time as the surrender at Stalingrad. India seemed secure and argument chiefly turned on how and when operations to recapture Burma should be conducted, and what part in them would be played by the Chinese forces of Generalissimo Chiang Kai-shek. In the Mediterranean it could only be a question of time before North Africa was cleared of Axis forces. 'Tightening the ring round Germany', an agreed concept of the ARCADIA Conference, was becoming a reality. Almost everywhere the enemy was on the defensive – including within Germany itself against the strategic bomber offensive whose importance in the general scheme of things had been reiterated in December by the Prime Minister himself, not without some demur from the CIGS and the First Sea Lord.

The latter had particular reason for concern over the primacy which the build-up of Bomber Command had acquired in British War Cabinet convictions. For in one vital area it could not yet be said that the enemy was on the defensive – in that part of the ring around him which for Western war effort was most vital, the Atlantic. Brooke's optimism had not extended to the Atlantic sealanes. In 1942 Allied shipping losses had exceeded new construction by 800,000 tons. Not only were more long-range aircraft required, but more escort ships; and to build more escorts it had been necessary to build fewer landing and assault craft, which would be critical in any amphibious operations against occupied Europe – or occupied territories in the Far East. Thus Brooke's absorption with shipping, as a vital prerequisite for offensive operations, led him always to concentrate on the free use of the Mediterranean – which saved tonnage on passage – and led him also to place supreme importance on the Battle of the Atlantic, not only for its own sake but because, until it went better, insufficient shipbuilding capacity could be devoted to amphibious craft.

With this important exception the enemy was at bay, and for the Allies the hour of the offensive had come. In North Africa and in Russia this offensive had started. But the great question for the British and the Americans was what to do next. And so they came to Casablanca.

Many arguments had taken place within the British War Cabinet and Chiefs of Staff Committee on this question of what to do next. On the general point of principle the Chiefs of Staff had accepted a concept of exploiting their gains in the Mediterranean with, as a first object, the aim of inducing the Italians to lay down arms. Such exploitation meant ROUNDUP would probably not take place in 1943 unless German power drastically and unexpectedly declined. But the Chiefs of Staff – and Brooke above all – doubted the practicability of ROUNDUP in 1943 anyway, because of logistic limitations and because, Brooke believed, German resistance was still inadequately weakened. To Brooke, although he did not put it in those terms, it was a question of a Mediterranean campaign – an exploitation of success in North Africa – during 1943 or no campaign in the West at all.

As to what form this 'exploitation' should take, opinion was divided between the merits of invading Sardinia or Sicily. Brooke – and Churchill – had come strongly to support Sicily as the target. Brooke believed that enemy counter-reinforcement would be more laborious than in Sardinia. This operation would be the first opposed landing in occupied Europe. Its success would be vital.

To what strategic objects should the expedition lead? Churchill's first paper, composed on his way to the ARCADIA Conference a year before, had referred to an Allied foothold on the mainland 'with reactions inside Italy which might be highly favourable'. This was the grand design – the detachment of Italy from the Axis. To Brooke it was self-evident that the defection of her Italian Ally would pose grave problems for Germany. The Germans might or might not seek to occupy and defend Italy itself:

if they did the cost to them would be high. More certainly they would need to replace Italian formations throughout the occupied Balkans. And wherever they were brought to battle in the Mediterranean theatre the limitations on European north-south communications might make German operational difficulties greater than those involved in concentration against an Allied beachhead in North West Europe. Their commitment might, therefore, be disproportionally large.

Brooke did not, however, at this stage put his influence unequivocally behind an Italian campaign of the kind which ultimately took place. Indeed he counselled caution on too great a military involvement in Italy itself. 'I wanted first,' he wrote in his diary at the end of the Casablanca Conference,

> to ensure that Germany should continue to be regarded as our primary enemy . . . secondly that for the present Germany can best be attacked through the *medium** of Italy and thirdly that this can best be achieved with a policy directed against Sicily.[4]

The prize was Italian surrender and its ensuing problems for Germany. The points of subsequent attack should be decided nearer the time, with the Balkans taken into account and with an eye always cocked on Turkey and the possibility of bringing her into the war on the Allied side.

To achieve Italian surrender – and Italian 'collapse' was spoken of in Whitehall as something which could certainly be brought about – success in North Africa must be first completed and then vigorously exploited. But all recognized that the crux with the Americans lay in the inevitable delay in ROUNDUP – ROUNDUP, that cross-Channel large-scale invasion on which American hearts were set, and which Marshall had always regarded as at risk from the North African adventure and involvement. The first and grand object of the British at the Casablanca Conference, therefore, was to secure American acceptance of a further step in the Mediterranean. To Brooke this was not only logical but inevitable, since he did not believe in the military practicability of a successful ROUNDUP in 1943 even if every available resource were switched from North Africa to Britain for a Continental invasion. But it was necessary to use this argument with care. To show too lukewarm an attitude towards ROUNDUP in 1943 might deepen the concern of those Americans who regarded the British as reluctant to contemplate cross-

* Author's italics.

Channel invasion at all: worse, it would weaken those who were trying loyally to hold the United States to the policy of 'Germany first'. American strategic policy might swing back to major emphasis on the Pacific, in default of effective land action against Germany. To help swing it back there would be at Casablanca the formidable figure of the Chief of the American Navy, Admiral Ernest King, to whom conduct of American operations in the Pacific had been virtually entrusted, who regarded it as an all-American matter, and who made little attempt to disguise his impatience with the policy of 'Germany first'. There were thus, at Casablanca, high stakes on the table and a false move could tear apart such fragile strategic unity as the Western Allies had achieved.

The British were greatly helped by preparation – both practical in terms of staff work and intellectual in terms of earlier dispute between themselves and with the Prime Minister. There was much to be said for the British Chiefs of Staff system of committee debate, and for the vigorous and often exhausting probes and interventions of their political head. It meant that minds were thoroughly prepared, and few counter-arguments were new. On the practical side Jacob had flown to North Africa in December to reconnoitre and prepare the ground for the Conference. He reported favourably on Casablanca as a venue, and set matters in hand before returning to Whitehall. At the Conference itself the British were supported not only by the indispensable presence of the Secretariat with Jacob at their head, but also by a ship with full clerical and communication facilities lying offshore. As near as possible the support the British Chiefs of Staff received in Whitehall, planners and all, was transferred to Casablanca.

American preparations did not seem so thorough and their support was by no means of the same order. It has been said that the United States Chief of Staff thought themselves out-generalled in argument at Casablanca largely because of British preparations, to which they felt their own measures unequal. There was a good deal in this; but if the British had the best of the debate it should not be ascribed only to preliminaries and staff support, however admirable. It must be attributed also to the vigour of the previous cut and thrust in London, to the strength of the British case where it differed materially from the American, and to the clarity of exposition shown by the principal British spokesman, Brooke. For it was Brooke who had to expound and convince.

313

The American position did not differ from the British in all particulars, but nor were they as generally united. Marshall and King represented the European and Pacific interests respectively. All agreed that the Battle of the Atlantic was crucial to that strategic offensive in the Western European theatre to which the Americans professed themselves loyal. This was common ground. In the Pacific theatre there should continue 'offensive and defensive operations': this admitted of considerable inter- pretation, but any interpretation was bound to involve landing craft. There should be offensive operations in Burma to help China and clear the only land line of support to Chiang Kai-shek's forces – the Burma road.

As expected, however, the vital difference between the two Allies lay in what form the 'strategic offensive in the Western European theatre' should take. True to his original view that the Mediterranean was a blind alley to which American forces had only been committed because of the President's insistence that they should fight the Germans somewhere: and reinforced in that view by the protracted nature which the campaign was assuming, Marshall considered that operations in North Africa should be closed down immediately Eisenhower's campaign in Tunisia had achieved victory. Thereafter all forces should be transferred to the United Kingdom for ROUNDUP as early as possible. The delicacy of the British position was that if they were too discouraging towards Marshall over ROUNDUP they would strengthen the hand of King. It was therefore important to show that operations in the Mediterranean could themselves be offensive in the spirit of the ARCADIA Conference; and also that the British shared enthusiasm for ROUNDUP, but that if ROUNDUP were postponed it would not simply be because of the commitment in the Mediterranean but through other causes. For Brooke, of course, these 'other causes' were first and foremost the unbroken strength of the German Army and the enemy's continuing ability to switch forces from East to West faster than the Allies' cross-Channel build-up could challenge. There were others: Brooke did not believe that the output of the Western Allies in materiel, particularly in landing craft and tanks, would suffice for a 1943 invasion, nor that the balance of air power – and the air interdiction programme, which demanded air supremacy, would ultimately be crucial – could yet assure victory. But the positive and offensive aspects of the British proposals needed emphasis, for the American Chiefs advanced the reasoned argument that if troops were to sit in England waiting for the Germans to be weakened by the Russians they would be better employed to decisive effect in the Pacific.

Closely relevant to these considerations was the pace and course of the campaign actually in progress in North Africa. The great successes of autumn in the desert seemed to have lost their momentum. October and November had been glorious months for the British Army. Their professional head, Brooke, had received the Grand Cross of the Order of the Bath in recognition of British victory in North Africa. But in the west a quick seizure of Tunis after the TORCH landings – described by Brooke as 'a great gamble for a great stake'[5] – had been frustrated by the speed of German reaction, and by a certain confusion – even chaos – in the command of this most delicate of Allied operations. The Eighth Army, in the east, was still short of Tripoli after its triumphant march from Alamein. An Axis force in Tunisia had been built up. It was to be crunched between the forces of Eisenhower and Montgomery, but in Tunisia the weather had intervened, while logistic problems would set the pace of the British advance from Libya. The crunching jaws were still a long way apart. Furthermore Brooke had already shown himself apprehensive over what he regarded as Eisenhower's lack of operational grip, and the uncoordinated nature of some of his attacks.[6] He had an opportunity during the Casablanca Conference to impress his views on the Allied Commander.[7] Nor was it only the high command which appeared defective. Alexander wrote to Brooke gloomily of the United States Corps in North Africa.

> They simply do not know their job as soldiers and this is the case from the highest to the lowest, from the General to the private soldier. Perhaps the weakest link of all is the junior leader, who just does not lead, with the result that their men don't really fight.[8]

Brooke had often had harsh things to say of the early softness of British officers and soldiers compared to their forebears of the First World War, but as experience was gained his confidence revived. The Americans, now, were at their beginning; but they had a resilience and openness which lay at the heart of their national genius, and when they learned they learned fast. Meanwhile, Brooke felt yet more confirmed in his belief that time must elapse before the decisive battles of the war could be faced.

*

Whatever Allied performance, however, the end in Tunisia was
not going to come quickly. Hitler had decreed that it should be
held, and, however strategically impracticable this might be in the
longer term, his Commanders in the field were giving effect to his
directives with their usual opportunism and professional skill.
Until the campaign was over, consideration of the next step by the
Allies would remain at the planning stage. The timing of the
campaign would affect the content of that planning.

At the Casablanca Conference, as at all such times, the
contribution and counsel of Dill were of huge value. The British
Chiefs of Staff would co-ordinate their own position between
themselves and with the Prime Minister before leaving London,
and be indispensably assisted in so doing by the flow of telegrams
to and fro across the Atlantic with the British Military Staff in
Washington. But the physical presence of Dill was vital. His
relations with Marshall were excellent, his own vision grand and
his patient tact unlimited. Before a meeting of the Combined
Chiefs of Staff the British would first meet with Dill. He would
explain to them how the Americans saw matters and what were
the internal pressures in Washington. Because, like all great
Ambassadors, he could interpret each side to the other, and
understand other points of view while loyal to that of his own
authorities, he could balance the uncompromising realism of
Brooke with greater sympathy and intuition.

At Casablanca the British Chiefs met Dill on the first afternoon
of the Conference, 13th January. Brooke had flown from London
in a converted Liberator bomber, uncomfortably sharing the floor
of the small cabin in the rear with Mountbatten. 'I had to use my
knees and elbows to establish my rights to my allotted floor space!'
he wrote later. At their preliminary meeting Dill underlined
American fear of commitments in the Mediterranean, and their
suspicion that the British did not understand the Pacific problem.
The Americans feared, furthermore, that after the defeat of
Germany – and Dill emphasized that the United States were
sincere in commitment to the defeat of Germany as the prime
enemy – the British would not bestir themselves too much over the
ultimate defeat of Japan.[9] Dill also described the dissension in
Washington, created not only by different opinions in the Army
and the Navy but also by the organizational quirk that operations
in the Pacific were planned exclusively by the Navy Department.

Thus the allocation of resources such as landing craft required in all theatres was a catch-as-catch-can affair. That said, the Americans had, like Brooke, come to see shipping as the dominant factor.

Later that day Brooke and his colleagues, Dill with them, met Churchill. The Prime Minister had a clear view of the tactics to employ with the Americans. There should be no hurry, no ultimatum; 'the dripping of water on a stone'.[10] Churchill made clear that he wished there to emerge from the Conference a programme of operations which might, on military grounds, appear beyond our powers. The end of the North African campaign should be followed by the capture of Sicily. Burma should be recovered, and there should be an invasion of France, perhaps as a limited operation. In the Pacific operations should be kept within bounds which would not inhibit such a programme.

On 14th January the Combined Chiefs of Staff of the United States and United Kingdom met for the first time in plenary session. The Chiefs met in a light and charming semi-circular room, leading off the hall of the hotel in which most of the business of the Conference took place – an important help on these occasions, when a depressing atmosphere can turn discussion morose. Brooke opened with a presentation of the British position. He led with the shipping question, the key to all Allied offensive operations, and thus gave the pride of place in his remarks to the Battle of the Atlantic, the one theatre where the Axis Powers were not yet on the defensive. In all other theatres, Brooke said, the Allies had the initiative. The point of main effort against Germany was on the Russian front, and Allied operations should be such as to divert and weaken German resistance to Russia. This would be done by air bombardment – an uncontentious issue between Britain and America – and by amphibious operations. As to where these should take place, Brooke deployed the thesis now generally accepted among the British that the immediate targets for such operations should be in the Mediterranean, whither German communications were poor and build-up against landings slow. (On the British side only Pound, the First Sea Lord, still had reservations, since he suspected that the escorts required for amphibious operations might have to be drawn from what all agreed should be the prime task in the Atlantic.) As to the strategic advantages, as well as the practicability, of Mediterranean operations Brooke referred to the aims of knocking Italy out and bringing Turkey in.

On the points which were known to be most sensitive, the timing of a major invasion against North West Europe, and the effort to be made against Japan – Brooke was noncommittal, without giving hostages to fortune. On ROUNDUP he said that build-up of British and American forces in the United Kingdom – BOLERO – must continue – so that advantage could be taken of any 'crack in Germany in the late summer' – thus not excluding ROUNDUP in 1943, while making timing, as he had always made it, dependent on the condition of the enemy. As to the Pacific, Brooke spoke of the reconquest of Burma but pointed to the lack of naval forces and landing craft necessary for those amphibious operations against Lower Burma – ANAKIM – which the British then regarded as likely to be an integral part of a campaign for the country's liberation.

Now Brooke requested a presentation of American views on the Pacific. His abrupt manner and staccato speech: the speed of his mind combined with his rapid delivery: his absolute mastery of the facts, and his inexorable and uncompromising presentation of them; all united to make the Americans somewhat wary, a wariness they never entirely lost. This was very different from the emollient diplomacy of Dill who could express an idea by inducing his companion to advance it as his own, and who could without humbug express disagreement as if it were a compliment. 'I think,' wrote Jacob at the time, 'CIGS' extremely definite views, ultra swift speech, and at times impatience, made them keep wondering whether he was not putting something over on them.' This may indeed have been the Americans' concern. Nevertheless the British Chiefs of Staff – and Dill – were necessarily complements of each other at these Conferences. Portal's transparent honesty, professional knowledge and courteous, quiet wit enchanted them. Dill they already admired and loved. Pound, they suspected, had less influence through declining powers. In all this there had to be one element of granite, the voice on occasion to say the harsh things harshly; the mind to think them. It was Brooke's, and in dealing with Allies, just as in dealing with Ministers at home, he won the absolute regard of his colleagues in the Chiefs of Staff Committee. To them, the best and most critical of judges, he was indispensable.

The Casablanca Conference, like all such, seemed at first an essay in reconciling the irreconcilable. Responding to the British invitation to expound plans for the Pacific King suggested that 30% of the Allied war effort should be devoted to the Pacific and

Alanbrooke's children: Tom, Pooks and Ti

'He told them stories, drew for them . . .'

The Casablanca Conference. *Front Row* Air Marshal Portal, Admiral Pound, Mr Churchill, Field Marshal Dill, General Brooke *Back Row* Brigadier Dykes, General Alexander, Admiral Mountbatten, General Ismay, Lord Leathers, Mr Macmillan, Brigadier Jacob

With General Marshall

Benita Pelly,
Lady Alanbrooke

With Generals Alexander
and Montgomery –
December, 1943. 'Monty
is tired out and Alex fails
to grip the show.'

Commander-in-Chief. St Paul's School, 1940

70% to the rest. 'We pointed out,' Brooke wrote in his diary that night, 'that this was hardly a scientific way of approaching war strategy! After considerable argument got them to agree to our detailing the Combined Planners to examine and report on the minimum holding operations required in the Pacific and the forces necessary for that action.' This was no more than a formula to keep business moving. The American component of the 'Combined Planners' had no mandate to do other than state what were American plans and what resources they would require, without attempt at debating the plans or pruning the resources to make more available for the war against Germany.

This was not as obstinate as it appeared. King's plans for the Pacific were, in the view of the British planners, very sound. The problem was to relate the resources they required to an agreed overall concept consistent with the idea of 'Germany first'. It seemed to the Americans that the European end of such a concept was still unsubstantial. They were reluctant to draw resources from positive plans against Japan unless they were to be devoted to equally positive – and ambitious – projects against Germany. It was therefore necessary for the British to approach the matter constructively and to engage stronger American interest in amphibious operations against the European enemy. Once the interest was sufficiently aroused the resources would follow. That, at any rate, was the policy adopted by the British planners. Brooke was sceptical about any attempt to get resources from King. 'Nothing we ever said,' he wrote later, 'had much effect in weaning him away from the Pacific. That is where his heart was, and the bulk of his Naval forces. The European war was just a great nuisance that kept him from waging his Pacific war undisturbed.'[11] Certainly at the end of the first day of Conference the British Chiefs were concerned that the claims of the Pacific could be pitched so high as to make resources everywhere inadequate. The Americans did not disguise the huge bill in men, aircraft, warships and shipping which would, in their view, be needed against Japan if she were to be prevented from consolidating her gains. This was all convincingly demonstrated – but how could it be done without a shift of the entire main point of effort to the Far East theatre?

The arguments went on daily – five days of incessant debate. At all times the British rested not on any argument against American Pacific plans for their unsoundness but on scarcity of resources, which demanded hard choices. Yet Churchill's injunction to be like 'water dripping on a stone' was followed, and in his diary on 16th January, the third day, Brooke wrote: 'I think we are beginning to make some progress, and that they are getting interested in our proposals.'

With typical volatility his diary the following evening started: 'A desperate day! We are further from obtaining agreement than we ever were!' But on the 19th some light broke, and in his letter to Benita that evening, Brooke wrote: 'At last things have been going better in our discussions. I was beginning to despair this morning.'

The light was largely induced by a paper produced by Portal and drafted by Air-Marshal Slessor. It addressed the relative priorities of the Pacific and European theatres in a way which would re-emphasize the priority of the war against Germany without emasculating that maintenance of pressure on Japan, that retention of the initiative in the Far East which the Americans would certainly – and rightly – not forgo.

From Brooke's point of view the paper – which found ready acceptance[12] – gave him all he wanted. It specifically committed the Allies to the occupation of Sicily – HUSKY: that was for him the great, the concrete achievement. As to ROUNDUP there would take place in the United Kingdom 'the assembly of the strongest possible force . . . in constant readiness to re-enter the Continent as soon as German resistance is weakened to the required extent'.

This assembly, whose object and timing entirely coincided with Brooke's thoughts, was subject to the overrides that the occupation of Sicily, operations to gain the Alliance of Turkey and operations in the Pacific 'with the forces allocated' must not be jeopardized. On the latter the paper stated:

> These operations [in the Pacific] must be kept within such limits as will not, in the opinion of the Combined Chiefs of Staff, jeopardize the capacity of the United Nations to take advantage of any favourable opportunity that may present itself for the decisive defeat of Germany in 1943.

Subject also to this proviso planning for ANAKIM* was to go ahead. The Americans had undertaken to produce massive assistance with naval forces and landing craft for this expedition against occupied Burma.

Thus, after much argument, the next step began to emerge. The Portal paper was ingenious in its wording. By deferring with

---

* ANAKIM denoted the whole campaign for the recapture of Burma of which the proposed amphibious landings were part.

the language of compromise all that did not need immediate action it won agreement on the latter. It did not look at operations beyond the occupation of Sicily (HUSKY) – and that was consistent with Brooke's own mind for nobody could tell how events in Italy might go. It gave the United States Navy sufficient of what they wanted, by not taking anything immediately from them and by reserving for the future scrutiny of the Combined Chiefs of Staff – in which forum King's voice would always be loud and strong – any limitations on action in the Pacific. It underwrote planning for ANAKIM. On this Brooke felt sufficiently optimistic to write to Wavell on 23rd January:

> The prospects of starting ANAKIM in 1943 seem much brighter. The Americans . . . are now prepared to assist ANAKIM with Naval and assault landing craft drawn from the Pacific. I feel we should keep them up to this and that it would be better to direct some of the effort they propose devoting to the Pacific to the more profitable Burma front. I do not see how we are ultimately to make any real headway against Japan without reopening Burma and possibly bringing Russia in as well.[13]

Whatever the accuracy of this prophecy it showed Brooke content with what had been set down at Casablanca about the war against Japan.

The words used about ROUNDUP did not make any commitment to action in 1943, but did not preclude it. Brooke feared, above all, unrealistic plans for premature invasion of North West Europe. Those constituted his private nightmare. Operations, step by step, in the Mediterranean were, for him, practical, prudent and consistent with that overall strategy of the war to which both the great Western Allies had originally subscribed. As to the ultimate invasion, it was agreed at Casablanca to set up a Chief of Staff and Planning Staff in London, and this significant step provided an impetus and gave a certain reality to that final act in the drama towards which the British, in American eyes, appeared sometimes lukewarm.

'I have seldom had a harder week or one with a heavier strain,' Brooke wrote to Benita on 20th January. It had been lightened by some bird-watching.

> Went for another good walk during which I found a new white heron, quite distinct from the Egrette [sic] and a new small owl which we could not place.[14] Went . . . out early with John Kennedy for a bird walk. We saw all our wader friends on the beach and then found a stonechat on the way home.[15]

These were precious and vital interludes.

Brooke had fought hard, but in his view personal contacts had prospered. He was privately critical of the attitudes of each of the American Chiefs (as they frequently were of him). He regarded Marshall as an organizer without strategic vision, King as biased entirely towards the Pacific, and General Arnold, the American Air Chief, as limited to air matters in his outlook. But 'as a team' he wrote in his diary on 20th January, 'they are friendliness itself, and although our discussions have become somewhat heated at times yet our relations have never been strained'. It is virtually impossible to assemble powerful and responsible men in conclave during a crisis without their forming critical views, in the instancy of the moment, about those with whom they disagree. The best that could be hoped for was sufficient agreement on the next concrete steps to take, combined with personal rapport; and this was achieved. A stimulus towards it lay in the wise words of Dill to Brooke when the CIGS seemed despondent. Dill pointed out that if the Combined Chiefs of Staff approached President and Prime Minister without agreement, the two political leaders would start resolving the strategic dilemma themselves, with what outcome none could foresee. It was a telling argument.

During the Casablanca Conference, Brooke was not clear of difficulties with his own British colleagues. That 'exploitation' of North African victory, which was accepted by all on the British side, had initially left open whether Sicily or Sardinia should be the first target. Brooke had studied the question closely and, supported by Churchill, had put his weight behind Sicily. It was on this basis that he had dealt with the Americans. Sicily would add something to the security of Allied sea communications through the Mediterranean, for which the clearance of Tunisia was the principal factor. Sardinia would add nothing. The British Planners, however, pointed strongly to the advantages of Sardinia, and both Portal and Mountbatten had been persuaded. Mountbatten's view was relevant. He attended most Chiefs of Staff meetings (on the questionable basis that virtually all operations were, under some definition, 'combined operations') but his role and voice, in Brooke's firm view as Chairman, should properly be confined to amphibious matters. Yet the choice between Sardinia and Sicily would certainly be such, and Mountbatten had a right to have his say.

Thus, after full meetings with the Americans all day on 21st January, Brooke spent three hours from 9 p.m. to midnight dealing with his own colleagues. 'In my own mind there is not the least doubt Sicily should be selected,' he wrote in his diary that night, 'but on the whole the majority of opinion is hardening against me.' 'We started at 9 a.m. and have been at it non-stop till midnight except for meals,' he wrote the same night to Benita, 'and even at meals arguments never stop.' Brooke was, however, determined to stop the Sardinia-Sicily argument dead, and he wrote later:

> I had a three hour hammer and tongs battle to keep the team together and to stop it from wavering. I told them that I flatly refused to go back to the American Chiefs of Staff and tell them that we did not know our own minds and that instead of Sicily we now wanted to invade Sardinia! I told them such a step would irrevocably shake their confidence in our judgement. What is more I told them frankly that I disagreed with them entirely and adhered to our original decision to invade Sicily and would not go back on it.[16]

Sicily it was. Whether or not Brooke's original reasoning was justified by subsequent events his view was surely sound that the matter was one of judgement, and the essential was to show united and steadfast judgement rather than dissension, uncertainty or half-heartedness.

Alexander had been summoned to Casablanca, arriving on 14th January, to assist with the discussions. He was to play a vital part in the troubled business of Command relationships in the North African campaign where, although the British Army was providing by far the strongest element, the French would not serve except directly under Eisenhower (in default of the appointment of Giraud himself as Commander of all forces, which he had first mooted and for which he was entirely unsuited). To harmonize these political sensitivities with the facts of the battlefield and the deployment of troops was difficult. Eisenhower had had to attempt two simultaneous jobs, that of a Supreme Commander, in fact if not name, at Algiers, and of a field commander at an improvised Headquarters at Constantine. The device was agreed of appointing Alexander Deputy to Eisenhower, so that the latter could concentrate upon the political and strategic problems which beset Algiers, and a field commander could – as his Deputy and in his name – co-ordinate the actions of the various national forces, including the British Eighth Army when it broke into Tunisia from the east. Meanwhile Air-Marshal Tedder was appointed

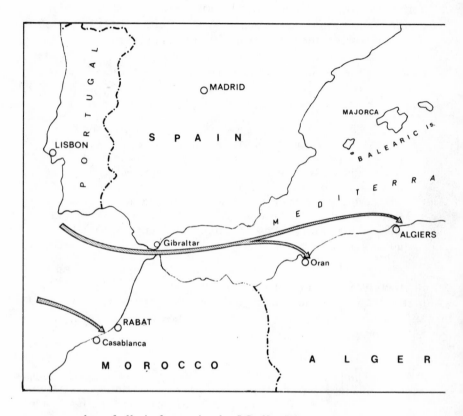

commander of all air forces in the Mediterranean.

The move of Alexander 'could not help flattering and pleasing the Americans in so far that we were placing our senior and experienced commander to function under their commander who had no war experience', wrote Brooke later.[17] 'We were pushing Eisenhower up into the stratosphere and rarefied atmosphere of a Supreme Commander . . . whilst we inserted under him one of our own commanders to deal with the military situations and to restore the necessary drive and co-ordination which had been so seriously lacking of late.' In spite of this move, Brooke sounded his not unusual note of scepticism: 'I had some doubts as to whether Alexander would have the ability to handle this difficult task.'[18] Nevertheless the North African campaign seemed set on course, although Brooke's doubts of Eisenhower's military gifts remained and he did not anticipate a quick conclusion.

The Conference over, the great men dispersed. To Brooke's

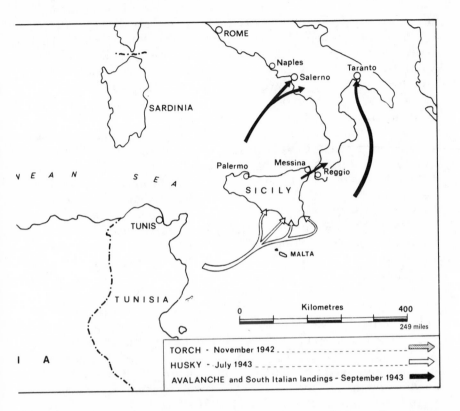

ROME

Naples
Salerno
Taranto

SARDINIA

Palermo   Messina
V E A   N   S   E   A   Reggio

SICILY

TUNIS

MALTA

T U N I S I A

Kilometres
0   400
                                    249 miles

I   A

TORCH · November 1942 ....
HUSKY · July 1943 ....
AVALANCHE and South Italian landings · September 1943

delight Churchill proposed to go to Marrakesh for a few days'
relaxation and painting and to take the CIGS with him. Brooke
quickly organized a day's partridge shooting, and both left
Casablanca on 24th January. 'We moved out of the place we were
yesterday to a most lovely spot,' Brooke wrote to Benita on the 25th
– 'a lovely change after the last 10 days' work. It did me the world
of good as I felt a sort of flat feeling as a reaction after the strain.'
These great Allied Conferences, sometimes accompanied by
internal dissension, put immense pressure on all participants and
on none more than the Chairman of the Chiefs of Staff Committee.
Upon the decisions reached depended the future conduct of the
war and the chances of victory of British servicemen everywhere.
The strain, however, had brought achievement, and from Brooke's
viewpoint Casablanca was a success. On no point that he thought
vital had he had to yield. The next steps forward, albeit short, were
those he desired. The Secretary sees meetings more clearly than

most. 'When I came to write the final document,' noted Jacob in his diary,[19] 'indicating the decisions taken and the agreement reached on all the separate matters dealt with, I found that if I had written down before I came what I hoped that the conclusions would be I could never have written anything so sweeping, so comprehensive, and so favourable to our ideas as in the end I found myself actually putting down. Our ideas had prevailed throughout.'

Furthermore, President and Prime Minister accepted what the Combined Chiefs of Staff had hammered out. Only on the question of timing did the political leaders balk. Although Churchill was strongly in favour of HUSKY, the invasion of Sicily, he was appalled to hear that the military men reckoned it could not be mounted until August – with, as possible target, 'the favourable July moon'. This assumed North Africa would be cleared in April. Churchill fiercely questioned the need of a fallow period between the end of April and the end of July. He pressed the Chiefs of Staff of both nations to aim for the 'June moon' instead. Eisenhower's directive was amended accordingly. In the event North Africa was not finally cleared until May, yet the landings took place on 10th July. Churchill's vigour was justified.

Brooke's respite at Marrakesh was short. His hope of a day after partridges was soon shattered. As he left his hotel on 25th January he was summoned by telephone to the villa where Churchill was staying. 'He greeted me,' Brooke recorded,[20] 'by telling me that we were off at 6 p.m.' Brooke demurred. Had not the Prime Minister promised himself (and others) a few days' rest? Was he not proposing to paint at Marrakesh – his paints had been specially brought? Churchill was adamant. The party would leave at 6 p.m. 'All right,' said Brooke, 'if we are off at 6 p.m. where are we going?' 'I have not decided yet,' Churchill replied.[21] He either wished to return to London, to be in his place in the House of Commons the following day, or to fly to Cairo. They flew to Cairo.

Now came the first step in a project dear to the Prime Minister's heart. He was anxious for a meeting with the Turkish President General Ismet Inonu. He felt that with Allied successes in North Africa and Russian victories on the Eastern Front Turkey might be amenable to friendly overtures. He had, a few months earlier, raised with Roosevelt the possibility of some sort of 'Black Sea offensive' against the deep flank of the German forces facing the Red Army in Southern Russia, an idea which the Chiefs of Staff had not instantly opposed and to which, although now overtaken by events, the attitude of Turkey would have been of great significance. Churchill wanted to build up Turkey's strength and secure her friendship, even though the time might not be ripe for Alliance. He had put this to the Cabinet while he was at Casablanca and had received a cool response. The Foreign Office feared that such a meeting was premature, and might court rebuff or produce embarrassment. Churchill returned to the charge, with Roosevelt's support, and obtained his colleagues' approval in a telegram which reached him shortly after his first meeting with Brooke on 25th January at Marrakesh. Brooke had a few hours' relaxation, driving in the Atlas mountains in the afternoon; and in the evening the party flew to Cairo. The proposal for a meeting had now been passed to Turkey, and in Cairo the Prime Minister would be poised to take advantage of a favourable response if one came.

Brooke, flying separately, arrived at Cairo a few minutes before Churchill on the morning of 26th January. It was an enjoyable contrast to his last visit. He wrote in his diary that night:

> It is very strange being back here after little more than 5 months and so much has happened in that time. When I was here last I kept wondering if the day would come when the Germans would be firing across the Nile into the Embassy gardens, and now they are on the point of being driven out of Tripoli.

Indeed the tide had turned and nowhere was that sensation more vivid than in Cairo, which still housed General Headquarters Middle East. 'Your Alex/Monty combined did the trick nicely,' the Ambassador, Sir Miles Lampson, had written to Brooke in December, 'you never saw such a change. Confidence everywhere and the earlier dry rot cut right out.'[22] In his diary of 27th January, Brooke referred to 'that nightmare of a first week last August with all the unpleasantness of pushing Auchinleck out and of reconstituting the Command and Staff'.

During 27th January, the telegram arrived which showed that the Turks would much welcome a visit from Churchill. The fears of the British Foreign Office appeared groundless. This naturally delighted the Prime Minister. His delight was later increased when he learned on arrival that the German Embassy in Ankara had heard of the projected meeting, and enquired of the Turkish Foreign Ministry whether this presaged a new alignment by Turkey – a démarche which did not in the least discomfort the

Turks. Churchill was also, wrote Jacob who was with him when he read the telegrams, 'not unhappy at the thought of how right he had been and how wrong the Cabinet and their advisers had proved'.[23] Prime Minister and CIGS flew on 30th January to meet the Turkish President and his principal advisers, including the Chief of the Turkish General Staff, at Adana in Southern Turkey. Brooke had usefully spent the time in Cairo discussing the Sicily operation with Alexander, shortly off to become Eisenhower's Deputy: and in briefing the various senior commanders on prospects in the Mediterranean theatre. He also paid a happy visit to the Siwa Oasis, site of that oracle consulted by Alexander the Great.

The meetings with the Turks took place in a railway carriage. The first phase, as is customary, was devoted to long speeches of welcome and courtesy. When the President of Turkey and the Prime Minister withdrew Brooke was left to conduct discussions with Field-Marshal Cakmak. Not unnaturally, considering the course Turkish history had taken in the last two decades, Brooke found Cakmak, as he expressed it, 'had no conception of the administrative aspects of handling modern armies'.[24] The military side of the talks would, it was hoped, clarify Turkish strengths and weaknesses and thus show in which areas help might be most useful.

According to Brooke's diary note that evening Cakmak showed that 'he had not prepared his case'. This may have been so, but a first meeting between principals of such different background and without preliminary work was unlikely to make the conduct of business easy. It was hardly surprising that Cakmak found it necessary to conduct long discussions with his own staff in Turkish: nor, perhaps, that Brooke found this infuriating, a test to his Irish temper.[25] There was also a linguistic difficulty. It had been agreed that the talks would be conducted in French and English. Cakmak's French was indifferent while Brooke, as Jacob put it, 'speaks perfect French, at his usual lightning speed!' Although Cakmak's supporters also spoke excellent French there could be no direct rapport between principals such as helps a meeting become warm. Nevertheless those present reckoned that Brooke handled the Turks very well. He declined to go into details on the (considerable) Turkish demands for materiel. Instead he pressed the Turks to improve their communications and mechanical training and, where appropriate, to invoke British help to do so.[26] It was also agreed that a British Military Staff would be established in Ankara.

The meetings were considered successful. It was clear to all that the Turks had been agreeably surprised that there was no British attempt to push them into Alliance and war: and equally clear that their chief preoccupations were with the post-war world and the position in it of the Soviet Union.

Whilst sitting opposite Cakmak during the discussions in the railway carriage Brooke's eyes picked up through the window behind the Turkish Chief of General Staff 'what I thought was a pallid harrier busy quartering over the plain. I had never seen a pallid harrier and was not certain whether what I was looking at was one or a hen harrier. I was consequently very intent in looking out of that window much to Cakmak's discomfiture, who kept looking round . . . It was not possible for me to explain through the interpreter that I was only "bird-watching".'[27] Nevertheless Brooke entered in his diary for 31st January, 'Turkey's neutrality will, from now on, assume a more biased nature in favour of the Allies, I hope somewhat similar to that of the Americans prior to their entry into the war.' This, as he appreciated afterwards, was unduly optimistic and took little account of the skills of the German Ambassador, Franz Von Papen. Nor did the euphoria with which the British party left Turkey sufficiently reflect Turkish anxieties about what would happen in the Balkans and Eastern Mediterranean following a German defeat.

On 31st January the party flew to Cyprus for an unscheduled stop at Government House. 'After dinner,' Brooke wrote that night, 'had a long talk with Government official who is an expert on birds. Finally, after PM had gone to bed, Lady Woolley* played two Liszts [sic] on the piano which were quite lovely. Now to bed for a good sleep. I feel very tired.' Next day they returned to Cairo.

During the last week of Brooke's Mediterranean Odyssey he savoured some of the fruits of victory. On 3rd February he and Churchill flew to Tripoli, to meet Alexander and Montgomery and again to visit the Eighth Army, last seen before Alamein. That day is best described in Brooke's words in his diary that night and in his later note.

> At 9.30 a.m. we all assembled and started off by car for Tripoli. It was most interesting seeing the place for the first time. The

* Wife of the Governor of Cyprus.

streets and house-tops were lined with sentries which held back the local inhabitants.

When we arrived on the Main Square and Sea Front we found there the bulk of the 51st Division formed up on the sea front and main square. The last time we had seen them was near Ismalia just after their arrival in the Middle East. Then they were still pink and white; now they were bronzed warriors of many battles and of a victorious advance.

I have seldom seen a finer body of men or one that looked prouder of being soldiers.

'This had been a memorable day,' Brooke wrote afterwards, 'and one I shall never forget, but what stands out clearest among all those stirring events was the march past of the 51st Div. in Tripoli. As I stood alongside of Winston watching the Division march past, with the wild music of the pipes in my ears, I felt a large lump rise in my throat and a tear run down my face. I looked round at Winston and saw several tears on his face, from which I knew that he was being stirred inwardly by the self-same feelings that were causing such an upheaval within me.'

From Eighth Army Brooke flew on 5th February to Algiers, where both he and Churchill talked to Eisenhower, Giraud, Anderson and the other principal actors on the North African stage. In Eisenhower's garden he 'discovered the same African blue-tit that I saw in Marrakesh'. That evening was spent unexpectedly in Algiers because of aircraft engine trouble, but next day Brooke flew to Gibraltar where he dined and watched a defensive fire demonstration organized by the Governor, General Mason Macfarlane. At 1.15 a.m. he left the Rock and an hour later was airborne on the final stage of his journey home, where his aircraft arrived within half an hour of Churchill's.

Jacob, who had accompanied the party throughout, flew direct from Algiers to England with the Prime Minister. 'It seemed that his mind was thinking of crashes,' Jacob recorded, 'he said to me "it would be a pity to have to go out in the middle of such an interesting drama without seeing the end. But it wouldn't be a bad moment to leave. It is a straight run in now, and even the Cabinet could manage it!" '[28] More prosaically Brooke entered in his diary that night, 7th February:

I now foresee some hard work ahead to convert some of the paper work of the last 3 weeks into facts and actions.

With Churchill he had flown 10,200 miles, settled the major outlines of Allied strategy for the next phase of war, made contact with the Turks, smoothed the path of Eisenhower in Tunisia, given wise advice on future operations to Alexander, and inspected some of the victorious Army for which he was responsible. Travelling by rail from a West Country airfield he reached London by 1 p.m., 'where to my great joy you met me'[29] he recorded in his diary, his communication for Benita's eyes. Next day he returned to the War Office.

Brooke was the most intransigent of the British military leaders on the question of timing of the 'Second Front' and of the necessity first to clear North Africa, then threaten Southern Europe, enable shipping to passage the Mediterranean and seek to produce the dispersal of German forces which otherwise could reinforce the Western Front facing a cross-Channel invasion. Was the British High Command justified in the stand which effectively postponed that invasion until 1944? What might have occurred had a different policy been adopted, the Mediterranean left in the situation of mid-1942, and all the force later committed to North Africa and to Italy been concentrated in Britain for a great adventure not later than summer 1943? Or, later, had the Allies closed Mediterranean operations at the end of the Tunisian campaign in May 1943?

Much must be speculation but surely certain things are clear. In the first place the events of late summer 1942 showed that the threat to Egypt was real, and it was by no means impossible that it could have been so intensified as to put the whole Middle East at risk. At the least there would have still needed to be significant reinforcement of the Desert Army, even to stand on the defensive in such a way as to make Egypt secure. Presumably, had operations in French North Africa not been undertaken, slower progress in the Western Desert was all that could have been hoped for: and had this not at all times covered the Cyrenaica airfields the position of Malta would have again become untenable. The British would surely, therefore, have been committed to a strong position in Libya, and the passage of the Mediterranean would have been at worst impossible, at best contested, with all that implied for the availability of shipping. Second, the argument for closing down Mediterranean operations after Eisenhower's victory in Tunisia in May 1943 was strongly affected by timing. At least in theory, an invasion of Western Europe in 1943 was conceivable had Eisenhower's final triumph been in January. By May it could not

331

have been mounted during the remaining fair weather months of 1943.

There are further and equally cogent points. Certainly an invasion with all available forces in 1943 would have meant a larger and concentrated British Army, forming a greater proportion of the Anglo-American force than it ultimately did. Certain economies would have resulted for the British: supply, compared to the supply of the Italian front, would have been simplified. But the American formations were still in the stage of build-up and development, and it is questionable whether the united force would have been of sufficient size or quality to reach a favourable decision in Western Europe. The Joint Planning Staff concluded that it would not. The extra year was of great value. Furthermore, the effect of the air offensive had become far more devastating by 1944, as accuracy improved.

Last and most important, however, was the relative position of the enemy forces. In 1943, had no North African campaign been undertaken by Anglo-American Armies or no Sicilian campaign in exploitation of victory in North Africa, Italy would still presumably have been an adversary. Large numbers of German formations diverted to Italy or Southern Europe to contain or replace Italian troops could have remained on the Eastern Front or reinforced the 'West Wall'. The German situation in Russia was by no means so serious, even after the fall of Stalingrad, as it was in 1944: indeed in mid-1943 a fresh German offensive in the East was in preparation, the battle of Kursk, CITADEL; and had the Germans instead resorted to the defensive, and transferred troops to the Western Front on a large scale their communications would undoubtedly have enabled them to build up at a much faster rate than the Allies could have disembarked, even had the initial landings been successful. Again, the extra year's attrition of the German Army on the Eastern Front was crucial, just as was the extra year's attrition of the Luftwaffe and the cumulative effect on German communications. It should also be remembered that the Battle of the Atlantic was not won until the summer of 1943, with all that implied for the timing of Allied build-up in the United Kingdom.

When all these factors are taken together they point inexorably to the impracticability of SLEDGEHAMMER 1942, and of ROUNDUP 1943. Brooke did not need persuading of the theoretic benefits of earlier invasion. He simply knew that it would not work. Once the decision was taken to invade Sicily the die was cast, for that operation required all available resources for an opposed landing, and must exclude a similar attempt on Western Europe in the same year. The decisions of Casablanca meant that invasion of North West Europe must inevitably be deferred until 1944; and thus ensured success.

CHAPTER XIV

The Beginning of the End

FOR BROOKE the next three months were largely spent in keeping his colleagues, his political masters and his American counterparts firm to what he regarded as the best interpretation of the Casablanca decisions.

The most immediate business lay in Tunisia, where victory must be final before the next step could be taken – the first great leap across the water, the invasion of Sicily. Although Brooke knew that as much as possible had been done to improve command in Tunisia he was still unhappy about progress, and about the performance of commanders. 'I had anxious moments at this time,' he wrote afterwards:[1]

> It had been made quite clear by what had happened up to date that Eisenhower had not got the required ability to ensure success in this theatre. Alexander, his Deputy, had many very fine qualities but no very great strategic vision. He had been carried by Montgomery through North Africa as regards the strategic and tactical handling of the situation. Monty was now far from him and Anderson certainly had not got the required qualities to inspire Alex. It was very doubtful whether he was fit to command his Army. The only comfort rested in the fact that Dick McCreery was still Alex's Chief of Staff and I had the very greatest confidence in his ability.

Not until Montgomery's Eighth Army had broken into Tunisia and the two wings of the Allied forces had united would Brooke feel easy about the North African front, where on 14th February, Rommel, in his last African battle and with something of his old quality, inflicted a sharp defeat on the Americans at the Kasserine Pass and threatened Anderson's communications with Algiers. But Rommel's heart had not been in it. He believed the Axis position in North Africa untenable. The situation was restored, and in late March Montgomery, by manoeuvre, forced the enemy out of the Mareth line on the Tunisian/Libyan frontier, having failed with heavy casualties to carry it by direct attack. On 7th April the two Allied Armies joined hands and the Axis forces,

334

TUNISIA – ALLIED ADVANCE MARCH – MAY 1943

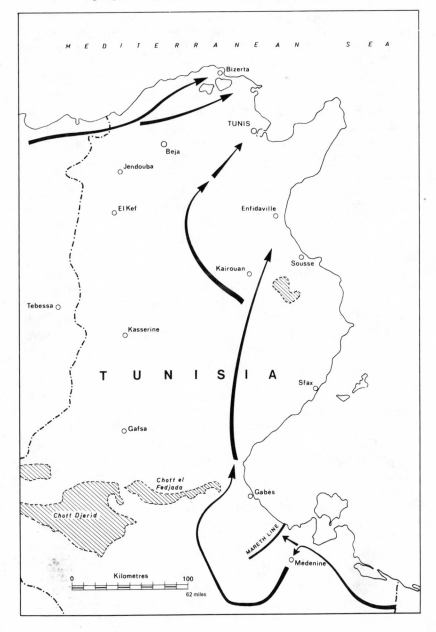

MEDITERRANEAN SEA

Bizerta

TUNIS

Beja

Jendouba

El Kef

Enfidaville

Kairouan

Sousse

Tebessa

Kasserine

T U N I S I A

Sfax

Gafsa

Chott el Fedjada

Chott Djerid

Gabès

MARETH LINE

Medenine

Kilometres
0   100
62 miles

now under the command of General Von Arnim, were hemmed into the mountain massif in the north-east, between Enfidaville and Beja.

Thereafter there took place the final Allied offensive in North Africa of which the first ten days saw some of the fiercest fighting of the whole war. The American, French and British forces were facing an enemy to whom they were greatly superior in numbers and in materiel. They had complete ascendancy in the air. Their command of the central Mediterranean was such that few seaborne supplies were reaching Tunisia from Italy, and those only at considerable shipping loss. Nevertheless the Axis forces were well-deployed, skilful and brave. No chances could be taken with them. None were: in the high command caution rather than manoeuvre was the hallmark of the campaign. Not until 13th May could Alexander – now in actual field command as an Army Group Commander, with a Staff and Headquarters, as well as acting as Deputy to Eisenhower – send his final report: 'The Tunisian campaign is over. All enemy resistance has ceased. We are masters of the North African shore.'

It was just over six months from the launching of TORCH and the breakout at Alamein. Nearly 240,000 prisoners were taken. The Mediterranean was clear to Allied shipping. The grand design could proceed. The early delays and fumbling in the Allied advance on Tunis had brought uncovenanted benefits, since they enabled the Germans greatly to reinforce and thus ultimately to suffer a major defeat with losses comparable to Stalingrad. Hitler's determination to hold Tunisia as long as possible had, however, a considerable effect on Allied strategy. Because it led to a sustained campaign it delayed all other European operations, as Marshall had explicitly feared. And because it helped deny to the Allies free passage of the Mediterranean it compounded that strain on Allied shipping which was the chief limiting factor on their operations.

Nevertheless Brooke remorselessly asserted that for the Allies there was no alternative. The arguments had been set out and he never saw reason to change his mind about them. Above all things Brooke feared a premature attempt on the defended coastline of Western Europe, before the German Army had been much further weakened. He was determined to win time – time for Germany to be increasingly bled by the Eastern Front, time for Italy to be detached from the Axis with consequential dispersal of the Germans, time to wear down Germany by further bombing and time to build up irresistible force in the United Kingdom. All this, in the context of 1943 and in Brooke's mind, predicated not only North African success but the exploitation of it for which he had fought at Casablanca. Perhaps he was not sorry that Alexander's *coup de grâce* in Tunisia had not been delivered at the speed of a Rommel.

Another commitment of Casablanca to which Brooke was determined to hold the Allies was BOLERO – the American build-up in Britain. 'Something has gone wrong with our Casablanca agreements,' wrote Brooke in his diary on 17th February, 'and the flow here not started at all.' 'They are entirely breaking down over promises of American Divisions to arrive in this country' (25th February). He signalled to Dill on 24th February: 'I am very disturbed by American failures to implement Casablanca agreements concerning BOLERO.'[2] And on 6th May he wrote an exasperated note:

> Up to the present the bulk of the American Navy is in the Pacific and larger land and air forces have gone to this theatre than to Europe in spite of all we have said about the necessity of beating Germany first!

Brooke associated the disappointing performance of BOLERO with American preoccupation with the Pacific, and with the influence of King on resource allocation, despite the cautious (but ambivalent) wording of the Casablanca agreement in that regard.

In this he was less than fair. The shipping situation was immensely complex. Britain lived by imports, and the British Government were not prepared to reduce them beyond a certain point – but to keep above this point needed American assistance. Then again the British had been promised shipping support for ANAKIM. The bill for this was considerable, and when presented caused consternation in Washington. Eisenhower reported in February that if he were to meet the target date for HUSKY to which the President and Prime Minister aspired he would need considerably more shipping. HUSKY, ANAKIM, BOLERO and the sustenance of the United Kingdom – all these were in competition not only with the Pacific theatre but with each other. Furthermore, part of the BOLERO commitment included the build-up of American air forces in Britain for the increased strategic air offensive against Germany agreed at Casablanca, so that decision, too, was at risk.

Brooke's concern about BOLERO was understandable. In the end BOLERO was performed to the necessary extent and the invasion itself took place – by no means later than Brooke would have thought sound. But the reason was not a change of heart or priority in Washington in 1943. It lay in victory in the Atlantic, which transformed the shipping situation. Meanwhile, in the first months of 1943, it became clear to all that the commitments undertaken at Casablanca were beyond the resources of the Allies. That BOLERO suffered was virtually inevitable. It did not suffer alone.

The next, and to Brooke most vital, step deriving from Casablanca was HUSKY – the invasion of Sicily.

Here Brooke had to contend with the impatience of Churchill. The Prime Minister had only reluctantly accepted the agreements of Casablanca on the timing of that operation, and the Chiefs of Staff had to deal with this reluctance in February. They had to examine again the possibilities of bringing the date forward to June. But, timing apart, there seemed no sign of second thoughts in any quarter on HUSKY although some pessimistic conclusions of Eisenhower had to be briskly dealt with in April. Eisenhower had given his view that if two German divisions were found to have reinforced Sicily the invasion would be unlikely to succeed and should not take place. Churchill's rage was understandable, and Brooke did not seek to contradict him when he minuted that 'If the presence of two German divisions is held to be decisive against any operation of an offensive or amphibious character open to the million men now in North Africa it is difficult to see how the war can be carried on.'[3] The point was taken, and the war was carried on. HUSKY took place.

But the crucial question was what to do after it. Brooke's eyes were, as Churchill's had always been, fixed on the detachment of Italy from the Axis. He knew well that the question 'what after Sicily?' would raise again, in sharp form, those differences of perception which most divided the Western Allies. As the end in North Africa drew nearer and the day for HUSKY approached this question could not be left uncertain for long.

As to commitment against Japan, Brooke and his colleagues could not greatly influence the interpretation placed by the United States on the Casablanca agreement insofar as American forces were concerned: 'Operations in these theatres [the Pacific and the Far East] shall continue with the forces allocated.' They could, however, invoke the subsequent paragraph:

These operations must be kept within such limits as will not, in the opinion of the Combined Chiefs of Staff, jeopardize the capacity of the United Nations to take advantage of any favourable opportunity that may present itself for the decisive defeat of Germany in 1943.[4]

The formulation had ingeniously cut the knot of disagreement at Casablanca. Could it provide sufficient guidance or common ground?

To Brooke the matter was one of spirit rather than letter. In cold print the Casablanca agreement referred to an opportunity 'for the decisive defeat of Germany in 1943'. Since Brooke had no belief in the possibility of the invasion of Western Europe in 1943 – a point of view to which he was only able finally to persuade Churchill in March; and since he also firmly believed that such an invasion would be essential to the 'decisive defeat of Germany' it was clear that he could not, with consistency, argue that an opportunity to inflict it was being jeopardized by operations in the Pacific; or, indeed, by anything else. But the spirit of Casablanca, in Brooke's view, was a reaffirmation of the principle of 'Germany first'. Again and again in the first months of 1943, he complained in his diary that the Americans did not believe in their hearts that Germany must be defeated before Japan.

Meanwhile matters were not going well in Burma. On 22nd April, Wavell and his colleague Naval and Air Commanders-in-Chief arrived in London. A limited offensive in Arakan had been thoroughly unsuccessful. It was necessary now to examine future operations there, and in particular ANAKIM. This examination effectively killed the enterprise. ANAKIM was judged impracticable, in that shipping resources were totally inadequate without a much increased American contribution. It was regarded as tactically questionable in terms of air cover and the possible defensive measures open to the enemy. It was – most significantly, if not of most immediate effect – described as strategically unsound, because the reconquest of Burma was not essential to the ultimate defeat of Japan. As for the Burma road to Chungking, hitherto regarded as vital to the support of China, the examination concluded that its capacity was so small that it could not be improved to take the sort of tonnage thought necessary until 1945. Seldom can an operation whose planning and preparation had been formally agreed by the highest authorities of two nations have been so damagingly indicted within a few months. There is no reason to suppose that Brooke was disturbed. He was unsurprised, although naturally disappointed, by the size of the gap in shipping which planning revealed for all the Casablanca projects. But he certainly preferred losing ANAKIM to losing anything else.

ANAKIM, however, was damned not only because of shortage of shipping but for strategic irrelevance and tactical unsoundness, and nothing had happened since Casablanca to affect this. Why Brooke was not more concerned with this contradiction is uncertain. It does not seem to have altered his regard for Wavell. 'You know as well as I do that drive is not Archie's strong suit. It never was,'[5] wrote Dill to Brooke at about this time, after a tour of India. There is no record that this particularly worried Brooke. The explanation probably lies in the fact that after India was clearly safe – after the tide of Japanese victory had been turned, notably at the battle of Midway – Brooke put the defeat of Japan into a compartment of his mind which he did not frequently inspect. His earlier remark to Wavell, about not seeing how Japan could be beaten without reconquering Burma, suggests a lack of the sort of exhaustive thought he brought to every aspect of the war against Germany. So it would remain for some time.

Nevertheless matters between the United States and United Kingdom clearly had to be resolved once again. Two great issues were on the table. The British Empire could only make a small-scale effort against Japan in 1943. What effect would this have on combined strategy? And what major operation against Germany should follow the invasion of Sicily, now due to take place in two months' time? On 5th May, Prime Minister and Chiefs of Staff set out in the *Queen Mary*, currently used for troop transport, to meet their American colleagues in Washington.

Brooke had found particularly trying the months between the return from North Africa in early February, and the embarkation for the second Washington Conference – to be named TRIDENT – in May. He had had a disagreeable attack of influenza in March and had had ten days in bed. He took some time to get over it. Churchill had suffered an attack of pneumonia at the same time. Brooke's expressions of irritation that the Americans were failing to live up to their undertakings were to some extent the outcome of ill health, as well as of realization of the gravity of the shipping position. Colleagues and subordinates alike tended to get short shrift in his diary, and whether visiting a major Home Forces Exercise in March or the Secret Service organization later in the same week he found major inadequacies and wrote them down.* His unfailing solace was in his ornithology. 'Now a quiet evening with bird books and I feel better,' he wrote to Benita on 30th March. And two days later:

> I have now got my Gould books!! and I feel like stopping at home turning the pages over and over again!! They are quite lovely and I can't get over how lovely they are.

Later he bought a complete set of these superb volumes. He sometimes shopped at Sotheran's in Sackville Street, where he would take off his uniform jacket and sit in the shop, in his red braces, thoroughly relaxed, deep in ornithology. On one occasion an officer on leave saw what he rightly thought to be the CIGS in the shop, boldly approached him and stated that he had a complaint to make. 'Put it through the proper channels,' grunted Brooke, thoroughly absorbed in birds.[7] Perhaps it was walking to Sotheran's one day that Brooke found his way into a memorable fictional portrait. In Anthony Powell's *The Military Philosophers*;

> This was the CIGS. His quite remarkable and palpable extension of personality, in its effect on others, I had noticed not long before, out in the open. Coming down Sackville Street, I had all at once been made aware of something that required attention on the far pavement and saw him pounding along. I saluted at admittedly longish range. The salute was returned. Turning my head to watch his progress, I then had proof of being not alone in acting as a kind of receiving-station for such rays – which had, morally speaking, been observable, on his appointment to the top post, down as low as platoon commander. On this Sackville Street occasion, an officer a hundred yards or more ahead, had his nose glued to the window of a bookshop. As the CIGS passed (whom he might well have missed in his concentration on the contents of the window), this officer suddenly swivelled a complete about-turn, saluting too. No doubt he had seen the reflection in the plate glass. All the same, in its own particular genre, the incident gave the outward appearance of exceptional magnetic impact.

The journey in the *Queen Mary* was busy. Brooke complained how exhausting were the incessant meetings in preparation for the Conference; the voyage also provided a certain break.

* In the case of the Secret Service Brooke wrote that there were no agents of any use in Sicily, Sardinia or Italy just when they were needed. In his view this arose from overdependence on ULTRA.[6]

Inevitably it also provided incident. Life near Churchill could not be void of drama. While at sea Wavell, who was accompanying the party, proposed to resign his command, so upset was he at the Prime Minister's criticisms of operations in Burma. Brooke told him that if he, Brooke, took offence when abused by Churchill he would resign once a day. The matter was dropped. The British party disembarked at New York on 11th May and travelled by train to Washington.

As at Casablanca, the second Washington Conference started with what seemed an impasse. To Brooke the American position, stated by the Chairman of the United States Joint Chiefs of Staff, Admiral Leahy, at the opening meeting in the Federal Reserve Building, was unsound for the same two reasons as hitherto. It was put in words which, as he wrote in his diary, allowed 'too much latitude for the diversion of force to the Pacific'. Second, it reverted to the conviction that victory could be attained more quickly by an early Western front being opened in France. The Americans evinced the same hostility towards extended operations in the Mediterranean as Brooke reckoned he had to some extent overcome at Casablanca – hence HUSKY. This hostility ran deep. Brooke recalled afterwards a private talk with Marshall at this time which perhaps went to the heart of their disagreement. Marshall said that he was still unreconciled to what he called 'your North African strategy'. When Brooke asked what alternatives there were Marshall said, with conviction, that an earlier invasion of North West Europe with concentrated forces could end the war quicker. Brooke replied caustically that it would probably finish it in an undesirable way.[8] The fundamental difference was not primarily about the logistic impracticability of assembling the forces and resources for invasion before 1944, although the argument largely took place on that basis. To Brooke it derived more from his conviction, so often expressed in his diary, that the invasion would only succeed against a German defender much more seriously weakened. In the final analysis, therefore, the difference was in the estimate of the enemy. On such questions nothing can be proved except in the event and by the sword. Whether Marshall's more sanguine views were justified will never be known. They were not tested.

Meanwhile there was again hard fighting between Allies. Brooke wrote in his diary on 18th May that the Americans were 'taking up the attitude that we led them down the garden path by taking them to North Africa. That at Casablanca we again misled them by inducing them to attack Sicily. And now they do not intend to be led astray again. Added to that the swing towards the Pacific is stronger than ever, and before long they will be urging that we should defeat Japan first!' To Brooke, who was conscious that a cleared Mediterranean released a million tons of shipping and who had just received the news of the final triumphs in Tunisia, criticism of the North African concept was hard to bear. As to the war against Japan, Brooke wrote after the war of his sense of 'absolute hopelessness' at TRIDENT over getting in step withe the Americans. 'The Americans,' he said, 'were trying to make us undertake an advance from Assam into Burma without adequate resources. In fact an advance which was only ultimately made possible by the provision of air transport for supply purposes.' For the first time he met General Joseph Stilwell, 'Vinegar Joe'. 'He is a small man,' he wrote at the time, 'with no conception of strategy.' And later, 'Except for the fact that he was a stout-hearted fighter suitable to head a brigade of Chinese scallywags I could see no qualities in him. He was a Chinese linguist, but had little military knowledge and no strategic ability of any kind.'[9] Stilwell was a considerable leader of men. Slim,* who saw plenty of him and had at least his share of the sour side of Stilwell, nevertheless saw his virtues very clear. But Stilwell's personality was not of a kind to appeal to Brooke. Also his involvement with Chiang Kai-shek represented an aspect of the war which Brooke found dangerously prominent in Washington thinking.

As the Conference continued the rough edges of each side's position were worn a little smoother, and in the end sufficient agreement emerged to carry on the war in something like harmony, although further conference would soon be needed.

There would, it was agreed, be 'continuance of pressure' on Italy in the Mediterranean. Brooke regarded this as a triumph, since the opening American position had been that all operations in the Mediterranean should be closed down after the capture of Sicily. The Americans regarded it as satisfactory because the wording of the agreement limited Mediterranean operations by specifically 'subordinating' them to the claims of ROUNDUP – the invasion of North West Europe. The agreement also set a date on ROUNDUP in 1944; and since the formal American position had been to press for ROUNDUP at the earliest practicable date, and Sicily had not yet been attacked let alone captured, it would have

* Wavell also liked Stilwell.

been hard at that stage to reconcile a target date for ROUNDUP in 1943 with an agreement (which was inevitable) to await the successful outcome of HUSKY. As between the Mediterranean and cross-Channel operations, therefore, an adequate consensus was reached. The specific form that 'pressure on Italy' should take would clearly need settling – but not yet. Certainly Brooke did not yet press for an invasion of the mainland. He wanted to see how events developed, and the ultimate decision to leap across the Straits to Italy was not taken until the middle of July. There was, therefore, something for both sides at TRIDENT. Brooke felt that he had got most of what he wanted. Above all the date of invasion of Western Europe was not unacceptably advanced.

Brooke did not believe anybody's inner convictions were affected. 'King,' he wrote in his diary on 25th May, 'still remains determined to press Pacific at the expense of all other fronts. Marshall wishes to ensure a cross-Channel invasion at expense of Mediterranean.' This gives an inadequate impression of his feelings. Brooke would not have defended the idea that a Mediterranean campaign could be a substitute for the final invasion, or that the latter should not have ultimate priority – although in the short term he reckoned (without persuading Marshall) that some shipping could be diverted from BOLERO to feed immediate needs in the Mediterranean. But he saw Mediterranean operations as progressively weakening Germany, each step cautious, a limited liability and attractive thereby. He saw alternative possibilities for the Allies in the Mediterranean, so that different options could be pursued and a wide range of problems posed to the enemy – in Italy, in Greece, in the Balkans, in the courtship of Turkey. In the final invasion of North West Europe, on the other hand, all cards would be simultaneously dealt and turned face upwards on one table. It would be all or nothing, and in one crucial theatre. It had to be all.

In the war against Japan the British Chiefs of Staff had not found it easy to reach previous agreement with the Prime Minister. Churchill had accepted the proposal to abandon ANAKIM, but he pressed for some major amphibious diversion, pointing to Sumatra and Java as possible targets. He believed that success in the Mediterranean would liberate major maritime forces for concentration in the Far East. They could use their command of the sea in classical form, and land a force wherever the Allies chose.

Brooke, supported by his colleagues, strongly opposed such ideas. It was inevitable that they would involve landing craft and escorts on a large scale. They would dissipate resources and would distract attention from the main enemy, Germany, and the main theatres of decision – Europe and the Atlantic. The utmost that should be done against Japan was to increase the airlift to China, and to undertake very limited operations from Assam.

When these conclusions were put to the Americans the principal opposition came from Roosevelt himself. He was always particularly sensitive to the pressures exerted by the Chinese and their friends in the United States, and he was determined that some dramatic effort, or at least an effort of dramatic appearance, should be made to help them. He had already heard the forceful representations of Stilwell that bold operations should be conducted by the British from Assam to open the Burma road: the airlift alone would not do. Roosevelt, therefore, was the prime mover in getting the opening of the Burma road written into the final resolution as one of the ultimate aims of operations – and this despite the fact that, in examining ANAKIM, the strategic value of Burma as well as the logistic value to China of the Burma road had been called into question. The truth was that a purely defensive policy in Burma might have been sound strategy: the reconquest of Burma did little towards the ultimate defeat of Japan, and the Chinese, whether or not helped by the Burma road, did a great deal less. But such a policy was impossible to present in America and impossible for the President to contemplate. Subsequent operations reflected that fact – and in the process, by a certain paradox, produced in Burma one of the most successful and intelligently conducted Allied campaigns of the war.

The ultimate resolution of the TRIDENT Conference was that air operations, both against the Japanese in Burma and to sustain China by supplies, should be intensified: that Japanese sea communications to Burma should be interrupted where possible; and that land operations from Assam should be vigorously conducted in combination with Chinese operations from the north in order to tie down Japanese forces. These operations were described 'as an essential step towards the opening of the Burma road'. Stilwell, in pressing for these, had imprudently referred to Chinese suspicion of British inaction and drew the fire of Churchill – the Prime Minister was officially recorded as saying that he was not prepared to undertake something foolish purely in order to placate the Chinese. All this was not too far from the British position. It did not demand the diversion of resources required against Germany, and Brooke was content. He was content even

345

when he heard the ambitious and impressive plans presented by the Americans for their 'island hopping' strategy, of gaining bases for fleet and air forces ever nearer Japan. This strategy involved only American forces, but it represented a great bill in amphibious resources. Nevertheless the improved position in the Atlantic; the agreed abandonment of ANAKIM; and the imminent (it was hoped) removal from the chess board of the Italian fleet should mean that maritime resources were equal for the tasks the Combined Chiefs had agreed. Unlike the aftermath of Casablanca, Brooke did not feel the bill for the plans agreed could not be paid. The swaying coach of Allied strategy was kept on the road.

It was agreed that the next steps in the Mediterranean should be discussed with Eisenhower – next steps after the invasion of Sicily, for which Eisenhower was now preparing himself, his troops of many nations and his somewhat temperamental commanders. On 26th May, Brooke, therefore, left Washington with Churchill, bound for Algiers. They had successfully persuaded Roosevelt and Marshall that the latter should join the party. Brooke feared that if he and Churchill visited Eisenhower without such a companion there would be subsequent suspicion that the British had privately nobbled him.

Brooke had disliked TRIDENT, and in spite of the comparatively successful outcome he found the failure of minds to meet depressing. There had been agreeable moments. He visited Williamsburg and loved it, and the Mellon gallery in Washington which stunned him with its splendour. He also visited the Pentagon – recently completed. 'A vast building,' he wrote to Benita –

> . . . another story goes that a lady was discovered in one of the passages in great distress asking to be taken off in an ambulance as she was on the point of childbirth. When she was told that she really ought not to come to the building in that condition she replied that she was not even pregnant when admitted to the building.

He was astringent over what he reckoned the size, wastefulness and excessive bureaucracy of American military headquarters, and he enjoyed the story. But his letter of 21st May recorded:

> After lunch I had 1½ hours off and went to a book shop to look at American bird books. I had great fun and forgot war and conferences for a bit and came away with two bird books.

346

Brooke's mission to Eisenhower was concerned with the longer term rather than the immediate future. On the latter there had been plenty of storms in Algiers. Plans for the invasion of Sicily had not gone through on the nod. There had been dissension between the Services over the relative priorities of a concentrated landing (Montgomery) and the capture of the West Sicilian airfields (Admiral Cunningham and Air-Marshal Tedder). There had been dissension over the priority to be given to a southern landing near Syracuse (Montgomery) and one in the west directed on Palermo (Patton*). Whatever Brooke's reservations, frankly expressed, on Eisenhower's capacity as a field commander he always recognized his ability to orchestrate an often temperamental and wayward group of players. On this, as on subsequent occasions, it was Eisenhower who brought about harmony, however temporary. It sufficed. All, and particularly Alexander who was now commanding 15th Army Group formed to co-ordinate Allied land forces for the invasion of Sicily, paid generous tribute to Eisenhower's service. The various operational Headquarters for the Sicilian landings had been moved to Malta, in close proximity to each other. 'Reports have reached me,' Maitland-Wilson† wrote to Brooke on 11th May –

> 'of bearings being inclined to heat already: the root of it all is the personality of Monty. I feel that with the location of most of the operational Headquarters in Malta there is going to be grave risk of open quarrels unless someone can go round daily with a lubricating can.[10]

This came as little surprise to Brooke. But he had faith in Alexander's skill with a lubricating can, and he was acquiring even more in Eisenhower's. While at Algiers, however, he saw Montgomery himself, summoned by Brooke from leave in England.

> 'He required a lot of education,' Brooke wrote in his diary on 3rd June, 'to make him see the whole situation and the war as a whole outside the 8th Army orbit. A difficult mixture to handle, brilliant commander in action and trainer of men but liable to commit untold errors due to lack of tact, lack of appreciation of other people's outlook. It is most distressing that the Americans do not like him, and it will always be a difficult matter to have him fighting in close proximity to them. He wants guiding and

* General George Patton, Commander US Seventh Army.
 † Maitland-Wilson had been appointed Commander-in-Chief Middle East when Alexander was sent to Tunisia.

watching continually and I do not think that Alex is sufficiently strong and rough with him.'

'I had to haul him over the coals for the trouble he was creating with his usual lack of tact and egotistical outlook,' Brooke wrote afterwards.[11] He accused Montgomery to his face of 'crass stupidity' – but from Brooke, Montgomery accepted the rebuke with contrition and gratitude for the forthright speaking.[12] It was Brooke's way, and none were spared if it was necessary.

In Algiers Churchill pressed Eisenhower towards the invasion of the mainland after Sicily was conquered. This was an interpretation of 'continuing pressure on Italy' which the Prime Minister made his own – and, of course, it happened. But in June Eisenhower – and Marshall supported him – believed it wise to 'wait and see'. Better to watch events after Sicily was invaded, and to watch the effect on Italy, than to plan too precisely more than one step ahead. Brooke did not dissent. He wrote in his diary on 2nd June that the three main points to be aimed at were the securing of North Africa (now accomplished): the elimination of Italy; and to 'bring Turkey in'.* But he did not press Eisenhower or Marshall further towards a definite invasion plan for Italy itself. They had covered that ground at Washington. Instead Eisenhower was invited to produce recommendations for the Combined Chiefs of Staff. Not until this was received at the end of June did the British Chiefs of Staff decide that Eisenhower should be impelled towards the mainland (his appreciation was still indeterminate). On 3rd July they so informed Washington. There the American Chiefs still – and understandably – wished to await the HUSKY landings, due within days.

Churchill and Brooke returned to London from Algiers on 5th June. The next two months were anxious. In retrospect Allied operations in the last two years of the Second World War have a certain inevitability. It did not seem so at the time. A landing operation on the scale of HUSKY, with over 1300 amphibious craft involved, was without precedent. For Brooke it had the added significance that if it met disaster there would be no hope of continuing with his policy – 'his' because he had not only made it his own through conviction but was personally so associated with it

* Turkish entry into the war played a great part in the strategic thinking of Churchill and sometimes of Brooke. It is hard, at least with hindsight, to make practical sense of the idea, and the scepticism of many, including the Americans, is easy to defend.

by the Americans – of concentrating on the defeat of Italy in a Mediterranean campaign.

Discussion continued on the best way of prosecuting the war against Japan. It is striking how seldom the Far East appears in Brooke's diary, his letters, his preoccupations. He had been deeply anxious when India seemed threatened in the dark winter and spring of '41–'42. But after the tide in the Far East turned, and it was clear that India was safe, it was equally clear that Japan would take a long time to beat and British possessions a long time to recover. The chief issue, for Brooke, was to ensure that that war did not poach resources or divert concentration from the war against Germany.

An American planning team visited London during the summer to help in the search for that elusive thing; an overall Allied strategic concept. It was agreed that it might be necessary in the end to invade Japan itself. Meanwhile there must be a Far Eastern version of 'closing the ring'. Japanese sea communications must be attacked, and her lines to her sources of supply and conquered territories increasingly disrupted. This meant a continuing build-up of maritime superiority. It also meant the progressive capture of bases for the fleet. Japanese possessions and ultimately the heartland of Japan must be attacked from the air. This involved a relentless progress of American forces from island airbase to island airbase, ever nearer Japan.

This was a slow-moving strategy, but none better was suggested. The Western Powers were already lifting their eyes beyond the defeat of Germany. It seemed clear, in those pre-atomic days, that the resources necessary to press this amphibious strategy to its conclusion would demand a regrouping from the European and Atlantic theatres. It was equally clear that this should happen as early as was consistent with victory in the West, and it was agreed that as a planning guideline resources should be transferred to the Far East some four to six months before the forecast date of Germany's defeat.

For Brooke and his British colleagues the immediate issue was where a campaign in Burma fitted into this pattern. Two primarily political factors affected the matter.

First, China and Chinese morale were particularly important to the American President and Administration. It was generally agreed that little could be expected from the Chinese Army. Nevertheless there had been undertakings towards Chiang Kai-

349

shek which involved supply, to whatever use it would be put. Supply, at least in the established view in Washington, meant opening the Burma road to augment the airlift; and the Burma road meant a campaign in Burma.

Second was the question of the restoration of the British Empire. Here Churchill showed more commitment and insight than his professional advisers. They tended to regard strategic options in the context of how they affected the ultimate defeat of Japan. So did Churchill. But he also kept his eyes on certain national objectives, of which one of the most important was to reconquer, and be seen to reconquer, British Imperial possessions or associated territories in the Orient.

The line-up of opinion swayed to and fro. The Americans believed that Burma should be cleared of Japanese by the British in two campaigns, in two successive campaigning seasons. The first of these would be in the winter of 1943, and on this Auchinleck wrote home in July a cautious appraisal of what could be done. Brooke had modified his earlier condemnation of Auchinleck who had taken up the Command-in-Chief in India, on Wavell's appointment as Viceroy, on 18th June. Two expeditions were under study: one a triple offensive in Upper Burma, co-ordinated between the British from the west, Stilwell's forces from the north and the Chinese from the east; and the other an amphibious operation against Akyab in lower Burma.

Auchinleck reckoned that the operation in Upper Burma should be very limited because of logistic factors: it should be little more than the preparation, by advancing communications, of a later campaign. The amphibious operation would require more resources than were available. It would anyway be hazardous. Auchinleck described the delays which he regarded as necessary between various phases of operations. A few weeks later, on 13th August, he recommended that, in view of the difficulties and limited value of possible objectives, no offensive at all should be undertaken in the forthcoming winter.

Churchill's reaction was predictable. He found all this deplorably timid and unimaginative. Some bold project should be undertaken with our greatly superior maritime forces in 1944, a project to seize territory and one which would exploit sea power. A 'slow push' through Burma would be a poor way of waging war for an Alliance with such command of the sea as the Western Powers now enjoyed. He favoured a landing in North Sumatra. Discussion on this had already been acrimonious. 'An unpleasant evening with Winston,' Brooke wrote to Benita on 29th July, 'which lasted till 1.30 a.m. and which became somewhat heated at times!'

Brooke's views were characteristic. First he was determined that no plans should be endorsed, whatever American pressure, which could draw effort from the Mediterranean, and in this he obtained his colleagues' support. Second he was thoroughly sceptical of Churchill's Sumatra project. He found Churchill with no coherent vision beyond Sumatra, no idea of what to do after getting there. It was also, of course, evident that any ambitious project of that kind would need more shipping than was available in the Far East theatre.

Nevertheless Brooke and the Chiefs of Staff rejected Auchinleck's proposal to postpone offensive operations altogether. They did not find his reasoning convincing, and they knew that such a policy would be completely unacceptable to Prime Minister and to Allies alike. It is likely, too, that Auchinleck's position was weak and his advice more sceptically received than those of some Commander who had caught a successful tide. Certainly this would be consistent with Brooke's simultaneous acceptance of the recommendations of General Wingate. Wingate was suggesting certain methods of organization and command for his Long Range Penetration Groups, against the representations of Auchinleck, the Commander-in-Chief. Auchinleck's representations were orthodox but cogent. It would not generally have been in Brooke's character to dismiss them. Although he had been impressed by Wingate's personality and ideas this did not extend to all his proposals. But Auchinleck's stock was low, and to be right in logic or justified by the event was not enough. So it was with his strategic recommendation. It was thus agreed that an offensive campaign should be undertaken in Burma.

There was another factor. Auchinleck would not now exercise command in the field. New command arrangements were in hand for the Far East. It was proposed to create a new South East Asia Command under a Supreme Allied Commander. Brooke thought of several names. His preference was for Air-Marshal Sholto Douglas who was proposed to the Americans and declined by them. Churchill then persuaded them to accept Mountbatten, an officer of great energy and enthusiasm, as yet inexperienced in senior command. Brooke was sceptical. 'He will require a very efficient Chief of Staff,' he noted in his diary on 6th August.

Brooke did, however, have his way over the appointment of an Army Commander, who would command the principal land forces in the Burma campaign. Churchill for some time contended that such an appointment would not be necessary. Brooke knew that it would – not least because of what he heard of poor morale of British troops and their sense of inferiority in the face of the Japanese. The appointment was soon to be filled by perhaps the most gifted and imaginative British Commander of the Second World War, Slim.

On the two fronts which Brooke always regarded as crucial – the Atlantic and the Eastern Front in Russia – Allied fortunes were prospering. The first six months of 1943 saw the climax of the anti-submarine war. There were two measurements of progress. First was the excess of new shipping construction over tonnage sunk by the enemy. Second was the excess of U-boat sinkings over U-boat construction. By both measurements the first part of the year went worse and worse for Germany, not least because the increasing range and effectiveness of the aircraft of Coastal Command and those operating from Canada ultimately covered the whole North Atlantic. In May, Admiral Dönitz withdrew his U-boats from the Atlantic, and reported to Hitler in July that German submarine warfare was ineffective and that no forecast could be made as to whether or when this would change. As the next step in the Mediterranean took place, and the ultimate invasion of North West Europe appeared on the horizon with an agreed date, its essential prerequisite – victory in the Atlantic – was achieved. Now the European theatre could be sustained with the materials of war without interruption or serious dispute.

Brooke's other and unchanging preoccupation was with Russia. It was in Russia that a German operational success could again change the situation. In Russia in July the Wehrmacht launched a great concentric attack on the Red Army, in the largest tank clash yet seen in war, the battle of Kursk, Operation CITADEL. The German attacks from north and south against the Kursk salient started on 5th July – five days before HUSKY.

The attacks were unsuccessful, in that no quick decisive result was achieved. Mobility – hitherto often something of a German monopoly – was now at the disposal of the Soviet troops.[13] The latter reacted vigorously. Hitler called off the operation on 13th July. He told the two Commanders concerned (Field-Marshals Von Manstein and Von Kluge) that the Allied landings in Sicily compelled him to find forces from the Eastern Front. With the end of CITADEL 'the initiative in the Eastern theatre of war', wrote

Von Manstein, 'finally passed to the Russians'.[14]

On Monday 15th June Brooke, complete with a streaming cold which had marred the weekend, attended a Cabinet Meeting. He wrote that night in his diary:

> PM called me in just before the meeting to tell me that he had been wanting to let me know during the last few days that he wanted me to take the Supreme Command of operations from this country across the Channel when the time was suitable.
>
> He said many nice things about being full of confidence in me, etc.

To Brooke this was the most rewarding and stimulating news imaginable. It 'gave me', he wrote later, 'one of my greatest thrills during the war. I felt that it would be the perfect climax to all my struggles to guide the strategy of the war into channels which would ultimately make a re-entry into France possible to find myself ultimately in command of the Allied Forces . . .'

He was sworn to secrecy, so that this particular diary could not be delivered to Benita for a while. The promise was reiterated by the Prime Minister on 7th July, after he had entertained the King to dinner. Brooke was of the party –

> After the King had left the PM kept us on till 1.30 a.m. Finally when we were saying goodbye he took me off into the garden of 10 Downing Street in the dark, and again told me that he wanted me to take over the Supreme Command of operations out of this country. But that I was to stop on as CIGS till January or February, and that I should only take over if it looked pretty certain that the operation was possible. He could not have been nicer, and said that I was the only man he had sufficient confidence in to take over the job.

It would, of course, be an appointment of which American endorsement was necessary.

'I realized well,' Brooke wrote afterwards, 'all the factors that might yet influence the decision and did not let my optimism carry me off my feet.' Nevertheless it was understandable that he should write at the same time, 'I was too excited to go to sleep when I returned home.'

This was the second time that a major command was proposed to Brooke in the Second World War. On the first occasion – when he was offered the command of the Middle East theatre in preference to Alexander – he suffered pangs from his refusal but he knew that he was right. It was essential in 1942 that he should stay

353

as CIGS. Now it was different. The command itself was on a much grander scale – the command of an Allied expedition launched on the greatest invasion operation across water in the history of the world. The central direction of the war could, Brooke was confident, be left without qualms to others. The ship of strategy would be on course. By the time the great invasion – now christened OVERLORD – was set in hand there would be no deviation possible from the policy which Brooke had so patiently pursued. And he was sick of Whitehall, and longed for the challenge of decision, and freedom from Cabinet and cabal.

A week later Brooke and Benita both attended a sherry party at 10 Downing Street. Churchill then asked Benita how she liked the idea of Brooke's becoming Supreme Commander of the invasion of France. He had not yet told her anything about it 'as it was still all so distant and indecisive'.[15] Distant and indecisive it might be but such frankness from Churchill could only give Brooke a sense that the thing would be settled. He knew the problems, but with such assurance in Churchill he could and did begin to feel sure himself that a new destiny awaited him. It seemed particularly enticing as night after night the meetings with colleagues and the Prime Minister went on. 'You look tired CIGS, are you doing too much?' Churchill said at 1.30 a.m. on 16th July. 'Don't go flying about too much.' Such a remark, Brooke wrote in his diary, 'means a lot and more than compensates for any extra strain'.

Yet the strain was incessant. Meeting after meeting, interview after interview, the days raced on towards the moment of the landings in Sicily, long days of exhaustion and anxiety into which Brooke as usual packed the work of several lesser men. 'We had a desperate session last night which lasted till 1.30 a.m.,' he wrote to Benita on 16th June, 'by which time I was dropping with sleep – I again had a Cabinet at 5.30 p.m., which lasted till near 8.00 p.m. and now I am just off for another night party with PM!' This was a little disingenuous of Brooke. 'The 'desperate session' had been preceded by the 'unmentionable' offer of Supreme Command. But he was kept painfully short of sleep now as ever. 'During dinner PM called up to say he wanted a meeting at 10.30 p.m. and we have another tomorrow night'. (21st June). So his letters to Benita would run. He drew on his usual consolations. On 22nd June:

> Went and invested capital in a set of Gould's Birds. It remains to be seen whether my forecast of the set going up in value comes true.

It did come true – he sold these superb volumes after the war at doubled price but with great sadness. In the meantime he described them as 'wonderful value . . . as an antidote to the War and to Winston! While looking at Gould's wonderful pictures I was able to forget everything connected with the War.'[16]

Brooke made a new and cherished friend. His diary for 21st July records:

> Dined with John Kennedy who had the Devonshires and Bannerman to dine. The latter is busy preparing a new book of birds to be illustrated by Lodge and brought with him some lovely pictures which Lodge has been painting for this book.

The book, *The Birds of the British Isles*, was published in 1954 and the first volume carried a foreword by Brooke, by then a Field-Marshal, a Peer and a Knight of the Garter. In Dr David Bannerman, an ornithologist of international renown, Brooke found a kindred spirit. Bannerman would advise him on purchases, exchange recollections with him, and give Brooke the benefit of his enormous expertise. Brooke responded with enthusiasm. His letters to Bannerman were warm, frequent and full of underlinings and emphasis. Here was a subject which really engaged his heart. Whatever the exigencies of business he would always find time to write a letter of enquiry or fellowship, or, as occasion sometimes demanded, of sympathy to Bannerman. Nor were these letters hasty scrawls demanded by courtesy; they were full, gentle, and above all considerate. In such letters Brooke could pour out that part of himself which was stifled by the unrelenting pace of war and of Whitehall – and find not added fatigue but respite in so doing.[17]

Brooke also lost a valued comrade at this time. 'Heard today,' he wrote in his diary on 5th July, 'the tragedy of Sikorski's death in an aeroplane accident at Gibraltar. He is a terrible loss and I feel I have lost a great friend.' Only later did Brooke fully realize what a loss Sikorski's death was to Poland. He thought after the war that Sikorski might have been able to do something 'to prevent the ghastly massacres of the Warsaw Underground Army'.

On 9th July the diary entry is brief. After a short account of an interview Brooke wrote: 'Tonight the attack on Sicily starts and thank heaven the suspense will be over . . .'

HUSKY went well. The only disaster was the airborne landing, which went sadly awry. There was little opposition to the seaborne landings and it was soon clear that the Italians had no stomach for the fight. Hitler immediately ordered two reinforcing German divisions to the island (there were already two, 'underpinning' the ten Italian divisions) and showed some initial signs of extending to Sicily his general, and generally fatal philosophy, of not yielding a yard of ground.

Brooke, as was his custom, had withheld comment on the operational plans. The Allied Commanders in HUSKY have been criticized, whether fairly or not, on a number of counts. It has been said that a failure to land on the mainland side of the Messina Straits enabled the Germans to reinforce more easily, and to escape when it was decided to evacuate the island. The bottle was uncorked. It has been said that the operations in Sicily itself lacked grip from the top. On such issues it was not Brooke's way to interfere, unless interference was invited or appeared necessary to prevent trouble. This was an Allied operation and Eisenhower was responsible to the Combined Chiefs of Staff. It seemed to go as planned, and Brooke was content to watch from afar, and to concentrate on the next step.

On this he had reason for satisfaction. The British Chiefs of Staff had already decided that an invasion of the Italian mainland should follow HUSKY, in order to accelerate the collapse of Italy. Their American colleagues had been cautious and had wished to see how matters would go in Sicily. Now, on 16th July it was agreed by all that Eisenhower should be pointed towards Italy as his next task. Exactly how and where landings on the mainland should be made – and with what resources – was to be the subject of study, planning and sometimes acrimony throughout July and early August.

Eisenhower was now convinced of the merits of the invasion of Italy itself. As to where, a landing near Naples, in the Gulf of Salerno, was remitted for examination and given the code name AVALANCHE. Brooke, as ever, was wary. He told Churchill on 19th July that he was convinced of the rightness of an assault on the mainland but he was concerned at the possible speed of German build-up against such an expedition compared to the rate at which the Allies could put troops ashore.[18] Also 'Air cover bad and dependent on carriers', he noted in his diary on 19th July. However on 22nd July he referred to AVALANCHE as 'a gamble but probably one worth taking'.

On 25th July Brooke and Benita were staying at Chequers. 'After dinner,' he wrote that night –

we had a film – *Sous les toits de Paris*. In the middle came news of Mussolini's abdication!!! Winston dashed off to talk with Eden. A memorable moment and at least a changeover from 'the end of the beginning' to 'the beginning of the end'!

Two days later the Joint Intelligence Committee warned that Italy might soon treat for an Armistice. The progress of HUSKY, the agreement to invade the mainland, and the fall of Mussolini all produced a situation where Allied consultation was again vital. On 5th August the Prime Minister and Chiefs of Staff, with a similar entourage to that which had accompanied them to TRIDENT, again boarded the *Queen Mary* lying in the Clyde. This time their destination was Halifax in Nova Scotia. The Conference was to be held at Quebec.

The first Quebec Conference was called QUADRANT. Like its predecessor TRIDENT it took place when a campaign – in the earlier case Tunisia and now Sicily – was nearing victory and urgent decisions were necessary on the way ahead. In each case the campaign ended during the Conference. Little jubilation found its way into Brooke's record. He loathed QUADRANT while it was going on, and he loathed it in anticipation. 'The nearer I get to this next Conference,' he wrote in his diary on 5th August, 'the less I like it. I know we shall have hard fighting with our American friends. I know too well what these Conferences are like and how much they take out of one.'

The QUADRANT Conference was arranged in the hotel Château Frontenac, superbly placed above the St Lawrence at Quebec. The British party disembarked from the *Queen Mary* at Halifax and continued their journey by train arriving on 10th August. The whole hotel was taken over for the Conference so that both living and business took place under one roof – an excellent device. The first meeting of the Combined Chiefs was due on 14th August, and the Conference followed its usual course – a prior meeting with Dill on 11th August, the presentation of what appeared hard and antagonistic positions in plenary sessions, a private session to discover where minds rather than words really differed, and a solution, with some elements of compromise, to which both sides could subscribe.

At QUADRANT the question largely turned on trust. The Americans had formed the view, once again, that British hearts were not in OVERLORD – the invasion of North West Europe. They believed that in spite of the specific agreement in

357

Washington in May to undertake this invasion in 1944, and to give
it a planning date, there was still strong British reservation. This,
to the Americans, lay behind a recent act of the British Chiefs of
Staff which they stigmatized as 'unilateral' and found particularly
suspicious – an order to retain certain forces and landing craft in
the Mediterranean *sine die* which it had been previously agreed
should disperse to the United Kingdom for OVERLORD and to
India for operations in Burma. These forces included seven
divisions at present under Eisenhower's command. To the
Americans the British were once again playing the Mediterranean
hand without regard to agreed priorities or to a sound strategy of
concentration. They were probably doing so with an eye on the
post-war situation in Europe and the Balkans, whereas OVERLORD
was, to Marshall's mind in particular, a straightforward military
operation for straightforward military results.

Had the argument between the two nations really turned on
this sort of difference of perception nothing could more decisively
justify the British and condemn the American position. War is a
political activity, and where strategy (about means) is not directed
by policy (about ends) there is an absence of what Clausewitz called
'the intelligent factor' in war. It would be agreeable but untrue to
suggest that on this occasion the British had a clear vision of the ends
to which means might lead, and a view about them. Some writers
have regarded British policy as consistently far-sighted, concerned
with the post-war world, and American policy as blind in this
respect.[19] At Quebec – and after – this was not so. The British
position was sound, but it did not derive from any profound cause as
suspected by Marshall. It rested on purely military factors. Brooke
and his colleagues saw no reason to change their opinion that a
Mediterranean campaign, vigorously prosecuted, would do more
to help Russia immediately and OVERLORD later than would the
concentration of larger forces in England now. They saw fresh and
attractive possibilities for such a campaign in the aftermath of
Mussolini's fall and with Italy's total collapse likely to be imminent.
Aboard *Queen Mary*, Brooke wrote to Maitland-Wilson,
Commander-in-Chief Middle East in Cairo, on 6th August: 'My
present thoughts are along the lines of building up a balanced
Anglo-American Field Force of some eighteen divisions from the
resources now in the Mediterranean to operate in Northern Italy.'[20]

This letter was of course subsequent to a definite Anglo-
American agreement to invade the mainland of Italy, and
subsequent to Mussolini's fall, but before specific plans for that

invasion had been made or approved, and before Italy had collapsed or the Germans had intervened in the massive way which was to come. It showed Brooke considering an Italian campaign wherein Allied forces reached, by whatever means, North Italy – presumably soon. It was not Brooke's way to talk of 'building up a . . . Field Force . . . to operate in North Italy' if what he meant was a Force to operate in Central Italy and fight its way through to the north in due course. The letter, therefore, suggests either further and more ambitious amphibious landings against resistance in the north, or a rapid advance to North Italy in the face of Italian forces in disarray. The former is not consistent with Brooke's reservations voiced then and subsequently about the Salerno landings. He would hardly have spoken of AVALANCHE as a gamble on 22nd July and then envisaged larger landings further north in a letter on 6th August. It is thus clear that when he wrote to Wilson he hoped that Italian collapse would 'open up' Italy to the Allies, by what route was uncertain. The Germans, after Italian defection, might sacrifice much of Italy without defence (and indeed the High Command of the Wehrmacht was known by the Allies to be considering this option). But it is equally clear that Brooke regarded this as a modest campaign. He wrote of eighteen divisions, and this was consistent with simultaneous build-up for OVERLORD. Indeed twenty-three divisions, apart from four French, had been reserved for operations in the Mediterranean after HUSKY – and this assumed the departure of the disputed seven to Britain.

Churchill's mind had ranged more ambitiously over the Mediterranean theatre. He had written to the Chiefs of Staff in July that operations in Italy in 1944 should be 'certainly to the Po, with option to attack westwards in the South of France or north-eastwards towards Vienna'. But he had at the same time written that the forces earmarked for OVERLORD might be inadequate, and he had adverted to his old love, an invasion of Norway. Brooke had shown no sort of encouragement for this idea, nor for the suggestion that OVERLORD was in doubt. There is no basis for the belief that Brooke at this time was lukewarm about OVERLORD. He was determined that it should occur, should succeed, and should not be premature. For its success he regarded Mediterranean operations as very important. He fought, for what seemed to him the thousandth time, a battle to convince his American colleagues of the connection between the two theatres. He also fought to convince them of his own and British good faith in the whole question of OVERLORD. After two days of plenary session the matter was resolved only by a private session, at which Brooke said flatly that the Americans doubted British faith and frankness. Once again he took them through the strategic argument. 'In the end I think our arguments did have some effect on Marshall,' he wrote in his diary on 16th August, and he wrote to Benita that night: 'We are over the first fence.'

The day before, 15th August, had been both professionally and personally black. At the Conference itself it had seemed to Brooke no headway was made. 'We left matters,' he wrote to Benita, 'in a strained condition. After dinner I spent 3 hours with Dill looking for solution to our difficulties. Worked too late and found myself looking for solutions in my sleep.'

Earlier that day Churchill had summoned Brooke to discuss certain appointments. One of them was that of Mountbatten to South East Asia. Another was that of Brooke himself. The Supreme Command for OVERLORD had been discussed with Roosevelt. The President had pressed for an American officer – Marshall himself. Churchill had acquiesced. The ostensible reason was the numerical superiority which American forces would have in the operation. Another reason, and one that echoed the battle Brooke was fighting in another room in Quebec, was the American view that Brooke shared with Churchill a scepticism about OVERLORD itself. The United States Secretary of the Army, Mr Stimson, had written to the President on the subject on 19th June. It was a forceful and persuasive letter. The British, Stimson said, were drawn to the Mediterranean for national and traditional reasons. He wrote again on 10th August. Neither British Prime Minister nor CIGS had their hearts in OVERLORD. Only an American officer could throw his soul into it, and inspire the confidence and the effort of the United States. In the United States Marshall was more respected and admired than any other soldier.

It was a dark moment. Brooke had probably depended more than he admitted to himself on the prospect of both challenge and release which return to Field Command would bring. He felt in his heart that he could see strategic factors and manage a great campaign better than any man in the Allied camp. He knew that he could dominate the diverse and talented subordinates likely to command the Armies and Air Forces of the invasion. He was sick to the point of exhaustion with Whitehall, with conferences, with the late night rehearsal and repetition of familiar argument. He wrote with bitterness of what seemed Churchill's insensitivity:

'Not for one moment did he realize what this meant to me. He offered no sympathy, no regrets – '[21] and in his diary – 'Dined by myself as I wanted to be with myself.' Then, however, he carried on with the same intelligence, dignity and remorseless application that he had shown from his first day in office. Nor did disappointment distort his view of the extraordinary genius he served, angry though the vagaries and obstinacy of that genius sometimes made him. 'He is quite the most difficult man to work with that I have ever struck,' he wrote in his diary the day after return to England, on 29th August, 'but I would not have missed the chance of working with him for anything on earth.' Still, the wound went deep.

QUADRANT produced its success. There was, thereafter, less doubt about British commitment to OVERLORD. A form of words was found about the level and significance of the operations to be undertaken in the Mediterranean which would make clear the primacy of OVERLORD, but would make equally clear that the success of the campaign in Italy – 'unremitting pressure on German forces in Northern Italy' – was directly connected to the invasion of North West Europe itself. Eisenhower must give up his 'seven divisions', and the 'unilateral' British embargo on the dispersal of forces from the Mediterranean was revoked. The 'full resources' of Britain and America were to be directed against Japan 'upon the defeat of the Axis in Europe'. The bomber offensive would continue. OVERLORD would take place as agreed at TRIDENT. JUPITER (the invasion of Norway) was agreed for planning 'in case circumstances render the execution of OVERLORD impossible' – a sop to Churchill who, to Brooke's considerable annoyance, had insinuated this idea in spite of the disagreement of his Chiefs of Staff and the suspicions it could arouse in his Allies. In the Far East major decisions were deferred, but preparations for a campaign in Upper Burma and an amphibious operation – somewhere – in 1944 would continue. Note was taken of American plans in the Pacific and 'studies' were approved, as generally happens on these occasions, including (again with a nod to Churchill) one for an operation against Northern Sumatra. An operation (which became the contentious ANVIL) was forecast, to assist OVERLORD in Southern France. None of this ran counter to Brooke's philosophy although he foresaw further debates on objectives and resources when an Italian campaign progressed, and OVERLORD and ANVIL drew nearer. But the main principles in which he believed had been unaffected by QUADRANT. There was no switch of resources towards the Pacific, nor any attempt to advance the date of OVERLORD. For the Americans QUADRANT cleared the air. It might be easier thereafter to go forward in harmony.

In spite of this rather tame ending to what Brooke had accurately prophesied would be a disagreeable meeting, he himself felt only exhaustion. His writings in letter and diary are of flatness and depression; and, inevitably in such a condition, 'I could almost have sobbed with the loneliness.' Clearly his great disappointment coloured his feelings, but he was very tired. He did not have the periodic – sometimes the frequent – relaxations which a Field Commander could enjoy between battles, or in his Mess in the evening with the camaraderie and elation of a campaign, like Wellington with his military 'family'. He had other consolations. His true family were everything to him, and when in England he generally saw his wife once a week. But the tempo of his life was implacable and there was seldom the smallest relief from responsibility. A merciful moment came during the QUADRANT visit itself when he enjoyed both before and after the Conference a happy truancy fishing in Quebec Province. All the Chiefs of Staff and Mountbatten joined in this on 12th August. On the 24th Brooke went alone with Portal – as keen a fisherman and ornithologist as he – and had two splendid days.

Yet those who saw something of Brooke at this time, away from his duties, remember most strikingly a man who seemed completely unabsorbed in his own anxieties, always ready to give his whole attention to others, to give advice, and to show understanding, wisdom and warmth. He had the gift, so rare and so irresistible, of concentrating absolutely upon the person he was with. He was an admirable listener. It was this intense human sympathy behind so austere a public mask that those who knew him best recalled most clearly, and for which they loved him.

During the Quebec Conference there had been many exchanges with Eisenhower on a momentous subject – peace overtures from Italy. Mussolini's successors were determined to finish the war. The question was how. The conditions of surrender were not too difficult to agree. More intractable were the circumstances. The Italians, very understandably, did not wish to deliver themselves to the Germans, throats bared to the knife; and the Germans were very conscious of what moves were in the air. In addition to the

German troops in Sicily and Southern Italy a substantial German Army was swiftly assembled in Southern Germany after the fall of Mussolini. It was placed under command of Rommel, and on 16th August began to move over the Brenner Pass. Contingency plans – Operation ACHSE – were prepared against an independent peace made by the new Italian Government. Italian forces would be replaced, disarmed or – if willing – embodied into the German Order of Battle. If it came to this point action would be swift and ruthless.

On the same day the last Axis forces were evacuated from Sicily. The Sicilian campaign was over. Now the Italian campaign was about to begin. Landings were planned at Salerno, south of Naples, and at Reggio opposite Sicily. The Reggio landings took place early on 3rd September. Later that day an Italian plenipotentiary secretly signed terms for an Armistice – an armistice which would not, however, be announced until a few days had elapsed. In the interval agonized exchanges took place between the Italian Government itself and Eisenhower on behalf of the Allies. The Italian Government, to defend themselves from the savage German retaliation they dreaded, had asked for an airborne landing near Rome. This operation was prepared, but at the last moment the Italians asked for deferment of the Armistice itself. They felt more exposed, hour by hour, to German action. In face of this Eisenhower firmly told the Italians that he was about to announce the Armistice, and on 8th September he did so. The Italians had few alternatives but to go ahead with the Armistice, and face or evade what the Germans would do; and the King of Italy took the decision for capitulation. The Italian Prime Minister, Marshal Badoglio, broadcast to the Italian people at 7.45 p.m., the same evening as did Eisenhower. Italy was out of the war. Early next morning the Allied Armies started landing at Salerno.

Thus the first act in the final consummation of the strategy Brooke had pursued so vigorously and tenaciously was completed. Allied forces returned to the mainland of the Continent. One of the major partners of the Axis, defeated and disillusioned, made peace. The time was approaching when one in every five German divisions would be tied to the Mediterranean theatre. The ring round Germany was not only tightened but lay at last upon the shores of Europe. It was indeed the beginning of the end.

CHAPTER XV

'Two's Company'

APART FROM ONE DAY in the War Office on 8th September, attending a lunch given by Eden for the departing Soviet Ambassador and a dinner given by the Army Council for Wavell, Brooke spent the period from 4th to 12th September 1943 on leave, with a few days' shooting on the Durham moors – 'The first real spell of leave,' he wrote on the 13th, 'that I have had since taking over the jobs of CIGS.' The days and nights continued as before, packed with meetings, interviews and entertaining which was itself more often than not full of business, and not always easy. 'Wavell came to dinner,' Brooke wrote in his diary on 14th September, 'and we had a long talk till 11.30 p.m. during which I gave him full details of the Quebec Conference and the most recent developments of the new South East Asia Command. He was as delightful and charming as usual . . .' although to Benita that night: 'I don't suppose he spoke more than 100 words while he was here. Heaven knows how many thousands I produced to keep the evening going!'[1] The diary tended to be frank, but the letters franker.

The months which followed the invasion of Italy were particularly marked by Brooke's irritation with what he regarded as American inability to perceive the chances now open to the Allies. He fumed at this in his diary and he stuck to his thesis in retrospect – that a more imaginative exploitation of the situation in the Mediterranean in the autumn of 1943 had been possible, had been frustrated by American policy and would, if carried out, have shortened the war.

A number of questions arise. Did Brooke consistently hold and voice this view? Some diary entries imply a whole-hearted policy of 'knocking away the props' and the inevitable devotion, therefore, of more resources to the Mediterranean than successive Allied Conferences had agreed. To what extent was this supported by his colleagues and by the Prime Minister? Was it a fair thesis? And can it be reconciled with Brooke's whole-hearted commitment to cross-Channel invasion?

As to Brook's consistency he certainly believed and argued

throughout that a 'forward policy' in the Mediterranean was a necessary step in the defeat of Germany and a fruitful exploitation of victories already won. It was a natural part of this concept that the Germans should be given no respite in the Mediterranean. If they were permitted to stabilize the situation there, and economize their defensive resources, Allied operations would fail in their objective of drawing German soldiers in large numbers to Southern Europe and keeping them there, to weakening effect in France opposite OVERLORD, and on the Eastern Front. In the Mediterranean the Allies had to attack, or fail in their strategic object. At first this went well. The Allies made good their landings at Salerno in mid-September. Brooke suffered the usual anxieties of a distant spectator. In retrospect he believed that the landings so far north had been too great a gamble, in view of the relative anticipated rates of build-up of forces in and against the beachhead, although he supported the gamble at the time. On 18th September, however, he wrote: 'The Salerno landing now seems safe.' Brooke's caution – 'I still do not think that we were right in taking such risks at that juncture of the campaign' – was typical. He was a prudent general, and whatever he wished in the Mediterranean it was not greater hazard.

But hopes of a rapid advance to Rome were quickly dashed, not by American recalcitrance but by a change of German plan. The Germans now appreciated that the most probable Allied action would be to open a campaign in the Balkans from an Italian base. They feared this. In Yugoslavia the Partisans had taken swift advantage of the Italian collapse, and the German Army had had to move considerable reinforcements southward, not only to repel the Allied invasion they anticipated but also to deal with a ferocious Balkan insurrection.

Now, therefore, the Germans decided that in Italy it would be right to stand south of Rome. It would complicate that Allied invasion of the Balkans they expected and dreaded. A front in the mountains of Central Italy would be easier to hold than one in the plains of the north. The further to the south the front the further would Allied bombers be from Southern Germany. Both flanks of a German position would rest on the sea; and although Allied amphibious capability meant that German reserves must be held in depth against possible landings, the experiences of Sicily and Salerno indicated that landings were likely to be cumbrous, and vulnerable to swift and resolute counter-stroke.[2]

Yet all this meant that the strategy in which Brooke believed was working admirably. The North African campaign had paved the way for the Sicilian invasion. From that had followed the Italian collapse, the invasion of Italy, the Yugoslav Partisan successes – and massive German reinforcement of Italy and the Balkans. A great Russian offensive in the Ukraine was again stretching German defence to the limit: the reinforcement of Southern Europe had drawn off numerous divisions otherwise available for the Eastern Front. Nevertheless, shortage of resources – principally shipping – meant that simultaneous Allied operations in the Aegean were impracticable, which particularly grieved Churchill. On 6th October Brooke recorded – 'PM by now determined to go for Rhodes without looking at effects on Italy.' 'It was another of those typical examples,' he wrote afterwards 'of dispersal of effort for very problematic gains.'[3] 'Another day of Rhodes madness,' he wrote on 7th October.

For the collapse of Italy, and the volatile situation which arose in consequence throughout the Mediterranean, together with the savage and often successful actions of Partisans in the occupied countries of Yugoslavia and Greece, presented fresh opportunities. Churchill was as keen as ever not to lose the chance of small-scale as well as larger action. With Brooke's somewhat grudging assent he stimulated Wilson, at Headquarters Middle East, to install British garrisons in place of the surrendering Italians on the islands of Cos and Lemnos in the Dodecanese. These garrisons could not be supported. Swift German seizure of Rhodes, with its airbase, meant that no reinforcements or supplies could reach Cos and Lemnos. Only the ejection of the Germans from Rhodes, or their forestalling, could have enabled the two islands to be held. As it was, Brooke had gloomily to note that the British garrisons of the Dodecanese Islands could be neither sustained nor evacuated, for he had had to oppose Churchill's eager hope to capture Rhodes, through lack of resources, if the main campaign in Italy was to be carried forward. This was a rare example of Brooke accepting a bad risk – and Cos and Lemnos were bad risks unless Rhodes could be taken – in hope of a strategic prize. The gamble was out of character.

The Dodecanese were Greek and the Greek situation was perplexing. In Greece, as in Yugoslavia, the local insurgents were split into Communist and anti-Communist groups. As in Yugoslavia the former had some claim to be regarded as more effective, and initially Brooke wanted British policy to support more unequivocally that faction whose military effort was of greatest immediate assistance to the Allied cause. He criticized those in the Foreign Office, who, on this occasion at least, were more alive to the Communist threat. He also grumbled that any commitment for British troops might become 'open-ended'. He withdrew this criticism unreservedly after the war, acknowledging that policy demanded more discrimination between Partisan factions than purely military reasoning could supply. But underlying Brooke's attitude to Greece and the Greek Islands was his belief that the best way of exploiting the Italian collapse was to press the Italian campaign itself as hard as possible, and that nothing should draw forces from this.

In early October Brooke gave no impression that he personally felt strategy was being disastrously frustrated by lack of American vision. On the contrary he himself, at that time, was very alive to the dangers of arousing American mistrust. Churchill had sought Roosevelt's support in the matter of Rhodes and received a cold reply. 'The whole thing is sheer madness,' Brooke wrote on 8th October, 'and he is placing himself quite unnecessarily in a very false position. The Americans are already desperately suspicious of him.' At that moment he felt that, by and large, matters were on course. The Allied strategy was working. Concentration should be on the Italian campaign and not on Aegean adventures however tempting. He explicitly disclaimed any belief in an Allied campaign in the Balkans, since he was perfectly clear that it could not be nourished simultaneously with a campaign in Italy. Churchill had an eye on possibilities in the Balkans of which the Americans were suspicious, but practicalities kept Brooke from giving him any encouragement. Indeed on 22nd October Dill wrote to him:

> 'I had a talk to Marshall and he was very touched at your consideration of him in this matter of Aegean. He told me to let you know privately that he never doubted you and that he knew well all the time whence the urge for ventures in the Balkans came.[4]

It does not, therefore, seem that Brooke consistently held the view – or, at least, held it with anything like the emphasis he gave to it later – that the Mediterranean in autumn 1943 was a lake of lost opportunities and that the Americans were to blame. What, indeed, was their sin? They were sticking to the QUADRANT agreements which had ordained a progressive move of some troops and much shipping to the United Kingdom for OVERLORD, after the invasion of Italy had been accomplished. But between 8th October and 1st November a general sentiment that the Americans were unenthusiastic about the Mediterranean – a sentiment with which the British had learned to live – turned into a cry of indignation which needed expression.

Brooke's diary entry for 1st November 1943:

> We are to discuss plans for another Combined Chiefs of Staff meeting, and the stink of the last one is not yet out of my nostrils! My God! How I hate those meetings and how weary I am of them! I now unfortunately know the limitations of Marshall's brain and the impossibility of ever making him realize any strategical situation or its requirements. In strategy I wonder if he can even see the end of his nose.

> When I look at the Mediterranean I realize only too well how far I have failed in my task during the last two years. If only I had had sufficient force of character to swing those American Chiefs of Staff, and make them see daylight how different war might be.

> We should have been in a position to force the Dardanelles by the capture of Crete and Rhodes. We should have had the whole Balkans ablaze by now, and the War might have been finished in 1943!!

> Instead, to satisfy American short-sightedness we have been led into agreeing to the withdrawal of forces from the Mediterranean for a nebulous Second Front and we have emasculated our offensive strategy. It's heart-breaking!

And on 20th November (during the Cairo Conference):

> Their drag on us has seriously affected our Mediterranean strategy and the whole conduct of the War. If they had come whole-heartedly into the Mediterranean with us we should by now have Rome securely, the Balkans would be ablaze, the Dardanelles would be open, and we should be on the highway to get Rumania and Bulgaria out of the War. I blame myself for having had the vision to foresee these possibilities and yet to have failed to overcome the American short-sighted views, and to have allowed my better judgement to be affected by them.

Brooke reckoned afterwards that he had been near nervous breakdown at the beginning of November and that this to some extent accounted for the intemperate nature of these entries. But Brooke was not alone. The change of mood in London had been brewing for some weeks. During the first fortnight in October the view came to be formed with increasing strength that the decisions of QUADRANT were inhibiting, and that opportunities created by the collapse of Italy might still not be fully exploited. If this were so, the chief inhibiting factor, on which all questions turned because it governed the movement of resources, was the target date of OVERLORD. On 14th October the Chiefs of Staff addressed the Prime Minister in that sense. Nevertheless Brooke's view was one of realism. 'We received a note from the PM wishing to swing round the strategy back to the Mediterranean,' he wrote in his diary on 19th October. 'I am in many ways entirely with him but God knows where this may lead us as regards clashes with the Americans.' They had, after all, been over this ground at QUADRANT many times, and matters had turned out as hoped for at that Conference. The new developments which, as the British suggested, had overtaken QUADRANT were, arguably, only the consummation of what had at Quebec been planned.

Probably the catalyst was a report by Alexander written on 21st October. In this Alexander correctly argued that if the objects of the Italian campaign – to pin German divisions to the ground and prevent their movement to France – were to be met there must be no relaxation of pressure. An inactive strategy in a country so defensible would enable the Germans to hold a front with minimum force, while compelling the Allies to exert considerable effort simply to maintain themselves in Italy secure against counter-offensive. It was necessary, therefore, to take the offensive ourselves. With the balance of ground forces near equal, a frontal offensive would best be helped by amphibious attack in the enemy's deep flank. On the west coast this implied a seaborne assault near and threatening Rome. Brooke agreed, and believed that there should be amphibious attacks in both east and west.[5] Yet shipping was due to leave the Mediterranean for OVERLORD, and shipping was also required for a major project of the Combined Chiefs of Staff, the move of bomber groups into Italy from North Africa. Alexander in a personal telegram to Brooke,[6] and Eisenhower, in a signal of 31st October underlined the problem. If certain shipping could be held in the Mediterranean until early January the Armies could be maintained the bomber groups moved and an offensive, including amphibious operations, undertaken. If not, Alexander's appreciation and Eisenhower's assessment combined to make clear that offensive pressure could not be exercised on the German Army at a critical moment, the Italian front would stagnate and the objects of the Italian campaign be frustrated. The matter of assault shipping was therefore dominant; and overshadowing it was the date of OVERLORD, which would need re-examination if assault shipping were to be held in the Mediterranean to support exactly those operations without whose performance OVERLORD itself might not succeed.

This was a perfectly clear thesis. Nor did it by implication run counter to the QUADRANT report, with its agreement to maintain 'unremitting pressure on German forces in Northern Italy' and its recognition of the connection between OVERLORD and operations in Italy. Indeed Eisenhower's proposal to retain shipping to assist Alexander's offensive gained partial acceptance in Washington as well as immediate endorsement in London. By now, however, both Churchill and the Chiefs of Staff felt that a wide gulf separated their minds from those of their American Allies. Churchill addressed Roosevelt on 23rd October in an exchange about the forthcoming Conference between the British, Americans and Russians. 'We do not feel,' he said, 'that such agreement [QUADRANT] should be interpreted rigidly and without review in the swiftly changing situations of war.' 'The present situation could not be tolerated,' Churchill told the Chiefs of Staff on 4th November, and Brooke told him that in general terms they agreed.

The Chiefs of Staff put a paper in the same sense to their American colleagues on 12th November. Since QUADRANT, they argued, there was a new situation caused by the collapse of Italy, fresh successes on the Russian front, the presence of an Allied Army on the Italian mainland and the German response. In these circumstances operational policy should be flexible. The date of OVERLORD should not be sacrosanct. Every opportunity should be taken to attack the Germans wherever possible. 'To sum up' the Chiefs of Staff wrote:

> Our policy is to fight and bomb the Germans as hard as possible all through the winter and spring; to build up our forces in the United Kingdom as rapidly as possible consistent with this: and finally to invade the Continent as soon as German strength in France and the general war situation gives us a good prospect of success.'

The first sentence may seem self-evident for a nation at war, but it was part of the British case that too rigid an adherence to the letter of QUADRANT, by depriving the Mediterranean of some essential sinews of war, would condemn the Armies to inaction.

To a paper with the ominous preamble – 'For some time past it has been clear to us and doubtless also the US Chiefs of Staff that disagreement exists between us' – to such a paper, following as it did some private fulminations of Brooke and preceding others, this conclusion was remarkably mild. The practical recommendations barely went beyond the QUADRANT decisions. It was proposed to unify command in the Mediterranean: to 'nourish and maintain' the offensive in Italy (one can compare with QUADRANT's 'unremitting pressure'): to place 'on a regular military basis' help to the Partisans in Balkan countries (QUADRANT had limited such operations to 'supply by air and sea transport', and to operations by 'minor Commando forces'): to 'aim to open the Dardanelles' and 'to bring Turkey into the War this year' – interdependent aims likely to rest as much on diplomatic as on military action. The only sting was in the penultimate paragraph:

> 'If the above measures necessitate putting back the date upon which the forces agreed to be necessary for OVERLORD will be available in the United Kingdom this should be accepted.

And the paper added that such delay would not necessarily and automatically delay OVERLORD itself to the same extent.

It may reasonably be asked what all the fuss was about. Here were no proposals for Balkan campaigns, nor for the mounting of new expeditions. Here was a suggestion for a little flexibility, no more, in considering the date of OVERLORD. Here, indeed, was merely written, in language forceful but vague, what was more or less already agreed should be done. Perhaps Brooke and his colleagues – and Churchill, who marked the paper 'I cordially agree' – had come to feel that unless the purpose in the Mediterranean were again emphasized it would quickly become ignored. Certainly the paper reflected Brooke's views. He recorded in his diary on 9th November a 'rough outline to go for' which exactly matched the formal paper put to the Americans a few days later.

But this was far from the almost despairing sense of division from Allies which Brooke's private words convey. It does not seem that the thesis of 'lost opportunities' when translated into specific proposals for action was taken very far between Allies.

Nor should it have been. The 'new situation' was hardly astonishing since it was that which previous operations had been designed to bring about. Indeed when Brooke described in his diary on 10th October Churchill telephoning him that 'the situation was so changed in Italy that we must readjust our thoughts' he added three exclamation marks in his diary, and the words 'I cannot stick much more of these eel-like tactics'. Virtually the only practical points at issue were the retention or provision of more landing craft in the Mediterranean in order to enable an amphibious landing to take place in support of an offensive in Italy; and a delay, possibly of some weeks, in the timing of OVERLORD. Both these points were difficult and substantive. Both were in the event satisfied. It is true that agreement emerged only from another great Conference. But it could not have emerged had there been so deep a division between minds as sometimes appeared in the months between Quebec and the next summit meeting in Tehran.

Yet this is only to dispose of the practical questions of how consistent Brooke was, how much support he had with his colleagues, and how positions were taken with the Americans and business carried on. Did Brooke nevertheless have a vision of campaigns in the Mediterranean which went further than anything he inwardly knew to be practicable within the limits of Anglo-American agreement? And might such a vision, had the Americans seen it too, have illumined a shorter path to victory?

Perhaps, like Churchill, he sometimes hankered for a real concentration on the Mediterranean, but he never explicitly argued for it. He was discouraging to Churchill over Aegean adventures, not only on grounds of practicability. He saw the advantages of possible effect on Turkey, but to him such operations must be subordinated to the Italian campaign and there is no evidence that he regarded them as so strategically significant that he would have risked or sacrificed much for them. He strongly believed in support for guerrillas, and had much correspondence with Wilson at this time on the subject; but he never proposed a Balkan campaign, and indeed wrote afterwards that it would not have been necessary – yet probably only a major offensive campaign in the Balkans could have provided the decisive victories in Southern Europe or achieved the sort of wholesale defections from the Axis his diary entries imply. Such a shift in strategy was not, of course, negotiable between Allies. Its political attractions, which have been well argued in retrospect, did not commend themselves to many at the time (Field-Marshal Smuts, whom Brooke greatly admired, was a far-sighted exception). It would have meant the abandonment of OVERLORD. It would have been particularly difficult to justify in view of what was long known of

German V weapon preparations against England, weapons which would demand counter-measures in the West. Its military practicability is questionable, and Brooke never mooted it. Thus it is not possible to find in Brooke's arguments a positive line of action to justify his diary entry: 'We should have had the whole Balkans ablaze by now and the War might have been finished in 1943.'

It would be wrong to labour a point from diary entries. Brooke always insisted that they were spontaneous, unmeasured, often unfair. But in this case, on reading after the war what he had written, he took care to reiterate the general theme. It remains an enigma.

On the question whether Brooke's views and actions at this time can be reconciled with a whole-hearted commitment to OVERLORD the answer must be 'Yes – but it did not appear so to the Americans'. In spite of Brooke's reference (1st November) to a 'nebulous Second Front', and in spite of his admirable determination that OVERLORD should not take place until conditions were right, there is no reason to doubt his resolution. But the general impression received by the Americans was different. To them Brooke was the man who always drew them step by step further into the Mediterranean morass. Brooke had no mind to propose or procure a major reversal of grand strategy. He simply wanted to get enough flexibility applied to the QUADRANT agreements to permit the Italian campaign to be carried forward offensively and effectively, even if this meant a slight delay in OVERLORD. To the Americans this attitude smacked of 'running out' on agreements through half-heartedness. Perhaps the more extreme version of Brooke's views did not remain a complete secret between him and his diary. There was probably again a suspicion in Washington that Brooke would fling everything into the Mediterranean if he could, caring little for other theatres, with inflated ideas of what could be done strategically in Southern Europe and with the influence of Britain, and the paramountcy of British interests, in the front of his mind.

It was clearly necessary once again to dispel mistrust at the forthcoming summit meeting – for it had been agreed during October that the Allies would meet again, and this time with Stalin and the Soviet Chiefs, at Tehran on 28th November. The timing of this particular round of suspicion was unfortunate. Allied relationships were taking a new and ominous turn. The Americans, with the President leading them down this particular track, had come to believe that Soviet-American understanding could be achieved more easily if there were neither the appearance nor the reality of too close an Anglo-American accord. For the first time, in 1944, American forces would outnumber British in the European theatre. The influence of Britain would be increasingly hard to maintain. Soviet-American relations might even receive a gentle impetus from discreet suggestion that British zeal in the common cause was less than American. The British might be brought to order, where recalcitrant, by Soviet-American concord in debate. Stalin knew well how to exploit such a situation. Only with difficulty were the Americans persuaded to meet the British for any length of time in Cairo, en route to Tehran.

It was tempting to take for granted how comparatively easy had been American acceptance of British suggestions hitherto. Dill had written in a perceptive letter to Brooke on 16th October that the latter should count his blessings: 'The American Chiefs of Staff have given way to our views a thousand times more than we have given way to them.'

But he continued:

> Our difficulties with the Americans are going to increase rather than diminish with their growing strength and a Presidential Election approaching. The President's enemies attack him through us and so his advisers feel that they must do everything to prove that they are not in our pockets.

Major changes in Allied Command arrangements were either imminent or proposed, discussion of which would continue to the year's end. The first, and the most immediate to Brooke's responsibilities as CIGS, was the selection of the man to command all British and Dominion forces in Operation OVERLORD. Paget was in command of all forces in the United Kingdom, having taken over from Brooke himself. It had been intended that this command should become that of British forces for OVERLORD – ultimately to be 21st Army Group. Paget, who had been Brooke's Chief of Staff, was an excellent trainer. Through no fault of his 'he had no experience in this way of commanding a large formation in action'[7] Brooke wrote. Brooke was determined that Montgomery should have this command. He regarded him as Britain's outstanding tactical Commander, and sufficiently ruthless in pursuit of victory. He knew that this appointment – which would be immediately subordinate to an American Supreme Commander – would not find universal favour. He suspected, accurately, that there would be pressure for Alexander whom the Americans greatly liked. There would be similar pressure from Churchill, who was devoted to Alexander. Brooke was determined to resist such pressure. He believed that Alexander was not the man for the task.* Meanwhile the Secretary of State, Grigg, was himself concerned at the proposal to bring in Montgomery, for he greatly admired Paget. In due course Brooke had his way. Paget, when sending Brooke his tribute after the war, referred to his substitution in characteristically generous terms. 'Like everyone else I stood too much in awe of you' he wrote, speaking surely for the senior officers of the Army as a whole. And 'I never questioned your wisdom in replacing me by Monty who proved himself an outstanding leader in battle'.[8]

In the Mediterranean the British Chiefs of Staff believed it necessary that all operations in the Mediterranean, the Aegean and against Southern Europe generally should be directed by one Allied Commander, responsible ultimately to the Combined Chiefs of Staff. Hitherto operations in the Eastern Mediterranean – and in spite of shortage of resources some small operations had been undertaken against German garrisons which had replaced Italian in the Dodecanese Islands – had been directed from the British GHQ Middle East in Cairo. This proposal would, in effect, mean widening the responsibilities discharged by Eisenhower in Algiers to include much that now lay with Maitland-Wilson in Cairo, while leaving to the latter continued national responsibilities for Palestine, Syria and other landward parts of his huge command. This was one of the points pressed by the British on their American colleagues in their note of 12th November, and already put to them ten days earlier. It happened: and Maitland-Wilson himself was soon to succeed Eisenhower in the Allied Command of the 'Mediterranean theatre of operations'.

The third command, of the utmost significance to all, not settled until the aftermath of the Tehran Conference, was that of OVERLORD itself. It had been Roosevelt's original proposal, when Brooke was disappointed of that high post, that it should go to Marshall. It was even suggested by some that Marshall could continue in the constitutional position of Chief of Staff of the United States Army, his responsibilities in Washington being

* When Eisenhower was later appointed Supreme OVERLORD commander and, as expected, expressed a wish for Alexander to be with him, Brooke on 11th December noted 'I don't much mind', although convinced it should be Montgomery. He later wrote with perplexity of this diary entry, 'I certainly minded a great deal.'

discharged by Eisenhower as a Deputy acting in his name. But in early December, before leaving Cairo for home, Roosevelt was to tell Churchill that Eisenhower and not Marshall was his choice for OVERLORD. The nomination gave Brooke satisfaction. He believed that Eisenhower's experience of command – Allied command – now made him an incomparably better choice than Marshall.

The reasons for Marshall's replacement by Eisenhower as Commander designate of all OVERLORD forces were largely political, and matured in the period between QUADRANT and the Cairo Conference, SEXTANT. Marshall's prestige in his own country was very high. He 'cuts more ice in America than any other man,' wrote Dill to Brooke on 16th October.[9] It was rumoured that Marshall was being 'removed' to Europe because of dispute. This was disturbing the President. 'I think the President is beginning to realize how difficult it will be to part with Marshall at the present time because of the fierce opposition on all sides,' Dill wrote on the 22nd.[10] He had sent a signal three days earlier: 'Had talk with Marshall today. He has no idea when President will allow him to take OVERLORD command.'

To allay criticism the idea was now mooted that Marshall could be appointed to a post greater even than OVERLORD. On 5th November, in Combined Chiefs of Staff session in Washington, the Americans proposed a 'European Supreme Command'. Marshall (assuming it were he) would direct operations both in North West Europe and in the Mediterranean, thus ensuring the right relationship between the two. The British response was predictable. The Prime Minister said at once and officially that he would never agree.[11] Brooke simply recorded in his diary '. . . a ridiculous suggestion by Leahy that Marshall should be made Supreme Commander of European theatre, to combine North Africa and cross-Channel. Luckily PM was entirely with us and sent back strong telegram to Dill with his views as to the absurdity of the proposal.' The suggestion was certainly of a sort to turn Brooke choleric. It was probably fortunate that he was able that evening to record: 'Dined with Doctor Bannerman and had a glorious evening of bird talk which I thoroughly enjoyed.'[12]

The proposal for a Supreme Commander with such wide authority rested on a fallacy. War is a political act, and strategy but the executant function of policy. It is dangerous and unwise to delegate to an Allied Commander major decisions in which political considerations must play a major and perhaps the dominant part. Of course the Commanders of the Second World War had to take certain such decisions: to assist them Political Advisers were appointed by one or both Western Allies. But the function of deciding strategic priorities throughout the European theatre, and as between Mediterranean and North West Europe, was of a different kind, a function in which matters of high policy and global strategy were critically involved. It could only be discharged at the military level by the Combined Chiefs of Staff, who were the direct agents of national governments sitting in a representative capacity in committee.

There was a further, more plainly military, point. Priorities between theatres could not be resolved simply by placing them under one man, because they affected other, external theatres; and they affected agencies which could not possibly be placed under that one man's control. Because certain resources were always scarce every major decision on priorities could have world-wide implications. Such decisions, therefore, could only be taken by the authority charged with the supreme direction of the war. The proposal was dropped and Marshall remained in Washington to the end.

A further American proposal on the higher direction of the war was made at this time. On 23rd November, in Cairo, the United States delegation suggested that there should be a Committee of 'United Chiefs of Staff', including Russia and China, on which each of the four principal Allies would be represented. Although the Americans did not suggest that this body would supersede or drive out of business the existing Anglo-American Combined Chiefs of Staff, the British feared that it might, in the event, turn into some sort of high court of strategic appeal with deplorable results. Brooke was firmly opposed to the idea and it only survived for twenty-four hours.

In the war against Japan an important change had taken place in the Command arrangements. The new South East Asia Command was now in being, Mountbatten as its chief. His deputy, lively watchdog of American interests, was Stilwell. His Naval Commander, Commander-in-Chief Eastern Fleet, was Admiral Somerville: General Giffard commanded the Eleventh Army Group of most land forces assigned to the Command; and Air-Marshal Peirse commanded all air forces. The command structure, with a 'supremo', and three Single Service Commanders, was the first of its kind to be designed specifically for the task. Other arrangements, hitherto, had to varying degrees grown from some existing order, or been haphazard and experimental. Brooke believed strongly in the theory of Unified Command. He believed equally strongly, however, that certain authority could never be devolved by the head of a Service. Brooke was asked after the war whether Mountbatten could have dismissed an Army Group or Army Commander. He replied that this could most certainly not be. He would, he said, have told a Unified Commander: 'If you should find any change necessary let me know your wishes and I shall do all I can to see that they are met.'[13] But the decision would rest with the Secretary of State and the Minister of Defence, and the CIGS was their adviser.

So tidy a unity generally has to be stretched to accommodate special situations, and nowhere was this more true than in the South East Asia land forces command, which was Brooke's particular concern. Giffard was not a commander of Allied forces. His 11th Army Group excluded Chinese forces organized and equipped by the Americans and based in India. A further anomaly existed whereby these troops were commanded by Stilwell (the Deputy Supreme Commander) although for a while they operated under, and Stilwell agreed to accept, the operational control of Slim, Commander of Fourteenth Army. South East Asia Command excluded India itself, which remained under Auchinleck as Commander-in-Chief, with Wavell as Viceroy.

Finally, at home, the Chiefs of Staff Committee itself needed new blood. The gallant old First Sea Lord, Pound, died on 21st October. He had long been ill and Churchill had been minded to appoint Admiral Fraser in his place. To Brooke's considerable pleasure, when he had got to know him well, the choice was made of Admiral Andrew Cunningham. The team of Brooke, Cunningham and Portal would now last until ultimate victory and beyond. As for Cunningham, he was, for Brooke, 'the most attractive of friends, a charming associate . . . the staunchest of companions . . . His personality, charming smile and heart-warming laugh were enough to dispense at once those miasmas of gloom.'[14]

For Brooke was growing and feeling old. His sixtieth birthday had passed in July. He found at this time an increasing distaste for work and a weariness of the whole business. He sometimes confessed to facing each Committee meeting with inner repulsion. His business with Churchill, and especially the sessions late at night, tried his composure and his strength increasingly. He felt tired much of the time. None of this showed, nor did he ever give to others any sense of the 'great man', overborne by preoccupations of state and without time to devote to people. On the contrary, his diary is full of small services done for others, their troubles confided, their lives if possible assisted by what influence or advice he could offer. He hoped it might be possible to obtain for his cousin 'Boy' Brooke – always, with his nephew Basil, Brooke's favourite relation – the post of Commissioner of the Metropolitan Police in succession to Sir Philip Game: the interest of Grigg, the Secretary of State, was invoked (without success). Then Brooke was sought by old friends, distraught parents whose daughter had volunteered, against their knowledge and wish, for service with the French Resistance: he immediately made personal enquiries. He was the instinctive choice of his family and close friends to consult, not for his position but for his humanity, concern and wisdom. Such human contacts were not only expressions of his natural gentleness and kindness. They were also necessary to him. They helped remind him of relationships beyond Whitehall and war.

The meetings in Cairo and Tehran (SEXTANT and EUREKA), which occupied the last ten days of November and the first ten days of December 1943, were, as ever, dreaded by Brooke. The interval between QUADRANT and SEXTANT was short – too short for much recovery. 'I wish our conference was over,' Brooke wrote in his diary on 20th November – 'It will be an unpleasant one, the most unpleasant one we have had.' If not the most unpleasant, it bid fair to be the least satisfactory in its preparation and staging. Instead of careful Anglo-American co-ordination it was all too likely that the Western Allies would arrive in Tehran and meet the Russians with their difficulties unresolved. There was a further difficulty. Roosevelt had arranged that Generalissimo Chiang Kai-shek should attend the meeting at Cairo. Thus, instead of devoting precious and limited time to co-ordinating Anglo-American positions in the war against Germany, before meeting the Russians, early discussion would inevitably have largely to be concerned with the Far East. The Americans were, indeed, anxious to limit the time for preliminary discussion of the European war before the three Power gathering in Tehran. There must be no appearance of undue collusion. Stalin must not be provoked. The omens were bad. Asia would take inevitable precedence, in an atmosphere likely to be confused by Chinese presence.

On 23rd October Mountbatten had received his directive from

Churchill. It placed emphasis on the maritime forces with which it was intended to reinforce the Command, and thus on amphibious operations:

> You will utilize to the full the advantage of the sea power and air power which will be at your disposal, by seizing some point or points which
> a. induce a powerful reaction from the enemy
> b. give several options for a stroke on your part in the light of the enemy's aforesaid reaction.

On land Mountbatten was enjoined 'to engage the Japanese as closely as possible in order by attrition to consume and wear down the enemy's forces'. He was also directed to 'maintain and broaden our contacts with China' and to establish 'direct contact [with China] through Northern Burma'.

Brooke had of course approved this directive. Although it clearly contained seeds of argument it had, from his point of view, advantages. As to amphibious operations it placed emphasis on forces and resources which would be at Mountbatten's disposal in the future. It implicitly limited those operations to those resources – and there could be flexibility about whence and when they should come. It was clear that at the forthcoming Conference much discussion would be concentrated on what form these operations should take, what the Chinese could hope from them and what Mountbatten could hope from the Chinese. Churchill had pressed the virtues of his favourite Sumatra operation, CULVERIN, on Mountbatten at Quebec and after, with some success. But, as at Quebec so now, amphibious operations turned on shipping; and shipping, while promised ultimately, was not yet to hand except to a very limited degree. Because of these limitations, a less ambitious operation was now proposed, which would require less shipping than CULVERIN (of whose merits Brooke was thoroughly sceptical) and less than that assault on the west coast of Burma which the Chiefs of Staff regarded as at least making operational sense. This lesser operation was christened BUCCANEER – a seaborne expedition to capture the Andaman Islands.

When BUCCANEER was turned into a firm plan by Mountbatten's staff it formed part of a programme which included an advance down the Arakan coast, an advance by one Corps across the Chindwin, and an advance by Stilwell's three Chinese divisions in North Burma accompanied by a southward march of a Chinese force from Yunnan in the far north. All would be assisted by depth operations carried out by Wingate's Chindits. It was with these plans in his pocket that Mountbatten was now invited to join the Chiefs of Staff in Cairo. To Brooke all this had yet to be set in a comprehensive Allied concept of overall strategy for the war against Japan. Such a concept certainly did not yet exist.

On 17th November Brooke left Northolt aerodrome at 1 a.m. Stopping for breakfast at Gibraltar he flew on to Malta. That evening Churchill and his party arrived, including the American Ambassador in London Mr John Winant. Next day the Chiefs of Staff conferred with the Prime Minister in the morning, and later held 'a long military discussion at dinner . . . which filled me with gloom'.[15] The same reaction was inspired by Alexander who joined the party from Italy: 'Charming as he is [he] fills me with gloom. He is a very, very small man and cannot see big . . . I shudder at the thought of him as a Supreme Commander.'*[16] These entries show a depression which increasingly marked Brooke's inner mood. His 'gloom' at Churchill's dissertation was largely caused, as he made clear afterwards, by his sense that Churchill was becoming ever more irritated by American predominance in the war and in Allied counsels. 'There lay at the back of his mind,' Brooke wrote, 'the desire to form a purely British theatre when the laurels would all be ours.'[17] Brooke was here playing the part of the loyal Ally, and with complete sincerity. Whatever his private outbursts he recognized how vital was Anglo-American accord, and he rarely gave it anything but first place in his mind. But Churchill's emotion was understandable and healthy, and he was true to Allied concepts and notably to OVERLORD, sometimes in face of his private convictions.

On Alexander Brooke reaffirmed his view later, although more graciously.

He held some of the highest qualities of a Commander, unbounded courage, never ruffled or upset, great charm and a composure that inspired confidence in those around him. But when it came to working on a higher plane and deciding matters of higher tactics and of strategy he was at once out of his depth; had no ideas of his own and always sought someone to lean on.[18]

* To replace Eisenhower in the Mediterranean as desired by Churchill. Brooke successfully opposed this, at this stage.

But he gave Alexander his confidence, and he was right to do so for Alexander held the confidence of his own command and attracted the loyalty and affection of troops of many nations.

One shaft of brightness helped pierce the 'gloom'. While in Malta he got to know Winant and discovered a man after his own heart. He found Winant deeply reserved, profound and, like Brooke, one who drew comfort and inspiration from nature. He later presented to Brooke not only Earl Grey's *Fallodon Papers* but Audubon's twelve volumes of *Birds of America* – gifts greatly treasured as was the friendship.

The British party arrived in Cairo on 20th November. The President and his Chiefs of Staff had sailed from the United States on 13th November, all determined to pin the British down on the date of OVERLORD, to hear Mountbatten's plans and if need be to apply, once again, pressure on their Allies for a Burma campaign providing more effective support to China. Chiang Kai-shek and his powerful and attractive wife had already arrived in Cairo. Above all, Roosevelt keenly anticipated his meeting with Stalin.

The Cairo Conference – SEXTANT – followed, as closely as time and the Chinese permitted, the pattern established for these occasions. The Mena House Hotel had been taken over for the Conference. The preliminary British meeting with Dill took place on the morning of 22nd November, and the first plenary session with the Americans in the afternoon. A meeting with both President and Prime Minister was held after dinner, and Brooke then accompanied Dill and Portal to the villa where Churchill was staying, to continue discussion. The first meeting with the Chinese was held on 23rd November. Brooke was interested to see the Chinese leadership. Chiang Kai-shek reminded him 'of a cross between a pine marten and a ferret, a shrewd, foxy sort of face. Evidently with no grasp of war in its larger aspects.' Madame Chiang Kai-shek was 'a queer character in which sex and politics seemed to predominate, both being used indiscriminately and individually or unitedly to achieve her ends'.[19]

It was not only, however, the skill and charm of Madame Chiang Kai-shek which distorted the business at SEXTANT, and produced an agenda in which operations in South East Asia were discussed, with Chinese participation, before those in Europe. The Americans argued that since Russia was not at war with Japan, and since the Chinese would not, therefore, be at Tehran, it was logical to dispose of immediate issues in the war in the Far East and then to turn to that war against Germany in which the United

States, the United Kingdom and the Soviet Union were all concerned. Debate on the latter would primarily take place at Tehran – with whatever previous Anglo-American discussion the British found essential. The Americans wished to limit the time for this last. Although, therefore, 'the war against Japan' was listed as Item 4 on the Agenda after 'OVERLORD and the Mediterranean' (Item 3), Item 2 was 'South East Asia operations'.

To Brooke all this was clear, illogical and distasteful. He disliked the primacy of operations against Japan which the order of consideration implied. But, more to the point, to agree about South East Asian operations with the Chinese implied resource allocation, and hands could be to that extent tied thereafter. He disliked the prospect of being short of time for what he reckoned was a prime point of dissension between British and Americans – the course of future operations in the Mediterranean. He disliked the evidence, as he saw it, of American mistrust. He particularly disliked all of this before a tripartite meeting with the Russians.

The first Cairo Conference lasted five days, the British meeting by themselves in the morning and with the Americans – with or without the Chinese – in the afternoon. The first part of the Conference was predictably dominated by the American determination to give Chiang Kai-shek some substantial part of what he wanted. He wanted supplies, and, although it was impossible to meet his requirements in full, it was agreed to increase the tonnage delivered by air from India. He wanted operations in Burma and the Bay of Bengal: it was here that the British were concerned. Churchill and the Chiefs of Staff maintained a united front. Although it was intended to bring a substantial British fleet into the India Ocean (as forecast in Mountbatten's directive) there could be no firm undertaking, as the Generalissimo requested, that amphibious operations would be carried out in March. They would be 'taken into consideration . . . when amphibious operations in all parts of the world are reviewed in about a week's time'. The American Chiefs of Staff accepted this wording, which met Brooke's principal concern that such operations should not be set in hand as part of an overall concept of war against Japan and in the context of the allocation of resources world-wide. Unfortunately, in private conversation, Roosevelt gave Chiang Kai-shek a promise of such operations 'within the next few months', and thus on 26th November the American Chiefs said that they had 'orders' that BUCCANEER (the operation against the Andaman Islands) was to be carried out at 'the appointed time'. Roosevelt was throwing in his big battalions, binding the hands of his Chiefs of Staff and inhibiting totally any objective professional discussion. It was a curious proceeding, a Presidential 'diktat' to which Churchill was not a party, a move which could not help relations. But by this stage the influence of Roosevelt, so brave and beneficent when Britain stood alone and friendless, tended to be either inept or malign. Had this particular promise not been reversed, as it later was, the effect on all other operations requiring landing craft would have been deplorable. As to the Chinese participation in staff discussions, Brooke found it a waste of time, a meaningless ritual. The only effective Chinese participants were Chiang Kai-shek and his formidable partner.

British and Americans were due to take off for Tehran very early on 27th November. First discussions of the war against Germany took place on 24th November. In spite of Brooke's concern, the Americans raised few problems on the note they had recently received from their British colleagues – that note which had grimly stated 'disagreement exists between us'. There did not seem to be a major issue between the parties. Indeed the Americans seemed to accept the postponement of OVERLORD with equanimity. Now it was BUCCANEER, on Presidential orders, which was sacred. On the European war matters went surprisingly well. True, Brooke had on 26th November what he described as 'the father and mother of a row' with Marshall, but one of the indispensable 'off the record' meetings restored calm. Nevertheless it was without attempting formal agreement, and thus in a certain disarray, that the participants left for Tehran on 27th November.

Throughout SEXTANT-EUREKA Brooke's chief aims were clear and constant: to prevent any diversions to the Bay of Bengal or elsewhere on a scale which could drain resources from the war against Germany, whatever Roosevelt had promised Chiang Kai-shek: to exploit the unexpected, and perhaps temporary, flexibility in the American position on OVERLORD's timing, so that a realistic date might be agreed, a date which could enable shipping resources somehow to be retained in the Mediterranean to assist Alexander's offensive; and to gain American support for that offensive and its implications. The second and third of these aims could probably only be attained with Soviet goodwill.

The comparative ease with which the British carried their points on OVERLORD and the Mediterranean at the first Cairo Conference may have owed something to the sense that the real fighting would begin at Tehran. It may have been helped, in spite of the concomitant irritations, by the Chinese presence and Roosevelt's pressure to help China – for this induced a sense that something else would have to 'give' and produced a certain limited flexibility of mind about OVERLORD. Probably, however, it also reflected the fact that the British had exaggerated their differences with their Allies and did not face so intractable a task as Brooke feared. Probably, too, this exaggeration had bred in the Americans a suspicion that the British would be more radical than was the case.

For Brooke the Tehran Conference – EUREKA – ended in success. It required a very clear head and considerable speed and adroitness in debate. Brooke had both.

From the start he saw how the land lay. Alone of the political leaders Stalin saw clearly both the connection between policy and strategy and the realities of military operations. He gained Brooke's high regard. 'Never once,' Brooke wrote, 'in any of his statements did he make any strategic error, nor did he ever fail to appreciate all the implications of a situation with a quick and unerring eye.'[20] Brooke appreciated vividly Stalin's view of where Soviet interests lay. He saw that Stalin was now reasonably content with the operational situation of the Red Army. Immediate diversionary operations were no longer required. Nor was Stalin prepared to endorse any campaign which might bring Allied forces into territories which he had mentally reserved for Communism. 'He had by then,' wrote Brooke, 'pretty definite ideas as to how he wanted the Balkans run after the War, and this would entail, if possible, their total inclusion in the future Union of Soviet Republics. British and American assistance was therefore no longer desirable in the Eastern Mediterranean.'[21] Nor was Stalin anxious for Allied advance to the north of Italy since, as Brooke wrote afterwards, 'such an advance led too directly towards Yugoslavia and Austria on which, no doubt, he had by now cast covetous eyes'.[22] Brooke saw clearly at Tehran, if not before, that Stalin's strategy and the strategy he would always seek to press on his Allies would be directed towards the long-term interest of the Soviet Union, an interest which he did not, like Roosevelt, confuse with that of the Western Allies. 'This War,' Stalin remarked privately in a very different company, 'is not as in the past: whoever occupies a territory also imposes on it his own social system. Everyone imposes his own system as far as his Army has power to do so. It cannot be otherwise.'[23]

Accordingly, for Brooke, 'we were reaching a very dangerous point where Stalin's shrewdness, assisted by American short-sightedness, might lead us anywhere.'[24] Stalin's two main thrust lines during the Conference were for OVERLORD – a massive operation bound to attract maximum German strength, and suitably distant – and a landing in the South of France, Operation ANVIL, to which he quickly responded when it was suggested by Roosevelt, as one of the options to which six divisions from the Mediterranean might be directed in support of OVERLORD. Since Roosevelt had posed this as an alternative to 'moving from the head of the Adriatic north-east towards the Danube' Stalin had no difficulty in expressing his preference. Roosevelt had suggested ANVIL might precede OVERLORD by a month.

Brooke regarded this latter proposal as lunatic. 'May God help us in the future prosecution of this War,' he wrote in his diary on 29th November. 'We have every hope of making an unholy mess of it and of being defeated yet.' Afterwards he wrote of ANVIL:

> This plan allowed for the whole of the month of April for the annihilation of these six divisions whilst fighting in Italy was at a standstill and OVERLORD had not yet started.
>
> I feel certain that Stalin saw through these strategical misconceptions, but to him they mattered little, his political and military requirements could now be best met by the greatest squandering of British and American lives in the French theatre.[25]

Compared with the clearcut views of Stalin, President and Prime Minister were at a considerable if unacknowledged disadvantage. Roosevelt was primarily concerned in agreeing with Stalin at virtually whatever cost, and Churchill was in an automatic and awkward minority. Churchill also had a private scheme to press some sort of endorsement of the desirability of operations in the Aegean, one of his favourite enterprises towards which his Chiefs of Staff were lukewarm. Stalin quickly scented that this, with its associated emphasis on the importance of getting Turkey into the war, was a subject of Churchill's rather than the Western Allies' conviction. He was suitably cold towards it.

Brooke measured his main aims against the opening positions and the circumstances of the battle – for each of these Conferences was like a battle with its ebbs and flows, its successes at first unperceived or dangers only late apprehended, and needing the same mixture of tenacity and opportunism. He reckoned that there was enough flexibility in the situation to get certain agreements, of which the most important should be an offensive in Italy, starting with the capture of Rome and to be directed on the Pisa-Rimini line – the Apennine barrier to Northern Italy. These operations would need to be supported by an amphibious assault, and therefore presupposed acceptance of the retention of landing craft in the Mediterranean until mid-January 1944; and from that must follow a date of OVERLORD 'not before 1st June'. For those gains he was prepared, at least for the time being, to accept ANVIL provided its date were left suitably indefinite. Indeed ANVIL would ensure that an amphibious capability remained in the Mediterranean. The Combined Chiefs of Staff agreed these points after a long discussion on the morning of 30th November. 'Not before 1st June' was changed to 'during May' (it being agreed that the latter, more palatable to the Russians, could for the purposes of EUREKA be equated with the former) and the agreement gained political acceptance as an Anglo-American position of which the Russians should be informed. Thus the Western Allies came together on an offensive in Italy, within strict limits, but one which would maintain pressure on the Germans of which otherwise there would be none: on ANVIL 'on as big a scale as landing craft permit', with 'for planning purposes D-day to be the same as OVERLORD D-day'; and on OVERLORD 'during May'. None of this encountered difficulty with Stalin.

Although this would need further refinement with the Americans before it could be considered safe, as far as it went it was a considerable triumph. The war against Japan had not, of course, featured on agendas at EUREKA, but one great step had been achieved. Stalin had intimated that when Germany was finished Russia would join in the war against Japan.

Brooke had one revealing experience. At a military Staff meeting Marshal Voroshilov, clearly acting under instructions, asked 'whether he [Brooke] regarded OVERLORD as the most important operation", saying that the Russians regarded it as vital and so, he believed, did the Americans. Brooke assented – with one reservation. The circumstances must be right. Unless what Voroshilov had described as 'auxiliary operations' were carried out – in this case in the Mediterranean – circumstances would not be right. Voroshilov 'had heard that operations in other areas were to be undertaken which might interfere with or delay OVERLORD'.

This pressure suggested collusion at some level. It was not Marshall. Not only was Marshall the straightest of men, but

Brooke had at Tehran had a heartening experience when Voroshilov said that OVERLORD was, after all, only a large-scale river-crossing. The English Channel was not wide. The Russians had much experience at crossing rivers. Marshall replied to him. 'I used to think that,' he said, 'but since then I've been taught the strategy of oceans.' Brooke's spirits rose. He suspected, however, that Mr Averell Harriman, the new United States Ambassador in Moscow, had implanted in Russian minds the idea that he, Brooke, was cool towards OVERLORD – and, perhaps, toward the Soviet Union. At the closing banquet when Brooke's health was proposed Stalin intervened, saying, as Brooke recalled: 'That as a result of this meeting and of having come to such unanimous agreement he hoped that I should no longer look upon the Russians with such suspicion . . .' Brooke, in turn, rounded on Stalin and affirmed his friendship but told him not to mistake appearance, if it was harsh, for underlying reality. He approached Stalin after dinner and told him that he resented his accusations. This went well. Stalin shook him warmly by the hand. He always spoke of Brooke with admiration, and with a deliberate respect he did not extend to all Allied senior military men he knew. The Russians acknowledged the Anglo-American proposals, and raised no difficulties. British and Americans returned to Cairo.

It was now necessary to put flesh on the bones, and to clear up unfinished business. The process was disturbed by news that the Americans intended to leave for home in forty-eight hours, a plan which appalled Brooke, who anticipated that there would still be hard negotiation and who suspected that once again the British were being placed under pressure of time. At the first plenary session back in Cairo Brooke was frank about the whole Conference.

> I said that this Conference had been most unsatisfactory. Usually at all these meetings we discussed matters till we arrived at a policy which we put before the PM and the President for approval and amendment. And that we subsequently examined whether ways and means admitted of this policy being carried out. Finally putting up a paper for approval which formed our policy for the future conduct of the War. This time such a procedure had been impossible. We had straight away been thrown into high level conferences with Stalin and now that we were back we were only given two days to arrive at any concerted policy.[26]

Yet the two sides did not seem far apart if at all. The principal point of dissension was now BUCCANEER – the invasion of the Andaman Islands – on which the American Chiefs of Staff were under firm Presidential direction. The British position was that this had been conceived before the strategy against Germany had been agreed with the Russians: that they, the British, had always considered that BUCCANEER could be carried out if, but only if, OVERLORD were significantly delayed and shipping diverted to the Indian Ocean – a major strategic switch to which they had not agreed but on whose implications they were clear; and that after EUREKA, because of firm intentions disclosed to the Russians, OVERLORD could not be delayed, except marginally, beyond the end of May. Furthermore ANVIL had been agreed at EUREKA, and agreed as an assault in the South of France of two divisions, with all that implied for shipping. These two circumstances, the British asserted, effectively eliminated BUCCANEER, whose own shipping requirements, following a reassessment by Mountbatten, had greatly grown.

The American Chiefs of Staff accepted that BUCCANEER was an operation whose (legitimate) motive was to show support for China. On 6th December, however, faced with a straight clash which his own Chiefs of Staff admitted existed between BUCCANEER and the OVERLORD date promised to the Russians, Roosevelt agreed to BUCCANEER's cancellation. Brooke was delighted, for, in the words of the British Historian of the war, the British Chiefs of Staff had been asked:

> to sponsor an operation to which they had not agreed and of whose merits they were not convinced, on a larger scale than before, at a time when other agreed operations were demanding fresh resources.[27]

With BUCCANEER cancelled, and to ensure that ANVIL could take place now that OVERLORD was delayed by a few weeks, King announced that after 1st March he could send some fifty tank landing ships and craft to the Mediterranean. Brooke's aims were achieved. OVERLORD's date was practicable. Operations in Italy could continue, including, subject to more detailed examination, amphibious operations. They should continue with the impetus necessary to maintain pressure on the Germans and keep them in Italy rather than France – or do so at least significantly more than if they had not been under that pressure. And there were, for the time being, to be no ambitious seaborne initiatives in the Bay of Bengal. Faced with the new situation Mountbatten proposed that in his area of command there should be a limited advance in Burma, as far as the Chindwin, and in Arakan.

Before the Allies dispersed, the Command arrangements which had been for some weeks under discussion were finally agreed. Eisenhower to command OVERLORD: Maitland-Wilson to be Supreme Commander, Mediterranean: Alexander to command Allied forces in Italy under Maitland-Wilson; Montgomery to command the British, British sponsored and Commonwealth troops under Eisenhower, and to command land forces in the actual assault. Churchill had wished for Alexander as Supreme Commander in the Mediterranean. He was supported by Mr Harold Macmillan, British Resident Minister, Mediterranean, whose motive Brooke distrusted:

> [Macmillan] knew he could handle Alex, and that he would be as a piece of putty in his hand; but on the other hand Jumbo Wilson was made of much rougher material which would not be so pliable . . .[28]

What he regarded as Macmillan's interference made Brooke angry. He considered that Macmillan, for whom he sent, had very inadequate comprehension of the duties of a Supreme Commander, and Brooke asked him always to discuss such matters with him, the CIGS, before approaching the Prime Minister.

For a series of conferences which started with misgiving, mistrust, rough words and rougher thoughts SEXTANT-EUREKA ended very harmoniously. In the official record:

> Sir Alan Brooke said he would like to express on behalf of the British Chiefs of Staff their deep gratitude for the way in which the United States Chiefs of Staff had met their views . . .
>
> General Marshall said that he very much appreciated Sir Alan Brooke's gracious tributes.

The last session took place on 7th December. 'Most of the heavy work here is over now,' Brooke wrote to Benita on the 8th, 'and it won't be long before I turn my nose towards home.'

Brooke's tactics at SEXTANT-EUREKA were thoroughly effective: 'Brooke's' tactics, because as Chairman of the Chiefs of Staff Committee he was their voice and leader in Allied discussions, although he always emphasized that both substance of argument and method of deploying it were essentially team matters.

He appreciated that to achieve his first aim – to prevent diversions to the Far East theatre – the 'Russian card' would play itself. Stalin would approve of concentration of resources against Germany, and Roosevelt, whatever his commitments to Chiang Kai-shek, wished to please Stalin. The best device, therefore was to defer decision on ambitious operations against Japan until their incompatibility with operations promised to Stalin could clearly be shown. Brooke's second aim was to get a realistic date set for OVERLORD. This was more difficult because here both Russians and Americans, suspicious of his 'Mediterranean diversions' could unite against him. He was able to use two points. First, the Americans were still, by Roosevelt's direction, committed to amphibious operations in the Bay of Bengal, whatever the British opposition. Although the effect of these on resources planned for OVERLORD had yet to be finally assessed there was bound to be such an effect, and this uncertainty to some extent inhibited opposition to OVERLORD's delay.

The second point was familiar and straightforward. Unless there were offensive operations in the Mediterranean continuing through the forthcoming months there would be no Western offensive anywhere. This was no way to help the Soviet Union; and if the geography of Italy and the facts of shipping implied consequential flexibility in the date of OVERLORD this should be accepted.

Finally, on ANVIL, Brooke reckoned that as an amphibious operation it would need resources which Alexander, once they were to hand, might use to better effect as the situation developed. ANVIL demands must not be allowed to prejudice OVERLORD: but ANVIL, together with OVERLORD's now agreed date, must make inevitable the cancellation of the amphibious operation against the Andamans – BUCCANEER. Brooke played his cards in the right order and with justification felt that the rubber had gone well.

He probably exaggerated the difficulties of getting agreement. Did he exaggerate the dangers which he believed, with fervour, rejection of his views would produce? Would OVERLORD a month earlier have been calamitous, and would it have failed had the Germans been able to stabilize the front in Italy and withdraw more divisions to France than in fact they did? Answers can never be known. It may even be that it was the persistent advocacy of Marshall which prevented OVERLORD from being yet further delayed. It may be significant that, to the Americans, Tehran and Cairo were the Conferences at which they successfully pinned the British for the first time to a firm OVERLORD date, a real commitment. All that can be said is that what done was successful, and there can be no certainty that equal success would have attended any other way.

CHAPTER XVI

'Consummation'

THREE MATTERS dominated Brooke's attention in the first five months of 1944.

First came the operations in Italy, for which he had fought so hard. Would they exert that pressure on the enemy for which they were designed? Would they hold German divisions to the Italian front by the threatening vigour displayed?

Second was the question of operations against Japan. In the short term these were planned by the British to be on a small scale compared to the ambitious projects first discussed: but they assumed a Japanese Army on the defensive, and a British initiative. Mountbatten, indeed, debated whether there could not even now be some offensive operation, using the limited sea and amphibious power left to him, more imaginative than the slow push in Burma to which SEXTANT had condemned him. Yet before the end of January all signs were of a renewed Japanese offensive brewing. To frustrate that offensive, turn it ultimately to the victorious account of the Allies and carry out, splendidly, the SEXTANT decisions of the Combined Chiefs of Staff was to be the function in the next few months of the Indian and British Army in Burma – Fourteenth Army, Slim's Army.

But more far-reaching than the next Burma campaign was the question of what the grand strategy should be against Japan, and what part the British should play. It had already been recognized that, well before the defeat of Germany, resources should be diverted to the Far East so that as little time as possible should be lost in undertaking the great offensive which should ultimately win the war – when the Allied slogan could at last become 'Japan first – Japan last'. The British Chiefs of Staff had not concentrated on Pacific and Far Eastern strategy since the early and desperate days after Pearl Harbor. Now they did so, as did the Prime Minister. The views of their Committee did not coincide with those of Churchill, and as the months raced by they grew ever angrier with each other.

The third matter to fill Brooke's thoughts was the preparation of the greatest act in the war: OVERLORD.

Every other operation was now unequivocally considered in terms of its relation to OVERLORD – what help could it afford to or what resources might it subtract from the main operation? Spanning Brooke's first and third preoccupations, designed to help OVERLORD but condemned to be a rival to the Italian campaign for scarce resources, was the planned landing in the South of France – ANVIL.

In Italy Alexander's offensive was going slowly. It was already clear that the planned amphibious assault south of Rome in the area of Anzio – Operation SHINGLE – could not be carried out as planned in mid-December. The progress of General Mark Clark's Fifth Army was not such as to create expectation of rapid link-up with a landing, which was the concept. SHINGLE was planned as a left hook, a landing to coincide with a Fifth Army offensive in the area of Cassino. Now it would be necessary to delay the operation until mid-January, if not cancel it. This immediately brought into question again the matter of landing craft, for the hard won agreements of SEXTANT assumed this operation complete and shipping released in mid-January for the OVERLORD build-up. Here promised again to be a manifestation of what the Americans regarded as the Mediterranean syndrome: always a little more needed, for a little longer and achieving a little less than previously agreed.

Brooke visited the Italian battlefront on his way back to London from Cairo in December. He travelled via Tunis, where the Prime Minister fell victim to a disagreeable bout of influenza with risk of pneumonia. Churchill was determined to go to Italy as well, but Brooke persuaded him for once to stay and look to his health. He had difficulty, and unwisely said that the Prime Minister's personal doctor, Sir Charles Wilson,* agreed that the Italian journey would be a grave mistake. Churchill shook his fist furiously in the CIGS's face. 'Don't you get in league with that bloody old man!'[1]

Brooke spent four days on the Italian front. The visit depressed him. 'Monty [Eighth Army] is tired out and Alex fails to grip the show,' he wrote in his diary on 14th December. He felt fresh impetus was needed. SHINGLE might provide it. It might loosen

* Lord Moran.

up the front and enable the Allies to break through the mountain positions around Cassino and advance on Rome. 'We are stuck in our offensive here,' he wrote, 'and shall make no real progress unless we make greater use of our amphibious power.' A visit to Clark's Headquarters did not heighten Brooke's spirits: 'No more inspiring than Eighth Army,' he noted. Brooke was disappointed by the delay on SHINGLE, but was confirmed in his view that it was necessary, and satisfied that his work at Tehran and Cairo had laid its foundations. The shipping question was solved by some revised calculations, by some 'borrowing forward' against shipping earmarked for ANVIL, and by proposing that some craft stay in the Mediterranean rather than, as planned for ANVIL, be later replaced from the Pacific. These devices, together with the cancellation of a small seaborne operation planned by Mount-batten with his residual amphibious resources, met the bill in full. SHINGLE would definitely take place.

Brooke flew back to Tunis on 18th December to find Churchill somewhat recovered, but condemned to a further week in bed followed by a convalescence at Marrakesh. The Prime Minister was anxious to hear all details – in responding to which Brooke was sparing of the more discouraging aspects of his Italian tour. For his part Churchill told Brooke that the King had approved his promotion to Field-Marshal, to take effect from New Year's Day 1944. On 19th December, Brooke set off on the journey home. 'It feels more like five years [away],' he wrote, 'so much has been done during the period, so much ground covered, so many visits and so many impressions. My brain is feeling tired and confused, and a desperate longing for a long rest.' He reached London on 20th December and reported next day to the King. Brooke's audiences were an unfailing source of support, with King George's sympathy, absorbed interest in men and events, and perceptive understanding of the course of the war and of what the CIGS was trying to achieve.

On Saturday 1st January 1944 Brooke was promoted to the rank of Field-Marshal. His family, and the Colebrooke employees, sent enthusiastic messages once again. His future peerage was anticipated light-heartedly and accurately. 'I've arranged for you to take the title of Alanbrooke – all in one – like that it's more distinguished than Allenby or Northbrooke and would come easy to your hand,' wrote his niece, Lady Mulholland. As usual, Gort sent a generous and friendly letter. Brooke himself wrote: 'It gave me a curious, peaceful feeling that I had at last and unexpectedly succeeded in reaching the top rung of the ladder,' and he spent a relaxed afternoon shooting in Hampshire, with a weekend at home to follow. The word 'peaceful' implies that there had always been a strong and restless strain of ambition in his character. In whatever he did he aimed high. Few modern soldiers avow ambition with the explicitness of a Wolfe – 'I shall be a hero' – but success seldom crowns those who lack the desire to rise and to excel. Brooke had increasingly felt that he could understand issues better and could guide events more firmly and perceptively than his contemporaries. He always set himself to master anything to which he set his hand. This sober self-knowledge, without trace of vanity, and this self-imposed perfectionism were the elements of his ambition. It was ambition, however, accompanied by scruple and by humanity.

For the first few days of the year Churchill was still convalescing in Marrakesh, whence a stream of telegrams issued on the conduct of campaigns, and whither he summoned Commanders for consultation, happily free from the inhibiting bonds of Whitehall. 'Winston sitting in Marrakesh is now full of beans and trying to run the war from there,' Brooke noted on 4th January. His diary for the rest of the War became increasingly a safety valve for his irritation with the Prime Minister. Both men were tired. Churchill, nine years older, had borne enormous burdens, and if Brooke's references to him sometimes showed more exasperation than recognition they reflected the fact that Brooke, too, had borne great strains. The days of the CIGS were very long. A letter to Benita on 8th March:

> I have had a tiring day and have not finished yet. A long COS followed by meetings with S of S and MS,* then Swayne to lunch to discuss his new duties as Chief of Staff to Auchinleck. Then Moran at 3.30 to discuss Winston's health followed by King of Greece at Claridges at 4 p.m. He kept me ¾ hour, I then had QMG† and DMO‡ at 5 to 5.45. At 6 p.m. went on to Cabinet meeting which lasted till 8.00 p.m. After dinner worked off some files and am now off to a meeting of PM at 10 p.m. which will last long and be very heated!!

Both Churchill and Brooke were sensitive and emotional, and

* Military Secretary.
† Quartermaster-General.
‡ Director of Military Operations.

this helped to make both at times excessively irritable. Churchill could find outlet for emotion in rhetoric, and in girding at his advisers. Brooke fumed to his diary. Fortunately the day was generally saved by some shaft from Churchill which delighted as it struck, especially when CIGS and Prime Minister saw the target alike. Brooke left one long meeting with Churchill dissolved in chuckles and mimicry. Discussion had turned to de Gaulle. 'What can you do with a man,' Churchill had growled, 'who looks like a female llama surprised when bathing?'[2] But he relished Churchill more in retrospect or at a distance, and after a very happy weekend on 14th January, staying at Sandringham with the King and Queen to shoot, he recorded on the 18th: 'The morning was somewhat upset by the return of the PM'; and on the 19th:

> The PM is starting off in his usual style! We had a Staff meeting with him at 5.30 p.m. for 2 hours and a Defence Committee from 10.20 p.m. for another two hours. And we accomplished nothing! I don't think I can stand much more of it.

'I fought Winston hammer and tongs till 7.30!' he wrote to Benita a few days later. It was a recurrent theme. Sometimes the fight brought Brooke to the point of outrage. In February, under four months before OVERLORD, the culminating operation of all, Churchill one evening felt a surge of alarm. Would not this great opposed landing produce terrible casualties, perhaps destroy a generation like the battles of 1916 and 1917? The Prime Minister suddenly said to his personal staff, 'Why are we trying to do this? Why do we not land instead in friendly territory, the territory of our oldest ally? Why do we not land in Portugal?' A minute was sent to the Chiefs of Staff that this should be discussed in the morning, and all through the night the General Staff Planners worked on a paper about the port capacity of Lisbon, the forces necessary if Spain were hostile, friendly or neutral, the capacity of the Trans-Pyrenean routes for the passage of an army. Next morning Brooke's brief on the subject was ready.

Brooke knew nothing of this. He had been kept up by Churchill until two o'clock in the morning listening to a disquisition on the strategic significance of the South Sea Islands, and in particular, the island of Bali, during which some of those meeting, including the Foreign Secretary, had fallen asleep. Thus, at his morning briefing, Brooke slumped at his desk and suddenly awoke to hear mention of Portugal.

'What's all this nonsense?'

It was explained to him that Churchill wished, at their forthcoming meeting with him, to discuss this matter with the Chiefs of Staff.

'Do you *know* the Pyrenees?' snapped Brooke. 'I do. I've been all over those tracks as a boy. And if you think we're going to conduct the invasion of Europe across the Pyrenees, you're an even bigger fool than I thought you were!'

At the meeting with Churchill, however, the CIGS spoke for twenty minutes. For fifteen he gave, with convincing clarity, the facts, exactly as researched and set out by his faithful staff. Then he changed style, and for the last five minutes he told Churchill in his most trenchant way what he thought of wasting time on so idiotic an idea. No more was heard of it.

Eight years later, General Simpson, who had briefed him on the 'Portuguese' occasion, told the story in his presence. 'You must be an even bigger fool . . . I never really said that did I? You must have known I didn't mean it?'

'I wasn't sure,' said Simpson.

'We shall make no real progress unless we make greater use of our amphibious power.' Later in life Brooke sometimes referred to the Mediterranean strategy he supported so vigorously, as a strategy which exploited command of the sea. By the ability to threaten different points Allied sea power stretched the German forces defending the coasts of Southern Europe. The enemy held reserves in North Italy against descents from the sea: or he anticipated landings from the Adriatic and reacted accordingly. This was the strategic concept of threatening diverse objectives.

Once undertaken, however, amphibious operations in modern times suffered from disadvantages which set limits to their strategic value. These disadvantages were seldom perceived by Churchill. 'This is a time,' he had wired exultantly to Wilson in the Middle East at the moment of the Italian surrender, 'to think of Clive and Peterborough and of Rooke's men taking Gibraltar,' and although this was in the context of the capture of Rhodes, the same spirit informed many of his exhortations. It was a spirit which took little account of operational and logistic realities in the twentieth century. Unlike the eighteenth century a modern land power in the Second World War had means of movement by rail and road – and in the case of the German Reich on interior lines – which enabled concentration by land to be much faster than that of any force built up from the seas and moving upon it. Unlike the eighteenth century the complexity of war demanded equal complexity – and capacity – in the vessels assembled to land and support a force. Unlike the eighteenth century the necessity for air cover limited the range of possible landing places – and made evident that limitation. Brooke, of all men, understood and calculated with great precision how such operations might turn out, and had the ceaseless task of urging these realities on a Churchill who, since the days of the mis-managed Norwegian campaign, had nourished a strong taste for dramatic interventions remote from the logistic possibilities of modern war. In the case of Anzio the logistics were well calculated. Strategic opportunity existed, but to exploit strategic opportunity there must be tactical success; and tactical success demands an unambiguous operational concept.

'Oh! How I hope that the Rome amphibious operation will be a success!' Brooke wrote in his diary on 20th January. 'It may fail but I know it was the right thing to do.'

The Anzio landings – Operation SHINGLE – took place on 22nd January and achieved complete surprise. The United States VI Corps under General Lucas, including the British 1st Division, landed in an initial strength similar to the force put ashore at Salerno – and landed unopposed. There was no immediate obstacle to an advance to Rome had that been the aim: and no obstacle to an advance to the Alban Hills beneath whose shadow ran the German north-south communications to their forces confronting the Allies round Cassino. Lucas had been instructed to advance 'on' the Alban Hills – an obscure phrase; but it was also made clear to him that the German reaction might force him to take the defensive, protect his beachhead and hope to attract the enemy reserves, while the rest of the Fifth Army, taking advantage of the diversion, broke through the German lines and marched on Rome. Churchill hoped for great things and was irritated by the United States character of the SHINGLE command. 'It is a short-sighted policy,' he wired to Wilson on 18th January, 'by all these means to conceal the fact that more than half the troops engaged, even on the Fifth Army and SHINGLE fronts, will be British, that the Eighth Army is also in action, and that Alexander and his Staff are responsible for the whole planning and control.'[3] Loyal ally though the Prime Minister was, he had a powerful feeling for British interest and honour, and the increasing preponderance of American strength caused him chagrin. Wilson had taken over from Eisenhower as Supreme Allied Commander, Mediterranean,

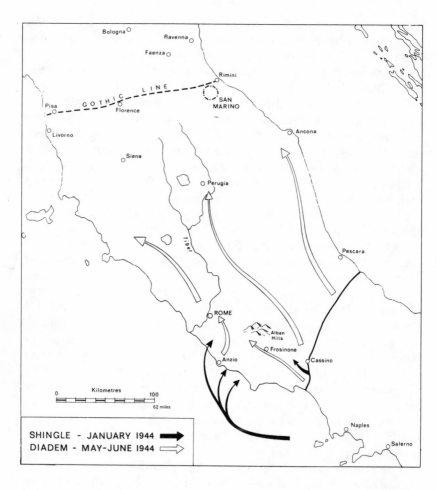

SHINGLE - JANUARY 1944
DIADEM - MAY-JUNE 1944

but Churchill often addressed him unashamedly as a British officer.

In the event there was no exploitation of initial success at Anzio: no drive to or 'on' the Alban Hills: no breakout by the rest of Fifth Army on the main front; and no march on Rome for a further four months. Lucas's decision not to advance quickly inland has been long debated. Lucas himself had no faith in such a move, which he thought would have been disastrous. Later he experienced the strength and speed of the German reaction, the fierce counter-attacks in the last ten days of February which came near to beating him back to the beaches, and he remained convinced that had these blows struck not a defensive perimeter but an extended pencil-like advance his force would have been cut off and destroyed. Churchill could not resist a sharp tactical probe in a signal to Wilson, asking him 'why no attempt made to occupy the high ground . . . twelve or twenty-four hours after the unopposed landing'. Wilson replied that it was 'not due to lack of urging from above, as Alexander and Clark visited beachhead in first 48 hours to speed up advance'.[4] This was a poor excuse if excuses were appropriate, and in fact Lucas claimed his decisions were supported on that occasion by both Alexander and Clark.

Instead the Allies formed a defensive beachhead, the German attacks were held and repulsed and the front was ultimately stabilized. But as an offensive SHINGLE failed. Clark's alternate concept was to break out on the main front using SHINGLE as an anvil for his hammer. That, too, failed.

Brooke, watching matters anxiously from afar, recorded Churchill's doubts about the handling of the enterprise. 'I had some job quietening him down again,' he wrote in his diary on 28th January: 'unfortunately this time I feel there are reasons for uneasiness.' He did not share the confidence of Wilson, who wrote from the Mediterranean on 31st January:

> Given our possession of that feature [the Cassino massif] and progress from the beachhead plus the disruption of his communications, I do not see how he can possibly hang on South of Rome.[5]

Brooke drew what comfort he could as the situation hardened. 'I feel,' he wrote on 14th February in his diary, 'the bridgehead south of Rome may hold all right and that ultimately we may score by not having had an early easy success.'

He was giving vent to his hope that the operation would 'suck in' more German divisions than otherwise would have been committed to the Italian front, and his words reflected his similar thoughts after the swift German reaction to the North African landings, in spite of his early disappointment at progress in Tunisia. But the story of SHINGLE had a different ending. Victory in Tunisia had been decisive, and an equally dramatic disintegration of the German front, with possible ultimate encirclement, had been looked for in consequence of the Anzio landings. It did not occur.

Lucas, the Corps Commander, has been excoriated, but Alexander's own part in the matter is unconvincing. In a signal to Brooke in November he had written '[SHINGLE] will not take place until *Fifth Army have reached Frosinone and are in a position to support the landing rapidly'** – a condition which certainly was not met. There is little in his own correspondence to indicate that he felt, early, a sense of missed opportunities. In a letter to Brooke on 26th January he referred to three phases of such an operation – the landing, the 'build-up to withstand a counter-attack', and a third phase 'when the counter-attack has been beaten off and we can thrust forward from a secure base in strength to reach a vital objective'. This was all very deliberate in tone. *Post facto*, on 22nd March, Alexander wrote to Brooke:

> What we were aiming at was to get astride the enemy's lines of communication. If we didn't want to face disaster six divisions (in the first wave) were necessary.[6]

But that is not what was planned or practicable.

Brooke had put much faith behind SHINGLE. He had to cast the balance sheet. Was it worthwhile? Because an operation does not attain its objective it is not necessarily wrong to have tried it. Failure to achieve decisive results may still mean that on balance useful gains have been made. The Anzio landings had the effect of somewhat widening the front the Germans had to defend, of giving the enemy a task of flank protection. To that extent SHINGLE stretched the enemy front and weakened his defence to the ultimate main attack. Until the front was stabilized in March the Germans conceived themselves threatened. Initially, they committed fresh forces to Italy. This last benefit, however, was short-lived. SHINGLE would only have contributed directly to the strategic object of the Italian campaign – to keep sufficient pressure on the Germans to assist OVERLORD – had the operations of the Allies at Anzio and Cassino, seen as a whole, forced upon the Germans a general retreat under relentless pressure, or a major and permanent reinforcement of Italy.

    The actual benefits, therefore, were arguable, indirect and deferred. For these benefits the Allies had to sustain for several months a commitment very onerous in shipping and landing craft, with the usual unsettling effect on inter-Allied negotiation and harmony. They also suffered considerable anxiety, as well as losses. The Allied forces at Anzio were outnumbered, and placed in a critical situation. Whereas both the Germans facing

---

* Author's italics.

southward and those fronting the beachhead were operating on interior lines, and could concentrate or economize force as the hour demanded, the Allies' two fronts were too remote for tactical interaction and movement between them was laborious. Because it was neither exploited directly, nor led to success on the main front, SHINGLE played no decisive part in the operations south of Rome. It did not trap the enemy by a move across his communications. It did not force him to withdraw on the main front. Instead it exposed a large Allied force to considerable danger and imposed a logistic burden for a long time. Yet surely the concept – of using amphibious power to assist a direct assault – was unexceptionable. The question that remains, and will continue long to be debated, is whether SHINGLE should not and could not have had a bolder and more explicit mission, one which would have included clear orders to a commander to drive inland and to exploit success. It is insufficient to say that this might have led to a disaster which did not occur. By that reasoning it would have been better not to begin; and perhaps that must remain the verdict – either to build up such strength as would make exploitation sure or not to start at all.

1944 was a Leap Year and the Prime Minister celebrated the extra day with a mordant comment on SHINGLE at an evening meeting on 29th February. 'We hoped,' he said, 'to land a wild cat that would tear out the bowels of the Boche. Instead we have stranded a vast whale with its tail flopping about in the water.'[7]

Whatever the course of events at Anzio it was, to Brooke, inconceivable that the Italian front should be allowed respite in the months before OVERLORD. If the Fifth Army offensive had failed to achieve a breakthrough, as by the end of March it clearly had, there must be a further major effort planned. Thus fighting continued round Cassino, fighting which Wilson and Alexander recognized would not be decisive but which would, they believed, win a springboard for the next attempt on Rome and the roads to North Italy which lay beyond. Brooke was sceptical about some of what he heard. 'I am not a believer in the use of heavy bombers on forward defences, he signalled to Wilson on 6th April, 'it is a great pity that Freyberg did not make a freer use of infantry.'[8] He reckoned that on this occasion the New Zealand commander, General Freyberg, was inevitably but excessively conscious, under pressure from his Government, of the need to minimize the casualties of the limited New Zealand manpower. 'It is hard in war to make omelets without breaking eggs,' Brooke wrote, 'and it is often in trying to do so that we break most eggs.'⁹

The Allies had the benefit of knowing the text of Field-Marshal Kesselring's appreciation of the situation by means of ULTRA. Brooke described it on 10th March as 'a most useful document giving his outlook on the whole of the fighting in Italy'. He regarded continuing offensive operations as vital. He believed that provided the Allies continued vigorously to attack in Italy the Germans would react, seek to hold ground and retain, perforce, a major Italian commitment. The opposed point of view, often advanced by Marshall, was that the Germans could decide to withdraw slowly, covered by minimal rearguard forces, and remove the bulk of their divisions. Brooke argued the case then and afterwards:

> Had this happened we should have been left with redundant forces in Italy. This was quite a sound argument strategically but it failed entirely to take Hitler's mentality into account. Nowhere yet had he retired voluntarily on any front and in not doing so had committed grave strategic blunders which led to his ultimate defeat. First Stalingrad . . . secondly Tunisia . . . thirdly the Dnieper river bend where he might have materially increased his reserves by shortening his front. It was not in Hitler's character to retire, he certainly would not give up Italy unless he was driven out of it and he would fight against such a contingency.¹⁰

In this assessment, broadly accurate, Brooke may have turned a slightly blind eye to the known fact that Hitler had approved an original German plan to stand only in North Italy and not to fight for the centre of the country. It had been the optimistic Kesselring who carried the day, something of a reversal of normal roles between the Führer and his Field Commanders. But that had been in the first confused days of the Italian volte-face. Now that the front had been formed, and much blood spilt in hard fighting south of Rome, Brooke's appreciation proved sound. To turn the factor to useful account, however, it would be necessary to keep attacking, for the Italian front would always lend itself to economic defence unless under pressure. Brooke, therefore, eagerly awaited Alexander's next major offensive – DIADEM. He had to fight for its genesis. Since the start of the year the shadow of ANVIL, the withdrawal of troops for a landing on the Mediterranean coast of France, had begun to lie over the Italian campaign. Despite what had been agreed with Americans and Russians in Tehran, was ANVIL to be sacrosanct, whatever the general situation in the

Mediterranean theatre, and the particular situation confronting Commanders and troops in Italy?

Brooke had never liked ANVIL. In Tehran it had been sufficiently remote to be accepted *sine die* albeit with a planning date. He had recognized its advantages. It underwrote the principle of amphibious operations in the Mediterranean in 1944. Without the concept of ANVIL it is unlikely that enough shipping would have been negotiated for the Anzio landing – and although this had turned out disappointingly Brooke never abandoned his belief that an offensive in Italy early in 1944 presupposed an amphibious element or threat. But now that ANVIL was imminent Brooke and his colleagues had to look at the operation with realism, and they did not like what they saw.

In the first place the British were sceptical as to the possible effects on OVERLORD. OVERLORD plans had hardened and committed the Allies to a major assault across the beaches of the Baie de la Seine. The whole extent of France would separate the battlefields of Normandy from any Mediterranean debouchment. Second, if ANVIL were to be more than a poised threat or feint, it would require a major force and a major effort in amphibious shipping for the assault echelon. At the same time the demands of OVERLORD, now that Eisenhower and Montgomery had taken control and scrutinized the plans, had increased, as had the planned width of initial assault. There was, therefore, inherent conflict between the claims of OVERLORD and ANVIL, although the latter's purpose was entirely to assist the former.

Third, and most urgent, ANVIL was in direct competition with the claims of the Italian campaign. If the Allies, as Brooke believed they must, were to keep pressure on the Germans in Italy: if they were to give full support to Alexander's offensives, first SHINGLE and now DIADEM, then it was surely essential not to withdraw troops in mid-campaign for an amphibious expedition of questionable value and for which time was short. The 'Italian dimension' to the argument seemed to Brooke conclusive. He was in regular correspondence with Wilson, who was in the best position to show the incompatibility of ANVIL with the sustenance of an offensive in Italy. There were also questions of the scope of ANVIL – limitations of resources meant a limited assault and build-up – and of timing. The demands of SHINGLE and its aftermath made it unlikely that ANVIL could in any case be launched to chime

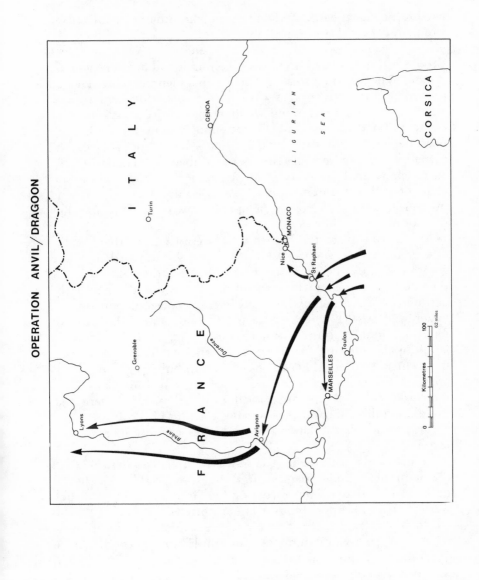

OPERATION ANVIL/DRAGOON

with OVERLORD, its main justification. Wilson to Brooke, 9th February:

> If we are to be committed to a reduced ANVIL it will be up to us to fit in our plan for the same with the Italian battle; which may well mean that our one assault loaded division could not be used until later than 'Y' date, [OVERLORD].

Wilson added that 'barking and not biting could be our role prior to that'.[11] This referred to the concept of reducing ANVIL to a threat for the time being, a concept to which Eisenhower himself had reluctantly agreed. In the same letter Wilson pointed to the risks of ANVIL – the security of the force once landed. One Allied assault division could be built up to three, in six days. It was anticipated that the Germans, on the other hand, could concentrate against them three divisions in three days.

To Brooke it was increasingly important not to understate the main point – the effect on the immediate future of the Italian campaign. He signalled to Wilson on 6th March: 'For Heaven's sake get ANVIL killed as early as you can.'[12]

To which Wilson replied on 8th March that he agreed. He had himself recommended cancellation on 22nd February. This had led to reluctant American agreement to postpone and review in the middle of March: if it were then decided that ANVIL could not be done, all landing craft would be sailed from the Mediterranean to be used for OVERLORD. But as the middle of March approached the problem was to find means to induce the Americans to swallow the pill. Wilson suggested that simply to declare the expedition unsound would drive the Americans back upon the Tehran and Cairo agreements. The Russians had been promised ANVIL as an attack, not a threat. It would be better to move step by step – he called it 'strangulation' – pointing to the negative effects on the Italian campaign which at that moment was going badly. But nine days later Wilson signalled that Alexander was now more optimistic about the outcome of the Cassino battle, and this made him equivocal about recommending the abandonment of ANVIL. He had based his argument upon the dangers of withdrawing troops from a losing battle. Now success made him hoist with his own petard.

This found little favour with Brooke who replied on the same day (17th March):

> I cannot understand why you cannot now make cast-iron case

against ANVIL. Even if the present attack is successful there is no prospect of being able to make available the number of divisions required for ANVIL . . . You will also need your landing craft for operations in conjunction with the main battle in Italy.[13]

For while the Anzio beachhead was isolated from the Fifth Army it raised a substantial landing craft requirement for maintenance.

The British then prepared a draft directive to Wilson, and American agreement to it was sought on 22nd March. In it Wilson would be ordered to continue the battle in Italy, to capture Rome if possible by the first week in June and to continue to advance. Unsurprisingly the Americans adverted to ANVIL, which they demanded should be covered by the same directive. To get over the shipping problem they said that they would make a substantial number of landing ships and craft available from the Pacific – but only if ANVIL were carried out, on a date which they now recognized must be well after OVERLORD. They suggested a target date of 10th July for the operation, and the maintenance of an amphibious threat during the period of OVERLORD itself. Meanwhile the Italian campaign should not be pressed beyond a certain point. This last was regarded as completely unacceptable by the British Chiefs of Staff:

Telegram from American Chiefs of Staff quite impossible to accept. Again arguing that after uniting Anzio bridgehead and main front we should go on the defensive in Italy and start a new front in Southern France. They fail to realize that the forces available do not admit of two fronts in the Mediterranean.[14]

The British concentrated their fire on the Americans' apparent unwillingness to keep up the battle in Italy, and in this they had success. The Americans, however, had made an offer of shipping from the Pacific, of which the Prime Minister was anxious to take advantage. He believed that with such resources committed to the Mediterranean any success in Italy could be exploited – in whatever direction or at whatever time seemed appropriate, ANVIL or otherwise. He hoped he might get the ships while still leaving vague the commitment to ANVIL. He entered the debate with a personal telegram to Marshall, without success: 'Waste of time,' wrote Brooke, 'as I feel certain the reply will be in the negative.' For the Americans reckoned that ANVIL had been agreed, and that it was thus the only just claimant for resources from the Pacific. If it had to be postponed, for reasons of which they were only reluctantly persuaded, no resources could be offered for other unspecified ventures, even if such ventures might (as Marshall recognized) in the event present superior attractions to ANVIL. The British were hostile to ANVIL but would, with reluctance, accept it if postponed. The Americans were determined that it should be carried out but would, with reluctance, accept its postponement. In that case there would be no additional shipping – although on this they later relented.

In the immediate argument the British were successful. ANVIL was postponed and made a matter for later decision. Wilson received his directive according to the British text. As to ANVIL he was simply instructed to 'make plans for the best possible use of the amphibious lift remaining to you, either in support of operations in Italy or in order to take advantage of opportunities arising in South of France or elsewhere'. But this was not to detract from his main task – 'Launch, as early as possible an all-out offensive in Italy.' 'At last all our troubles about ANVIL are over,' wrote Brooke in his diary on 11th April. 'We have got the Americans to agree, but have lost the additional landing craft they were prepared to provide. History will never forgive them for bargaining equipment against strategy and for trying to blackmail us into agreeing with them by holding the pistol of withdrawing craft at our heads.'

History may, instead, suggest that the case for these craft in default of ANVIL had not been made. As to 'troubles being over' this was far from so, but for the time being Brooke had his way. ANVIL, as considered at that time, would have been a dangerous and ineffectual distraction. Instead, the Italian campaign, vigorously prosecuted, was to be the only Mediterranean operation to pave the way to OVERLORD. Nevertheless, ANVIL remained alive, and once it was agreed that it should not draw off resources from Alexander's next offensive it was looked at by the British with less hostility. On 27th April the British Chiefs of Staff told the Americans that they would favour some such operation after OVERLORD, and Admiral King responded that in that case he would make available the shipping from the Pacific whose earlier retention had so aroused Brooke's wrath. Wilson, who returned to London for a few days on 3rd May, was told to look at a number of possibilities for post-OVERLORD operations, of which ANVIL was only one. Another was a landing in the Bay of Biscay which carried some familiar hallmarks. 'A great deal of this,' Brooke had noted of a meeting on 8th February, 'was concerned with a proposed wild venture of his [Churchill's] to land 2 Armoured Divisions in Bordeaux . . . I think we have ridden him off this for the present.'

Meanwhile on 11th April Alexander returned to London to present his plans. There was to be a major offensive, Operation DIADEM, finally to break into the Liri Valley and advance to Rome itself. The bulk of the Eighth Army were to be concentrated with Fifth Army in the West Italian sector. Both Armies would carry out the offensive. Alexander declared he could attack any time after 10th May.

Brooke made clear in his diary and private correspondence how much the problems of operations in Europe – SHINGLE, ANVIL, OVERLORD – dominated his mind. Once again it is striking how few are the direct references to the campaign in Burma. The course of events there in the first few months of 1944 was dramatic, yet even the Chiefs of Staff Committee only periodically took note without comment. If Burma did not compare to Europe in the personal concern it evoked, the reason probably lay not only in the paramount importance of events in the war against Germany, but also in the reluctance with which Brooke and his colleagues regarded offensive operations in Burma at that stage. He had fought to reduce their scope, and he regarded the limited land attacks Mountbatten had been empowered to undertake as concessions to American sentiment, rather than as opportunities directly linked to the central theme and drama of the war.

He made, however, plenty of comment on the future of the war against Japan, the wider strategic picture of which the Burma campaign was a small but vivid part. 'Long COS meeting with planners discussing Pacific strategy,' he wrote in his diary on 21st February:

> and deciding on plan of action to tackle the PM with to convince him that we cannot take the tip of Sumatra for him. We shall have very serious trouble with him over this. But we have definitely decided that our strategy should be to operate from Australia with the Americans and not from India through the Malacca straits.

A mighty storm was brewing.

It had been agreed in Cairo, in general terms, that the main effort against Japan must take place in the Pacific. Churchill had initialled the agreement, but had not fully debated it nor discussed its implications at that time with his advisers.

The war in the Pacific demanded a main effort at sea and in the air. Japan's conquests had been attained by the use of sea, air and amphibious power. The war could only be brought to Japan itself by the reconquest of bases from which air strikes and ultimately invasion could be launched. This meant a major maritime effort.

Such an effort admitted of choices. The principal choice lay between the occupation of a number of the great islands of the South Pacific, culminating in the Philippines and Formosa; and, alternatively, a more direct seaward line of advance, less costly in land forces, which would be directed on Formosa by the line of the Caroline and Mariana islands, isolating the Japanese forces in the Philippines and Dutch East Indies, and obviating the need to assault them directly. The forces involved, and the strategic choices, would be largely if not solely American. The most vigorous proponent of striking at the Japanese Army island by island with amphibious force, was General Douglas MacArthur. The most convinced protagonist of a primarily maritime approach was Admiral Ernest King. 'To arrive at a concerted plan with the Americans of a defeat of Japan is not going to be easy,' Brooke wrote to Wavell on 22nd February.

> There is dissension in many places, King and MacArthur have different points of view as to how the war in the Pacific should be run, the PM . . . still passionately in love with the tip of Sumatra . . . Curtin and the Australians have fairly definite views as to the assistance they expect from us when Germany is beaten . . . to steer the ship on a strategic course through all those rocks is not going to be an easy matter.[15]

For now the question in London was how British forces should be involved. At SEXTANT it had been settled that, during 1944, the British effort by land should be in Burma. Looking further ahead it had also been proposed that as large a fleet as Britain could produce should be brought to the Pacific and based on the Solomon and Bismarck islands: while an Army, initially of four British divisions, should be based in Australia as soon as possible after Germany's defeat – generally assumed to be before the end of 1944. These forces, with Australian and New Zealand Allies and supported by powerful air forces, would then co-operate with the American Army and Navy on the left flank of a mighty amphibious advance towards Japan. The role of South East Asia Command, somewhat analogous to that of the Mediterranean Command in the European theatre, would be to threaten, draw off and contain the maximum number of Japanese forces which could otherwise reinforce the Pacific or defend the homeland. The Americans were as clear that this could best be done by the British concentrating on the land offensive in Burma, as Brooke had been clear over the part played by an Italian campaign. Roles were reversed.

The concepts discussed at SEXTANT began to take the form of a British plan early in 1944. The Chiefs of Staff considered a paper on 3rd February and minuted the Prime Minister thereafter.[16] They emphasized that operations in South East Asia should be minor. Any amphibious action must be 'with available resources' – no more could be looked for; virtually all such shipping would be concentrated in the Pacific. Suggestions made by South East Asia Command that there should be a major advance mounted from the west, from the Bay of Bengal, were scouted. Such an advance would be too slow, too laborious. Judging by the pace of recent American advance it could also be irrelevant. The same considerations applied to Churchill's pet project of seizing the tip of Sumatra – CULVERIN – which was described as certain, on balance, to draw off more of our own forces from the Pacific 'of the type that is required' than those of the enemy, and for longer. For the British Chiefs of Staff were committing themselves firmly to a Pacific strategy – to join the Americans in the Pacific. Brooke put the matter in a letter to Dill a few weeks later[17] – 'I am quite clear,' he wrote

> in my own mind that strategically it is right for us to use all our forces in close co-operation from Australia across the Pacific in the general direction of Formosa. By operating our forces alongside of MacArthur we can pool resources at sea and in the air for various closely connected steps. Whereas by retaining our forces in the Indian Ocean we operate independently, incapable of close co-operation, with the result that operations will be more protracted.

Churchill was profoundly opposed to the Pacific strategy. It had been discussed in the Defence Committee of the Cabinet in January, and he had launched his preliminary bombardment. He declared that the matter had not been fully put to him at SEXTANT, and he disassociated himself from any agreements there made. He pointed out that American plans were still ambiguous, as between Army and Navy, MacArthur and Admiral

Nimitz. He queried (as it turned out with prescience) whether a British fleet was in fact required by the Americans in the Pacific at all. He envisaged the base installations of India as wasted assets in such a strategy. Above all, however, Churchill wished to open up a British offensive, with British forces, in a British theatre of operations, supported from British bases. He wished, with these forces, to liberate British possessions or protected states. He did not relish sending large forces of all three Services to act as an adjunct, possibly not even a very welcome and certainly not a vital adjunct to great American forces in a great American campaign. Churchill believed that we should operate from our main Imperial base, India; and should be seen in South East Asia as liberators not as auxiliaries.

The argument continued through February and March with remarkable bitterness. No issue caused more ferocious battles between the Prime Minister and the Chiefs of Staff Committee than the Pacific strategy.

> 'I very much regret,' the Prime Minister minuted angrily on 20th March, 'that the Chiefs of Staff should have proceeded so far in this matter and reached such settled conclusions upon it without in any way endeavouring to ascertain and carry the views of the civil power under which they are serving.'[18]

As often happened a point of major principle was somewhat smothered by argument over a detailed plan. Churchill, as part of his general concept that we should operate from the Bay of Bengal and aim to free Malaya, not only pressed the claims of Sumatra – CULVERIN – but also supported Mountbatten's idea that we should thereafter move from base to base along the Asiatic coast. It was not difficult for Brooke to argue that there could not be resources for three convergent lines of advance – King's, MacArthur's and Mountbatten's.[19] Nor was it hard to criticize the relevance, the practicability and the possible timing of CULVERIN. Churchill, in this acrimonious debate with his professional advisers, took position as a strategist, where he was vulnerable: on weak ground, where Brooke and his colleagues could strongly attack with military reason.

Yet the underlying arguments of those defending a Pacific strategy or opposing it were essentially political. Brooke wrote after the war:

> The first of these alternatives [operations based on India] was

the easiest to stage *but limited itself to the recapture of British possessions** without any direct participation with American and Australian forces in the defeat of Japan. I felt that at this stage of the war it was vital that British forces should participate in direct action against Japan in the Pacific. First of all *from a Commonwealth point of view to prove to Australia** our willingness and desire to fight with them for the defence of Australia as soon as the defeat of Germany rendered such action possible. Secondly, I felt it was important that *we should operate with all three Services alongside of the Americans in the Pacific against Japan in the final stages of the war.** I therefore considered that our strategy should aim at the liberation of Burma by South East Asia Command based on India, and the deployment of new sea, land and air forces to operate with bases in Australia alongside of forces in the Pacific.[20]

This was a positive policy, but as he stated it Brooke's motive was broadly political – the effect on Australian sentiment, the sharing of victory in the Pacific with the United States. Yet Churchill also had a political motive, at least as defensible and perhaps a good deal more so. British influence and prestige, British post-war interests, would not automatically be restored by American policy and American arms. There was clearly much in favour of a strategy which would have made clear that in South East Asia, at least, it was for the British to avenge Singapore.

Yet if the issue of principle was political, the immediate point was one of timing. Even had the Chiefs of Staff accepted the overriding political importance of what became known as the 'Bay of Bengal' strategy – and on a political point Churchill not only constitutionally had standing but was almost invariably more perceptive – they could and did still argue that it was impracticable to do anything effective in time. It was common ground that no major moves could be made, nor major enterprises be undertaken until Germany's defeat was certain within measurable time. Even assuming, as all did, that this meant before the end of 1944, the Americans looked to be at final grips with Japan before any independent and ambitious offensive could possibly be mounted from the Bay of Bengal. It would be irrelevant. It would be too late. All that could be done in time would be to join a campaign already underway, to the best of our ability and in what strength could be mustered.

* Author's italics.

Successive battles were bloody. A diary entry by Brooke on
25th February:

> I am quite exhausted after 7½ hours with Winston today and most
> of that time engaged in heavy argument. He was still insisting on
> doing the north Sumatra operation and would not discuss any
> other operation and was in a thoroughly disgruntled and bad
> temper. I had a series of heated discussions with him.
>
> Then a hurried lunch and at 3 p.m. we met again. This time he
> had packed the house against us, and was accompanied by
> Anthony Eden, Oliver Lyttleton and Attlee in addition the whole
> of Dickie Mountbatten's party . . .
>
> The whole party were against the Chiefs of Staff!
>
> We argued from 3 p.m. to 5.30 p.m. I got very heated at times,
> especially when Anthony Eden chipped in knowing nothing
> about Pacific strategy! Winston pretended that this was all a
> frame-up against his pet Sumatra operation and almost took it as
> a personal matter. Furthermore his dislike for Curtin and the
> Australians at once affected any discussion for co-operation with
> Australian forces through New Guinea towards the Philippines.
>
> Dickie chipped in and talked unadulterated nonsense, and I lost
> my temper with him. It was a desperate meeting with no
> opportunity of discussing strategy on its merits.

Yet after one such day, with interviews, meetings, attendance
at a two-hour Cabinet until 8 p.m. and with another session with
the Prime Minister starting at 10 p.m. continuing late as ever,
Brooke not only wrote up his diary and scribbled a long letter to
Benita between meetings but also sent a charming letter to
Bannerman with thanks for an evening of dinner and ornithology.
He had, as ever, found solace in an hour or two looking at superb
bird pictures, and nothing restored him more.

Nor was it ever all darkness with Churchill. The diary entry for
25th February continued:

> PM called up and asked me to dine. I thought it was to tell me
> that he couldn't stick my disagreements any longer and proposed
> to sack me! On the contrary we had a tête-à-tête dinner at which
> he was quite charming, as if he meant to make up for some of the
> rough passages of the day . . .
>
> At 10 p.m. another COS meeting which lasted till 12
> midnight. PM in much more reasonable mood and I think that a
> great deal of what we have been doing has soaked in.

This was sadly optimistic and March proved a dreadful month. On
3rd March Brooke recorded that in Committee:

I had to discuss the very difficult problem which is brewing up, and in which the PM is trying at present to frame up the War Cabinet against the Chiefs of Staff Committee. It is all about the future Pacific strategy, it looks very serious and may well lead to the resignation of the Chiefs of Staff Committee.

Ismay, at this point, suggested to Churchill that he should break the 'deadlock' with the Chiefs of Staff by stating that the matter turned on political considerations which in this case must be paramount. A meeting was held between the Chiefs of Staff Committee on the one hand and Churchill, supported by Attlee, Eden, Lyttleton and Lord Leathers on the other. It did not bring relief or harmony. On 8th March:

Dear old Cunningham so wild with rage that he hardly dared to let himself speak! I therefore had to do most of the arguing, and for $2\frac{1}{2}$ hours from 10 p.m. to 12.30 a.m. I went at it hard, arguing with the PM and 4 Cabinet Ministers. The arguments of the latter were so puerile it made me ashamed to think that they were Cabinet Ministers. It was only too evident that they did not know their subject and had not read the various papers connected with it, and had purely been brought along to support Winston. And damned badly they did it, too! I had little difficulty in dealing with any of the arguments they put forward.

The matter was not put on to a political basis, as Ismay had suggested. Instead, perhaps inevitably, the meeting tussled with strategy, and on the practicability, timing and consequences of alternate strategic courses Brooke was easily master. It was resolved to 'assemble more data'.

Matters went from bad to worse. Churchill had obtained from Roosevelt a view that no planned operations in the Pacific would suffer from the absence of a British fleet. This was ammunition against the Chiefs of Staff.Armed with it he addressed to each of the Chiefs of Staff a paper in which he expressed his 'duty as Prime Minister and Minister of Defence to give certain rulings'. These amounted to orders for a 'Bay of Bengal' strategy directed ultimately to the reconquest of Malaya and Singapore, discarding any idea of deploying the fleet or any other forces in the Pacific.

This caused consternation. An old friend wrote to Brooke on 19th March: 'Hard though it may be you have to keep your balance and your position. You said yourself you are sometimes tempted to speak your mind freely.'[21]

It was certainly not a temptation which Brooke resisted on professional matters. However the Chiefs of Staff wisely took some time in framing their response on this occasion. In the diary on 21st March:

> We discussed . . . how best to deal with Winston's last impossible document. It is full of false statements, false deductions and defective strategy. We cannot accept it as it stands and it would be better if we all three resigned sooner than accept his solution.

But the Chiefs of Staff temporized, neither accepting nor resigning. Instead they pointed out that the additional data required after their previous confrontation with the Prime Minister was not yet to hand. Only when it was could they make a formal recommendation – which, they delicately but firmly pointed out, was their inescapable duty. Churchill did not push the matter to crisis at that stage. He knew well that the resignation of all Chiefs of Staff in the period immediately before the invasion of Europe would have been an intolerable blow to public confidence. Nevertheless he had the Cabinet behind him on the political issues involved in the strategic choice, and the situation was dangerous.

Ultimately some sort of compromise emerged, and in early April the Chiefs of Staff agreed that an alternative strategy should be examined. It came to be called the 'Middle Strategy'. Under this, as in the Pacific Strategy, a British, Australian and New Zealand Army would be based in Northern and Western Australia. There would be an advance on the general axis Timor-Celebes-Borneo-Saigon. No British resources would be allocated to the parallel American operations. This marked a step in the argument, it threw the shadow of a compromise when one was sadly needed. 'Examined the possibility and advantages,' wrote Brooke on 14th April,

> of a line of advance on an axis from Darwin towards Borneo. This might give us *a chance of running an entirely British Imperial campaign*** instead of furnishing reinforcements for American operations.'

The Middle Strategy – and variations of it which successively appeared – at least reconciled some of Churchill's desire for national reassertion with Brooke's wish to stand together with the Australians at the end and to avoid impracticable undertakings in the meanwhile. The 'Middle Strategy' brought reluctant minds nearer to each other, and althouth it was never carried out it played its own peculiar part in history. Discussion, sometimes with

* Author's italics.

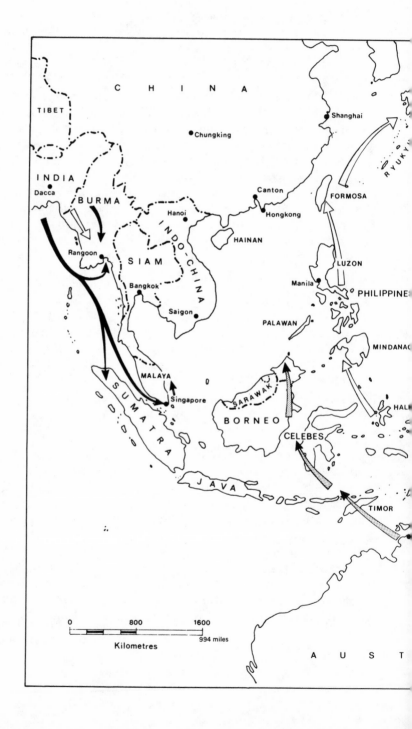

THE PACIFIC THEATRE

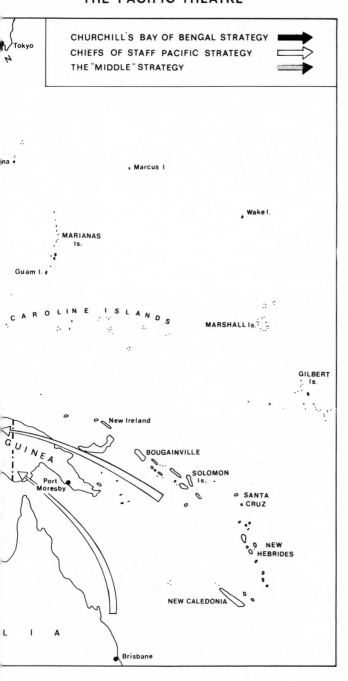

CHURCHILL'S BAY OF BENGAL STRATEGY
CHIEFS OF STAFF PACIFIC STRATEGY
THE "MIDDLE" STRATEGY

Tokyo

N

na

Marcus I

Wake I.

MARIANAS
Is.

Guam I.

C A R O L I N E   I S L A N D S

MARSHALL Is.

GILBERT
Is.

New Ireland

G U I N E A

BOUGAINVILLE

SOLOMON
Is.

Port
Moresby

SANTA
CRUZ

NEW
HEBRIDES

NEW CALEDONIA

L   I   A

Brisbane

acrimony, continued for the next few months – indeed until the second Quebec Conference in September – but matters were never as bad between Brooke and Churchill as they had been in February and March. As always light would break through the clouds of their relationship. Brooke stayed at Chequers on 7th May. Churchill talked late.

> He then said some very nice things about the excellent opinion that the whole Defence Committee and War Cabinet had of me, and that they had said that we could not have a better CIGS.[22]

At such moments, Brooke wrote after the war,

> You left him with the feeling that you would do anything within your power to help him carry the stupendous burden he had shouldered.[23]

The 'Middle Strategy' ultimately withered, largely through American scepticism of its usefulness. The United States Chiefs of Staff made it plain that they would not welcome with much warmth the presence of a British fleet in the South Pacific. They considered that the British should concentrate on the land campaign in Burma and should stay in the Indian Ocean. The only useful contribution the British could make to their grand strategy, they believed, was to help China by a Burmese campaign, and thus keep her in arms against Japan. Meanwhile the Japanese reinforced Burma strongly in response to Slim's successful operations, and it was clear that by whatever plan – and several were now considered – the campaign in Burma would itself constitute a major effort. A last initiative towards British participation in the Pacific was taken in August, with renewed suggestion of a British fleet to act under American command – with, as a possible alternative, a 'British Empire Task Force' to be placed under MacArthur. Some six Australian, one New Zealand and four British divisions were envisaged. At the plenary meeting of the Combined Chiefs of Staff in September it was finally agreed that the fleet should participate in Pacific operations, in spite of Admiral King's angrily expressed reluctance;[24] but there would be no 'Task Force'. There would be thus no independent line of advance from Australia. Britain's part in the war in the Pacific would be essentially maritime. Burma would be reconquered. The 'Pacific Strategy' quietly died.

It is ironic that the most serious battles between Churchill and the Chiefs of Staff in the Second World War, producing the only occasions when Brooke seriously discussed mass resignation, were, as matters turned out, irrelevant. Japan was to fall with a suddenness which owed nothing to British choice of strategy whether primarily contributive to American effort, as the Chiefs of Staff first wished, or more independently driven through Britain's liberated territories as Churchill fiercely desired.

Even in such turmoils the Chiefs managed to keep their heads about priorities. On hearing that the Royal Air Force were about to use Scotts Head Island, off the Norfolk coast, as a bombing range, an anxious Bannerman explained to Brooke that this would disturb the nesting season of the rare roseate tern unless carefully timed and controlled. Brooke was appalled and spoke to Portal immediately. An alternative was found.[25]

Brooke's third great preoccupation in the first five months of 1944 was the preparation of OVERLORD. Many other matters filled his day. The situation in Greece, where there could well arise a major requirement for British troops: the first V weapons, 'pilotless planes' as they were first called, of which threat the Chiefs of Staff had long been aware, and had regularly discussed at weekly sessions, and of which the first fell on London on 13th June: the continuing fitness of commanders for their posts: but OVERLORD dominated.

The operational plan for the invasion was, Brooke reckoned, in good hands. Eisenhower, he thought, was 'Just a co-ordinator, a good mixer, a champion of inter-Allied co-operation and in those respects few can hold the candle to him. But is that enough? Or can we not find all the qualities of a Commander in one man?'[26] And after the war Brooke wrote that he would, in the light of further experience, reiterate every word of that judgement. Yet 'a champion of inter-Allied co-operation' was exactly what the hour would demand.

But Montgomery would command the initial landing, and had been working on the detail of the plans since taking command at the beginning of the year. In consequence the width of assault had been substantially extended. It was still constricted – by resources – and Brooke suffered the periodic agony of every commander in like situation. 'I do wish to Heaven that we were landing on a wider front,' he wrote in his diary on 7th June. But Brooke retained complete faith in Montgomery's tactical sense and confidence. 'He is making good headway in making plans,' he wrote in March, adding with typical asperity 'and equally successful in making enemies as far as I can see'.[27] 'I had to tell him off,' he wrote in May, 'and ask him to concentrate more on his own job and not meddle himself in everybody else's affairs . . . as usual he took it well.'[28]

Other major commands had fallen into place, and Brooke had few misgivings. MacNaughton had now been replaced at the head of the Canadian Army by Crerar, to Brooke's profound relief. He grieved that MacNaughton then and in later life appeared to bear rancour, but he never wavered in his view that the change was essential for the well-being and performance of the Canadian troops themselves.

The hardest preparatory step of all lay in the waiting. Alexander's offensive in Italy was due to start on the night of 11th May. Brooke took a blessed week's leave at the end of April, fishing in Scotland and catching twelve salmon with a dear friend.* As always it restored him. 'I am feeling worlds better,' he wrote to Benita on 30th April, but consumed by

> a terrible longing to give up work and settle down in some spot far from humanity to enjoy to the utmost the better things in life such as birds, fishing, nature, gardening during the remaining years of my life!

Back in London, 'Attack started up to time,' he noted at 11.30 p.m. on 12th May, 'but no news all day. I am awaiting message.' 'Spent Sunday at home photographing a Marsh Tit,' he wrote next day.

Operation DIADEM, the attack on the West Italian front, was to sweep the Allies at last into Rome and towards the north. Cassino fell on 18th May and on the 24th Eighth Army broke through the German line, VI American Corps striking from the Anzio beachhead the following day. On 4th June the Allied Armies entered Rome. The Germans avoided encirclement, and withdrew. 'I never want to go through a time like the present one,' Brooke wrote on 27th May:

> The cross-Channel operation is just eating into my heart. I wish to God we could start and have done with it.

> 'This prolonged waiting period before the operation was shattering,' he added after the war. 'I remember having all the same feelings as I used to get before starting in a point to point race, an empty feeling at the pit of one's stomach and a continual desire to yawn!'

---

* Lieutenant-Colonel Ivan Cobbold, Scots Guards, a friend to whom Brooke was devoted and whose hospitality and shooting whether in Scotland or Suffolk he greatly enjoyed, was killed when the Guards Chapel was destroyed by air raid on 18th June 1944.

Brooke had tended, however, to win point-to-point races, but delayed starts are hard to bear. After agonizing deferments through unexpected weather he wrote to Benita on 5th June. 'The attack is definitely starting tomorrow.'

On 6th June, D-Day, the Allies landed on the coast of France. This was the consummation of all plans. By 7.30 (a.m.) Brooke began to receive first news of the invasion. As the morning dragged on he could stand his office no more and went for a walk in St James's Park to find some solace looking at the ducks. He encountered the King's Private Secretary, Sir Alan Lascelles, on exactly the same mission:[29] 'A most unreal day during which I felt as if I were in a trance, entirely detached from the war.'[30]

With typical misgivings he wrote in the following days that he was unhappy at progress: 'We are not gaining enough ground and German forces are assembling fast.'[31] On 9th June he noted that the news was better. Later that day the American Chiefs of Staff arrived in London from Washington, anxious themselves to inspect progress of the greatest operation yet undertaken.

On 12th June Brooke crossed the Channel by destroyer to visit the beachhead. He accompanied the Prime Minister, Smuts and the American Chiefs of Staff. His only regret was that Dill, his dearest friend and most valued colleague, was not of the party. Dill was unwell, and never fully recovered. The party toured the beaches, visited the Headquarters of 21st Army Group (Montgomery) and Second (British) Army (Dempsey). Touring the invasion front offshore, and watching the progress of disembarkation, in a convoy of small craft in line astern, Brooke pointed out to the captain of the vessel in which he was travelling that Churchill was in the lead patrol boat. He was solicitous. There were still mines about:

'Shouldn't the Prime Minister be in the one behind us?'

He was assured that if Churchill's boat hit a mine it would be Brooke's which consequently would sink. He grunted, presumably satisfied.[32]

Thus Brooke once more returned to France. He had left it four years ago with the bitter taste of defeat, and with a future uncertain and dark. Now he had been for two and a half years at the head of Britain's Army. He had ceaselessly, and with unrelenting firmness and candour, pressed a strategy which would prepare for this moment and would ensure its success. He had always, and without apology, been the chief of those who refused to contemplate a premature 'Second Front'. Through years of vigorous debate he had maintained the necessity of distracting Germany by forcing her to disperse her forces, and by so threatening Southern Europe and fighting in Italy as to prevent the maximum concentration against the invading Allies. He had, often to the profound irritation of Government, been strong as steel that the British Army must not be committed to operations unless and until conditions were right: and this had meant victory in the Battle of the Atlantic, and the prosecution of the bomber offensive which played so vital a part in the weakening of the enemy. He had, throughout, demanded time. He believed in attrition. It was attrition achieved in the skies over Germany, and above all on the Eastern rather than the Western front. This made no difference to the principle. There must be a wearing down. As firmly as Haig before him, and with the same logic, Brooke believed in attrition and preached it; and with the same ultimate triumph.

CHAPTER XVII

In the Shadow of the Future

ALEXANDER'S TROOPS entered Rome on 4th June. The Germans in Italy were in full retreat. A spirit of confidence and triumphant advance animated the Allied Armies. Temporarily, at least, the Italian campaign appeared one of opportunity and movement, while operations in North West Europe were still in a condition of build-up, of edging forward. The British and American Chiefs, in the immediate aftermath of successful OVERLORD landings, conferred on 11th June and discussed the Mediterranean theatre.

They had before them two documents. Wilson, Supreme Allied Commander Mediterranean, had been directed to examine future amphibious operations either in France or the Adriatic. On 17th May he had produced a report favouring, of several alternatives, a descent on the Riviera in mid-August. This, again, was ANVIL – now to be rechristened DRAGOON. Its aim was directly to assist the campaign in Normandy by threatening the German flank or rear in France.

Wilson had been specifically told to consider the amphibious dimension. In very different vein Alexander, commanding the Allied forces in Italy, sent Brooke on 7th June his views on future operations by his victorious troops. Alexander reckoned he could do one of three things. He could advance to and stand at the line Pisa-Rimini, which he expected to be able to attack about the end of July. This would enable forces to be economized on the Italian front. It was the only alternative he discussed which would be compatible with DRAGOON or any like operation. Second, the Armies could be directed not only to the Pisa-Rimini line but beyond it into North West Italy, developing thence operations into Southern France. As a third possibility, there could be an Allied advance from the Apennines to North East Italy with a view to mounting a campaign towards the Danube Valley and Vienna, moving by the 'Ljubljana Gap'. This was 'The Vienna Alternative'. Thus, when the Americans and British met in June, they had to hand Alexander's appreciation of the opportunities the Italian campaign appeared now to present as well as Wilson's on

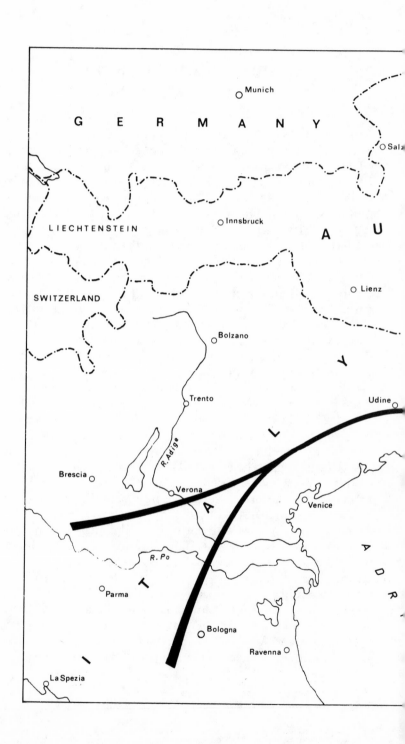

THE "VIENNA ALTERNATIVE"

the narrower question of ANVIL/DRAGOON and the amphibious alternatives to it.

Debate on these options has been clouded rather than illumined by wisdom after the event. The political and grand strategic advantages of a move into Central Europe, perhaps before the Red Army, are so evident that this particular concept has acquired greater retrospective merit than was then argued for it. At this stage – June and July 1944 – Churchill expressed the matter as clearly as circumstances allowed. In a personal wire to Roosevelt on 1st July he referred to a 'nice' telegram he had received from Stalin, and pointed out in connection with the 'Vienna Alternative':

> On a long-term political view he [Stalin] might prefer that the British and Americans should do their share in France in this very hard fighting that is to come, and that East, Middle and Southern Europe should fall naturally into his control.'[1]

But Churchill knew well that the argument for pre-empting the Soviets in Central Europe was not one of whose wisdom he could easily persuade Roosevelt. When the Combined Chiefs of Staff met on 11th June their debate was not about the political factors affecting Alexander's alternatives – his more ambitious alternatives – but on how best to help Eisenhower's campaign in Northern France with troops at present in the Mediterranean.

Brooke had little trouble with this. He believed, as ever, that Alexander's pursuit should be kept at full pressure – the Germans in Italy must be allowed no respite. It was accepted by both sides that this implied a rapid advance to the Pisa-Rimini line – Alexander's first alternative. Thereafter, Brooke was content that the spotlight should swing to DRAGOON – a landing of some ten divisions, many of them French, probably on the Riviera. He noted that night:

> Decided Italian campaign to stop at Apennines on Pisa-Rimini line and an amphibious operation to be prepared to land either in Southern France or Bay of Biscay.

And he wrote later:

> Now at last, we had put the South France operation in its right strategic position. By the time we reached the Pisa-Rimini line the Italian theatre should have played its part in holding reserves away from Northern France. We could then contemplate the landing in Southern France to provide a front for French forces

from North Africa and to co-operate on the southern flank of OVERLORD operations.[2]

In mid-June, therefore, Brooke was unconcerned about DRAGOON, and had no sense of missed opportunity arising from the fact (agreed by all) that DRAGOON, if undertaken, would severely limit other operations in Italy by withdrawing forces. Indeed, Brooke was and remained sceptical on military grounds of Alexander's vision of an advance north-eastward on Vienna. The latter he referred to as Alexander's 'dreams'[3] or 'wild hopes'.[4] He was strongly in favour of pressing the Germans as far as the Pisa-Rimini line, but as to a Danubian adventure:

> We should embark on a campaign through the Alps in winter. It was hard to make him [Churchill] realize that if we took the season of the year and the topography of the country in league against us we should have three enemies instead of one.[5]

Brooke was not impressed by the suggestion that the Julian Alps could be easily circumvented by way of Ljubljana. 'The proposals he has made,' he wrote of Alexander, 'are not based on any real study of the problem.' Since this was Brooke's mind, the British and Americans had little trouble in agreeing a telegram sent to Wilson on 14th June. In it Wilson was instructed that nothing should be allowed to impede a victorious advance to the Pisa-Rimini line (to be named the Gothic Line by its defenders) and that no forces should be withdrawn from Alexander which would place this achievement at risk. Thereafter, however, there would be an amphibious operation; whether in the Bay of Biscay or on the Riviera was left for later decision. In spite of Wilson's recommendation, the Combined Chiefs recorded that the most likely area to help the main OVERLORD front would be a landing near Bordeaux. It is a measure of Brooke's relaxation on the matter that he was prepared to acquiesce in this option although as sceptical of it as he had previously been. It was as if he was content to get American support for Alexander's immediate pursuit in Italy, and to join battle with the Americans over subsequent operations only if and when that battle became necessary.

It soon did. The main blow to the fragile Anglo-American consensus was dealt by Kesselring. Wilson's instructions had included a passage which the British quoted with force and indignation:

> We must complete the destruction of the German Armed Forces

in Italy south of the Pisa-Rimini line. No Allied forces should be withdrawn from the battles that are necessary for this purpose.[6]

This effectively made the decision about, and the timing of, DRAGOON dependent on the progress of operations in Italy. Now, however, Kesselring decided to stand well south of the ground Allied plans had assigned him. Instead of withdrawing, so that the Pisa-Rimini line could be attained and followed by DRAGOON in the timescale assumed by the Allies at their June meeting, Kesselring hastily prepared defensive positions in the hilly country south of that line and north of Perugia. Although, by Allied reckoning, the Germans could be forced out of this position or destroyed therein without too much delay, the British calculated that it would require all the forces at Alexander's disposal. Thus DRAGOON could not be carried out unless Alexander were to be deprived of troops, and his advance reined in well south of the line previously agreed.

Once again, bitter argument ensued. The Americans regarded DRAGOON as an agreed operation. In their view the exact line reached in Italy must be of less significance than a new landing specifically to assist Eisenhower's operations, and open a new port of entry to the Northern European front. The British, they thought, were, as ever, 'dragging their feet' and invoking the letter of the law (in the case of the paragraph in the telegram to Wilson which adjured him to reach the Pisa-Rimini line) to disguise their undiminished and only temporarily concealed hostility to DRAGOON. The Americans were clear, and so signalled on 24th June, that the best way to help OVERLORD and to exploit success was to concentrate more forces in the decisive theatre – France.

The British, on the contrary, reckoned that the Americans wished to carry out an operation whose usefulness had always been questionable at the expense of a front where the Germans were unexpectedly standing and inviting defeat well south of the line anticipated. By favour of ULTRA Kesselring's intentions in transcript were to hand on 27th June. In Brooke's eyes they strongly reinforced the sense of a telegram sent to the Americans the day before:

> We are convinced that the Allied forces in the Mediterranean can best assist OVERLORD by completing the destruction of the German forces with which they are now in contact, and by continuing to engage, in maximum strength, all German reinforcements deployed to oppose their advance.[7]

and Brooke wrote that evening:

> We are up against the same trouble again, namely saving
> Alexander from being robbed of troops in order to land in
> Southern France.[8]

To Brooke, it was a straightforward matter of forcing a winning
Commander to break off battle before reaching the objective he
had been instructed to attain, in order to mount a problematical
operation, some weeks later, in another theatre whose situation
might be wholly different when the time came and the troops
arrived. Furthermore, there were now greater prizes to be won on
the Italian front. The Germans had offered a chance, and they
might be smashed before they could withdraw. Kesselring's
intentions were clear – and not only Kesselring's. ULTRA was
having its proper effect not only on operations but on strategy.
Brooke wrote:

> We had now interrupted this all-important message from Hitler
> to Kesselring giving him instructions to fight south of the
> Apennines to cover preparation of a line on the Pisa-Rimini
> alignment. There could now be no argument that the Germans
> were about to retire in front of us in Italy. To my mind it was all-
> important to keep them occupied there at this juncture, and
> prevent withdrawal of force from Italy to Northern France. We
> had the forces deployed ready for action, surely it was better to
> continue employing them there . . .[9]
>
> 'Kesselring's Army,' Brooke wrote in his diary on 28th June, 'is
> now a hostage to political interference with military direction of
> operations, it would be madness to fail to take advantage of it.'

Brooke reckoned the subjection of his enemies to political
interference was a key factor in Allied victory. 'I'd like to meet
Hitler,' he said to a surprised colleague after the war, 'I'd like to
shake his hand. I'd thank him. He was worth forty divisions to
us!'[9a]

To the Americans this was familiar ground. Once again, as they
saw it, the Italian campaign was providing disappointing news of
the battle or advance actually under way, and by offering
chimerical perceptions of the future was frustrating the performance of an agreed programme elsewhere. On 27th June, they
demanded a decision on DRAGOON.

Exchanges were bitter. Churchill took a very personal hand,
reproaching Roosevelt with going back on agreement to reach the
Gothic Line before diverting troops to DRAGOON, and with

failing to recognize the opportunities the situation in Italy offered. It was, in Brooke's eyes, unfortunate that at this point Churchill introduced again the 'Vienna Alternative'. He did not confine himself to arguing for the destruction of Kesselring's forces, with which Brooke agreed. He also pressed the glittering prospects of Alexander's more ambitious proposals; and not only had these been declined at the Anglo-American meeting on 11th June, but they were not supported by Brooke professionally. Brooke, therefore, greatly regretted Churchill's intervention – not least because he thought it inconceivable that at that stage the Americans would agree to consider the 'Vienna Alternative' or find it a persuasive debating point. 'It is very unfortunate,' he noted on 30th June, 'that Alex and Winston ever started this wild scheme about going to Vienna. This has made our task with the Americans an impossible one.'

Roosevelt's reply was as Brooke expected. If only for political reasons no American troops could possibly be committed to operations 'with a Balkan flavour' as Brooke put it, while the issue in Normandy was still in the balance. Roosevelt, with some justice, made the further point that French troops should return to France as liberators. Under DRAGOON they would do so. The President further suggested that Alexander, despite British protestations and even after the withdrawal of DRAGOON forces, would have enough troops to 'chase Kesselring north of Pisa-Rimini and maintain heavy pressure against his Army at the very least to the extent necessary to contain his present force'.[10] The President made clear that he regarded the 'Vienna Alternative' as inconsistent with the agreed strategy for conducting the war, and intrinsically unsound if only because of the time likely to be involved and the difficulty of the terrain.

Brooke counselled that the British should yield gracefully. For him the argument was very definitely not about the 'Vienna Alternative'. It was about DRAGOON's effect on Alexander's chances of smashing Kesselring's forces south of the Gothic Line. Possibly, Brooke thought, Alexander might do better than he surmised with the forces left to him. The stakes were not now such that Anglo-American accord should be placed at further risk. Churchill was becoming ever more irritated by American views, and Brooke found himself frequently acting as an influence for compromise rather than, as previously, for intransigence. It was thus in the case of DRAGOON, and on 1st July he sent a personal signal to Wilson telling him with regret that instructions to launch

DRAGOON were about to be issued. Next day, Wilson's directive was dispatched. Target date for the operation was 15th August. Churchill's delicate reference, in his telegram* also on 1st July, to Stalin's possible 'long-term political view', drew no response.

This was not, however, the end of the matter. The British had formally acquiesced in DRAGOON, but the Prime Minister was unreconciled. Throughout July he used again the familiar arguments of lost opportunities and a possible stalemate in the Mediterranean theatre. He deployed now a third argument – the progress of operations in North West Europe. By the end of July, the German front in Normandy had started to crumble. Soon thereafter there began that great breakout and advance which would bring the Allies within weeks to the Meuse. DRAGOON, Churchill argued, might have had some relevance in helping loosen a North West European front in danger of stabilizing. It could play little or no part in a campaign likely to move too fast for it. He made one last attempt, which Brooke regarded as perhaps strategically desirable but diplomatically impossible of success, to get American agreement to divert the DRAGOON landings from the Mediterranean to Atlantic ports thus, he suggested, bringing the forces embarked into the North West European battle with more dispatch.† It is not clear how the complexities of so radical a switch could have been handled. Unsurprisingly, the Americans were not prepared to contemplate the change of plan. DRAGOON took place on 15th August. A month later the DRAGOON forces, moving north against little opposition, had linked up with the Americans debouching from Normandy across Northern France and passed as a separate Army Group to Eisenhower's command.

Brooke had little stomach for the battle against DRAGOON in its later form, save for a week at the end of June when he thought mounting the operation might force Alexander to give Kesselring the respite he needed. He had little faith in DRAGOON's effectiveness, but nor did he believe in the 'Vienna Alternative'. He thought the latter impracticable, and that any such operation must be too distant in time to be relevant to the DRAGOON debate. He saw the force of the points put by Roosevelt, while not accepting them in their entirety. Whatever the weaknesses of DRAGOON, he thought the matter insufficiently clearcut and

---

* See page 428
† Eisenhower was claimed by Churchill to support this, but disavowed it. Churchill also sought the support of Montgomery, who thought the idea nonsense.[11]

important to be allowed to poison Anglo-American relations as the players took their stations for the closing act of the great drama. 'Alex's wild talk about his advance to Vienna killed all our arguments dead,' he wrote to Wilson on 2nd August. 'However, I do not feel that ANVIL [sic] can do much harm at this stage of the War.'[12]

In all this Brooke may have yielded too easily. DRAGOON has been described as a deplorable mistake, as bad as any made by the Allies in the war.[13] Certainly, the American Fifth Army in Italy lost to DRAGOON some 40% of its strength, and the Allied forces were weakened at a time when Kesselring was reinforced. Certainly the advance to and attack upon the Gothic Line were somewhat delayed. The Italian campaign became temporarily static. Possibilities of a decisive victory, let alone a great strategic advance thereafter, vanished with the Italian summer and as swiftly. But to Brooke there was anyway no possibility of a great strategic advance, while operations lasted. There was a battle to fight in Italy and another, decisive, battle in France and if the Americans were absolutely set upon moving their troops from the former to the latter it was wiser at this stage to make the best of it. In Brooke's view, although not in Churchill's, the best of it was by no means bad. The original plan and Directive to Wilson of 14th June had aimed no further than the Gothic Line, and although the Armies of Italy were robbed of the divisions for DRAGOON before they reached that line, reach it they did and made a preliminary attack at the end of August. Meanwhile Kesselring had been first reinforced by eight German divisions and then had four removed: thus German forces had been on balance increased, those of their opponents diminished. The Italian campaign was still playing its part. But new questions were now again arising of what that part should be; of what, in fact, should be the pattern of operations throughout the Mediterranean. For now the situation throughout the war theatres was moving rapidly. The German Army might be on the point of collapse, the Balkans would be in a highly disturbed state following German disintegration or withdrawal. Strategic opportunities and responsibilities might suddenly appear, and yesterday's appreciation or instruction be wholly inadequate for tomorrow.

On 18th August, Brooke flew to Italy for discussions with Wilson and Alexander. He found relations between them and their respective Headquarters strained, a matter which bothered him.

On 23rd August he stayed with Alexander. The 'Vienna Alternative' was again discussed – this time in connection with a proposal by Alexander to constitute an all-British front in Italy, replacing American divisions by British drawn from France. Brooke characterized the scheme put to him as 'fantastic'. Apart from the shipping and logistic effort required for such a switch, he pointed out forcefully that it would leave the main effort on the principal front in North West Europe to an all-American Army. As to the advance on Vienna which Alexander suggested such an all-British Army of Italy would carry out, Brooke again pointed to the physical difficulties. Nevertheless, he accepted that it was necessary to consider courses of action and lines of advance in case of the melting of resistance. The occupation of Austria had already been approved as one such course. Meanwhile, Alexander was still confronting resistance which had certainly not melted. Orders for the main attack on the Gothic Line were given on 7th September. Churchill, meanwhile, was by no means ready to drop the 'Vienna Alternative'. he told Smuts on 31st August:

> I hope to turn and break the Gothic Line, break into the Po Valley, and ultimately advance by Trieste and the Ljubljana Gap to Vienna.[14]

But to an ever-greater extent this was becoming a final aspiration as victory entered the grasp, a matter of end play rather than a strategic alternative against an active enemy. A great surge of optimism was sweeping the West, and the end did indeed seem near. Turkey broke off diplomatic relations with Germany early in August. The Soviet Union declared war on Bulgaria on 5th September, and Soviet troops entered the country unopposed three days later, followed immediately by Bulgarian capitulation. Rumania had already changed sides and declared war on Germany. In Greece the impending collapse of occupation gave a new edge to British preparations to replace it with British forces, and to forestall a Communist take-over: Wilson was ordered to prepare a division for entry into Greece (Operation MANNA) but only, as he and Brooke made clear to a disappointed Churchill, if the Germans had actually withdrawn. In Yugoslavia there appeared at least a temporary truce between Tito's Partisans and the Royal Government in exile – a truce which the British had no desire to complicate by proposing the entry of British troops. Throughout the Balkans there was disintegration, collapse of those elements which supported the German connection and a good deal of fear of the arrival of the Red Army. For a great Soviet offensive was under way. Soviet troops reached the Rumanian/Yugoslav border on 6th September. Nor was it only the Eastern Front and the Balkans which seemed to promise to the Allies imminent triumph in the field. On 5th September, the Joint Intelligence Committee in London assessed that 'the process of final military defeat leading to the cessation of organized resistance has begun in the West'.[15]

In France throughout June and July, British and American troops had edged their way forward, pushing and straining the desperate German defence that hemmed the Normandy beachheads. Their strength was colossal. The concentration of troops and vehicles was such that much of the combat zone more closely resembled the car parks at a race meeting than a modern battlefield. This was the ultimate reward of the long years of strategic air bombardment, which had driven the Luftwaffe so completely to the defensive that German air power could do little against the congested fields and orchards behind the Allied lines. Now rich in materiel, able to use machines wastefully because confident of replacement, the Allies drove the Germans from hedge to hedge of the close *bocage* country, from the woods and orchards and cornfields of Normandy. They were supported by an immense force of bombers, switched now on occasion to direct support of the land battle.

Outnumbered, mastered in the air, unable to move their reserves where such existed, short of men, ammunition, fuel and every requirement of war, the Germans' front cracked.

The great breakout began on 25th July. In the next six weeks the Allies smashed their way out from the beachhead, trapped and destroyed a large part of the German Army in the West at Falaise on 20th August, entered Paris on the 25th and Brussels on 3rd September. The Armies raced across the map like the Germans in 1940. They had not yet, however, secured any major ports beyond those won in the initial Normandy attack. The Germans had left strong garrisons in the Channel ports* and on the north bank of the Scheldt, controlling the approach to Antwerp. The huge tonnages required to support modern mobile forces – and made all the huger by the lavish attitudes permitted – were still laboriously carried from Normandy and through the funnels of the earliest captured ports or beaches.

* Ostend, however, fell on 8th September, and Le Havre on the 12th.

THE ALLIED BREAKOUT FROM NORMANDY   AUGUST - SEPTEMBER 1944

On 29th August Brooke visited Montgomery in France, and had a long talk about what he called the 'recent crisis with Eisenhower'. This was the first phase of the so-called 'broad front versus narrow thrust' controversy. Montgomery, who until this time was still commanding all land forces of the Allies in the West, believed that the logistic situation as well as the principle of concentration demanded one main effort with prime support behind it. German forces in the West appeared on the point of collapse. They could well rally, with that resilience and genius for organization and improvisation they had so often shown; but they would only rally if they were given respite. To keep up the pressure it was, in Montgomery's view, essential to use a sword rather than a bludgeon, to pierce rather than batter. He suggested concentrating the whole of 21st Army Group (British and Canadian Armies) together with the 12th Army Group (Bradley's Americans) as a great Allied left wing which would advance north-east with the right flank north of the Ardennes, the left directed on the Pas de Calais and Antwerp. Such a massive operation could hardly be described as a 'narrow' thrust as its detractors have done. Montgomery called it a punch. It should, he said, be under one commander, and the implication was that it should be Montgomery. Eisenhower, on the other hand, believed that several parallel advances, with the ability to exploit whichever showed most promise, were within the capacity of his forces. Furthermore, Eisenhower reckoned that logistics must limit any advance, so that the deep thrust into Germany to end the war must wait on an improvement in the supply situation, whether made on one front or several. At the same time (1st September) Eisenhower assumed from Montgomery personal control of all land forces. He appreciated that only he could hold the balance between what were not only competing strategies but competing national and political pressures: for the Americans were far from content that there should be a liberation of Western Europe largely led, as the public would see it, by Montgomery but with massive American resources withal.

This issue did not come to the Combined Chiefs of Staff. It was for the time being resolved by Eisenhower himself, and by a certain compromise in which the American First Army operated north of the Ardennes on Montgomery's right although not under his orders. Brooke was content with any compromise which Eisenhower and Montgomery could work out. His judgement favoured Montgomery, but 'This may work', he noted.[16] At the time and on the spot the German Army in the West appeared on the point of collapse, and to the troops themselves calculations of port capacity and of supply seemed less significant in slowing victorious advance than did limited road and bridge space in relation to the vast number of motor and tracked vehicles competing for it. There were, however, major obstacles ahead. To those with larger maps than the leading Tank Commanders the Rhine and its major tributaries still remained to be crossed.

One dreadful event clouded the summer sky, a portent of the future. On 1st August, the Polish Home Army, the Patriotic Underground movement commanded by General Bor-Komorowski, began the tragic insurrection against the German occupation forces known as the Warsaw Rising. It had been made clear to the Poles that large-scale help from the West would be out of the question. But now the Red Army had advanced rapidly in Eastern Poland. Their troops had reached the south-east suburbs of Warsaw, and this not only provided military opportunity by the pressure it placed on the German front but also produced a powerful political incentive to face the advancing Russians with a national Polish authority which had itself freed its capital, inflicted a defeat upon the invader and emphasized its legitimacy with the sword.

What followed is well known. In spite of their proximity, and their position as the only Ally with the forces and facilities to help the Poles, the Soviet Command declined to give help, and prevented others from so doing. A plea from Churchill to Stalin was met by chilling indifference. The German counter-measures in Warsaw were savage and remorseless. No Russian move disturbed them. The Warsaw Rising was characterized by Moscow as 'the work of adventurers'. A request to Stalin for Western aircraft to use Russian airfields for recovery, after dropping supplies to the Poles, was rejected categorically. Some supply sorties, latterly only with Polish aircraft, flew from Italy, whence the round-trip could be made. The Rising was crushed by the beginning of October. The Polish Home Army, containing as it did the most courageous and patriotic elements, was destroyed. A large proportion – about one-fifth – of the population of Warsaw, men, women and children, were killed. Russian complacency with German butchery of the flower of occupied Poland is easily understood. It served the same purpose as their own murder of thousands of Poland's leaders at Katyn some years before.

439

Brooke watched events with sympathy and gloom. General Sosnokowski, who had taken over command from Sikorski, saw him on 9th August to plead for physical assistance. He asked for an Airborne Brigade to be sent to Warsaw. Brooke had nothing to give, and well understood Sosnokowski's despair.

If the end was near in Europe, how soon could forces be moved from Europe to the Far East? Brooke wrote to Wavell on 3rd August. They were frequent and warm correspondents:

> With the situation they now are in in Russia and Italy the Germans have nowhere to turn to for reinforcements and have inadequate forces on each front. It cannot last very much longer and I doubt whether they last to the end of the year.[17]

He wrote again on 31st August. First, there came some sympathy at the Viceroy's handling by the Prime Minister.

> You are right about the PM's feelings towards you! But you are not the only one in such a privileged position! He spends his time being furious with me and we have had a few royal battles of late. However, they blow over and we move on a calm sea occasionally between storms. But it is a wearing life and I am ageing fast under it. It is going to be a race whether I or the War collapse first.

And then:

> I am very doubtful whether the Germans can now put up any form of co-ordinated defence in France. The difficulty now is to judge the moment when we are justified in withdrawing forces from Europe to move to Asia. I believe the moment is very near . . .[18]

In the war against Japan, the Japanese had strongly reinforced Burma in response to the successful offensive of Fourteenth Army at Imphal. Far to the east Stilwell's forces on 3rd August took Myitkina, whose airfield was a critical factor in increasing air supply to China. Now Mountbatten advanced two alternative plans. One (CHAMPION, later CAPITAL) was a direct advance towards the Irawaddy. The Chiefs of Staff regarded this as unsatisfactory – a continuation of what they described as a 'long-drawn out struggle in the jungles and swamps against an enemy who has superior lines of communication to those which we possess'. The second plan (VANGUARD, later DRACULA) involved an airborne assault on Rangoon, followed by the opening of that port to seaborne follow-up and supply. The British Chiefs of Staff thought DRACULA practicable and desirable and Brooke wrote of it as the obvious thing to do. It would, they reckoned, cut Japanese communications to Burma, and set a term to the Burmese commitment, which they found increasingly onerous – and now likely to be increasingly irrelevant to the ultimate defeat of Japan. The British, therefore, put DRACULA to their American colleagues. It does not seem, however, that Brooke was whole-heartedly opposed to CAPITAL, although its disadvantages were described to the Americans on 18th August. He considered that DRACULA would need to be accompanied by at least some operations in Upper Burma, and had difficulty with Churchill over it.

> 'He was quite impossible to argue with,' he wrote afterwards, 'as for instance his idea of taking Rangoon and leaving the rest of Burma, when the main idea of the Burma campaign was to re-open communications through Burma to China.'[19]

Nevertheless, Brooke assented to a message saying that the British felt bound to reject CAPITAL.

The Americans did not favour DRACULA, although they were content that planning should proceed, recognizing that resources for it would depend upon the situation in Europe. As for CAPITAL they took, predictably, a contrary view to the British. To the Americans, CAPITAL was consistent with what they regarded as the prime function of operations in Burma – to help open a land route to China. They recommended that CAPITAL should be set in hand also, always provided that it did not draw forces from Europe or the Pacific. As to British proposals for participation in the Pacific itself, the matter was left for resolution at the forthcoming OCTAGON Conference to start on 12th September at Quebec.

Some of Brooke's sharpest exchanges with Churchill came during this time, when their efforts were so soon to be rewarded by victory. He was tired and often intolerant. The stimulus of dangerous crisis was gone. Churchill, too, was increasingly unstable, less the rock of defiance he had so magnificently been, more the erratic dilettante of genius he always had it in him to be. Brooke's patience was again at breaking point, and his comments often were uncompromising and harsh. He wrote on 6th July, after what he called 'a frightful meeting with Winston . . . quite the worst we have had with him':

441

He began to abuse Monty . . . I flared up and asked him if he could not trust his generals for five minutes instead of continuously abusing them and belittling them. He said that he never did any such thing. I then reminded him that during two whole Monday Cabinets, in front of a large gathering of Ministers, he had torn Alexander to pieces . . . He was furious with me . . .

Cunningham wrote of the same meeting:

Meeting started unprofitably by Brooke calling him to order for undermining Generals in command by his criticisms at Cabinet meetings. This obviously hurt him badly. But he was in a terrible mood.[20]

The note recurred often.

'I feel that we have now reached the stage,' Brooke wrote on 15th August 'where for the good of the nation and for the good of his own reputation it would be a Godsend if he could disappear out of public life. He has probably done more for this country than any other human being has ever done, his reputation has reached its climax, it would be a tragedy to blemish such a past by foolish actions during an inevitable decline which has set in during the last year. Personally, I have found him almost impossible to work with of late and I am filled with apprehension as to where he may lead us next.'

And an entry of 10th September (the day of arrival in Canada for the OCTAGON Conference) which he later described as 'unnecessarily hard':

Three quarters of the population of the world imagine that Winston Churchill is one of the strategists of history, a second Marlborough, and the other quarter have no conception of what a public menace he is, and has been throughout this war . . . Without him England was lost for a certainty . . . with him England has been on the verge of disaster time and again . . . Never have I admired and despised a man simultaneously to the same extent.

It was indeed unnecessarily hard, and showed Brooke at his most intolerant. Two days earlier Churchill had commented on the Intelligence appreciation already noticed* in a memorandum which showed little sign of failing faculties. Brooke had told him that while the Chiefs of Staff reckoned that German resistance might be prolonged into the winter they were favourably

---

* On page 436.

influenced by the optimism of the JIC Report. Churchill remained sceptical. The last four paragraphs of his memorandum deserve reproduction in full:

> 3. One can already foresee the probability of a lull in the magnificent advances we have made. General Patton's Army is heavily engaged on the line Metz-Nancy. Field-Marshal Montgomery has explained his misgivings as to General Eisenhower's future plan. It is difficult to see how the 21st Army Group can advance in force to the German frontier until it has cleared up the stubborn resistance at the Channel ports and dealt with the Germans to the North at Walcheren and to the North of Antwerp.
>
> 4. On the other side, the Russians have made no progress into East Prussia and the Germans have re-established contact with their armies cut off in the Baltic States. The turning-over of Rumania to the Allied cause has given the Russians a great advantage and it may well be that they will enter Belgrade and Budapest, and possibly Vienna, before the Western Allies succeed in piercing the Siegfried Line. However desirable militarily such a Russian incursion may be, its political effect upon Central and Southern Europe may be formidable in the last degree.
>
> 5. It would have been of great value had this report been accompanied by a table, showing the disposition of the various German Divisions as they are now and as they are expected to be at the end of September.
>
> 6. No one can tell what the future may bring forth. Will the Allies be able to advance in strength through the Siegfried Line into Germany during September, or will their forces be so limited by supply conditions and the lack of ports as to enable the Germans to consolidate on the Siegfried Line? Will they withdraw from Italy, in which case they will greatly strengthen their internal position? Will they be able to draw on their forces, at one time estimated at between 25 and 35 divisions, in the Baltic States? The fortifying and consolidating effect of a stand on the frontier of the native soil should not be under-rated. It is at least as likely that Hitler will be fighting on the 1st January as that he will collapse before then. If he does collapse before then the reasons will be political rather than purely military.[21]

Such a prescient and practical note should be set in the balance against Brooke's less temperate strictures. There is no doubt which way the balance tips; Churchill wins at all points. The fundamental trouble, the factor which again and again drove

Brooke to anger and consequent injustices was Churchill's fascination with the details of operational planning and his determination to act as if he were himself a Chiefs of Staff Committee personified. For this he was unsuited by temperament and by knowledge. The British system of running the war, however efficient, enabled him freely to indulge this particular appetite. It has been said that in the Second World War there was none of that dissension between military leaders and politicians which marked some of the Government's relations with the Services in the First World War. To a large extent this is true, and much of the truth derives from system, above all from the fact that Churchill held at once the offices of Prime Minister and Minister of Defence, as well as from the unity which the Chiefs of Staff Committee enabled the Military to achieve; so that strategic matters could be argued between the constitutionally responsible Minister (who could then, as Prime Minister, 'carry' the Cabinet in so far as that is possible) and the Chiefs of Staff whose prior deliberations had resolved professional difficulties. The system produced great strength in the direction of the war effort. It was very effective vis-à-vis Government, Parliament and the country. It did not, however, eliminate tensions. By largely concentrating them within the closed circle of Churchill and his professional advisers it made them private, albeit as fierce as anything in the earlier war. It is certain that this was preferable; but it was, for the chief participants, at least as exhausting and as exasperating.

The second Quebec Conference – OCTAGON – has been called the last of the great Anglo-American Conferences which formulated the grand strategy. It was held, as so often such Conferences had been held before, in the shadow of fast moving events on the war fronts. The possibility of imminent victory was in the air. The British and Americans had to be ready for that victory, but had so to take station that if it were deferred they would not be caught off balance. The voyage in *Queen Mary* was particularly trying to the tempers of all concerned, and Brooke wrote afterwards that he had the 'bitterest memories' of the journey. Churchill was suspicious that the British and American Chiefs of Staff would make common cause against him, particularly in the matter of the war against Japan where, although for different reasons, both teams of Chiefs opposed Churchill's determination to place emphasis on an Indian Ocean strategy. Two days out from Halifax, Nova Scotia, Churchill told the Chiefs of

Staff that there was no single point on which he and they seemed in agreement.[22] It was an unpromising start. The first two days of the Conference were as disorganized in terms of a co-ordinated British position as any could remember. A harmonious meeting was held between British and American Chiefs of Staff on 12th September, in which the latter agreed to leave American divisions in Italy until the end of Alexander's current offensive – agreed as the attainment of the Po Valley. However the following day, in a plenary meeting, Churchill suggested, as the two main objectives of Allied arms, an advance on Vienna and the capture of Singapore. 'Neither of them in our plans,' commented Brooke ruefully.

The day was probably saved by Admiral King. He showed himself thoroughly intransigent in the matter of a British fleet co-operating in the Pacific. He did not want it, and said so. Since this, at least, was by now a common objective of Churchill and the British Chiefs, King's bad-tempered opposition had useful effect in restoring some unity to the British side. It was one of those occasions which provoked even the friendly and urbane Portal to reflect that the American aim sometimes seemed to be to cripple the British Empire regardless of all else.[23] Even a suspicion of this was, of course, sufficient to bring Churchill charging to his Chiefs of Staff's support. King was reluctant to see the British play any major part in the war against Japan, and both Churchill and the British Chiefs of Staff were determined that they should. The American President and other Chiefs were sympathetic to the British viewpoint. King was isolated. There emerged a general agreement on prosecution of the war against Japan, a subject which dominated the Conference. The campaign in Burma should be pressed. CAPITAL, in four phases, should start in November; DRACULA – the capture of Rangoon – be executed if possible in March 1945, before the next monsoon. A British fleet should participate in 'main operations against Japan in the Pacific'. The 'planning date' for the defeat of Japan was agreed to be eighteen months after the defeat of Germany. In Italy the Americans were happy that the present offensive should reach its objectives, and that thereafter the plan to advance towards Vienna after victory in Italy should be developed – as a plan. Wilson was sent a Directive accordingly. Brooke acknowledged the advantages, particularly the political advantages, of this, contenting himself with saying that he did not visualize it as a possibility during the winter.

In North West Europe the zones of occupation of Germany were agreed as between British and Americans. Eisenhower's plans for the next steps on the Western Front were approved, involving a two-thrust advance towards Germany, and the essential capture of the port of Antwerp. The greater potential of the northern thrust into Germany was accepted by both sides and written into the proceedings.

While, however, this general endorsement was being given to Eisenhower's plans they were already being to some extent modified. Mongtomery did not believe in a two-thrust or 'broad front' strategy. He believed that the logistic situation meant that only one main thrust line should be developed, and produced his plans for an advance in the north combined with airborne assault. This became Operation MARKET GARDEN, the ill-fated attempt to seize Arnhem and a bridgehead across the Rhine in Holland. The merits, risks, and misadventures of the operation have been frequently recounted. All was over at Arnhem by 27th September. To Brooke, in retrospect, it was one of Montgomery's few mistakes. Brooke reckoned that Antwerp should have been brought into service and the Scheldt cleared before all else. The failure of MARKET GARDEN dispelled hopes of victory in Europe in 1944, and this inevitably delayed movement of resources to the Far East. In particular, it made inevitable the delay of DRACULA until after the 1945 monsoon.

After some agreeable days fishing in Quebec Province, Brooke flew back by Clipper from Canada on 21st September. For a Conference which had started with such depression and lack of harmony OCTAGON had gone well. At the beginning even the patient Ismay had handed his resignation – promptly refused – to the Prime Minister. Ill-temper and misunderstandings flourished. At the conclusion, Brooke and Portal, while fishing, received a typical Churchill signal: 'Please let me know how many captives were taken by land and air forces respectively . . .'* The sun was out again.

Brooke was only in London for a few days after his return from OCTAGON and before setting out again on his travels. At the beginning of October he visited Eisenhower at his Headquarters at Versailles. Considering the strictures passed by Brooke before and later it is good to read his warm appreciation of the Supreme Commander in the aftermath of MARKET GARDEN. 'Ike nobly took all blame on himself,' Brooke recorded on 5th October, 'as he

---

* The catch was 250.

MARKET GARDEN ~ SEPTEMBER 1944.   VERITABLE ~ FEBRUARY 1945.

had approved Monty's suggestion to operate on Arnhem.' The atmosphere was friendly, and Brooke noted how well Eisenhower ran the Conference. It was a lull before storms.

Two days later Brooke took off from England for Russia. Another meeting was essential, now that it was clear the war would last into 1945. The Western Powers were anxious to discover Soviet intentions on the Eastern Front, and if possible co-ordinate their own. Brooke flew by way of Naples and Cairo, reaching Moscow on 9th October. The Moscow Conference of October 1944 – TOLSTOY – was the most personally agreeable which Brooke attended. Much of the work to be done was political, and many meetings were held at which he was not required. So far from feeling excluded he was delighted. He spent as much time sightseeing as possible. Junior members of the delegation found him the most relaxed of companions, always asking whether there was not some party to attend.[24] He found the necessary banquets with their insincere speeches as tedious as ever, but he was taken frequently to the opera which he loved – the magnificent Moscow opera, with stage nearly as large as an auditorium, and with productions of a lavishness unknown for years to wartime London. Most important, the Russians were, for the first time, forthcoming about their own plans. It was the first meeting since the invasion of France. British and American Armies now hammered at the western gates of Germany. Perhaps in consequence, the Soviet military chiefs, following Stalin's personal example, were described by Brooke as friendly and communicative. They explained their intentions accurately in what Brooke called 'a really satisfactory discussion on the whole of the German Eastern front, including future moves. The whole was on a most open and free basis of discussion.'[25]

Furthermore the Russians were prepared now to discuss the war against Japan, which they intended to join immediately Germany was defeated. Brooke was once again impressed by Stalin's complete mastery:

> I asked them whether they considered that they could maintain 60 divisions and their strategic air forces over their Trans-Siberian railway. Antonov replied in the affirmative, but he was corrected by Stalin who thought this was doubtful. The railway had a capacity of 36 pairs of trains per day, but of these only 26 could be counted on for military traffic, and the capacity of each train was from 600 to 700 tons. He [Stalin] considered that assistance from America across the Pacific would be required.[26]

Stalin, wrote Brooke later, 'displayed astounding knowledge of technical railway details, had read past history of fighting in that theatre, and from this knowledge drew very sound deductions'.[27]

To Wavell he wrote afterwards how, 'On our last trip . . . Stalin could not have been more pleasant and more free in his talks and his plans.'[28]

The final great converging moves towards Hitler's Reich from West and East were agreed.

Hitherto, the British Chiefs of Staff had not been particularly concerned with the aims of the war. Theirs had been a clear and sufficiently testing task – to avoid defeat in one of the greatest crises of national history, and to win every campaign in which their forces were engaged. A 'Post Hostilities Planning Staff' had been set up to report on immediate post-war problems, but it attended primarily to practical matters – zones of occupation, the garrisons required for liberated or occupied territories, the administrative problems likely to meet Commanders in situations where authority had collapsed or fled – rather than matters of high policy. Now, however, the expectation of an early end to hostilities concentrated minds wonderfully. The object of any war, it has been said, is a better peace. Unless the conduct of operations is directed towards ultimate political ends war becomes simply an exercise in slaughter, offering to the strategist the chance to 'win' – but without coherent object thereafter.

When they considered the course of operations, particularly in Asia, the British were daily reminded of a fact of life which they had to accept but resented: and none more so than Churchill. The United States, because of its military effort and its wealth, was a dominant partner; and an ally by no means friendly to the British Empire. As they came to terms with their near-exclusion from the Pacific theatre, and as they perceived Roosevelt's hostility to the legacy of the European Empires in the Far East, the British Chiefs of Staff ruefully recognized that they had fought for an Empire whose future was in serious doubt. The end of that Empire would mark the end of Britain as a World Power. They struggled in the twilight.

In Europe, too, it now seemed that the fruits of victory would be sour. In the Second World War the political leaders of the Western Powers have been understandably criticized for their lack of long-term policy. Roosevelt and (although to a lesser extent)

449

Churchill were victims of their own illusions or rhetoric. Victory –
particularly after the slogan of 'unconditional surrender' was
coined – became an end in itself. The sort of world which that
victory might produce unless conscious steps were taken was, until
a late hour, shifted to a separate and cloudy part of the collective
mind. It was easier to look on the war in primarily military terms;
and easier still, when political questions of the future forced
themselves upon official attention, to believe that all would
ultimately be well between wartime Allies.

Only Stalin was consistently realistic. He knew what he
wanted. But although Soviet conduct and reputation might give
cause for disquiet the concord produced by comradeship in arms
would, in the view of many, tame the Russian appetite. Thus ran
the cradle-song with which the West sang itself to sleep. Such
views, held with obduracy by some in high places, were without
justification whether with hindsight or at the time. To destroy
Nazism and the horrors it imposed was admirable but it was not
enough. Russian seizure of the Baltic States, the Russians'
brutality in occupied Poland before they were themselves invaded,
and every facet of Soviet doctrine and history made clear that
Central Europe, if occupied by a victorious Red Army, would be
subjected to enforced Bolshevization and atrocity. The praise-
worthy object of destroying Nazism carried an obligation to
consider what would replace it. The obligation had so far been only
cursorily or ineptly discharged. The political element in strategy –
what Clausewitz called 'the intelligent factor of which war is but
the instrument' – seemed entrusted all too often to those who
either ignored it or got it wholly wrong. This absence of policy
was of considerable assistance to Nazi propagandists who
represented the Western Allies, not without plausibility, as bent
on the indiscriminate destruction of Germany regardless of its
politics. The ultimate beneficiary, of course, was the Soviet
Union.

Nevertheless, the Western democracies, even where they were
not blind, had an intractable political problem. Popular support
for the war and for the Allies, once aroused, had an inertial force.
Governments were subject to political pressures of an uninformed
but still potent kind – everybody admired Russian fortitude, and
many contrived to deceive themselves or others that Russia was
some sort of working man's Paradise.

The Chiefs of Staff, who had the experience of trying to work
with the Soviet leaders and do business with them, were by no

means blind, but their tasks had been military, and strategic only in the military sense.

Brooke had a long conversation with the Secretary of State for War on 27th July 1944. He recorded it that night in his diary:

> Should Germany be dismembered or gradually converted to an Ally to meet the Russian threat of twenty years hence? I support the latter and feel certain that we must from now onwards regard Germany in a very different light. Germany is no longer the dominating power in Europe – Russia is. She has . . . vast resources and cannot fail to become the main threat in fifteen years from now.
>
> Therefore, foster Germany, gradually build her up and bring her into a Federation of Western Europe.

The matter was now in the military as well as political arena. Of a paper discussed with the Foreign Secretary himself on 2nd October, Brooke wrote:

> We had considered the possible future, and more distant threat to our security in the shape of an aggressive Russia. Apparently, the FO could not admit that Russia might some day become unfriendly.[29]

With what seemed a paradox, the Chiefs of Staff suspicion of 'an aggressive Russia' led them towards supporting the 'dismemberment' of Germany on the basis that at least the western parts of that country would then be held clear of Soviet control. 'The dismemberment of Germany,' their paper had concluded, 'would be to our strategic advantage,

a. as a measure for the prevention of German rearmament and renewed aggression

b. as an insurance against the possibility of an eventually hostile USSR.'[30]

Brooke wrote after the war that this paper created a considerable stir in the Foreign Office: 'We might even have been asked to withdraw this paper had we not asked for an interview with Anthony Eden who approved our outlook.'[31]

Eden minuted 'This is very bad' on the signed paper, so his approval was probably of parts of the Chiefs of Staff reasoning rather than all.

In general, their attitude found no support in the Foreign Office. The paper was re-written, while the Chiefs were away in Moscow, under new direction by the Vice-Chiefs:

It was desirable that the new paper should be written in such a way as to leave no room for *the misconception which had apparently arisen** in connection with the previous paper that our principal aim in advocating dismemberment was to secure the North West part of Germany as our Ally against any future threat to our security.[32]

A recantation! But the battle and the illusions ebbed and flowed until events imposed their own grim solution. The Prime Minister shared the Chiefs of Staff concern with ever fewer inhibitions, in contrast to the Foreign Office, or much of it. This concern unfortunately led Churchill up some paths – such as The 'Vienna Alternative' – where Brooke as professional military adviser could not conscientiously follow. But the mood was now taking form which would dominate the future, and as so often it was the Prime Minister who articulated it. 'We shall finish,' Churchill would sometimes growl, 'with the barbarians in the heart of Europe.'[33]

* Author's italics.

CHAPTER XVIII

End Game

BROOKE WAS SAID BY SOME, both at the time and after the war, not to get on well with the Americans. This is questionable. There are plenty of quotations in a contrary sense. Nevertheless, one of the sharpest points of contention between Brooke and his American colleagues came now. It did not concern grand strategy. The strategic arguments were virtually over. It concerned operations in one theatre – North West Europe – and it assumed the form of a serious criticism, made by the British and disputed by the Americans, of Eisenhower. Since the criticism concerned the conduct of land operations Brooke was the principal party. It is a rare example of an attempt by Brooke to interfere in the business of a Field Commander, when no factors outside his theatre of command were involved. The Commander, an Allied Supreme Commander, was American. The majority of forces under his command were American. The matter could only become international in flavour, and combative at that.

After the Allied breakout from Normandy the enemy on the Western Front was in complete disarray. Operations took the form of a pursuit, limited by logistics and road capacity rather than opposition. In September and October the Germans staged a remarkable recovery. The German age for recruitment to the Army was lowered to sixteen. The nation was scoured for men and boys. By a 'crash programme' of organization and training, the experienced staffs of the Wehrmacht were somehow able to create and to command a substantial number of additional divisions. These divisions, many of them formed of the very young, the old and the sick, were of uneven quality, but they fought under the iron discipline of the German Army and they fought for their homeland. They sufficed to impose a check. The Allies' pursuit flagged after the great victories of August and early September. Their own logistic situation was overstrained. There was a certain sense of the war being won, a slackening of that tempo absolutely necessary to the exploitation phase of war. Euphoria bred delay.

The Allies had three Army Groups on the Western Front. From the north were 21st (British-Canadian) Army Group under Montgomery; 12th (United States) Army Group under General Omar Bradley; and 6th (United States-French) Army Group under General J. L. Devers. The co-ordination of these three and the direction of land operations were in the hands of Eisenhower, who now directly commanded all land forces. Montgomery had commanded them for the invasion and early battles; and as the pursuit from Normandy developed, Montgomery had preached with vehemence the need to concentrate force and channel logistic support. An attempt to advance on too broad a front would, he predicted, lead to inadequate strength at the point of decision.

Then in mid-September Montgomery had been permitted to launch MARKET GARDEN, the attempt to seize the Rhine bridge at Arnhem, cross the Lower Rhine and outflank the German defensive barrier in the far north. To support the operation advances elsewhere were checked. The decision was Eisenhower's and he loyally accepted all responsibility thereafter. It was a decision which seemed to signify acceptance by Eisenhower of Montgomery's thesis – concentration on one thrust, that thrust to be in the north. In fact, their minds were not close. Montgomery reckoned that after crossing the Lower Rhine his forces could swing east and south, past and towards the Ruhr, a grand strategic objective. His eyes were on the Ruhr, the Rhine an obstacle to leap on the way. Eisenhower appeared sometimes to share this view. On 20th September he wrote to Montgomery:

> The envelopment of the Ruhr from the north by 21st Army Group supported by First (US) Army is *the main effort of the present phase of operations**[1]

But at other times Eisenhower wrote and spoke of MARKET GARDEN as a strictly limited operation, at most to secure a bridgehead across the Rhine as part of operations to close up to it. Eisenhower was ambivalent.

MARKET GARDEN failed. German resistance stiffened everywhere. The front stabilized. Throughout October and November Montgomery returned with growing insistence to his central theme – that the Allies were not strong enough to dissipate their offensive effort in a number of uncoordinated advances. There had to be, he put to Eisenhower, a new masterplan, a fresh concept. It was necessary to define the most significant geographic

* Author's italics.

objective, and to concentrate all available force in a main thrust to seize it. All other operations should be relegated to a subsidiary role. Montgomery suggested that the Ruhr was the obvious strategic objective. Deprived of the Ruhr industries, Germany could no longer make war. On the point of principle, Montgomery felt even more strongly about concentration in the attritional battles now likely before the Rhine could be reached than he had when arguing for concentration in pursuit. He suggested that the Ruhr could and should thereafter be 'pinched out' by two great attacks across the Rhine, north and south of the Ruhr itself, both launched from north of the Ardennes. This had been Montgomery's concept for MARKET GARDEN and it remained valid. Now, however, there must be deliberate, phased operations to close up to the Rhine in the first place.

Eisenhower, in September orders, had placed emphasis on the operations in the north. Indeed, he had been directed to do so by the Combined Chiefs of Staff. But, unlike Montgomery, he did not believe that the principle of concentration on one point of effort, which he had accepted for MARKET GARDEN, applied to subsequent conditions and a possible stalemate. Instead, Eisenhower believed, there had to be a general 'tidying up' of the front, elimination of German bridgeheads west of the Meuse and – more importantly – revolutionary improvement in the logistic situation which only the clearance of the Scheldt and a general pause would produce. There was, therefore, a 'push' in all Army Group sectors, a punch in none. In Montgomery's view little was being accomplished at relatively high cost.

Eisenhower received Montgomery's admonitions with a good deal of irritation. He also strongly resented a favourite, additional idea of Montgomery's – that there should again be a separate land force Commander to run the land battle, subordinate to Eisenhower and freeing him for what Brooke called 'the true duties of a Supreme Commander'[2] – including those myriad and complex quasi-political and civil administrative questions with which the Supreme Commander, operating in recently liberated territories, had necessarily to cope. Eisenhower regarded this suggestion as criticism of his capacity. Montgomery kept Brooke informed of his exchanges with Eisenhower. Brooke agreed that there was inadequate 'grip'. 'I doubt,' he noted in his diary on 8th November, 'whether we will even reach the Rhine.' But although Brooke agreed with Montgomery's criticism of the command arrangements he recognized that this would be no easy matter to change.

'The Americans,' he wrote on 8th November, 'with pre-
ponderating strength of land and air forces very naturally claim
the privilege of deciding how the forces are to be organized and
commanded.'

Furthermore, Brooke suspected a strong element of egotism in
Montgomery's strictures. He wrote the following day:

> I had a talk with Montgomery before he returned to France. He
> still goes on harping over the system of command in France and
> the fact that the war is being prolonged. He has got this on the
> brain as it affects his own personal position, and he cannot put up
> with not being the sole controller of land operations.

Nevertheless, Brooke realized that it was exasperating for
Montgomery, a soldier of brilliant professional instincts, to see
what he reckoned to be opportunities lost, lives squandered, a
campaign awry. Brooke accompanied Churchill to France on 10th
November and visited the French First Army under General de
Lattre de Tassigny, about to undertake an attack as part of
Eisenhower's 'broad front' push towards the Rhine, in Alsace. He
regarded the operations as futile, an opinion shared by the French.
Brooke did not dispute Eisenhower's general thesis about the value
of reaching the Rhine on a broad front. He objected to how it was
being attempted. His heart was with Montgomery. But he knew
how easy it was to exacerbate matters. When Montgomery wrote to
him on 17th November that the situation was going from bad to
worse – 'I think we are drifting into dangerous waters'[3] – Brooke
firmly advised him not to approach Eisenhower again, and to
remain silent. Montgomery then suggested another option to put
to Eisenhower – that the command should be organized in two
rather than three groups, with Montgomery as one of the two,
commanding all forces north of the Ardennes; the suggestion of a
'land commander' subordinate to Eisenhower to be dropped.
Brooke thought little of this idea. He told Montgomery that if
Eisenhower's co-ordination of three Army Groups was unsatisfactory he did not see why he should do particularly better
with two. Furthermore:

> You are asking for the command of the Northern Group. You
> must remember that you have repeatedly affirmed that the
> northern line of advance is the one and only one that has any
> chance of success . . . You are, therefore, proposing yourself for
> the one and only front that can play any major part in the
> Western offensive on Germany. Have you considered whether

you are likely to be very acceptable in American eyes for this Command?[4]

Next, Brooke discussed an option whereby Bradley might command all land forces, the latter divided into two groups as suggested by Montgomery. With an overall American land force commander, Brooke thought that the Americans might – just – accept Montgomery as Commander of the Northern Group. Montgomery was authorized to discuss this with Eisenhower and did so on 28th November. Montgomery thought the meeting went well. He followed it up with a letter setting out his opinions with brusque clarity. The meeting had, in fact, gone far from well. Eisenhower agreed with little, and was incensed by Montgomery's letter. He held a meeting with his Army Group Commanders on 7th December, and from Montgomery's point of view this went no better. Eisenhower did not believe in a major operation to 'pinch out' the Ruhr with maximum strength under one Commander. Instead, he believed that the Ruhr should be by-passed to the north by Montgomery; that Bradley's left-hand Army – Ninth Army – should assist this operation, under Montgomery's command; that Bradley's 12th Army Group should have two tasks, to threaten the southern Ruhr as a support to Montgomery, and to advance with its right wing – Third Army – on the axis Frankfurt-Kassel. This concept gave Montgomery a formidable Anglo-American force, but in his view it still failed to meet the principle of concentration. Bradley, he suggested, would still be looking two ways; and if the northern thrust were to be made sufficiently strong, the southern could not possibly succeed. Brooke was by now fully behind Montgomery. His objection was to a second, southern, deep thrust which must inevitably draw off resources and for which there was not sufficient strength overall. It was, Brooke agreed with Montgomery, essential to regard the Ruhr as a strategic objective, and to operate against it in such strength that the Germans would be reluctantly but inevitably drawn into a battle of manoeuvre in Northern Germany for which they had neither the fuel nor the residual armoured strength. Brooke believed that the difference of opinion was fundamental. He sought Churchill. Eisenhower was invited to London to present his views. He came on 12th December.

At this meeting Brooke launched a vigorous criticism of Eisenhower's conduct of operations. It was the first time this had taken place, face to face. The cards were on the table. Eisenhower

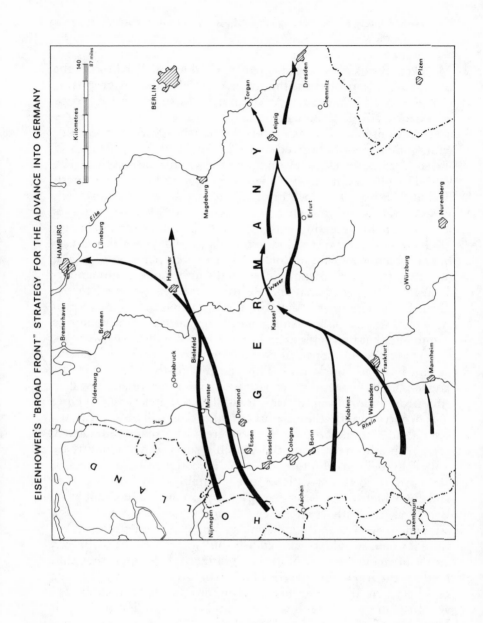

EISENHOWER'S "BROAD FRONT" STRATEGY FOR THE ADVANCE INTO GERMANY

explained his plan for two parallel advances after the Rhine was crossed, an event he did not anticipate before May 1945. This date, Eisenhower later explained, derived from faulty information about the Rhine itself. It appalled British Ministers. Brooke then attacked. He said that the Supreme Commander's plan violated the principle of concentration, and that neglect of this principle had led to the disappointments of the last two months. Eisenhower's forces were inadequate for the two thrusts he proposed; neither would be decisive. Churchill did not engage in debate on Brooke's side. He treated Eisenhower as a guest. He did not wish to present to the Supreme Commander an antagonistic and united British front, although next day he accepted Brooke's thesis. 'At 6 p.m. meeting with Eisenhower,' Brooke wrote to Benita a few hours later, 'lasting till 8 p.m. during which I disagreed with all Ike's plans. Dinner at 10 Downing Street during which I continued to disagree with Ike's plans.'[5]

Ministers now became alarmed. The Chiefs of Staff were instructed to produce a paper about the problems of the Western Front for Cabinet consideration. They did so on 18th December, and recommended that the Americans should be asked to join in requesting from Eisenhower his detailed plans for the winter and spring – a necessary preliminary to taking the matter to the crunch, since the Supreme Commander was responsible to the Combined Chiefs of Staff. But that day Eisenhower gave orders to cancel an attack in the Saar – one of those isolated operations which Brooke and Montgomery so criticized. It was cancelled because the astonishing had happened. The German Army in the west had attacked. Three Armies, with twenty-eight divisions, twelve of them Panzer, were rumbling towards the Meuse through the Ardennes.

The German December offensive, brainchild of the Führer but conducted with considerable skill, shook the Western Allies. They had been preparing for and arguing about the final battles which should complete the destruction of the German Army. They had been engaged in a slow push towards the Rhine. Suddenly, they had to meet a counter-attack, violent, concentrated and directed through country where only four American divisions lay in the attacker's path.

The attack came at a critical moment in the controversy about Eisenhower's conduct of the campaign. It was inevitable that the initial disasters should be taken as supporting evidence for views formed in a different context. Brooke considered that the German

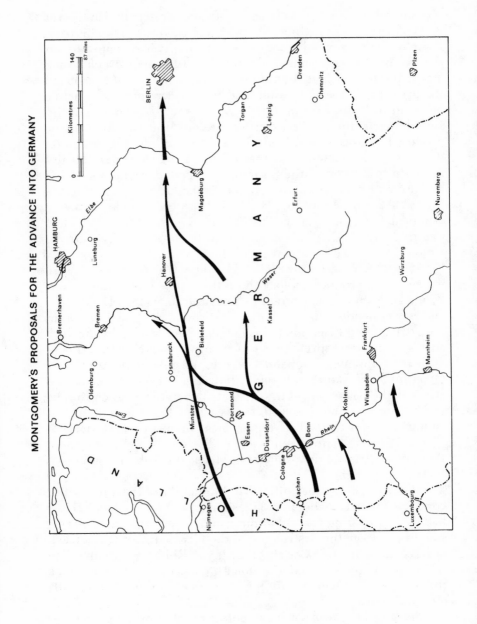

MONTGOMERY'S PROPOSALS FOR THE ADVANCE INTO GERMANY

success was largely due to Eisenhower's faulty disposition 'spread out on a long front with no adequate reserves'.[6] He also reckoned that events showed the weakness of the command organization. He was relieved when Montgomery was given command of all forces, American and British, north of the German penetration, thus producing for the defensive battle the sort of concentration of force in one pair of hands which Brooke and Montgomery had sought for the offensive. There were obvious diplomatic hazards here, and Brooke saw them clear. He warned Montgomery to avoid an attempt to show that events had justified his previous arguments. He wrote to him on 21st December:

> Events and enemy action have forced on Eisenhower the setting up of a more satisfactory system of command. I feel it is most important that you should not even in the slightest degree appear to rub this undoubted fact in.[7]

But he had gloomily to record in his diary two days later:

> It looks to me as if Monty, with his usual lack of tact, has been rubbing into Ike the results of not having listened to Monty's advice.

Not only had Eisenhower's command arrangements been temporarily and perforce changed, but (according to Montgomery's impressions) his strategic concept. Eisenhower now apparently agreed that only one-large scale offensive would be possible – when the Allies passed to the offensive once again.

Brooke's recorded criticism of Eisenhower in connection with the Ardennes offensive was twofold. First, that his deployment had been faulty, with too equal a strength along the front, with inadequate weight in the north and no reserves. A disposition anyway wrong for the offensive had, he said, positively invited the sort of blow it received. He wrote to Wavell: 'The American policy of always attacking everywhere and never having any reserves provided very tempting situations for the enemy.'[8] It is, of course, true that, had Eisenhower held more strength in the north of his front for the future offensive, there would have been more divisions closer to hand when the Germans attacked. It is equally true that to help the situation in the Ardennes Eisenhower had to plan to move divisions from 6th Army Group in the south, and order them to shorten their line by withdrawing in Alsace thus provoking a crisis with the French Government. Clearly, too, had a much stronger northern wing also possessed a strong and

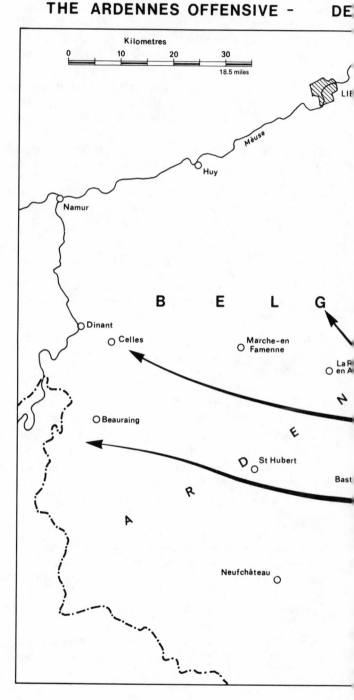

1944

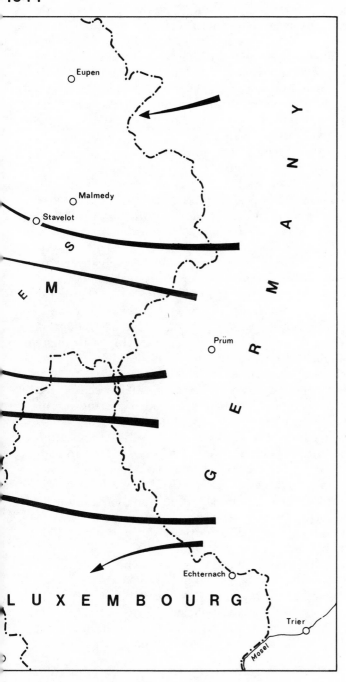

Eupen

Malmedy

Stavelot

S

E M

Prüm

M

E

R

G

LUXEMBOURG

Echternach

Trier

Mosel

uncommitted reserve, that reserve would have been in hand to intervene in the Ardennes battle. None of this would necessarily have led to more defensive strength actually in the Ardennes. Such arguments are speculative, and Brooke kept them for his diary. Had the Allied dispositions been different as to balance who can say that the Germans would have struck as and where they did? The criticisms of Eisenhower's deployment related to the offensive battles he was planning to conduct. Whether they can have direct bearing on Allied unreadiness for the German attack in December 1944 is doubtful.

Brooke's second criticism related to command. He felt instant relief when the scope of Montgomery's responsibilities was widened at the height of the battle. He was surely right. The skill, energy and confidence Montgomery immediately displayed were characteristic. Yet Brooke spoke of 'a more satisfactory command system' as if to imply that the previous system had contributed to the initial disasters. This is harder to demonstrate. An offensive is often most successful when directed – often deliberately directed – at the junction of two commands, thus posing to the defence an immediate problem of co-ordination and decision. In December 1944, the entire German *Schwerpunkt* was within the area of Bradley's Army Group. In theory the defensive and counter-offensive measures should have been simpler to co-ordinate because of this fact. Of course, the Army Group had a wedge driven into it which made command the harder, but it is not self-evident that, if all forces north of the Ardennes had been placed under one command before the battle instead of during it, the German task would have been more difficult.

Thus far theory. In fact, it was surely the practical application of theory and the nature of personalities which counted in Brooke's assessment. His strictures are not entirely convincing in logic; there is a touch of *post hoc ergo propter hoc*. But Brooke did not trust Eisenhower's ability to 'grip' such a situation, and that opinion lay at the heart of his criticism of Eisenhower's arrangements. He did not trust his will to concentrate decisive power for an offensive. He did not believe in his ability to override his Army Group and Army Commanders where necessary, nor in his consistency of decision. Conversely, he trusted completely Montgomery's ability to get control of events and turn them towards success. For, from the start, Brooke was sure that if the German offensive failed, the whole situation in the west would be transformed. 'There is no doubt,' he wrote on 18th December, 'that this might turn out to be a heaven sent opportunity.' Brooke's criticisms of Eisenhower over the Ardennes battle were based in part on military principle, but to a larger extent on personality and on Brooke's disagreement with Eisenhower's appreciation and plans for the campaign as a whole.

By Christmas, the situation was stabilized, Allied counter-attacks in preparation. The dogged courage of the American fighting man played the chief part in the matter. Now the British returned to the charge on the whole question of the 'broad front', the 'second thrust' after the Rhine had been crossed. They took up with their American colleagues the business left unfinished with Eisenhower after the London meeting of 12th December. On 3rd January, Brooke accompanied Churchill to visit Eisenhower at Versailles, a visit overshadowed by the powerfully voiced objections of de Gaulle (who was present) to Eisenhower's proposed withdrawal in the area of Strasbourg in order to free American divisions for the north. Brooke also visited Montgomery. He had reassuring news of the course of operations, but nothing he heard or saw altered his critical view of Eisenhower's strategy. Thus on 6th January, the British Chiefs of Staff sent to Washington the memorandum they had presented to Churchill on 18th December. In it they proposed a meeting of the Combined Chiefs of Staff, and requested that Eisenhower's appreciation and plan for future offensive operations be obtained and discussed at that meeting. The memorandum ended starkly:

> The combined Chiefs of Staff can then fully satisfy themselves that the basic essentials of our strategy in the west are fulfilled, namely:
>
> (a) All available offensive power must be allotted to the Northern front, – i.e. from about Prum northwards; and
>
> (b) One man must have power of operational control and co-ordination of the ground forces employed on this front.[9]

The question was to be discussed at or en route to a summit meeting ARGONAUT to be held at the beginning of February at Yalta in the Crimea.

Two weeks later Eisenhower produced what the Combined Chiefs required. The battle of the Ardennes was over. The Germans were withdrawing. Eisenhower set out in his plan the three phases to be undertaken in 1945 in order to finish the war. First, the Rhine had to be reached; second, it had to be crossed;

third, Germany had to be invaded thereafter. With regard to the first phase Eisenhower said that the Rhine must be reached – 'closed' – throughout its length. Only then could it provide a defensive obstacle for those sectors in which the Allies would need to stand on the defensive, while the offensive was conducted elsewhere. Not unnaturally, Eisenhower was concerned that the enemy should not be left with any possibility of counterstroke, and he therefore believed that no major enemy bridgeheads should be left west of the Rhine. Eisenhower reckoned it was so much easier to defend the Rhine than to contain the enemy west of it, that to attain the whole of the west bank would liberate a further mass of divisions for the offensive. He proposed to conduct methodical operations first in the north and then in the south to reach the Rhine.

The crossing operation, Eisenhower's second phase, was clearly linked to his concept for the campaign thereafter, and this was the contentious issue. Eisenhower unrepentantly proposed two main lines of advance east of the Rhine – one north of the Ruhr across the North German plain, and one on the axis Frankfurt-Kassel. He therefore proposed to seize two main bridgeheads across the Rhine from which these advances could be launched, one north and one south; one in Montgomery's sector, one in Bradley's. Yet Eisenhower gave an interpretation to this concept which largely met British anxieties. He said that he planned to deploy north of the Ruhr the maximum force which could be maintained (estimated at some 35 divisions), and he said that the southern advance was not intended to compete with the northern but to provide an alternative if the main punch were held up. On the command organization Eisenhower conceded nothing – yet the northern advance, while not the sole advance, would be under unified command.

Brooke described this as an 'awful' appreciation.[10] There was a good deal of American indignation at what they regarded as gratuitous mistrust of Eisenhower's ability, yet when the Combined Chiefs discussed the question at Malta on 1st February, on their way to Yalta, they accepted the plan. Brooke refused formally to endorse the appreciation, since he still believed that a southern advance might weaken the decisive character of the northern punch. He thought it unsound. But Eisenhower's emphasis and interpretation (which only became clear at the Malta meeting) meant that in practice, if not in theory, the two sides to the debate were not far apart. The Americans reckoned that

Eisenhower had been vindicated. In a closed session and with forthright speaking they made clear to the British that the Supreme Commander had the Joint Chiefs of Staff unequivocally behind him. Brooke and his colleagues had no alternative but to bow, since they reckoned that the practical application of Eisenhower's plans, with their emphasis on the north, gave them most of the substance of what they wanted. Furthermore, the condition of the German Army meant that liberties could probably be taken with impunity. The matter was closed.

Since the British position in December had been that a second, southern line of advance was beyond the power of Eisenhower's forces, and that it would inevitably weaken to a dangerous extent the advance in the north, was their acceptance of the 'parallel advance' in February a recantation? Or made without a whole heart? Certainly Brooke continued for a while to be concerned that strength might be dissipated. But the crossing of the Rhine and subsequent operations were entirely successful, and it may reasonably be asked what he was fussing about, why he doubted. He has been reported as watching the Rhine crossing with Eisenhower in March 1945 and saying to him —[11] 'I am sorry if my fear of dispersed effort added to your burden . . . Thank God you stuck by your guns.' Did this imply contrition? It is unlikely. In his 'Notes on my Life' Brooke quoted this alleged remark to Eisenhower and simply commented that he must have been misquoted. He reported in his own diary on 25th March:

> He [Eisenhower] also wanted to know whether I agreed with his present plans for pushing in the south for Frankfurt and Kassel. I told him that with the Germans crumbling as they are the whole situation is now altered from the time of our previous discussion. Evidently the Boche is cracking and what we want now is to push him relentlessly, wherever we can, until he crumples. In the present condition, we certainly have the necessary strength for a double envelopment strategy, which I did not consider as applicable when he was still in a position to resist strongly.

The crux lay in the overall war situation. When Brooke first seriously questioned Eisenhower's policy, in the autumn of 1944, the German Army had shown remarkable powers of recovery. Brooke was too wary a huntsman to take chances with a wounded beast. The principles of war still applied, and in his view Eisenhower's concept breached them. Then the situation changed. The Red Army offensives brought Soviet power to the heart of the

Reich. The strategic air offensive of the Western Allies, its effect intensified by technical improvements and a coherent Anglo-American targeting policy, had reached a mighty pitch of accuracy and destructive power. Lastly, the German December offensive itself had fatally weakened the Wehrmacht.

When the Rhine was ultimately crossed the German Army in the west was capable of little more than brave but uncoordinated defence of defensible ground, with virtually no capacity for manoeuvre. The arguments which Brooke advanced in 1944 against Eisenhower's strategy are not diminished by the fact that the final act took place against a different background. Nor is his welcome of an opportunist general advance in March evidence of inconsistency or change of heart. Brooke was always empirical. He formed his views on the situation as it was at the time.

On balance, Brooke was probably right to criticize an absence of firmness in Eisenhower's command, which showed itself in a certain lack of will to impose solutions, and too great a readiness to change his priorities under pressure. The effect was an operational concept which may have been faulty, and might have failed if put to the test – none can say, because the German Ardennes offensive transformed the situation. The matter must remain speculative. The Supreme Commander's problems were great. His capacity to attract loyalty from men of many nationalities was also great. He governed by consent. It might have been possible to devise more impeccable solutions, yet simultaneously produce a Command simmering with resentment. After the war was over, Eisenhower was presented with the Freedom of the City of London. On 12th June 1945 Brooke wrote in his diary:

> Ike made a wonderful speech and impressed all hearers . . . I had never realized that Ike was as big a man until I heard his performance today.

Brooke disagreed with Eisenhower on professional grounds. He proceeded from that disagreement to underrate him as a soldier and a man. Eisenhower was trusted by those who served him. In war that is a very great deal. And he won.

In the Mediterranean theatre Brooke's problem was, as ever, how much strength should be kept there in order to pin down German divisions: what, if any, opportunities the theatre offered outside the Italian front; and how to deal with the political dimension, which so often demanded military means.

Brooke visited Italy on his way to Moscow in October and again on his return. By now he, hitherto so stout a champion of the Mediterranean strategy, was as much a 'Westerner' as Marshall had been. 'I did not consider that there was much future now left in this theatre,' he wrote in his diary on 3rd October. The situation in Italy was inevitably one of slow progress. The Allies had removed forces as a matter of deliberate policy. They had mounted Operation DRAGOON in Southern France. They had relegated Italy to a secondary place in their calculations. An attack on the Gothic Line in September had yielded no decisive results. Alexander described some of his divisions, both British and American, as being 'pretty well whacked'.[11a] It was unsurprising that after a quick conference with Alexander in Naples on 8th October Brooke noted:

> Alex is getting stuck in the Apennines with tired forces and cannot spare any for amphibious operations . . . It is therefore hard to estimate what the situation will be when Alex can find forces, namely in February.[12]

For the Allies had again turned to the idea of amphibious operations – against Istria, against Trieste – to threaten the enemy's deep flank. The problems here were twofold. First, the situation in the Balkans and particularly in Yugoslavia was so volatile that there could be no certainty of welcome for the Allies, even if an operation thither were judged operationally sound. Second, logistics and the need to rest tired troops meant that there must be fresh forces and some delay, probably until the first week in February. Even so, the availability of troops would depend upon events in Greece – for the situation in Greece was beginning to come to the boil.

The prospect of delay in any Mediterranean amphibious operation irritated the Prime Minister. He always liked the imaginative and the instant, and he resented the logistic factors which had put brakes on every such enterprise from the beginning. His comment was refreshingly typical:

> One of the absurd things in all the plans submitted by AFHQ [Mediterranean] is the idea that if they move in February they will be in time to affect anything. In the three months which they say must elapse before they are capable of movement, the whole of Yugoslavia will be cleared of the Germans, who will either have been overwhelmed or made their escape to the north. Very likely this will take place in six weeks. The Yugoslavs will then

occupy Trieste, Fiume and other towns which they claim. So what will be the need of an expedition and all the landing craft and so on? The days of these slow-moving, heavy footed methods are over, but we still cling to them with disastrous consequences.[13]

Brooke had been less enamoured than Churchill of the possibilities amphibious operations could anyway present, more aware of their difficulties. He believed that the right course was to stand on the strategic defensive in Italy, while keeping up as much pressure on Kesselring as resources permitted; to be prepared to exploit any changed situation; but to transfer as many divisions to North West Europe as might be done without enabling the Germans easily to do the same. With this in mind a new Directive to the Mediterranean theatre was prepared.

Meanwhile, there were major changes of command. On 5th November, Field-Marshal Sir John Dill died in the United States. It was a sad blow to Brooke who loved him, and valued his counsel as pearl beyond price in this most 'allied' of all historic struggles. 'His loss is quite irreparable,' Brooke wrote that evening, 'he is irreplaceable in Washington.' But Dill had to be replaced, *pace* Churchill who at first disputed this necessity. Wilson, Supreme Commander of the Mediterranean theatre, was selected. He had been appointed Field-Marshal on 3rd November. Now he was instructed to hand over his command to Alexander. The American General Mark Clark was appointed to command the Allied Armies in Italy, renamed 15th Army Group, in Alexander's place. These changes were the subject of sustained and acrimonious argument between Churchill and the Chiefs of Staff, as well as an exchange of telegrams between Churchill and Alexander which the former hoped Brooke would not see. They provide an example of the sort of problems which sometimes arose between Prime Minister and CIGS, and for that reason the exchanges are set out in more detail in Appendix III. Brooke won his point but it took time. Such matters were not petty or procedural. If they miscarried, the ultimate effect would be felt in the field, the cost counted in soldiers' lives.

The Italian front continued to play its role in the grand design, and the Germans withdrew no forces from it to take part in the Ardennes offensive. At Malta, in early February, in the same phase of their meeting in which they approved Eisenhower's instructions, the Combined Chiefs of Staff agreed their policy for the Mediterranean theatre. Alexander was to keep up pressure on the

German forces in Italy, and to 'remain prepared to take immediate advantage of any weakening or withdrawal of the German forces'.[14] He was not to undertake amphibious operations except for the introduction of 'light forces through liberated Dalmatian ports in order to harass and exert pressure and attrition on the Germans withdrawing in the Balkans', as an earlier Directive instructed him; now phrased as 'such minor operations on the Eastern shores of the Adriatic as your resources allow'.[15] The Mediterranean theatre was to find five divisions to be transferred to North West Europe – three Canadian and two British.

This move was forecast to take two and a half months, an estimate which also – understandably – enraged Churchill. He asked what purpose the troops would be likely to serve in April, in view of the rate matters were now likely to move in North West Europe, and how such a protracted exercise could justify removing them from Italy where they could continue to fight. The estimate was reduced to six weeks, but the point was yet another demonstration of a fact Churchill had tended to resist throughout the war – the extreme slowness of strategic mobility based on sea power in modern times, compared to movement on land. The central position of Germany and her satellites gave them interior lines of communication and a power of concentration which only the Russians could match. It also gave them a major degree of self-sufficiency. Only land blockade by invasion and conquest, or bombardment by ever increasing air power, could stem the movement of necessities to the Reich. The Western Powers, in contrast, were dependent upon the sea for their existence.

Alexander's instructions had referred to the Germans withdrawing in the Balkans. On 7th October 1944, the German High Command gave orders for the total evacuation of Greece. This created for the Allies an opportunity to interfere with this withdrawal, whether by more ambitious operations in the Adriatic or by the continued advance of the Russian Armies from the east. The former were refused for lack of time and resources. The latter might yet take place. But meanwhile the situation in Greece itself demanded attention.

It was rightly feared by the British, who held the direct responsibility on behalf of the Allies for the Mediterranean theatre, that chaos and revolution would follow German evacuation of Greece. The British had had prolonged dealings with the various factions, both in Greece and among the Greeks in exile. They had prepared a plan – Operation MANNA – to introduce British troops immediately into Greece when the Germans withdrew. Some sort of external disciplined force would be needed in Greece, it was believed, to see fair play. Churchill, indeed, had wished for British troops to go to Greece to assist in driving the Germans out; in fact, he had told the Greeks in August that this would occur. It was a prospect immediately scouted by Brooke, who made plain throughout that any British presence must follow not precede the enemy's departure.

Brooke was very concerned by MANNA. It was a 'political' operation in the sense that it had a direct political aim unconnected to the war against Germany – and his strictures on that account were not particularly far-sighted. Wilson's letters to him from the Mediterranean had shown little awareness of the dangers to Greece from Communism, and had placed emphasis on purely military considerations – on which faction could most harm the Germans – with little thought to their motives or to the consequences.[16] But Brooke's predominant concern was that British troops, who could ill be spared, would be 'sucked in' to a situation which would end by needing many times the first estimate of force requirement. In this he was right; but he was wrong to grumble at it and with hindsight he acknowledged the fact. 'All my worst forebodings coming true,' he wrote in his diary on 3rd December – 'Anthony Eden had originally asked for 5000 soldiers. I had told him that he would end by wanting some four divisions which he denied flatly.'

Communist guerrilla forces (ELAS) had occupied many towns in Greece when the Germans withdrew. It was soon clear that the Communists would next try to seize power throughout the country by force. British reinforcement was vital. A British Commander, General Scobie, was appointed. At the beginning of December he had on his hands a full-scale armed Communist revolt. The British Embassy itself was under siege.

Throughout this episode the United States authorities behaved with ostentatious neutrality. The British had to act independently and vigorously. Opinion in the United States was ill-informed and hostile, and Roosevelt tacked with the domestic wind. Admiral King, without reference to the Combined Chiefs of Staff or the Allied Supreme Commander, forbade American naval vessels to carry men and supplies to Greece. Meanwhile within that country a constitutional impasse and a military deadlock – marked by savage atrocities – were only broken by the arrival on

End Game

Christmas Day of Churchill himself, accompanied by Eden. When he left, a Regent, Archbishop Damaskinos, had been accepted. A ceasefire was ultimately agreed. The semblance of peace was achieved. The scars went deep and under threats of civil war of varying intensity British troops remained in Greece in some force until October 1949. Brooke was right to fear an unlimited commitment in both size and time. He was mistaken, and later admitted it, in making the commitment a matter for complaint at his Government. Churchill saved Greece.

The war in South East Asia had taken a turn for the better. One of Brooke's rare references in his diary to the struggle against Japan was on 17th January:

> We had a specially long COS meeting as we had Boy Browning*
> back from Kandy, having been sent by Dickie to plead his case
> for more transport aircraft for Burma operations.
> There is no doubt that the operations there have taken quite a
> different turn, and there is now just a possibility of actually
> taking Rangoon from the north. This is due to the Japanese
> beginning to crumple up and to be demoralized.
> One of our difficulties arises through the fact that the
> transport aircraft belong to the Americans and that the
> reconquest of lower Burma does not interest them at all. All they
> want is north Burma and the air route and pipe-line and Ledo
> road to China.

The entry reflected accurately an American preoccupation. Their forces in SEAC were there to help China, and certainly not to be drawn into enterprises more attuned (in American eyes) to the reconquest of the British Empire than the defeat of Japan. It also reflected a remarkable and brilliant development.

Operation CAPITAL, approved by the Combined Chiefs of Staff at the OCTAGON Conference in September, had four phases, of which the first was planned to be complete by the end of January and to take Slim's Fourteenth Army to the River Chindwin, in Central Burma; while the second phase was scheduled to continue until mid-March, and to gain ground which would enable subsequent operations to take place in the plain of Mandalay. These operations in Central Burma were to be accompanied by a continuing southern thrust in Arakan in West Burma, and by attacks in the north aimed to open the Burma road. All were crucially dependent on air transport.

* General Browning was now Chief of Staff to Mountbatten.

Yet South East Asia Command did very much better than this. Offensive operations were continued in monsoon conditions through September and October. Fourteenth Army cleared the Imphal Plain and reached the Chindwin by the end of November rather than January. Swift successes thereafter brought them to the Irawaddy. Operations went well in Arakan. On the northern front, the Burma road was open by 22nd January. Slim now prepared a highly imaginative plan for the crossing of the Irawaddy and the capture of Mandalay itself. The Allies' battle was well ahead of programme. CAPITAL was overtaken by victorious events.

Meanwhile, however, operations were nearly brought to a standstill by an American demand for transport aircraft to be transferred to China, where a Japanese offensive had caused some alarm. The British Chiefs of Staff immediately remonstrated with their colleagues in Washington. They received partial satisfaction, and by transferring some resources of their own they enabled Mountbatten's operations to continue. But it was necessary to agree with the Americans a new basis for planning. The Allies had a clear initiative in Burma. Their battles were going fast and well. The enemy was hesitant and unsettled. It was essential, in the British view, to take advantage of the situation and to give Mountbatten a new and more ambitious Directive. The forthcoming meetings of the Combined Chiefs of Staff in Malta, on the journey to the Crimea, would give an opportunity to discuss it. The British produced a draft. In it Mountbatten would simply be directed to liberate Burma at the earliest possible date.

When this was discussed at the ARGONAUT Conference in Malta the Americans did not dispute the aim. They did, however, enter a strong reservation over the means. In Mountbatten's Command were American troops, Chinese divisions and massive American resources, particularly of transport aircraft. In the American view the first task of these was the direct support of China. Mountbatten might use them – but if they were to be needed in China at any time they would have to go. The Americans accepted a formula whereby, if the removal of such resources placed current operations of Mountbatten in jeopardy (in the opinion of the British Chiefs of Staff), the matter should be discussed by the Combined Chiefs. With this the British had to be content. It provided an uncertain basis for planning, whose first requirement is some assurance of specific resources. But it enabled a new Directive, albeit with this reservation, to be sent to

Mountbatten. ARGONAUT marked the beginning of a new chapter in the war against Japan.

Brooke and his colleagues arrived for the second phase of the ARGONAUT Conference, at Yalta in the Crimea, on 3rd February. The preliminary meetings with the Americans in Malta had been occasionally acrimonious when Eisenhower's strategy was discussed, or Montgomery's personality; but they had cleared the air. The next steps in North West Europe and Italy, and a new aim for the campaign in South East Asia had all been agreed. When the Combined Chiefs of Staff next met in plenary session Germany would have been defeated. Yalta was the last major consultation before that defeat.

The very word 'Yalta' has become a symbol of surrender by the Western Powers of much they had – or should have – fought the war to obtain or protect for others: liberty, democracy, self-determination, decency, justice. 'Yalta' has become a synonym for betrayal, whether of those parts of Europe now irremediably to be assigned to Soviet power; or of the wretched multitudes conscripted by Germany and now to be transferred to Soviet authority and likely death, although surrendered to the Western Allies; or of ideals themselves. 'Yalta' has come to stand for Western naïvety or indifference, and Soviet brutality and cunning.

This was not the Yalta Brooke knew in those February days. The Russians were certainly in a mood of elation. Taking advantage of the obvious German preoccupation with their Ardennes battles, the Red Army had mounted a great offensive in January. In three weeks they had advanced nearly three hundred miles towards the heart of the Reich. They were now only forty miles from Berlin, and at the gates of Budapest. The Russians knew that Germany was beaten. Their object was to dominate as much of Europe as possible thereafter. Military operations, whether their own or their Western Allies', should be conducted to that end. They meant to incorporate the eastern half of Poland and the Baltic Republics into the Soviet Union, part of their bargain with Hitler in 1939. They intended to ignore Britain's and America's pledges to Poland and to subordinate the rest of that suffering country to Communist rule. Similar satellite status would be imposed on Rumania, Bulgaria, Hungary, Albania, Yugoslavia; with Czechoslovakia, and perhaps other morsels, marked for possible subversion and swallowing once Soviet military power was established in the heart of an impotent and demoralized Europe.

None of this, sensed beneath the surface rather than explicit, was surprising to Brooke. As early as the Quebec Conference of 1943 he had speculated on the dangers of the Russians seizing the opportunity of war to further international Communism.[17] When the Chiefs of Staff had voiced such concern, they had been greeted with Ministerial indignation. Yet in spite of their confidence and their ambitions, the Russians knew that the dying German beast could still bite. They had far outrun their supplies, and had halted their Armies to consolidate. They were anxious that the Western Powers should continue to press the Germans in the west until they themselves could resume a final and decisive offensive later in the year. Stalin, Brooke noted, thought that fighting might last well into the summer.[18] The Yalta Conference – ARGONAUT – was not particularly informative on the military side (Brooke said that the Western Allies learned little they did not know before), but it went easily and pleasantly. Brooke recorded that Stalin 'was full of fun and good humour' – as well he might be. The Allied zones of occupation of Germany and Austria after victory were agreed. Some co-ordination of plans was necessary, notably of air policy to prevent Allies bombing each other, but although there were difficulties there was little contention. There was Anglo-American harmony, the irritations of Malta now past. Marshall gave the briefing for the Western side and Brooke contented himself with saying that General Marshall had fully covered the war situation and he had nothing to add. Only one curious note was struck. Stalin raised with Churchill and Eden the possibility of troops from Italy advancing through Northern Yugoslavia and operating on the left flank of the Red Army, a contingency which his earlier efforts had undoubtedly been aimed to frustrate. By February such an operation was inconceivable within the next few months unless the German defence in Italy crumbled. Stalin's motive was unclear. Perhaps he was seeking confirmation that no advance towards the Danube would, in fact, occur before he could get there himself.

There was then the question of Japan. The President and Prime Minister were advised that Japan might not be defeated until eighteen months after victory over Germany. This naturally stimulated the need to ensure a full Soviet part in the war against Japan as soon as the German war was over. The conditions for this were set out in a secret agreement signed by Roosevelt, Churchill and Stalin. It provided for the entry of the Soviet Union into the war 'two or three months' after Germany surrendered.[19] Important concessions by Japan to Russia – Stalin's price – were agreed for enforcement after final victory.

Thus the grim associations of 'Yalta' had little impact on Brooke. He had no particular difficulties at the Conference in terms of professional problems or Allied relationships.

> 'The Military side of the Yalta Conference,' he wrote later to Wavell, 'was a great success and we settled all we wanted. I am not quite so certain whether we shall find that the result of the political conference turns out to be all that was hoped for.'[20]

The dangers of Soviet policy in the future, the ruthlessness of Soviet conduct and the naïvety of the American President were entirely familiar to him. He did not record them as phenomena connected in particular with Yalta. They were the depressing currency of much Allied commerce, and had for a long time so been. He spent some fascinating hours at Sebastopol studying the battlefields of the Crimean War as well as the scenes of recent fighting. On 10th February he left Russia for the last time, and 24 hours later reached home.

In one important respect the Conference had been tragic for Brooke. On 2nd February, while in Malta on his way to the Crimea, he had learned that his Aide-de-Camp, Captain Barney Charlesworth, had been killed in an air crash near Pantelleria. Charlesworth had been his constant companion through most of the years of war. He had looked after and shared the flat in Westminster Gardens. 'He was,' wrote Brooke that evening, 'always cheerful and in good humour no matter how unpleasant situations were.' Charlesworth had been the soul of discretion as well as efficiency, the perfect confidant. Brooke missed him grievously. In his place he brought an old friend into his front office on 26th February, Brigadier 'Rollie' Charrington, a comrade from Staff College days, a Hampshire neighbour. Charrington, a 12th Lancer, had been a General and had commanded a brigade in Greece in the earlier years of war. Ill health had stopped his career in its tracks. He accepted reversion to the temporary rank of Lieutenant-Colonel in order to serve Brooke, and was his constant companion until the end.

ARGONAUT confirmed for Mountbatten a new and simple aim for

his campaign. He was to reconquer Burma. His command organization was changed. He now had one Land Force Commander, General Leese, for the whole command. Leese had commanded Eighth Army in Italy after Montgomery and had handed over to General McCreery. Two operations had been previously approved by the Combined Chiefs of Staff – CAPITAL and DRACULA (a very resource-hungry operation) of which the first had been overtaken by events and the second might be no longer necessary if Fourteenth Army could reach Rangoon overland without it.

DRACULA presented problems. Mountbatten was directed to follow the reconquest of Burma by the liberation of Malaya and Singapore. He gave orders to capture Rangoon before the monsoon – interpreted as before 1st June. The subsequent tasks would demand an advanced base for amphibious operations. It was decided that to seize Phuket Island, west of the Kra Isthmus in Southern Siam, would best meet this need. But unless it were to be unacceptably deferred, to carry out this intermediate operation would draw off essential forces from DRACULA – the amphibious operation against Rangoon. Both could not be done. Slim, therefore, suggested a solely overland advance on Rangoon by Fourteenth Army. The battles for Meiktila and Mandalay were at their height. Slim believed that he could win them, manoeuvre the Japanese out of Central Burma and advance direct on Rangoon. On 23rd February this was agreed. DRACULA was cancelled. Slim's operations across the Irawaddy, EXTENDED CAPITAL, were a complete success.

By the end of March the Japanese, after one vigorous counter-attack, were in full retreat. At that moment there was another crisis over air transport – a crisis which could have placed at risk not only Slim's operations, which were now fast becoming a triumphant march on Rangoon, but the actual maintenance of the Armies at the point they had reached. The British Chiefs of Staff strongly supported Mountbatten's representations. Churchill wired personally to Marshall and was reassured. Provided that Mountbatten's programme – to capture Rangoon before 1st June – was not delayed the Americans would do nothing to upset it. The strain on air transport was, however, acute. It was vital, by whatever means, to seize and open Rangoon for supply. In spite of the later need to operate towards Malaya with amphibious forces, delay in that direction was now accepted, and a reduced form of DRACULA was quickly organized at the end of March, in order to

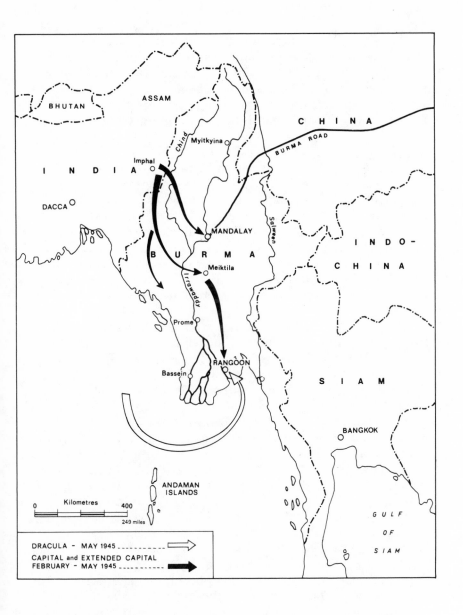

BHUTAN

ASSAM

C H I N A

Chind

Myitkyina

BURMA ROAD

Imphal

I N D I A

DACCA

Salween

MANDALAY

B U R M A

Meiktila

I N D O -
C H I N A

Irrawaddy

Prome

RANGOON

Bassein

S I A M

BANGKOK

ANDAMAN
ISLANDS

Kilometres

0   400

249 miles

G U L F

O F

S I A M

DRACULA – MAY 1945 ....

CAPITAL and EXTENDED CAPITAL
FEBRUARY – MAY 1945 ....

assist Fourteenth Army by a complementary assault on Rangoon from the sea.

Thus, in the end, DRACULA took place, just ahead of a victorious culmination to Slim's campaign. Brooke's next diary entry about Burma was a laconic note on 2nd May: 'Meanwhile in Burma the landings south of Rangoon are going well.' The Japanese had already fled. The first part of the ARGONAUT Directive was already obeyed. Burma was purged of the enemy.

ARGONAUT produced no dissension between British and Americans over the Mediterranean. In Italy Alexander had been told to contain the enemy by exerting sufficient pressure, but to take advantage of any change in the situation. He and Clark, his Army Group Commander, interpreted this instruction broadly and boldly. They believed the Allies could mount an offensive with their existing resources. As in Burma the land forces of the combatants were about equal. There were 27 enemy divisions of which 23 were German, and 17 larger divisions on the Allied side. The critical disparity was in the air. The Allies had virtual air supremacy.

But Alexander also knew that there was a strong movement on the German side in favour of surrender. SS General Wolff, responsible for administration in Italy, put out feelers at the beginning of March. Meetings were arranged in Switzerland. These dragged on – Wolff's authority was suspect. 'It does not seem very plausible,' Brooke noted on 10th March, and on the 14th, 'the whole business looks pretty fishy.' These soundings indicated, however, that a strong push might bring down the house of cards, although the German soldier was fighting as well as ever.

Alexander's object was to break out from the Apennines and into the Po Valley and Northern Italy where Allied superior mobility and air power could be decisive. The British Chiefs of Staff agreed that the last two divisions of the five demanded from the Mediterranean for Eisenhower's command need not be withdrawn, in view of the situation in Greece with its contingent effect on the forces in Italy. On 27th March Brooke wrote in his diary – 'Situation is now such that one additional division in the Western Front won't make much difference.'

Thus between 9th and 14th April, towards and across the River Reno running from the Apeninnes east into the Adriatic, 15th Army Group attacked. They were completely successful. By 20th April the front was at last clear of the Apennines. Operating on a two-Army front the Allies crossed the Po on the 22nd and the Adige on 27th April. These battles coincided with a general uprising in Northern Italy. Mussolini was shot by Partisans on 28th April.

At the same time, the Yugoslav Partisans were achieving notable successes against the fifteen German and twelve Croatian divisions still in Yugoslavia. A major Partisan offensive had been launched on 20th March. Arms and ammunition in quantity had been reaching them through the liberated Dalmatian ports. By the end of April the Partisans under Tito had occupied Istria and the port of Fiume, and were in the suburbs of Trieste.

On 24th April two representatives from General Von Vietinghoff, Commander of the German forces in Italy, reached Switzerland with authority to negotiate an unconditional surrender. Alexander was given permission to receive them, and they reported to his Headquarters in Italy. On the 28th all German forces surrendered, the capitulation to be effective on 2nd May, the same day the Allies entered Rangoon.

Brooke had, from the beginning, been the strongest proponent of a Mediterranean strategy. Without his skilful advocacy, there might have been no Italian campaign at all. From first to last that campaign fulfilled its purpose. Throughout the years since the landings at Salerno (apart from a short period in 1944), the Germans had always maintained more fighting formations in Italy than the Allies, and this continued until the end. In a country well-suited to defence, against an enemy whose flanks rested on the sea, the Allies had nevertheless attacked continuously. They pinned the Germans to the peninsula by fighting. That was their task. They were, additionally and finally, completely victorious in the field.

On 8th February, two days before the end of ARGONAUT, Montgomery's attack to clear the Lower Rhineland and close up to the Rhine opened with the biggest artillery barrage of the war. On the left the offensive was conducted by First (Canadian) Army, with divisions of Second (British) Army under command. Two days later, Ninth (United States) Army was due to begin a great convergent advance across the River Roer and to the banks of the Rhine. But before the Americans could open their attack the Germans smashed the discharge-valves of the last uncaptured Roer dam and flooded the valley delaying the Americans for a fortnight. Initially, therefore, the British and Canadians had to advance unsupported along a narrow corridor between two rivers, which Hitler had ordered to be defended to the death. Fighting their way eastward through the Reichswald Forest and across the Siegfried Line, over mined and sodden fields, through the rubble of historic towns shattered by bomb and shell, they engaged eleven German divisions, half of them armoured or composed of fanatical and skilful young Paratroops. This was Operation VERITABLE.

Eisenhower told Montgomery, to his satisfaction, that General Simpson's Ninth Army of twelve divisions would remain under Montgomery's command to the end of the war. That, anyway, was the Supreme Commander's intention in February.[21] On the 23rd, Simpson was able to start his attack. Smashing through Roermond Ninth Army advanced east and north-east and broke clean through the Siegfried Line. By 2nd March they reached the Rhine at Dusseldorf. By 10th March, Montgomery's command had cleared the west bank. 50,000 prisoners had been taken. On Montgomery's right, Bradley's left-hand Army – First Army – moved through the Eifel mountains, reached the Rhine, and on 7th March seized a bridgehead south of Bonn at Remagen. Further to the south, on 22nd March, Patton's Third Army won a further bridgehead at Oppenheim in the Palatinate. Eisenhower had, as he had determined, 'closed' the Rhine.

Brooke visited the Army on 2nd March. He saw the American Ninth Army, fresh from the capture of Roermond. He saw the Canadian First Army, led by his old friend Crerar. He saw the British 51st Division, out of the line and with their pipes and drums parading, that Highland division he had thrilled to watch march past in Tripoli in those seemingly long past days when the tide had just turned. Now he saw them parade on German soil.

Churchill was a fellow visitor, already making plans to be present when the British crossed the Rhine. Brooke remembered well the resentment Churchill had shown when, soon after the OVERLORD landings, Montgomery had apparently not welcomed a proposed visit from the Prime Minister – resentment Brooke had quickly dispelled by quietly telling Montgomery to issue an invitation and how to phrase it. On this occasion, immediately after his return, he wrote to Montgomery:

> ... as regards the PM's proposals for his next visit do not take this matter too light heartedly; there are the seeds of serious trouble ahead ...
>
> I can tell you he is determined to come out for the crossing of the Rhine and is now talking of going up in a tank! I feel the safest

way would be to find some reasonably secure viewpoint (not too far back or there will be hell to pay) to which he can be taken and from which he can see and have explained what is happening.[22]

Montgomery was happy to concur. His invitation was accepted with alacrity and delight. The operation was due to take place on the night of 23rd March – this great operation across a swollen watercourse 500 yards wide, supported by parachute and airborne landings in the enemy's rear.

Churchill and Brooke arrived at Montgomery's advanced headquarters on 23rd March. After dinner Montgomery went, as usual, early to bed. The Prime Minister took the CIGS for an evening stroll.

> We walked up and down in the moonlight. It was a glorious night and we discussed the situation . . . We went back over some of our early struggles, back to Cairo when we started Alex and Monty off. How he had had to trust my selection at that time. The part that the hand of God had taken in removing Gott at the critical moment etc. He was in one of his very nicest moods, and showed appreciation for what I had done for him in a way which he has never done before.[23]

In the next two days they together watched the airborne operation, and then drove to the Rhine itself for numerous visits and encounters. Brooke recorded some memorable vignettes.

> Winston then became a little troublesome and wanted to go messing about on the Rhine crossings and we had some difficulty in keeping him back. However, in the end he behaved well and we came back in our armoured cars.[24]

And next day:

> We found that Wesel was still occupied and that considerable sniping was going on inside the town . . . shells began to fall some 300 yards downstream, reports then came in that the Germans were shelling the road behind us, at the same time shells began to fall about 100 yards upstream of us. We decided it was time to remove the PM, who was thrilled with the situation and very reluctant to leave.[25]

Brooke wrote later of:

> General Simpson, on whose front we were, coming up to Winston and saying 'Prime Minister, there are snipers in front of you, they are shelling both sides of the bridge and now they have

started shelling the road behind you. I cannot accept the responsibility of your being here, and must ask you to come away.'

The look on Winston's face was just that of a small boy being
called away from his sandcastles on the beach by his nurse. He
put both his arms round one of the twisted girders of the bridge
and looked over his shoulder at Simpson with pouting mouth
and angry eyes.[26]

By 27th March, Montgomery was ready for the rapid advance to the Elbe which he had always planned. 'My tactical
headquarters moves,' he signalled to Brooke that day, 'will be
Wesel–Munster–Herford–Hanover – thence via the autobahn to
Berlin, I hope.'[27] Meanwhile, far to the south, Patton broke out
of his bridehead at Oppenheim; while at Remagen Bradley
exploited his opportunity and passed the whole of First Army
to the east bank by 24th March. On 28th March First and
Third Armies made contact at Giessen and on the 29th the
Americans entered Frankfurt. The southern thrust was under
way.

The last barrier to the heart of Germany had been crossed.
During April the Western Allies drove eastward into a shattered
Reich on two main parallel courses, their advance delayed, though
never for long, by the isolated, desperate but hopeless actions of a
brave enemy. The last weeks of the war in Europe witnessed yet
another altercation between British and Americans, one which,
with the benefit of hindsight, has acquired the same sort of
significance as the earlier arguments over 'the Vienna alternative'.
The altercation once again took the form of a British criticism of
Eisenhower. The issues went deeper.

On 28th March Eisenhower sent a signal direct to Stalin. In it
he forecast his own operations. First his Armies would complete
the encirclement of the Ruhr. Next he described his task as 'to
divide the remaining enemy forces by joining hands with your
forces'. To achieve this he proposed to drive on a main axis Erfurt
– Leipzig–Dresden. This would take the Allies to the upper Elbe.
No mention was made of North Germany, none of Berlin. A
secondary advance would be made in the Danube Valley as far as
Linz. Eisenhower suggested the need for co-ordination, and asked
for Soviet intentions – the Red Army was temporarily halted.
Stalin replied that Eisenhower's plan seemed admirable. He added
that Berlin had lost its strategic importance and that it would be
invested by a 'secondary' Soviet operation.

This exchange found no favour in London. First, there was the procedural point. Brooke wrote next day – 'To start with he has no business to address Stalin direct. His communications should be through the Combined Chiefs of Staff.' Such a criticism was not pettifogging or irrelevant. Few things make more trouble and ill feeling than attempts to cut out responsible authorities. But Eisenhower could and did plead that experience showed Stalin alone to have sufficient authority in such military matters.

Brooke continued:

> He has produced a telegram which was unintelligible and, finally, what was implied in it appeared to be entirely adrift and a change in all that had been previously agreed on.[28]

Eisenhower had also directed Simpson's Ninth Army to revert from Montgomery's to Bradley's command for the eastern drive. Montgomery and the British appeared relegated to a secondary role. Indeed, Eisenhower was now explicit that Bradley's 12th Army Group should make the running in the centre of the front. But Brooke was, on the whole, philosophic. He reckoned that national prestige was a factor in the plans and he felt that to be inevitable. Montgomery had indignantly represented that the new plan was an unexplained overturning of what had been agreed and planned. Brooke told him that he should make no further representations to Eisenhower.[29] Eisenhower, then and later, strongly denied that his plan implied change from what had been agreed – a matter which turned on clarity and interpretation. It is not demonstrable that Eisenhower changed his mind or his intentions, but he could sometimes express these in ways which proponents of different philosophies could each claim supported their case.

The British Chiefs of Staff had a number of exchanges (some with disagreeable undertones) with their American colleagues. In no way would the latter agree to limit Eisenhower's right to order his Armies as he wished or correspond with Stalin if he desired. Eisenhower maintained, and the American Chiefs strongly supported him, that his plans were based on purely military considerations; and, in the absence of any political direction in a contrary sense, rightly so.

The British were not on strong ground. On military considerations (although, as ever, alternative solutions could be argued) Eisenhower's plan seemed perfectly likely to achieve its object. Germany was obviously at her last gasp. The British argued for more emphasis to be placed on reaching northern ports on the unconvincing basis that German U-boat activity might at this stage be renewed. Brooke's heart was not in such a case. Nor was Churchill's. He found such arguments feeble.[30] As for Berlin, the Combined Chiefs of Staff had never explicitly pointed Eisenhower towards it, although it had long been recognized as probably the crowning prize of victory, and in September Eisenhower himself had written of 'concentrating all our energies and resources on a rapid thrust to Berlin'.[31]

The issue was essentially political. Soviet behaviour was becoming ever more ominous. Churchill believed with increasing conviction that it would be an excellent thing for the Allies to enter Berlin before the Red Army. As, through April, the Armies advanced (the Russian final offensive began on the 17th) Churchill believed that it would be highly desirable for the Western Allies to meet the Russians as far to the east as possible. Eisenhower's arrangements with Stalin had the effect of reining in the American advance and leaving territory – including the Czechoslovak capital, Prague – to be occupied first by the Russians, by default. Churchill chafed at this. He also chafed at what looked a slow and undramatic part assigned to British troops, by Eisenhower's plans, at the ultimate moment of triumph.

Yet Eisenhower, who has been criticized for his 'halt on the Elbe' agreement with Stalin, could not reasonably have taken into account such political factors unless told to do so by the Combined Chiefs of Staff, themselves acting under political directive. Even had the Allies advanced further, as would have been militarily easy in the event, they would have had later to withdraw unless the Yalta agreement were to be torn up; for ARGONAUT had already assigned the zones of occupation. It was, of course, Churchill's view that relations with the Soviet Union had reached a point where possession of territory should be used as a bargaining counter, and where adherence by the Western Allies to the ARGONAUT agreements on occupation zones should be balanced by Soviet fulfilment of their pledges – notably towards Poland – which they were already flagrantly disregarding. It was a reasonable view. It was, however, formed late. Brooke had no illusions in the matter. In February his friend, the Polish General Anders, had poured out his heart.

> The root of the trouble lay in the fact that he could never trust the Russians after his experiences with them, whilst Winston and Roosevelt were prepared to trust the Russians. After having been a prisoner and seeing how Russians could treat Poles, he

considered he was in a better position to judge what Russians were like than the President or the Prime Minister.[32]

But on the question of using the Allied advances for political leverage Brooke took a simple and perhaps simplistic view.

'We have already agreed with the Russians,' he wrote in his diary on 23rd May, 'as to zones of occupation in Germany. I consider that Winston is fundamentally wrong in using this as a bargaining counter.'

Clearly though Brooke saw the future Soviet menace, his straightforward nature jibbed at the idea of abandoning agreements so recently attained – whatever Soviet behaviour.

It would certainly have been defensible, farsighted and militarily practicable, to recognize the Soviet threat to the security of Europe in April 1945 and to act thereon – so to direct operations that the Western Allies were in the best posture to deal from strength thereafter. But Eisenhower was never given a Directive remotely in that sense. Furthermore, neither in Britain nor in the United States was public opinion ready for such a démarche. Government propaganda in the Western democracies had been directed towards helping Western–Soviet relations. Soviet actions which would have appalled Western opinion received little publicity, or were represented as understandable in view of Russian suffering. Such sentiments cannot be switched overnight. It was far too late for the Prime Minister to ask the President, as he did, to agree that there was great political merit in meeting the Red Army as far to the east as military operations could secure. It was far too late, as happened, to suggest to the President on 30th April that the liberation of Prague by American forces might 'make the whole difference to the post-war situation in Czechoslovakia'. The time for that had passed. Roosevelt died on 12th April, but nothing of his record in the last years of war gives reason to suppose he would have accepted what was now Churchill's line.

The Armies from east and west surged towards each other as the last manifestations of Nazi power collapsed in Germany. The American and Russian Armies met on the Elbe at Torgau on 25th April. On the 30th Hitler committed suicide in Berlin. On the 4th Seventh (United States) Army, having advanced through Bavaria and into Austria, joined hands with the American Fifth Army from Italy on the Brenner Pass. On the same day, Brooke recorded in his diary:

Monty met Keitel this morning, who surrendered uncondition-
ally all North Germany, Schleswig-Holstein, Denmark, Friesian
Islands and Heligoland.

Brooke spent 6th May, a Sunday, at home.

A quiet Sunday, during the afternoon went over to meet Bertie
Fisher and to put up hides for nightingales, bullfinch and
blackcap nests.

Next day was full of telegrams and meetings on the complexities of
surrender. 'So this is at last the end of the war,' Brooke wrote:

I can't feel thrilled, my sensation is one of infinite mental
weariness . . . The most acute feeling is one of deep depression
such as I have experienced at the end of the strain of each
Combined Chiefs of Staff Conference.

The Cabinet and the Chiefs of Staff reported to the King at
Buckingham Palace at 4.30 next afternoon. It was VE – 'Victory in
Europe' Day. The German war was over.

Brooke felt little elation. Personal sadnesses and a strong sense
of the futility and suffering of war filled his heart. His great-
nephew, Harry Brooke, Basil Brooke's youngest son, had just been
killed in action in Italy: the eldest son had been killed two years
before. His heart went out to their parents, and to so many others.
At such times he found himself thinking of losses rather than
triumphs. It was like 11th November 1918, of which he had
written: 'I felt untold relief at the end being there at last, but was
swamped with floods of memories of those years of struggle. I was
filled with gloom that evening and retired to sleep early.' Thus it
was again, but there was one difference. Brooke's diary entry for
8th May 1945 ended:

I must leave behind me the German War, and now turn my
energies, during my few remaining days as CIGS, towards the
final defeat of Japan.

CHAPTER XIX

Checkmate

THE GERMAN WAR was finished. Western Europe was devastated, impoverished and demoralized. Central and Eastern Europe was occupied by Soviet troops and in process of forcible Communization. The Yugoslav Partisans were threatening Western authority and interests in Venezia Giulia. Victory in Europe marked deliverance of a sort, although in no sense a triumph for the values of Western civilization. Brooke found the problems of peace even more intractable than those of war. There were no fewer meetings, no fewer interviews, visits to make, gratitude to express. In June he visited Bletchley Park to thank the tireless workers responsible for ULTRA, that remarkable Intelligence source which had done so much to help the strategic and operational decisions of the Allies. There were anxieties on the home front. 'I had tea with Croft,' he wrote on 16th May, 'who is worried about the security of MI5 and 6. So am I!'

Public pressure in Britain and America was for some demobilization, consistent with dealing the final blows at Japan – and Japan seemed a very long way away. The Americans spoke of an occupation of Germany lasting perhaps as little as two years. Everywhere was a sense of weariness and a yearning for tranquillity and homecoming. The mood of the West was against any thought of assuming new burdens or contemplating fresh dangers. Brooke was instructed by Churchill to investigate the possibility of 'taking on' Russia before American and British forces were demobilized, if Soviet behaviour became too outrageous. He found the idea fantastic. He wrote in his diary on 24th May – 'There is no doubt that from now onwards Russia is all powerful in Europe.'

Brooke had clear views on the menace of the future, but at that moment the entire political climate made such a démarche impossible to conceive. He was told to concentrate on the purely military problem. The resultant study 'made it clear that the best we could hope for was to drive the Russians back to about the same line the Germans had reached. And then what? Were we to remain mobilized indefinitely to hold them there?'[1]

The Chiefs of Staff regarded such operations as unthinkable. Nevertheless, Churchill stood his ground with grim patience. Brooke's diary on 11th June:

> Winston gave a long and very gloomy review of the situation in Europe. The Russians were further west in Europe than they have ever been except once. They were all powerful in Europe. At any time that it took their fancy they could march across the rest of Europe and drive us back into our island. They had a 2 to 1 superiority over our forces and the Americans were returning home. The quicker they went home, the sooner they would be required back here again. He finished up by saying that never in his life had he been more worried by the European situation.

This was indeed a hollow victory. It was thus unsurprising that Churchill greeted the news of the first major Atomic Bomb Test with jubilation. Brooke countered with a scepticism which was a great deal less justified. He afterwards freely acknowledged Churchill's vision and what he criticized as his own 'reactionary sentiments which led me into a failure to fully realize the importance of the new discovery'.[2] In his diary on 23rd July he recorded:

> I was completely shattered by the PM's outlook. He had seen the American reports of results of the new TA* Secret Explosive [atomic bomb] which had just been carried out in the States. He had absorbed all the minor American exaggerations, and as a result was completely carried away. It was now no longer necessary for the Russians to come into the Japanese War, the new explosive alone was sufficient to settle the matter!
>
> Furthermore, we now had something in our hands which would redress the balance with the Russians. The secret of the explosive and the power to use it would completely alter the diplomatic equilibrium, which was adrift since the defeat of Germany . . .
>
> I tried to crush his over optimism based on the result of one experiment, and was asked with contempt what reason I had for minimizing the results of these discoveries. I was trying to dispel his dreams and as usual he did not like it.

Meanwhile, as Brooke ruefully reflected, there was still some of the present war to finish before contemplating the next.

When the British Chiefs of Staff concentrated on the Japanese war they were forcibly reminded that to the Americans the Pacific

* Code name TUBE ALLOYS

was an American theatre, and the war an American war. This was just. A mighty effort had been put forward by the United States. Two parallel advances had been driven, in some competition, towards Japan, the one in the south by the island-hopping strategy of MacArthur through New Guinea and the Philippines, the other by Nimitz in the Central Pacific by way of the Marianas. These had gone splendidly, and faster than anticipated. Japanese maritime power had been virtually destroyed at the battle of Leyte Gulf in October. The Americans landed in Luzon in the Philippines in January. Manila fell at the end of February. Whatever the British might do in the future they could have played little or no part in these great operations although, further to the OCTAGON decisions, a small United Kingdom Pacific fleet was continuously in action from mid-March under American command. These operations were crucial. They were directed against Japan itself.

The principal British contribution had been in South East Asia, where they had every reason for safisfaction at the recent course of the campaign. But they had been periodically and sometimes unpalatably reminded by their Allies that operations in SEAC were only useful in so far as they helped support China. With the liberation of Burma and the projected liberation of Malaya, Singapore and other lands in South East Asia the Americans were little concerned. They tended to associate them with European Empires and to disapprove of those Empires in principle. Brooke had observed in Roosevelt an aversion to restoring Indo-China to French rule.[3] The Americans wished to beat Japan, and for them the quickest way to do it was to drive at the Japanese homeland itself by the progressive use of maritime and air power. This would culminate in an invasion.

There had been, and there continued, doubts about the necessity of ultimate invasion. As early as the Casablanca Conference Portal had enquired whether the United States Chiefs of Staff did not think it would be possible to gain a decision over Japan by air bombardment alone. At the QUADRANT Conference of August 1943 Brooke had asked the question: 'Might we not obtain the collapse of Japan without invasion?' and it had been agreed that blockade and air bombardment alone might, conceivably, produce victory. Nevertheless, when the war in Europe ended in May 1945, the assumption of the American planners was that Japan would need to be invaded. On 14th June the United States authorities finally agreed that the operation must be carried out.

The British did not wish to be left out of this decisive enterprise, but there was a tussle of priorities with both military and political implications; to some extent a re-enactment of the earlier quarrel between Churchill and the Chiefs of Staff over the 'Pacific Strategy'. On the one hand the British wanted to enable Mountbatten to exploit success in Burma. They looked favourably, therefore, on projected operations against the Japanese in Malaya and Singapore, which might now be mounted earlier than hitherto planned. On the other hand, they did not want Britain to be excluded from the final act in the Central Pacific – yet any contribution there might need to be at the expense of SEAC, and spoil or delay Mountbatten's operations. The Americans also proposed a new British Commonwealth Command area in the South West Pacific, supported from Australia; a command which would be exercised through the Australian Chiefs of Staff. Brooke and his colleagues liked the idea, but they – and the Australians – looked with caution at any arrangement which might seem to relegate their forces to a subsidiary role.

There was another major point at issue. The British thought themselves excluded from decisions about the central strategy of the war against Japan. Hitherto they had been reasonably content. Now, with South East Asia the only active British theatre of operations, they were not. They were determined to participate in the final action. They wished also some share of its preparation and control. These matters now seem academic. At the time, however, the approved assumption was that hostilities would last a further eighteen months. Nobody expected an instant end to the war. It was not unnatural that the Americans were impatient at any attempt to share responsibility in this theatre, so vital to them. On 17th April, Wilson had written to Brooke from Washington:

> It is going to be difficult to get acceptance that the Pacific operations should become a Combined Chiefs of Staff instead of a Joint [US] Chiefs of Staff responsibility, which is, I take it, what you would like to see accomplished.[4]

The matter was to be resolved at Potsdam. Meanwhile, the British continued to feel that they were left out of planning, and that decisions were communicated to them late, if at all, despite Wilson's best efforts. Typical of this, Brooke felt, was an American proposal in April to attack North Borneo, and obtain a base for the British Pacific fleet at Brunei – a proposal which went some way before the British themselves heard of it, and of which they thought little! But the problem lay as much with inter-Service rivalry in Washington as with mistrust of Allies. Marshall, who apologized handsomely over the Borneo incident, explained that King arrogated to himself much of the responsibiltiy for the Pacific theatre, and was congenitally reluctant to share information.

Behind the issue of sharing formal control between Allies lay another, intangible but irritating. On 23rd April Wilson wrote again:

> I have now been here long enough to see that . . . the belittling of what our forces are doing, as compared to the US Forces, is on the increase, and, in addition, there is continual sniping at our policy, intentions and administration in every theatre. This will, I fear, have a tendency to increase when the war changes completely to the Pacific.[5]

These undercurrents strengthened Brooke's determination, after VE Day, to be 'in at the kill'. On 11th May he replied to Wilson:

> We feel that it is most desirable that we should take a definite part in the defeat of Japan proper through the medium of naval, land and air forces employed in the operations against the island of Japan.
>   . . . we do feel that from every point of view it is most desirable that we should take a direct part in operations against Japan itself as opposed to operations for the recapture of lost colonies.[6]

This was the British resolve. At the end of June the Chiefs of Staff put a paper in that sense to the Prime Minister. They formally proposed the size and shape of a British Imperial contribution to the Allied invasion force. Churchill endorsed the proposal, on 4th July, and on the 17th the Combined Chiefs in principle agreed that a British Commonwealth land force should participate 'in the final phase of the war against Japan'. The force would operate under MacArthur's command. The British would also contribute their Pacific fleet and ten squadrons of Long Range bomber aircraft, later to be increased to twenty.

Meanwhile, all was not well in South East Asia Command. The first difficulty was administrative and delicate.

When Germany surrendered, the Government had decreed that the period of service for British Servicemen overseas would be limited to three years and eight months. Those who had served this long would be repatriated, and so it would continue. The ruling had a significant effect in reducing the strength of units being prepared for SEAC operations against Malaya (Operation ZIPPER), and the planned date for the operation was deferred a fortnight, until 9th September, in consequence. In June, however, the War Office decided to reduce the qualifying period by a further four months. Grigg, the Secretary of State for War, announced this in the House of Commons, and it received due publicity. In future, men who had completed three years and four months service overseas could come home.

Mountbatten immediately commented that this – on which he had not been consulted – would delay ZIPPER indefinitely by an unacceptable weakening of the strength of units. Furthermore, he pointed out, the shipping situation was such that the men, having been withdrawn from units, could not be repatriated for some time anyway. An operational penalty was being incurred for the sake of a measure intended to boost morale, but likely to do the reverse as the delay sank into disappointed men.

The Chiefs of Staff reckoned that Mountbatten was over-stating the operational risk of carrying out ZIPPER with weakened formations. Japan was known to be *in extremis*. Mountbatten, on reconsideration, accepted that ZIPPER could be done on the date fixed, albeit with greater risk. Some eight divisions were involved. But the question of delay in shipping men home was harder. Brooke, in his diary on 19th June, accused the Government of electioneering (Parliament had been dissolved and a General Election called). He referred to Grigg's announcement as a 'votecatching statement'. Eventually, a corrective statement was made by Grigg, warning the men concerned of the likely delay.

It was not the War Office's finest hour. Brooke had clearly not been apprised of the problem from the operational point of view – and was personally unaware of the statement before it was made. Statements of that kind were and are 'cleared' with the General Staff, although, under strong political imperatives, exceptions have been known; and this must have been an exception. Brooke sympathized with Mountbatten and thought him right in the matter; and the authorities having got into the mess, the only way out was by political recantation, which took place. If it was electioneering it was singularly unsuccessful.

The other problem in South East Asia Command was personal. In Burma, Slim had conducted a campaign of remarkable success. Burma was free. A suggestion was now made to replace him as Commander of Fourteenth Army, which would carry out the invasion of Malaya under another leader. Slim would, instead,

OPERATIONS PLANNED BUT NOT UNDERTAKEN
IN THE INDIAN OCEAN

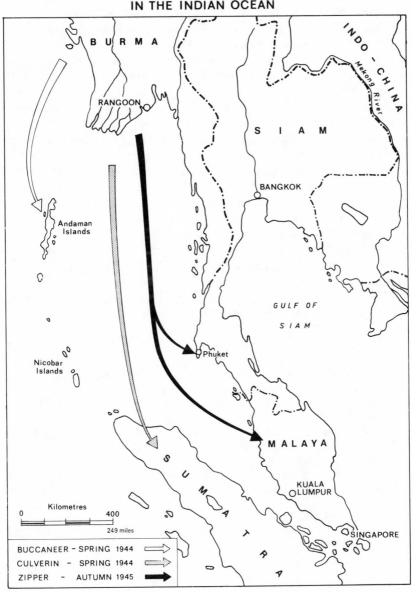

BURMA

RANGOON

Andaman
Islands

Nicobar
Islands

INDO - CHINA

Mekong River

S I A M

BANGKOK

GULF OF
SIAM

Phuket

MALAYA

KUALA
LUMPUR

S U M A T R A

SINGAPORE

Kilometres

0   400

249 miles

BUCCANEER – SPRING 1944

CULVERIN – SPRING 1944

ZIPPER – AUTUMN 1945

command a new (and very small) army – Twelfth Army – responsible for 'mopping up' in Burma itself; for garrison rather than campaign. It was a peculiar proposal, made within days of the capture of Rangoon. To give effect to it – with, it was hoped, Slim's acquiescence – Leese, Commander-in-Chief Allied Land Forces South East Asia, and Slim's immediate superior, was authorized to 'sound him out'; to discover whether he would find the idea palatable. Slim was thought to be tired. Leese, whose idea all this was, visited Slim with Mountbatten's approval, on 7th May, with this in mind. Before doing so, but after seeing Mountbatten, he sent a signal to Brooke. In advance of any approval from home – or any reaction from Slim – he also told General Christison* that he was to take over Fourteenth Army. Slim reacted sharply to the interview. He made no complaint, but he received the impression that he was being replaced, and he told Leese that he would prefer to retire. Although Slim behaved with total dignity and discretion the news spread and Fourteenth Army was soon in a ferment of astonishment and rage.

British Army Commanders were not to be dismissed or relieved without the approval of the CIGS and Ministers. Brooke had received no recommendation from Mountbatten, and needed no prompting to go into action. The correspondence which followed gives a taste of Brooke when dealing with matters of the kind.

He sent two personal signals on 18th May. To Leese:

> I wish to make it quite plain that I consider the manner in which you have attempted to carry out changes in highest appointments under your command has been most unsatisfactory and highly irregular.
>
> You are serving under a Supreme Commander to whom you should make proposals, and in whom the responsibility rests for making official recommendations. No definite action could even then be taken without my approval and that of the Secretary of State, and possibly even Prime Minister . . .

and more in the same vein.

To Mountbatten:

> I have told Leese that if he has any proposals to make he should submit them to you . . .

* Commander XV Corps.

Meanwhile I have expressed my surprise and displeasure that he should have discussed the matter with Slim at all. I have also made it clear that I have every confidence in Slim whose record has been outstandingly successful, and that unless very strong arguments can be adduced I have no repeat no intention of agreeing to his supercession by Christison.

After receiving this Mountbatten wrote two very long letters to Brooke, on 23rd May and 7th June. He described every conversation held during this curious episode. He made clear that he had authorized Leese to approach Slim, but entirely disassociated himself from the impression Leese had created during that approach, as well as from Leese's offer to Christison. Leese had exceeded his instructions. Mountbatten gave in his letters a catalogue of other failings and asked Brooke's advice. It might not look good, he said, if he appeared to procure the dismissal of a second Commander-in-Chief (the first had been General Giffard). There could only be one answer. Brooke quoted Mountbatten's own letter back to him in a letter of 19th June:

> Taking all these facts into consideration I can only assume that you yourself have not the confidence in Leese which you ought to have in one who is probably your principal subordinate commander.
>
> You ask for my advice. I can only tell you what action I should take if I was in your place. I should feel that there was no alternative but to replace Oliver Leese at the earliest possible moment.

Leese returned home. Brooke was not entirely surprised by the muddle which had led to the unwittingly offensive treatment of a victorious Army Commander. As early as 13th March he had noted in his diary: 'We may possibly have trouble later between Oliver Leese and Dickie. If we do, it will be Oliver's fault.' Nevertheless he remained uneasy over the whole business. Leese had undoubtedly blundered, but Mountbatten had agreed that Leese should see Slim in the first place, which Brooke regarded as highly improper without authority from London. Mountbatten's subsequent letters had been elicited by Brooke's reaction, and had a loud self-exculpatory ring.[7]

Brooke's diary entry for 10th July ran: 'Poor Oliver Leese came to see me, having just arrived back. Very sad and repentant. He took it all wonderfully well.' And after the war he wrote:

497

That interview has remained vividly impressed on my mind owing to the wonderful, manly way in which Oliver faced up to the blow that had hit him. There was not a word of abuse from him against anyone, or any suggestion that he had been roughly treated. And yet at the bottom of my heart I had a feeling, and still have a feeling, that, although he may have been at fault, he had a raw deal at the hands of Mountbatten.[8]

In Leese's place, Slim was made Commander-in-Chief! However, before Fourteenth Army, under whatever Commander, could invade Malaya in September; and before a British Commonwealth Corps could be assembled to participate in the invasion of Japan, an historic event occurred. Events moved faster than plans foretold.

The last great Allied Conference took place at Potsdam in July. It was named TERMINAL. It marked the end of the German war. It was followed within three weeks by the end of the Japanese war.

Brooke arrived in Potsdam on 15th July. Eric Hosking recalled after Alanbrooke's death how he had visited the CIGS at Ferney Close to ask about building a hide nearby to photograph a hobby. Alanbrooke had said 'I'm off to the Potsdam Conference in two days' time – when I get home will you let me use the hide?'[9] and he telephoned from Potsdam, before the Conference ended, to ask how things were going. Brooke arrived home from Potsdam on 25th July, and on the 28th climbed the pylon tower and spent four enchanted hours with his cine camera twelve feet from the hobby nest. It was, as ever, the perfect restorative.

The Conference itself was peaceful. Anglo-American discussion was concentrated on the Pacific war, on questions soon to be proved academic. The question of shared strategic responsibility for the Pacific theatre was resolved. Decision would be left with the United States Chiefs of Staff – the Pacific was not to be a 'Combined Chiefs of Staff Theatre'; but a mechanism was agreed whereby the United Kingdom could reserve or deny the employment of British forces if there was disagreement with the overall plan. It was a small crumb from a very rich man's table, and it seems doubtful if it would have proved substantial if ever put to the test. Brooke was not dissatisfied at the time. He recognized the preponderance of American might[10] in the Pacific, and the realities of power. He recognized that the Americans would not, and could not be compelled to, establish consultative machinery which might fetter their discretion or divide their authority. Hard fighting was still anticipated. At Potsdam the agreed planning date for the end of Japanese resistance was still set at mid-November 1946.

There were discussions with the Americans about the passage of information to the Russians. A co-ordinated Anglo-American policy was settled – on operations and Intelligence the United States would decide, on all other matters there would be Anglo-American consultation. Portal asked 'What about the considerable technical information which has been developed by joint effort?'[11] and was assured that this would not be subject to unilateral American decision. There were ceremonies. There were banquets. As so often, Brooke felt, at the end, little but flatness and weariness.

'I am feeling very tired and worn out,' he wrote on 24th July. Within a fortnight all was changed.

On 6th August 1945 Wilson wrote from Washington to Brooke:

> We have just got news that the first TA [atomic] bomb was dropped on Japan this morning.

Co-operation between Britain and America in the production of an atomic bomb, the project TUBE ALLOYS, stemmed from the QUADRANT Conference of August 1943. A Combined Policy Committee had been established in Washington. Dill, and then Wilson, were members of that Committee. Wilson was there as a representative of the Prime Minister rather than the Chiefs of Staff. He answered to Sir John Anderson, Chairman of the British Committee responsible for atomic matters. Anderson reported to Churchill. Wilson periodically spoke about progress to Brooke, but the British Chiefs of Staff were not formally involved in the project. Nor were they, in the event, involved in the momentous decision to use the bomb against Japan. The QUADRANT agreement had established between the United States and the United Kingdom: 'We will not use it against third parties without each other's consent' and this agreement was honoured. The Chiefs of Staff, however, did not discuss it. Wilson learned in April from Marshall and others that the Americans had reached the point of production where the bomb could soo┆ they intended to use it. Wilson reported to ┆ guidance on how the agreement about British ┆ applied. It was agreed that British endorsen ┆ appear in a record of proceedings of the ┆

Committee, and Churchill initialled a Minute to that effect on 1st July, saying that he would wish to discuss the matter further with President Truman at the forthcoming Allied Conference at Potsdam, due to begin on 17th July.

Meanwhile a peace party had surreptitiously formed within the Supreme War Council of Japan, with the strong but necessarily discreet encouragement of the Emperor himself, who was determined that Japan must sue for peace. There were powerful forces within the Japanese Army which would oppose peace to the last. Nevertheless instructions were sent early in July to the Japanese Ambassador in Moscow to seek the good offices of the Soviet Union as an intermediary. These exchanges between Tokyo and the Japanese Embassy in Moscow were known by interception to the Americans. The Japanese overtures were reported by the Soviet authorities to Stalin and Molotov, who were already in Potsdam. Discussions with Churchill and Truman took place, and a Declaration, agreed between the major three combatant powers at war with Japan – Britain, America and China, – was broadcast on 27th July. In this, the 'Potsdam Declaration', the Allied Powers called for unconditional surrender of all the Japanese Armed Forces. The language of the Declaration, although stern, did not call for the end of the Government of Japan, nor the end of the Imperial dynasty. The Soviet Union meanwhile replied to Japan that since there had been no concrete proposal by Japan they could take no action. They had privately assured Britain and America that they would declare war soon after 8th August.

Within Japan the reaction to the Declaration was confused. There was still some hope of Soviet good offices. The Japanese Prime Minister told the Press on 28th July that the Government intended to ignore the Declaration – which had not been formally communicated to Japan. This apparent rejection was taken by the Allies as evidence that the Emperor and the 'peace party' had insufficient power. Their hands should be strengthened by further demonstration of the inexorable power of the Allies. On 6th August the first bomb was dropped on Hiroshima. On 9th August, the second bomb was dropped on Nagasaki. On 9th August the Soviet Union declared war on Japan.

The future appeared still uncertain. On 9th August Brooke wrote in his diary: 'Quite a long COS meeting with the Planners in to discuss final actions necessary to put into action the preparations of the Corps for the invasion of Japan.' Next day, however:

'Just before lunch, BBC intercepts of Japanese Peace offers were received in the shape of an acceptance of the Potsdam offer,' and papers were commissioned to examine the immediate steps, such as the rapid occupation of Hong Kong, that would need to follow Japanese surrender.

The British part in the defeat of Japan had not been so well publicized as had the European or desert campaigns. Nor did the British Empire's overall contribution to the Japanese war approach that of the United States. They had, however, fought in Burma a long and arduous campaign ending in complete victory. In that campaign they had inflicted on the Japanese Army the largest single defeat it suffered in war. Brooke accepted the Burmese campaign as a necessary price to pay for Allied goodwill. After it accomplished its first object – the defence of India – he tended to look at it askance. The Americans were frank in regarding its purpose as to help keep China in the war; and most of the time Brooke looked on the liberation of Burma as peripheral to the defeat of Japan. Nevertheless, for the Japanese it had been a drain on resources, an awkward and expensive effort to sustain. For the British it meant the liberation by British Imperial forces of Imperial territory, the swift deliverance of Malaya and Singapore in the aftermath, the presence of a British Commander, Mountbatten, at the final ceremonies of victory. For at 3 a.m. on 10th August the Japanese Cabinet, which had been in session for several hours without reaching definite conclusions, heard from the Emperor himself his opinion that the war must end. They accepted it, despite a final attempt by elements in the Army to stage a *coup d'état*. On 14th August the Japanese finally and formally surrendered. The Second World War was over.

The most dramatic turn of the Potsdam Conference, as far as Brooke was concerned, lay in domestic politics. On 26th July, Brooke noted in his diary:

> The Conservative Government has experienced a complete landslide and is out for good and all! If only Winston had followed my advice he would have been in at any rate till the end of the year.

Brooke had been strongly against the election, for the straightforward reason that it would divide and distract the country at a time when its energies and unity were still needed to finish the war. Now it was over. The partnership was over. Churchill was out. On 27th July the Chiefs of Staff went to 10 Downing Street at

6.30 p.m. to confer for the last time with the man with whom they had experienced so much, at whom they had complained so often, whom they had resisted on occasion so stoutly, whom in the last resort they loved so warmly. They were not adroit at graceful gesture, and at least one onlooker was infuriated at their stiffness. They did not raise a glass to Churchill's health. They had no elegant words of sympathy or affection.[12] Brooke, however, felt deeply as ever, and this constraint was the result of much rather than little emotion. He wrote that night:

> It was a very sad and very moving little meeting at which I found myself unable to say much for fear of breaking down. He was standing the blow wonderfully well.

On such occasions he could communicate better by letter than speech. Three days later, Churchill wrote back:

> My dear Brookie,
>   I am deeply grateful for all you have done for me and for the country. Your charming letter has touched me deeply and cheered me. I shall always value your friendship, as I do my memories of Ronnie and Victor in those young and far off days.
>   Our story in this war is a good one, and this will be recognized as time goes on.[13]

Brooke's note after the war gave the last word and the best word on their relationship:

> I shall always look back on the years I worked with him as some of the most difficult and trying ones in my life. For all that, I thank God that I was given an opportunity of working alongside of such a man.[14]

CHAPTER XX

'Envoi'

THE SECOND WORLD WAR was over. Professional life was as demanding as ever for the CIGS. For Brooke increasing distaste for the routine of office, as well as plain exhaustion, tempered relief. At Potsdam, Churchill had asked him to stay at his post for a further year, and on 6th August wrote that he had told Attlee of this request 'putting on record my invitation to you and your acceptance of it'. Attlee had replied that he had the greatest confidence in Brooke.[1] Brooke was less happy. 'I am very doubtful if I can stick it out,' he wrote in his diary on 6th September.

He longed for private as well as public peace. An appeal to his sense of duty, however, could only be met with one response. Furthermore, it was put to him that the new Labour Secretary of State for War, Mr Lawson, had no knowledge whatsoever of the Army or of Defence matters and would need a CIGS of Brooke's experience. He acquiesced the more readily since he found Lawson the most charming of men, although he missed the wisdom and firmness of Grigg.

It was not until January of 1946 that Brooke got the Prime Minister's agreement to his handing over to Montgomery in June. For nearly a year he was occupied with a world over much of which had been fought the most devastating war in human history; and with the reorganization, deployment and demobilization of an Army spread across that world. He set out to tour it.

With clear ideas about what he needed to examine, Brooke began, on 27th October, a journey which covered some 42,000 miles.[2]

Brooke thought in Imperial terms. Even at so comparatively recent a point in time it was natural for him to regard British responsibilities as spanning the world. The nations of the British Empire looked to each other for mutual support in defence, and to the areas in which their influence was paramount for most of the raw materials necessary for life, prosperity or war.

In a great struggle, just over, the Empire had been the only combatant force on the Allied side from the first to the last day. It was reasonable to look to the future as a time when such bonds should be strengthened not loosened. Brooke had a concept of Imperial zones of interest, each zone centred on a Commonwealth nation with strategic direction from its own Chiefs of Staff, zones linked with one another by an Imperial Chiefs of Staff committee. It was the sort of organizational problem and solution with which his mind had been so frequently occupied in the past four years. He envisaged an Indian Zone, to include Ceylon and Burma and with links to Iran and Afghanistan; a Far East Zone comprising Singapore, Malaya, Borneo and Hong Kong and linked with French Indo-China and the Dutch East Indies; and an Australian Zone to include New Zealand, New Guinea and the Solomons. Most important of all, he believed that there should be some sort of Zone or Federation for mutual defence in the Middle East.

Only vestiges of such ideas are discernible in later arrangements. The most dramatic problems soon to arise were not about methods of organization for external defence but about the relationships within the Empire itself. The very concept of Empire was being questioned. The new British Government had to adjust to new realities, not unwelcome to some, odious to others. Brooke, too, had to adjust. The world tour greatly helped him to do so. His philosophy was always to accept and understand change where changed circumstances imposed it: to nourish the Commonwealth as an ideal, an association of free men bound by certain common moral and political ideas: to appreciate where power – and danger – lay in the new world which had emerged from the war, and work towards a new balance; and to avoid overcommitment and the undertaking of duties beyond the power of Britain, unaided, to perform.

Brooke's first visit was to Greece. He felt the need for a clearcut policy, a definition of aims. The country had suffered a Communist bid for power of deplorable ferocity, and the part played by British troops in frustrating it was greatly appreciated. 'Scobie, Scobie!' Brooke heard the Athenian crowd roar in salute to the popular British General. But Brooke had no illusions about the problems and dangers. Three months earlier he had discussed with his colleagues in London what he called 'the gathering clouds on the northern Greek frontier', Yugoslav divisions, Bulgarian divisions, Russian divisions in Bulgaria; young Communist regimes ready to test their muscles. He had looked gloomily at the possibility of British forces having actually to defend the frontiers of Greece as well as assist in the rehabilitation of the country – and all at a time when the British Government was pressing for rapid demobilization. 'What is Greece going to cost us in treasure and men?' he wrote in his diary on 29th October in Athens. 'Can we afford to meet this liability? Will America take a share?'

Brooke only spent two days in Greece. It was enough, however, for him to take a favourable view of the development of the young Greek Army. Next he visited a number of Middle Eastern States, returning to some of them on the way home. Everywhere he put to his hosts the concept of a Middle East Federation underpinned by British arms and presence.

On the whole he found receptive ears. In Iraq, Transjordan and Saudi Arabia there was a general sense that the great danger of the post-war world lay in Soviet expansion. Some of Brooke's hosts believed danger from that direction to be not only inevitable but imminent. The Emir Abdullah of Transjordan was particularly cogent on the subject, leaving with Brooke the feeling of true friend to Britain in foul weather as in fair, and one who would support the sort of Federation he had in mind. In Iraq, too, the Regent expressed welcome for such a plan. In Saudi Arabia, which Brooke visited on his return journey a month later, King Ibn Saud immediately brought up the subject of Russia. 'Their doctrines in this world,' Brooke quoted him as saying, 'are like a cancer in a man's stomach.'[3] Ibn Saud was receptive to ideas of defence co-operation. The King showed every sign of cordiality. After a magnificent banquet, Brooke wrote:

> Ibn Saud sprayed my hands with special scent and said that once equipped this way it was no longer possible to remain alone in bed! However, he did not provide me with any companion. He presented me with a very fine sword.[4]

In Palestine Brooke saw Gort, the High Commissioner, and was deeply troubled to see him look so ill. Gort collapsed the evening Brooke was with him, and had to be flown to England where he died five months later. It was the same evening that Jewish terrorists carried out multiple attacks on the railway, the Haifa Oil Refinery, the station at Lydda. Brooke had no illusions about the future problems of Palestine, the disturbances which would attend the end of the Mandate. He did not foresee the strength of the poison which would be injected into relations between the Western and Arab worlds by the Palestine question. Few did.

In Egypt, whither he travelled immediately after Greece and

on his journey home, there was a more ambivalent attitude to Brooke's ideas of a Federation for defence. King Farouk, of whose intelligence and goodwill Brooke formed a high opinion (believing him to have been mishandled by the British), was strongly in favour. The Prime Minister, however, made it clear that no Egyptian Government could accede to such an idea – or any other – until British troops had been withdrawn.

From the Arab States Brooke flew to Abadan. His visit to Iran was to see oil installations and to talk to oil men – that oil whose defence absorbed so much of his mind in 1942. 'Is it intended,' he wrote in the aircraft flying from Abadan to Karachi, 'that in the evolution of humanity atomic energy should ultimately replace that generated by coal or oil?'[5] He flew on to Delhi, for the most nostalgic part of his tour.

Brooke, as ever on his travels, was lonely, speculating in his daily letters on whether at the next port of call there might be mail from England, calculating when he was past the half-way point of his journey and could legitimately regard himself as on the way home. 'It was a *frightful* wrench leaving you,' he wrote to Benita on his first evening away, in Athens, 'Heaven knows how I hate these departures.'[6] He was already longing for return. Yet India brought different emotions. 'Bombay brought back floods of memories of my old Indian days and gave me a desperate longing to be 25 again, landing there for the first time with my whole life in front of me again.'[7] In Calcutta he stayed in the house he remembered from the distant days of Lord Minto as Viceroy, Victor resplendent on Minto's staff, Alan agonizing over whether to try for the Staff College. It had all seemed very permanent, the great, central, Imperial strategic factor – India, the need to defend it, to keep open the routes to it. Now in his long talks with Wavell, the Viceroy, and Auchinleck, the Commander-in-Chief, there was a sense of impending storm. Wavell was gloomy about the political future. Auchinleck believed that the Indian Army would, on the whole, remain loyal to the Raj. Both agreed with Brooke that it was impracticable to think of Indian troops for long assisting in the myriad tasks which still had to be done elsewhere in Asia in the aftermath of war. None, at that time, spoke of evacuation – of the end of British India – except as something one day inevitable, but in no way as a solvent of the present problem. Yet when it came, and when the decision was made six months later to grant independence quickly and to accept the possibility of partition, Brooke reckoned it entirely right. It did, however, remove one of the fundamental elements of his concept of Imperial defence. Indeed, it finally annulled the concept itself.

In Burma Brooke found native apathy about restoring the country. He felt this fitted ill with aspirations for independence. He looked at such matters as one of his generation, regretting the absence in Britain of the youthful idealists who once took up the challenge of Imperial administration. However, Burma gave him the opportunity to see the scenes of some of the recent fighting. His elder son, Tom, was an Artillery officer stationed at Mandalay, and together they toured some Burma battlefields. On 15th November, he flew to Hong Kong, where he assessed the correct size of the future garrison. Thence to Japan, to be greeted at Tokyo Airport by the Supreme Commander, General Douglas MacArthur. They had never met before.

Brooke was anxious to discuss with MacArthur the concept and the command of a British Commonwealth force contributing to the occupation of Japan. There had been difficulties, which he was quickly to understand and then to remove in his visits to Japan and Australia. Most of all, however, he was anxious to see MacArthur himself. He had formed the highest opinion of the American General as a strategist, with ability, in Brooke's words, 'in a class by its own' (sic).[8] He was not disappointed by the meeting. He found MacArthur a man of striking personality and dignity, with a penetrating mind. Brooke saw that he might have defects; he clearly had a theatrical streak, which Brooke reckoned might be no bad thing. But 'a very big man' he recorded in his diary on 21st November, the night before leaving Japan and after many long discussions with MacArthur, 'and the biggest General I have yet seen during this war'. Subsequent events, when MacArthur fell from grace during the Korean War, in no way dimmed Brooke's admiration.

He was also impressed by the firmness MacArthur expressed on the Russian menace, and what he then and later regarded as the farsightedness of the man. They discussed Korea to which Brooke paid a fleeting visit, finding the same sense of an Iron Curtain rung down, what he called an 'impenetrable wall', as he had seen in Europe.[9]

Brooke's next visits were to Australia and New Zealand. It was an essential part of his scheme for Commonwealth Independence that in each zone there should be a 'lead' country with a Chiefs of Staff committee, all such committees operating on roughly similar lines. He found Australia inadequate in that respect, and that his

Australian colleagues did not resent but welcomed a frank talk on the subject. The Australian Chiefs of Staff were geographically separated from the seat of Government by the distance from Melbourne to Canberra; and they had allowed the Permanent Secretary to the Minister to become, in effect, their mouthpiece to Government. 'He takes it upon himself,' Brooke noted with horror on 26th November, 'to reply to telegrams from the British Chiefs of Staff without referring the matter to the Australian Chiefs of Staff and he represents military views in the Cabinet for the Australian Chiefs of Staff. There is no doubt that he is most capable but it is equally certain that he has been allowed to assume far too much power.'

Such comments may appear, in modern times, an intrusion. Those times were very different. Australia and the United Kingdom were not distant, friendly Commonwealth members maintaining courteous relations. They were, instead, intimately joined – until very recently by shared bloodshed and suffering – in great military enterprises which demanded trust and frankness. Plain talk was preferable to cool correctitude.

The matter was the more important because Brooke sensed a lack of realism in the Australian Government and in their attitude to what he regarded as the dangers of the future. This sense was to be reinforced four months later at an Imperial Conference in London, where Brooke described Australian Ministers showing 'blind faith' in the United Nations organization and a total failure to realize the nature of the Soviet threat, 'trying to prove' he was to write in his diary on 23rd April, 'that we were endangering the security of the world and likely to cause a war with Russia by looking at her as a possible aggressor'.

New Zealand was of particular interest to Brooke, because, twenty years before, he had considered leaving the Army and making his home there. He found the country delightful. There was also moments of satisfying relief from business. 'We went out to a sanctuary – where I had a lovely time looking at birds. I nursed a Duck-billed platypus in my arms – Pooks would have loved it. Also saw those little Koala Bears that look like Teddy Bears.'[10]

Of all the problems with which Brooke had to wrestle, none were more intractable than those facing South East Asia Command. Mountbatten's Headquarters were now at Singapore where Brooke arrived on 5th December. Memories of the terrible days of its surrender, the greatest single defeat inflicted on British arms, almost 'stifled' him, he wrote that evening. Those days had been among his first as CIGS. Now, as he stepped from the aircraft to be greeted by Mountbatten, he found a Tri-Service Guard of Honour.

> Somehow this Guard of Honour seemed to be an outward and visible sign of the culmination of all my work. Germany beaten, Japan beaten, and all the lost bits of Empire restored. I felt 'well, now I can return quite peacefully after having seen this'.[11]

It was pleasing to him to find that Mountbatten, whom he had so often criticized savagely in his diary for preoccupation with trivia and lack of perception of essentials, had 'come on in a most astonishing way', handling meetings with assurance and skill. It was as well, for mutual confidence was certainly needed in handling the problems of the Command, combinations as they were of the politically sensitive and the militarily complex. The worst was the matter of the Netherlands East Indies. In Brooke's view the Dutch were unreasonable, expecting their former possessions to be restored to them in exactly their former condition; an expectation which, to be met, would have demanded a large-scale campaign by British Commonwealth forces to suppress Indonesian nationalists. Brooke wrote, on his first evening in Singapore:

> (a) The problem of using Indian troops in Java, owing to impending trouble in India and the fact that there are no British troops available, does not admit of our contemplating any extensive operations to restore Dutch rule.
> (b) Therefore, the Dutch must be told that unless they are prepared to grant Dominion status to N.E.I. of a nature acceptable to the Indonesians we are not in a position to support them.
> (c) Should they disagree to do so then we should inform them that we have no alternative but to disassociate ourselves entirely from them, and to deal with N.E.I. purely from the aspect of concluding the war by disarming the Japanese, returning them to Japan and freeing the prisoners they had made. Should the Indonesians interfere with this policy we should inform them that any resistance they offered could only be classified as co-operation with the Japanese and treated accordingly. They all agreed that this was the line to take, and the one I should represent to the Government.

Brooke was more optimistic – as it turned out excessively so – about the future of French possessions in Indo-China. The responsible French General was Leclerc, a man Brooke took to immediately as the finest kind that France produces. It seemed to Brooke that the French, unlike the Dutch, were prepared to solve their own problems.

From South East Asia, via another short visit to India, Brooke reached Africa. Anticipating the move of British troops from Egypt, the British Government had decided to investigate the possibilities of Kenya as a base for a Middle East Reserve. Brooke was not impressed. Kenya, to him, had every advantage save one; it was in the wrong place. Communications were such that the place was likely to stay wrong, in spite of strong support for the concept by some Ministers, including Attlee. But he loved Kenya. He visited the Masai Game Reserve south of Nairobi, and was happy as always with his camera among wild beasts and birds.

After visits to the Sudan and Saudi Arabia Brooke flew to Italy. In Rome on 20th December he had a wretched mishap. As he was being taken round the excavations in the foundations of St Peter's he stepped, in the dark, into an open drain with a two-foot drop, and wrenched his calf and Achilles tendon. The doctor prescribed an immediate X-ray, but Brooke was determined not to miss an audience with the Pope which had been arranged for 6 p.m. He was in great pain, but found it possible to walk with two sticks. His excellent batman, Lockwood, had given him what he described as the largest brandy he had ever drunk, to keep him going. 'But when I entered the room,' he wrote afterwards – 'swaying on two sticks and breathing brandy I am certain that the Pope wrote me off as one of those drunken Orangemen from the North of Ireland that are beyond praying for . . . In any case he was certainly quite charming and never disclosed his feelings.'[12]

Brooke landed in England on 23rd December. He had visited some twenty-two different countries or Imperial Territories. He had discussed the world and the times with the Pope, with Rulers, Prime Ministers, Governors, Supreme Commanders. It was a vast exercise in liaison and communication. Everywhere he went where British troops were stationed he had been able to talk, to explain how he saw the problems of the Army, to listen to their own anxieties and experiences. He now felt equipped to face what turned out to be his six final months of office.

Brooke had reservations about some aspects of the Labour Government's policies. He voiced them clearly and frankly as was his wont, seeing it as his task to tell Ministers plainly, whether asked or not, the strategic implications of what they proposed.

Personally, however, he found his political masters most
congenial. He knew them well from their years in the Wartime
Coalition. He had always admired Attlee's shrewdness and
economy of words. He came to be ever more impressed by Bevin,
and what he described as his 'great qualities', and on 18th March
he noted – 'He is a most wonderful, helpful individual always full
of ideas. It is astonishing the ease with which he absorbs
international situations and the soundness of his judgement.'

On others he was less charitable. But on the whole his
judgement after the war showed a certain mellowness, a relaxation
of strain. Nevertheless, these were months of deterioration of the
situation in India. They were also months in which the decision
was taken to quit the Delta in Egypt. Brooke recognized the
inevitability of this; he parted company on the point from his old
friend Smuts, whom he so greatly admired but who on this issue,
he thought, was 'inclined to take rather a diehard attitude'.
However, he was not satisfied that the Government were exacting
sufficient concessions from Egypt and he declined the Prime
Minister's suggestion that, immediately after leaving office, he
should join the British negotiating team in Cairo. Nor was he yet
free of correspondence with one to whom such developments were
wholly deplorable. Churchill wrote to him on 8th May:

> I am profoundly sorry that you should be associated, I am told,
> with the Government's policy of evacuating all British forces,
> naval, military and air from Egypt and that your name and
> technical reputation should be quoted in support of this deadly
> policy.
>
> There is no way whatever of guarding the Canal, in the sense
> of keeping it open, except by the permanent presence of British
> personnel in the Nile Valley.
>
> I fear you have been sadly misled.

Brooke was within weeks of giving up the post of CIGS. 'It
was,' he replied:

> so very kind of you to write and let me have your views on the
> question of evacuating Egypt and I was so grateful for all the
> trouble you took. I can assure you that I am fully aware of all the
> facts you refer to and have given them due consideration in
> arriving at any conclusion.[13]

It was like old times.

Victory had brought high honours. In the Peerage he was created

Baron in September 1945, taking the title of Alanbrooke of Brookeborough in Fermanagh. Churchill wrote, in the context of his 'resignation list' of recommendations:

> It is my earnest desire that my three great friends the Chiefs of Staff should receive some recognition on my initiative of the work we have done together in those long and anxious years.

Some thought the Barony inadequate reward. The new Prime Minister apparently agreed; in January 1946 Alanbrooke and his colleagues were advanced to the rank of Viscount. In December he was invested as a Knight of the Garter. His part in a great alliance was recognized by large-scale award of foreign decorations. He was made Grand Commander of the Legion of Honour of France; Knight Grand Cross of the Orders of Dannebrog of Denmark, of the Netherlands Lion, of the Royal Order of North Star of Sweden and of the Military Order of Christ, of Portugal. He received the Grand Cross of the Victorian Order in his own country. When he gave up the appointment of CIGS he was given the Order of Merit. He held the United States Distinguished Service Medal. Universities bestowed honorary Doctorates and Degrees upon him.

These honours were gratifying. Yet Alanbrooke had little taste for public applause. He remained largely unknown by the many, hugely valued by the few. He preferred it thus. A friend, Sir George Giffard, wrote:

> At the end of the war in Europe, the Commanders of the Allied Forces are being properly and warmly congratulated upon their splendid successes but I have not seen anywhere an adequate tribute to you whom I regard as the architect and builder of our victory over Germany.[14]

The note was often struck. 'Few people,' wrote Sir Charles Loyd, 'will ever realize what you have achieved in this war and how much it [Alanbrooke's Peerage] is deserved,'[15] and some years later Sir Archibald Nye, then United Kingdom High Commissioner to Canada and the man who had watched Alanbrooke daily from the next door office of the VCIGS, expressed the same thought:

> You yourself have been indifferent to what people think . . . only a handful of people begin to realize all you did . . . you are more responsible for the winning of the war on the Allied side than any other individual with the sole exception of Winston himself.[16]

A great Victory Parade was held in London on 8th June 1946. The Chiefs of Staff insisted in riding together in one car. In war they had been united after many debates, through many tribulations, and countless anxieties. Now they were determined to be seen publicly united in the bright sun of victory. Yet, thankful for victory, heavy with honours, Alanbrooke remained the unknown Field-Marshal. He handed over the appointment of CIGS to Montgomery in June 1946, having ensured that Montgomery should inherit and use a balanced team within the General Staff, rather than surround himself with some of his 'faithful', his 'military family' as he had shown some intention of doing.

Alanbrooke wrote the last entry in his wartime diary on 25th January 1946. His final 'Note on my Life' related not only to the day he left the War Office but to his whole time in office. The concluding sentence is appropriate:

> As for Winston I thank God from the bottom of my heart for having been allowed to work with him for $4\frac{1}{2}$ long and momentous years.

Alanbrooke then settled at Ferney Close, for the first time in forty-three years a private man.

A Field-Marshal never retires. His service or counsel are always at the disposal of Government without any special instrument of recall. He is expected to assume many honorific positions, to dignify institutions by his presence, to make speeches. Alanbrooke was always ready to assume duties, to encourage and to help, particularly in connection with Charities and with ex-Servicemen. He was President of the Forces Help Society, of the Royal United Kingdom Benevolent Association, of the Star and Garter Home for Disabled Servicemen, of the London Union of Youth Clubs, and many more. In every case he took profound interest in the details of the institutions. He was never perfunctory. By temperament a private man who disliked public occasions and platform orations, he nevertheless took infinite trouble with each. He spoke widely – to military audiences, to naturalists, to Universities, to City companies, to schools, to the police. His speeches would be written out in full, and then reduced to a list of main points on a smaller sheet of paper. He could be an enthralling speaker. At the unveiling of a portrait of Churchill in the Junior Carlton Club in 1950 the Press reported his audience 'spellbound' at the insights that he eloquently conveyed of the higher direction of war. Anecdotes were kept in a stocklist of stories – most of them good stories, and always told with his excellent gift of mimicry and sense of timing. When it was appropriate to mention the war to an audience he often adverted to a favourite theme – the part played by the Chiefs of Staff Committee and the fact that the conduct of war means teamwork.

When the Chiefs of Staff were given the freedom of the City of London they followed the habits they had formed in office and 'cleared' the drafts of their speeches with each other. They formed a Trinity and Alanbrooke constantly hammered the fact home. He would quote as the soldier's ideal:

> The patience of a Saint in hardship
> The tenacity of a bulldog in adversity
> The courage of a lion when roused
> The chivalry of a Knight in all his dealings[17]

and he would apply this as much to work in the battlefields of Whitehall as in the field. His other constant theme was the necessity for the nations of the Commonwealth to grow closer rather than diverge. And when he spoke of the future it would often be in pessimistic terms. On one occasion he spoke of the Soviet Union 'sitting as a great pianist facing his keyboard' and said that 'collision must inevitably come' unless the Soviet Union were ultimately to break up. The answers, he believed, lay in spiritual revival, in the economic recovery of Western Europe and in the strengthening of Commonwealth bonds.[18]

A Field-Marshal never retires; but he goes on half-pay. Alanbrooke worried about money. As the youngest son of a large Irish family he had very limited means, and the half-pay of a Field-Marshal was inconsiderable. Ferney Close was sold, and the family moved out into the converted gardener's cottage. The collection of Gould bird books was sold – a sad wrench, although he recorded satisfaction at doubling the purchase price. Alanbrooke needed some activity which carried emolument.

It was not long in coming. First he was appointed Government-nominated Director of the Anglo-Iranian Oil Company, an appointment which started immediately he left Whitehall. He took up a large number of Directorships, both in industry and in the City. He was a Director of the Midland Bank, the National Discount Company and the Belfast Banking Company, as well as of the Triplex Glass Company, the Lowland Tanker Company and Hill, Thomson. Those who served on

Boards with him recorded their huge admiration for the qualities he showed – perception, quickness at grasping essentials; decisiveness and clarity; above all a forthright determination to speak the truth as he saw it, however contrary to previous fashions of thought. He was valued for his experience of the international world of Governments, for his intelligence and strength, for the warmth of his personality and for the delight of his company. His colleagues in the Boardroom esteemed him and wrote to him in terms remarkably similar to those used by his military associates. Clearly there was a certain element of reward in these Directorships, at first; there was a sense among many that the Service Chiefs deserved something tangible from their fellow citizens, and this was a way to provide it. But equally clearly Alanbrooke came to be valued for what he contributed and it was exactly what he always had – thoroughness, sureness of grasp, integrity.

No commercial activity gave him more happiness than the Hudson Bay Company of which he became a Director in 1948. He served for eleven years, and in July 1949 paid an extensive visit to the Company's bases in Canada. He revived his wartime habit and kept a diary. His approach to everything he was shown was just as in the Army – meticulous, observant and shrewd. He preceded the tour with a short visit to the United States, where he saw some old friends in Washington, dined with Marshall, and visited Dill's grave and splendid equestrian statue, erected by the Americans in the Field-Marshal's honour in the cemetery at Arlington.

Alanbrooke's tour of Canada gave him the sort of experiences he most treasured – something of the wild, something of sport, witnessing the enthusiastic and successful professional activity of men who knew what they were doing. He visited Ottawa, Winnipeg, Calgary, Edmonton, Vancouver, Victoria and Montreal. He went to the remote posts on the Hudson Bay, moving by air and then by sleigh. The sleighs were each drawn by a team of sixteen dogs, and Alanbrooke wrote with delight of 'the guttural noises from the Eskimos to manage their team'. A good deal of distance at Hudson Bay had also to be covered on foot – from time to time in thigh-deep water. After over five miles of this, on one occasion, Alanbrooke described himself as 'very cooked'. He had to follow his walk with a sleep of only one and a half hours before flying to his next stop at six o'clock in the morning. He was sixty-six and loved it all. At Churchill 'a visiting ornithologist helped me with some of my identifications'.

In British Columbia there was some memorable salmon fishing. But Alanbrooke treated the inspection of posts as a military operation. He had hoped that his tour would be entirely as a 'civilian' – under Company auspices and without Governmental overtones. This was too much to expect. Inevitably, in 1949, a visiting Field-Marshal, the wartime CIGS, would find himself carrying out at least some military duties on such a tour. He was to some extent the guest of the Canadian Government, and not purely a commercial visitor.

Furthermore, the Governor-General was none other than Alexander, who joined him for part of the tour. This was delightful. But, throughout, Alanbrooke regarded himself as essentially on business. He saw everything. When he visited a Company store he looked at everything and he met everybody. His recorded assessments of individuals were as pungent as on visits to wartime commands. 'He never interferes in the various branches except to advise and help. In fact, he believes in a military chain of command,' he noted approvingly of one local head of Company operations, 'and no interference with subordinates except through the head of their branch.' In commercial as in military matters Alanbrooke was always adamant on the necessity for a clear and well-defined channel of responsibility, and on the duty of all to use it – both up and down. 'The organization,' he jotted down on the Hudson Bay Company, 'very much like any military one, namely decentralization of command, sales represent operational side, Military Secretary Branch for selection of personnel, Intelligence Branch and Training Branch.' He was on familiar ground in some comments: 'Felt young blood required and more method'.[19]

Alanbrooke had still plenty of military activity. He had been a Colonel Commandant of the Royal Artillery since 1939 and of the Royal Horse Artillery since 1940. In November 1946 he was appointed Master Gunner of St James's Park, an office traceable at least to the thirteenth century in the annals of England, but in modern times effectively the Colonel and presiding authority over the whole of the Royal Regiment – its history and traditions, its standards, its benevolent institutions, its present, its future and its past.

Eminence in other and broader spheres never blurred Alanbrooke's love for the Regiment and absorption in every aspect of its life. To them he was, as he always had been, 'Brookie'. In his most formative years he had served, and only served, as a Gunner.

He now derived more satisfaction from his service to the Royal Artillery than from any other dignity or position. He always exhorted his brother officers to keep their minds open, to learn from the past but not to live in it, above all not (as he expressed it in a speech at Woolwich in 1946) 'to stand aloof from other arms'; but instead 'to be inquisitive'. In the same speech he speculated on Artillery responsibilities in the future, citing the possibilities of rockets, guided weapons and 'Homing Projectiles'. He was tireless in correspondence about Regimental problems. Alanbrooke was a man for whom no human question could be trivial, or beneath a Field-Marshal's attention. He was charming and considerate to younger men. On one occasion, at a great dinner at Woolwich attended by King George, a young officer was allotted a place to dine and was travelling back from his duty station at Trieste. Held up on the journey he arrived too late, so that his place was taken by a 'first reserve'. Alanbrooke heard at dinner that this had happened – the officer had just arrived and had been told that although too late for dinner he could 'take brandy' with the assembled company. Immediately after dinner Alanbrooke went went up to him and put an arm round his shoulder: 'Come along. I'll present you to the King.'[20]

Alanbrooke was also, from 1946 to 1954, President and Colonel Commandant of the Honourable Artillery Company, that ancient and unique military establishment which has brought such distinction to the association between the Armed Services and the City of London. He greatly enjoyed it, joining with zest in the correspondence which then, as often, arose about the structure, recruitment and roles of this most senior element in the Volunteer establishment of the country. In 1950 he became Lord Lieutenant of the County of London, and in the same year Constable of the Tower.

In 1953 came the highest military dignity of all. The office of Lord High Constable of England is, in modern times, only exercised at Coronations. At the Queen's Coronation Alanbrooke was Lord High Constable. He was thus in command of all troops taking part. He rode in the procession and attended the splendid ritual in Westminster Abbey as one of the great officers of State.

Now Alanbrooke could give plenty of time to the things he loved. He went on frequent fishing trips to Scotland, Ireland and Norway, describing every triumph or disappointment to Benita in the sort of detail he had long ago given to his mother, in describing the annual hunting expeditions in the Himalayas. But although he always loved to fish his real passion now was cine photography – the photography of birds. He had endless correspondence with fellow ornithologists about photographic equipment as well as about the birds themselves, and how to approach and observe them.

Thus some of Alanbrooke's happiest appointments were in this field. He was President of the London Zoological Society; President of the Severn Wildfowl Trust and Vice-President of the Royal Society for the Protection of Birds. From the start of this association he was always active in the making of films, giving a showing of his own films to the British Trust for Ornithology in 1945 and enjoying more with every year the adventures and the achievements of ornithology. He was not a professional, but he was in the first rank of gifted and knowledgeable amateurs. He was, above all, enthusiastic. Ornithological expeditions now took the place of those Indian treks of youth.

Alanbrooke undertook expeditions to the Hebrides, to Farne Islands, to the Bass Rock, to Hilbre Islands in the Cheshire Dee. He was particularly fond of wading birds. He would say 'I don't want any bloody little brown birds!' He made four very rewarding journeys to Holland, guided by a Dutch fellow-enthusiast, M. Van Tienhoven. These trips were very thoroughly prepared, not only administratively but in terms of the birds particularly sought. He would say that he was 'after Golden Oriole, Little Bittern, Reedwarbler, Great Crested Grebe, Blacknecked Grebe, Avocet and Spoonbill', and a detailed commentary on the requirement with suggested places, dates, possibilities or improbabilities of success would come back for further thought and proposal. Ultimately, a programme would be composed. These expeditions were physically arduous to a man in his late sixties or seventies – or, indeed, to anybody – and Alanbrooke had a number of mishaps which led his doctor on occasion to counsel more restraint. He seldom let the counsel affect his ornithology. He would climb to the loftiest hides in dirty weather. On one occasion in the Camargue in France he was determined to film flamingoes in a particular place of which he had heard only indirectly and accidentally, the flamingoes not being in their anticipated spot. Alanbrooke tracked them down, and cajoled permission from the Salt Mine authority in whose territory it lay. He 'used rank' – '*Je suis Maréchal*' – for the only time his friends ever recalled. Then, at the age of sixty-eight, he stood many hours knee deep in water.[21] He was indefatigable.

Probably Alanbrooke's most enthralling expeditions were two he made to Spain, in 1956 and 1957. These expeditions to the Coto Doñana started from Jerez, whence a long and arduous journey brought the party to that remarkable home of birds. They were led by two great experts, both revered by Alanbrooke, Mr Eric Hosking and Mr Guy Mountfort. The various members of the expedition had responsibility for photography, medical care and all the other aspects of planning. Alanbrooke loved it all. He made a particular contribution by obtaining some anti-mosquito lotion from the Quartermaster-General at the War Office. He derived great satisfaction from his own considerable contribution to the resultant films and report. As in Holland, the Spanish hosts to the expedition were generous, knowledgeable and charming.[22] Alanbrooke wrote the introduction to Mountfort's book describing the Coto Doñana. Next to the practice of ornithology he loved writing and talking about it to or for kindred spirits – Bannerman, Hosking, Mountfort, Van Tienhoven and others who shared his passion for this most compelling of studies. He was quick to take up with President Eisenhower in 1959 an American ornithologist's suggestion that the albatross was at risk from United States naval activity in the area of Midway in the Pacific; and received a helpful reply.

Alanbrooke did not brood about the war. Sometimes he gave a professional assessment of some of its course. Sometimes he adverted to a favourite theme (and what some would regard as a very debatable proposition) – that Hitler had made a great strategic error in 1942 in persisting with the Stalingrad offensive instead of diverting his thrust southward through Persia and Iraq; debatable because the left flank of such an extended advance would surely have been as vulnerable as was the German Sixth Army at Stalingrad to a Soviet counter offensive and on at least as unfavourable terms. He was full of anecdotes about the war, all recounted with zest and humour and impeccable timing. Just as he knew how to judge the right point of intervention at a Cabinet Meeting, so his stories were expertly inserted into a conversation and brilliantly told. He spoke annually, for many years, at the Staff College at Camberley on the life of a CIGS in war. But on the whole he did not wish to write memoirs, although he enjoyed some memoirs of others, saying that Montgomery's, in particular, gave 'a true picture'. He did, however, assent to the writing of a book based on his diaries. The story of the genesis and production of that book is told by Sir Arthur Bryant in his Epilogue to this volume.

Alanbrooke chose to live in England rather than Ireland. His home had long been in Hampshire and his children had grown up there. The Ireland he had known and loved as a young officer, whose stories he told with perfect timing and intonation, whose songs he sang – that Ireland had passed for ever.

But no connections were closer to Alanbrooke's heart than those he was now able to strengthen with his native Ulster. A Freeman of the Cities of both London and Belfast, he was made President of the London Ulster Association, and Chancellor of Queen's University , Belfast. He was also Chairman of the Belfast Banking Company, of which he was long a Director. He produced for the Midland Bank in 1959 a very thorough note on 'Banking and Economic Conditions in Northern Ireland'. His nephew Basil was Prime Minister of the Province. All doors were open to him, through his family, his great record in a great tradition, his character as a fighting man. But he was primarily valued not for his origins, nor even for his achievements but for his character and personality. Whatever he did, as always, he did thoroughly and well. He dignified every occasion. In Ulster, there was an extra dimension of love and pride. The Field-Marshals and Generals of Ulster were given a dinner in Belfast, and Alanbrooke responded to Lord Castlereagh's toast:

> If feelings of pride exist in mother Ulster's heart for her soldier sons these feelings are more than reciprocated by them, not only through filial motives but principally on account of the glorious part she played in the winning of the war.[23]

He spoke of his emotion in wartime, returning from one of the great conferences across the Atlantic, looking down upon a darkened land and knowing it was Fermanagh; and he talked uncompromisingly of the strategic importance of Ulster. He was given the 'Boyne Medal' in 1960. It was a replica, presented to outstanding public figures, of a medal presented to a gallant officer by William III after the Battle of the Boyne. In response to an address on that occasion he spoke simply and movingly of his love for Ulster, his boyhood memories of Colebrooke. Ferney Close was his personal sanctuary. Ulster represented childhood and tribe.

There were other and poignant reminders of childhood in his

later years. On 22nd May 1940, while the Commander of II Corps was engaged in the agonizing business of retreat, the Municipal Council of Bagnères-de-Bigorre held a meeting. Somebody had noticed in a French newspaper that a British General, commanding an Army Corps, apparently spoke Gascon and had been born at Bagnères. It was resolved by the Council to invite General Brooke to visit his birthplace. Then came the collapse of France, and ultimately the liberation. In 1946, the Mayor took the matter up. Through the British Embassy an invitation was issued. Bagnères-de-Bigorre wished to confer upon the British Field-Marshal the freedom of the town of his birth. Pau, his earliest home, wished to do the same. In February 1947, Alanbrooke returned to the places inextricably linked in his mind with his beloved mother. His sister wrote to him afterwards . . . 'I don't wonder that it was almost more than you could stand up to with the waves of memories flooding over you.'

Accompanied by Benita, Alanbrooke arrived at Pau on 21st February. He was a guest of the Municipality. The *Société France-Grande Bretagne* had organized the visit and Alanbrooke was delighted to find their President, Vicomte de Vaufreland, one who had hunted with him in the days of the Pau Hunt, when the country around was known as the Leicestershire of France; the days of the fashionable English society of Pau, of Alice Brooke, the days before 1914. Next morning, Alanbrooke and Benita were first driven to the Avenue Thiers where he had been to school, and thence along the road he had so often walked to the Villa Jouvence.

Opposite the Villa a covered stand had been erected, and drawn up on three sides of a square were soldiers of a French Parachute Regiment and detachments of ex-Servicemen, while cheering schoolchildren packed the pavements. After speeches of welcome the Préfet unveiled the plaque let into the garden wall of the Villa Jouvence.

Dans cette villa a habité pendant
les 10 premières années de sa vie
Alan Francis Brooke
Fils de Sir Victor Brooke Baronet
Maître d'Equipage à Pau 1885–1888
actuellement
Field Marshal Viscount Alanbrooke
Chef du GQG Impérial Britannique 1942–45

The crowds cheered, the children waved their little paper Union Jacks. Alanbrooke stepped down from the stand and crossed the road to the plaque. He turned and started to speak. As always, he had composed his speech in detail before. He thanked them for the honour done. He spoke, as so often, of his *deux patries*:

> J'étais tout de même à demi Français. De tous côtés je retrouve des précieuses mémoires de ma jeunesse . . .

The crowd relaxed with relief and approval of his fluent French. But suddenly something happened. He paused, and then broke into their local Béarnais. In Béarnais, he spoke of his memories of childhood during the darkest days of war. Then he quoted his favourite verse from their local song. There was a great gasp from hundreds of Béarnais throats – and then the crowd went mad. He was one of them, this Maréchal. He spoke their tongue like they did, he knew their songs. The song was taken up by thousands, and Alanbrooke left them, to lay a wreath at the War Memorial, to pay visits to two old friends who had known his mother, to revisit the Villa Jouvence itself. On 23rd February he drove to Bagnères-de-Bigorre.

Bagnères is a small village in rough and beautiful country in the foothills of the Pyrenees. Something of its comparative remoteness and solitude must have penetrated Alanbrooke's own character in infancy, breathing into him his love of nature, wildness, silence. The Chalet Geruset is on the western outskirts of the village. Alanbrooke and Benita were met by a Guard of Honour of French Paratroops. The small streets of Bagnères were decked with the flags of Britain and France. At the Mairie a copy of Alanbrooke's birth certificate was given to him. The Sous-Préfet spoke with emotion.

> *Vous êtes, M. le Maréchal, l'un des artisans les plus efficaces de cette victoire que votre pays a poursuivi au long de six douloureuses années avec cette tenacité inalterable et cette unanimité dans l'acceptation des plus grands sacrifices, marque invariable de son destin national . .*

It was a notable tribute. The party walked to the Chalet Geruset where a plaque was set into the wall.

> *Dans ce chalet est né le 23 Juillet 1883*
> *le Field Marshal Viscount Alanbrooke*
> *Chef de l'Etat Major Impérial Britannique*
> *de 1942 à 1945*

Then the Mayor of Bagnères crossed to the entrance gate of the Chalet and started to speak. He spoke of the common suffering of Britain and France, of the need for that common suffering to light a torch for future generations. A child, he said, would one day read the inscription and his mother would say 'He was a man of much honour, who rendered great service to his country and the world. Like you, little one, he came here to see the house of his birth because he had a great and good heart. He dedicated his life to his country and the triumph of just causes, his name is honoured and his life shines as an example to all.'

In Alanbrooke's heart there could not fail to be recalled those moments long ago, unknown to the Mayor, when his own mother, seeking to spur him, had said that she wished there to be earned, one day, a plaque on the place of his birth with such words as those. As he slowly walked towards the plaque those near him saw the tears glisten in his eyes. He started his prepared reply in perfect French. Then he faltered; and this time, with complete spontaneity, threw out his arms, smiling, and broke into the patois of Bigorre to express his feelings.

The people of Bigorre, hardy and vigorous, are used to travel in search of fortune or livelihood, but they always return. There was nothing strange in a distinguished son revisiting Bagnères. Alanbrooke walked slowly up the drive to the Chalet through lines of cheering villagers and children. He spent some quiet minutes in the house, in his mother's room, where he had been born. Then he came on to the balcony and schoolchildren sang 'Home Sweet Home' in English, and again his companions saw tears well into his eyes. His mother's 'Benjamin' had come home.[24]

Alanbrooke's last seventeen years of life, between leaving the War Office and his death, were happy, tranquil years. He was very active. He maintained a huge number of interests and commitments, but he could regulate his own life and was seldom at the call of others. He saw more of his family than had ever been possible in office, for even after the war he had often been alone in his London flat while Benita managed matters at Ferney Close. In his last years he savoured the contentment and ease of an unhurried family life for the first time since 1939. Those who only knew him at home or at this time would have found unrecognizable the image of the stern and uncompromising military man who had done more than any other to bring victory. They knew him as essentially gentle, as humble, as charming, and as exceptionally good with the young.

He was as he always had been to his chosen circle, the best and most entertaining of companions. He stalked and filmed his young grandchildren with the same skill as in his ornithology. His family, of all generations, gave him enormous happiness. His handwriting changed from a severe and formal vertical hand to something much more flowing and relaxed. He was adept at putting people at their ease. This was the true Alan, the imprisoned bird which had so often had to beat its wings against the iron cage of duty he had so firmly constructed. He was never idle, eternally active in house or garden if not working in his study.

One appalling tragedy marked the last years. Both Alanbrooke's daughters had married, Rosemary in 1945, the younger, Kathleen – 'Pooks' – in 1953. In November 1961 Kathleen died as a result of a riding accident. Alanbrooke was shattered. From her earliest days his letters to Benita had been filled with his adoration of her, and he never really recovered from the blow.

He was already retiring from certain Boards and occupations, for the first time excusing himself from functions and appointments. In the summer of 1963, however, he keenly anticipated two particular occasions. One was the Garter Service in St George's Chapel, Windsor on 17th June. The second was the intended presentation to him of a number of the Gould bird books he had so loved and had felt compelled to sell. A generous friend had learned the facts, and had organized a subscription to get at least some of these volumes together, as a present to Alanbrooke by eighty of his friends and admirers on his eightieth birthday.[25]

Alanbrooke missed both occasions. As the Knights of the Garter assembled with their Sovereign for the solemn annual congregation of the highest Order of Chivalry in Christendom they learned that Alanbrooke, one of the greatest of their number, had suffered a heart attack and died at his home a few hours before. He had been lying quietly in bed, drinking a cup of tea in the middle of the morning with Benita in the room. The cup slipped from his hand, he fell back on the pillows and died without pain or struggle, surrounded by the love which had been so very much the greatest thing in his life.

Nine days later, amid all the ceremony that attends the funeral of a Field-Marshal and a Knight of the Most Noble Order of the Garter he was brought to Windsor for the last time. Then he was taken to lie near the home which had brought him so much gentle peace.

CHAPTER XXI

Alanbrooke

LORD ALANBROOKE'S ACHIEVEMENT was to take the lead in infusing realism into the Western Allies' supreme direction of the Second World War, and to do so unremittingly and unflinchingly. It was a remarkable achievement. 'No one will ever know,' said Admiral Sir Bertram Ramsay shortly before his own death in January 1945, 'what the country owes to Alanbrooke. His worth is quite uncalculable.'[1]

He had to deal and play three separate hands – with Allies, with colleagues and subordinates, and with the War Cabinet of the United Kingdom.

With Allies – which chiefly meant the Americans – Alanbrooke has been described as only partially successful. He drove a hard bargain, and in the words of his beloved Dill: 'The American Chiefs of Staff have given way to us a thousand times more often than we to them.' It was been said that they did not feel easy with him, did not trust him not to 'outsmart' them. With his sharp, rapid, rather nasal delivery, his ability to talk fluently and accurately on complex issues without notes or assistance, and his impatient, inexorable logic, he was formidable. Was he the master of Allied Councils his admirers believed?

Almost certainly he was. So critical a participant as Admiral King was reported by Admiral Somerville in Washington as becoming expansive when in relaxed mood about Alanbrooke.[2] The American Chiefs of Staff, said King, were tremendously impressed by the ability of the CIGS to present a case with brilliant clarity. They noted with astonishment his mastery of a detailed subject, often involving figures and data, without reference to any notes, simply having before him a piece of paper with three or four words thereon. The Americans were wary of him, but their respect was profound.

Alanbrooke's own recorded preoccupations give an impression of remarkable absorption in the problems of the Mediterranean theatre. The Americans certainly thought this reflected a mind excessively concerned with traditional British interest – the

Mediterranean as a route to India and the East, the Middle East as an important *place d'armes* for sea and air communications thither, British direct responsibilities and paramount influence in the Arab world itself.

Alanbrooke did not think in those terms, although it would have been perfectly rational to do so; as late as 1951 one of only three pillars of British Defence Policy was defined as a firm base in the Middle East. But when Alanbrooke became CIGS the War against Germany had produced its own imperatives. Rightly or not – and he would certainly have said rightly – the British were in Egypt and the Middle East, and he saw their position as an essential 'long stop' counter to enemy penetration of the Causasus and pressure on Iran, and thus to threats from the north-west to India and to oil.

He saw the Middle East as a forward base for the defence of India and the protection of vital oilfields. This was the defensive function. But simultaneously Egypt provided an offensive function – a base for conquest of the North African littoral, with the possibilities that in turn offered for operations against Southern Europe. Thus the strategic potential of the Mediterranean theatre and the questions of priority it posed were always complex. As the war went on, and those questions embraced the future of the Balkans as well as North Africa, the Middle East and Italy, the matter certainly became no simpler. Because of this complexity Alanbrooke devoted much thought to the Mediterranean. But that did not mean that he regarded its priority as paramount. He recognized that the war would be won on the direct approaches to Germany, in Western Europe, in France and in the Low Countries.

The war against Japan posed strategic problems of a different order. In terms of military decision these were overwhelmingly American. The British, of course, had military problems in the defence of India and the reconquest of Burma. But in terms of overall war strategy, the British problem chiefly consisted in balancing the need to stand with the Americans in the final defeat of Japan against the obligation – and national interest – to play a significant national part in the eyes of those who felt dependent upon British power and looked, with some uncertainty, for its restoration. Yet the war against Japan created less problems between Allies than it did between Prime Minister and Chiefs of Staff at home.

Alanbrooke's differences with the Americans were often

strong. Although these differences were generally felt by his colleagues as well, Alanbrooke came to epitomize the obstinate British to the Americans. He was not only the chief spokesman of the British Chiefs of Staff, but was also the most convinced exponent of strategic policies which differed from the Americans' most sharply. These principal differences lay in attitudes towards the Mediterranean, and in the timing of the invasion of North West Europe; and these differences make up a significant part of Alanbrooke's story.

Was he always right? Probably not. No man is. Some have disputed the logic which impelled the Allies towards exploiting British presence in the Western Desert, by extending the campaign to North Africa and thus threatening the whole southern flank of occupied Europe. It is probably true that the expedition – TORCH – finally made an invasion of North West Europe in 1943 impossible. In Brooke's view it would anyway have failed, launched with inadequate forces against an enemy undistracted elsewhere in Europe. But he did not have to make that case on its merits. He was assisted by the pattern of events and their timing. For Roosevelt made clear there was a political imperative for American forces to be engaged somewhere against the Axis before the end of 1942. That could only be in North Africa. Failing SLEDGEHAMMER 1942 – manifestly impracticable – TORCH was a political necessity.

Once the North African campaign was under way, the turning point was the Casablanca Conference and the decision to invade Sicily. Once that decision had been taken the pace of the North African campaign meant that further operations in 1943 could only be in the Mediterranean. Was Alanbrooke right not only to accept this but to press it? What would have been the outcome of a decision to move all forces from North Africa to the United Kingdom for a 1943 ROUNDUP – to undertake TORCH, but thereafter to leave Sicily and Italy to their own devices? If it were really practicable successfully to start the decisive battles of the West in 1943 rather than 1944 the strategic and political advantages were clear for all to see. Brooke thought the invasion would have failed once ashore. Could it have been launched at all? It is doubtful. Logistic advice at the time was against, and Alanbrooke certainly did not challenge it. The Battle of the Atlantic was not finally won until midsummer, and victory in Tunisia did not come until May. But even had the enterprise been practicable there were overwhelming arguments against it.

First, a great strategic advantage would have been neglected. Alanbrooke argued throughout 1942 for relentless pressure on Italy, so that the German Army should be driven to replace the Italian throughout the Mediterranean theatre, and possibly be induced to spend effort on defending Italy itself. To leave Italy unmolested – and combatant – after the victories of Tunisia would have relaxed a point of pressure on Germany. To Alanbrooke this would have been indefensible. To him the pressure had to be exerted and constantly maintained until North West Europe was invaded.

Second, the policy of concentrating in the United Kingdom for an invasion of North West Europe in 1943 would only have been sound if that invasion had had the near certainty of operational success which existed in 1944. Nothing could have been more damaging than an unsuccessful invasion, with Italy still in arms against the Western Allies, Germany free to concentrate against a second attempt and Western morale shattered by expensive failure. To Alanbrooke all this was perfectly possible. He did not believe the German Army and Air Force would be sufficiently weakened before 1944: that weakening had to come from a further year's subjection to air bombardment and from a further year's campaigning in the appalling conditions of the Eastern Front. The German Army in the East was still deep in Russia in the summer of 1943, and still capable of a major offensive, as at Kursk. Great though the distances were there was little impediment to those forces being switched, instead, to defeat an invasion of the West. Alanbrooke, furthermore, did not believe that American production and American training would be adequate to the main task before 1944.

Nobody can say whether this assessment was impeccable because it was not put to the test. It can surely be said, however, that the fighting in Normandy, when it ultimately occurred, was not such as to contradict it. It seems unlikely that smaller and less well-trained forces than those who undertook OVERLORD would have had certain success against a German resistance materially more powerful and less inhibited by air power as to operational movement. Yet such would have been the case in 1943. Alanbrooke regarded his judgement in 1943 as vindicated by the subsequent course of the war, and it seems hard to gainsay him.

Alanbrooke was respected by the Russians. From Stalin downwards they recognized his strength. Churchill has left record of Stalin's appreciation of the CIGS's directness and intelligence.[3]

'A very clever military leader,' Stalin remarked to him thoughtfully as he gazed at Brooke. Alanbrooke took the line from the start that it was folly to give the Russians anything without demanding a *quid pro quo*. He had a clear vision of what their long-term aims were, and of the methods they would use to achieve them. He thought Western policy weak towards the Soviet Union, and it is likely that no small part of Russian respect for him stemmed from their appreciation of this. Strangely, in spite of his sense of the Russians as enemies under the skin and ultimately, he may have handled them better than he did the Americans.[4]

With his colleagues Alanbrooke was a superb chairman, representative, counsellor and comrade. 'I take away with me,' Portal wrote to him in 1945, 'what I know will be an enduring memory of your friendship and of what I learned from you. I can honestly say that I have an unbounded admiration for the way you handled our COS affairs and for the forcefulness and complete sincerity and the clearsightedness and soundness with which you always dealt with Ministers on our behalf – no one could ever hold a candle to your record in that respect and it was about the biggest factor in getting results.'[5]

Alanbrooke was *primus inter pares*. He was not a 'supremo' and he completely rejected the concept. To him it was necessary to win the sincere agreement of the professional leaders of the three Services, who were responsible in the last resort for the lives of Service men and women, for the sound deployment of ships and aircraft and divisions, for the outcome of battles. He often railed in private against some of the views of his fellow Chiefs of Staff when they did not agree with him – and they probably railed at him. But he passionately believed that they had to reach agreement, and on every point of substance they did.

In reaching these agreements, in presenting that united military advice which was so signal an achievement of the British system in the Second World War, the Chiefs of Staff were managers of a machine. Points of view become associated with great men but they are generally evolved by a process. It was not the least of their successes that the British Chiefs of Staff presided over a highly efficient process. The Joint Planning Staff, who drafted each version of a paper, would obtain at each edition the views of each of the Chiefs, produced by his Department – in the case of Alanbrooke by the General Staff. The Department had to be completely sensitive to the views of the Chief – but prepared to argue objectively and fearlessly and thus to influence those views. There was thus an internal and vertical dialogue in each Department, and a lateral and interdepartmental discussion in the Joint Planning Staff. Out of this would emerge the successive versions of papers gradually more acceptable to all, until the search for agreement necessitated debate by the Chiefs of Staff themselves. The process was adaptable and flexible. It was worked under enormous pressure, day and night, year in year out. It was essential and effective, and not Alanbrooke nor any of his colleagues could have played their part without it.

In terms of strategic outlook Alanbrooke had few major differences with the Royal Navy. He thought Pound ineffectual, but recognized that his health was at the root of much. He was devoted to Cunningham. On the principal issues he was absolutely convinced of the primacy of the Battle of the Atlantic. The free passage of the Mediterranean, with all that demanded in maritime effort, was a keystone of his strategic philosophy. He recognized with as heavy a heart as any sailor the political imperatives behind the Arctic convoys, although he believed that the British should have been harsher towards the Russians and less accommodating in the matter. As to the 'Pacific Strategy' the Chiefs of Staff stood together against Churchill in their strange battle of early 1944.

With the Royal Air Force matters were sometimes different. Alanbrooke found Portal a most agreeable companion and charming colleague; they shared tastes for fishing and country pursuits, both were skilled ornithologists. But both were completely professional; and as a professional soldier and strategist Alanbrooke considered that excessive claims were made for and priority given to the strategic air offensive. He recognized the critical part it could play in weakening Germany, but he reckoned that Harris had too much influence with Churchill and that his claims for the achievements of Bomber Command were exaggerated. The result, in Alanbrooke's view, was an excessive priority given to building up the strategic bomber force at the expense of aircraft and pilots for close support of the Army, and at the expense of the Battle of the Atlantic. The detailed argument has been conducted often and at length. In the author's view the first of these points – support for the Army – had little validity; while the second – on the Battle of the Atlantic – was a fair criticism of our Air Policy.

Alanbrooke did not believe in meddling with how Commanders in the field ran their campaigns. He sometimes offered advice, and sometimes uttered criticism, but he always made clear that the Commander on the spot, provided that he had all relevant information, must be free to decide his course of action and must be supported. This principle of trust and non-interference extended to some of the most momentous decisions of the war from the Western Allies' point of view. The decision, for instance, to land on D-Day in Normandy and not in the Pas de Calais was not one in which Alanbrooke interfered. Crucial though it was, to him it was an operational decision, one for the responsible Commander. The application of this principle was easy with some, like Montgomery, in whose operational judgement he had complete faith. He would say of Montgomery, 'I don't interfere with him. He is an incomparable tactician. He's right – and doesn't let people forget it!'[6] Montgomery wrote to him after the war: 'I can only say again that any success I may have achieved in the field is due basically to you: it is all your doing.'[7]

The principle was harder with others, like Auchinleck or even like Alexander, who were, he felt, out of their depth in some situations. Nevertheless, while they were in command, and unless there were sound reason to lose confidence in them and replace them, the CIGS backed them to the hilt. Few passages of arms were more savage than when, for instance, Alanbrooke turned on Churchill and told him roundly that he had no business to abuse British Commanders before the Cabinet. On the reverse of the coin, if he thought subordinates inadequate or mistaken, whatever their position he made his view icy clear.

Alanbrooke's greatest achievement was in his handling of Ministers. The word 'Ministers' masks the heart of the matter. Every Chief of Staff is Chief of Staff to a superior, he is professional adviser and executant to one with more authority than he. In Alanbrooke's case this superior was a very great and remarkable man, the Prime Minister and Minister of Defence, Winston Spencer Churchill. Their relationship inevitably dominated the years which Alanbrooke spent at the summit of his profession. In this relationship Alanbrooke was, by general verdict, fearless, formidable, articulate and in the end, convincing.

It was a stormy relationship. Alanbrooke profoundly admired Churchill yet found his ideas often unrealistic, his habits of mind irrational and infuriating, his method of work frustrating and exhausting, and his temper sometimes vile. He found some characteristics of Churchill intolerable – his unfairness, his pettishness, his fondness for unsound advice and advisers, his dislike of any but palatable facts when pursuing a favourite scheme. Yet he loved him. He loved his courage, his humour, his readiness to bear huge burdens for England. From all this stress Alanbrooke found relief in his diary. For his part, Churchill probably found Alanbrooke a trying subordinate. The latter's uncompromising negatives, his bleak resistance to cajolery, his practical approach, his reliance on facts alone were often tedious to Churchill.[8] Yet Churchill loved Alanbrooke, and to others often said so. He had implicit trust in him.[9] Where others would be tongue-tied or resentfully inarticulate beneath the bludgeoning of Churchillian invective or exhortation, Alanbrooke was eloquent, cogent, persuasive. Alanbrooke's was a dissective, Churchill's a romantic mind. To Churchill the war was a great drama, often terrible, generally exhilarating, tragic and triumphant by turns, but never dull. He lived it to the full. To Alanbrooke, the soldier, it was a grim and distasteful business, a matter for exact calculations, hard logical thought, lonely constancy and iron will. He wrote in his diary on VE Day, 8th May 1945, 'I would not have missed the last three and a half years of struggle and endeavour for anything on earth,' and yet he loathed them.

The sides of Churchill which Alanbrooke found hard to bear pushed him at times to despair. The Prime Minister had no understanding of operational details, nor of logistic constraints and opportunities; but he had a great passion for them. He pestered Commanders in the field for information and bombarded them with exhortations which went well beyong his responsibilities. He thus wasted a great deal of time, not least his own, and much impeded the war effort thereby. He also placed subordinates, by these tactics, under considerable nervous strain. He could be implacable, he could be unjust, he could appear vindictive, although seldom for long. All this Alanbrooke found a sad trial. He had to protect British Commanders against interference and defend them against diatribes, and he did so with energy and without equivocation. It was a running battle, never lost or won. Yet outwardly, with rare exceptions, Alanbrooke was, in the words of Eden, 'patient, even tempered and untiring'; and Eden also recorded that Alanbrooke 'never left Prime Minister and President in any doubt as to what militarily he and the Chiefs of Staff considered right . . . and would never be bullied into compromise'.[10] It is likely that as CIGS his trials were less than those of the First Sea Lord, because the comparatively centralized system of controlling naval operations makes them particularly vulnerable to the sort of interference to which Churchill was prone. Such interference undoubtedly fed the Prime Minister's appetite for martial exploits, his sense that he was like Marlborough 'riding in the whirlwind'. But as Chairman of the Chiefs of Staff Committee, in matters of grand strategy Alanbrooke bore the brunt.

This was not all. As the war progressed, and particularly in its last eighteen months, Alanbrooke felt that Churchill was deteriorating physically and mentally, that the enormous strains of war had taken too high a toll, and that the Prime Minister was less and less capable of reaching a timely and coherent decision, or of accepting rational argument. He also felt that Churchill's resentment of American predominance was so bitter that it distorted his judgement. His later diary abounds with views that Churchill was no longer master of himself. He reiterated those views after the war when he reconsidered them. Some of this was probably fair, but some of it reflects the irritation of an equally exhausted and certainly sensitive man, one who reacted to both public and personal circumstances with an intensity of feeling which his exterior belied, and which could lead to private exaggeration. Alanbrooke was perfectly aware that Churchill was and remained unique. He knew that Churchill was indispensable – his profound anxiety whenever Churchill was ill[11] shows a lively sense of that.

In spite of some exasperated diary entries to the contrary he knew that Churchill's fall or departure from the scene would have shaken public confidence and given immense comfort to Britain's enemies. Alanbrooke realized that the pressure under which Churchill had lived since 1940 made most things comprehensible, even forgivable. He had no regard for Churchill as a strategist in the military sense; but he knew that Churchill could lead as none other and that he epitomized Britain at war. His rages with Churchill – no other word is adequate to the degree of irritation and condemnation – were understandable but they were private luxuries. They found vent in a diary which can mislead as to character. A reader of Alanbrooke's diary and nothing else would find an emotional, hasty and intolerant man, immoderate in expression. On the contrary, in his professional dealings, Alanbrooke was an excellent listener, calm, rational and persuasive.

Nor were his rages always just. The relationship became so difficult from Alanbrooke's side that he was often in danger of damning the best of Churchill's thought with the worst. This danger became more acute as time and the war progressed. One has only to read Alanbrooke's comment on Churchill's reaction to the atomic bomb, for instance, to see how prescient was Churchill, how unwisely dismissive was Alanbrooke. For at its best Churchill's grand strategic vision was superior to that of his professional advisers. Alanbrooke was not a visionary. He saw the next step clearly, and those beyond only as far as they could be inspected and measured. For the rest he liked to wait and see. He was cautious. He knew how unpredictable are events which turn on battle. This made him place a great premium on flexibility, and gave him a deep dislike of strategic agreements regarded like contracts. Churchill shared this view; but he also liked to paint great pictures, to which events might be made to conform. When he looked at a detail he often saw it awry. And if he did not like it he preferred not to look at it at all. Nevertheless, Churchill sometimes saw visions, and sometimes they came true. It was Churchill who first expressed the opportunities of the Mediterranean campaign in authoritative form; and it was Churchill's vigour – even at the time, imprudence – which made certain the North African enterprise and all that flowed from it. Furthermore, in the debate on the Pacific strategy, the most bitter internal debate of the war, Churchill's instincts were probably sounder than Alanbrooke's. In his reaction to the heady optimism of September 1944 and his sense that hostilities could continue into 1945 and that we should be ready for them Churchill's judgement was vindicated by events.

Perhaps above all, Alanbrooke could not get on terms with Churchill's method of conducting argument. It was the way of a great Parliamentary performer, rather than a Commander or an Administrator. Churchill would attack a proposition with savagery because he felt that only under that sort of attack would truth emerge or survive. Truth, for Churchill, had to be tempered in the fire of his own critical rhetoric, his own ferocious cross-examination. It is curious how often, to the end of his days, Alanbrooke commented with exasperation that Churchill had apparently 'come round' to an idea and produced it as his own having bitterly attacked it the previous day. To Alanbrooke this was evidence of vacillation. For Churchill, it was the way he worked.

All in all, Churchill and Alanbrooke formed a remarkable

combination. To be chief adviser to a genius demands a certain genius of its own sort, and Alanbrooke possessed it.

As professional head of the Army, Alanbrooke gave complete confidence to all. It was overdue. Dill, although Alanbrooke greatly and rightly admired him, had been out of his depth with Churchill. He lived on his nerves. The relationship of Dill with his superiors coloured, as always happens, relationships to and within subordinate echelons.

Strength, clarity and authority were needed at the end of 1941, when Alanbrooke became CIGS. He immediately displayed them, and throughout his term of office his subordinates, although they often feared him and without exception went in awe of him, were profoundly relieved that he was where he was. The conscience of the Army was sound, its confidence much restored.

Alanbrooke was certainly not infallible in his judgements of men. He was by temperament remote, and he did not find it easy to get on terms with those he did not already know well. To a few of the latter he was probably too indulgent, to others too intolerant. When he rejected a man, he did so emphatically – sometimes over-emphatically. He was somewhat ungenerous to and about Gort. He may have been accurate in his estimate of Alexander, but he perhaps showed insufficient appreciation of the selflessness of a man who could so naturally and quietly forgo much credit which was his strict due – and the serene quality of one who could effortlessly attract so much devotion. He saw Auchinleck's weakness clearly, but less clearly the fundamental nobiltiy of his character. He grumbled at Mountbatten, and showed little sense of Mountbatten's remarkable achievement, his inspirational quality. His intimates at the top of the Army were Dill, Wavell and Adam. To most senior soldiers he was formidable, although to those who got to know him well he was also both entertaining and kind. But all knew that he was his own man, uncompromising and direct, no mouthpiece of another. Furthermore, Alanbrooke had a great man's gift of acknowledging fault in himself. He once rebuked General Anderson for an error of tact in North Africa and later found that he had been misinformed; he immediately wrote to Anderson a charming letter of apology and self-criticism. This was typical. Alanbrooke in his professional dealings was a stern man but he was both just and humble. All knew that self-justification had no part in his character. All knew that he would stand up for them when they needed it. In the tributes paid to him at his death, whether in the Press or in letters to Benita, a frequent note was struck by soldiers: 'Of all I ever met or soldiered with he was in all respects the greatest.'[12]

As a soldier, Alanbrooke was cautious and inherently conservative. He was a well-read and thoughtful student of history and exponent of the military art, and he knew that risks are the stuff of war: there are no certainties. But by conviction he was prudent and calculating. He would only take a risk when all the factors had been explored, every assessment made which could be made, everything quantifiable measured. In the Second World War, in fighting the Germans, Alanbrooke was particularly reluctant to offer hostages to fortune. He respected his adversary too much. His caution owed much to experiences at two places only a few miles apart, experiences divided by only twenty-three years: Ypres and Dunkirk. They coloured his mind. Such a general may sometimes miss opportunities, and none can say whether as a Commander in the field Alanbrooke would have shown that divine spark which could inspire a Wellington, for instance, to see in a flash at Salamanca the one fleeting chance for delivery of a crushing blow at a critical moment; to say 'By God, that will do', and ride off to transform history. It may be so.

Alanbrooke's command of his Corps in 1940 was impeccable, and his speed of apprehension was as great as that of the Duke himself. Had he been given his heart's desire, the supreme command of the OVERLORD forces, none can say how it would have gone. Paget said afterwards – 'He would have won the war in Europe a year earlier. He would have been decisive and have closely directed the campaign.'[13] There is hyperbole here – a 'year earlier' the campaign had not started. Certainly, Alanbrooke would have exercised strong control, and his strategic sense and experience were greater than Eisenhower's. But he would have met as many political difficulties at that stage in the war, and it is doubtful whether his tact would have matched Eisenhower's; and tact was essential. Alanbrooke's character, like Wellington's, was of the kind which saves lives by thought and study, and by disdain of gesture. His prudence and self-discipline were the consequence of devoted study of his profession. They did not stem from a cold temperament. He was not afraid of his feelings, and he felt deeply. He had a streak of melancholy. He wept freely. He could be impulsive and exaggerated: but he kept this for his diary and for his private moments. In those, he could express extremes of emotion, including personal loathing for public figures, which he sometimes but not always modified on reflection.

Alanbrooke's instincts were orthodox. He found, for instance, Mountbatten's conduct of affairs and relationships in South East Asia Command novel and unsound. He was sceptical of the whole concept of supreme and joint-Service Command as untried and dubious unless anchored by strong single-Service Commanders. Thus, he instinctively supported General Giffard* – describing him to Wavell as 'one of the few with any stability and commonsense'[14] in SEAC – when it is more likely that imagination as much as sense was required, and Giffard had too little of the former. Alanbrooke liked 'sound' men. He quickly became impatient if they worked with him and he found them pedestrian; but his taste was for the familiar and tried rather than for the original and the irregular. He was supremely rational rather than imaginative – a conservative cast of mind, needing occasionally to be mixed with its obverse.

Above all, Alanbrooke was strong. It was a highly intelligent strength. His particular qualities as a soldier stemmed from this strength and this intelligence. Of these qualities, first was shrewdness. His mind was sharp. He took a point exactly, and he gave a factor its right weight, no more and no less. Next, he was quick. Both his realistic acuteness and his speed of mind reflected upbringing more than blood, were more Gallic than Anglo-Saxon. In rapid speech his words tripped over each other, as if they could not keep pace with the movement of his mind. Finally, he was decisive and thus convincing. When he summed up, or gave orders, or presented a case there was no doubt in any mind what was required. He carried this gift through life and at every military level, whether in Staff Conference and Cabinet, or in command. The gift so admired by his colleague Chiefs was as marked in the Commandant at Larkhill – or in the Corps Commander of 1940, remembered then by his own Chief of Staff as one whose orders never conceivably needed written confirmation, they were so unequivocal and so clear.[15] Mr Robert Casey, the distinguished Australian Statesman, summed it up admirably in his own Memoirs:

> Alan Brooke is a man of unusual quality and intensity. I know of
> no Service Leader who contributed more to the winning of the
> Second World War than he did, by his military capacity, by his

* Who crossed swords with Mountbatten.

judgement and by his complete honesty of thought and expression.[16]

Alanbrooke was not perfect in act, in judgement or in charity. He was simply the outstanding soldier of his generation, a superb professional and the prime military architect of Britain's successes in the Second World War.[17]

In one respect, the qualities which made Alanbrooke a great soldier were carried into his personal life. He was thorough. His nephew, Lord Brookeborough, remarked:

> He was never one to leave things to chance. Any mortal thing he did he did well. In his hobbies, his private life or his profession he would study his subject with meticulous attention to details.[18]

In all he did he made himself expert, whether meditating on a new fishing device or tactic, perfecting his photography, preparing his early hunting trips in India or learning a new language. But, in the main, the private man was completely in contrast with the professional. To many of those who only knew him in the Army he was, or could be, forbidding although he was totally without pomposity or affectation. To those whose acquaintance or friendship was other he was a different human being, warm, amusing, and affectionate. Moran, who saw much of him in the war years, described him as 'a simple, gentle, selfless soul – a warning to us all not to give up hope about mankind'.[19] He was an admirable listener, one who gave his whole attention. His thoughtfulness for others was immense. He took great trouble with the young or the materially unimportant. He loved his family and his own true friends and they loved him deeply in return. He attracted love from the few, awe from the many, admiration from all.

Alanbrooke's love of nature was an integral part of his character. It found its principal expression in ornithology, where he was described by the greatest experts as being in the first rank of non-professional ornithologists.[20] This love of nature, of birds, of colour and beauty and the high, wild places gave him that extra dimension any great professional needs if he is to be a whole man. Alanbrooke was a great man and a whole man. He could love and be moved, as well as fight and decide. He had passion and compassion as well as strength and will. With this inside him, he needed to confide. He had to pour out his feelings, hopes, fears, hates and frustrations. He needed to do so to someone he loved, and to do so every day. Hence his daily letters to his mother until she died, his later diary and letters to Benita. If he were not with a beloved confidante, he had to write. That alone could alleviate the pangs of solitude, and the melancholy which accompanied his gaiety and his intensity of feeling. In such outpourings, he was self-questioning, impulsive, turbulent and exaggerated, while the public man was confident, calm and judicious. This dichotomy imposed a considerable strain, for Alanbrooke was a man of transcendent honesty. To those who knew him and worked with him it was impossible to imagine him saying an evasive thing.

The Field-Marshal had first wished to be a surgeon. Perhaps it was simply a boy's fancy, but it is significant. His mind was dissective. In accord with the traditions of his family, attracted by the possibilities of sport, travel and action within his slender means, he became a soldier. Because of his natural abilities, and ingrained compulsion to master what he took up, he became a superb soldier. But he was not a 'born' soldier in the sense of only caring for a warrior's pursuits or finding a thrill in war – as some do even in modern war – unmatched by other challenges. Such, perhaps, was Montgomery, or Rommel or Patton in their differing ways. Such, certainly, was not Brooke. Like Wellington, circumstances impelled him towards the military profession; he would have excelled in any sphere. He happened to be a soldier. Perhaps inevitably he became the chief of all.

His life's climax was as professional head of the British Army and Chairman of the British Chiefs of Staff Committee in the Second World War. As such he was without peer.

He fought with tenacity, courage and skill for a realistic strategy and for a path that would lead most surely and most economically to victory. He fought colleagues, he fought Allies, he fought Ministers, he fought Churchill. He fought successfully.

Because his battles were successful, British soldiers were able to hazard their lives in other battles with more chance of victory. He wished nothing more. He was the best Chief of the Imperial General Staff ever produced by the Army, and he was produced at the vital hour. Britain was fortunate indeed.

EPILOGUE

by Sir Arthur Bryant

The Making of *The Turn of the Tide*

ON THE LAST DAY of his five and a half years as Chief of the Imperial General Staff, Sir Alan Brooke wrote in his diary, 'My feelings were so mixed that I found it hard to disentangle them. But, above everything, the longing for rest predominated over all other feelings.' Then he had driven down to Norfolk to stay with a fellow ornithologist and spend what he described as 'two lovely days, one on Scolt Head Island and one on Hickling Marshes, making a film of a roseate tern which had just hatched off her family'. 'I spent this morning in complete peace mending an old rabbit hutch,' he had recorded after one of his rarely uninterrupted wartime Sundays at home with his wife and children; 'after lunch I went to Turgis Green where . . . I spent $1\frac{1}{2}$ hours in hide photographing bullfinch. Came home for late tea and more work at rabbit hutch.' The last thing he wanted to do when release at last came to him was to re-live, let alone write about, the burden of unremitting toil and responsibility he had borne for so long.

Yet, five years later, after rejecting every suggestion that he should write his memoirs, Lord Alanbrooke – then the Royal Regiment of Artillery's greatest living son – acceded to its request that he should allow his life to be written after his death if I would agree to write it. Knowing the universal regard in which he was held by the Army, I did not feel I could refuse his Regiment's invitation provided it proved compatible with future commitments, including a multi-volume history of England on which I had just started work.

At the time, therefore, of this mutual provisional acceptance of the Royal Regiment's proposal, we exchanged letters, I writing, 'I hope that the prospect of being your Boswell does not fill you with too much dismay', and he replying, 'I am delighted that you will be undertaking my memoirs a little later on, and shall try and get some notes worked out that may help you.' During that spring of 1951, I attended, at his invitation as Master Gunner, a Guest Night at Woolwich, while in the following year he gave away the prizes at an exhibition organized by the St John and Red Cross

Hospital Library of which I was then Chairman. And in the summer of 1954, he kindly arranged for me to be present at the Garter Service in St George's Chapel, Windsor, when Winston Churchill was installed as his fellow Knight of the Garter.

But at the end of that year our acquaintanceship, and the long working partnership and friendship which were to follow, suddenly ripened. It had been arranged that, until I was in a position to commence work on his biography, a research student – Mrs 'Buster' Long, a former member of the Chiefs of Staff secretariat – should prepare material on his early life and on recollections of their work together by his wartime colleagues. In the autumn of 1954 the Royal Regiment asked me if I would examine what she had done with a view to deciding whether she should continue amassing more. It then transpired that, in order to help me in my future task, the Field-Marshal had started to copy from his wartime diaries passages which he felt might be of use to me. In doing so he had become so absorbed that, with his habitual perfectionism, he had transcribed in his own hand almost the whole of his wartime diary, adding to it a running commentary of autobiographical notes and memories which its re-reading had recalled. Much of this Mrs Long had typed for me to consider with the other material she had collected.

At that time, having just published the first volume of my history of England, I was preparing material for its successor, *The Age of Chivalry*. But I was so struck by what the reading of Alanbrooke's autobiographical notes and diary entries made clear that, unknown to the world, it had been the strategic perception and genius of this unassuming and reticent soldier at Churchill's side which, more than any other single factor, had turned the triumphant tide of Axis victory in 1942 – the year in which he became Chairman of the Chiefs of Staff Committee. And that, thereafter, playing a leading part in guiding and influencing the decisions of the British and American military leaders, his strategic genius had been largely instrumental in bringing about the defeat of Nazi Germany's bid for world dominion. Here, lying before me, was one of the great original documents of military history. And unless I could do something about it quickly, rather than wait until its author's death before making its contents known, it might be many years, even centuries, before his decisive contribution to the Western Allies' victory became recognized.

For neither Winston Churchill's widely acclaimed six volumes of his *Second World War* – the last of which had recently appeared

– nor any of the official War Histories so far published had given any indication of what this great British soldier had achieved. And, as a result, a false legend of how the War in the West had been directed and won was already becoming established, and in a few years' time might no longer be possible to alter.

Important though my unfinished history of England might seem to me, here was something historically far more urgent. Accordingly, on November 30th 1954, I wrote to him.

'I have re-read your very remarkable Notes most carefully and have thought a great deal about them. What they contain seems so important to this country that, if only a small part of it can now be made available in a form which will neither hurt nor create division and ill-feeling, I feel that there is much to be said for making the attempt. It is nearly ten years since the War ended and thirteen since you set in motion the train of events which led – after 1942, as I see it, almost inevitably – to victory. Through that wonderful and very moving partnership between you and the Prime Minister this country contributed in that year something even greater than its stand in 1940: the implementation of Churchill's brave definition in May 1940 of our war aim: "Victory in spite of all terrors." I have always felt that Alamein was, strategically speaking, almost the most dramatic victory in our history – the nearest parallel is the Battle of the Nile, so similar in many of its circumstances. And your Notes and narrative put it in its true setting and make it seem even more moving than before.

'The truth about it which they reveal – one which, if presented rightly and with discretion, could reflect nothing but credit on those concerned and, most of all, on this country – ought to be told while people, here and in America, are still sufficiently interested in the War to be receptive. If it is not told now, it may be too late. In that case, as with Haig and the British Army's achievement in 1916–18, a false legend will have been established which it may take a century or more to shake. And that legend will rob this country, as it has already partly done, of the credit of a magnificent achievement.

'Because of their complete truth and frankness, and partly because of their very brilliance the diary and Notes obviously cannot be published in full for many years. Even the full-length biography that the Royal Regiment wants written cannot be published within any foreseeable period, for, if it is to be regarded as definitive, it should not be published or even written in your lifetime – and even a Field-Marshal can scarcely be expected to commit suicide in order that a false legend should be combated before it is too late! Yet I feel that there is room, if you agree, for something to be done now – a work based on your diary and Notes – to make people realize how Britain in 1941–2 laid the foundations for victory.

'I should like to suggest the publication of a short book, to be called, say, *The Turn of the Tide,* telling the story of what happened between the fall of France and Alamein and, in particular, in your first decisive year as CIGS. If you decided it should be written, I should like to write that book and I regard it as so important that I would be prepared to lay aside what I am doing now in order to write it. After studying your Notes very carefully, I think it could be done in such a way as to cause no controversy or offence, and yet, by quoting from them wherever practicable, to present the story with something of the same vividness as you tell it. It would not, I admit, be easy, but I think I could do it.

'The object of the book as I see it, would be to tell the story of (a) how Britain held the ring of sea-power round Germany and Italy in Europe, first alone, and then with a desperately stricken Russia and a still unarmed America by her side, prevented them from breaking out to form with their Japanese ally a solid Axis block from the Pacific to the Atlantic; (b) how, while struggling herself for survival, she prepared the way for the Allied counter-attack which began with Alamein, Torch and Stalingrad. That story would be the setting, as it were, for the jewel which I should extract from your diaries and Notes . . . It would make no attempt to deal with the details of operations (the business of the official war histories) but would, from the time you became CIGS, focus the light solely on that little pinnacle of high strategic decision on which you and the Prime Minister, the COS Committee and the British and, later, American war leaders lived.

'The presentation of the story should, I suggest, be completely objective. I should make no comments and pass no judgments, even by implication, but let the story tell itself, as you and the PM wrestled with events, and slowly, and in the face of so many difficulties, wrested the initiative from the enemy. The principle that I think should be followed is that as much of the truth as can be told now should be told, and in as vivid a way as possible (that is, wherever practicable, by quoting from your diary and Notes) subject to the proviso that nothing should be said or used that could hurt or give offence to those who were your colleagues and companions. And, though this might somewhat modify the prevailing conception of the PM's omniscient part in directing and dictating the entire course of the War – one which, if left uncorrected, will almost certainly be followed by a violent and damaging reaction after his death – it would not, I feel, diminish his stature, but, in the long run, enhance it. For the effect of your Notes has been to make me see him as, not a lesser, but a greater, man – because so much more real and human than the rather boring and infallible image which a stupid propaganda is creating. Your pages, for all the natural and transient irritations of the hour, reveal, better than anything I have ever read, his courage, wonderful vitality and, above all, underlying magnanimity. I don't know which of the two I am left admiring more at the end – he for never overriding you when you stood firm despite all his passionate attempts to convince you against your will, or you, not only for your unerring strategic sense, but for both standing firm and staying put, when any other man would have lost his balance under the strain and thrown in his hand. You must often have almost hated one another yet you finished the journey together. There seems something very fitting, after that companionship, that today you should both be Knights of the Garter.

'For the rest, the book would give me the chance to do what I had hoped to do in the unfinished official shorter *War History of Sea-power 1939-45*, on which I worked in my spare time for seven years for the Admiralty and Air Ministry: to present, free from all the cluttering mass of detail of the full official War Histories, the broad strategic perspective of the War which you, and you alone, I think, always saw clearly. In one of my chapters in *The Age of Elegance*, I called Wellington "Neptune's General" and the title might apply as aptly to you. Had Hitler seen the strategic truth as you saw it, I don't see how we could have held and turned the tide in that year of decision, 1942.

'I shall more than understand,' I concluded, 'if you decide against it.' But hurt, I think – though he never spoke of it – by Churchill's unconscious failure in his *Second World War* to acknowledge the full part played by the Chiefs of Staff Committee, Alanbrooke welcomed this proposal to anticipate this part of his posthumous biography. With his agreement I communicated what was in my mind to General Lund of the Royal Regiment, and, a week before Christmas, the Field-Marshal, his wife and Sir Otto and Lady Lund, dined at my house in Rutland Gate to discuss our course of action. By this time, with his permission, I had in confidence shown the diary accounts of his 1942 American,

Egyptian and Moscow journeys to my trusted and much loved publisher, Billy Collins who – as moved by them as I – approved my proposal to lay aside my unfinished history of England in order to write, as the framework in which to set and elucidate the diary, a strategic narrative of the War.

On the day after our dinner Alanbrooke wrote to me, 'I am so pleased that you can now start straight in on the book . . . Meanwhile I shall get on with 1943 so that you may judge whether any of it should be included.' To which I replied, 'Thank you for your kind promise to help me answer questions. It is a strange and very exciting sensation for a historian to communicate with the subject of his history. I am used to living with the acts and works of the great men of the past until they become as real to me as my own contemporaries. But I have never been able to question them, and I shall certainly avail myself of this unwonted luxury!'

Thus began, by the light and with the aid of Alanbrooke's diaries, the five years' collaboration between us, on his part of re-living and, on mine, of recording his day-by-day struggles with his colleagues, chief and allies so brilliantly epitomized by General Fraser:

'He fought with tenacity, courage and skill for a realistic strategy and a path that would lead most surely and most economically to victory. He fought with colleagues, he fought with Allies, he fought Ministers, he fought Churchill. He fought successfully.'

Henceforward for the next five years, until the publication in the autumn of 1959 of *Triumph in the West* – the sequel to the book on which we embarked that Christmas – he and I were in continuous communication by letter and word of mouth. In all that long association, during which I constantly sought his guidance, submitting to him everything I wrote in my repeated re-drafts of the thirty chapters and more than a thousand pages of our two books, we never had the slightest difference.

The only occasion on which I ever had to over-persuade him was, characteristically, – for he was the least mercenary of men – over the financial arrangements for our co-operation – he maintaining that, as a writer by profession, I ought to keep whatever the book earned. At first, as there was some difficulty in predicting what this would be, or what obstacles, or even total stop, our venture might encounter, and, as I was relinquishing a form of historical writing which I had made remunerative for a speculative venture in a contemporary and controversial field, I suggested a formula under which I should keep a major share of the profits until the sales approached those normally earned by my books, after which all further profits should go to him until they equalled mine, when we should share on a fifty-fifty basis. In the end, after it had become clear that the book was likely to attract a wide readership, this fifty-fifty formula was adopted at all levels. By then, at my suggestion, Collins were negotiating, on Alanbrooke's behalf, the formation of a Trust under which, in return for the conveyance to them of the copyright of all passages from the diary and autobiographical Notes used in my two books, his Trust should receive his half share of the royalties as a tax-free capital sum, since he was neither a professional author nor himself writing the books. By this means *The Turn of the Tide* and its successor were able to go far to redress the injustice done Alanbrooke by an egalitarian-minded Socialist Government's refusal to vote the traditional parliamentary grant promised by Churchill to the nation's victorious commanders. For his sole financial recognition from the State for his services had been a war gratuity of £311.5.0.

One uncertainty which faced us both from the start of our collaboration was the precarious state of Alanbrooke's health. By now in his early seventies, the strain imposed on his heart by the prolonged overwork of the War years was taking increasing toll. Just a month after our dinner party, he wrote, 'I have been in bed for the last two weeks, and with a sentence of one or two more weeks in bed followed by some four to six resting with no engagements. The trouble was brought on by a go of 'flu which disclosed a tired and distended heart and a congestion of the lungs. I had been suspecting that the heart was at times resenting what I was asking it to do, but felt that, as long as it did not make too much fuss over it, it had better carry on.

'I am getting on well,' he continued, 'the congestion of the lungs is clearing and the pulse behaving rather better. The specialist made me cancel my trip to Canada in March, which is sad as I was looking forward to it. I am, however, having a chance to get on with the diary notes. I have now reached November 21st '43 and am having a very interesting time with Malta – Cairo – Teheran – Cairo – Tunis – Italy, meetings with Chiang Kai-shek, Inonu, the beginning of Winston's illness, etc. It is a period of special interest to look back on and to realize the extent to which the Americans crippled the end of the Mediterranean [campaign] (a) by wanting to shift to cross-Channel operations too soon (b) withdrawing landing-craft etc. from the Mediterranean to please that useless Chiang Kai-shek.'

A week later he wrote again. 'The doctor seems quite pleased with the way I am progressing, but has not yet decided when he is going to let me up. I have finished another small book for Buster to type which has carried me to December 3rd '43. I have been dealing yesterday with Winston's 69th birthday in Teheran, attended by Roosevelt, Stalin, Eden, Harry Hopkins and many others. I am now just returning to Cairo for the last stages before Winston is ill in Tunisia and I go on to see Alex. It is all stirring up amusing and interesting memories.' 'I handed over another volume of Notes to Buster yesterday,' he added at the end of January, 'and am half way through the next volume. I have reached January 20th '44. My illness at any rate gives me a chance of getting on with the Notes.'

For it was becoming increasingly clear that, for all his earlier wish to put his intolerably burdensome and harassing wartime experiences out of his mind, he was now ready, and even anxious, to re-live them in retrospect. And what made our collaboration such a rewarding experience for us both was that he took as much interest in the technical problems of researching and writing my explanatory historical narrative of the war's course as I in his strategic plans and vision and his day-by-day struggles, as recorded in his diary, to make them acceptable to his colleagues, chief and allies and translate them into sustained victorious operations. At the start of our joint venture he was still contributing to the material placed at my disposal by continuing to supplement his diary by the autobiographical memories or Notes its re-reading evoked. While he did so, eager to lose no time I was already at work on the introductory chapters. Thus, in one of the earliest of our many exchanges of letters, I find myself writing, 'By the end of the weekend I hope to have draft of a first chapter I have called "Defenceless Island" and, in another week or ten days, the start of a second which I am calling "The Saving of the Army". I feel it is important to set the scene of our story: the long neglect of our arms and belated attempts to repair that neglect and the strategic problems created by it – which is, in effect, the situation you were called upon, first in a subordinate capacity, and then in a supreme one, to solve.'

A month later, on February 17th, I wrote again. 'I am writing to tell you how moved I have been this evening reading the story – which Buster brought in this afternoon – of the second Quebec

Conference, of your terrible personal disappointment, of your triumph with the Americans (all the more moving because of the hardness and loneliness of it and the misery you must have been suffering) and then, so unexpectedly and exquisitely told, the wonderful climax of the Habakkuk story! . . . Reading all this wonderful later stuff (so much of it, of course, that we can't yet use, yet a lot of it that we can) I keep wondering whether it is worth while struggling as I'm doing at present, and not too successfully trying to preface it all by telling the story of those dreary days of unpreparedness, unrealism, defeat and disaster in which your story begins. We needn't do it, and yet deep down I feel we ought to – and that those who won the triumphs of the later years were standing on the shoulders of those who died so forlornly through absurd mistakes that might have been avoided, and yet which were so gloriously redeemed in the dark days of 1940. Reading of your struggles and triumphs in (how unlike triumphs they must have seemed at the time, as your diary makes so clear) Casablanca, Washington and Quebec, I am reminded of that very early entry in your diary – for November 15th 1939 – where you write, "While talking to them I always have the horrible feeling that I may at one time or another be instrumental towards the issue of orders that may mean death to them." And, in the wisdom of those decisions you won others to with so much patience and skill, and at such a cost to yourself, you were all the time saving countless lives as well as winning victory for your country. I don't see how anything can ever compensate you for that great command in the field for which you were so superlatively fitted and for which your whole life seemed the training and prelude. For it must have seemed like the loss of half your being – and yet the supreme service you did, almost unknown to ninety-nine out of a hundred of your countrymen, could never have been equalled, let alone surpassed, by any victories in the field, however brilliant.'

On which writing two days later, he commented, 'The Quebec disappointment was a desperately bitter one, but I think the decision was a right one. A British Commander would have been in a difficult position with the bulk of his forces made up by Americans. This was made evident by Monty's position. He started in Normandy as the Commander of the land forces under Eisenhower who was Supreme Commander (the job I was to have had). Owing to the outcry in the American Press . . . by September 1st Eisenhower assumed the dual role of Supreme Commander and Commander of the Land Forces, while Monty resumed command of British Forces.' Some months later, when I had reached the point in my draft chapters where he had been offered command of the Middle East and refused it, he added, 'It means so much to me that you should so fully realize what I went through when turning down the M.E. Command and when the promise of Overlord was withdrawn. They were two of the major events in my life, and very few people have fully realized how bitter the disappointment was. This was probably due to the fact that in both cases it was essential to keep my true feelings to myself. But, even in after years, few of my friends seemed fully to realize what the decision cost me and how deeply the disappointment hurt.'

In continuing his earlier letter of February 19th, Alanbrooke again mentioned how his illness was helping him to progress with his autobiographical Notes. 'I have now reached September 20th '44, the end of the 2nd Quebec Conference. I am afraid that in the 1944 diaries you will find me rather embittered against Winston. I do hope you will make allowances for the fact that they were written at a time when I was getting very tired, and also at a time when repeated goes of pneumonia, treated with M & B, had made him more difficult than ever to handle. There is no doubt that at this time my criticism of him was often unkind and unfair.

'I can well imagine,' he added, 'what a difficult time you must be having with those early chapters. I hope for your sake that you may soon be out of the bocage and in the open country.' This was a reference to an admission of mine in a letter about the phoney winter of 1939/40, that I was still, as it were, 'fighting in the bocage with the open country beyond still eluding me'. 'One thing about which I am pleased, dissatisfied though I am with my own work,' I replied, 'is that the typescript of your early diary volumes, which my secretary has nearly finished transcribing, is going to enable me to keep much closer to the diary and so keep you much more continuously in the centre of the picture than I had thought possible from Buster's original transcripts. It isn't that your Notes aren't invaluable for this, as for the later and more important periods, but the continuous diary gives me a line to work along which at this point would otherwise be lacking.' 'I am still struggling in France,' I wrote on March 16th, as I continued with my work on the pre-Dunkirk diary volumes, 'and am beginning to feel that, unlike the BEF, I shall never get out of it!'

By the middle of April 1955 Alanbrooke was beginning to comment on the first draft chapters as he received them. 'It has been a matter of intense interest,' he wrote, 'to see how you work at a book, the immense amount of labour you put into it, and the way portions of it suddenly burst into flame like flowers . . . I have made a few minor suggestions in pencil in the margin to discuss with you when we meet . . . The Prelude is a wonderful picture of the years leading up to the War, and an excellent introduction to the book. It is perhaps a bit on the long side and you may be able to condense it, but I must confess that I read it twice to see what could be cut and did not find much.'

For the start of the book was taking, as always, much longer than I had anticipated. 'It is still slowly – very slowly – taking shape,' I wrote at the beginning of July. 'I am still not writing the book itself but only the chapters out of which I shall reconstruct it when all are written and I can treat the whole . . . chronologically and as a unity. But I am quite clear, if you agree, that the book should lead up to give consecutive and long – very long – passages from your own narrative,

(i)   The flight to Washington in June 1942
(ii)   The Middle East and Moscow journey of August 1942
(iii) Casablanca
(iv) The 1943 Quebec Conference.

Apart from my telling the story of the course of the War and so leading up to the problems you sought to solve, the whole object of the book should be to make it possible to quote as extensively as possible and with as few omissions from these remarkable passages. They are all being typed out by my secretary so that you can consider them, together with my introductory chapters and the omissions I am suggesting making. I propose to do a little interweaving with the Winston, Hopkins and other parallel narratives, but as little as possible beyond what is necessary to give background, and be just. In other words I want the climax of the book and the explanation and vindication of your strategy, and of what you were striving to do and did, to come, not from my words, but yours. Whether I can reduce the scale of the rest of the book in the final rewriting to carry the story as far as Quebec I still don't know.'

Four weeks later I wrote again: 'I have now reached the point where I can use the diary and Notes in sufficiently long extracts to form a continuing narrative – in other words, I am at long last through and in the open country. And, though I shall probably need to make a certain number of cuts, this wonderful description of your travels is one that I should like, if you agree, to use as much

in extenso as possible. For it will grip and hold the reader and
reveal, better than any paraphrase of mine, what you achieved and
how you achieved it. You have already approved the June 1942
Washington journey and of the Americans' visit to London in July.
Broadly speaking, whereas, up to the end of the chapter I sent you
last week, I can only use the diary in small illustrative passages to
point my own narrative, after June 17th 1942 it should mainly, I
feel, be the other way round. Though confined to the accounts of
the great international Conferences – Moscow, Casablanca,
Washington, Quebec, etc. – the story can then become in a large
measure yours, and I should only, I feel, for the remainder of the
volume intervene at intervals, to let the reader realize anything of
importance and relevance that was happening simultaneously and
continue my story of the course of the war – e.g. Alamein – between
your accounts of the Conferences.

'Everything, of course, must turn on how far my introductory
chapters lead adequately up to yours and so render their use *in
extenso* possible. But, provided I can make the former good enough
and set the relationship between you and Winston in its broad
background of a magnificent national achievement under his
superb leadership, I feel convinced that that is the most effective
form the book can take. If you agree, what we have now to do is to
decide what long passages I am to use, and I can then rewrite the
early, or rather intermediate, chapters on 1939/41 on the scale
required to lead up to them . . . I shall write the Alamein chapter at
once before going back to the early part of the book, and we shall
then be able to form a rough idea of the size of the volume. I should
like, if possible, to include Washington and the decision to invade
Italy with the news of the Sicily landings – an obvious moment to
end a book called *The Turn of the Tide*. In that case Quebec would
have to wait and become the beginning of Vol. II.'

For imperceptibly we had already begun to envisage a far
wider chronological canvas than that which I had originally
conceived and proposed. And it was his desire to re-live and see
recorded the whole of his three and a half years' traumatic
experience of shaping, in committee, council, conference and daily
argument, the strategic direction of the War – an experience so
exacting at the time as to seem almost unbearable and for which his
nightly diary entries had been his only outlet. And this had now
caused him, and myself with him, to wish to enlarge a canvas, at
first stretching only from the 'Phoney Winter' and Dunkirk to
Torch and Alamein, and to substitute for it one which, taking in

the victories of 1942 and the reopening of the Mediterranean, extended from the day when he assumed chairmanship of the Chiefs of Staff Committee to the final defeat of the Axis in 1945.

As the book progressed, so did our friendship. During the April of 1955 my wife and I were able to pay a brief visit to our country home on the Dorset coast, which we had been unable to visit since the previous autumn, partly because of the demands made by *The Turn of the Tide* and partly because of the terror our aged stray terrier had conceived at the sound of the guns on the nearby Bovington tank range. A few days' cessation of firing over Easter had given us the chance of a brief stay in Dorset, and on April 11th Alanbrooke, who had been unable to come up to London to see me owing to a bad cold, wrote, 'I do hope that you are able to have a little rest while you are at Smedmore and that you will not be bombarded with queries about cows, trees, poultry etc. If you are coming back by car would you care to drop in here for lunch or tea. We are right on your road, and it will give the dog a chance of a run round.' Thereafter, whenever we managed a visit to Dorset, we would break our journeys at Hartley Wintney, where he and his wife, Benita, were living in their former gardener's cottage. That May he and I spent a weekend together at Stanway, the Gloucestershire home of his friends, Guy and Lady Letty Benson. During it, in addition to working with him on the book, I accompanied him to the bird sanctuary at Slimbridge, where we lunched with the Peter Scotts, looking out from their lovely picture window at the swarming bird life outside and where the great soldier with his camera completely forgot everything, including myself, the book and his own heart trouble, while I vainly tried to restrain him from exhausting himself in his pursuit of his elusive photographic quarry!

That August, the Bovington gunnery range being closed for Bank Holiday, the Alanbrookes stayed two days with us at Smedmore. Afterwards he wrote, 'My dear Arthur, I do hope that you will agree that through my diaries you know me better than most people and that consequently we might well drop formalities and use Christian names. Sitting in the lovely surroundings of your beautiful garden and reading those enthralling chapters of your book made the time fly all too fast. I was thrilled by what you gave me to read, and would not have thought it possible to deal with the delicate relations between Winston and myself so admirably' – a reference to a first draft of an introductory chapter I had just written called 'A Partnership in Genius'. 'If he should take offence at anything you have written he would certainly fall in my estimation, but I feel such a contingency is most unlikely. In all you have written you have shown such understanding of what I was trying to achieve and of the difficulties I met. It is a wonderful feeling having a historian dealing with one's diaries who has such acute strategic sense and such wide vision. I am afraid that I was of little help to you in going through those chapters, but there was nothing that I wanted to alter.'

A few days later I nearly lost him – and the book! On August 13th, writing to thank me for two more chapters, he added, 'I hope you will be able to read this, but my hand is all bandaged up which makes my writing worse than ever. I had a narrow shave last week, I electrocuted myself with my Tarpen Hedge Trimmer and took a full 230 volts! Luckily the connection came apart just as I passed out. As no one was there' – for Benita being out, he was alone in the garden – 'I think it would have been the end of me if the current had gone on passing through me. I am lucky to have got off with some bad burns on my hands, and my heart none the worse for it.'

Yet neither the shock nor his miraculous escape from death nor the pain he was suffering, caused him to postpone, even by a day, the round of ornithological visits and public engagements he had planned for the autumn. 'I am off tomorrow for Norfolk,' he continued, 'for a week's bird photography, and should have time while I am away to go through Chapters 2 and 3 and have them ready to return to you when I get back on August 21st.' Six weeks later he was still writing, 'The hand is going on very slowly but I have been warned to expect that an electric burn always goes deep. Luckily it does not hurt much unless I bump it, but it makes life a little difficult . . . It has now been bandaged for 7 weeks and the doctor says another 5 will be required. I have quite got over the shock and the heart has now settled down again to its pre-accident behaviour.' Until the winter his work on my draft chapters, which I continued to unload on him, was interspersed with similar excursions. 'Have practically finished Chapter V and feel that it is a great improvement on what I saw before,' he wrote on September 29th. 'Shall finish it tonight so as to return it before we start for Cheshire . . . I leave here tomorrow afternoon and shall be away till the evening of October 6th. That will finish my bird photography for the year and from then I shall be at home.'

Every summer during the five years we worked together, except one – when an equally alarming and far more painful accident with a rotary scythe resulted in a fracture to eight of his ribs* – this dauntless septuagenarian embarked on a programme which would have deterred a far younger man. 'We start on Thursday morning early,' he wrote at the beginning of the second spring of our collaboration, 'and return on the evening of the 17th May, only to start again for Holland on May 21st! By June 4th the Holland trip will be over, and I shall be at home till July 9th, when I am due in Belfast for Queen's University graduation ceremonies' – he was its Chancellor – 'and then on to Mayo to see my daughter till July 20th. I am giving these dates so that you should know when I am available.' Once, aware of what fatal havoc a collapse of his overstrained heart could have on our joint venture, I half jestingly protested, 'I am appalled by your itinerary! It sound as bad as the War! I should do exactly the same thing in your shoes, but what will happen to your poor collaborator if you drop down dead, rushing diagonally up and down the length of Britain in this weather? If you haven't by then settled the copyright question with Billy Collins' – a reference to the negotiations with his newly appointed Trustees, from whom Collins were now buying the copyright of his diary extracts to save them from tax, and the consequent necessity of safeguarding my right to use them in the event of his premature death – 'Anne and I will starve, I shall be thrown into prison for not paying last year's surtax, and my farm employees will be rendered homeless! So *please*, for our sakes, be careful.'

By the early months of 1956 the main part of the book had assumed the broad shape in which it was to appear a year later. 'My final chapter "Trident",' I wrote on January 28th, 'has been one of the hardest of the lot, involving constant rewriting to twine all the various converging threads into an intelligible pattern. In a way it's the most important chapter in the book, for it shows what your strategy was achieving. I have been most impressed by its fatal effects on Hitler's attempts to create a central strategic reserve. Guderian's book throws some particularly interesting light on this.

'It seems clear to me now that, having taken the story right up to the fall of Italy – I had originally, you will remember, thought only of going to Alamein, though you always thought Casablanca,

---

* Commenting on this and an accident to my foot through which I had driven a scythe while weeding my beech plantations, he wrote, 'As you say, we seem to be a little unfortunate at times in our agricultural pursuits! you with cold steel, and I with modern mechanization.'

and perhaps Trident, should be included – my first idea of the book, as a story of the hard part of the war and a frame in which to set such of your diaries as I could use to illustrate your achievement, has imperceptibly changed into something rather different – a study of your strategy both during *The Turn of the Tide* and later on, causing the turn of that tide, so confining it to what no other *War* history – not even Winston's (one might almost say, least of all Winston's!) – has told them. It will mean, of course, scrapping that first pre-war part, "Defenceless Island". It seems a pity to have wasted two months or more on the former last winter, but perhaps I shall one day be able to use it; for it's a story that wants telling.'

'I do feel that those early chapters are just what was wanted to deal with the start of the War,' Alan wrote on April 30th, 'and that you have succeeded in condensing all that mass of material in a masterly way. Benita is still reading it, but I shall be posting it back to you before we leave on Thursday.' Benita, however, was more critical. 'I must send you a little note,' she wrote to me, 'to tell you how enthralled I am with the Introduction, Prelude and Chapter 1, which Alan is taking back to you tomorrow. May I remark in one or two places on his characteristics as they strike me. The Prelude in its pictures of him seems to me somewhat too austere, a side that *does* appear in his make-up, especially when putting over convictions – but under stress. Though he did not put out the hand of friendship lightly, he has the gift of making his friends very real ones, both among those who work for him and with all whom he has the opportunity of getting to know. Here his gift as a raconteur holds his listeners with his inimitable manner of description and humour. Again, knowing so well his approach to others, I should not term his manners as "aloof" – in fact it would be contrary to his regard for his fellow men, and of his friendly contact as exemplified on p. 11, "always talks as if he were still a Brigadier!" These are minor points, of course, but do have a bearing on the impressions that readers will get of Alan as a man; and I feel that posterity should know of the kindly and human make-up, concealed only when duress and circumstances compelled his sterner attack.'

The relevance – and justice – of Benita's criticism I could well appreciate, enjoying as I now did the warmth and delight of his friendship. His enchanting gift of mimicry – always good-humoured and never unkind – I had experienced during our first dinner party together at Rutland Gate when the exquisite humour of it had reminded me of a much loved Irish aunt, who in my youth had often kept me in fits of laughter by this accomplishment and who I later discovered had been Alan's first cousin, Laura Smythe. As one got to know him better it was difficult to associate the formidably correct and immaculate Field-Marshal, with his abrupt speech, quick decisive manner and rapier-like mind, with the simple and utterly kind and considerate being he was in private life. His letters were seldom without some expression of concern or gratitude for the work I was doing, which he always insisted was for him. 'I do hope that you will soon have a real good rest,' he wrote that July, 'you must be worn out with all you have put into the book.' And in August, when I was staying in London to see it through its final stages, 'I am very distressed thinking of you writing in the Park surrounded by humanity when, if it had not been for all the work I caused you, you might have been resting peacefully in one of your two large gardens.' One of them – the one in which he had read my first draft chapters a year earlier – passed out of my life that autumn. 'I do hope you are not entirely worn out with all the work of completing the book and leaving Smedmore on top of it all,' he wrote, 'I do feel for you leaving that lovely place.' And he showed the same tender solicitude over my old dog's closing months of pain and death. 'I do so agree with you that they have souls like us.'

By then I was sending him the final drafts of each of my successive chapters for his approval before they went to press. 'I am returning herewith the first seven chapters,' he wrote on October 11th: 'we have both been thrilled by them. It was such an experience reading them in their consecutive order and in their completed form. I had never realized when reading odd chapters the wonderful way they all blend into one marvellous narrative . . . In my wildest dreams I had never visualized anything like this.' 'I have now only got one more chapter to read,' he added ten days later, 'and feel very depressed that I have got to the end of the book. It has been a matter of intense interest reading through the whole from end to end and in its right sequence. When you started I had no idea that you would be able to produce anything like this. You have seen so clearly what my strategy was and looked at the War through the self-same spectacles as I did.' By the 23rd, he had finished the last chapter. 'I do not feel that I have ever half expressed my feelings of the most deep-rooted gratitude for having so well understood what I aimed at during the War and my reasons for doing so. It has always been a source of some sadness to me that so very few have realized this. I do feel that your book will assist others to understand what my strategy was and why I stuck to it so fast.' Twice in the closing week of 1956 he wrote again to thank me for what he called 'the stupendous work put into it. I shall never be able to find adequate words to express what the book has meant to me . . . It has added a tremendous interest to the last years of my life.'

The time had now come for others to read – and approve or disapprove – what together we had written, he in his diary and I in my strategic narrative of the War's course. During the past year we had sought advice from several of those who had worked with or under him – from Sir James Grigg, the Secretary of State for War during the years when the tide was turned; General Archie Nye, who had been his trusted Vice-Chief of Staff; Ian Jacob, whose own diaries the latter had kindly allowed me to use; and Field-Marshal Montgomery who, more than any other, had been his wartime protégé and was now at work on his own memoirs; as well as my own close soldier friends – Bernard Paget, who had been his Chief of Staff when the country was facing invasion in 1940 and later his successor as Commander-in Chief Home Forces, and Dick O'Connor, who had won our first desert victories in the dark winter of 1940/41.

During that summer, news of the book, until now a close secret, had been percolating to the Press. As early as the previous Christmas, I had had to write a letter correcting a misleading paragraph about it in a gossip column. 'I have deliberately made it very short,' I told Alan, 'to ensure that they put it *all* in and not merely part of it . . . The longer I live, the more I dread Press publicity! though for authors, unlike Field-Marshals, it is in a sense a necessity of life, for, if people never hear of one, they don't read one's books! I fancy we shall get a good deal of it, much of it unwanted, before we're through with the *Turn of the Tide*.'

For it was already clear that it was going to prove something of a sensation. 'I am delighted that Collins is getting excited about the book,' Alan had written on July 22nd, 'though it is sad that it will not be out till after Christmas. However, it is excellent news that he is prepared to put it out in a big way.' Already there were suggestions of serialization; our earlier decision to opt, not merely for an account of Alan's turning of the tide in 1942, but of the entire strategy of how victory in the West was won, postulated serious problems of presentation which had now to be faced. In October I sent him a copy of a letter from Sir Norman Brook – the all-powerful Secretary of the Cabinet to whom, as also to the War Office, I had applied for official clearance of what Alan had written while in the Crown's service. Sir Norman, who had been in close touch with Churchill during his final premiership, had strongly advised omitting from the book any criticism by Alan of Winston's strategy. 'Norman Brook,' I reported, 'dined with me after writing the letter and agreed that he was looking at it purely from Winston's point of view and that there was another and equally legitimate one – yours – as well as that of historical truth. He felt that anyone reading the book as a whole, including the Prelude, would regard it as a fair picture, and he said that if Winston didn't do so he, for one, would consider Winston wrong; but that what he feared was the Press giving terrific publicity to isolated passages in which you have criticized Winston, and ignoring the rest. He has offered to advise us a little later on as to what, in his view, would be the best way to prepare Winston for such criticism – either a letter from you to him or in some other way. My own view is that you should, apart from any other step, write a very brief Foreword of five or six lines to be printed at the very beginning of the book in which you say that it sets out the story of the events you describe as you know it; but, though it deals with controversies in which you were sometimes critical of your American and British colleagues and of the great man who saved England from disaster and rallied her forces, such criticism pales into insignificance compared with the intense feeling of admiration you have for him and your sense of the privilege of having served him in such a crisis of our history. And you could end, I suggest, with one of the great passages from the Diary or Notes about your admiration for Winston.'

'I did not find Norman Brook's arguments very impressive,' was Alan's comment; 'those intended to refute suggestions that Winston interfered with commanders showed surprising short-sightedness. I do, however, see the danger that the Press may well give great publicity to extracts which in their isolation from the rest may give offence. I do not like the idea of writing a letter to him beforehand, as this will only arouse the suspicious side of his nature and make him look for offence from the book. I whole-heartedly agree with your view that I should write a brief Foreword . . . on the lines suggested in your letter. I would be most grateful if you would very kindly try your hand at making a rough draft.'

He thought even less of a suggestion of Montgomery's – with whom I had been staying and who had expressed a fear that *The*

Turn of the Tide would cause Churchill 'a lot of hurt' – that he should act as an intermediary. 'I shudder at the thought of his preparing Winston for the book when he stops with him over the New Year! Tact is not his strong point, and I fear he would be much more likely to put Winston in a suspicious mood in which he might be looking for offence.' But he was touched by the kind references to himself in Monty's memoirs, which I had been reading in typescript while at Isington. 'I am so glad as a result of your visit you found your heart warming to him. There is a tremendous amount of good in Monty once you get inside that somewhat troublesome and unattractive exterior which some people are never able to see beyond.'

Publication date had been fixed for February 5th 1957. Billy Collins and his brilliant publicity manager, Ronald Politzer, had excelled themselves in their preparations for promoting – indeed it almost seemed over-promoting – the book. The banqueting hall of the Dorchester was booked for a launching ceremony, over which Alanbrooke and his fellow Chiefs of Staff were to preside, attended by nearly everyone who had played a leading part in the war, including several hundred high-ranking officers from all three Services. And an exacting programme of public broadcast and television appearances was arranged for Alan himself, including a Foyle Luncheon at which he was to take the chair and Lady Churchill to represent her husband, now in his eighty-third year.

Yet only a month before the book's ceremonial launching doubts arose as to whether its principal figure would be able to attend. For at the beginning of January Alan went down with congestion of the lungs and a racing heart. 'I am planning to give it almost complete rest,' he wrote on the 13th, 'I hope it will respond to it, in which case all will be well. If not, I am afraid I may have to cut some of the functions. We were both so touched by your charming letter telling me not to overtax my strength. It's just like you wanting to take as much of the load off me as possible, as if you had not been carrying far too much of it already. I am delighted to hear that you are to take the Chair at the Foyle Luncheon, for though as you say, it will be another free meal, it weighs very heavily on me.'

A more ominous letter from Benita followed. 'Alan is hoping so much to be able to carry out the engagements of the 5th and 8th' – the second a broadcast debate – 'but the doctor will give a final ruling. I doubt his being up to both myself – this is for your eye alone as I don't want him to feel discouraged at this lack of progress. He can do so little, even moving about the house, without a reaction by his heart. And I think he had a set-back when, determined to look at the first snowdrops, he went out for about 10 minutes the other day. If it turns colder I don't think he should attempt either engagement.'

A week before the Dorchester meeting, Alan wrote again. 'I have been doing everything I possibly can to give my heart a chance to calm down, but without any marked success so far! I remain in bed till 12 noon, I hardly ever go out and spend most of the day resting in a chair with my feet up. Although we have not made much impression on the heart yet, we have succeeded in clearing the chest considerably. I now cough very much less, had my chest X-rayed this morning, and am, therefore, praying that if we clear the chest up the heart may settle down a bit. The doctor comes again on Friday, when we shall have to make a final decision. I shall be *bitterly* disappointed if I am not able to be with you on the 5th, and have far from given up hope.'

The doctor's verdict came three days later. Though strongly against the broadcast, he agreed to the Dorchester. There were two other items in the letter Alan wrote next day with the good news. One was that Collins had telephoned to tell him that *The Turn of the Tide* had been chosen by the American 'Book of the Month' Club. The other was that he had received the first copy of the book.

> I felt it hard to believe my eyes as I unwrapped it; since then I have never let it out of my sight! Long ago, when I was about six years old, I caught a very small fish about 2 inches long. I wrapped it in my handkerchief, carried it round with me all day, periodically looking at it, and finally put it on a saucer on the table beside my bed so that I might look at it the last thing before going to sleep and the first thing on waking up!! It was one of the very big events of my early life and one that left such a mark that I remember all details of it as if it were yesterday.
>
> Well now in my old age the arrival of that book in its red paper cover this afternoon is a proportionately bigger event in my life. And yet it wakens all those juvenile tendencies of mine with my small fish! I wish to carry the book about with me the whole time and I want to see and touch it whenever I want. It will certainly come up to bed with me tonight so that I may have one last look at it before settling down, so that I may touch it if I wake, and that finally when I wake tomorrow it may be one of the first things I shall see!
>
> There is of course just the chance that on reading this letter

you will think I have gone soft in the brain! I take that risk willingly because I know you well enough to feel that you will be able to read between the lines and in doing so perhaps realize what this book means to me . . . What a *tremendous* part you have taken in making these last years of my life full of interest and thrills! I do bless you and thank you for what you have done. Your very, very grateful Alan.'

The writer, then in his seventy-fourth year, was a Knight of the Garter, a Field-Marshal, holder of the Order of Merit and a score of other high honours, and had recently filled the great office of Lord High Constable of England.

This letter, so characteristic of him – for all his genius so unassuming, simple and selfless, with his gentle playful humour and self-mockery, and, rarest of virtues in the successful and famous, his touching capacity for gratitude – completes my story of the making of *The Turn of the Tide*. That of its sequel, *Triumph in the West*, could add no more to David Fraser's definitive biography, though perhaps one day the letters that passed between us during our five years' collaboration – from which I have quoted only the briefest fraction – may seem worth preserving.

That the immediate reaction following the publication of *The Turn of the Tide*, with its vast sales on both sides of the Atlantic, was partly controversial was of little lasting import compared with the fact that it made Alanbrooke's achievement part of the continuing history of our country. It was the personal allusions in his diary to contemporary personalities which struck the headlines rather than the accompanying narrative of the war and its transformation which enabled the ordinary reader to follow the strategic decisions which, thanks to the diarist's genius, foresight and patient persistence, played so vital a part in the victory of the Western democracies. Four weeks after the Dorchester meeting, which he had so narrowly missed but had been able, at the eleventh hour, to attend and enjoy, I wrote to him: 'The worst of the excitement attending the publication now seems over, thank heaven, and the rest will depend on the book and what people think of it when they've ploughed through it – quite a long job for most, as we've given them more than a quarter of a million words to digest! The first of the new impressions reached the shops yesterday – a wonderful achievement on the publishers' part – and Billy has just ordered the printing of a third impression, which, I think, makes 135,000 copies.'

The only thing which hurt Alan over the book's sensational

reception was the injury it did to Churchill's *amour propre*. For it was natural that, having all his life taken so passionate an interest in all matters affecting his first profession, soldiering, and having been so humiliatingly rejected in the hour of victory by the people he had saved from defeat and disaster, Winston in his old age and retirement should have set such store on the popular belief that he had personally directed all the principal military decisions of the War. What Norman Brook and Monty had feared had come to pass, and the great War Minister and his private friends, fastening on passages in the diary – particularly those taken from their context in the serialized extracts – had resented as derogatory whatever fell short of the fashionable adulation of the hour.

At first Alan hoped against hope that Churchill's delay in acknowledging the copy of the book he sent him, with its deeply sincere inscription and Foreword, was only unintentional. 'I was lucky,' he wrote after the Foyle Luncheon on February 17th, 'in sitting next to Lady Churchill and sent many messages through her to him.' Even when a week later no reply had come, he was still hoping to receive a word from him. But when it came, it left him in no doubt of his old chief's and comrade's displeasure.*

'I thought Winston's letter to you very lacking in generosity,' I wrote after seeing it. 'It is a pity that his greatness is marred by this grudging side. But, of course, he is very old and he can scarcely be expected to be above it all. Yet I am sure in the long run the picture you have drawn of him will enhance his historical stature more than anything except his wonderful speeches. You have revealed his greatness in action as no one else has done, and it is all the more convincing and unanswerable because it is set in criticism and your own natural frustration and impatience with his ways . . . I enclose a letter from G. M. Trevelyan – the doyen of my profession – which I think you may like to have. It is the real answer to the foolish criticism about Winston.'**

But when later I apologized to Alan for that criticism, feeling that I was to blame in not having guarded him more against it, he would have none of it. 'You must not worry yourself about the attacks made on me. I have a thick hide, Kipling's "If" has been a great help to me through life. "If you can bear to hear the truth you've spoken twisted by knaves to make a trap for fools" seems

---

* Five months later, however, when the two met at the Garter Service at Windsor, Alan wrote to me, 'I am glad to say that Winston was quite pleasant, and I could see none of the anger that Monty had mentioned.'   ** (See p. 24)

specially applicable at present.' Nor did he cease to reiterate what the book had meant to him. 'As we come to the last day of the present year,' he wrote eleven months after its publication, 'I cannot let it slip away without once more thanking you for all those hours of toil and labour which you devoted to it . . . It has added a tremendous interest to the last years of my life.' And when a year later the draft chapters of *Triumph in the West* were beginning to reach him, he wrote, 'I am just thrilled going through it all . . . Benita and I are immersed in them and having a wonderful time . . . I always thought that the odds were heavily against my being spared to see this second volume. You can therefore imagine what a joy it is to read these pages.'

Then, at the end of the month – December 1959 – in which our second volume was at last published, he wrote to me again. 'I cannot let this year slip by without once more thanking you for the immense work you put into the last five years in writing those two books based on my diaries . . . Until you wrote them the role and work of the Chiefs of Staff organization was not understood nor even realized, which is not surprising as it had not existed in previous wars. I think you have also brought home to the reader how inevitable clash of personalities must be in the conduct of a war, especially amongst allies, and what a tremendous part these clashes play in the ultimate forming of a policy for the conduct of operations . . .'

'Do not dream of bothering to answer this, it requires no reply. I just had to write it as a safety-valve to those feelings of unbounded gratitude that are boiling over as I look back on your work of the past five years . . . I wonder how you ever had the courage to undertake it and the heart to carry it through.'

Had Alan lived to read the Life which his fellow soldier has now written, completing what I began a quarter of a century ago, I feel he would have been even more grateful.

APPENDIX I

Anti-aircraft Artillery

In 1938 there was a conflict of view over the type of gun. The choice lay between the mobile 3·7″ guns, first coming into production in the year Brooke took over, and the static (and older) 3·7 and 4·5 guns. The question turned on a number of factors of which one was clearly how relevant the mobility of the gun would be.

It was contended by some that the mobile gun would confer few advantages. A mobile column would take hours or days to move from one threatened position or town to another, whereas the attacking aircraft had absolute flexibility. The concept of 'mobile reserves' – what the subsequent Commander-in-Chief of Anti-Aircraft Command was to call 'a travelling circus' – of anti-aircraft guns was indeed found in the light of actual experience to be futile.

However, the idea of a near-tactical reserve of anti-aircraft guns which was admittedly ill-founded in logic was not the only or prime reason why some – and Brooke was of their number – wished for a higher proportion than that planned of mobile to static guns in production. It was, rather, that the pattern of every attack and the tactics the Royal Air Force would find necessary to combat it could change and evolve as operations developed: and that guns must be capable of movement in order not to respond to an instant tactical situation but to a possibly changing concept of threat and response.

The decisive factor, however, was speed of production. The static gun and mounting took only about half the time to produce of its mobile counterpart. The need was for guns and there was a growing sense that time was running out.

APPENDIX II

Chief of the Imperial General Staff

The sense that British military organization lagged well behind that of Continental nations – and particularly that of Prussia and thus Imperial Germany – was strong in the closing decades of the nineteenth century. Cardwell, who as Secretary of State for War sponsored major changes in Army organization and in the British Regimental system, had proposed, in the 1870s, the creation of a General Staff. Subsequent commissions also recommended such a body. The General Staff was conceived as a Corps of officers who would be specially educated and trained for two prime tasks. First at 'Army Headquarters' – at the War Office in London – they would provide a policy-making cell for operations, Intelligence, training and organization. Second, in field formations or in Commands and Districts, officers filling General Staff appointments would, by virtue of their own training under a common system, be equipped to undertake the preparation and transmission of orders and the whole regulation of military activity in accordance with the general wishes of the commander – and also enforce that uniformity of tactical doctrine and staff procedures which were rightly seen to be more and more important, as military operations covered ever wider areas remote from the personal intervention of the higher commander, and were increasingly dependent upon the initiative of subordinates and the unambiguity of communications.

Matters moved at less than lightning pace. Nevertheless when, at the beginning of the century and soon after the conclusion of the South African War, the office of Commander-in-Chief was abolished and the affairs of the Army entrusted to an Army Council, the senior Military Member was designated Chief of the General Staff. He was a head without a body, for there was no General Staff, recognized as such. Soon thereafter, however, the idea of a 'General Staff list' was approved – qualified officers who would fill designated appointments both in London and in the field. The officers so selected should (under the Army order putting the scheme into effect) 'be considered most likely to prove capable for forming a school of progressive military thought'. They would have graduated at the Staff College (but not all graduates would be so selected) and be placed on the list (kept secret) by the Army Council. Actual appointments would be made by the Secretary of State in consultation with the Chief of the General Staff, and would normally be for four years. Officers below the rank of Lieutenant-Colonel would then return to Regimental duty for not less than one year: this followed the German pattern whereby members of the General Staff could only be confirmed in promotion after a successful (albeit comparatively short) period of command with troops in the new rank.

There was then the question of extending the system, so that in case of war officers from the Dominions would be so trained as to supervise the co-operation of forces from all parts of the Empire. The principle of an Imperial General staff was adopted at an Imperial Conference in 1907, a detailed plan was approved in 1909, the title of Chief of the General Staff was broadened to include the adjective 'Imperial', and officers from the Dominions regularly attended the Staff College, and qualified as members of the General Staff.

By the start of the First World War, therefore, the concept was still shallow rooted. Unlike the heirs of the long Prussian tradition, deriving from Scharnhorst in the ferment of the 'Freiheitskrieg' against Napoleon, British General Staff Officers had barely had time to digest the idea still less to develop a corporate ethos when the Army was swamped by a huge expansion to meet the needs of Continental war. Most of the General Staff at the War Office were taken away in 1914 and embodied in the Expeditionary Force. The tiny number of officers already on 'The List' had to be augmented by an enormous number of less experienced and less thoroughly trained assistants. The 'red tabs' on the lapels of a Staff Officer's jacket, first conceived as a distinction which would be as coveted as the broad red stripe down a German General Staff Officer's breeches, soon became so widely worn as to forfeit regard; and the comparative safety and comforts of life on the Staff as opposed to that of the Regiments in the trenches came to produce dislike and ribaldry rather than respect. The concept of a professional élite hardly survived 1914.

Between the wars the concept was to some extent reborn, although the poor regard for 'the Staff' which was one of the first war's heritages to the Army militated against the original concept, and the general mistrust of the British for unabashed professionalism and for any but well-concealed intelligence also worked against it. The increased self-reliance and the formal independence of the Dominions diminished the significance of the 'Imperial' connection. The Chief of the Imperial General Staff may not have been exactly a head without a body once again, but his actual function was to supervise the policy, operations, organizational, Intelligence and training branches in the War Office and to act as *Primus inter pares* of his military colleagues on the Army Council. He thus was senior military adviser to the Secretary of State for War and the recognized professional head of the Army.

APPENDIX III

An Instance of Professional Advice

Having obtained the agreement of the Secretary of State for War that Wilson should replace Dill and Alexander replace Wilson, the Prime Minister sought on 6th November 1944 the concurrence of the Chiefs of Staff to a telegram on the subject to the President. The opening paragraph, concerning Wilson's move to Washington, survived intact to the final telegram. Very different was the fate of the paragraphs which referred to Alexander. Churchill's first draft:

> In these circumstances I propose to you that General Alexander should become Allied Supreme Commander in the Mediter-ranean with General McNarny as his Deputy with headquarters in Italy, and should also carry on the Command-in-Chief of the Anglo-American Armies on that front. I have been much disturbed by the immense staffs which have grown up, one for the Armies at the front, and the other for the Allied Supreme Command at Caserta. These Commands should be combined and telescoped with economy and advantage.

This appeared to be a proposal to merge the functions and headquarters of the Supreme Commander, Mediterranean (responsible for the whole theatre, including Greece, Yugoslavia and so forth) with those of the Commander-in-Chief of the Armies in Italy, an Army Group Commander. Brooke regarded this as fundamentally unsound, and had consistently so advised. He was, therefore, irritated to find the idea advanced by inclusion – for quick agreement, since Churchill said he needed to wire Roosevelt immediately – in a draft telegram. On 6th November, the Prime Minister received a Minute from Ismay beginning:

> The Chiefs of Staff feel that the telegram . . . raises issues of such grave moment that they would welcome an opportunity of discussing it with you both in its organizational and its personal aspects.

The Minute acknowledged need for economy in staffs, but set out cogently the reasons why there were two distinct functions requiring two men. Brooke's diary that evening (7th November):

> He went on to suggest Alexander should combine the duties of Supreme Commander and his own present one at the same time. He went further to suggest that Greece should return to Middle East where we have just taken it from, and in every possible way proposed upsetting the organization of Command in the Mediterranean . . . we had to pull it to pieces badly and sent it back mutilated with our reasons. He has been unable to send it off, but has decided to have a 10.30 p.m. meeting with us which promises to be a fairly heated one.

At 1.00 a.m. Brooke opened his diary again:

> Just back from our meeting with the PM. Anthony Eden attending, and, as I had suspected , he was responsible for the change in the PM's plans. He had just come back from Italy where he had been seeing Alexander who had as usual whined about being crushed by Wilson's HQ, the great duplication of work, etc. As a result he had recommended combining the Supreme Commander and [Army] Group Commander into one, and wanted in fact to commit the error which Eisenhower has just made in France . . . After much arguing I made my point, namely Wilson to replace Dill, Alex to replace Wilson, and Clark to replace Alex . . .

Next day, 8th November, the Chiefs of Staff discussed an amended telegram, and reckoned that it was clear for Churchill to send to Roosevelt. It was not sent. Churchill and Brooke visited the French in Paris and in Alsace between 10th and 14th November, and on the day after return Brooke noted:

> *November 15th* started the old COS life again, and worried about PM's fantastic ideas as to what command implies, he has never yet understood the system of a chain of command . . . Winston had wired to Alexander through secret channels without telling me. Alex, who has got somewhat of an inflated idea of his position, has wired back a lot of very incomprehensible stuff . . .

For Churchill had held up the telegram to Roosevelt and on 8th November had sent it secretly in draft to Alexander (an Army Group Commander, not then a Supreme Commander) with a covering signal which started, 'This has not been sent yet because I should like your opinion on it.' Churchill's signal then reported briefly his exchange with Brooke, and continued:

On the other hand we are all anxious that you should plan, inspire and direct any large battle that may have to be fought. Let me know what you think of the arrangement we propose . . . *It is not until I have heard from you that I shall address General Wilson'** [Alexander's superior Commander].

Churchill marked the telegram 'through C' (i.e. through Secret Intelligence channels which would not be seen by the Chiefs of Staff). On 10th November, Alexander signalled back to Churchill:

> I like your suggestion . . . I urge strongly that Mark Clark becomes only Commander of a group of Armies directly under me as C.-in-C. This will be the same set up as I understand Eisenhower has in France. It must not be as we have here at present where I am, in addition to being an Army Group Commander, also C.-in-C., AAI [Allied Armies in Italy] of the whole Italian theatre.

This was the 'very incomprehensible stuff', and Brooke found it helped blur rather than clarify Churchill's mind. Brooke urged that the telegram drafted after the meeting on 7th November be sent to Roosevelt unaltered. On the same day (15th November) Churchill was minuted:

> The Chiefs of Staff have discussed your Minute . . . and your suggested amendments to the draft telegram to the President.
>
> They also do not see that any change in your original draft telegram is necessary. General Alexander's point is not quite clear, but at any rate by appointing him Supreme Commander you confer on him all the power he requires to control the operations of the Army Group . . .

On Churchill's method of communication Brooke wrote afterwards:

> Winston had a very unpleasant habit of occasionally sending private telegrams to Commanders by SIS route without telling me that he was doing so. These telegrams were usually connected with some subject I had fully discussed with him and had disagreed with him. He then tried to get Commanders to agree with him and consequently to disagree with me. Fortunately all the Commanders-in-Chief throughout the War served me with exceptional loyalty. I had a rule with them that if they ever sent a telegram to the PM they always sent me a copy. In this case, and in a few similar ones, my staff on applying to the Cabinet office were unable to trace the PM's original wire . . .

* Author's italics.

Once I had obtained the original I took it, together with a copy of Alex's reply, to the PM and said that I was surprised that he considered it necessary to send this wire as we had previously fully discussed the matter and he knew my views. He showed some surprise that I had secured the original, but never any shame over what he had done!

On 16th November Churchill returned to the charge:

I still do not understand your point of view. Clearly there are three offices:
a) The Supreme Commander in the Mediterranean.
b) The Commander-in-Chief in Italy and
c) The Commander-in-Chief of the 15th Group of Armies.
Hitherto b) and c) have been held by the same person. Now it is a) and b) which are to be held by the same person. Is not this what we all mean?

This must be cleared up before I can send any telegram to the President. It is quite clear that Alexander sees the position as I do.

WSC

Later the same day the patient Ismay signed another Minute:

Prime Minister:
The Chiefs of Staff had a long discussion about your Minute this morning and I am sorry to say that they still do not see eye to eye with you. They point out that there has never been such an appointment as 'Commander-in-Chief in Italy' . . .

There were in fact only two offices not three, namely:
I)   The Supreme Commander in the Mediterranean, and
II) The Commander-in-Chief of the 15th Group of Armies, who had the title of 'Commander-in-Chief of the Allied Armies in Italy'.

However, by now Churchill was both confused and angry and minuted back that a meeting next day would be necessary. 'I am in full agreement,' he wrote, 'with General Alexander.' What that meant was, however, obscure to the Chiefs of Staff.

Next day, 17th November, the Minutes of the Prime Minister's meeting with the Chiefs of Staff simply recorded:

The Conference considered the revised draft telegram from the Prime Minister to the President which had been prepared in the light of their previous discussion of this question.

The Conference

a) approved the terms of the revised draft telegram subject to amendments agreed in discussion;

b) took note that the Prime Minister would send the telegram to the President.

Brooke noted in his diary that night:

> We had to meet at 4 p.m. and after laborious explanations I at last got him to accept matters as they are. Finally, the telegram was sent off to the President.

The telegram sent to Roosevelt conformed exactly to the draft agreed with such premature relief by the Chiefs of Staff on 8th November!

Codewords Mentioned or Relevant in Text

ACHSE	German takeover of Italian Armed Forces.
ANAKIM	Plan for recapture of Burma.
ANVIL	Landings in South France (later DRAGOON).
ARCADIA	First Washington Conference, December–January 41/42.
ARGONAUT	Conference in Crimea Feb 45, and in Malta en route.
AVALANCHE	Allied landings at Salerno.
BOLERO	Build-up in United Kingdom of United States forces for subsequent operations in Europe.
BUCCANEER	Planned operation against Andaman Islands.
CAPITAL	Advance in Central Burma 1944.
CHAMPION	Early name for CAPITAL.
CITADEL	German offensive against the Kursk Salient, 1943.
CRUSADER	Eighth Army operations in Desert Nov 41–Jan 42.
CULVERIN	Planned operations against Sumatra.
DIADEM	Offensive in Italy May 44.
DRACULA	Airborne and seaborne attack on Rangoon May 45.
DRAGOON	Later name for ANVIL.
EUREKA	Tehran Conference, Nov 43.
EXTENDED CAPITAL	Extended operations in Central Burma 1944/45.
GYMNAST	Allied operations to occupy French North Africa.

HERCULES	Planned German/Italian invasion of Malta, 1942.
HUSKY	Invasion of Sicily July 43.
IMPERATOR	Planned large-scale Allied raid on Continent 1942.
IRONCLAD	Capture of Diego Suarez, Madagascar, March 42.
JUPITER	Suggested operation against North Norway.
MANNA	Introduction of British forces into Greece on German withdrawal.
MARKET GARDEN	Allied operation to seize bridges over the Rhine in the Netherlands, September 44.
MICHAEL	German offensive, March 18.
OCTAGON	Second Quebec Conference, Sep 44.
OVERLORD	Allied invasion of France, 44.
POINTBLANK	Allied strategic bomber offensive from United Kingdom.
PYTHON	Scheme for repatriation of time expired servicemen and women from overseas.
QUADRANT	First Quebec Conference, Aug 43.
ROMULUS	Operation for clearance of Arakan, Dec 44.
ROUNDHAMMER	Plan for invasion of Continent, compromise between ROUNDUP and SLEDGEHAMMER.
ROUNDUP	Major Allied invasion of Europe 1943.
RUTTER	Dieppe raid, 42.
SEELÖWE	Invasion of England, 1940.
SEXTANT	Cairo Conference, Nov 43.
SHINGLE	Landings at Anzio, Jan 44.
SICHELSCHNITT	German offensive, June 40.
SLEDGEHAMMER	Limited Allied invasion of Europe, 1942.
SUPERCHARGE	Last phase of battle of El Alamein, Nov 42.
SYMBOL	Casablanca Conference, Jan 43.
TERMINAL	Potsdam Conference, July 45.
TOLSTOY	Moscow Conference, October 44.
TORCH	Later name for GYMNAST, Nov 42.
TRIDENT	Washington Conference, May 43.

TUBE ALLOYS	Atomic Bomb programme.
ULTRA	Enemy signal interception and decoding.
VANGUARD	Capture of Rangoon from the sea.
VERITABLE	21st Army Group operations to clear up to the Rhine, Feb 45.
ZIPPER	Planned Allied operations in Malaya and Singapore, autumn 45.

Note on Sources and Bibliography

The Alanbrooke Papers, access to which is controlled by the Trustees of the late Viscount Alanbrooke's Settlement, and by the Executors of his Will, are deposited in the Liddell-Hart Centre at King's College, London. They contain a great deal of material, including Alanbrooke's manuscript diaries in the Second World War, his early letters to his mother, and the notes he made on re-reading his wartime diaries, which he called 'Notes on my Life'. All these are duplicated in typescript in the Alanbrooke papers. In all cases where I have referred to his diary the original manuscript version (Section 5 of the Alanbrooke Papers) has been used: the typescripts differ in some cases. The 'Notes' are called 'Notes for my memoirs' in Section 2 of the Alanbrooke Papers and are in manuscript, covering the period from birth to 1943, and the post-war period. Typescripts of these, as well as of the period 1943 to 1946 are in Section 3, and I have used Section 3 throughout where 'Notes' are given as a reference: the particular volume will in each case be clear from the date and context. These 'Notes' are, in the later years, interspersed with selections from his diaries made by Alanbrooke himself.

Also in the collection are numerous letters and documents both from and about Alanbrooke, both in early life and later: as well as the record of a number of interviews about him with men and women who knew him well. The Alanbrooke Papers also contain the Field-Marshal's personal copy of the records of the great International Conferences of the Second World War.

A separate series of boxes contains further letters and personal signals written or made by or to Alanbrooke during the Second World War. These have been described as 'Alanbrooke Personal Files': were loaned by the Trustees to Sir Arthur Bryant and were used by him together with the diaries and 'Notes on my Life' in writing *The Turn of the Tide* and *Triumph in the West* (Collins, 1957 and 1959). Documents from this collection were quoted in these books; and have also been available to and quoted by me in the same form. The collection is due ultimately to be reunited with the main body of the Alanbrooke Papers.

The *Grand Strategy* volumes of the *History of the Second World War*, written as they were with full access to the documents lodged in the Public Record Office, are an indispensable aid for any biographer of Alanbrooke. Not only do they represent the culling of a mass of official documents, memoranda and Minutes of meetings, but they address the subject of grand strategy, and in particular the differences between Allies, with an exactness as to fact and a judicious objectivity as to comment which put issues into better perspective than do the less temperate observations of participants, however distinguished. For those volumes published before general access was permitted to the documents in the Public Record Office, annotated copies are held by the Historical Section of the Army Department.

The letters between Lord Alanbrooke and his wife are the property of the present Lord Alanbrooke. Sir Ian Jacob's diary is unpublished.

A short and selective bibliography is attached.

Finally, I have, without acknowledgement or apology, drawn in some cases on my own recollections and reflections.

SELECTED BIBLIOGRAPHY

ANON   *The Dark Side of the Moon.* Faber and Faber 1946.

BARKER, Elisabeth   *Churchill and Eden.* Macmillan 1978.

BARNETT, Corelli   *The Desert Generals.* William Kimber 1960.

BOND, Brian   *Chief of Staff.* Diaries of Lt. Gen. Sir Henry Pownall. Leo Cooper 1972 and 1974. *France and Belgium 1939–1940.* Davie-Poynter 1975.

BRYANT, Arthur   *The Turn of the Tide.* Collins 1957. *Triumph in the West.* Collins 1959.

BUTLER, J. R. M.   *Grand Strategy.* Vol. II, H.M.S.O. 1957. *Grand Strategy.* Vol. III, Part 2, H.M.S.O. 1964.

CHURCHILL, Winston   *The Second World War.* Cassell 1948–1954.

COLVILLE, J. R.   *Man of Valour.* Collins 1972.

CONNELL, John   *Wavell, Soldier and Statesman.* Collins 1964. *Auchinleck.* Cassell 1964.

DAVIDSON, Major-General Sir John   *Haig, Master of the Field.* Sanders, Phillips and Co. 1953.

DE GUINGAND, Major-General Sir Francis   *Operation Victory.* Hodder and Stoughton 1947.

DEICHMANN, General der Fliegen a.d. Paul   *German Air Operations in Support of the Army.*

DJILAS, M.   *Conversations with Stalin.* Rupert Hart-Davis 1962.

EHRMANN, John   *Grand Strategy.* Vol. V, H.M.S.O. 1956. *Grand Strategy.* Vol. VI, H.M.S.O. 1956.

EISENHOWER, General of the Army Dwight   *Crusade in Europe.* William Heinemann 1948.

FARRAR-HOCKLEY, A. H.   *The Somme.* Batsford 1964.

GUDERIAN, Colonel General Heinz   *Panzer Leader.* Michael Joseph 1952.

GWYER, J. M. A.   *Grand Strategy.* Vol. III, Part I, H.M.S.O. 1964.

HORNE, Alistair   *To Lose a Battle.* Macmillan 1969.

HOWARD, Michael   *Grand Strategy.* Vol. IV, H.M.S.O. 1972.

ISMAY, General Lord   *Memoirs.* Heinemann 1960.

JOURNAL of the ROYAL ARTILLERY.

KENNEDY, Major-General Sir John   *The Business of War.* Hutchinson 1957.

LEIGHTON, R. M. and COAKLEY, R. W. *Global Logistics and Strategy*. History of the U.S. Army in the Second World War. U.S. Department of Defense 1955.

LEWIN, Ronald *Churchill as Warlord*. Batsford 1973. *Slim, the Standard Bearer*. Leo Cooper 1976.

LIDDELL-HART, Sir Basil *Memoirs*. Cassell 1965. *History of the Second World War*. Cassell 1970.

MATLOFF, M. and SNELL, E. M. *Strategic Planning and Coalition Warfare*. History of the U.S. Army in the Second World War. U.S. Department of Defense 1953.

MONTGOMERY, Field-Marshal Viscount *Memoirs*. Collins 1958.

MORAN, Lord *Winston Churchill. The Struggle for Survival 1940–1966*. Constable 1966.

NICHOLLS, O. H. *The 18th Division in the Great War*. Blackwood 1922.

NICOLSON, Nigel *Alex*. Weidenfeld and Nicolson 1973.

RICHARDS, Denis *Portal of Hungerford*. Heinemann 1977.

ROSKILL, Stephen *Churchill and the Admirals*. Collins 1977.

SAINSBURY, Keith *The North African Landings 1942*. Davis-Poynter 1976.

SLESSOR, Marshal of the Royal Air Force Sir John *The Central Blue*. Cassell 1956.

SLIM, Field-Marshal Viscount *Defeat into Victory*. Cassell 1956.

SPEER, Albert *Inside the Third Reich*. Weidenfeld and Nicolson 1970.

STATIONERY OFFICE, H.M. *History of the Second World War*.

STEPHEN, O. Leslie *Sir Victor Brooke, Sportsman and Naturalist*. John Murray 1894.

TEDDER, Marshal of the Royal Air Force Lord *With Prejudice*. Cassell 1966.

TERRAINE, John *General Jack's Diary*. Eyre and Spottiswoode 1964.

TREVOR-ROPER, Hugh *Hitler's War Directives*. Sedgwick and Jackson 1964.

TRYTHALL, A. J. *Boney Fuller*. Cassell 1977.

UNITED STATES Department of the Army, Office of Chief of Military History *Command Decisions*. Harcourt, Brace 1959.

VON MANSTEIN, Field-Marshal Erich *Lost Victories*. Methuen 1958.

WILMOT, Chester *The Struggle for Europe*. Collins 1952.

NOTES

CHAPTER II

1 An account of the early history of the Brookes of Colebrooke is given in the Alanbrooke Papers (section 12).
2 Alanbrooke Papers. For notes on childhood see Lady Wrench's letters (section 10 – also section 12).
3 'Notes on my Life' (section 3). Hereafter 'Notes'.
4 Alanbrooke letters to his mother throughout the period between his childhood and her death are in the Alanbrooke Papers (section 1). Hereafter 'Early letters'.
5 Many extant in the Alanbrooke Papers.
6 *Sir Victor Brooke, Sportsman and Naturalist*. O. Leslie Stephen (John Murray 1894).
7 Notes.
8 Lord Brookeborough. Alanbrooke Papers (section 12).
9 Early letters.
10 Reproduced in Alanbrooke Papers (section 4).
11 Alanbrooke Papers (section 4).

CHAPTER III

1 Notes.
2 Early letters.
3 *Ibid.*
4 Alanbrooke Papers (section 4).
5 Notes.
6 *Ibid.*
7 *Ibid.*
8 Early letters.
9 Alanbrooke Papers (section 4).
10 Notes.
11 *Ibid.*
12 *Ibid.*
13 *Ibid.*
14 Early letters.
15 *Ibid.*
16 Communicated by General Sir Ronald Adam.
17 Notes.

CHAPTER IV

1 Notes.
2 *Ibid.*
3 *Ibid.*
4 Early letters.
5 Early letters.
6 Notes.

7 Alanbrooke Papers (section 4).
8 Notes.
9 *War Diary of an Artillery Officer 1914–1918*. Major P. H. Pilditch. (unpublished).
10 Notes.
11 *The 18th Division in the Great War*. O. H. F. Nicholls, Blackwood 1922. Hereafter 'Nichols'.
12 Notes.
13 Notes.
14 Alanbrooke Papers (section 12).
15 Nichols.
16 Quoted in *General Jack's Diary 1914–1918*. Ed. John Terraine (Eyre & Spottiswood 1964).
17 Notes.
18 *Ibid.*
19 Early letters.
20 *My War Memories*. Ludendorff. Hutchinson & Co.

21 Early letters.
22 'Evolution of Artillery', a series of articles by Brooke published in the journal of the Royal Artillery. Hereafter 'E. of A.'
23 Alanbrooke Papers (section 12).
24 Notes.
25 *Ibid.*
26 Alanbrooke Papers (section 12).
27 *History of the Great War.* H.M.S.O. 1948.
28 Notes.
29 Early letters.
30 Extant in Alanbrooke Papers (section 4).
31 Early letters.
32 *Ibid.*
33 Quoted from *Heerführer des Weltkrieges*, in preface to the British Official History, Vol. II, 1917.
34 Notes.

CHAPTER V

1 Communicated to author.
2 Notes.
3 Notes.
4 Alanbrooke Papers (section 12).
5 Notes.
6 For recollections of Alanbrooke's family at that time see Alanbrooke Papers (section 12).
7 Personal communications to author.
8 For papers from Alan-

brooke's period at Imperial Defence College see Alanbrooke Papers (section 4).
9 For recollections of Alanbrooke's command at Larkhill see Alanbrooke Papers (section 12).
10 Notes.
11 Letters between Alanbrooke and Viscountess Alanbrooke throughout their lives, property of Viscount Alanbrooke. Hereafter 'Letters'.

CHAPTER VI

1 Alanbrooke Papers (section 4).
2 *Ibid.*
3 *Ibid.*
4 Alanbrooke Papers (sections 4 and 12).
5 Notes.
6 *Ibid.*
7 Alanbrooke Papers (section 4).
8 *Ibid.*
9 Communicated by Lt.-Colonel F. E. Drake-Briscoe.
10 Notes.
11 See *Boney Fuller* by A. J. Trythall. Cassell 1977.
12 Quoted in *Memoirs* Liddell-Hart. Cassell 1965. Henceforth 'Liddell-Hart'.
13 Notes.
14 Liddell-Hart.
15 *Ibid.*
16 Notes.
17 *Ibid.*
18 *Ibid.*
19 *Ibid.*
20 Alanbrooke Papers (section 12).
21 Notes.
22 Liddell-Hart.
23 Notes.
24 *Ibid.*
25 Alanbrooke Papers (section 12).
26 *Ibid.*
27 *Ibid.*
28 Notes.
29 All in Alanbrooke Papers (section 5).
30 Communicated by Sir Alan Lascelles to the author.
31 Alanbrooke Papers (section 12).

CHAPTER VII

1 Diary. 15th January 1940.
2 Notes.
3 *Ibid.*
4 *Chief of Staff.* Diaries of Lt. Gen. Sir Henry Pownall. Ed. Brian Bond. Leo Cooper.
5 Diary. 5th February 1940.
6 Communicated by General Sir Cecil Blacker.
7 Letters.
8 *Memoirs* by Field Marshal Viscount Montgomery of Alamein. Collins 1958.
9 See Official History of the Second World War *France & Flanders 1940* See also *France & Belgium 1939–1940* Brian Bond. Davis-Poynter 1975.
10 Communicated in conversation with author.
11 Diary. 12th May 1940.
12 Diary. 19th May 1940.
13 Diary. 25th May 1940.
14 *History of the Second World War: Grand Strategy* Volumes. H.M.S.O. Henceforth *Grand Strategy*.
15 Notes.
16 *Ibid.*
17 *Ibid.*
18 Communicated by Field-

Marshal Viscount Montgomery.
19 Communicated by General Sir Ronald Adam.
20 Notes.
21 *Ibid.*
22 *Ibid.*
23 Alanbrooke Papers (section 10).
24 Notes.
25 Alanbrooke Papers (section 12).

26 Alanbrooke Papers (section 8 – 'Archdale').
27 Notes.
28 *The Second World War* Winston Churchill. Cassell 1949. Henceforth 'Churchill'.
29 Notes.
30 *Ibid.*
31 *Ibid.*
32 Archdale.

CHAPTER VIII

1 Notes.
2 Diary. 1st–2nd July 1940.
3 Diary. 30th June 1940.
4 *Hitler's War Directives*. Ed. H. R. Trevor-Roper. Sidgwick & Jackson 1964.
5 *Ibid.*
6 Notes.
7 *Ibid.*
8 *Ibid.*
9 Diary. 17th October 1940.
10 Notes.
11 Letters.
12 *Ibid.*
13 Notes.
14 *German Air Operations in Support of the Army*. General der Fliegen a.d. Paul Deichmann.
15 *Ibid.*
16 Notes.

17 Communicated by Sir Alan Lascelles.
18 Notes.
19 *The Central Blue* Marshal of the Royal Air Force Sir John Slessor. Cassell 1956.
20 Diary. 9th July 1941.
21 Notes.
22 *Ibid.*
23 *Memoirs* Lord Ismay. Henceforth 'Ismay'. Heinemann 1960.
24 Alanbrooke Papers (section 12).
25 Letters.
26 Communicated by the Hon. Richard Beaumont.
27 Notes. In fact his diary entry records birds not brace!
28 Letters.

CHAPTER IX

1 *Archie Nye – A Memoir*. Anthony Harrison (unpublished).
2 Alanbrooke Papers (section 12).
3 *Ibid.*

4 *Ibid.*
5 Notes.
6 Communicated by General Sir Frank Simpson. Henceforth 'Simpson'.
7 Communicated by

Lieutenant-Colonel Jones of the CIGS Private Office. Henceforth 'Jones'.
8 Notes.
9 Alanbrooke Papers (section 6).
10 Jones.
11 Simpson.
12 Alanbrooke Papers (section 12).
13 Communicated by Viscount Head.
14 *Ibid.*
15 For views of each see Alanbrooke Papers (section 12).
16 *Ibid.*
17 *Ibid.*

CHAPTER X

1 Notes.
2 Communicated by Viscount Alanbrooke.
3 Communicated by Sir Ronald Adam.
4 Alanbrooke Papers (section 12).
5 Diary. 9th December 1941.
6 Notes.
7 Alanbrooke Personal Files.
8 Ismay.
9 Grand Strategy. Vol. III.
10 *Ibid.*
11 Alanbrooke Personal Files.
12 Communicated by Colonel Peter Dunphie.
13 Alanbrooke Papers (section 6).
14 *Ibid.*
15 *Ibid.*

CHAPTER XI

1 For Inter-Allied Debate see *Grand Strategy*. Vols III & IV.
2 Diary. 13th April 1942.
3 Notes.
4 *Ibid.*
5 *Ibid.*
6 Diary. 16th April 1942.
7 Notes.
8 Diary. 10th April 1942.
9 Alanbrooke Personal Files.
10 Notes.
11 *Ibid.*
12 *Ibid.*
13 *Grand Strategy.*
14 Notes.
15 *Ibid.*
16 See also *Portal of Hungerford* Denis Richards. Heinemann 1977.
17 Letters.
18 See *Inside the Third Reich* Albert Speer. Weidenfeld & Nicolson 1970.
19 Quoted in *Churchill and Eden.* Elisabeth Barker. Macmillan 1978.

CHAPTER XII

1 Diary. 31st December 1941.
2 Alanbrooke Papers (section 6).
3 *Ibid.*
4 *Ibid.*
5 *Ibid.*
6 *Ibid.*
7 *Ibid.*
8 *Ibid.*
9 *Ibid.*
10 *Ibid.*
11 Alanbrooke Personal Files.
12 Alanbrooke Papers (section 6).
13 Diary. 8th July 1942.
14 Alanbrooke Papers (section 6).
15 *Ibid.*
16 Letters.
17 Notes.
18 Diary. 16th April 1942.
19 Notes.
20 Alanbrooke Papers (section 12).
21 *Ibid.*
22 Diary. 6th August 1942.
23 Notes.
24 Simpson. Brooke accepted that Montgomery was cautious and methodical (even, in some German eyes, predictable): but he knew that Montgomery would produce victories.
25 Alanbrooke Papers (section 6).
26 Alanbrooke Papers (section 12).
27 Notes.
28 *Ibid.*
29 Alanbrooke Papers (section 10).
30 *Ibid.*
31 Alanbrooke Papers (section 10).
32 Alanbrooke Papers (section 6).
32a Simpson.
33 Alanbrooke Papers (section 10).
34 Letter to Wavell, 10th September 1945. Alanbrooke Personal Files.
35 Notes.
36 Col. Peter Dunphie.
37 Diary. 13th August 1942.
38 Notes.
39 *Winston Churchill. The Struggle for Survival* Lord Moran. Constable 1966. Henceforth 'Moran'.
40 Alanbrooke Papers (section 12).
41 Alanbrooke Papers (section 12).
42 Moran.
43 Letters.
44 *Ibid.*
45 Alanbrooke Papers (section 12).
46 Letters.
47 Letters.
48 Notes.
49 Letters.
50 Jones.
51 Diary. 22nd October 1942.
52 Notes.
53 Simpson.
54 Alanbrooke Papers (section 12).
55 Notes.
56 Notes.
57 Quoted in *Grand Strategy.*
58 Notes.
59 Notes.
60 Diary. 16th December 1942.
61 Recorded in Alanbrooke Papers.
62 *History of the U.S. Army in the Second World War. Global Logistics & Strategy.* Leighton and Coakley.

CHAPTER XIII

1 Ismay.
2 Diary. 25th May 1943.
3 Diary of Lt. Gen. Sir Ian Jacob. Hereafter 'Jacob'.
4 Diary. 3rd January 1943.
5 Diary. 22nd January 1943.
6 COS (43) (o) 5th January 1943. Secretary's standard file.
7 Diary. 16th January 1943.
8 Alanbrooke Personal Files.
9 Jacob.
10 *Ibid.*
11 Notes.
12 *Grand Strategy.* Vol. IV Appx III(D).
13 Alanbrooke Papers (section 12/XII).
14 Diary. 17th January 1943.
15 Diary. 18th January 1943.
16 Notes.
17 Notes.
18 *Ibid.*
19 Jacob.
20 Notes.
21 *Ibid.*
22 Alanbrooke Papers (section 12/XII).
23 Jacob.
24 Notes.
25 Diary. 30th January 1943.
26 Jacob.
27 Notes.
28 Jacob.
29 Diary. 7th February 1943.

CHAPTER XIV

1 Notes.
2 Alanbrooke Personal Files.
3 *Grand Strategy.* Vol. IV.
4 CCS 155/1: 19th January, 1943.
5 Alanbrooke Personal Files.
6 Notes.
7 Communicated by Mr L. G. Simpson.
8 Notes.
9 *Ibid.*
10 Alanbrooke Personal Files.
11 Notes.
12 Notes.
13 Communicated by participants.
14 Von Manstein: *Lost Victories* Methuen 1958.
15 Notes.
16 Notes.
17 Letters communicated by Dr David Bannerman.
18 COS (43) 165.
19 For example – *Great Mistakes of the War.* Hanson W. Baldwin. Alvin Redman. London 1950.
20 Alanbrooke Personal Files.
21 Notes.

CHAPTER XV

1 Letters.
2 General Nye, Brooke's Vice-Chief of the General Staff, had anticipated this German plan as early as August, at which time British Intelligence had argued that it would be unsound for the Germans to hold even the Pisa-Rimini line. Nye thought they would make every effort 'to hold the line of the Apennines'. He was right.
COS (43) 186 – 12th August 1943.
3 Notes.
4 Alanbrooke Personal Files.
5 COS (43) 267 (o) – 2nd November 1943.
6 Alanbrooke Personal Files.
7 Notes.
8 Alanbrooke Papers. (section 12).
9 Alanbrooke Personal Files.
10 *Ibid.*
11 For the Prime Minister's admirable Minute on the subject see *Grand Strategy*. Vol. V p. 172.
12 Diary. 8th November 1943.
13 Alanbrooke Papers. (section 12). See also Chapter XIX.
14 Notes.
15 Diary. 18th November 1943.
16 *Ibid.*
17 Notes.
18 *Ibid.*
19 Diary. 23rd November 1943.
20 Notes.
21 *Ibid.*
22 *Ibid.*
23 *Conversations with Stalin.* Milovan Djilas. Rupert Hart-Davis. 1962.
24 Notes.
25 Diary. 30th November 1943.
26 Diary. 4th December 1943.
27 *Grand Strategy.* Vol. V p. 185.
28 Notes.

CHAPTER XVI

1 Diary. 11th December 1943.
2 Communicated by Colonel Peter Dunphie.
3 Alanbrooke Personal Files.
4 *Ibid.*
5 *Ibid.*
6 *Ibid.*
7 Diary. 29th February 1944.
8 Alanbrooke Personal Files.
9 Diary. 31st March 1944.
10 Notes to Diary. 19th May 1944.
11 Alanbrooke Personal Files.
12 *Ibid.*
13 *Ibid.*
14 Diary. 31st March 1944.
15 Alanbrooke Papers (section 6).
16 COS (44) 32nd Meeting: 3rd February 1944.
17 Alanbrooke Personal Files.
18 *Ibid.*
19 COS (44) 48th Meeting: 14th February 1944 – attributed by CIGS as 'Admiral King's plan' though more properly that of Nimitz.

20 Notes.
21 Alanbrooke Papers (section 10).
22 Diary. 7th May 1944.
23 Notes.
24 Diary. 14th September 1944.
25 Communicated by Dr Bannerman.
26 Diary. 15th May 1944.

27 Diary. 10th March 1944.
28 Notes. 5th June 1944.
29 Communicated by Sir Alan Lascelles.
30 Diary. 6th June 1944.
31 Diary. 7th June 1944.
32 Communicated by Air Commodore The Hon. Sir Peter Vanneck.

CHAPTER XVII

1 *Grand Strategy*. Vol. V.
2 Notes.
3 Diary. 21st June 1944.
4 Diary. 22nd June 1944.
5 Diary. 23rd June 1944.
6 Quoted in *Grand Strategy* Vol. V.
7 *Ibid.*
8 Diary. 26th June 1944.
9 Notes.
9a Simpson.
10 Quoted in *Grand Strategy* Vol. V.
11 Letter Montgomery–Brooke 6th August 1944. Alanbrooke Personal Files.
12 Alanbrooke Personal Files.
13 For example Field-Marshal Lord Harding quoted in *Alex*. Nigel Nicolson. Weidenfeld and Nicolson 1973.
14 Quoted in *Grand Strategy*. Vol. V.
15 *Grand Strategy*. Vol. V.
16 Diary. 29th August 1944.
17 Alanbrooke Papers (section 6).

18 *Ibid.*
19 Notes.
20 Quoted in *Churchill and the Admirals*. Stephen Roskill. Collins 1977.
21 Quoted in *Grand Strategy*. Vol. V.
22 Notes.
23 Alanbrooke Papers (section 12).
24 Communicated by Mrs Bright Astley. See *The Inner Circle*. Joan Bright Astley. Hutchinson 1971.
25 Diary. 14th October 1944.
26 Diary. 15th October 1944.
27 Notes.
28 Alanbrooke Papers (section 6).
29 Diary. 2nd October 1944.
30 COS (44) 822 (o).
31 Notes.
32 COS (44) 336 (o) 12th October 1944.
33 Communicated by Sir Ian Jacob.

CHAPTER XVIII

1 Quoted in *Command Decisions* from U.S. Office of the Chief of Military History (OCMH) files. Harcourt, Brace and Co. New York 1959.
2 Diary. 25th November 1944.
3 Alanbrooke Personal Files.
4 Letter 24th November 1944. Alanbrooke Personal Files.
5 Letters. 12th December 1944.
6 Notes.
7 Alanbrooke Personal Files.
8 Alanbrooke Papers (section 12).
9 *Grand Strategy*. Vol. VI.
10 Diary. 31st January 1945.
11 *Crusade in Europe*. Eisenhower. William Heinemann 1948.
11a Letter Wilson–Brooke 4th October 1944. Alanbrooke Personal Files.
12 Diary. 8th October 1944.
13 30th October 1944. *Grand Strategy*. Vol. VI.
14 *Grand Strategy*. Vol. VI.
15 *Ibid*.
16 Alanbrooke Personal Files.
17 Alanbrooke Papers (section 6).
18 Diary. 4th February 1945.
19 *Grand Strategy*. Vol. VI.
20 Alanbrooke Papers (section 12).
21 Montgomery to CIGS 14th February 1945. Alanbrooke Personal Files.
22 Alanbrooke Personal Files.
23 Diary. 23rd March 1945.
24 Diary. 24th March 1945.
25 Diary. 25th March 1945.
26 Notes.
27 Alanbrooke Personal Files.
28 Diary. 29th March 1945.
29 Alanbrooke Personal Files.
30 Churchill. Vol. VI.
31 Alanbrooke Personal Files.
32 Diary. 22nd February 1945.

CHAPTER XIX

1 Notes.
2 *Ibid*.
3 Diary. 6th April 1945.
4 Alanbrooke Personal Files.
5 *Ibid*.
6 *Ibid*.
7 The whole episode is clearly set out in *Slim* by Ronald Lewin. Leo Cooper 1976. The papers on the case are with The Slim Papers at Churchill College, Cambridge (copies).
8 Notes.
9 Eric Hosking's Appreciation in *Bird Notes* after Alanbrooke's death in 1963.
10 Notes. 24th July 1945.
11 Alanbrooke Papers (section 6).
12 Communicated by Lt. Gen. Sir Ian Jacob.
13 Alanbrooke Papers (section 7).
14 Notes.

CHAPTER XX

1 Alanbrooke Papers (section 8).
2 Notes on my Life.
3 Diary. 16th December 1945.
4 Alanbrooke Papers (section 7).
5 Diary. 4th November 1945.
6 Letters. 27th October 1945.
7 Letters. 9th December 1945.
8 Notes on my Life.
9 *Ibid.*
10 Letters. 27th November 1945.
11 Diary. 5th December 1945.
12 Notes on my Life.
13 Alanbrooke Papers (section 7).
14 Alanbrooke Papers (section 10).
15 *Ibid.*
16 Alanbrooke Papers (section 8).
17 Alanbrooke Papers (section 9).
18 *Ibid.*
19 Alanbrooke Papers (section 8).
20 Alanbrooke Papers (section 12).
21 Communicated by General Lathbury. Alanbrooke Papers (section 12).
22 Don Mauricio Gonzalez and his family.
23 Alanbrooke Papers (section 9).
24 Alanbrooke Papers (section 12).
25 They were presented to Benita on 26th July 1963.

CHAPTER XXI

1 Alanbrooke Papers (section 10).
2 *Ibid.* Somerville to Ismay 5th December 1944.
3 Churchill V. See also Alanbrooke Papers (section 7).
4 So Portal thought. Alanbrooke Papers (section 12).
5 Alanbrooke Papers (section 10).
6 Simpson.
7 Alanbrooke Papers (section 10).
8 See, for example, Moran.
9 See views of Eden. Alanbrooke Papers (section 12).
10 *Ibid.*
11 See frequent diary entries.
12 Alanbrooke Papers (section 8).
13 Alanbrooke Papers (section 12).
14 Alanbrooke Papers (section 6).
15 Communicated by General Sir Neil Ritchie.
16 *Personal Experience.* Rt Hon. Robert Casey. Constable 1962.
17 Eden referred to him as 'the greatest of the Allied military leaders'. Alanbrooke Papers (section 12).
18 *Ibid.*
19 Moran.
20 Communicated by Dr David Bannerman.

INDEX

INDEX